# The Second Jewish Commonwealth

FLAVIUS JOSEPHUS

# The Second Jewish
# Commonwealth

*From the Maccabaean Rebellion
to the Outbreak of the Judaeo-Roman War*

EDITED BY NAHUM N. GLATZER

SCHOCKEN BOOKS · NEW YORK

This volume comprises *Jewish Antiquities,* Books XII.iv–XX, translated by William Whiston, as revised by A. R. Shilleto, 1889.

First SCHOCKEN edition 1971

Manufactured in the United States of America

# CONTENTS

## THE SECOND JEWISH COMMONWEALTH

## LIST OF MAPS

# PREFACE

WHEN, in the eighth decade of the first Christian century, Josephus started to work on the *Jewish Antiquities,* the forty-year-old historian could look back on a colorful career. Scion of a noble, priestly Jerusalem family, he had studied the heritage of his people and its contemporary representations, had decided to attach himself to the Pharisees, had journeyed to Rome on a diplomatic mission, had taken a stand against the anti-Roman Jewish revolutionaries, had lamely "defended" Galilee against the Romans and surrendered to Vespasian to become his and his son Titus' military adviser, had accepted Roman citizenship and residence after the destruction of Jerusalem and a royal grant that enabled him to write (in Greek) the history of that war: *De bello Judaico,* the *Jewish War.* The imperial patrons were well pleased with the performance of their client.

Josephus devoted the next period of his life, a span of about eighteen years, to what was to become his *magnum opus:* a presentation of the entire history of the Jewish nation from the biblical period (even starting with the creation of the world) to the outbreak of the rebellion against Rome in 66. The work appeared in 93–94 under the title *Joudaike archaiologia,* Jewish Archaeology, or, as the work is commonly known, *Jewish Antiquities.* Emperor Titus had died in 81; his successor, Domitian, was an enemy of literature and learning. Josephus' sponsor became a certain Epaphroditus, apparently a scholar himself and a man who found it important to foster the scholarship of others in a time of stress.

Josephus the author of the *Antiquities* differs from Josephus the author of the *War.* The strong pro-Roman sentiment of the latter (who put all the blame for the war on the fanaticism of the zealots) has cooled; in the *Antiquities* he "figures solely as Jewish historian and apologist" (H. St. John Thackeray). He has lived in Rome long enough to be aware of the unsavory aspects of the Empire's civilization; he has had time enough after the fall of his nation to reflect on its history as a whole—a subject that was on his mind even when he was writing the *War.*

Josephus composed his work—assisted by Greek stylists and editors—for the benefit of the educated pagan reader. He thought, "it will appear to the whole Greek-speaking world worthy of their study" and noted that "there were persons who desired to know our history and exhorted me to go on with it" (*Antiquities*, Preface). He promised his reader "to have nothing so much at heart as this, that I may omit no facts, either from ignorance or fault of memory." While appreciating the fact that readers expect "a proper beauty of style," he stressed as his principal aim "to speak accurately and truly" (*ibid.*, XVI.i.1). Alas, Josephus must have found it difficult to adhere to this high standard of historical presentation.

The first part of the work (Books I–XI.vi) is devoted to the biblical period up to the end of the fifth century B.C.; this is followed by a brief section (XI.vii–XII.iii) on the time leading up to about 200 B.C. Josephus then tells the story of Joseph, son of Tobias, and the rise of his house, placing the events after the conquest of Palestine by the Seleucid Antiochus III. However, as shown by V. Tcherikover, the account must be ascribed to the period when the country was controlled by Ptolemaic Egypt, i.e., to the decades before 200 B.C. The detailed account of the Tobiads (the origin of which was either a family chronicle or a source friendly to the Ptolemaic dynasty) was meant to document the new force that entered Judaean public life: Hellenism and its emphasis on the self-asserting personality, political action, international relations, and rejection of traditional beliefs and mores. Josephus concludes the story by crediting Joseph the Tobiad with "having brought the Jews out of a state of poverty and weakness to one that was more splendid" (XII.iv.10). In the present volume the story of the Tobiads is reprinted as a foil to the Maccabaean rebellion.

The section of the *Antiquities* that follows recounts the story of Jewish affairs from the accession of Antiochus IV, Epiphanes, in 176 B.C. and the Maccabaean rebellion to the events that led to the fateful break with Rome in A.D. 66. Josephus relates the struggle of the Maccabaean brothers for freedom, the rule of the Hasmonaean kings, the rise of King Herod, the drama of his achievements and failures, the division of the land under Herod's sons, the government of the Roman procurators, the benign and

peaceful rule of Herod's grandson, Agrippa I, and the resump-
tion of the increasingly intolerable Roman rule. Into this story
Josephus inserted accounts of Roman decrees concerning Jews,
of the Jews in Babylonia, of Emperors Gaius Caligula and
Claudius, of the conversion of the royal house of Adiabene to
Judaism.

As his sources for the second part of the *Antiquities,* Josephus used the *First Book of Maccabees;* Jewish and pagan
accounts of the Hasmonaean period; the works of Herod's
court historian, Nicolaus of Damascus, of which fragments have
been preserved; Herod's *Memoirs,* and the no longer extant
*Historical Sketches* of Strabo; as well as collections of Roman
official documents, a number of no longer identifiable reports,
and, of course, the author's own recollections of events.

The most powerful (and the most detailed) narrative in the
work is the story of King Herod. Joseph, who had previously
told of King Herod in his *War,* had access to more sources for
his *Antiquities.* Furthermore, he had acquired a more critical
attitude. Now, he blames Nicolaus for having written his history
"so as to please and serve him [Herod], touching upon nothing
but what redounded to his glory and openly excusing many of
his notorious crimes and very diligently concealing them."
Whereas he, Josephus, reminding the reader of his royal Hasmonaean and priestly background, thinks "it unbecoming to say
anything that is false . . . and accordingly we have described
the actions in an honest and upright manner" (XVI.vii.1).

Throughout the work we find references to divine providence
manifested in history and in individual lives, to schools representing various Jewish views, to "our ancestral traditions," and
to just divine laws. But we miss an awareness of the religious
pathos, of Messianic passion, of the process of internalization
alive in that period of history. Hillel, secret anti-king to Herod,
is not mentioned; neither is Yohanan ben Zakkai, who during
the last years of Jerusalem prepared for Israel's reconstruction.
Writing for a Gentile audience, Josephus must have considered
such issues and such men as having no general import and no
place in his history. That he was personally and deeply committed to his ancestral faith is evidenced by his exposition of
Judaism in the second part of his treatise *Against Apion* and

by his plan to write a work in four books "about God and His essence as well as concerning the laws" (XX.xi.3). In the *Antiquities* he chose to plead for universal tolerance and humanism: "Justice is most for the advantage of all men equally, both Greeks and barbarians, to which our laws pay the greatest regard, and so render us . . . benevolent and friendly to all men. On which account we have reason to expect the like return from others . . ." (XVI.vi.8).

Writers on Josephus point critically to the weaknesses of his presentation. Quite often, they say, he is overly dependent on his sources, reproducing both facts and the underlying tendency, regardless of his own views. His construction tends to be uneven, his data are not always correct, his digressions numerous. His work is thus a compilation rather than a balanced, structured composition. Though this criticism is largely correct, it does not substantially affect Josephus' position in Jewish historiography. His work—the *Antiquities* and the *War*—is the only major source for our knowledge of the last centuries of the Second Jewish Commonwealth, a period of crucial significance as both the historical basis of postbiblical Judaism and the historical background of early Christianity. Despite the deficiencies (which Josephus shares with other historians of antiquity), what emerges is an absorbing portrait of a period rich in drama, intrigue, despair, and heroism.

The works of Josephus, like those of Philo of Alexandria, were early forgotten by the Jewish community but eagerly preserved by the Church. Josephus, the non-Christian who mentioned Jesus (in a passage of disputed authenticity) and other events in the earliest period of Christianity, deserved close attention. Translations into Latin spread the knowledge of Josephus in the West. In the seventeenth century the first English translation was made from the Greek text by Thomas Lodge (London, 1640). A later translation (Dublin, 1736–41) by the Unitarian scholar William Whiston of Cambridge, England, became the standard English rendition and was frequently reprinted; a revision by A. R. Shilleto, also of Cambridge, appeared in London in 1889–90. The best scholarly edition of the Greek text with full *apparatus criticus* is the work of Benedictus Niese (Berlin, 1885–95).

The present volume utilizes the Whiston–Shilleto version. The old geographical notes of the Palestine explorer Sir C. W. Wilson have been retained. A "Guide through the Work," a chronological summary, and a bibliography have been added for the convenience of the reader.

NAHUM N. GLATZER

Brandeis University
January 1971

# CHRONOLOGICAL SUMMARY

B.C.

| | |
|---|---|
| 330 | [Alexander the Great conquers the Persian Empire, including Palestine] |
| 3d cent. | Palestine under the rule of the Egyptian Ptolemies |
| mid–3d cent. | Joseph, son of Tobias. The Tobiads |
| 198 | Antiochus III of Seleucid Syria conquers Palestine |
| 176–173 | Antiochus IV, Epiphanes, of Syria |
| 166–164 | Maccabaean rebellion. Mattathias. Judas and his brothers |
| 140 | Judaea regains independence under the rule of Simon the Hasmonaean |
| 140–63 | Rule of the Hasmonaeans. Pharisees and Sadducees |
| 2d–1st cents. | The Essenes; Dead Sea sect |
| 135–104 | John Hyrcanus; conquests east of the Jordan; subjection of the Samaritans and the Idumaeans |
| 104–103 | Aristobulus I; conquests in Galilee |
| 103–76 | Alexander Janneas; conquests east of the Jordan; destruction of Gaza; defeat by the Nabataeans |
| 76–67 | Salome Alexandra |
| 67 | Civil war between Aristobulus II and Hyrcanus II |
| 67–63 | Aristobulus II |
| 63 | Pompey captures Jerusalem; strong position of Antipater of Idumaea |
| 63–40 | Hyrcanus II, high priest and ethnarch |
| 55–54 | [Caesar invades Britain] |
| 51–30 | Cleopatra VII, last queen of Egypt |
| 49 | Assassination of Aristobulus II, by friends of Pompey |
| 48 | Pompey killed in Egypt; Herod turns to Caesar |
| 47 | Antipater procurator of Judaea; Herod governor of Galilee |
| 47–46 | Execution of Hezekiah |
| 44 | Assassination of Julius Caesar; Herod turns to Cassius |

xii

| | |
|---|---|
| 43 | Antipater poisoned by Malichus |
| 42 | Cassius defeated at Philippi by Antony; Herod turns to Antony |
| ca. 40 | [Hillel comes to Jerusalem] |
| 40 | Invasion of Palestine by the Parthians; Herod flees to Rome; appointed king of Judaea |
| 40–37 | Antigonus, son of Aristobulus II, high priest and king |
| 37 | Herod and Sossius capture Jerusalem; Herod marries Mariamne; purge of the Synhedrion |
| 37–4 | Herod the Great |
| 35 | Murder of Aristobulus III, high priest; building of Antonia |
| 34 | Execution of Joseph, husband of Herod's sister Salome |
| 34 | Cleopatra with Herod in Jerusalem |
| 32 | Herod's war with the Arabians (Nabataeans) |
| 31 | Earthquake in Palestine |
| 31 | Antony's downfall at Actium; Herod turns to Octavian |
| 31 B.C.–A.D. 14 | Octavian (Augustus). Augustan age: Vergil, Horace, Ovid, Livy, Strabo |
| 30 | Execution of Hyrcanus II; Herod visits Augustus |
| 30 | Suicide of Antony and Cleopatra |
| 29 | Execution of Mariamne |
| 28 | Execution of Alexandra |
| 27 | Herod rebuilds Samaria (Sebaste) |
| 25 | Execution of Costobarus, second husband of Salome, and the sons of Babas |
| ca. 24 | Herod builds palace and Tower Antonia |
| 23 | Herod receives from Augustus Trachonitis, Batanaea, and Auranitis |
| 23 | The sons of Mariamne, Alexander and Aristobulus, sent to Rome |
| 22 | Building of Caesarea begun |
| 20 | Augustus in Syria, presents to Herod territory of Zenodorus |
| 20 | Reconstruction of the temple begun |
| ca. 20 | [Birth of Philo of Alexandria (d. ca. A.D. 50)] |
| 15 | Marcus Agrippa visits Herod in Jerusalem |
| 14 | Antipater, son of Herod by Doris, recalled to the Court |
| 10 | Celebration of the completion of Caesarea |

| | |
|---|---|
| 9 | Expedition against the Nabataeans |
| 7 | Execution of Alexander and Aristobulus; Antipater's power at the Court |
| 5 | Herod learns of Antipater's hostile schemes |
| 4 | Revolt of the people by Judas and Matthias |
| 4 | Execution of Antipater |
| 4 | Death of Herod |
| 4 B.C.–A.D. 6 | Archelaus, ethnarch of Judaea, Samaria, and Idumaea |
| 4 B.C.–A.D. 39 | Herod Antipas, tetrarch of Galilee and Peraea |
| 4 B.C.–A.D. 34 | Philip, tetrarch of Batanaea, Trachonitis, and Auranitis |

A.D.

| | |
|---|---|
| 6–41 | Judaea, Samaria, and Idumaea, a Roman province, governed by procurators |
| 6 | The enrollment of Quirinius; Judas the Galilean, rebel leader |
| 14–37 | Tiberius, emperor |
| 26–36 | Pontius Pilate, procurator |
| ca. 27 | Preaching of John the Baptist |
| ca. 30 | Crucifixion of Jesus by Pontius Pilate |
| 37–41 | Gaius Caligula, emperor |
| 37–44 | Herod Agrippa I, king over the territory of Philip; from 41 on, over the former realm of Herod the Great |
| 40 | Jewish embassy to Caligula, led by Philo |
| 41–54 | Claudius, emperor |
| 44–? | Cuspius Fadus, procurator, executed Theudas, a false prophet |
| ?–48 | Tiberius Alexander, procurator; crucified sons of Judas the Galilean, rebel leaders |
| 44–66 | Kingdom of Agrippa becomes a Roman province |
| 48 | Herod Agrippa II, son of Agrippa I, becomes king of Chalcis, later king of Trachonitis, Batanaea, Gaulanitis, parts of Galilee and Peraea (d. 100) |
| 51–60 | Felix, procurator; rise of the Sicarii, extreme zealots; the false prophet from Egypt |
| 51–57 | [Missionary travels of Paul] |
| 54–68 | Nero, emperor |
| 60–66 | Festus, Albinus, Gessius Florus, procurators |
| 64 | [Josephus' journey to Rome] |

66              Cessation of temple offering for the emperor;
                revolt against Rome
70              [Fall of Jerusalem. Josephus in Rome]
73              [Fall of fortress Masada]
ca. 75–79       [*The Jewish War*, by Flavius Josephus]
93              [*Jewish Antiquities*, by Flavius Josephus]

# THE HOUSE OF THE HASMONAEANS

(all dates are B.C.)

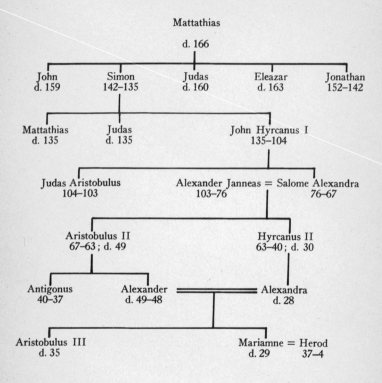

Mattathias
d. 166

John | Simon | Judas | Eleazar | Jonathan
d. 159 | 142–135 | d. 160 | d. 163 | 152–142

Mattathias | Judas | John Hyrcanus I
d. 135 | d. 135 | 135–104

Judas Aristobulus | Alexander Janneas = Salome Alexandra
104–103 | 103–76 | 76–67

Aristobulus II | Hyrcanus II
67–63 ; d. 49 | 63–40 ; d. 30

Antigonus | Alexander | Alexandra
40–37 | d. 49–48 | d. 28

Aristobulus III | Mariamne = Herod
d. 35 | d. 29 | 37–4

# THE HOUSE OF HEROD

(m.—married)

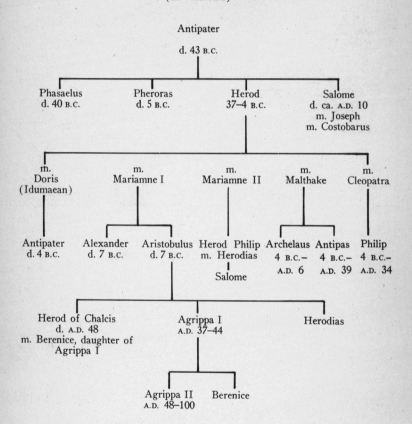

Antipater
d. 43 B.C.

Phasaelus
d. 40 B.C.

Pheroras
d. 5 B.C.

Herod
37–4 B.C.

Salome
d. ca. A.D. 10
m. Joseph
m. Costobarus

m.
Doris
(Idumaean)

m.
Mariamne I

m.
Mariamne II

m.
Malthake

m.
Cleopatra

Antipater
d. 4 B.C.

Alexander
d. 7 B.C.

Aristobulus
d. 7 B.C.

Herod Philip
m. Herodias

Archelaus
4 B.C.–
A.D. 6

Antipas
4 B.C.–
A.D. 39

Philip
4 B.C.–
A.D. 34

Salome

Herod of Chalcis
d. A.D. 48
m. Berenice, daughter of
Agrippa I

Agrippa I
A.D. 37–44

Herodias

Agrippa II
A.D. 48–100

Berenice

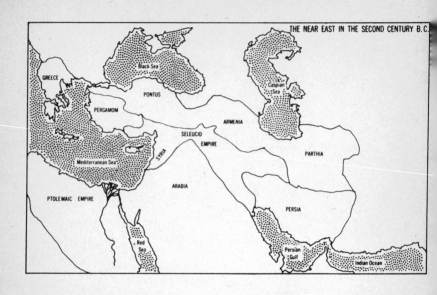

THE NEAR EAST IN THE SECOND CENTURY B.C.

GREECE

Black Sea

PONTUS

Caspian Sea

PERGAMOM

ARMENIA

SELEUCID

EMPIRE

PARTHIA

Mediterranean Sea

SYRIA

PTOLEMAIC EMPIRE

ARABIA

PERSIA

Red Sea

Persian Gulf

Indian Ocean

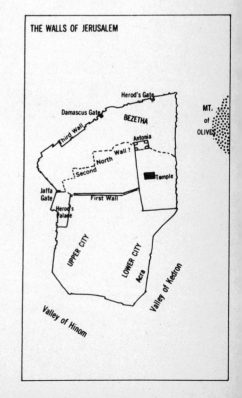

THE WALLS OF JERUSALEM

Herod's Gate

Damascus Gate

BEZETHA

MT. of OLIVES

Third Wall

Antonia

North Wall ?

Second

Temple

Jaffa Gate

First Wall

Herod's Palace

UPPER CITY

LOWER CITY

Acra

Valley of Kedron

Valley of Hinom

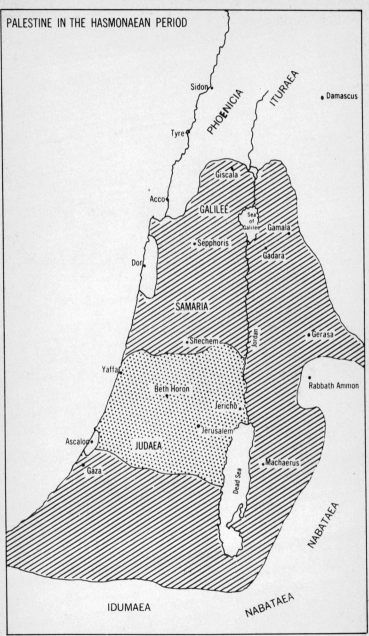

PALESTINE IN THE HASMONAEAN PERIOD

Sidon

PHOENICIA

ITURAEA

Damascus

Tyre

Giscala

Acco

GALILEE

Sea of Galilee

Gamala

Sepphoris

Gadara

Dor

SAMARIA

Jordan

Gerasa

Shechem

Yaffa

Beth Horon

Jericho

Rabbath Ammon

Jerusalem

Ascalon

JUDAEA

Gaza

Machaerus

Dead Sea

NABATAEA

IDUMAEA

NABATAEA

 Territory under Simon, ca. 135 B.C.

Territory under Alexander Jannaeus, ca. 76 B.C.

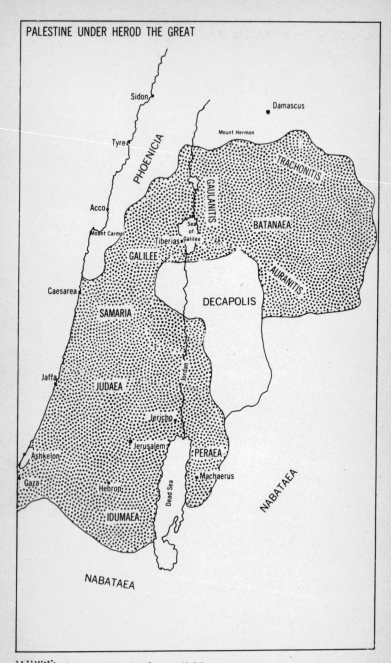

PALESTINE UNDER HEROD THE GREAT

Sidon

Damascus

Mount Hermon

Tyre

PHOENICIA

TRACHONITIS

GAULANITIS

Acco

BATANAEA

Mount Carmel

Sea of Galilee

Tiberias

GALILEE

AURANITIS

Caesarea

DECAPOLIS

SAMARIA

Jaffa

Jordan

JUDAEA

Jericho

Jerusalem

PERAEA

Ashkelon

Machaerus

NABATAEA

Gaza

Hebron

Dead Sea

IDUMAEA

NABATAEA

Territory under Herod the Great, ca. 10 B.C.

# GUIDE THROUGH THE WORK

## Book XII

## Book XIII

### JONATHAN, BROTHER OF JUDAS

# BOOK XII.

## CHAP. IV.

### *The House of Tobias.*

#### § 1.

AFTER this, Antiochus made a friendship and league with Ptolemy,[1] and gave him his daughter Cleopatra in marriage, and yielded up to him Cœle-Syria and Samaria and Judæa and Phœnicia by way of dowry. And upon the division of the taxes between the two kings, all the principal men farmed the taxes of their several countries, and, collecting the sum that was assigned to them, paid the same to the two kings. Now at this time the Samaritans were in a flourishing condition, and much harassed the Jews, ravaging their land, and carrying off slaves. This happened when Onias was high priest, for after Eleazar's death, his uncle Manasseh took the priesthood, and when he too had ended his life, Onias received that dignity. He was the son of Simon, who was called the Just, and Simon was the brother of Eleazar, as I said before. This Onias had a little soul, and was a great lover of money; and for that reason, because he did not pay the tax of

---

[1] Ptolemy V., Epiphanes, 205-181 B.C.

twenty talents of silver for the people, which his fore-fathers paid to these kings out of their own estates, he provoked to anger king Ptolemy Euergetes,[1] who was the father of Philopator.[2] Euergetes sent an ambassador to Jerusalem, and complained that Onias did not pay the taxes, and threatened that if he did not receive them he would parcel out their land, and send soldiers to dwell upon it. When the Jews heard this message of the king, they were confounded: but so avaricious was Onias, that nothing of this put him about.

§ 2. Now there was one Joseph, young indeed in age, but of great reputation among the people of Jerusalem for character, sense, and uprightness. His father's name was Tobias, and his mother was the sister of Onias the high priest. She informed him of the coming of the ambassador, for he was then sojourning at a village called Phicol,[3] his native place. And he went to Jerusalem, and reproved Onias for not seeing to the preservation of his country-men, but bringing the nation into dangers, by not paying this money, though it was for their benefit that he had received the authority over them, and had been made high priest: but if he was so great a lover of money, as to have the heart to see his country in danger on that account, and the citizens suffering the greatest damage, he advised him to go to the king, and petition him to remit either the whole or a part of the sum demanded. Onias's answer was that he did not care for his authority, and was ready, if it were possible, to lay down his high priesthood, and that he would not go to the king, for he cared nothing at all about the matter. Joseph then asked him, if he would give him leave to go as ambassador on behalf of the nation? He replied that he would. Thereupon Joseph went up into the temple, and called the multitude together to an assembly, and exhorted them not to be disturbed or alarmed because of his uncle Onias's carelessness, but desired them to be at rest, and not to terrify themselves with fear about it; for he promised them that he would be their ambassador to the king, and persuade him that

---

[1] Ptolemy III., Euergetes, 247-222 B.C.
[2] Ptolemy IV., Philopator, 222-205 B.C.
[3] Not identified.

they had done him no wrong. And when the multitude heard this, they returned thanks to Joseph. So he went down from the temple, and treated Ptolemy's ambassador in a hospitable manner, and presented him also with rich gifts, and feasted him magnificently for many days, and then sent him on to the king before him, and told him that he would soon follow him. For he was now still more desirous to go to the king, from the encouragement of the ambassador, who urged him to go to Egypt, and promised him that he would take care that he should obtain everything that he desired of Ptolemy, for he was highly pleased with his liberality and the gravity of his deportment.

§ 3. When Ptolemy's ambassador reached Egypt, he told the king of the thoughtlessness of Onias, and informed him of the good disposition of Joseph, who was coming to him to excuse the multitude, as not having done him any harm, for he was their champion. In short he was so very profuse in his encomiums upon the young man, that he disposed both the king and his wife Cleopatra to have a kindness for him before he arrived. And Joseph sent to his friends at Samaria, and borrowed money of them, and got ready what was necessary for his journey, clothes and cups and beasts of burden, which cost about twenty thousand drachmæ, and set out for Alexandria. Now it so happened that at this time all the principal men and rulers went up from the cities of Syria and Phœnicia to buy the taxes; for every year the king sold them to the well-to-do men in each city. And these men saw Joseph journeying on his way, and jeered at him for his poverty and meanness. But when he got to Alexandria, and heard that king Ptolemy was at Memphis, he went up there to meet him. And as the king was sitting in his chariot with his wife and friend Athenion (who was the very person who had been ambassador at Jerusalem, and been entertained by Joseph,) directly Athenion saw him, he at once made him known to the king, saying this was the person about whom on his return from Jerusalem he had told the king how good and generous a young man he was. So Ptolemy saluted him first, and desired him to come up into his chariot, and as Joseph sat there, began to complain of the behaviour of

Onias. To which Joseph answered, "Forgive him on account of his age, for thou canst not certainly be unacquainted with this fact, that old men and infants have their minds exactly alike; but thou shalt have from us, who are young men, everything thou desirest, and shalt have no cause to complain." The king was so delighted with the grace and pleasantry of the young man, that he began already, as though he had had long experience of him, to have still greater affection for him, insomuch that he bade him lodge in his palace, and be a guest at his table every day. And when the king was come to Alexandria, the principal men of Syria saw Joseph sitting with the king, and were much offended at it.

§ 4. Now when the day came, on which the king was to farm the taxes of the cities, and those that were the men of principal dignity in their several countries bid for them, the sum of what was bidden for the taxes of Cœle-Syria and Phœnicia and Judæa and Samaria amounted altogether to eight thousand talents. Thereupon Joseph accused the bidders of having agreed together to estimate the value of the taxes at too low a rate, and promised that he would himself give twice as much for them, and for those who did not pay, he would send the king their whole substance, for this privilege was also sold with the taxes. The king was pleased to hear that offer, and because it augmented his revenues, he said he would confirm the sale of the taxes to him. But when he asked him the question, Whether he had any sureties, that would be bound for the payment of the money? he answered very cleverly, "I will give as security persons good and honourable, whom you shall have no reason to distrust." And when he bade him name who they were, he replied, "I give thee no other persons, O king, for my sureties than thyself and thy wife; and you shall be security for both parties." Then Ptolemy laughed at the proposal, and granted him the farming of the taxes without any security. This was a sore grief to those who had come into Egypt from the cities to be thus outbid, and they returned home everyone with shame.

§ 5. And Joseph took with him two thousand foot-soldiers of the king's, for he desired to have some assistance, in order to force such as were refractory in the cities to pay. And borrowing five hundred talents from the king's friends at Alexandria, he started for Syria. And when he got to Ascalon,[1] and demanded the taxes of the people of Ascalon, they refused to pay anything, and insulted him also, upon which he seized about twenty of their principal men, and slew them, and gathered their substance together, which amounted to a thousand talents, and sent it all to the king, and informed him of what he had done. And Ptolemy admired the prudent conduct of the man, and commended him for what he had done, and gave him leave to do as he pleased. When the Syrians heard of this, they were dismayed, and having before them a sad example in the men of Ascalon that were slain, they opened their gates, and willingly admitted Joseph, and paid their taxes. And when the inhabitants of Scythopolis[2] attempted to affront him, and would not pay him the taxes, which they formerly used to pay without any hesitation, he slew also the principal men of that city, and sent their effects to the king. By this means he got much wealth together, and made vast gains of this farming of the taxes, and made use of what he had thus got to support his authority, thinking it prudent to keep what had been the occasion and foundation of his present good fortune. And he privately sent many presents to the king, and to Cleopatra, and to their friends, and to all that were powerful at the court, and thereby purchased their good-will.

§ 6. This good fortune he enjoyed for twenty-two years, and was the father of seven sons by one wife : he had also another son, whose name was Hyrcanus, by his brother Solymius' daughter, whom he married on the following occasion. He once went to Alexandria with his brother, (who took with him a daughter already marriageable, in order to give her in wedlock to some of the Jews of chief dignity there,) and supping with the king, and falling in love with a dancing girl of great beauty that came into the room where they feasted, he told his brother of it, and entreated him, because a Jew is forbidden by their law to lie with a foreign woman, to conceal his offence, and to be kind

---

[1] *'Ascalân.*                    [2] *Beisân.*

and subservient to him, and to give him an opportunity of fulfilling his desires. Upon this his brother willingly entertained the proposal of serving him, and disguised his own daughter, and brought her to him by night, and put her into his bed. And he being in drink knew not who she was, and so lay with his brother's daughter, and this he did many times, and loved her exceedingly, and said to his brother, that he loved this dancing girl so well, that he would run the hazard of his life for her, for probably the king would not give him leave to have her. But his brother bade him be in no concern, and told him he might enjoy her whom he loved without any danger, and might have her for his wife, and opened the truth to him, and assured him that he chose rather to have his own daughter abused than see him come to disgrace. Then Joseph commended him for his brotherly love, and married his daughter, and by her had a son, whose name was Hyrcanus, as I said before. And as this his youngest son at thirteen years old showed great natural courage and wisdom, and was greatly envied by his brothers, as being much above them and such a one as they might well envy, Joseph had a mind to know which of his sons had the best natural parts, and so he sent them each to those that had at that time the best reputation for instructing youths, but all the others, by reason of their sloth, and unwillingness to take pains, returned to him foolish and unlearned. After them he sent out Hyrcanus, the youngest, and gave him three hundred yoke of oxen, and bade him go two days' journey in the wilderness, and sow the land there, but kept back privately the leather harness of the oxen. When Hyrcanus came to the place, and found he had no harness, he scorned the idea of the drivers of the oxen, who advised him to send some of them home to his father to bring them harness, for thinking he ought not to lose time waiting for the return of those who might be despatched, he invented a kind of stratagem that showed wisdom greater than his age. For he slew ten yoke of the oxen, and distributed their flesh among the labourers, and cut their hides into several pieces, and made harness, and yoked the oxen with them; by which means he sowed as much land as his father had ordered him to sow, and returned to him. And when he was come back, his father was mightily pleased with his sagacity, and commended the sharpness of his understanding, and his boldness in what he did, and loved him still more, as if he were his only genuine son, and his brothers were much troubled at this.

§ 7. And when one told him that Ptolemy had a son just born, and that all the principal men of Syria, and the other countries subject to him, intended to keep a festival on account of the child's birthday, and had set out with great retinues to Alexandria, he was himself indeed hindered from going by old age, but he tried to see whether any of his sons would go to the king. And when the elder sons excused themselves from going, and said they were not courtiers enough for such company, and advised him to send their brother Hyrcanus, he gladly hearkened to their advice, and called Hyrcanus, and asked him, whether he would go to the king, and if he was willing to do so. And upon his undertaking to go, and saying that he should not want much money for his journey, because he would live moderately, so that ten thousand drachmæ would be sufficient, Joseph was pleased with his son's moderation. A little while after the son advised his father not to send his presents to the king from there, but to give him a letter to his steward at Alexandria, that he might furnish him with money for purchasing what would be most excellent and most precious. So he, thinking that his presents to the king would come to about ten talents, and commending his son as giving him good advice, wrote to Arion his steward, who managed all his money at Alexandria, which money was not less than three thousand talents. For Joseph sent the money he received from Syria to Alexandria, and when the day appointed for the payment of the taxes to the king came, he used to write to Arion to pay them. Now when the son had asked his father for a letter to this steward, and had received it, he set out for Alexandria. And when he was gone, his brothers wrote to all the king's friends to kill him.

§ 8. Now when he was come to Alexandria, he delivered his letter to Arion, who asked him how many talents he would have, (hoping he would ask for no more than ten, or only a little more,) and when he said he wanted a thousand

talents, the steward was angry, and rebuked him, as one
that intended to live extravagantly, and let him know
that his father had got together his wealth by carefulness
and by resisting his inclinations, and wished him to imitate
the example of his father: he also said that he would give
him only ten talents, and that for a present to the king.
The lad was irritated at this, and threw Arion into prison.
And when Arion's wife had informed Cleopatra of this,
and entreated that she would rebuke the lad for what he
had done, (for Arion was in great esteem with her,) Cleopatra told the king of it.   And Ptolemy sent messengers to
Hyrcanus to tell him that the king wondered, when he was
sent to him by his father, that he had not yet come into
his presence, but had put the steward in prison.   He gave
order, therefore, that he should come to him, and explain
why he had acted so.   And they report that the answer
he made to the king's messengers was that there was a
law of the king's that forbade a child that was born to taste
of the sacrifice before he had been to the temple and sacrificed to God.   According to which reasoning he had not
himself come to him as he was waiting for the presents he
was to make to him who had been his father's benefactor:
and he had punished the slave for disobeying his commands, for it mattered not whether a master was little
or great.   "Unless, indeed, we punish such as these, thou
mayst thyself also expect to be despised by thy subjects."
Upon hearing this answer of his, Ptolemy fell a laughing,
and wondered at the great wit of the lad.

§ 9.  When Arion learned that this was the king's disposition, and that he himself had no other alternative, he
gave the lad a thousand talents, and was let out of prison.
And after three days had elapsed, Hyrcanus came and
saluted the king and queen.   They saw him with pleasure,
and feasted him in a friendly manner, out of respect to his
father.   And he went to the merchants privately, and
bought a hundred boys that were well educated and in the
flower of their age at a talent a-piece, and also bought a
hundred maidens at the same price.   And when he was invited to feast with the king among the principal men of the
country, he sat down the lowest of them all, because he was
little regarded, as still a lad in age, by those who placed

every one according to their dignity. Now when all those
that sat at meat with him had laid the bones of their por-
tions on a heap before Hyrcanus, (for they had themselves
cleared the meat off them,) till the table where he sat was
full of bones, Trypho, who was the king's jester, and was appointed to joke and laugh at revels, was now called for by
the guests that sat at table. So he stood by the king, and
said, "Dost thou see, my lord, the bones that lie by Hyrcanus? By this thou mayst conjecture that his father has
made all Syria as bare as he has made these bones." And
the king laughing at what Trypho said, and asking Hyrcanus, "How he came to have so many bones before him?"
he replied, "No wonder, my lord : for dogs eat the flesh
and bones together, as these have done, (looking at the
king's guests,) for there is nothing before them ; but men
eat the flesh, and cast away the bones, as I, who am a man,
have now done." Upon this the king admired his answer,
which was so wisely made, and bade all the company
applaud, as a mark of their approbation of his facetious
jest. On the next day Hyrcanus went to every one of the
king's friends, and to the men powerful at court, and
saluted them, and inquired of their servants, what present
their masters would make the king on his son's birthday ;
and when they said that some would give twelve talents,
and that others of greater dignity would give more according to the quantity of their riches, he pretended to every
one to be grieved that he was not able to offer so large a
present, for he had no more than five talents. And when
the servants heard what he said, they told their masters ;
and they rejoiced at the prospect that Joseph would be
lightly esteemed, and would offend the king by the small-
ness of his present. When the day came, the others, even
those that brought the most, offered the king not more
than twenty talents, but Hyrcanus gave to every one of the
hundred boys and hundred maidens that he had bought a
talent a-piece for them to carry, and led the boys up to the
king, and the maidens to Cleopatra ; everybody, even the
king and queen themselves, wondering at the unexpected
munificence of the present. He also presented to the
friends and courtiers of the king gifts worth a great number
of talents, that he might escape the danger he was in from

them: for it was to them that Hyrcanus' brothers had written to kill him. Now Ptolemy admired the young man's loftiness of soul, and commanded him to ask what gift he pleased. But he desired nothing else to be done for him by the king than to write to his father and brothers about him. So when the king had paid him very great respect, and had given him very fine gifts, and had written to his father and brothers and all his commanders and officers about him, he sent him away. But when his brothers heard that Hyrcanus had received such favour from the king, and was returning home with great honour, they went out to meet him and kill him, and that with the knowledge of their father; for he was angry at him for the large sums of money that he had bestowed as presents, and so had no concern for his preservation. However, Joseph concealed his anger to his son from fear of the king. And when Hyrcanus' brothers fought with him, he slew many others of those that were with them, as also two of his brothers, but the rest escaped to Jerusalem to their father. And when Hyrcanus came to the city, as nobody would receive him, he was afraid, and retired beyond the river Jordan, and there dwelt and levied tribute on the barbarians.

§ 10. At this time Seleucus, who was called Philopator,[1] the son of Antiochus the Great, reigned over Asia. And [now] Hyrcanus' father Joseph died. He was a good man and high-souled, and brought the Jews out of a state of poverty and meanness to one that was more splendid. He farmed the taxes of Syria and Phœnicia and Samaria twenty-two years. His uncle Onias also died, and left the high priesthood to his son Simon. And when he also died, Onias his son succeeded him in that dignity, to whom Areus, King of the Lacedæmonians, sent an embassage with a letter, a copy whereof here follows.

"AREUS, KING OF THE LACEDÆMONIANS, TO ONIAS, GREETING.

"We have met with a certain writing, whereby we have discovered that both the Jews and Lacedæmonians are of

[1] Seleucus IV., 187-175 B.C.

one stock, and are derived from the kindred of Abraham.[1]
It is but just, therefore, that you, who are our brethren,
should send to us about any of your concerns as you please.
We will also do the same, and esteem your concerns as
our own, and will look upon our concerns as yours. Demoteles, who brings you this letter, will bring your answer
back to us. This letter is square, and the seal is an eagle,
with a dragon in its claws."

§ 11. Such were the contents of the letter which was
sent by the king of the Lacedæmonians. Now upon the
death of Joseph, the people grew seditious, because of
his sons. For whereas the elder ones made war against
Hyrcanus, who was the youngest of Joseph's sons, the
multitude was divided, but most joined with the elder
ones, as did Simon the high priest because of his kins-
manship to them. However, Hyrcanus determined not to
return to Jerusalem any more, but stationed himself
beyond the Jordan, and was at perpetual war with the
Arabians, and slew many of them, and took many of them
captive. He also erected a strong castle, and built it
entirely of white stone to the very roof, and had animals
of a prodigious size carved on it. He also drew round it
a great and deep canal of water. He also made caves
many furlongs long by hollowing a rock that was opposite, and made large rooms in it, some for feasting, and
some for sleeping and living in. He introduced also a
quantity of water which ran through it, and was very delightful and ornamental in the court-yard. However, he
made the mouths of the caves so narrow, that no more
than one person could enter them at once ; and that on
purpose for his own preservation, lest he should be besieged by his brothers, and run the hazard of being taken
by them. Moreover, he built courts of greater size than
ordinary, which he adorned with spacious gardens. And
when he had brought the place to this state, he called it

[1] Whence it comes that these Lacedæmonians declare themselves here
to be akin to the Jews, as derived from the kindred of Abraham, I
cannot tell, unless, as Grotius supposes, they were derived from the
Dores, that came of the Pelasgi. These are by Herodotus called ' Barbarians,' and perhaps were derived from the Syrians and Arabians, the
posterity of Abraham by Keturah. See Antiq. xiv. 10, § 22, and
Jewish War, i. 26, § 1, and Grot. on 1 Maccab. xii. 7.—W.

Tyre.[1] It is between Arabia and Judæa, beyond the Jordan, and not far from the country of Heshbon.[2]   And he ruled over those parts for seven years, even all the time that Seleucus was king of Syria.   But when Seleucus was dead, his brother Antiochus, who was called Epiphanes,[3] took the kingdom.   Ptolemy, also, the king of Egypt, died, who was also called Epiphanes, and left two sons, both young in age, the elder of whom was called Philometor,[4] and the younger Physcon.   As for Hyrcanus, when he saw that Antiochus had a great army, and feared lest he should be taken by him, and punished for what he had done to the Arabians, he ended his life by suicide, and Antiochus seized upon all his substance.

## CHAP. V.

*How, upon the Quarrels of the Jews with one another about the High Priesthood, Antiochus made an Expedition against Jerusalem, and took the City and pillaged the Temple, and distressed the Jews.  Also how many of the Jews forsook the Laws of their Country; and how the Samaritans followed the Customs of the Greeks, and called their Temple on Mount Gerizim the Temple of Zeus Hellenius.*

### § 1.

ABOUT this time, on the death of Onias the high priest, the king gave the high priesthood to Jesus his brother; for the son whom Onias left [or Onias IV.] was yet but an infant.   I shall, in its proper place, inform the reader of all the circumstances that befell this child.   Now this Jesus, the brother of Onias, was deprived of the high priesthood by the king, who was angry with him, and gave it to his younger brother, whose name also was Onias, for Simon had these three sons, to each of whom the high

[1] The ruins of the palace of Hyrcanus are still to be seen, at '*Arak el-Emir*, in the position described.

[2] Now *Hesbân;* the capital of Sihon, king of the Amorites, near the border between Reuben and Gad.

[3] Antiochus IV., 175-164 B.C.

[4] Ptolemy VI., Philometor, 181-146 B.C.

priesthood came, as I have already informed the reader. This Jesus changed his name to Jason, and Onias was called Menelaus. Now as the former high priest, Jesus, formed a party against Menelaus, who was appointed after him, the multitude were divided between them both. And the sons of Tobias took the side of Menelaus, but most of the people assisted Jason: so that Menelaus and the sons of Tobias got the worst of it, and fled to Antiochus, and informed him that they were desirous to leave the laws of their country, and the Jewish way of living according to them, and to follow the king's laws, and the Greek way of living. So they desired his permission to build for themselves a Gymnasium at Jerusalem.[1] And when he had given them leave, they drew their prepuce forward, that when they were naked they might appear to be Greeks. They also left off all the customs that belonged to their own country, and imitated the practices of other nations.

§ 2. Now Antiochus, as the affairs of his kingdom were in a prosperous condition, resolved to make an expedition against Egypt, both because he had a desire to make himself master of it, and because he despised the sons of Ptolemy, as still weak, and not yet of abilities to manage affairs of such consequence; so he marched with a great force to Pelusium, and circumvented Ptolemy Philometor by treachery, and occupied Egypt. He then went to the parts about Memphis, and when he had taken Memphis, he set out for Alexandria, in hope of taking it by siege, and of subduing Ptolemy who reigned there. But he was driven not only from Alexandria, but out of all Egypt, by the Romans, who charged him to let that country alone, as I have elsewhere stated before. I will now give a particular account of what concerns this king, who took Judæa and the temple; for in my former work I mentioned these things very briefly, and therefore now

---

[1] This word, Gymnasium, properly denotes a place where the exercises were performed naked, which because it would naturally distinguish circumcised Jews from uncircumcised Gentiles, these Jewish apostates endeavoured to appear uncircumcised, by means of an operation, hinted at by St. Paul, 1 Cor. vii. 18, and described by Celsus, vii. 25, as Dr. Hudson here informs us.—W.

think it necessary to go over the history again at greater length.

§ 3. King Antiochus then, returning out of Egypt for fear of the Romans, made an expedition against the city of Jerusalem, and in the hundred and forty-third year of the kingdom of the Selucidæ,[1] took the city without fighting, those of his own party opening the gates to him. And when he had got possession of Jerusalem he slew many of the opposite party, and when he had carried off a great deal of money, he returned to Antioch.

§ 4. Now it came to pass two years after, in the hundred and forty-fifth year, on the twenty-fifth day of the month, which is by us called Chasleu, and by the Macedonians Apellæus, in the hundred and fifty-third Olympiad, that this king went up to Jerusalem with a large force, and pretending peace, got possession of the city by treachery;[2] at which time he spared not so much as those that admitted him into it, on account of the riches that were in the temple ; but owing to his covetousness (for he saw there was in the temple a great deal of gold, and many votive offerings of very great value), in order to plunder its wealth, he ventured to break the league he had made. And he stripped the temple bare, and took away the vessels of God, as the golden candlesticks, and the golden altar of incense, and the table of shew-bread, and the altar of burnt-offering, and did not keep his hands off even the veils which were made of fine linen and scarlet. He also emptied the temple of its secret treasures, and left nothing at all remaining, and so cast the Jews into great lamentation, for he forbade them to offer the daily sacrifices which they used to offer to God according to the law. And when he had pillaged the whole city, he slew some of the inhabitants, and some he carried away captive, together with their wives and children, so that the number of captives amounted to about ten thousand. He also burnt down the finest buildings, and when he had overthrown the city walls, he built a citadel in the lower part of the city,[3] for the place

---

[1] In 170 B.C., at the close of his second Egyptian campaign. See Daniel xi. 31.

[2] In 168 B.C. at the close of his fourth Egyptian campaign.

[3] This citadel, of which we have such frequent mention in the fol-

was high, and overlooked the temple, on which account he fortified it with high walls and towers, and put into it a garrison of Macedonians. None the less in that citadel dwelt the impious and wicked part of the [Jewish] multitude, at whose hands the citizens suffered many terrible things. And when the king had built an altar upon God's altar, he slew swine upon it, and so offered a sacrifice neither according to the law, nor the ancient Jewish religious worship. He also compelled them to forsake the worship of their own God, and to adore those whom he esteemed gods, and made them build temples, and raise altars in every city and village, and offer swine upon them every day. He also commanded them not to circumcise their sons, and threatened to punish any that should be found to have transgressed this injunction. He also appointed overseers, who should compel them to do what he commanded. And indeed many Jews complied with the king's commands, some voluntarily, others out of fear of the penalty that was denounced: but the best men, and those that had noble souls, did not regard him, but paid greater respect to the customs of their country than to care about the punishment which he threatened the disobedient with, so they every day died in great miseries and bitter torments. For they were whipped with rods, and their limbs were torn to pieces, and they were fixed to crosses while they were still alive and breathed; they also strangled, as the king had ordered, the women and those of their sons who had been circumcisel, hanging their sons about their necks as they were on the crosses. And if there were any sacred book or copy of the law found, it was destroyed, and those with whom they were found miserably perished also.

§ 5. When the Samaritans saw the Jews suffering these

lowing history, both in the Maccabees and in Josephus, seems to have been a castle built on a hill, lower than mount Zion, though upon its skirts, and higher than mount Moriah, but between them both; which hill the enemies of the Jews now got possession of, and built on it this citadel, and fortified it, till a good while afterwards the Jews regained it, demolished it, and levelled the hill itself with the common ground; that their enemies might no more recover it, and might thence overlook the temple itself, and do them such mischief as they had long undergone from it, Antiq. xiii. 6, § 6.—W.

things, they no longer alleged that they were of their kindred, or that the temple on Mount Gerizim belonged to Almighty God. This was according to their nature, as I have already shown. They now said that they were a colony of Medes and Persians: and indeed they were a colony of theirs. So they sent ambassadors to Antiochus, and a letter, whose contents were as follows. "To king Antiochus Epiphanes, god, a memorial from Sidonians who live at Shechem. Our forefathers, because of certain frequent plagues, and following a certain ancient superstition, made a custom of observing that day which by the Jews is called the Sabbath.[1] And when they had erected a temple without a name on the mountain called Gerizim, they offered upon it the customary sacrifices. Now upon thy just treatment of these wicked Jews, those that carry out thy orders, supposing us to be akin to them and doing as they do, make us liable to the same accusations, although we be originally Sidonians, as is evident from the public records. We therefore beseech thee, our benefactor and saviour, to give order to Apollonius, the governor of this part of the country, and to Nicanor, the manager of thy affairs, not to disturb us, or to lay to our charge what the Jews are accused for, since we are aliens from their nation and customs; and let our temple, which at present has no name at all, be called The Temple of Zeus Hellenius. If this be once done, we shall be no longer disturbed, but shall be more secure in attending to our own occupations and so bring in a greater revenue to thee." When the Samaritans had petitioned for this, the king sent them back the following answer in a letter. "King Antiochus to Nicanor. The Sidonians who live at Shechem have sent me the enclosed memorial. When therefore we were advising with our friends about it, the messengers sent by them represented to us, that they are no way concerned in the charges brought against the Jews, but choose to live after the customs of the Greeks. Accordingly we declare them free from such accusations, and order that,

---

[1] This allegation of the Samaritans is remarkable, that though they were not Jews, yet did they, from ancient times, observe the Sabbath-day, and as they elsewhere pretend, the Sabattic year also, Antiq. xi. 8, § 6.—W.

agreeably to their petition, their temple be called The Temple of Zeus Hellenius." He also sent the like letter to Apollonius, the governor of that province, in the forty-sixth year, on the eighteenth day of the month Hecatombæon.

## CHAP. VI.

*How, upon Antiochus prohibiting the Jews to make use of the Laws of their country, Mattathias the Son of Asamonæus alone despised the King, and overcame the Generals of Antiochus' Army ; as also concerning the Death of Mattathias, and the Succession of Judas.*

### § 1.

NOW at this time there was a man who dwelt at Modiim,[1] whose name was Mattathias, the son of John, the son of Symeon, the son of Asamonæus, a priest of the order of Joarib, and a native of Jerusalem. He had five sons, John who was called Gaddes, and Simon who was called Matthes, and Judas who was called Maccabæus, and Eleazar who was called Auran, and Jonathan who was called Apphus. Now this Mattathias lamented to his sons the sad state of their affairs, as the spoiling of the city, and the plundering of the temple, and the calamities of the people, and he told them, that it was better for them to die for the laws of their country, than to live so ingloriously.

§ 2. Now when those that were appointed by the king were come to the village of Modiim, to compel the Jews to do what was commanded, and enjoin those that were there to offer sacrifice as the king had ordered, they desired that Mattathias, a person of the highest repute among them, both on other accounts and because of his goodly family, would begin the sacrifice, because his fellow citizens would follow his example, and because such behaviour would make him honoured by the king. But Mattathias said he would not do so, and if all other nations obeyed the commands of Antiochus, either

---

[1] Now *el-Medieh*, about seven miles east of Lydda, and about sixteen miles north-west of Jerusalem.

out of fear or to please him, neither he nor his sons would leave the religious worship of their country.  But when he had ended his speech, one of the Jews came into the midst, and sacrificed as Antiochus had commanded.  At this Mattathias had great indignation, and ran upon him with his sons who had swords with them, and slew both the man himself, and Apelles the king's general, who was trying to compel them to sacrifice, and a few of his soldiers.  He also overthrew the altar, and cried out, "Whoever is zealous for the laws of his country, and for the worship of God, let him follow me."  And when he had said this, he went into the desert with his sons, and left all his property in the village.  Many others did the same also, and fled with their children and wives into the desert, and dwelt in caves.  Now when the king's generals heard of this, they took all the soldiers they then had in the citadel at Jerusalem, and pursued the Jews into the desert; and when they had overtaken them, they first endeavoured to persuade them to repent, and to choose what was most for their advantage, and not to put them to the necessity of treating them according to martial law.  But as they would not listen to their persuasions, but continued to be of a different mind, they attacked them on the Sabbath-day, and burnt them as they were in their caves, without their resisting, or even so much as stopping up the entrances of the caves.  And they abstained from defending themselves on that day, because they were not willing to break in upon the honour they owed the Sabbath even in such an evil case, for our law requires us to rest upon that day.  There were about a thousand, with their wives and children, who were smothered and died in those caves; but many escaped and joined themselves to Mattathias, and appointed him to be their ruler.  And he taught them to fight even on the Sabbath-day, and told them, that unless they would do so, they would become their own enemies, by observing the law so rigorously, for their adversaries would continue to assault them on that day, and if they would not then defend themselves, nothing could prevent their all perishing without fighting.  This speech persuaded them.  And this rule continues among us to this day, that if there be necessity, we may fight on the Sabbath-days.  So Mattathias got a great army about him, and overthrew the altars,

and slew all those that broke the law that he could get in
his power, for many of them were dispersed among the
nations round about for fear of him. He also commanded
that those boys who were not yet circumcised should
be circumcised now, and he drove out of the country those
that were appointed to hinder their circumcision.

§ 3. But when he had ruled one year he fell very ill,
and called for his sons, and set them round about him,
and said, " O my sons, I am going the way of all flesh,
and I commend to you my resolution, and beseech you
not to be negligent in keeping it, but to be mindful of
the wish of him who begat you and brought you up, to
preserve the customs of your country, and to recover your
ancient polity, which is in danger of being upset, and not
to be seduced by those that betray it, either from their own
inclination, or out of necessity, but to be sons worthy of
me, and to be above all force and necessity, and so to dispose your souls, as to be ready, if it shall be necessary, to
die for your laws, reflecting on this, that if God see that
you are so disposed he will not overlook you, but will
greatly value your virtue, and will restore to you again
what you have lost, and will give you back again that
freedom in which you shall live in security, and enjoy your
own customs. Your bodies are mortal and subject to fate,
but they receive a sort of immortality by the remembrance
of the actions they have done. And I would have you so
in love with this immortality, that you may pursue after
glory, and when you have undertaken the greatest things,
may not shrink from losing your lives. I exhort you
especially to agree with one another, and in whatever
point any one of you exceeds another, to yield to him so
far, and so to reap the advantage of every one's own virtues.
Esteem then your brother Simon as your father, because
he is a man of extraordinary prudence, and be governed by
him in the counsels he gives you. Take Maccabæus for the
general of your army, because of his courage and strength,
for he will avenge your nation and repel your enemies.
Conciliate the righteous and religious, and so add to their
power."

§ 4. When Mattathias had thus discoursed to his sons,
and had prayed to God to be their helper, and to restore to

the people their former manner of life, he died soon afterwards and was buried at Modiim,[1] all the people making
great lamentation for him.  And his son Judas called
Maccabæus took upon him the administration of affairs, in
the hundred and forty-sixth year : and by the ready assistance of his brothers and others, drove their enemies out of
the country, and put those of their own country to death
who had transgressed their laws, and purified the land from
all pollution.

## CHAP. VII.

*How Judas overthrew the Forces of Apollonius and Seron,
and killed those Generals; and how, when a little while
afterwards Lysias and Gorgias were beaten, he went up to
Jerusalem and purified the Temple.*

### § 1.

WHEN Apollonius, the general of the army of Samaria,
heard of this, he took his army, and marched against
Judas.   And he met him, and joined battle with him, and
beat him, and slew many of his men, and among them
Apollonius himself the general, whose sword (which he
happened to be wearing) he seized upon and kept for himself ; but he wounded more than he slew, and took a great
deal of spoil from the enemy's camp, and retired.  But when
Seron, who was general of the army of Cœle-Syria, heard
that many had joined themselves to Judas, and that he
had with him an army sufficient for fighting and making
war, he determined to march against him, thinking it
became him to endeavour to punish those that lawlessly
transgressed the king's injunctions.   So he got together
as large an army as he was able, and joined to it the
fugitive and wicked Jews, and marched against Judas,
and advanced as far as Bethhoron,[2] a village of Judæa, and
there pitched his camp.  And there Judas met him, and
intended to offer battle, and when he saw that his soldiers

---

[1] *el-Medieh*, thirteen miles west of *Beitin*, Bethel.  See p. 19, note 1.
[2] *Beit 'Ur el-Foka.*

were loath to fight, because their number was small, and because they wanted food, for they were fasting, he encouraged them by telling them that victory and conquest of enemies was not derived from numbers but from piety towards God; and that they had the plainest proof of this in their forefathers, who by their righteousness and by exerting themselves on behalf of their laws and children, had frequently conquered many ten thousands, for innocence was a mighty force. By this speech he induced his men to despise the multitude of the enemy, and to fall upon Seron. And upon joining battle with him, he routed the Syrians; and as their general fell they all ran away with speed, thinking flight their only chance of safety. And he pursued them to the plain, and slew about eight hundred of the enemy, and the rest escaped to the region which lay near to the sea.

§ 2. When king Antiochus heard of these things, he was very angry at what had happened, and got together all his own army, and many mercenaries whom he took with him from the islands, and made preparations to invade Judæa about the beginning of the spring. But when, upon his mustering his soldiers, he perceived that his treasury was deficient, and that there was a want of money, (for all the taxes had not been paid because of the insurrections of the various nations, and he was so munificent and liberal that his own revenues were not sufficient for him,) he resolved first to go into Persia, and collect the taxes of that country. So he left in command one whose name was Lysias, who was in great repute with him, and governor as far as the bounds of Egypt and Lower Asia from the river Euphrates, with part of the forces and elephants, and charged him to educate his son Antiochus with all possible care until he came back, and to conquer Judæa, and enslave its inhabitants, and utterly destroy Jerusalem, and annihilate the whole nation. And when king Antiochus had given these orders to Lysias, he went into Persia, and in the hundred and forty-seventh year crossed over the Euphrates, and went to the upper satrapies.

§ 3. Upon this Lysias chose Ptolemy (the son of Dorymenes) and Nicanor and Gorgias, very influential men

among the king's friends, and delivered to them forty
thousand foot and seven thousand horse, and sent them
against Judæa. And they came as far as the city Emmaus,[1]
and pitched their camp in the plain. Auxiliaries also
came to them out of Syria and the country round about,
as also many of the fugitive Jews. And besides these came
some merchants to buy those that should be captured
(having fetters with them to bind those that should be
made prisoners), with the silver and gold which they
were to pay for their price. And when Judas saw their
camp, and how numerous the enemies were, he urged his
own soldiers to be of good courage, and exhorted them to
place their hopes of victory in God, and to make supplication to him clothed in sackcloth according to the custom
of their country, and to show their usual habit of supplication in the greatest dangers, and so to prevail with
God to grant them the victory over their enemies. And
he set them in the ancient order of battle used by
their forefathers, under their captains of thousands and
commanders of divisions, and dismissed such as were
newly married, as well as those that had newly gained
possessions, that they might not fight in a cowardly
manner, from an inordinate love of life, in order to enjoy
those blessings. When he had thus marshalled his soldiers,
he encouraged them to fight by the following speech which
he made to them. "Comrades, no other time is more
necessary than the present for courage and contempt of
dangers; for if you now fight manfully you may recover
your liberty, which, as it is a thing for itself agreeable to
all men, so to us it proves much more desirable, by its
affording us the power of worshipping God. Since then
you are in such a case at present, that you must either recover that liberty, and so regain a happy and blessed way
of living, which is that according to our laws and the customs of our country, or submit to the most ignoble sufferings, nor will any seed of your nation remain if you play
the part of cowards in this battle, fight manfully. And
reflecting that you must die though you do not fight, and
believing that besides such glorious rewards as those of the

[1] *'Amwâs.*

liberty of your country, your laws, and your religion, you
shall obtain everlasting glory, prepare yourselves and resolve to be ready to fight with the enemy as soon as it is
day to-morrow morning."

§ 4. This was the speech which Judas made to encourage
his army. And when the enemy sent Gorgias, with five
thousand foot and one thousand horse to surprise Judas by
night, with certain of the fugitive Jews as guides for that
purpose, the son of Mattathias heard of it, and resolved
to fall upon the enemies in their camp, now their forces
were divided. When he had therefore supped in good time,
and had left many fires in his camp, he marched all night
to the enemy who were at Emmaus. Now as Gorgias
found no enemy in their camp, he suspected that they had
retreated and hidden themselves among the mountains,
and resolved to go and seek wherever they were. But
about daybreak Judas appeared to the enemy at Emmaus,
with only three thousand men, and those ill-armed by
reason of their poverty, and though he saw the enemy
very well and skilfully fortified in their camp, he encouraged the Jews, and exhorted them to fight though
with ill-armed bodies, for God had sometimes of old
given such men strength, and that against such as were
more numerous and better armed to boot, in delight at
their great courage. Then he commanded the trumpeters
to sound for the battle, and by thus falling upon the enemy
when they did not expect it, and so alarming and dis-
maying their minds, he slew many of those that resisted,
and went on pursuing the rest as far as Gadara[1] and the
plains of Idumæa[2] and Azotus[3] and Jamnia;[4] and of these
there fell about three thousand. And Judas exhorted his
soldiers not to be too desirous of spoil, for they must still
have a contest and battle with Gorgias and the forces that
were with him: but when they had once overcome them,
then they might securely plunder the camp, because they
were the only enemies remaining, and they expected no
others. And just as he was saying this to his soldiers,
Gorgias' men looked down from a hill at the army which

[1] *Umm Keis.*
[2] The southern portion of the plain of Philistia.
[3] *Esdûd.*                           [4] *Yebnah.*

they had left in their camp, and saw that it was routed, and the camp burnt; for the smoke that arose from it showed them what had happened, even though they were a great way off. When therefore those that were with Gorgias understood that things were in this posture, and perceived that those that were with Judas were ready to fight them, they also were panic-struck, and turned to flight; and now Judas having beaten Gorgias' soldiers without fighting, returned and seized on the spoil. He took a great quantity of gold and silver, and purple and blue raiment, and returned home with joy, singing hymns to God for this success; for this victory contributed not a little to the recovery of their liberty.

§ 5. But Lysias was confounded at the defeat of the army which he had sent out, and the next year he got together sixty thousand chosen foot, and five thousand horse, and invaded Judæa, and went up to the hill-country near Bethsura,[1] a village of Judæa, and pitched his camp there. And Judas met him there with ten thousand men, and when he saw the great number of the enemies, he prayed to God that he would assist him, and joined battle with the advanced guard of the enemy, and beat them, and slew about five thousand of them, and so caused panic in the rest of the army. Lysias indeed observing the great spirit of the Jews, and that they were prepared to die rather than lose their liberty, and being afraid of their desperate valour as real strength, took the rest of his army back with him, and returned to Antioch, where he stayed to enlist foreigners in his service, and made preparations to invade Judæa with a greater army.

§ 6. And now that the generals of Antiochus' armies had been beaten so often, Judas assembled the people together, and told them, that after these many victories which God had given them, they ought to go up to Jerusalem, and purify the temple, and offer the customary sacrifices. And as soon as he with the whole multitude had come to Jerusalem, and found the temple deserted, and its gates burnt down, and weeds growing in the temple on account of its desertion, he and those that were with him

---

[1] *Beit Sûr*, four miles north of Hebron.

began to lament, being quite confounded at the sight of the temple. And he picked out some of his soldiers, and gave them order to fight against the guards that occupied the citadel, until he should have purified the temple. And when he had carefully purged it, he brought in new vessels, as the candlestick, the table of show-bread, and the altar of incense, which were made of gold, and hung up veils at the doors, and added doors. He also demolished the altar, and built a new one of stones that he gathered together, not hewn with iron. And on the five-and-twentieth day of the month Chasleu, which the Macedonians call Apellæus, they lighted the lamps that were on the candlestick, and offered incense upon the altar of incense, and laid loaves upon the table of show-bread, and offered burnt-offerings upon the new altar. Now it so fell out, that these things were done on the very day on which their divine worship had ceased, and been changed to a profane and common use, three years before, for the temple that had been made desolate by Antiochus continued so for three years. This desolation happened to the temple in the hundred and forty-fifth year, on the twenty-fifth day of the month Apellæus, and in the hundred and fifty-third Olympiad: and it was dedicated anew on the same day, the twenty-fifth of the month Apellæus, in the hundred and forty-eighth year, and in the hundred and fifty-fourth Olympiad. And this desolation came to pass according to the prophecy of Daniel, which was given four hundred and eight years before; for he declared that the Macedonians would stop the temple worship.

§ 7. Now Judas celebrated the festival of the restoration of the temple sacrifices for eight days, and omitted no sort of pleasure, but feasted the people upon the very rich and splendid sacrifices, and honoured God, and delighted the people by hymns and psalms. Nay, they were so very glad at the revival of their national customs after a long time of intermission, now that they had unexpectedly regained the freedom of their worship, that they made it a law for their posterity, that they should keep a festival for eight days on account of the restoration of their temple worship. And from that time to this we celebrate this festival, and call it "Lights." I suppose the reason was, because this liberty appeared to us beyond our hopes, and hence the name was given to the festival. Judas also rebuilt the walls round about the city, and reared towers of great height against the incursions of enemies, and set guards therein. He also fortified the city of Bethsura, that it might serve as a citadel against any emergency caused by the enemies.

## CHAP. VIII.

*How Judas subdued the Nations round about; and how Simon beat the People of Tyre and Ptolemais; and how Judas overcame Timotheus, and forced him to flee away, and did many other things, after Joseph and Azarias had been beaten.*

### § 1.

WHEN these things had taken place, the nations round about the Jews were very uneasy at the revival of their power and strength, and rose up and destroyed many of them, gaining advantage over them by laying snares for them, and plotting against them. Judas had perpetual wars with these nations, and endeavoured to restrain them from their incursions, and to prevent the mischiefs they did to the Jews. So he fell upon the Idumæans, the posterity of Esau, at Acrabatene,[1] and slew a great many of them, and took their spoil. He also invested and besieged the sons of Baanus, who had laid ambush for the Jews, and burnt their towers, and slew the men that were on them. After this he marched against the Ammonites, who had a great and a numerous army, of which Timotheus was the commander. And when he had subdued them, he seized on their city Jazor,[2] and took their wives and children captives, and burnt the city, and then returned to Judæa. But when the neighbouring nations heard that he had returned, they mustered together in

---

[1] Probably the same place as the 'ascent of Akrabbim' of Josh. xv. 3.

[2] The Jazor, probably *Khurbet Sâr*, west of *'Ammân*, Philadelphia.

great numbers in the land of Gilead against the Jews
that were on their borders. And they fled to the fortress
of Dathema,[1] and sent to Judas to inform him that Timotheus was endeavouring to take the place where they had
fled. And as their letters were being read, there came
other messengers out of Galilee, who informed him that
the inhabitants of Ptolemais and Tyre and Sidon, and
the strange nations in Galilee, had concentrated their
forces.

§ 2. Then Judas, considering what was best to be
done with relation to the urgency of both these cases,
ordered Simon his brother to take three thousand picked
men, and go to the assistance of the Jews in Galilee, while
he and another of his brothers, Jonathan, marched into
the land of Gilead with eight thousand soldiers. And he
left Joseph (the son of Zacharias) and Azarias over the
rest of the forces: and charged them to guard Judæa very
carefully, and to fight no battles with anyone until his
return. Simon accordingly went into Galilee, and fought
the enemy, and put them to flight, and pursued them to
the gates of Ptolemais, and slew about three thousand of
them, and took the spoil of those that were slain, and
rescued those Jews who had been taken prisoners, and their
baggage, and then returned home.

§ 3. As for Judas Maccabæus and his brother Jonathan,
they crossed over the river Jordan, and when they had
gone three days' journey further they met the Nabatæans,
who came to meet them peaceably, and told them how
affairs within the land of Gilead stood, and how many of
them were in distress, and driven into the garrisons and
cities of Gilead, and exhorted him to make haste to go
against the foreigners, and to endeavour to save his own
countrymen out of their hands. To this Judas hearkened,
and returned into the wilderness, and fell first upon the
inhabitants of Bosorra,[2] and took the city, and beat the inhabitants, and slew all the males and all that were able to
fight, and burnt the city. Nor did he stop even when night
came on, but he pushed on to the garrison where the Jews
happened to be invested, and where Timotheus lay round
the place with his army, and Judas reached the city in the

---

[1] *Remtheh.*          [2] Bosorra, Bozrah, *Busrah.*

morning; and when he found that the enemy were just
making an assault upon the walls, and that some of them
were bringing ladders, by which they might get upon the
walls, and others engines to batter them down, he bade
the trumpeter sound his trumpet, and encouraged his
soldiers cheerfully to undergo dangers for their brethren
and kindred; he also divided his army into three, and fell
upon the rear of the enemies.   And when Timotheus' men
perceived that it was Maccabæus that was upon them, of
whose courage and success in war they had formerly had
sufficient experience, they turned to flight; but Judas followed them close with his army, and slew about eight
thousand of them.   He then turned aside to a city of the
foreigners called Malle, and took it, and slew all the males,
and burnt the city itself.   He then removed from thence,
and overthrew Chasphom,[1] and Bosor,[2] and many other cities
in the land of Gilead.

§ 4. And not long after this, Timotheus got together
a great army, and took others as auxiliaries, and induced some of the Arabians for pay to join him in his
expedition, and went with his army beyond the brook over
against the city of Raphon.[3]   And he exhorted his soldiers,
if it came to a battle with the Jews, to fight courageously,
and to prevent their crossing over the brook: for he told
them beforehand, "if they come over it, we shall be
beaten."   And when Judas heard that Timotheus prepared
himself to fight, he took all his own army, and marched in
haste against the enemy, and when he had crossed over the
brook, he fell upon the enemies, and some of them met
him, whom he slew, and others of them he so terrified, that
he compelled them to throw down their arms and flee;
and some of them escaped, others fled to what was called
the temple at Carnain,[4] in hopes of preserving themselves;
but Judas took the city and slew them, and burnt the
temple, and so contrived several ways of destroying the
enemies.

§ 5. When he had done this and gathered all the Jews

---

[1] The Casphon of 1 Macc. v. 26, not identified.
[2] *Busr el-Hariri*, five miles S.E. of Edrei.
[3] Possibly *Rafeh*.
[4] Ashteroth Karnaim, *Tell 'Asherah*.

in Gilead together, with their children and wives and the
substance that belonged to them, his intention was to bring
them back into Judæa.   And as soon as he was come to a
certain city, whose name was Ephron,[1] that lay upon the
road, (and as it was not possible for him to go any other
way, so he was not willing to go back again,) he sent to the
inhabitants, and desired that they would open their gates,
and permit them to go on their way through the city, for
they had stopped up the gates with stones, and cut off
their passage through it.   But as the inhabitants of
Ephron would not listen to him, he encouraged those that
were with him, and encompassed the city round, and
besieged it, and lying round it day and night took the city,
and slew every male in it, and burnt it all down, and so
obtained a way through it ; and the multitude of those that
were slain was so great, that they went over their dead
bodies.   They then crossed over the Jordan, and arrived at
the great plain, situate over against which is the city of
Bethshan,[2] which is called by the Greeks Scythopolis.[3]   And
marching on from thence, they came into Judæa, singing
psalms and hymns as they went, and indulging such tokens
of mirth as are usual in triumphs.   They also offered
thank-offerings, both for their success, and the preservation of their army, for not one of the Jews was slain in
these battles.

§ 6. But as to Joseph (the son of Zacharias) and Azarias,
whom Judas left in command of the rest of the forces at
the time when Simon was in Galilee fighting against the
people of Ptolemais, and Judas himself and his brother
Jonathan were in the land of Gilead, they also wished to
get the glory of being fine generals, so they took the army
that was under their command, and went to Jamnia.
There Gorgias, the general at Jamnia,[4] met them, and upon
joining battle with him, they lost two thousand of their
army, and fled away, and were pursued to the very borders

---

[1] Not identified.                                          [2] *Beisân.*
[3] The reason why Bethshan was called ' Scythopolis,' is well known
from Herodotus, Book i. ch. 105, and Syncellus, p. 214, that the Scythians,
when they overran Asia, in the days of Josiah, seized on this city, and
kept it as long as they continued in Asia, from which time it obtained
the name of ' Scythopolis,' or the ' city of the Scythians.'—W.
[4] *Yebnah.*

of Judæa. And this reverse befell them from their disobedience to the injunction Judas had given them, not to
fight with anyone before his return. For besides the rest
of Judas' sagacious counsels, one may well admire this
concerning the reverse that befell the forces commanded by
Joseph and Azarias, which he understood would happen, if
they broke any of the injunctions he had given them. But
Judas and his brothers did not leave off fighting with the
Idumæans, but pressed them hard on all sides, and took
from them the city of Hebron, and demolished all its fortifications, and set all its towers on fire, and ravaged the
country of the foreigners, and took the city of Marissa,[1]
They went also to Azotus,[2] and captured it, and laid it
waste, and took away a great deal of the spoil and prey
that were in it, and returned to Judæa.

## CHAP. IX.

*The Death of Antiochus Epiphanes. How Antiochus Eupator*
*fought against Judas, and besieged him in the Temple, and*
*afterwards made Peace with him and departed. Of*
*Alcimus and Onias.*

### § 1.

ABOUT this time king Antiochus, as he was going
through his upper provinces, heard that there was a
very rich city in Persia, called Elymais,[3] and a very
rich temple of Artemis therein, full of all sorts of votive
offerings, as also weapons and breastplates, which, he found
upon inquiry, had been left there by Alexander, the son
of Philip, king of Macedon. And being incited by this
news, he set out for Elymais, and assaulted it, and besieged
it. But as those that were in it were not terrified at his
assault, nor at his siege, but opposed him very courageously,
he was baffled in his hope, for they drove him away from
the city, and went out and pursued after him, insomuch

---

[1] Mareshah of Josh. xv. 44. *Kh. Mer'ash*, near *Beit Jibrin*, Eleu-
theropolis.

[2] *Esdûd.*

[3] There was no town called Elymais, possibly Ecbatana is intended.

that he fled away as far as Babylon, and lost many of his army.  And when he was grieving for this disappointment, some persons told him of the defeat of his commanders whom he had left behind to fight with the Jews, and what strength the Jews had already got.  When the concern about these affairs was added to the former, he was confounded, and from the anxiety he was in fell into an illness which lasted a great while, and his pains increased upon him, so at length he perceived that he should die, and called his friends to him, and told them, that his illness was severe, and confessed also that this calamity was sent upon him for the miseries he had brought upon the Jewish nation, in plundering their temple, and despising their god : and when he had said this, he gave up the ghost.  So one may wonder at Polybius of Megalopolis, though otherwise a good man, saying that " Antiochus died because he purposed to plunder the temple of Artemis in Persia," for the purposing to do a thing, and not actually doing it, is not worthy of punishment.  But if Polybius could think that Antiochus lost his life on that account, it is much more probable that the king died on account of his sacrilegious plundering of the temple at Jerusalem.  But I shall not contend about this matter with those who think that the cause assigned by Polybius of Megalopolis is nearer the truth than that assigned by us.

§ 2.  However this may be, Antiochus, before he died, called for Philip, who was one of his companions, and made him the regent of his kingdom, and gave him his diadem and royal robes and ring, and charged him to carry them and deliver them to his son Antiochus, and desired him to take care of his education, and to preserve the kingdom for him.  Antiochus died in the hundred and forty and ninth year : and Lysias declared his death to the multitude, and appointed his son Antiochus to be king, (for he had the care of him,) and called him Eupator.[1]

§ 3.  At this time the garrison in the citadel at Jerusalem and the Jewish fugitives did a great deal of harm to the Jews : for the soldiers in the garrison used to sally out upon the sudden, and kill such as were going up to the

---

[1] Antiochus V., Eupator, succeeded his father, whilst still a child, in 164 B.C.

temple to offer their sacrifices, for this citadel commanded
the temple.   When this had often happened, Judas resolved
to destroy that garrison, so he got all the people together,
and vigorously besieged those that were in the citadel.
This was the hundred and fiftieth year of the dominion of
the Seleucidæ.   So he made engines of war, and threw up
earthworks, and tried hard to take the citadel : but not a
few of the fugitives who were in the place went out by
night into the country, and got together some other wicked
men like themselves, and went to Antiochus the king, and
begged of him, that he would not suffer them to continue in
the great hardships they underwent from those of their own
nation, and that on his father's account, because they had
left the religious worship of their fathers, and adopted that
which he had commanded them to follow.   They said also
that there was danger that the citadel, and those appointed to garrison it by the king, would be taken by
Judas and those that were with him, unless he sent them
succours.   When Antiochus, who was but a boy, heard
this, he was angry, and sent for his captains and friends,
and ordered that they should get an army of mercenaries
together, and such men also from his own kingdom as
were of an age fit for war.   And an army was collected
together of about a hundred thousand foot, and twenty
thousand horse, and thirty-two elephants.

§ 4. So the king took this army, and marched from
Antioch with Lysias, who had the command of the whole
force, and came to Idumæa, and thence went up to Bethsura,[1] a city that was strong and not to be taken without
great difficulty, and sat down before the city, and besieged
it.   And as the inhabitants of Bethsura [1] courageously opposed him, and sallied out upon him, and burnt his engines
of war, a great deal of time was spent in the siege.   But
when Judas heard of the king's coming, he raised the siege
of the citadel, and met the king, and pitched his camp at a
certain pass, at a place called Bethzachariah,[2] at the distance of seventy furlongs from the enemy ; and the king
soon drew his forces away from Bethsura, and brought
them to that pass.   And as soon as it was day, he put his
men in battle array, and made his elephants follow one

---

[1] *Beit Súr.*            [2] *Beit Skária,* nine miles north of *Beit Súr.*

another through the narrow pass, for they could not go
abreast. Now round every elephant there were a thousand
foot, and five hundred horse ; and the elephants had high
towers and archers on their backs. And he made the
rest of his army go up the mountains on each side, and
put his friends in the van, and ordered the army to shout
aloud, and so attacked the enemy. He also exposed to
sight their golden and brazen shields, so that a glorious
splendour emanated from them ; and when the army
shouted, the mountains echoed again. When Judas saw
this, he was not terrified, but received the enemy with
great courage, and slew about six hundred of the front
ranks. And when his brother Eleazar, whom they called
Auran, saw the tallest of the elephants armed with royal
breastplates, supposing that the king was upon it, he
attacked it with great bravery. He also slew many of
those that were round the elephant, and scattered the rest,
and then went under the belly of the elephant, and smote
it, and slew it, but the elephant fell upon Eleazar, and by
its weight crushed him to death. And thus did Eleazar
come to his end, when he had first courageously destroyed
many of his enemies.

§ 5. Then Judas, seeing the strength of the enemy, retired to Jerusalem, and prepared to endure a siege. As
for Antiochus, he sent part of his army to Bethsura to besiege it, and with the rest of his army marched to Jerusalem. And the inhabitants of Bethsura were terrified at
his strength, and seeing that their provisions grew scarce,
they delivered themselves up on the security of oaths, that
they should suffer no harsh treatment from the king. And
when Antiochus had thus taken the city, he did them no
other harm than sending them out unarmed. He also
placed a garrison of his own in the city. But as for
the temple of Jerusalem, he besieged it a long time, for
those within bravely defended it, for whatever engines
the king set against them, they counter-contrived other
engines. But at last their provisions failed them, the
fruits of the ground they had laid up were spent, and
the land not being tilled that year continued unsown,
because it was the seventh year, on which, by our laws, we
were obliged to let it lie uncultivated. And so many of

the besieged deserted for want of necessaries, that only a few were left in the temple.

§ 6. Such happened to be the circumstances of those who were besieged in the temple. But when Lysias, the general of the army, and Antiochus the king, were informed that Philip was marching upon them from Persia, and was endeavouring to get the management of public affairs to himself, they determined to raise the siege, and march against Philip, yet did they resolve not to let this be known to the soldiers nor to the officers, but the king commanded Lysias to speak openly to the soldiers and the officers, without saying a word about the affair of Philip, and to intimate to them, that the siege would be very long, that the place was very strong, that they were already short of provisions, that many affairs of the kingdom wanted regulation, and that it was much better to make a league with the besieged, and to become friends of the whole nation, by permitting them to observe the laws of their fathers, since they broke out into this war only because they were deprived of them, and to return home. When Lysias had spoken thus to them, both the army and officers were pleased with the resolution.

§ 7. So the king sent to Judas, and to those that were besieged with him, and promised to give them peace, and to permit them to make use of and live according to the laws of their fathers. And they gladly received his proposals, and when they had taken security upon oath for their performance, they evacuated the temple. But when Antiochus went into it, and saw how strong the place was, he broke his oaths, and ordered his army that was there to raze the walls to the ground, and when he had done so he returned to Antioch: he also took with him Onias the high priest, who was also called Menelaus: for Lysias advised the king to slay Menelaus, if he would have the Jews be quiet and cause him no further disturbance, for he had been the origin of all the mischief by persuading his father to compel the Jews to leave the religion of their fathers: so the king sent Menelaus to Berœa,[1] a city in Syria, and there had him put to death, when he had been high priest ten years. He had been a wicked and im-

---

[1] *Aleppo.*

pious man, and, in order to get the government to himself, had compelled his nation to transgress their laws. After the death of Menelaus, Alcimus, who was also called Jacimus, was made high priest. But when king Antiochus found that Philip had already usurped the government, he made war against him, and beat him, and took him and slew him. Now, as to Onias, the son of the high priest, who, as I before said, was left a child when his father died, when he saw that the king had slain his uncle Menelaus, and given the high priesthood to Alcimus, who was not of the stock of the high priests, being induced by Lysias to transfer that dignity from his family to another house, he fled to Ptolemy king of Egypt; [1] and being held in great esteem by him and his wife Cleopatra, he asked and obtained a place in the district of Heliopolis, [2] wherein he built a temple like that at Jerusalem. But of these things I shall hereafter give an account in a place more proper for it.

## CHAP. X.

*How Bacchides, the General of Demetrius' Army, made an Expedition against Judæa, and returned without success; and how Nicanor was sent a little afterwards against Judas, and perished, together with his Army; as also concerning the Death of Alcimus, and the Succession of Judas.*

### § 1.

ABOUT the same time, Demetrius, [3] the son of Seleucus, fled away from Rome, and took Tripolis, a city of Syria, and set the diadem on his own head. He also gathered together certain mercenary soldiers, and entered the kingdom, and was joyfully received by all, who delivered themselves up to him. And when they had taken

---

[1] Ptolemy V., Epiphanes, 205-181 B.C. His wife was a daughter of Antiochus the Great.

[2] To the N.E. of Cairo. Possibly *Tell el-Yehûdi*.

[3] Demetrius I., Soter, son of Seleucus Philopator, and grandson of Antiochus the Great, was the rightful heir to the throne which had been usurped by Antiochus Epiphanes. He reigned 162-150 B.C.

Antiochus, the king, and Lysias, they brought them to
him alive; both of whom were immediately put to death
by the command of Demetrius, when Antiochus had reigned
two years, as I have already related elsewhere. And now
many of the wicked Jewish fugitives came together to him,
and with them Alcimus the high priest, who accused the
whole nation, and particularly Judas and his brothers, and
said, that they had slain all his friends, and that those in
the kingdom that were of his party, and waited for his
return, were put to death by them; and that these men
had ejected them out of their own country, and caused
them to be sojourners in a foreign land; and they desired
that he would send one of his own friends, and ascertain
through him what mischief Judas' party had done.

§ 2. At this Demetrius was very angry, and sent Bacchides, a friend of Antiochus Epiphanes, an able man, and
one that had been intrusted with all Mesopotamia, and
gave him an army, and committed Alcimus the high priest
to his care, and ordered him to slay Judas and those that
were with him. So Bacchides set out from Antioch with
his army, and when he was come into Judæa, he sent to
Judas and his brothers to treat on friendship and peace,
for he had a mind to take him by treachery. But Judas
did not believe in him, for he saw that he came with an
army such as men do not bring when they come to make
peace, but only when they come to make war. However,
some of the people crediting what Bacchides caused to be
proclaimed, and supposing they should undergo no great
harm from Alcimus, who was their countryman, went over
to them, and when they had received oaths from both
of them, that neither they themselves, nor those of the
same views, should come to any harm, they trusted themselves with them. But Bacchides troubled not himself
about the oaths he had taken, but slew threescore of them,
although by not keeping his faith with those that first went
over to him he deterred all the rest who intended to go over
to him from doing so. And when he was gone out of Jerusalem, and was at the village called Bethzetho,[1] he sent and
arrested many of the deserters, and some of the people

---

[1] The Bezeth of 1 Macc. vii. 19. Either the Mount of Olives or
Bezetha.

also, and slew them all, and enjoined all that lived in the country to submit to Alcimus, whom he left there, with some part of the army, that he might be able to keep the country in obedience, and returned to Antioch to king Demetrius.

§ 3. Then Alcimus wishing to have his power more firmly assured, and perceiving, that if he could make the people his friends, he would govern with greater security, ingratiated himself with all by kind words, and carried himself to everybody in an agreeable and pleasant manner, by which means he soon got a great body of men and an army about him, although the greater part of them were wicked and deserters. With these, whom he used as his servants and soldiers, he went all over the country, and slew all that he could find of Judas' party. And when Judas saw that Alcimus was already become great, and had destroyed many of the good and holy men of the nation, he also went all over the country, and destroyed those that were of the other's party. And when Alcimus saw that he was not able to oppose Judas, but was unequal to him in strength, he resolved to apply to king Demetrius for assistance ; so he went to Antioch, and exasperated him against Judas, accusing him of having suffered a good deal at his hands, and saying that he would do more mischief unless he were prevented, and brought to punishment, by a powerful force being sent against him.

§ 4. Then Demetrius, being already of opinion that it would be a thing injurious to his own interest to overlook Judas, now he was become so great, sent against him Nicanor, the most affectionate and faithful of all his friends (for it was he who fled away with him from the city of Rome), and also gave him as large a force as he thought sufficient to conquer Judas, and bade him not spare the nation at all. Now when Nicanor was come to Jerusalem, he resolved not to fight Judas immediately, but judged it better to get him into his power by treachery, so he sent him a message of peace, and said there was no necessity for them to fight and hazard themselves, and he would pledge him his oath that he would do him no harm, for he only came with some friends, in order to let him know what king Demetrius' intentions were, and what his views about

their nation. When Nicanor delivered this message,
Judas and his brothers listened to him, suspecting no
deceit, and gave him assurances of friendship, and received
Nicanor and his army. But while he was greeting Judas,
and they were talking together, he gave a certain signal
to his soldiers to seize Judas; but he perceived the
treachery, and ran back to his own soldiers and fled away
with them. And upon this discovery of his purpose, and the
trap laid for Judas, Nicanor determined to make open war
upon him, and gathered his army together, and made preparations for fighting him, and on joining battle with him
at a certain village called Capharsalama,[1] he beat him, and
forced him to flee to the citadel which was in Jerusalem.

§ 5. And when Nicanor came down from the citadel to
the temple, some of the priests and elders met him and
saluted him; and showed him the sacrifices which they
said they were offering to God for the king: upon
which he blasphemed, and threatened, unless the people
delivered up Judas to him, to pull down the temple
on his return. And when he had thus threatened, he
departed from Jerusalem, but the priests fell into tears
for grief at what he said, and besought God to deliver
them from their enemies. Now Nicanor, when he was
gone from Jerusalem, and was at a certain village called
Bethhoron,[2] pitched his camp there, another army from
Syria having joined him: and Judas pitched his camp at
Adasa,[3] another village thirty furlongs from Bethhoron,
having with him no more than a thousand soldiers. And
when he had encouraged them not to be dismayed at the
multitude of their enemies, nor to regard how many they
were against whom they were going to fight, but to consider who they themselves were, and for what rewards
they hazarded themselves, and to attack the enemy courageously, he led them out to fight, and joining battle
with Nicanor, overcame the enemy after a severe fight,
and slew many of them; and at last Nicanor himself fell
fighting gloriously. Upon his fall his army did not stay,
but having lost their general turned to flight and threw
down their arms; and Judas pursued them, and slew

[1] Not identified.                    [2] *Beit 'Ur.*
[3] *Kh. 'Adaseh,* eight miles south of *Jufna,* Gophna.

them ; and gave notice to the neighbouring villages by the sound of the trumpets that he had conquered the enemy. And when the inhabitants heard the trumpets they put on their armour quickly, and met their enemies as they were running away, and slew them, insomuch that not one of them escaped out of this battle, and there were nine thousand of them. This victory happened to fall on the thirteenth day of that month, which is by the Jews called Adar, and by the Macedonians Dystrus ; and the Jews celebrate this victory every year thereon, and esteem the day as a festival. After this the Jewish nation was for a whi'e free from wars, and enjoyed peace, but afterwards it returned to its former state of wars and perils.

§ 6. And now, as the high priest Alcimus meant to pull down the wall of the sanctuary, which had been there of old time and had been built by the holy prophets, he was smitten suddenly by God, and fell down speechless upon the ground, and after undergoing torments for several days, he at length died, when he had been high priest four years. And when he was dead, the people bestowed the high priesthood on Judas, who hearing of the power of the Romans, and that they had conquered in war Galatia and Iberia and Carthage in Libya, and that besides these they had subdued Greece, and the kings Perseus and Philip and Antiochus the Great, resolved to enter into a league of friendship with them. He therefore sent to Rome two of his friends, Eupolemus the son of John, and Jason the son of Eleazar, and by them begged the Romans to assist them and be their friends, and to write to Demetrius not to fight against the Jews. And the senate received the ambassadors that came from Judas to Rome, and discussed with them the errand on which they came, and granted them a league of assistance. They also made a decree concerning it, and sent a copy of it into Judæa. It was also laid up in the Capitol, and engraven on tables of brass. The decree itself was as follows. "The decree of the senate concerning a league of assistance and friendship with the nation of the Jews. It shall not be lawful for any that are subject to the Romans to make war against the nation of the Jews, nor to assist those that do so either with corn or ships or money. And if any people attack the Jews, the Romans

shall assist them to the utmost of their power. Again, if
any people attack the Romans, the Jews shall assist them.
And if the Jews have a mind to add anything to, or with-
draw anything from, this league of assistance, it shall be
done with the common consent of the people of the Romans.
And whatever addition shall thus be made shall be of force."
This decree was written by Eupolemus the son of John, and
by Jason the son of Eleazar, when Judas was high priest of
the nation, and his brother Simon general of the army.
And thus came about the first league between the Romans
and the Jews.

## CHAP. XI.

*How Bacchides was again sent out against Judas; and how*
*Judas fell fighting courageously.*

### § 1.

NOW when Demetrius was informed of the death of
Nicanor, and of the destruction of the army that was
with him, he sent Bacchides again with an army into
Judæa, who set out from Antioch, and came into Judæa,
and pitched his camp at Arbela,[1] a city of Galilee, and
having besieged and taken those that were in caves there [2]
(for many of the people had fled to them), he removed
from thence and made all the haste he could to Jerusalem. And when he learned that Judas had pitched his
camp at a certain village whose name was Bethzetho,[3] he
hurried up against him his army consisting of twenty thousand foot and two thousand horse. Now Judas had no more
soldiers than one thousand.[4] When these saw the number of
Bacchides' men they were afraid, and left their camp, and

---

[1] *Irbid*, west of the Sea of Galilee.

[2] The caves in the *Wâdy Hammâm*, below *Irbid*.

[3] In 1 Macc. ix. 4, Berea, probably *Bireh*, north of Jerusalem.

[4] That Josephus' copy had here not 1,000 but 3,000, with 1 Macc.
ix. 5, is very plain, because though the main part ran away at first even
in Josephus, as well as in 1 Macc. ix. 6, yet, as there, so here, 800
are said to have remained with Judas, which would be absurd, if the
whole number had been no more than 1,000.—W.

fled away, all but eight hundred. Now though Judas was deserted by his own soldiers, and the enemy pressed him hard and gave him no time to gather his army together, he was disposed to fight with Bacchides' army, though he had but eight hundred men with him; so he exhorted these men to undergo the danger courageously, and encouraged them to attack the enemy. And when they said they were not able to fight so great an army, and advised that they should retire now and save themselves, and that when he had got all his men together, he should then fall upon the enemy afterwards, his answer was this: "Let not the sun ever see such a thing as that I should show my back to the enemy; and even though this be the time that will bring me to my end, and I must die in this battle, I will rather stand to it courageously, and bear whatever comes, than by now running away bring reproach upon my former exploits, and tarnish their glory." This was the speech he made to those who remained with him, whereby he encouraged them to attack the enemy.

§ 2. Then Bacchides led his army out of their camp, and put them in battle array. He set the horse on both the wings, and posted the light soldiers and archers in front of the whole line, and stationed himself on the right wing. And when he had thus put his army in order of battle, and was going to engage with the enemy, he commanded the trumpeter to give a signal of battle, and the army to make a shout and to fall on the enemy. And when Judas had done the same, he joined battle with them, and both sides fought valiantly, and the battle continued till sunset, when Judas noticed that Bacchides and the strongest part of the army was on the right wing, so he took the most courageous men with him, and ran upon that part of the army, and fell upon those that were there, and broke their ranks, wedging himself into the middle, and forced them to run away, and pursued them as far as a mountain called Aza.[1] But when those on the left wing saw that the right wing was routed, they hemmed Judas in and pursued him, and came behind him, and got him in the middle of

[1] The 'Mount Azotus' of 1 Macc. ix. 15-18. Apparently the hill of *Bîr ez-Zeit*, near *Jufna*, Gophna.

their army; so not being able to fly, but surrounded by enemies, he stood still, and he and those that were with him fought desperately, and when he had slain a great many of those that came against him, he was at last wounded and fell, and gave up the ghost, and died in a way worthy of his former famous actions. When Judas had fallen, those that were with him had no one whom they could look to, so when they saw themselves deprived of such a general, they fled. But Simon and Jonathan, Judas' brothers, received his dead body from the enemy under a truce, and carried it to the village of Modiim, where their father had been buried, and there they buried him, and the people lamented for him many days, and performed the usual solemn funeral rites. And this was the end of Judas, a noble man and great warrior, and mindful of the commands of his father Mattathias, who endured all things, both in doing and suffering, for the liberty of his countrymen. And his character being so excellent, he left behind him a glorious reputation and memory by gaining freedom for his nation, and delivering them from slavery under the Macedonians. And when he had retained the high-priesthood three years, he died.

# BOOK XIII.

FROM THE DEATH OF JUDAS MACCABÆUS TO THE DEATH OF QUEEN ALEXANDRIA.

## CHAP. I.

*How Jonathan took the Government after his brother Judas, and with his brother Simon waged War against Bacchides.*

### § 1.

HOW the nation of the Jews recovered their freedom when they had been brought into slavery by the Macedonians, and how many and great struggles their general

Judas went through, till he was slain fighting for them, has been related in the previous book; but after he wes dead, all the wicked, and those that transgressed the laws of their forefathers, sprung up again in Judæa, and flourished, and distressed them on every side. A famine also assisted their wickedness and afflicted the country, till not a few, by reason of their want of necessaries, and because they were not able to bear up against the miseries that both the famine and their enemies brought upon them, deserted to the Macedonians. And now Bacchides gathered those Jews together who had apostatized from the way of living of their forefathers, and chose to live like other nations, and committed the care of the country to them. And they arrested the friends of Judas, and those of party, and delivered them up to Bacchides, who, when he had first tortured and tormented them at his pleasure, by that means at last killed them. And when this misery of the Jews had become so great, that they had never experienced the like since their return from Babylon, those that remained of the companions of Judas, seeing the nation perishing miserably, went to his brother Jonathan, and begged that he would imitate his brother and the care which he took of his countrymen, for whose general liberty he died, and that he would not let the nation be without a leader, especially in its present ruin. And when Jonathan said that he was ready to die for them, as he was indeed esteemed no way inferior to his brother, he was appointed to be the general of the Jewish army.

§ 2. When Bacchides heard this, and was afraid that Jonathan might be very troublesome to the king and to the Macedonians, as Judas had been before, he sought to slay him by treachery; but this intention of his was not unknown to Jonathan, nor to his brother Simon: and when these two were apprised of it, they took all their companions, and hastily fled into the wilderness which was nearest to the city, and when they were come to a lake called Asphar,[1] they abode there. But when Bacchides heard that they had shifted their quarters, and were in

---

[1] Probably one of the small reservoirs for collecting rain water in the desert. Xenophon (*Anab.* iv. 2, § 22) uses λάκκος for the subterranean chambers in which he stored his wine.

that place, he marched against them with all his forces,
and pitching his camp beyond the Jordan, recruited his
army. And when Jonathan knew that Bacchides was
coming upon him, he sent his brother John, who was also
called Gaddis, to the Nabatæan Arabs, that he might
deposit his baggage with them until the battle with Bacchides should be over, for they were the Jews' friends.
But the sons of Amaræus laid an ambush for John from
the city of Medaba,[1] as he was on his journey to the Nabatæans, and seized upon him, and upon those that were
with him, and plundered all that they had with them, and
slew John and all his companions. However, they were
adequately punished for what they now did by John's
brothers, as I shall relate presently.

§ 3. Now when Bacchides learnt that Jonathan had
pitched his camp among the marshes of the Jordan, he
watched for the Sabbath-day, and then attacked him, supposing that he would not fight on that day because of the
law. But Jonathan exhorted his companions to fight, and
told them that their lives were at stake, since they were
hemmed in by the river and by their enemies, and had no
way of escape, for their enemies pressed upon them in
front, and the river was behind them. And after he had
prayed to God to give them the victory, he joined battle
with the enemy, of whom he overthrew many; and as he
saw Bacchides coming up boldly to him, he stretched out
his right hand to smite him, but he foreseeing and avoiding the stroke, Jonathan with his companions leaped into
the river and swam across it, and by that means escaped
beyond the Jordan, as the enemy did not pursue them
over that river: but Bacchides returned at once to the
citadel at Jerusalem, having lost about two thousand of
his army. He also fortified many of the cities of Judæa,
whose walls had been demolished, as Jericho, and Emmaus,[2]
and Bethoron,[3] and Bethel,[4] and Timnath,[5] and Pharatho,[6]
and Tekoa,[7] and Gazara.[8] And he built towers in every one

---

[1] *Medeba*, east of Jordan, and four miles S.E. of *Hesbân*, Heshbon.
[2] Emmaus, Nicopolis, *'Amwâs*.          [3] *Beit 'Ur el-Foka*.
[4] *Beitîn*.                        [5] *Tibnah*.
[6] *Fer'ata*, about six miles W. of *Nâblus*, Shechem.    [7] *Kh. Tekû'a*.
[8] Gezer, *Tell Jezar*, four miles W. of *Amwâs*.

of those cities, and encompassed them with strong and high walls, and put garrisons into them, that they might issue out of them and do mischief to the Jews. He also fortified the citadel at Jerusalem more than all the rest. Moreover, he took the sons of the principal Jews as hostages, and shut them up in the citadel, and in that manner guarded them.

§ 4. About the same time a person came to Jonathan and his brother Simon, and told them that the sons of Amaraeus were celebrating a marriage, and bringing the bride, who was the daughter of one of the illustrious men among the Arabians, from the city of Gabatha,[1] and that the damsel was to be conducted with pomp and splendour. So Jonathan and Simon, thinking that a most favourable opportunity had presented itself for avenging the death of their brother John, and that they had forces sufficient to take satisfaction from them for his death, marched to Medaba, and lay in wait among the mountains for the coming of their enemies. And as soon as they saw them conducting the virgin and her bridegroom, and a great company of friends with them such as was to be expected at a wedding, they sallied out of their ambush and slew them all, and took their ornaments, and all the prey that then followed them, and so returned, after taking this satisfaction for their brother John from the sons of Amaraeus, for as well as those sons themselves, their friends and wives and children that followed them perished, being in all about four hundred.

§ 5. Then Simon and Jonathan returned to the marshes of the Jordan, and there abode. And Bacchides, when he had secured all Judaea with his garrisons, returned to the king: and now the affairs of Judaea were quiet for two years. But when the deserters and the wicked saw that Jonathan and those that were with him lived in the country very quietly because of the peace, they sent to king Demetrius, and besought him to send Bacchides to seize upon Jonathan, which they showed could be done without any trouble, for in one night, if they fell upon them before they were aware, they might slay them all.

---

[1] Possibly *Jeb'a*.

So the king sent Bacchides, who, when he was come into Judæa, wrote to all his friends, both Jews and allies, to seize upon Jonathan, and bring him to him; but when, upon all their endeavours, they were not able to seize upon Jonathan, for he was aware of the snares laid for him, and on his guard against them, Bacchides was angry at these deserters, as having imposed upon him and the king, and took and slew fifty of their leaders. Whereupon Jonathan, with his brother and those that were with him, retired to Bethalaga,[1] a village that lay in the wilderness, from fear of Bacchides. He also built towers, and encompassed it with walls, so that he should be safely guarded. Upon hearing this Bacchides led out his army, and took his Jewish allies besides, and marched against Jonathan, and made an assault upon his fortifications, and besieged him many days. But Jonathan did not abate his courage at the energy Bacchides displayed in the siege, but courageously opposed him, and leaving his brother Simon in the city to fight with Bacchides, he went privately out himself into the country, and got together a great body of men of his own party, and fell upon Bacchides' camp in the night-time, and destroyed a great many of them. His brother Simon also knew of his falling upon them, because he perceived that the enemies were slain by him, so he too sallied out upon them, and burnt the engines which the Macedonians used in the siege, and made a great slaughter of them. And when Bacchides saw himself intercepted by the enemies, some of them before and some behind him, he fell into dejection and trouble of mind, being confounded at the unexpected ill success of the siege. However, he vented his displeasure at this *contretemps* upon those deserters who got him sent by the king, as having deluded him; and wished to raise the siege in a dignified manner, if it were possible for him to do so, and then to return home.

§ 6. When Jonathan heard of his intention, he sent ambassadors to him, to propose friendship and mutual alliance, and that they should restore the captives taken on both sides. Bacchides thought this a dignified way of

---

[1] In 1 Macc. ix. 62, Beth-basi, apparently Beth-Hoglah, *'Ain Hajlah*, near the north end of the Dead Sea.

retiring home, and made a league of friendship with Jonathan, and they swore that they would not any more make war against one another. Accordingly they exchanged prisoners, and he returned to Antioch to the king, and after this departure never invaded Judæa again. Then Jonathan, having obtained this quiet state of things, went and lived in the city of Michmash,[1] and there governed the people, and punished the wicked and ungodly, and so purged the nation of them.


## CHAP. II.

*How Alexander, warring with Demetrius, granted Jonathan many Favours, and appointed him to be High Priest, and persuaded him to assist him, although Demetrius promised him greater Favours on the other side. Concerning the Death of Demetrius.*

### § 1.

NOW in the hundred and sixtieth year it so fell out that Alexander,[2] the son of Antiochus Epiphanes, went up into Syria and took Ptolemais,[3] the soldiers within having betrayed it to him, for they were vexed with Demetrius on account of his haughtiness and difficulty of access; for he used to shut himself up in a palace of his that had four towers, which he had built himself not far from Antioch, and would admit nobody. He was also slothful and negligent about public affairs, whereby the hatred of his subjects was the more kindled against him, as I have already related elsewhere. But when Demetrius heard that Alexander was in Ptolemais, he took his whole army and led it against him: he also sent ambassadors to Jonathan, to propose mutual alliance and friendship, for he resolved to be beforehand with Alexander, lest he should treat with Jonathan first, and gain assistance from him: and this he did from the fear he had that Jonathan would remember how ill he Demetrius had formerly treated him,

---

[1] *Mukhmâs.*
[2] Alexander Balas claimed the throne in 152 B.C.
[3] *St. Jean d'Acre,* '*Akka.*

and would join Alexander in the war against him. He therefore gave orders that Jonathan should be allowed to raise an army, and should get armour made, and should receive back those Jewish hostages whom Bacchides had shut up in the citadel at Jerusalem. When this good fortune had befallen Jonathan by the concession of Demetrius, he went to Jerusalem, and read the king's letter in the audience of the people and of those that kept the citadel. When this was read, those wicked men and deserters who were in the citadel were greatly afraid, on the king's permission to Jonathan to raise an army and to receive back the hostages. And he delivered every one of them up to their parents. And thus did Jonathan make his abode at Jerusalem, renewing the city to a better state, and arranging everything as he pleased, and he gave orders that the walls of the city should be built with square stones, that it might be more secure against enemies. And when those that kept the garrisons that were in Judæa saw this, they all left them, and fled to Antioch, except those that were in the city of Bethsura, and those that were in the citadel of Jerusalem, for most of these were of the wicked Jews and deserters, and so did not deliver up their garrisons.

§ 2. When Alexander knew what promises Demetrius had made Jonathan, and also knew his courage and what great things he had done when he fought against the Macedonians, and also what hardships he had undergone at the hands of Demetrius and Bacchides the general of Demetrius's army, he told his friends that he could not at the present conjuncture find any one that could afford him better assistance than Jonathan, who was not only courageous against his enemies, but also had a particular hatred against Demetrius, as having both suffered many injuries from him, and done many injuries to him. If therefore they were of opinion that they should make him their friend against Demetrius, nothing was more for their advantage now than to invite him to assist them. It being therefore determined by him and his friends to send to Jonathan, he wrote to him the following letter. "King Alexander to his brother Jonathan greeting. We have long ago heard of thy courage and thy fidelity, and for that reason have sent to thee, to make with thee a league of friendship and mutual alliance. We therefore appoint thee this day high priest of the Jews, and order that thou art to be called my friend. I have also sent thee, as presents, a purple robe and a golden crown, and beg, now thou art honoured by us, that thou wilt reciprocate our sentiments."

§ 3. When Jonathan had received this letter, he put on the high priest's robe at the time of the feast of Tabernacles,[1] four years after the death of his brother Judas, for since that time no high priest had been made. And he raised a large force, and had a quantity of arms made. This greatly grieved Demetrius when he heard of it, and made him blame himself for his tardiness in not anticipating Alexander in getting the good-will of Jonathan, and giving him opportunity to do so. However, he also himself wrote a letter to Jonathan and to the people, the contents whereof were as follows. "King Demetrius to Jonathan and to the nation of the Jews greeting. Since you have preserved your friendship for us, and though you have been tempted by my enemies, have not joined yourselves to them, I not only commend you for this your fidelity, but also exhort you to continue in the same, for which you shall be repaid, and receive rewards and favours from us. For I will free you from most of the tribute and taxes which you formerly paid to the kings my predecessors and to myself; and I do now set you free from those tributes which you have ever paid; and besides, I forgive you the tax upon salt, and the value of the crowns which you used to offer to me ;[2] and instead of the third part of

---

[1] Since Jonathan plainly did not put on the pontifical robes till seven or eight years after the death of his brother Judas, or not till the feast of Tabernacles in the 160th year of the Selucidæ, 1 Maccab. x. 21, Petitus's emendation seems here to deserve consideration, who, instead of four years after the death of his brother Judas, would have us read eight years after the death of his brother Judas. This would tolerably well agree with the date of the Maccabees, and with Josephus's own exact chronology at the end of the twentieth book of the Antiquities, which the present text cannot be made to do.—W.

[2] Take Grotius's note here : "The Jews (says he) were wont to present crowns to the kings [of Syria;] afterwards that gold, which was paid instead of those crowns, or which was expended in making them, was called the crown gold and crown tax." On 1 Maccab. x. 29.—W.

the fruits [of the field,] and half the fruits of the trees, I
give up my share of them from this day. And as to
the poll-tax, which ought to be paid me for every inhabitant of Judæa, and of the three toparchies that adjoin
Judæa, Samaria and Galilee and Peræa, this I concede
to you now and for all time to come. I will also that the
city of Jerusalem be holy and inviolable, and free from
tithe and taxes to its utmost bounds: and I permit your
high priest Jonathan to hold the citadel, that he may
place as garrison in it such persons as he approves of for
fidelity and good-will to himself, that they may keep it for
us. I also make free all those Jews who have been made
captives and slaves in my kingdom. I also give order that
the beasts of the Jews be not pressed for our service. And
let their Sabbaths, and all their festivals, and three days
before each of them, be free from any public burdens.
I likewise set free the Jews that dwell in my kingdom,
and order that no injury be done to them. I also give
leave to such of them as are willing to enlist in my
army, that as many as thirty thousand may do so,
which Jewish soldiers, wherever they go, shall have the
same pay that my own army has: and some of them I
will place in my garrisons, and some as guards about
mine own body, and some as rulers over those that are
in my court. I give them leave also to use the laws of
their forefathers, and to observe them, and I will that they
have power over the three toparchies that adjoin Judæa,
and it shall be in the power of the high priest to see that
not one Jew shall have any other temple for worship but
that at Jerusalem. I offer also out of my own revenues
yearly, for the expenses of the sacrifices, one hundred and
fifty thousand drachmæ, and what money is over I will
that it shall be your own. I also remit to you those ten
thousand drachmæ which the kings received from the
temple, because they belong to the priests that minister in
the temple. And whoever shall flee to the temple at
Jerusalem, or to its precincts, either owing the king money,
or on any other account, let them be set free, and let their
property be untouched. I also give you leave to repair
and rebuild your temple, and that at my expense. I also
allow you to build the walls of your city, and to erect high

towers, and let them be erected at my expense. And if there be any fortress that would be convenient to have very strong in the country of the Jews, let it be built at my expense."

§ 4. This was what Demetrius promised, and granted to the Jews, in this letter. But king Alexander raised a great army of mercenary soldiers, and of those that joined him from Syria, and marched against Demetrius. And in the battle that ensued, the left wing of Demetrius put those opposite them to flight, and pursued them a great way, and slew many of them, and spoiled their camp, but the right wing, where Demetrius happened to be, was beaten. And as for all the rest, they ran away, but Demetrius fought courageously, and slew a great many of the enemy, but as he was in pursuit of the rest, his horse carried him into a deep bog, where it was hard to get out, and there it happened, upon his horse's falling down, that he could not escape being killed; for when his enemies saw what had befallen him, they turned back, and surrounded Demetrius, and all threw their darts at him, and he being now on foot, fought bravely, but at length he received so many wounds, that he was not able to resist any longer, but fell. And this is the end that Demetrius [1] came to when he had reigned eleven years, as I have elsewhere related.

## CHAP. III.

*The Friendship between Onias and Ptolemy Philometor ; and how Onias built a Temple in Egypt like that at Jerusalem.*

### § 1.

NOW the son of Onias the high priest, who had the same name as his father, and who had fled to king Ptolemy, [2] who was called Philometor, lived now at Alexandria, as I have said already ; and when he saw that Judæa was ravaged by the Macedonians and their kings, desiring to purchase to himself eternal memory and fame, he resolved

[1] The defeat and death of Demetrius was in 150 B.C.
[2] Ptolemy VI., Philometor, 181-146 B.C.

to send to king Ptolemy and queen Cleopatra, to ask leave
of them that he might build a temple in Egypt like that
at Jerusalem, and might ordain Levites and priests out of
their own stock.   The chief reason why he was desirous to
do so was that he relied upon the prophet Isaiah, who
lived more than six hundred years before, and foretold that
there certainly was to be a temple built to the most high God
in Egypt by a man that was a Jew.   Onias was incited by
this prediction, and wrote the following letter to Ptolemy
and Cleopatra.   "Having done you many and great services in war by the help of God, and being in Cœle-Syria
and Phœnicia, and having gone with the Jews to Leontopolis[1] in the district of Heliopolis, and to other places of
your nation, I found that most of your people had temples
in an improper manner, and that on that account they
bore ill-will to one another, which happened to the
Egyptians because of the multitude of their temples, and
their different opinions about divine worship.   Now I
found a very fit place in a stronghold that has its name
from rural Bubastis,[2] the place is full of wood of various
kinds and sacred animals.   I desire, therefore, that you
will grant me leave to purge this holy place, which belongs
to no special divinity and is fallen down, and to build
there a temple to the most high God, after the pattern of
that in Jerusalem, and of the same dimensions, for the
benefit of yourself and your wife and children, that those
Jews who dwell in Egypt may have a place where they
may come and meet together in mutual harmony with one
another, and assist you in your needs.   For the prophet
Isaiah foretold that there should be an altar in Egypt to
the Lord God.   And many other such things did he pro-
phesy relating to the place."

§ 2.   This was what Onias wrote to king Ptolemy.
Now any one may conjecture his piety, and that of his
sister and wife Cleopatra, by the letter which they wrote
in answer to it; for they laid the sin and transgression of
the law upon the head of Onias.   For this was their reply.
"King Ptolemy and queen Cleopatra to Onias greeting.
We have read thy petition, wherein thou desirest leave to

[1] Probably *Tell el-Yehúdi*, near the *Shibin el-Kanater* railway station.
[2] *Tell Basta*, near the *Zagazig* railway station.

be given thee to purge the temple which is fallen down at Leontopolis in the district of Heliopolis, and which has its name from the rural Bubastis. So we cannot but wonder that it should be pleasing to God to have a temple erected in a place so unclean, and so full of sacred animals. But since thou sayest that Isaiah the prophet foretold this long ago, we give thee leave to do it, if it may be done according to your law, and so that we may not appear to have offended God at all in the matter."

§ 3. So Onias took the place, and built a temple, and an altar to God, like that in Jerusalem, but smaller and poorer. I do not think it needful for me now to describe its dimensions or its vessels, which have been already described in the seventh book of my Jewish War. And Onias found some Jews like himself, and priests and Levites to perform divine service there. But I have said enough about this temple.

§ 4. Now it came to pass that the Jews in Alexandria had a quarrel with the Samaritans, who paid their worship to the temple that was built in the days of Alexander on Mount Gerizim, and disputed about their temples before Ptolemy himself, the Jews saying that according to the laws of Moses the temple was to be built at Jerusalem, and the Samaritans saying that it was to be built on Mount Gerizim. They desired therefore the king to sit with his friends, and hear a debate on these matters, and punish those with death who were beaten in the argument. Now Sabbæus and Theodosius managed the argument for the Samaritans, and Andronicus, the son of Messalamus, for the people of Jerusalem and the Jews. And they swore by God and the king to prove their case according to the law, and they desired of Ptolemy, that he would put to death whoever he should find violated what they had sworn to. And the king took several of his friends into counsel, and sat down to hear what the pleaders said. Now the Jews that were at Alexandria were in great concern for those who were to contend for the temple at Jerusalem; for they took it very ill that any should try to take away the reputation of their temple, which was so ancient and celebrated all over the world. Now as Sabbæus and Theodosius gave leave to

Andronicus to speak first, he began to show, from the law
and the succession of the high priests, how every one had
received that dignity, and ruled over the temple in succession from his father, and how all the kings of Asia had
honoured that temple with their votive offerings and the
most splendid gifts, while as for that at Gerizim, no one
made any account of it, or regarded it, as if it had a being
at all.  By this speech and similar arguments Andronicus
persuaded the king to determine that the temple at Jerusalem was built according to the laws of Moses, and to put
Sabbæus and Theodosius to death.  And these were the
events that befell the Jews at Alexandria in the days of
Ptolemy Philometor.


## CHAP. IV.

*How Alexander greatly honoured Jonathan, and how Deme-
trius, the Son of Demetrius, overcame Alexander, and became King himself, and made a League of Friendship
with Jonathan.*

### § 1.

DEMETRIUS having been slain in battle, as I have
stated above, Alexander took the kingdom of Syria,
and wrote to Ptolemy Philometor asking his daughter in
marriage, and said it was but just that he should be
joined in affinity to one who had now recovered the throne
of his forefathers, and had been promoted to it by God's
providence, and had conquered Demetrius, and was on
other accounts not unworthy of being connected with him.
Ptolemy received this offer of marriage gladly, and wrote
him an answer, congratulating him on account of his
having recovered the throne of his forefathers, and
promising him that he would give him his daughter in
marriage, and desiring him to meet him at Ptolemais, as
he would bring his daughter there, for he would accompany
her so far from Egypt, and would there give her to him in
marriage.  When Ptolemy had written this, he soon went
to Ptolemais, and brought his daughter Cleopatra along
with him; and as he found Alexander there before him,

as he desired him, he gave him his daughter in marriage, and for her dowry gave as much silver and gold as became such a king to give.

§ 2. When the wedding was over, Alexander wrote to Jonathan the high priest, and desired him to come to Ptolemais. And when he came to the kings, and made them magnificent presents, he was honoured by them both. Alexander also compelled him to put off his own garment, and to put on a purple garment, and made him sit with him on his throne, and commanded his captains to go with him into the middle of the city, and proclaim that it was not permitted to any one to speak against him, or to cause him any trouble. And when the captains had done so, those that were prepared to accuse Jonathan, and who bore him ill-will, when they saw the honour that was done him by proclamation by the king's order, ran away, and were afraid lest some mischief should befall them. Nay, king Alexander was so very kind to Jonathan, that he registered him as the principal of his friends.

§ 3. Now in the hundred and sixty-fifth year Demetrius,[1] the son of Demetrius, came from Crete with a great number of mercenary soldiers, whom Lasthenes the Cretan furnished him with, and sailed to Cilicia. This news threw Alexander into great concern and anxiety, so he hastened immediately from Phœnicia to Antioch, that he might put matters in a safe posture there, before Demetrius should come. He also left Apollonius Daus governor of Cœle-Syria, who coming to Jamnia[2] with a great army, sent to Jonathan the high priest, and told him, that it was not right that he alone should live in security and authority, not being subject to the king, and that this brought him reproach among all men, that he had not yet made himself subject to the king. "Do not thou therefore deceive thyself (he continued), sitting among the mountains, and thinking thyself strong, but if thou hast any reliance on thy strength, come down into the plain, and let our armies be pitted together, and the event of the battle will prove which of us is the best man. Know, however, that the most valiant men of every city are in my army, and these are the

---

[1] Demetrius II., Nicator, landed in Syria in 148 B.C.
[2] *Yebnah.*

very men who have always beaten thy progenitors; but let us have the battle on ground where we may fight with weapons, and not with stones, and where there may be no place where those that are beaten may flee to."

§ 4. Jonathan was irritated at this message, and picking out ten thousand of his soldiers, marched from Jerusalem with his brother Simon, and went to Joppa, and pitched his camp outside the city, because the people of Joppa had shut their gates against him, for they had a garrison in the city put there by Apollonius. But as Jonathan was preparing to besiege them, they were afraid he would take the city by storm, so they opened the gates to him. And Apollonius, when he heard that Joppa was taken by Jonathan, took three thousand horse and eight thousand foot, and went to Azotus,[1] and removing thence made his journey silently and slowly, and going up to Joppa, feigned to retire, and so drew Jonathan into the plain, as he prided himself highly upon his horse, and placed his hopes of victory principally in them. And Jonathan sallied out, and pursued Apollonius to Azotus; and as soon as Apollonius perceived that his enemy was in the plain, he came back and gave him battle. Now Apollonius had laid a thousand horsemen in ambush in a valley, that they might take their enemies in the rear, and though Jonathan perceived this, he was in no consternation, but ordering his army to form a square he charged them to repel the enemy on both sides, and set them so as to face those that attacked them both before and behind. And as the fight lasted till the evening, he gave part of his forces to his brother Simon, and ordered him to attack the enemies' lines, but he himself charged those that were with him to cover themselves with their armour, and so receive the darts of the horsemen. And they did as they were commanded, so that the enemy's horsemen, though they threw their darts till they had no more left, did them no harm, for the darts that were thrown did not enter their bodies, as they lit upon their shields, that were joined and united together, the compactness of which easily resisted the force of the darts, which glanced off without

---

[1] *E*ṣdûd.

taking effect. But when the enemy grew tired of throwing darts from morning till late at night, Simon perceived their weariness, and fell upon the main body of the enemy, and as his soldiers fought with great vigour, he put them to flight. And when the horse saw that the foot ran away, neither did they stay themselves, but being very weary by the fight lasting till the evening, and their hope from the foot being quite gone, they ran away in great disorder and confusion, till they separated from one another, and were scattered over all the plain. Upon which Jonathan pursued them as far as Azotus, and slew a great many of them, and compelled the rest, who despaired of escaping, to flee to the temple of Dagon, which was at Azotus. But Jonathan took the city at the first onset, and burnt it and the villages round it, nor did he abstain from the temple of Dagon itself, but he burnt it also, and so killed those that had fled to it. Now the entire number of the enemies that fell in the battle, or were burnt to death in the temple, was eight thousand. Now when Jonathan had overcome so great an army, he removed from Azotus, and went to Ascalon,[1] and when he had pitched his camp outside the city, the people of Ascalon came out and met him, bringing him presents, and honouring him ; and he gratefully accepted their kindness, and returned thence to Jerusalem with a great deal of spoil which he got when he conquered his enemies. And when Alexander heard that his general Apollonius was beaten, he pretended to be glad of it, because he had fought with his friend and ally Jonathan against his directions. Accordingly, he sent to Jonathan, and bore testimony to his worth, and gave him honorary rewards,[2] as a gold pin, which it is the custom to give the king's kinsmen, and allowed him Ekron[3] and its toparchy as his own inheritance.

§ 5. About this time king Ptolemy, who was called Philometor, came to Syria with a land and sea force to the

---

[1] *'Askalân.*

[2] Dr. Hudson here observes, that the Phœnicians and Romans used to reward such as had deserved well of them, by presenting to them a ' gold pin.' See chap. 5, § 4.—W.

[3] *'Akir.*

assistance of Alexander, who was his son-in-law;[1] and all
the cities received him in a friendly manner, as Alexander
had commanded them to do, and conducted him as far as
Azotus, where all made loud complaints about the burning
of the temple of Dagon, and accused Jonathan of having
destroyed it and the adjacent country with fire, and slain
a great number of them. Ptolemy heard these accusations,
but said nothing. Jonathan also went to Joppa to meet
Ptolemy, and received from him handsome presents, and
all marks of honour. And when he had escorted him as
far as the river called Eleutherus,[2] he returned again to
Jerusalem.

§ 6. But when Ptolemy was at Ptolemais, most unexpectedly he was very near destruction, for he was plotted
against by Alexander, through Ammonius who was his
friend. And when the plot was detected, Ptolemy wrote
to Alexander, and demanded of him that he should bring
Ammonius to condign punishment, informing him of the
way he had plotted against him, and desiring that he might
be accordingly punished. But as Alexander did not comply with his demands, he perceived that it was he himself
who had laid the design, and was very angry with him.
Alexander had also formerly been on very ill terms with
the people of Antioch because of Ammonius, for they
had suffered very much at his hands. However Ammonius
at length underwent the punishment his insolent crimes
had deserved, for he was killed in an opprobrious manner
as a woman, having endeavoured to conceal himself in
feminine dress, as I have elsewhere related.

§ 7. And now Ptolemy blamed himself for having given
his daughter in marriage to Alexander, and for assisting
him against Demetrius, so he dissolved his connection with
him, and took his daughter away from him, and immediately sent to Demetrius, and offered to make league of
mutual alliance and friendship with him, and agreed to
give him his daughter in marriage, and to restore him to
the throne of his fathers. Demetrius was well pleased
with this message, and accepted his alliance, and his

[1] Alexander Balas had married Cleopatra, the daughter of Ptolemy
Philometor.
[2] *Nahr el-Kebîr*, north of Tripolis.

daughter's hand in marriage. But Ptolemy had still one more hard task to do, and that was to persuade the people of Antioch to receive Demetrius, because they were hostile to him on account of the injuries his father Demetrius had done them, yet he did bring it about. For as the people of Antioch hated Alexander on Ammonius' account, as I have related already, they were easily prevailed to cast him out of Antioch; and he, being thus expelled out of Antioch, went into Cilicia. Ptolemy then went to Antioch, and was made king by its inhabitants and by the army; so that he was forced to put on two diadems, the one of Asia, the other of Egypt. But being naturally a good and righteous man, and not desirous of what belonged to others, and, besides this being also wise in reading the future, he determined to avoid exciting the envy of the Romans; so he called the people of Antioch together to an assembly, and urged them to receive Demetrius; and assured them, that he would not be mindful of what they had done to his father, in case he should now be obliged by them; and undertook that he would himself be a good preceptor and governor to him; and promised that he would not permit him to attempt any bad actions; and said that for his part he was contented with the kingdom of Egypt. By these words he persuaded the people of Antioch to receive Demetrius.

§ 8. And now Alexander marched from Cilicia into Syria with a numerous and great army, and burnt and ravaged the country belonging to Antioch, whereupon Ptolemy and his son-in-law Demetrius (for he had already given him his daughter in marriage), led their army against him, and beat Alexander, and put him to flight, and he fled to Arabia. Now it happened, in the battle, that Ptolemy's horse was frightened at hearing the cry of an elephant, and threw him, and his enemies seeing this rushed at him, and gave him many wounds upon his head, and brought him into danger of death; for when his body-guards rescued him, he was so very ill, that for four days he was insensible and speechless. However, Zabel, a prince among the Arabians, cut off Alexander's head, and sent it to Ptolemy, who recovering of his wounds, and becoming sensible on the fifth day, heard at once most agree-

able news, and saw a most agreeable sight, namely heard of
the death and saw the head of Alexander; yet a little after
this joy and satisfaction at the death of Alexander, he
also departed this life. Now, Alexander, who was called
Balas, reigned over Asia five years, as I have related elsewhere.

§ 9. But when Demetrius, who was also called Nicator,[1]
had taken over the kingdom, he was so wicked as to treat
Ptolemy's soldiers very hardly, neither remembering the
alliance that was between them, nor that he was his son-
in-law and kinsman by his marriage with Cleopatra, so
the soldiers fled from his wicked treatment to Alexandria,
but Demetrius retained the elephants. And Jonathan the
high priest levied an army out of all Judæa, and attacked
the citadel at Jerusalem, and besieged it; it was held by
a garrison of Macedonians, and by some of those impious
men who had abandoned the customs of their forefathers.
These men at first despised the attempts of Jonathan to
take the place, relying on its strength; but some of those
wicked men went out by night and came to Demetrius, and
informed him that the citadel was being besieged; and he
was irritated with what he heard, and took his army, and
went from Antioch against Jonathan. And when he was
at Ptolemais he wrote to him, and commanded him to
come quickly to him there; upon which Jonathan did not
intermit the siege of the citadel, but took with him the
elders of the people and the priests, and carried with him
gold and silver and garments, and a great number of
presents, and went to Demetrius, and presented him with
them, and so pacified the king's anger. So he was
honoured by him, and received from him the confirmation
of his high priesthood, as he had got it by the grants of
the kings his predecessors. And when the Jewish deserters accused him, Demetrius was so far from giving
credit to them, that when Jonathan petitioned him that he
would demand no more than three hundred talents for the
tribute of all Judæa and the three toparchies of Samaria

---

[1] This name, ' Demetrius Nicator,' or ' Demetrius the Conqueror,' is
so written on his still extant coins, as Hudson and Spanheim inform
us; the latter of whom gives us here the entire inscription, ' King Demetrius the God Philadelphus Nicator.'—W.

Peræa and Galilee, he complied with the proposal, and gave him a letter whose contents were as follows. " King Demetrius to Jonathan his brother, and to the nation of the Jews, greeting. We have sent you a copy of the letter which we have written to Lasthenes our kinsman, that you may know its contents. ' King Demetrius to Lasthenes his father greeting. I have determined to return thanks, and to show favour, to the nation of the Jews, who have acted uprightly to us. Accordingly, I remit to them the three prefectures, Apherima,[1] Lydda,[2] and Ramatha,[3] which were added to Judæa out of Samaria, with their appurtenances, as also what the kings my predecessors received from those that offered sacrifices in Jerusalem, and what are due from the fruits of the earth and trees, and what else belongs to us, as the salt pits and crowns that used to be presented to us. Nor shall they be compelled to pay any of these taxes either now or henceforth.' Take care therefore that a copy of this letter be taken, and given to Jonathan, and be set up in some prominent place in the holy temple." Such were the contents of the letter. And now, when Demetrius saw that there was peace everywhere, and that there was no danger nor fear of war, he disbanded his army, and diminished their pay, and was bountiful only to such foreigners as had come with him from Crete and the other islands. However, this procured him ill-will and hatred from the soldiers, on whom he bestowed nothing from this time, whereas the kings before him used to pay them even in time of peace as much as they did in war, that they might have their goodwill, and that they might be very ready to undergo the perils of war, if occasion should require.

[1] Probably Ephraim, *Taiyibeh*.                    [2] *Ludd*.
[3] Probably the same as Ramathaim-Zophim, in Mount Ephraim; not identified.

## CHAP. V.

*How Trypho, after he had beaten Demetrius, handed over
the kingdom to Antiochus the Son of Alexander, and got
Jonathan for his Ally; and concerning the Actions and
Embassies of Jonathan.*

### § 1.

NOW a certain commander of Alexander's forces, an
Apamian by birth, whose name was Diodotus, though
he was also called Trypho,[1] took notice of the ill-will the
soldiers bore to Demetrius, and went to Malchus the
Arabian, who was bringing up Antiochus the son of
Alexander, and told him what ill-will the army bore to
Demetrius, and persuaded him to hand over to him Antiochus, for he said he would make him king, and restore
to him the kingdom of his father. Malchus at first opposed him in this, as he did not trust him, but as Trypho
urged him for a long time, he at last persuaded him to
comply with his views. Such was the state of affairs with
Trypho.

§ 2. Meantime Jonathan the high priest, being desirous
to get rid of those that were in the citadel of Jerusalem,
and of the Jewish deserters, and wicked men, as well as of
those in all the garrisons in the country, sent presents and
ambassadors to Demetrius, and entreated him to take
away his soldiers from the strongholds of Judæa. Demetrius made answer that after the war, which he was now
deeply engaged in, was over, he would not only grant him
that, but greater things than that also, and begged him to
send him some assistance, and informed him that his army
had revolted. So Jonathan picked out three thousand of
his soldiers, and sent them to Demetrius.

§ 3. Now the people of Antioch hated Demetrius, both
on account of the mischief he had himself done them, and
because they were his enemies also on account of his father
Demetrius, who had very badly treated them; so they

---

[1] Trypho, according to Strabo, was a native of Cariana, in the district
of Apamea, *Kal'ât el-Medyk*, in Syria.

watched for some opportunity which they might lay hold of, to fall upon him. And when they were informed of the assistance that was coming to Demetrius from Jonathan, and considered at the same time that he would raise a numerous army, unless they prevented him, they took up arms, and surrounded his palace as if besieging it, and occupied all the outlets, and sought to subdue their king. And when he saw that the people of Antioch were become his bitter enemies, and were thus in arms, he took the mercenary soldiers whom he had with him, and those Jews who had been sent by Jonathan, and assaulted the Antiochians; but he was overpowered by them and beaten, for they were many myriads. But when the Jews saw that the Antiochians were getting the better of it, they went up to the roof of the palace, and shot at them from thence, and because they were so remote from them by their height, that they suffered nothing on their side, but did great execution on them, fighting from such an elevation, they drove them out of the adjoining houses, and immediately set them on fire. Thereupon the flames spread over the whole city, and burnt it all down, by reason of the closeness of the houses, and because they were mostly built of wood; and the Antiochians, as they were not able to help themselves, or put out the fire, turned to flight. And as the Jews leaped from the top of one house to the top of another, and pursued them after that manner, it happened that the pursuit was very surprising. But when the king saw that the Antiochians were anxious to save their children and wives, and so did not fight any longer, he fell upon them in the narrow streets and fought them, and slew a great number of them, till at last they were forced to throw down their arms, and surrender to Demetrius. And he forgave them their insolent behaviour, and put an end to the rebellion: and when he had given rewards to the Jews out of the rich spoil he had got, and had returned them thanks as the authors of his victory, he sent them back to Jerusalem to Jonathan, testifying to the assistance they had afforded him. But he behaved ill to Jonathan afterwards, and broke the promises he had made, and threatened that he would make war upon him, unless he would pay all the tribute which the Jewish nation had paid the former kings. And he would have done so, if Trypho had not hindered him, and diverted his preparations against Jonathan into concern for his own preservation. For Trypho returned from Arabia to Syria with the lad Antiochus, for he was yet but a youth in age, and put the diadem on his head: and as the whole forces that had deserted from Demetrius, because they could get no pay, came over to him, he made war upon Demetrius, and joining battle with him, overcame him in the fight, and took from him both his elephants and the city of Antioch.

§ 4. Demetrius upon his defeat retired into Cilicia, and the lad Antiochus sent ambassadors and a letter to Jonathan, and made him his friend and ally, and confirmed to him the high priesthood, and yielded up to him the four prefectures which had been added to Judæa. Moreover, he sent him vessels and cups of gold, and a purple robe, and gave him leave to use them. He also presented him with a gold pin, and ordered him to be called one of his principal friends, and made his brother Simon general over his forces from the Ladder of Tyre to Egypt. And Jonathan was so well pleased with these favours of Antiochus, that he sent ambassadors to him and to Trypho, and professed himself his friend and ally, and said he would join him in a war against Demetrius, informing him that Demetrius had made no proper return for the favours he had done him, for though he had received many kindnesses from him when he stood in great need of them, he had for such good turns requited him with injuries.

§ 5. And as Antiochus gave Jonathan leave to enlist a numerous army in Syria and Phœnicia, and to make war against Demetrius' generals, he set out at once to the several cities, which received him splendidly indeed, but put no troops into his hands. And when he was come from thence to Ascalon,[1] the inhabitants of Ascalon came and brought him presents, and entertained him handsomely. He exhorted them, and every one of the cities of Cœle-Syria, to forsake Demetrius, and to join Antiochus, and to assist him in his endeavour to punish Demetrius

---

[1] *'Askalân.*

for the offences he had formerly been guilty of against themselves: and he told them there were many reasons for that step, if they had a mind to take it. And when he had persuaded those cities to promise their assistance to Antiochus, he went to Gaza, in order to induce it also to be friendly to Antiochus. But he found the inhabitants of Gaza much more alienated from him than he expected, for they shut their gates against him, and although they had deserted Demetrius, they resolved not to join themselves to Antiochus. This provoked Jonathan to besiege them, and to ravage their country, for he set a part of his army round Gaza itself, and with the rest he overran their land, and devastated it, and burnt what was in it. When the inhabitants of Gaza saw themselves suffering thus, and that no assistance came to them from Demetrius, and that what distressed them was at hand, but what might aid them was still at a great distance, and it was uncertain whether it would come at all or not, they thought it would be prudent conduct to leave off any longer adherence to Demetrius, and to cultivate friendship with the other; so they sent to Jonathan, and promised to be his friends, and afford him assistance. For such is the temper of men, that before they have had the trial of great afflictions, they do not understand what is for their advantage, but when they find themselves in any evil plight, they then change their minds, and what it had been better for them to have done before they had been at all hurt, they choose to do, but not till after they have suffered such hurt. And Jonathan made a league of friendship with them, and took from them hostages for their performance of it, and sent those hostages to Jerusalem, while he himself went over all the country as far as Damascus.

§ 6. But when he heard that the generals of Demetrius' forces were come with a numerous army to the city of Kadesh,[1] which lies between the land of the Tyrians and Galilee (for they supposed they should so draw him out of Syria to preserve Galilee, for they thought he would not allow war to be made upon the Galilæans, who were his

---

[1] *Kades*, on the hills west of the lake *el-Hûleh*.

own people), he went to meet them, having left his brother Simon in Judæa, who raised as large an army as he was able out of the country, and then sat down before Bethsura, and besieged it, it being the strongest place in all Judæa ; and a garrison of Demetrius' kept it, as I have already related.   And as Simon was throwing up earthworks, and bringing his engines of war against Bethsura,[1] and was very energetic in the siege of it, the garrison was afraid lest the place should be taken by Simon by storm, and they put to the sword ; so they sent to Simon, and desired the security of his oath, that they should come to no harm from him, and then they would evacuate the place, and go away to Demetrius.   Accordingly he gave them his oath, and so got them out of the city, and put therein a garrison of his own.

§ 7. But Jonathan removed out of Galilee from the waters which are called Gennesar,[2] for there he had encamped, and went into the plain that is called Asor,[3] without knowing that the enemy was there.   When therefore Demetrius' men knew, a day beforehand, that Jonathan was coming against them, they set men in ambush on the mountain, while they themselves met him with an army in the plain : and when Jonathan saw this army ready to engage him, he also got ready his own soldiers for the battle as well as he was able.   But those men that were set to lie in ambush by Demetrius' generals having appeared on the Jews' flank, they were afraid lest they should be taken between two fires and be exterminated, so they all fled headlong, and left Jonathan, except about fifty who stayed with him, and among them Mattathias the son of Absalom, and Judas the son of Chapsæus, who were leaders of the whole army.   And they advanced boldly, and like men desperate, against the enemy, and so attacked them that by their courage they daunted them, and by their valour put them to flight.   And when those soldiers of Jonathan that had retreated saw the enemy giving way,

[1] *Beit Sûr*, four miles north of Hebron.
[2] The springs at *et-Tabighah*, which watered the plain of Gennesareth ; or, perhaps, the Sea of Galilee.
[3] The plain near *Jebel Hadîrah*, not far from *Kades*, Kedesh Naphtali.

they rallied after their flight, and pursued them hotly as far as Kadesh, where the camp of the enemy was.

§ 8. Jonathan having thus won a glorious victory, and slain two thousand of the enemy, returned to Jerusalem. And when he saw that all his affairs prospered according to his mind by the providence of God, he sent ambassadors to the Romans, being desirous of renewing the friendship which their nation had had with them formerly. He also enjoined on his ambassadors as they returned to go to the Spartans, and remind them that they were their friends and kindred. So when the ambassadors got to Rome, they went into their senate, and said what they were commanded by Jonathan the high priest to say, how he had sent them to confirm their friendship. The senate then confirmed what had been formerly decreed concerning their friendship with the Jews, and gave them letters to carry to all the kings of Asia and Europe, and to the governors of the cities, that so they might get safe conduct back to their own country. And as they returned, they went to Sparta, and delivered the letter which they had received from Jonathan for them, a copy of which here follows. " Jonathan the high priest of the Jewish nation, and the senate and commonalty of the Jews, to the ephors and senate and people of the Lacedæmonians, who are their brothers, send greeting. If you be well, and both your public and private affairs be agreeable to your minds, it is according to our wishes ; and we are well also. When in former times a letter was brought to Onias, who was then our high priest, from Areus, who at that time was your king, by Demoteles, concerning the relationship between us and you, a copy of which is here subjoined, we not only joyfully received the letter, but were also well pleased with Demoteles and Areus, although we did not need such a testimony, because we were well satisfied about it from the sacred writings.[1] Yet

---

[1] This clause is otherwise rendered in the first book of Maccabees, xii. 9. " For that we have the holy books of scripture in our hands to comfort us." The Hebrew original being lost, we cannot certainly judge which was the truest version, only the coherence favours Josephus. But if this were the Jews' meaning, that they were satisfied out of their Bible that the Jews and Lacedæmonians were akin, that part of their Bible is now lost, for we find no such assertion in our present copies. —W.

we did not think fit first to claim this relationship to you,
lest we should seem premature in taking to ourselves the
glory which is now given us by you. It is a long time
since this our relationship to you was renewed; and when
upon holy and festival days we offer sacrifices to God,
we pray to him for your safety and victory. As for
ourselves, although we have had many wars that have
come to us through the covetousness of our neighbours, yet
we determined not to be troublesome either to you or to
others that were related to us; but since we have now
overcome our enemies, and had occasion to send Numenius
the son of Antiochus, and Antipater the son of Jason, who
are both honourable men belonging to our senate, to the
Romans, we gave them a letter to you also, that they
might renew our mutual friendship. You will therefore also do well yourselves to write to us, and send us an
account of what you stand in need of from us, since we are
in all things disposed to act according to your desires."
And the Lacedæmonians received the ambassadors kindly,
and made a decree for friendship and mutual alliance, and
sent it to them.

§ 9. At this time there were three sects among the Jews,
who had different opinions concerning human actions; one
was called the sect of the Pharisees, another the sect of the
Sadducees, and the third the sect of the Essenes. As for
the Pharisees,[1] they say that some, but not all, actions are

---

[1] Those that suppose Josephus to contradict himself in his three
accounts of the notions of the Pharisees, this here, and the earlier one
in the Jewish War, ii. 8, § 14, and the latter, Antiq. xviii. 1, § 3, as if he
sometimes said they introduced an absolute fatality, and denied all
freedom of human actions, is almost wholly groundless: he ever, as the
very learned Casaubon here truly observes, asserting, that the Pharisees
were between the Essenes and Sadducees, and did ascribe all to fate, or
divine providence, as much as was consistent with the freedom of human
actions. However, their perplexed way of talking about fate or providence, as overruling all things, made it commonly thought they were
willing to excuse their sins by ascribing them to fate. Perhaps under the
same general name some different opinions in this point might be pro-
pagated, as is very common in all parties, especially in points of meta-
physical subtility: however, our Josephus, who in his heart was a great
admirer of the piety of the Essenes, was yet in practice a Pharisee, as
he himself informs us, Life, § 2. And his account of this doctrine of
the Pharisees is certainly agreeable to his own opinion, who fully

the work of fate, and some are in our own power, either to
do or not to do. And the Essenes affirm that fate governs
all things, and that nothing befalls men but what is according to its decree. But the Sadducees take away fate,
and say there is no such thing, and that the events of
human life are not at its disposal, and suppose that all our
actions are in our own power, so that we ourselves are
the authors of what is good, and bring our troubles on ourselves by our own folly. But I have given a more exact
account of all these opinions in the second book of the
Jewish War.

§ 10. Now the generals of Demetrius, wishing to retrieve
the defeat they had had, gathered together a greater army
than they had had before, and marched against Jonathan.
And he, as soon as he was informed of their coming, went
quickly to meet them, to the district of Amathis,[1] for he
resolved to give them no opportunity of coming into
Judæa. So he pitched his camp fifty furlongs from the
enemy, and sent out spies to take a view of their camp, and
see how it was drawn up. When his spies had given him
full information, and had captured some men by night,
who told him the enemy intended to attack him, he, being
thus apprised beforehand, provided for his security, and
placed outposts outside his camp, and kept his men armed
all night ; and charged them to be of good courage and
resolve to fight even in the night-time, if they should be
obliged to do so, that their enemies' designs might not be
concealed from them. But when Demetrius' generals
found out that Jonathan knew what they intended they
were puzzled, and alarmed to find that the enemy had discovered their intentions, nor did they expect to overcome
them in any other way, now they had failed in the snare
they had laid for them ; for should they hazard an open
battle, they did not think they should be a match for
Jonathan's army. So they resolved to flee, and having lit
many fires, that when the enemy saw them they might
suppose they were there still, they decamped. And when

allowed the freedom of human actions, and yet strongly believed the
interposition of divine Providence. See concerning this matter a remarkable clause, Antiq. xvi. 11, § 7.—W.

[1] Hamath, *Hama* in Syria.

Jonathan came to their camp in the morning, and found it
deserted, and understood they were fled, he pursued them,
but could not overtake them, for they had already passed
over the river Eleutherus,[1] and were out of danger. And
when Jonathan returned from thence, he went into Arabia,
and fought against the Nabatæans, and drove off a great
deal of their cattle, and took [many] captives, and went to
Damascus, and there sold all that he had taken. And
about the same time Simon his brother went over all Judæa
and Palestine, as far as Ascalon, and fortified the strongholds; and when he had made them very strong, both by
works and the garrisons placed in them, he went to Joppa,
and when he had taken it, he introduced a strong garrison
into it, for he heard that the people of Joppa wished to
deliver up the city to Demetrius' generals.

§ 11. When Simon and Jonathan had arranged these
matters, they returned to Jerusalem, where Jonathan
gathered all the people together, and advised restoring the
walls of Jerusalem, and rebuilding the wall round the
temple precincts that had been thrown down, and making
the adjoining places stronger by very high towers; and
besides that building another wall in the midst of the
city, to exclude the garrison, which was in the citadel,
from the market-place, and so to hinder them from any
plentiful supply of provisions; and moreover making the
fortresses that were in the country much stronger and more
secure than they were before. And when this advice was
approved of by the multitude as good, Jonathan himself
superintended the building in the city, and despatched
Simon to make the fortresses in the country more secure
than before. But Demetrius crossed over and went
into Mesopotamia, wishing to occupy that country and
Babylon, and by becoming master of the upper satrapies
to get a *point d'appui* for recovering his entire kingdom;
for the Greeks and Macedonians who dwelt in those parts
frequently sent ambassadors to him, and promised, that if
he would come to them, they would deliver themselves up
to him, and assist him in fighting against Arsaces, the
king of the Parthians. Elated by these hopes he marched

---

[1] *Nahr el-Kebir.*

to them, having resolved that, if he once overthrew the
Parthians, and got a sufficient army of his own, he would
make war against Trypho, and eject him from Syria. And
as the people of that country received him with great en-
thusiasm, he raised forces, with which he fought against
Arsaces, and lost all his army, and was himself taken alive,
as I have elsewhere related.

## CHAP. VI.

*How Jonathan was slain by Treachery ; and how thereupon
the Jews made Simon their General and High Priest : and
what courageous Actions he performed, especially against
Trypho.*

### § 1.

NOW when Trypho knew what had befallen Demetrius,
he was no longer loyal to Antiochus, but devised how
he might kill him and take possession of his kingdom : but
his fear of Jonathan was an obstacle to this design, for
Jonathan was a friend of Antiochus. So he resolved first
to get Jonathan out of the way, and then to set about his
attempt on Antiochus ; and resolving to take him off
by deceit and treachery, he went from Antioch to Bethshan, which by the Greeks is called Scythopolis,[1] at which
place Jonathan met him with forty thousand picked
men, for he suspected he came to fight him. But when
Trypho perceived that Jonathan was ready to fight, he
attempted to gain him over by presents and by treating
him in a friendly manner, and gave order to his captains
to obey him, and by these means wished to make him
believe in his good-will, and to take away all suspicions
out of his mind, that so he might make him careless and
heedless, and take him off his guard. He also advised
him to dismiss his army, because there was now no occasion for bringing it with him, as there was no war but all
was in peace. However, he begged him to retain a few
men about him, and go with him to Ptolemais, for he

---

[1] *Beisân.*

would deliver the city up to him, and would bring all the
fortresses that were in the country under his dominion;
and he told him that he came there for that very purpose.

§ 2. Now Jonathan did not suspect anything at all of
his intentions, but believed that Trypho gave him this advice out of kindness, and in sincerity. Accordingly he dismissed most of his army, and retained no more than three
thousand, and left two thousand of these in Galilee, and
himself, with one thousand, went with Trypho to Ptolemais: but when the people of Ptolemais [1] shut their gates,
as they had been commanded by him to do, Trypho took
Jonathan alive, and slew all that were with him. He also
sent soldiers against the two thousand that were left in
Galilee, in order to kill them also, but they, having heard
what had happened to Jonathan, were too quick for them,
and before those that were sent by Trypho arrived, they
armed themselves, intending to depart from the country.
And when those that were sent against them saw that they
were ready to fight for their lives, they gave them no
trouble, but returned back to Trypho.

§ 3. Now when the people of Jerusalem heard that Jonathan was taken, and that the soldiers who were with him
were killed, they deplored his sad fate, and there was
earnest inquiry made about him by everybody, and a great
and reasonable fear fell upon them, and made them sad,
lest, now they were deprived of the courage and forethought of Jonathan, the nations about them should bear
them ill-will, and though they were before quiet on account
of Jonathan, should now rise up against them, and, by
making war against them, should put them into the
utmost dangers. And indeed what they suspected really
befell them, for when those nations heard of the death of
Jonathan, they began to make war against the Jews as
now destitute of a leader; and Trypho himself got an
army together, and was minded to go up to Judæa, and
make war against its inhabitants. But when Simon saw
that the people of Jerusalem were terrified at the circumstances they were in, he desired to make a speech to them,
and so to render them more resolute in opposing Trypho

[1] *Acre, 'Akka.*

when he should come against them. So he called the people together into the temple, and there began to encourage them as follows. "My countrymen, you are not ignorant that my father, and myself, and my brothers, have hazarded our lives, and that willingly, for the recovery of your liberty. Since I have therefore such examples before me, and we of our family have determined even to die for our laws and religion, no terror shall be so great as to banish this resolution from our souls, nor to introduce in its place a love of life and contempt for glory. Do you therefore follow me with alacrity wherever I shall lead you, not being destitute of a leader willing to suffer and dare the greatest things for you ; for neither am I better than my brothers that I should be sparing of my own life, nor worse than them so as to avoid and refuse what they thought the most honourable of all things, namely, to undergo death for your laws and worship of God. I will therefore give them sufficient proof that I am their very brother; and I am so bold as to expect that I shall avenge their blood upon our enemies, and deliver you all, with your wives and children, from the injuries they intend against you, and with God's assistance preserve your temple from destruction by them, for I see that these nations hold you in contempt, as being without a leader, and so are encouraged to make war against you."

§ 4. By this speech Simon inspired the multitude with courage, and as they had been before dispirited through fear, they were now raised to a good hope of better things, insomuch, that the whole multitude of the people cried out with one voice that Simon should be their leader ; and that, instead of his brothers Judas and Jonathan, he should have the government over them : and they promised that they would obey him whatever he should command them. So he got together immediately all his own soldiers that were fit for war, and made haste to rebuild the walls of the city, and to strengthen it by very high and strong towers, and sent a friend of his, one Jonathan, the son of Absolom, to Joppa, and gave him orders to eject its inhabitants, for he was afraid that they would deliver up the city to Trypho; but he himself stayed to look after Jerusalem.

§ 5. Now Trypho removed from Ptolemais with a great
army, and came into Judæa, and brought Jonathan with
him in bonds. And Simon met him with his army at the
city of Addida,[1] which is upon a hill, and beneath it lie the
plains of Judæa. And when Trypho knew that Simon had
been made their leader by the Jews, he sent to him, and
would have imposed upon him by deceit and treachery, and
bade him, if he would have his brother Jonathan released, to
send a hundred talents of silver, and two of Jonathan's
sons as hostages, that when he should be released, he
would not make Judæa revolt from the king, for at present he was kept in bonds on account of the money he had
borrowed of the king, and still owed. But although Simon
was aware of the craft of Trypho, and although he knew
that if he gave him the money he should lose it, and that
Trypho would not set his brother free, and that he himself
would also be delivering up the sons of Jonathan to the
enemy, yet because he was afraid that he would be calumniated among the multitude as the cause of his brother's
death, if he neither gave the money nor sent Jonathan's sons,
he gathered his army together, and told them what offers
Trypho had made, and added that the offers were a snare
and treacherous, and yet that it was preferable to send
the money and Jonathan's sons than to be liable to the imputation of being unwilling to save his brother through
not complying with Trypho's offers. Accordingly, Simon
sent the sons of Jonathan and the money; but when
Trypho had received them he did not keep his promise,
nor set Jonathan free, but took his army, and went all
about the country, and resolved to go afterwards to Jerusalem by way of Idumæa, and went to Adora[2] a city of
Idumæa. And Simon marched out against him with his
army, and still kept pitching his own camp over against
his.

§ 6. Now when those that were in the citadel sent to
Trypho, and besought him to make haste and come to
them, and to send them provisions, he got his cavalry ready,
as though he would be at Jerusalem that very night. But
so great a quantity of snow fell in the night, that it covered

---

[1] *Haditheh*, close to Lydda.
[2] Adoraim of 2 Chron. xi. 9. *Dûra*, five miles west of Hebron.

the roads, and lay so deep, that there was no getting on, especially for horses. This hindered him from coming to Jerusalem, so Trypho removed from thence, and went into Cœle-Syria, and made a hurried raid into the land of Gilead, and slew Jonathan there, and when he had given order for his burial, returned himself to Antioch. But Simon sent some to the city Basca [1] to bring away his brother's bones, and buried them in their own city Modiim, [2] and all the people made great lamentation over him. Simon also erected a very large monument of white and polished stone to his father and brothers, and raised it a great height, so as to be seen a long way off, and made porticoes about it, and set up pillars which were of one stone apiece, a work wonderful to see. Moreover, he built seven pyramids also to his parents and brothers, one for each of them, which were very wonderful both for size and beauty, and which have been preserved to this day. And we know that it was Simon who exhibited so much zeal about the burial of Jonathan, and the building of these monuments to his relations. Now Jonathan died when he had been high priest four years, [3] and had also been the ruler of his nation. And these were the circumstances of his death.

§ 7. But Simon, who was made high priest by the people, in the very first year of his high priesthood set the nation free from their slavery under the Macedonians, so that they paid tribute to them no longer; which liberty and freedom from tribute they obtained after a hundred and seventy years of the kingdom of the Assyrians, [4] which was

---

[1] The Bascama of 1 Macc. xiii. 23 ; not identified.

[2] el-Medieh.

[3] There is some error in the copies here, when no more than four years are ascribed to the high priesthood of Jonathan. We know by Josephus's last Jewish chronology, Antiq. xx. 10, that there was an interval of seven years between the death of Alcimus or Jacimus, the last high priest, and the real high-priesthood of Jonathan, to whom yet those seven years seem here to be ascribed, as a part of them were to Judas before, Antiq. xii. 10, § 6. Now since, besides these seven years' interregnum in the pontificate, we are told, Antiq. xx. 10, that Jonathan's real high priesthood lasted seven years more ; these two seven years will make up fourteen years, which I suppose was Josephus's own number in this place, instead of the four in our present copies.—W.

[4] These 170 years of the Assyrians mean no more, as Josephus explains himself here, than from the era of Seleucus, which, as it is known

after Seleucus,[1] who was called Nicator, got the dominion over Syria. Now the affection of the people to Simon was so great, that in their contracts with one another, and in their public records, they wrote, "In the first year of Simon the benefactor and ethnarch of the Jews:" for under him they were very successful, and overcame the enemies that were round about them. For Simon overthrew the cities of Gazara[2] and Joppa and Jamnia,[3] and took the citadel of Jerusalem by siege, and razed it to the ground, that it might not be any more a *point d'appui* for their enemies, when they occupied it, to do them a mischief, as it had been till then. And when he had done this, he thought it the best way, and for their advantage, to level the very mountain itself upon which the citadel happened to stand, that so the temple might be higher than it. And, indeed, when he had called the multitude to an assembly, he persuaded them to have it demolished, by reminding them what miseries they had suffered by its garrisons and the Jewish deserters, and what miseries they might hereafter suffer in case any foreigner should seize the kingdom, and put a garrison into that citadel. This speech induced the multitude to compliance, because he exhorted them to do nothing but what was for their own good  So they all set to work and levelled the mountain, and spent both day and night in that work without any intermission, and it took them three whole years before it was brought to a level with the rest of the city. After this the temple was the highest of all the buildings, now the citadel and mountain whereon it stood were demolished. And these actions were thus performed under Simon.

to have begun in the 312th year before the Christian era, from its spring in the first book of Maccabees, and from its autumn in the second book of Maccabees, so did it not begin at Babylon till the next spring, on the 311th year. And it is truly observed by Dr. Hudson on this place, that the Syrians and Assyrians are sometimes confounded in ancient authors, according to the words of Justin the epitomizer of Trogus Pompeius, who says that " the Assyrians were afterwards called Syrians," i. 11. See Jewish War, v. 9, § 4, where the Philistines themselves, at the very south limit of Syria, in its utmost extent, are called Assyrians by Josephus, as Spanheim observes.—W.

[1] In 312 B.C.; the first year of Simon was 143-2 B.C.
[2] *Tell Jezar.*          [3] *Yebnah.*

## CHAP. VII.

*How Simon confederated himself with Antiochus Pius, and made War against Trypho, and a little afterwards against Cendebæus, the General of Antiochus's Army ; as also how Simon was treacherously murdered by his son-in-law Ptolemy.*

### § 1.

NOW a little while after Demetrius had been captured, Trypho his governor murdered Antiochus [1] the son of Alexander,[2] who was called ' the god,' [3] when he had reigned four years, though he gave it out that he died under the hands of the surgeons. He then sent his friends and those that were most intimate with him to the soldiers, and promised that he would give them a great deal of money if they would elect him king. He represented to them that Demetrius was made captive by the Parthians, and that Demetrius's brother Antiochus, if he ever came to be king, would do them a great deal of hurt, in revenge for their revolting from his brother. So the soldiers, in expectation of the wealth they should get by bestowing the kingdom on Trypho, made him their ruler. However, when he had gained the management of affairs, Trypho showed his wicked disposition. For while he was a private person he paid court to the multitude, and pretended to great moderation, and so drew them on artfully to whatever he pleased, but when he had once got the kingdom, he laid aside any further dissimulation, and was the true Trypho.[4] And this behaviour made his enemies superior to

[1] Antiochus VI., Theos, son of Alexander Balas and Cleopatra, 145 B.C.

[2] How Trypho killed this Antiochus, the epitome of Livy informs us, chap. 55, viz. that he corrupted his physicians or surgeons, who falsely pretending to the people that he was perishing with the stone, as they cut him for it, killed him, which exactly agrees with Josephus.—W.

[3] That this Antiochus, the son of Alexander Balas, was called ' the god,' is evident from his coins, which Spanheim assures us bear this inscription, ' King Antiochus the God, Epiphanes the Victorious.'—W.

[4] A paronomasia or play on his name, which might signify *Haughty* or *Insolent*.

him, for the soldiers hated him, and revolted from him to Cleopatra the wife of Demetrius, who was then shut up in Seleucia[1] with her children. But as Antiochus[2] (the brother of Demetrius) who was called Soter was wandering about, not being admitted by any of the cities on account of Trypho, Cleopatra sent to him, and invited him to marry her, and to take the kingdom. The reasons why she invited him to do so were these, that her friends persuaded her to it, and that she was afraid for herself, in case some of the people of Seleucia should deliver up the city to Trypho.

§ 2. After Antiochus had come to Seleucia, as his forces increased every day, he marched out to fight Trypho, and having beaten him in battle, drove him out of Upper Syria into Phœnicia, and pursued him there, and besieged him in Dora[3] where he had fled, which was a fortress hard to be taken. He also sent ambassadors to Simon the high priest of the Jews, about a league of friendship and mutual alliance. And he readily accepted his proposal and sent to Antiochus great sums of money and provisions for those that besieged Dora, and supplied them very plentifully, so that for a little while he was looked upon as one of his warmest friends. And Trypho fled from Dora to Apamea,[4] where he was besieged and taken, and put to death, after he had reigned three years.

§ 3. Antiochus, however, because of his covetous and wicked disposition forgot the kind assistance that Simon had afforded him in his necessity, and handed over an army to his friend Cendebæus, and sent him to ravage Judæa, and to seize Simon. When Simon heard of Antiochus' iniquitous conduct, although he was now in years, yet, being exasperated at the unjust treatment he had met with from Antiochus, and with more spirit than his age warranted, he took like a young man the command of his army. He sent out his sons first with the bravest of his soldiers, and himself marched on with his army by another

---

[1] Near the mouth of the Orontes.
[2] Antiochus VII., Sidetes, 137 B.C.
[3] Dor, *Tantûrah*, on the sea coast, eight miles north of *Kaisarîyeh*, Cæsarea Palæstina.
[4] *Kal'ât el-Medyk*.

way, and laid many of his men in ambush in the narrow
mountain passes, nor did he fail of success in any one of
his manœuvres, but was too much for his enemies in every
one of them.   And he led the rest of his life in peace, and
also himself made a league with the Romans.

§ 4. And he ruled over the Jews eight years, and came
to his end at a feast through the treachery of his son-in-
law Ptolemy, who also arrested his wife and two of his
sons, and kept them in bonds, and sent some to kill
John the third son, whose name was also Hyrcanus.   But
the young man perceiving them coming avoided the danger
he was in from them, and made haste into the city [Jeru-
salem], relying on the good-will of the people, because of
the benefits they had received from his father, and because
of the hatred the mob bore to Ptolemy.   And when Ptolemy
endeavoured to enter the city by another gate, they drove
him away, having already admitted Hyrcanus.


## CHAP. VIII.

*Hyrcanus receives the High Priesthood, and ejects Ptolemy
from the Country.   Antiochus makes War against Hyrcanus, and afterwards makes a League with him.*

§ 1.

SO Ptolemy retired to one of the fortresses that was
above Jericho, called Dagon:[1] but Hyrcanus, having
taken the high priesthood that had been his father's before,
first propitiated God by sacrifices, and then marched against
Ptolemy, and when he attacked the fortress, he was in all
other respects too much for Ptolemy, but was overcome by
compassion for his mother and brothers.   For Ptolemy
brought them out on the walls, and ill-treated them in the
sight of all, and threatened that he would throw them
down headlong, unless Hyrcanus raised the siege.   And as
he thought that the more he relaxed his energy about
taking the place, the more did he show favour to those

[1] Not identified.

that were dearest to him by preventing their sufferings, he abated his zeal about it.  However, his mother stretched out her hands, and implored him not to grow remiss on her account, but to be enraged so much the more, and to do his utmost to take the place quickly, in order to get his enemy in his power, and revenge himself upon him for what he had done to those that were his dearest ones ; for death would be sweet to her, though with torment, if that enemy of theirs were but brought to punishment for his wicked dealings to them.  Now, when his mother said this, Hyrcanus resolved to take the fortress, but when he saw her beaten and lacerated, his courage failed him, and he could not but sympathize with his mother's sufferings, and so was overcome.  And as the siege was protracted owing to this, the year in which the Jews are wont to rest came on ; for the Jews observe this rest every seventh year, as they do every seventh day.  And Ptolemy, being for this cause released from the war,[1] slew the brothers and mother of Hyrcanus, and when he had so done, fled to Zeno, who was called Cotyla, the tyrant of the city of Philadelphia.[2]

§ 2. Now Antiochus, being very indignant at the miseries that Simon had brought upon him, invaded Judæa in the fourth year of his reign, and the first year of the rule of Hyrcanus, in the hundred and sixty-second Olympiad.[3] And when he had ravaged the country, he shut Hyrcanus

[1] Hence we learn, that in the days of this excellent high priest, John Hyrcanus, the observation of the Sabbatic year, as Josephus supposed, required a rest from war, as did that of the weekly Sabbath from work : unless in case of necessity, when the Jews were attacked by their enemies, in which case indeed, and in which alone, they then allowed defensive fighting to be lawful even on the Sabbath-day, as we see in several places of Josephus, Antiq. xii. 6, § 2 ; xiii. 1, § 3 ; Jewish War, i. 7, § 3. But then it must be noted, that this rest from war no way appears in the first book of Maccabees, chap. xvi., but the direct contrary ; though indeed the Jews, in the days of Antiochus Epiphanes, did not venture upon fighting on the Sabbath-day, even in the defence of their own lives, till the Maccabees decreed so to do, 1 Macc. ii. 32-41, Antiq. xii. 7, § 2.—W.

[2] Rabbath Ammon, east of Jordan, now 'Ammân.

[3] Josephus's copies, both Greek and Latin, have here a gross mistake, when they say that this first year of John Hyrcanus, which we have just now seen to have been a Sabbatic year, was in the 162nd Olympiad, whereas it was for certain the second year of the 161st.  See the like before, xii. 7, § 6.—W.

up in the city, which he surrounded with seven camps, but accomplished nothing much at first, because of the strength of the walls and the valour of the besieged, and also from want of water, which they were delivered from by a great downfall of rain at the setting of the Pleiades.[1] However, at the north part of the wall, where the ground happened to be level, the king raised a hundred towers, each three stories high, and placed bodies of soldiers upon them, and made attacks every day, and cut a double ditch deep and broad, and so shut the inhabitants in. But the besieged contrived to make frequent sallies out, and if the enemy at any point were not upon their guard, they fell upon them, and did them a great deal of hurt, and if the enemy perceived them, they then easily retired. And as Hyrcanus saw the inconvenience of having so great a number of men in the city, for provisions were sooner consumed by them, and yet, as one may well suppose, great numbers did nothing, he weeded the useless ones and excluded them out of the city, and retained those only who were in the flower of their age and fit for war. However, Antiochus would not let those that were excluded go away, so they wandered about among the walls, and wasted away by famine, and died miserably. But when the feast of Tabernacles was at hand, those that were within commiserated their condition, and received them in again. And when Hyrcanus sent to Antiochus, and desired there might be a truce for seven days because of the festival, he yielded to his piety towards God, and agreed to a truce, and also sent in a magnificent sacrifice, bulls with their horns gilded,[2] and all sorts of sweet spices, and gold and silver cups. And those that were at the

---

[1] This heliacal setting of the Pleiades, or seven stars, was, in the days of Hyrcanus and Josephus, early in the spring, about February, the time of the latter rain in Judæa ; and this, so far as I remember, is the only astronomical character of time, besides one eclipse of the moon in the reign of Herod, that we meet with in all Josephus, the Jews being little accustomed to astronomical observations, any further than for the uses of their calendar, and utterly forbidden those astrological uses which the heathens commonly made of them.—W.

[2] Dr. Hudson tells us here, that this custom of gilding the horns of those oxen that were to be sacrificed, is a known thing both in the poets and orators.—W.

gates received the sacrifice from those that brought it, and took it to the temple, Antiochus in the meanwhile feasting his army ; which was very different conduct from that of Antiochus Epiphanes, who, when he had taken the city, offered swine upon the altar, and sprinkled the temple with the broth of their flesh, violating the laws of the Jews, and the religion they derived from their forefathers; for which reason our nation made war upon him, and would never be reconciled to him. But all called this Antiochus Pious for the great zeal he showed in religion.

§ 3. And Hyrcanus took this moderation of his kindly, and when he saw how religious he was towards the Deity, he sent an embassage to him, and desired that he would restore their national polity. And Antiochus rejected the counsel of those that would have had him utterly destroy the nation because of their holding aloof from other nations, and did not regard what they said, but being persuaded that all they did was done from piety, he answered the ambassadors, that if the besieged would deliver up their arms, and pay tribute to him for Joppa and the other cities which bordered upon Judæa, and would admit a garrison of his, he would on these terms make war against them no longer. But the Jews, although they were content with the other conditions, would not agree to admit a garrison, because they did not associate with other people ; but they were willing, instead of the admission of a garrison, to give him hostages, and five hundred talents of silver, of which they paid down three hundred at once, and sent the hostages, whom king Antiochus accepted, one of whom was Hyrcanus' brother. Hyrcanus also demolished the fortifications that went round the city : and on these conditions Antiochus raised the siege and departed.

§ 4. Now Hyrcanus opened the tomb of David, who excelled all other kings in riches, and took out of it three thousand talents, and relying on this store, was the first of the Jews that kept foreign troops. There was also a league of friendship and mutual alliance made between him and Antiochus, so Hyrcanus admitted him into the city, and furnished him with whatever his army wanted in great plenty and with great generosity, and accompanied him

when he made an expedition against the Parthians. Nicolaus of Damascus bears me out as to this, who writes in
his history as follows. "When Antiochus had erected a
trophy at the river Lycus,[1] upon his conquest of Indates, the
general of the Parthians, he stayed there two days, at the
request of Hyrcanus the Jew, because of a national festival,
whereon the laws of the Jews did not allow them to
travel." And truly he did not speak falsely in saying so;
for the festival of Pentecost was the next day to the
Sabbath; nor is it lawful for us to journey[2] either on the
Sabbath-days, or on a festival day. But when Antiochus
joined battle with Arsaces the Parthian, he lost a great
part of his army, and was himself slain: and his brother
Demetrius[3] succeeded him in the kingdom of Syria, Arsaces
having freed him from his captivity when Antiochus attacked Parthia, as I have previously related elsewhere.

## CHAP. IX.

*How, after the Death of Antiochus, Hyrcanus made an
Expedition against Syria, and made a League with the
Romans. Concerning the Death of King Demetrius and
Alexander.*

### § 1.

BUT when Hyrcanus heard of the death of Antiochus,
he straightway made an expedition against the cities
of Syria, thinking, as was indeed the case, to find them
destitute of fighting men, and of such as were able to
defend them. However, it was not till the sixth month
that he took Medaba,[4] and that not without his army suffering great hardships. After this he took Samega,[5] and the

[1] Apparently the Lycus, *Nahr el-Kelb*, north of Beirût.
[2] The Jews were not to march or journey on the Sabbath, or on such
a great festival as was equivalent to the Sabbath, any further than a
'Sabbath-day's journey,' or 2,000 cubits.—W.
[3] Demetrius II., Nicator, reascended the throne in 128 B.C., after the
defeat and death of Antiochus VII., Sidetes.
[4] *Medeba*, east of the Jordan.
[5] In Jewish War, i. 2, § 6, Samaea; supposed to be near Lake
Merom.

places in its neighbourhood, and besides these Shechem[1] and
Gerizim, and the nation of the Cuthæans, who dwelt near the
temple (like the one at Jerusalem) which Alexander permitted Sanballat the general to build, for the sake of
Manasseh, who was son-in-law to Jaddus, the high priest,
as I have formerly related, which temple was now laid waste
two hundred years after it was built.   Hyrcanus took also
Adora[2] and Marissa,[3] cities of Idumæa, and subdued all
the Idumæans, and permitted them to stay in their own
country, if they would circumcise their foreskins, and conform to the laws of the Jews.   And they were so desirous
of living in the country of their forefathers, that they submitted to circumcision and the rest of the Jewish mode
of life;[4] since which time they have been accounted no
other than Jews.

§ 2.  Hyrcanus the high priest was also desirous to
renew the friendship they had with the Romans.   Accordingly he sent an embassage to them ; and when the senate
had received his letter, they made friendship with him
in the following manner.   "Fanius (the son of Marcus)
the prætor gathered the senate together on the eighth
day before the Ides of February in the Comitia, in the
presence of Lucius Manlius, the son of Lucius, of the

---

[1] *Náblus.*                              [2] Adoraim, *Dúra.*

[3] Mareshah, *Kh. Mer'ash,* near *Beit Jibrîn.*

[4] This account of the Idumæans submitting to circumcision, and the
entire Jewish law, from this time, or from the days of Hyrcanus, is
confirmed by their entire history afterwards.  See Antiq. xiv. 8, § 1 ; xv.
7, § 9 ; Jewish War, ii. 3, § 1 ; iv. 4, § 5.  This, in the opinion of Josephus, made them proselytes of justice, or entire Jews, as here and
elsewhere, Antiq. xiv. 8, § 1.   However, Antigonus, the enemy of
Herod, though Herod was derived from such a proselyte of justice for
several generations, will allow him to be no more than a 'half Jew,'
xiv. 15, § 2.  But still take out of Dean Prideaux, at the year 129, the
words of Ammonius, a grammarian, which fully confirm this account of
the Idumæans in Josephus.  "The Jews (says he) are such by nature,
and from the beginning, whilst the Idumæans were not Jews from the
beginning, but Phœnicians and Syrians ; but being afterward subdued
by the Jews, and compelled to be circumcised, and to unite into one
nation, and be subject to the same laws, they were called Jews."  Dio
also says, as the Dean there quotes him, from book xxxvi. p. 37.
"That country is called ' Judæa,' and the people ' Jews ; ' and this name
is given also to as many others as embrace their religion, though of
other nations."—W.

Mentine tribe, and Caius Sempronius, the son of Caius, of the Falernian tribe, to discuss what the ambassadors sent by the people of the Jews, viz. Simon the son of Dositheus, and Apollonius the son of Alexander, and Diodorus the son of Jason, all three good and virtuous men, came to treat about, namely the league of friendship and mutual alliance which existed between them and the Romans, and about other public affairs. For example, they desired that Joppa and its havens, and Gazara[1] and its springs, and the several other cities and places of theirs which Antiochus had taken from them in war contrary to the decree of the senate, might be restored to them, and that it might not be lawful for the king's troops to pass through their country, or the countries of those that were subject to them, and that whatever had been decreed by Antiochus during the war, without the consent of the senate, might be made void, and that the Romans would send ambassadors, who would take care that restitution should be made to them of what Antiochus had taken from them, and that they would make an estimate of the country that had been laid waste in the war, and that they would grant them letters of protection to kings and commonwealths for their security on their return home. It was decreed then as to these points to renew the league of friendship and mutual alliance with these good men, who were sent by a good and friendly people." But as to the letters desired, their answer was that the senate would consult about that matter when their own affairs would give them leave, and that they would endeavour for the time to come that no such injury should be done them; and that the prætor Fanius should give them money out of the public treasury to pay their expenses home. And thus did Fanius dismiss the Jewish ambassadors, and gave them money out of the public treasury, and gave the decree of the senate to those that were to conduct them on their way and to see that they got home safely.

§ 3. And thus stood the affairs of Hyrcanus the high priest. But as for king Demetrius, who wished to make war against Hyrcanus, he had no opportunity or chance

---

[1] *Tell Jezar.*

for it, as both the Syrians and soldiers hated him, because he was a bad man. And when they had sent ambassadors to Ptolemy[1] who was called Physcon, begging him to send them one of the family of Seleucus to take the kingdom, and he had sent them Alexander[2] (who was also called Zebina) with an army, and there was a battle between them, Demetrius was beaten in the fight, and fled to Cleopatra his wife to Ptolemais, but his wife would not receive him, so he went thence to Tyre, and was there taken, and when he had suffered much at the hands of those that hated him, he was slain by them.[3] And Alexander took over the kingdom, and made a league with Hyrcanus the high priest, but afterwards when he fought with Antiochus the son of Demetrius,[4] who was also called Grypus, he was beaten in the fight and slain.

## CHAP X.

*How, upon the Quarrel between Antiochus Grypus and Antiochus Cyzicenus about the Kingdom, Hyrcanus took Samaria, and utterly demolished it; and how Hyrcanus joined himself to the Sect of the Sadducees, and left that of the Pharisees.*

### § 1.

WHEN Antiochus had taken over the kingdom of Syria, he was afraid to lead an army into Judæa, because he heard that his uterine brother, who was also called Antiochus,[5] was raising an army against him from Cyzicus. So he stayed at home, and resolved to prepare himself for the attack he expected from his brother, who was called Cyzicenus, because he had been brought up in Cyzicus.[6] He was the son of Antiochus who was called Soter, who died in Parthia, and was the brother of Demetrius, the father of Antiochus Grypus, for it so happened that Cleopatra had married two brothers, as I have related

[1] Ptolemy VII., Euergetes II., 146-117 B.C.
[2] 128 B.C.                                    [3] 128 B.C.
[4] 126 B.C.                 [5] 114 B.C.
[6] Near *Panderma*, on the coast of the Sea of *Marmora*.

elsewhere. This Antiochus Cyzicenus went into Syria and continued many years at war with his brother. Now Hyrcanus lived all this while in peace. For after the death of Antiochus he revolted from the Macedonians, nor did he any longer pay them the least regard either as their subject or their friend, but his affairs were in a very improving and flourishing condition in the times of Alexander Zebina, and especially under the brothers Grypus and Cyzicenus. For the war which they had with one another gave Hyrcanus the opportunity of enjoying himself in Judæa quietly, insomuch that he amassed an immense quantity of money. However, when Antiochus Cyzicenus ravaged his land, he then openly showed his hand, and when he saw that Antiochus was destitute of Egyptian auxiliaries, and that both he and his brother were worn out by the struggles they had with one another, he despised them both.

§ 2. And he made an expedition against Samaria, which was a very strong city; of whose present name Sebaste,[1] and its rebuilding by Herod, I shall speak at the proper place. And he attacked and besieged it vigorously, for he was greatly displeased with the Samaritans for the injuries they had done to the people of Marissa, who were colonists and allies of the Jews, at the bidding of the kings of Syria. When he had therefore drawn a trench, and built a double wall fourscore furlongs long all round the city, he set his sons Antigonus and Aristobulus over the siege. And they brought the Samaritans to such great distress by famine, that they were forced to eat what is not usually eaten, and to invite Antiochus Cyzicenus to help them, who came readily to their assistance, but was beaten by Aristobulus, and pursued as far as Scythopolis by the two brothers, but got away. And they returned to Samaria, and shut up the Samaritans again within the wall, till they were forced to send for the same Antiochus a second time to help them, who procured about six thousand men from Ptolemy Lathurus, whom he sent without his mother's consent, so that she nearly turned him out of the succession. With these Egyptians Antiochus at first overran and ravaged the country of

[1] *Sebustieh.*

Hyrcanus like a robber, for he durst not meet him face to face to fight with him, not having an army sufficient for that purpose, but he supposed that by thus ravaging his land he should force Hyrcanus to raise the siege of Samaria. However, as he fell into ambush and lost many of his soldiers, he went away to Tripolis, and committed the carrying on of the war against the Jews to Callimander and Epicrates.

§ 3. As to Callimander, he attacked the enemy too rashly, and was put to flight, and slain immediately; and as to Epicrates, he was such a lover of money, that he openly betrayed Scythopolis and other places near it to the Jews, but was not able to make them raise the siege of Samaria. And when Hyrcanus had taken the city, which was not till after a year's siege, he was not content with that only, but he razed Samaria to the ground, and brought rivulets to it to swamp it, and by digging through it he made a lake of it, and took away all indications that there had ever been a city there at all. Now a very surprising thing is related of this high priest Hyrcanus, how God came to talk with with him. For they say that, on the very day on which his sons fought with Antiochus Cyzicenus, he was alone in the temple as high priest burning incense, and heard a voice saying that his sons had just overcome Antiochus. And he openly declared this to all the multitude upon his coming out of the temple, and it proved true. Such was the condition of affairs with Hyrcanus.

§ 4. Now it happened at this time, that not only were those Jews who were at Jerusalem and in Judæa in prosperity, but also those who dwelt at Alexandria and in Egypt and Cyprus. For Cleopatra the queen was at variance with her son Ptolemy who was called Lathurus, and appointed as her generals Chelcias and Ananias, the sons of that Onias who built the temple like that at Jerusalem in the district of Heliopolis, as I have elsewhere related. Cleopatra intrusted her army to these men, and did nothing without their advice, as Strabo of Cappadocia attests in the following words. "Now most, both of those that came to Cyprus with us, and of those that were sent afterwards there by Cleopatra, revolted to Ptolemy immediately; only those Jews that were called Onias' party continued faithful, because their countrymen Chelcias and Ananias were in chief favour with the queen." These are the words of Strabo.

§ 5. However, this prosperous state of affairs moved the Jews to envy Hyrcanus, and they that were the worst disposed to him were the Pharisees, who were one of the sects of the Jews, as I have stated already. And so great is their influence over the multitude, that when they say anything against the king, or against the high priest, they are at once believed. Now Hyrcanus was a disciple of theirs, and greatly beloved by them. And once he invited them to a feast, and entertained them very kindly, and when he saw them in a good humour, began to say to them, that they knew he was desirous to be a righteous man, and to do all things whereby he might please God, which was the very profession of the Pharisees. However, he desired, if they observed him offending in any point, and going out of the right way, that they would call him back and correct him. And as they testified to his being entirely virtuous, he was well pleased with their commendation. But one of his guests there, whose name was Eleazar, a man malignant by nature and delighting in faction, said, " Since thou desirest to know the truth, if thou wilt be righteous in earnest, lay down the high priesthood, and content thyself with the civil government of the people." And when he desired to know for what reason he ought to lay down the high priesthood, the other replied, " We have heard from old men, that thy mother was a captive in the reign of Antiochus Epiphanes." This story was false, and Hyrcanus was very angry with him, and all the Pharisees were very indignant.

§ 6. Now there was one Jonathan, a very great friend of Hyrcanus, but of the sect of the Sadducees, whose notions are quite contrary to those of the Pharisees. He told Hyrcanus that Eleazar had cast that slur upon him according to the general opinion of all the Pharisees, and that this would be made manifest, if he would but ask them the question, what punishment they thought Eleazar deserved for what he had said. And Hyrcanus having asked the Pharisees what punishment they thought Eleazar deserved (for he would feel sure that the slur was not laid on him with their approbation, if they were for punishing him as his crime deserved), the Pharisees made answer, that Eleazar deserved stripes and bonds, but that it did not seem right to punish his taunt with death.   And indeed the Pharisees generally are not apt to be severe in punishments.   At this mild sentence Hyrcanus was very angry, and thought that the man had reproached him with their approbation. But it was Jonathan who chiefly exasperated him against them, and influenced him so that he made him join the Sadducees and leave the party of the Pharisees, and abolish the decrees they had imposed on the people, and punish those that observed them.   From this source arose that hatred which he and his sons met with from the multitude; but of this I shall speak hereafter.   What I would now merely state is this, that the Pharisees have delivered to the people a great many traditional observances handed down from their fathers, which are not written in the laws of Moses, and for that reason it is that the Sadducees reject them, and say that we are to esteem those observances obligatory that are in the written word, but are not to observe what are derived from the tradition of our forefathers.   And great disputes and differences have arisen concerning these things among them, as the Sadducees influence none but the rich, and have not the populace on their side, but the Pharisees have the multitude to back them.   But as to these two sects and that of the Essenes I have given an accurate account in the second book of the Jewish War.

§ 7. But when Hyrcanus had put an end to this sedition, he afterwards lived happily, and administered the government in the best manner for thirty-one years, and then died, leaving behind him five sons.   He was esteemed by God worthy of the three greatest privileges, the government of his nation, the dignity of the high priesthood, and the power of prophecy, for God was with him, and enabled him to know and foretell the future.   Thus, as to his two eldest sons, he foretold that they would not long continue in the government of public affairs; and their unhappy fate will be worth description, that people may thence learn how very much they came short of their father's happiness.

## CHAP. XI.

*How Aristobulus, when he had taken the Government, put a Diadem on his Head, and was most barbarously cruel to his Mother and Brothers ; and how, after he had slain Antigonus, he himself died.*

### § 1.

NOW when their father Hyrcanus was dead, the eldest son Aristobulus, intending to change the government into a kingdom, for so he resolved to do, was the first after the captivity to put a diadem on his head, four hundred and eighty-one years and three months after the people had been delivered from the Babylonish slavery, and had returned to their own country again. This Aristobulus loved his next brother Antigonus, and treated him as his equal, but the others he held in bonds. He also put his mother into prison, because she disputed the government with him, for Hyrcanus had left her mistress of all, and proceeded to that degree of barbarity, as to starve her in prison. He was also estranged from his brother Antigonus by calumnies, and eventually slew him too, though he seemed to have a great affection for him, and made him partner with him in the kingdom. Those calumnies he did not at first give credit to, partly because he loved him and so did not give heed to what was said against him, and partly because he thought the charges proceeded only from envy. But when Antigonus once returned from an expedition, and the feast of Tabernacles was then at hand, it happened that Aristobulus was fallen sick, and Antigonus went up most splendidly adorned to the temple, with his soldiers about him in their armour, to celebrate the feast, and to put up many prayers for the recovery of his brother, and some wicked persons, who had a great mind to set the brothers at variance, made a handle of the pompous appearance of Antigonus, and of the great actions which he had done, and went to the king, and spitefully exaggerated his pompous show at the feast, and insinuated that all this behaviour was not like that of a private person, but an indication that he aspired to royal authority, and that his coming with a strong body of men must be with an intention to kill him, and that his way of reasoning was, that it was silly in him, when he might reign himself, to look upon it as a great favour that he shared in the honour of his brother.

§ 2. Aristobulus listened unwillingly to these insinuations, but took care not only that his brother should not suspect him, but also that he himself should run no risk of his own safety; so he posted his guards in a certain place that was underground and dark, (he himself then lying ill in the tower which was called Antonia,[1]) and commanded them, in case Antigonus came to him unarmed, not to injure him at all, but if he came armed, to kill him. And he sent to Antigonus, and desired that he would come unarmed; but the queen, and those that joined with her in the plot against Antigonus, persuaded the messenger to tell him the direct contrary, how his brother had heard that he had got a fine suit of armour for war, and desired him to come to him in that armour, that he might see it. And Antigonus, suspecting no treachery, and relying on the good-will of his brother, came to Aristobulus armed, as he was, in his entire armour, in order to show it him. But when he was come to a place which was called Strato's Tower, where the passage happened to be very dark, the guards slew him. Now this death of his proves that nothing is stronger than envy and calumny, and that nothing does more alienate the good-will and natural affections of men than these passions. But here one may take occasion to marvel at one Judas, who was of the sect of the Essenes, and who never missed the truth in his predictions; for when he saw Antigonus passing by the temple, he cried out to his companions and friends, who dwelt with him as his scholars in the art of foretelling things to come, that it was good for him to die now, since he had spoken falsely about Antigonus, who was still alive, for he saw him

---

[1] The tower Antonia, on the north of the Temple. Josephus here uses the later name; it was called Baris at this period, see Antiq. xv. 11, § 4, and was strengthened and partially rebuilt by Herod the Great.

passing by, although he had foretold that he should die that very day at the place called Strato's Tower, and the place where he had foretold he should be slain was six hundred furlongs off, and most of the day was already past, so that he was in danger of proving a false prophet. As he was saying this in a dejected mood, the news came that Antigonus was slain in a place under ground, which was also itself called Strato's Tower, having the same name as that Cæsarea[1] which lies on the sea. This event greatly disturbed the prophet.

§ 3. But Aristobulus repented immediately of this slaughter of his brother, on which account his disease increased upon him, and he was so disturbed in mind at such blood-guiltiness, that his inward parts consumed away owing to his intolerable pain, and he vomited blood, which one of the servants that attended upon him, when carrying it away, did, by divine providence, as I cannot but think, slip down and shed part of it at the very place where there were spots of Antigonus' blood there slain still remaining. And when there was a cry raised by the spectators, as if the servant had shed the blood in that place on purpose, Aristobulus heard it, and inquired what the matter was? And as they did not answer him, he was the more earnest to know what it was, it being natural to men to suspect that what is concealed in such cases is very bad. So upon his threatening, and forcing them by terrors to speak, they at length told him the truth: whereupon he shed many tears, in the mental agony which arose from his consciousness of what he had done, and gave a deep groan, and said, " I am not, I see, to escape the detection of God for the impious and horrid crimes I have been guilty of, but a quick punishment is coming upon me for shedding the blood of my relations. And now, most shameless body of mine, how long wilt thou retain a soul that ought to die to appease the ghosts of my brother and mother? Why dost thou not give it all up at once? And why do I deliver up my blood drop by drop, to those whom I have so wickedly murdered?" In saying these last words, he died, having reigned a year. He was called a

---

[1] The ancient name of Cæsarea Palæstina was Strato's Tower.

lover of the Greeks,[1] and had conferred many benefits on
his own country, having made war against Ituræa, and
added a great part of it to Judæa, and compelled the inhabitants, if they would remain in that country, to be circumcised, and to live according to the Jewish laws.  He
was naturally a man of equity, and of great modesty, as
Strabo bears witness on the authority of Timagenes in
the following words.  "This man was a man of equity,
and very serviceable to the Jews, for he added a country
to them, and obtained a part of the nation of the Ituræans
for them, and bound them to them by the bond of the
circumcision of their foreskins."


## CHAP. XII.

*How Alexander, when he had taken the Government, made an
Expedition against Ptolemais, and then raised the Siege
out of fear of Ptolemy Lathurus ; and how Ptolemy made
War against him, because he had sent to Cleopatra to persuade her to make War against him, though he pretended
to be in Friendship with him.*

### § 1.

WHEN Aristobulus was dead, his wife Salome, who
was called by the Greeks Alexandra, let his brothers
out of prison (for Aristobulus had kept them there, as I
have said already), and made Alexander Janneas king,
who was superior in age and in moderation.  He happened
to be hated by his father as soon as he was born, and was
never permitted to come into his father's sight till he died.
The reason of which hatred is thus reported.  As Hyrcanus
loved chiefly his two eldest sons, Antigonus and Aristobulus, he inquired of God, who appeared to him in his
sleep, which of his sons should be his successor ; and upon
God's showing him the countenance of Alexander, he was
grieved that he was to be the heir of all his goods, and
had him brought up in Galilee.[2]  However, God did not

---

[1] Philhellen.
[2] The reason why Hyrcanus suffered not this son of his, whom he did
not love, to come to Judæa, but ordered him to be brought up in Galilee,

deceive Hyrcanus, for after the death of Aristobulus he certainly took over the kingdom, and slew one of his brothers, who aimed at the kingdom, but held the other in honour, who chose to live a private and a quiet life.

§ 2. When he had settled the government in the manner that he judged best, he made an expedition against Ptolemais; and having overcome the enemy in battle, he shut them up in the city, and invested it, and besieged it; for of the maritime cities there remained only Ptolemais and Gaza to be conquered, and Strato's Tower[1] and Dora[2] which were held by the tyrant Zoilus. Now as Antiochus Philometor, and his brother Antiochus who was also called Cyzicenus, were warring against one another, and destroying one another's armies, the people of Ptolemais could get no assistance from them; but when they were hard pressed by this siege, Zoilus, who occupied Strato's Tower and Dora, and maintained a legion of soldiers, and, because of the contest between the kings, aimed at kingly power himself, came and brought some small assistance to the people of Ptolemais. Nor indeed had the kings such a friendship for them, as that they could hope for any aid from them; for both those kings were in the case of wrestlers, who finding themselves deficient in strength, and yet being ashamed to yield, put off the fight by laziness, and by resting as long as they can. The only hope they had remaining was from the kings of Egypt, and from Ptolemy Lathurus who now held Cyprus, and who went to Cyprus when he was driven from the government of Egypt by his mother Cleopatra. So the people of Ptolemais sent to him, and desired him to come as an ally to deliver them, now they were in such danger, out of the hands of Alexander. And as the ambassadors gave him hopes, if he would pass over into Syria, that he would have the people of Gaza on the side of those of Ptolemais, and also said that Zoilus, and also the Sidonians and

---

is suggested by Dr. Hudson, that Galilee was not esteemed so happy and well-cultivated a country as Judæa, Matt. xxvi. 73, John vii. 52, Acts ii. 7, although another obvious reason occurs also, that he was further out of his sight in Galilee than he would have been in Judæa.—W.

[1] Cæsarea Palæstina, *Kaisarîyeh.*

[2] *Tantûrah.*

many others, would assist him, he was sanguine at this, and got his fleet ready as soon as possible.

§ 3. Meantime Demænetus, one that had great powers of persuasion, and a leader of the populace, made the men of Ptolemais change their opinions, and said to them, that it was better, as the future was uncertain, to run all hazard against the Jews, than to accept evident slavery by delivering themselves up to a master, and besides that, to have not only a war at present, but to expect a much greater one from Egypt, for Cleopatra would not permit Ptolemy's raising an army for himself out of the neighbourhood, but would come against them with a great army of her own, for she was labouring to eject her son out of Cyprus even ; and while Ptolemy, if he failed in his hopes, could still retire to Cyprus, they would be left in the greatest danger possible. Now Ptolemy, although he heard of the change of mind in the people of Ptolemais, yet went on with his voyage all the same, and put in at a place called Sycaminus,[1] and there set his army on shore. His whole army, horse and foot together, amounted to about thirty thousand, with which he marched near to Ptolemais, and there pitched his camp ; but as the people of Ptolemais would neither receive his messengers, nor hear what they had to say, he was very anxious.

§ 4. But when Zoilus and the people of Gaza came to him, and desired his assistance, because their country was laid waste by Alexander and the Jews, Alexander raised the siege for fear of Ptolemy : and when he had drawn off his army into his own country, he played a double game afterwards, privately inviting Cleopatra to march against Ptolemy, but publicly pretending to desire a league of friendship and mutual alliance with him ; and he promised to give him four hundred talents of silver, and asked him in return to put out of the way the tyrant Zoilus and give his country to the Jews. Then Ptolemy gladly made such a league of friendship with Alexander, and subdued Zoilus, but when he afterwards heard that Alexander had privately made overtures to his mother Cleopatra, he broke his league of friendship with him, and besieged Ptolemais, because it

---

[1] *Haifa el-Atîkah*, close to Mount Carmel.

would not receive him; and leaving his generals, with some part of his forces, to go on with the siege, he set out himself with the rest to subdue Judæa.  And when Alexander understood that this was Ptolemy's intention, he also got together about fifty thousand soldiers out of his own country, or, as some writers have said, eighty thousand, and with this army went to meet Ptolemy.  But Ptolemy unexpectedly made an assault upon Asochis,[1] a city of Galilee, and took it by storm on the Sabbath-day, and captured about ten thousand people, and took a great deal of spoil.

§ 5. He next tried to take Sepphoris,[2] which was a city not far from that which had just been sacked, but he lost many of his men there, and marched on to fight with Alexander.  And he met him near the river Jordan, at a certain place called Asophon,[3] not far from the river Jordan, and pitched his camp near the enemy.  He had eight thousand in the van of his army whom he called Hecatontamachi,[4] who had shields of brass.  Those in the van of Ptolemy's army also had shields covered with brass: but Ptolemy's soldiers were in other respects inferior to those of Alexander, and therefore were more cautious in running hazard: but Philostephanus the tactician put great courage into them, and ordered them to cross the river which lay between the two camps. Nor did Alexander think fit to hinder their passage over it, for he thought if the enemy had the river on their back, he should the easier take them prisoners, as they could not then flee out of the battle,  At first the courage and daring on both sides were alike, and a great slaughter was made by both the armies; but Alexander had the best of it, till Philostephanus divided his troops, and reinforced those that were giving way; and as there was no reserve to help those Jews that gave way, they consequently fled, and those near them did not assist them, but fled with them.  But Ptolemy's soldiers acted quite differently, for they followed the Jews, and killed them, and at last those that slew them pursued after them, when they had made them all run away, and slew them till their weapons

---

[1] Probably *Kefr Menda*, see Life, § 45.
[2] *Sefûrieh.*                          [3] Not identified.
[4] That is, able each to fight one hundred men.

were blunted, and their hands quite tired with slaughter. And the report was that thirty thousand were slain, but Timagenes says there were fifty thousand slain. As for the rest, part of them were taken captive, and part fled to their own homes.

§ 6. After this victory, Ptolemy scoured all the country round, and when night came on, he took up his quarters in certain villages of Judæa, and as he found them full of women and children, he commanded his soldiers to cut their throats and hack them in pieces, and then to cast them into boiling caldrons, and devour their limbs as sacrifices. This command was given, that such as fled from the battle, and came to them, might suppose their enemies were cannibals, and so might be still more terrified at them upon such a sight. Both Strabo and Nicolaus affirm that they used these people in this manner, as I have already related. Ptolemy also took Ptolemais by storm, as I have shown elsewhere.

## CHAP. XIII.

*How Alexander, upon the League of Alliance which Cleopatra had agreed with him, made an Expedition against Cœle-Syria, and overthrew the City of Gaza; and how he slew many myriads of Jews that rebelled against him: also concerning Antiochus Grypus, Seleucus, Antiochus Cyzicenus, Antiochus Pius, and others.*

### § 1.

WHEN Cleopatra saw that her son was grown great, and laid Judæa waste with security, and had got the city of Gaza under his power, she resolved no longer to overlook what he did, as he was at her gates, and as he was so much stronger now than before, would probably desire to rule over the Egyptians. So she immediately advanced against him with both a naval and land force, and made the Jews Chelcias and Ananias generals of her whole army, and sent the greatest part of her riches, her grand-

children, and her will, to the people of Cos.¹ Cleopatra
also ordered her son Alexander to sail with a great fleet to
Phœnicia, when that country revolted, and herself went to
Ptolemais, and as the people of Ptolemais would not receive her, besieged the city. But Ptolemy went out of Syria,
and made haste into Egypt, supposing that he should
find it destitute of an army and so soon take it. But he
failed in his hope. At this time Chelcias, one of Cleopatra's
generals, happened to die in Cœle-Syria, as he was in pursuit of Ptolemy.

§ 2. When Cleopatra heard of her son's attempt, and
that his Egyptian expedition did not succeed according to
his expectations, she sent part of her army there, and
drove him out of that country. And when he had returned from Egypt again, he spent the winter at Gaza.
And meantime Cleopatra took the garrison that was in
Ptolemais as well as the city by siege, and when Alexander
came to her, he gave her presents, and paid her such marks
of respect as were but proper, since he had had no other
refuge but her in the miseries he endured under Ptolemy.
Now some of her friends urged her to seize Alexander, and
to overrun and take possession of the country, and not to
sit still and see such a multitude of brave Jews subject to
one man. But Ananias' counsel was contrary to theirs,
for he said she would do an unjust action, if she deprived a
man that was her ally of the authority which belonged to
him, and that a man who was related to them. "For
(said he) I would not have thee ignorant of this, that any
injustice thou doest to him, will make all us Jews thy
enemies." Cleopatra hearkened to this advice of Ananias,
and did no injury to Alexander, but made an alliance with
him at Scythopolis, a city of Cœle-Syria.

§ 3. Now when Alexander was delivered from the fear he
was in of Ptolemy, he at once made an expedition into
Cœle-Syria, and took Gadara,² after a siege of ten months.
He also took Amathus,³ a very strong fortress belonging
to those who dwelt beyond the Jordan, where Theodorus,

¹ Cos, *Stanko*, an island off the West Coast of Asia Minor, was the
birthplace of Ptolemy Philadelphus.
² *Umm Keis.*
³ Hamath, *Hama,* in the valley of the Orontes.

the son of Zeno, had his chief treasures, and what he esteemed most precious. This Zeno fell unexpectedly upon
the Jews, and slew ten thousand of them, and seized on
Alexander's baggage. But this misfortune did not terrify Alexander, but he made a raid on the maritime
parts, as Raphia[1] and Anthedon[2] (the name of which
last king Herod afterwards changed to Agrippiades), and
took even it by storm. And when he saw that Ptolemy
had retired from Gaza to Cyprus, and that his mother
Cleopatra had returned to Egypt, in his rage because the
people of Gaza had invited Ptolemy to assist them, he
besieged their city and ravaged their country. But when
Apollodotus, the general of the army of Gaza, fell upon the
camp of the Jews by night with two thousand mercenaries
and ten thousand of his own men,[3] the men of Gaza prevailed while the night lasted, as they made the enemy
believe that it was Ptolemy who attacked them : but when
day dawned, and that mistake was corrected, and the Jews
knew the truth, they rallied and fell upon the men of
Gaza, and slew about a thousand of them. But as the men
of Gaza stoutly resisted, and would not surrender either
for scarcity of provisions or because of the great numbers
that were slain (for they would rather suffer any hardship
whatever than come into the power of their enemies),
Aretas, the king of the Arabians, a very illustrious person,
encouraged them by promising that he would come to their
assistance. But before he came Apollodotus happened to
get slain, for his brother Lysimachus, envying him for the
great reputation he had among the citizens, murdered him,
and won over the army, and delivered up the city to Alexander. And he, when he entered first, was quiet, but afterwards set his army upon the inhabitants of Gaza, and gave
the city up to sack. So some went one way, and some
another, and slew the inhabitants of Gaza; but they did
not behave cowardly, but opposed those that came to slay

[1] See Ant. xiv. 5, § 3, and Jewish War, i. 8, § 4. On the edge of the
desert, twenty-two miles S.W. of Gaza, now *er-Rafâh*.
[2] See Ant. xiv. 5, § 3, and xv. 7, § 3; Jewish War, i. 4, § 2, i. 8, § 4,
and i. 21, § 8; it was twenty stadia, about two and a half miles, south
of Gaza, *Tell el-'Ajûl* or *Kefr Hette*.
[3] I read οἰκείων for the common reading οἰκετῶν.

them, and slew as many of the Jews. And some of them, when they saw themselves deserted, burnt their own houses, that the enemy might get none of their spoil; nay, some of them with their own hands slew their children and wives, having no other way but this of avoiding slavery for them. But the senators, who were in all five hundred, fled to Apollo's temple (for this attack happened to be made as they were sitting in council,) and Alexander slew them, and when he had utterly overthrown their city, he returned to Jerusalem, having spent a year in the siege.

§ 4. About this very time Antiochus, who was also called Grypus, was treacherously slain by Heracleon, when he had lived forty-five years, and reigned twenty-nine. His son Seleucus[1] succeeded him in the kingdom, and warred with Antiochus, his father's brother, who was also called Cyzicenus, and beat him, and took him prisoner, and slew him. But not long after Antiochus,[2] the son of Cyzicenus, who was called the Pious, came to Aradus,[3] and put the diadem on his own head, and warred against Seleucus, and beat him, and drove him out of all Syria. And he fled to Cilicia, and went to Mopsuestia,[4] and levied money again upon the people of Mopsuestia; but they were indignant and burnt down his palace, and slew him and his friends. But when Antiochus, the son of Cyzicenus, was king of Syria, Antiochus, the brother of Seleucus, made war upon him, and was beaten and slain, he and his army. After him his brother Philip[5] put on the diadem, and reigned over some part of Syria; but Ptolemy Lathurus sent for his fourth brother Demetrius, who was called Eucærus, from Cnidos,[6] and made him king at Damascus. Both these brothers did Antiochus vehemently oppose, but soon died; for when he was come as an ally to Laodice, queen of the Gileadites, who was warring against the Parthians, he fell fighting courageously. And his two brothers Demetrius and Philip governed Syria, as has been elsewhere related.

§ 5. As to Alexander, his own people were rebellious

---

[1] Seleucus Gryphus, 96 B.C.    [2] Antiochus X., 89 B.C.
[3] Arvad, the island *er-Rûad*.    [4] Now *Missis*, east of *Adana*.
[5] 87 B.C.
[6] The ruins are on Cape *Crio*, at the S.W. end of Asia Minor.

against him, for at a festival which was then being celebrated, as he stood at the altar and was going to sacrifice, the
nation rose in insurrection against him and pelted him with
citrons [which they then had in their hands,] because the law
of the Jews requires at the feast of Tabernacles that every
one should have branches of palm-trees and citron-trees,
as I have elsewhere related.   They also reviled him, as
descended from a woman who had been a captive,[1] and so as
unworthy of his dignity, and of sacrificing.   At this he was
in a rage, and slew about six thousand of them.   He also
constructed a wooden screen round the altar and the temple,
as far as the partition within which it was only lawful for the
priests to enter, and by this means he debarred the multitude from coming near him.   He also kept an army of
Pisidian and Cilician mercenaries ; but could not so utilize
the Syrians, as he was their enemy.   He also overcame
the Moabites and Gileadites, who were Arabians, and
made them pay tribute.   Moreover, he demolished Amathus, as Theodorus durst not fight with him.[2]   But en-
gaging in battle with Obedas, king of the Arabians,
he fell into an ambush in places that were rugged and
difficult to travel over, and was thrown down into a deep
ravine by a multitude of camels at Gadara a village of
Gilead, and barely escaped with his life.   From thence he
fled to Jerusalem, where because of his ill success the nation
attacked him, and he fought against them for six years,
and slew no less than fifty thousand of them.   And when
he begged that they would desist from their ill-will to him,
they hated him so much the more on account of what had
happened ; and when he asked them what he ought to do,
they all cried out that he ought to die, and sent to Demetrius Eucærus, and begged him to make an alliance with
them.

[1] This reproach cast on Alexander seems only the repetition of the
old Pharisaical calumny upon his father.   See chap. x. § 5.—W.
[2] This Theodorus was the son of Zeno, and was in the possession of
Amathus, as we gather from § 3, foregoing.—W.

## CHAP. XIV.

*How Demetrius Eucærus overcame Alexander, and yet in a
little time retired out of the Country for fear of the Jews.
As also how Alexander slew many of the Jews, and thereby
got rid of his Troubles.  Concerning the Death of
Demetrius.*

### § 1.

SO Demetrius came with an army, which he swelled with
those that invited him, and encamped near the city
of Shechem;[1] and Alexander, with six thousand two
hundred mercenaries, and about twenty thousand Jews
who were of his party, marched against Demetrius, who
had three thousand horse and forty thousand foot.  Now
there was much negotiation on both sides, Demetrius
trying to make the mercenaries that were with Alexander
desert because they were Greeks, and Alexander trying to
make the Jews desert that were with Demetrius.  However, neither of them could persuade the opposite side to
do as they wished, but a battle ensued, in which Demetrius
was the conqueror, and all Alexander's mercenaries were
killed, when they had given proof of their fidelity and
courage.  A great number of Demetrius's soldiers were
slain also.

§ 2. Now when Alexander fled to the mountains, six
thousand of the Jews mustered to him, moved by pity
at his reverse.  So Demetrius was afraid, and retired
out of the country; after which the Jews fought against
Alexander, and were beaten, and slain in great numbers
in the several battles which they had.  And when he
had shut up the most powerful of them in the city
of Bethome,[2] he besieged them therein; and when he
had taken the city, and got the inhabitants into his power,
he brought them to Jerusalem, and did one of the most
barbarous actions in the world to them: for as he was

[1] *Náblus.*
[2] In Jewish War, i. 4, § 6, the name is given as Bemeselis; the site is
unknown.

feasting with his concubines in the sight of all the city, he ordered about eight hundred of them to be crucified, and while they were still living ordered the throats of their children and wives to be cut before their eyes. This was indeed by way of revenge for the injuries they had done him, but this punishment which he exacted was inhuman, though we suppose him to have been ever so much distressed, as it is probable he was, by his wars with them, for he had by their means come to the last degree of hazard both as to his life and kingdom. For they were not satisfied to fight only by themselves against him, but introduced foreigners also for the same purpose; nay, at last they reduced him to that degree of necessity, that he was forced to deliver back to the king of Arabia the land of Moab and Gilead, which he had subdued, and the places that were in them, that they might not join the Jews in the war against him, and they also did ten thousand other things to affront and outrage him. However, this barbarity seems to have been without any necessity, and on account of that extreme savageness he got the name of Thracidas among the Jews.[1] And the soldiers who had fought against him, who were about eight thousand in number, fled by night, and continued in exile all the time that Alexander lived. And he, being now freed from any further disturbance from them, reigned the rest of his time in the utmost tranquillity.

§ 3. Now when Demetrius departed from Judæa, he went to Berœa,[2] and besieged his brother Philip, taking with him ten thousand foot, and a thousand horse. But Strato, the tyrant of Berœa and ally of Philip, called in Zizus the ruler of the Arabian tribes, and Mithridates Sinaces, the ruler of the Parthians. And they coming with a large force, and besieging Demetrius in his intrenched camp, into which they had driven him with their arrows, compelled those that were with him to surrender from want of water. And they took a great deal of spoil out of that country, and captured Demetrius himself, whom they sent to Mithridates, who was then king of Parthia, but as to

---

[1] Or Thracian. The Thracians were proverbial for savage barbarity, see for example Thucydides, vii. 29.

[2] *Aleppo.*

those of the people of Antioch whom they took captive, they restored them to the people of Antioch without any ransom. Now Mithridates, the king of Parthia, held Demetrius in great honour, till Demetrius ended his life by sickness. And Philip, directly the fight was over, went to Antioch, and made himself master of it, and reigned over Syria.

## CHAP. XV.

*How Antiochus, who was called Dionysus, and after him*
*Aretas, made Expeditions into Judœa; as also, how*
*Alexander took many Cities, and then returned to Jerusa-*
*lem, and died after an Illness of Three Years, and what*
*Advice he gave to Alexandra.*

### § 1.

AFTER this, Antiochus, who was called Dionysus, and was Philip's brother, aspired to the dominion, and went to Damascus, and got the power into his hands, and there reigned. But as he was making an expedition against the Arabians, his brother Philip heard of it, and went to Damascus, where Milesius, who had been left governor of the citadel, delivered up the city of the Damascenes to him; but as Philip was ungrateful to him, and bestowed upon him nothing of what he hoped for when he received him into the city, but wished to have it believed that it was rather delivered up out of fear of him than owing to the kindness of Milesius, and because he did not reward him as he ought to have done, he was suspected by him, and so lost Damascus again; for when he was going into the Hippodrome, Milesius shut him out of it, and kept Damascus for Antiochus. And he, hearing how Philip's affairs stood, came back from Arabia, and also immediately marched into Judæa, with eight thousand foot, and eight hundred horse. And Alexander, being afraid at his coming, dug a deep trench from Chabarzaba,[1] which is now called Anti-

---

[1] *Kefr Sâba.*

patris,[1] to the sea near Joppa,[2] where alone an army could be brought against him. He also raised a wall one hundred and fifty furlongs in length, and erected on it wooden towers and curtains, and waited for the coming of Antiochus, who burnt all those works, and made his army pass by that way into Arabia. The Arabian king [Aretas] at first retired, but afterwards suddenly appeared with ten thousand cavalry. Antiochus met them and fought desperately, but when he had got the victory in his part of the battle, and was bringing up reinforcements to the part of his army that was hard pressed, he got slain. And when Antiochus had fallen, his army fled to the village of Cana,[3] where most of them perished by famine.

§ 2. After him Aretas reigned over Cœle-Syria, being called to the government by those that held Damascus, because of the hatred they bore to Ptolemy the son of Mennæus. He also made thence an expedition into Judæa, and beat Alexander in battle, near a place called Addida,[4] but upon certain conditions agreed on between them retired from Judæa.

§ 3. But Alexander marched again to the city Dium,[5] and took it, and then made an expedition against Essa,[6] where most of Zeno's treasures happened to be, and surrounded the place with three walls, and when he had taken the city by assault, he marched on to Gaulana[7] and Seleucia.[8] And when he had taken those cities, he also took the valley which is called the valley of Antiochus, as also the fortress of Gamala.[9] He also accused Demetrius, who was governor of those places, of many crimes, and turned him out: and after he had spent three years in this war, he returned to his own country, and the Jews joyfully received him because of his good success.

---

[1] *Kul'at Râs el-'Ain.* For discussion on true site of Antipatris see Memoirs of Palestine Fund, ii. 258-262.

[2] That part of the Mediterranean off the coast at *Jaffa.*

[3] Apparently a village in the south of Palestine, and not one of the Canas of Galilee.                           [4] *Haditheh,* near Lydda.

[5] One of the cities of Decapolis, east of Jordan; the site has not yet been recovered.

[6] A town east of Jordan, site unknown.

[7] *Sahem ej-Jaulân,* east of the Sea of Galilee.

[8] See Life, § 37; Jewish War, iv. 1, § 1.        [9] *Kul'at el-Husn.*

§ 4. Now at this time the Jews were in possession of the following cities of the Syrians and Idumæans and Phœnicians; on the sea coast Strato's Tower,[1] Apollonia,[2] Joppa,[3] Jamnia,[4] Azotus,[5] Gaza,[6] Anthedon,[7] Raphia,[8] and Rhinocurura;[9] in the interior of the country towards Idumæa, Adora[10] and Marissa[11] and Samaria,[12] Mount Carmel and Mount Tabor, Scythopolis,[13] Gadara,[14] Gaulanitis,[15] Seleucia,[16] and Gabala;[17] in the country of Moab, Heshbon,[18] Medaba,[19] Lemba,[20] Oronas,[21] Telithon,[22] Zara,[23] the valley of the Cilicians,[24] and Pella[25] (which last they utterly destroyed, because its inhabitants would not change their religious rites for those peculiar to the Jews). The Jews also possessed others of the principal cities in Syria, which had been destroyed.

§ 5. After this king Alexander, although he fell ill from hard drinking, and was troubled with a quartan ague for three years, yet would not leave off going out with his army, till he was quite worn out with the labours he had undergone, and died on the borders of the Gerasenes,[26] while besieging Ragaba,[27] a fortress beyond the Jordan. But when his queen saw that he was on the point of death, and had no longer any hope of surviving, she came to him weeping and lamenting, and bewailed the desolate condition which herself and her sons would be left in, and said to him, "To whom dost thou thus leave me and my children, who are destitute of all other support, and that though thou knowest how much ill-will thy nation bears thee?" But he gave her the following advice, to do what he would suggest to her, in order to retain the kingdom

[1] Cæsarea Palæstina, *Kaisarîyeh*.
[2] *Arsûf*, between *Kaisarîyeh* and *Jaffa*.  [3] *Jaffa*.
[4] *Yebnah*.        [5] Ashdod, *Esdûd*.        [6] *Ghuzzeh*.
[7] See p. 100, note 2.        [8] *er-Rafâh*.
[9] *el-'Arîsh*, the border town between Egypt and Palestine.
[10] *Dûra*.        [11] *Kh. Mer'ash*.        [12] *Sebustieh*.
[13] *Beisân*.        [14] *Umm Keis*.        [15] *Sahem ej-Jaulân*.
[16] See p. 106, note 6.        [17] Probably for Gamala, *Kul'at el-Husn*.
[18] *Hesbân*.        [19] *Medeba*.        [20] Unknown.
[21] Possibly the Horonaim of Is. xv. 5, and Jer. xlviii. 3, 5, 54.
[22] Unknown.        [23] *Beit Zâra*.        [24] Unknown.
[25] *Tubakât Fâhil*.
[26] The borders of the district of Gerasa, *Jerâsh*.
[27] Not identified.

securely for herself and her children: namely, to conceal his death from the soldiers till she should have taken Ragaba, and after that to go in triumph as upon a victory to Jerusalem, and put some authority into the hands of the Pharisees, for they would commend her for the honour she did them, and would reconcile the nation to her; for they had great authority among the Jews, both to injure such as hated them, and to bring advantages to those who were friendly disposed to them, for they were believed most of all by the multitude when they spoke any severe thing against others, though it was only out of envy. And he said that it was owing to them, whom indeed he had insulted, that he had incurred the displeasure of the nation. "Do thou therefore," he added, "when thou art come to Jerusalem, send for the leading men among them, and show them my dead body, and with great show of sincerity, give them leave to use it as they themselves please, whether they will dishonour my corpse by refusing it burial, as having suffered much at my hands, or whether in their anger they will offer any other outrage to that body. Promise them also that thou wilt do nothing without consulting them in the affairs of the kingdom. If thou dost but say this to them, I shall have the honour of a more glorious funeral from them than I could have had from thee, for when it is in their power to abuse my dead body, they will do it no injury at all, and thou wilt rule in safety."[1] When he had given his wife this advice he died, after having reigned twenty-seven years, and lived fifty years save one.

[1] It seems, by this dying advice of Alexander to his wife, that he had himself pursued the measures of his father Hyrcanus, and taken part with the Sadducees, who kept close to the written law, against the Pharisees, who had introduced their own traditions, chap. 7, § 2, and that he now saw a political necessity of submitting to the Pharisees, and their traditions hereafter, if his widow and family were to retain their hold over the Jewish nation.—W.

## CHAP. XVI.

*How Alexandra, by gaining the good-will of the Pharisees, retained the Kingdom Nine Years, and then, having done many glorious Actions, died.*

### § 1.

AND Alexandra, when she had taken the fortress, acted as her husband had suggested to her, and spoke to the Pharisees, and put all things into their hands, both as to the dead body, and as to the affairs of the kingdom, and so pacified their anger against Alexander, and made them her friends and well-wishers. So they went among the multitude, and made speeches to them, extolling the actions of Alexander, and telling them that they had lost a righteous king; and by the commendation they gave him, they induced them to grieve and be in heaviness for him, so that he had a more splendid funeral than had any of the kings before him. Alexander left behind him two sons, Hyrcanus and Aristobulus, but committed the kingdom to Alexandra. Now as to her two sons, Hyrcanus was indeed unfit to manage public affairs, and delighted rather in a quiet life; but the younger, Aristobulus, was active and bold. And Alexandra herself was loved by the multitude, because she seemed displeased at the offences her husband had been guilty of.

§ 2. Now she made Hyrcanus high priest, because he was the elder, but much more because he did not meddle with politics, and she allowed the Pharisees to do everything, and also ordered the multitude to be obedient to them. She also restored those practices which the Pharisees had introduced, according to the traditions of their forefathers, and which her father-in-law Hyrcanus had abrogated. She had indeed the name of queen, but the Pharisees had all the authority; for it was they who restored such as had been banished, and set such as were prisoners at liberty, in a word, they differed in nothing from lords of the realm. However, the queen also looked after the affairs of the kingdom, and got together a great body of mercenary soldiers, and increased her own army to such a degree, that she became terrible to the neighbouring tyrants, and took hostages of them. And the country was entirely at peace, except for the Pharisees; for they disturbed the queen, and urged her to kill those who had persuaded Alexander to slay the eight hundred men ; after which they themselves cut the throat of one of them, Diogenes, and after him they did the same to several, one after another, till the leading men of the opposite party came to the palace, and Aristobulus with them (for he seemed to be displeased at what was done, and it appeared clear that, if he had an opportunity, he would not permit his mother to go on so), and reminded the queen what great dangers they had gone through, and what great things they had done, whereby they had demonstrated the firmness of their fidelity to their master, and had in consequence received the greatest marks of favour from him ; and they begged of her, that she would not utterly blast their hopes, as it now happened, that after having escaped the hazards that arose from their [open] enemies, they were cut off at home, by their [private] enemies, like brute beasts, without any remedy whatever. They said also, that if their adversaries would be satisfied with those that had been slain already, they would take what had been done patiently, on account of their natural love to their masters, but if they must expect the same for the future also, they implored of her dismissal from her service, for they could not bear to think of attempting any method for their deliverance without her, but would die willingly before the palace, if she would not forgive them. They said also that it would be a great disgrace both for themselves and for the queen, if when they were neglected by her, they should be welcomed by her husband's enemies, for the Arabian Aretas and the other monarchs would give any pay if they could get such men as mercenaries, whose very names, before their voices were heard, would be probably terrible to them. But if they could not obtain this their second request, and she was determined to prefer the Pharisees before them, let her place every one of them in her fortresses; for if some demon had a spite against Alexander's house, they would be willing to live in a lowly station.

§ 3. As these men used much language of this kind, and called upon Alexander's ghost to commiserate those already slain, and those in danger of being so, all the bystanders broke out into tears ; especially Aristobulus, who showed what his sentiments were, and used many reproachful expressions to his mother.   He said also that they were indeed themselves the authors of their own calamities, seeing they had unreasonably permitted a woman, who was mad with ambition, to reign over them, when there were sons in the flower of their age fitter to rule over the kingdom.   Then Alexandra, not knowing how to refuse with any decency, committed all the fortresses to them, except Hyrcania [1] and Alexandrium [2] and Machærus,[3] where her principal treasures were.   A little while after she also sent her son Aristobulus with an army to Damascus against Ptolemy, who was called Mennæus, who was a bad neighbour to that city ; but he did nothing considerable against him, and returned home.

§ 4. About this time news was brought that Tigranes,[4] the king of Armenia, had made an irruption into Syria with five hundred thousand soldiers,[5] and was coming to attack Judæa.   This news, as may well be supposed, terrified the queen and nation.   Accordingly, they sent him many and very valuable presents, as also ambassadors, as he was besieging Ptolemais.   For queen Selene, who was also called Cleopatra, ruled then over Syria, and had persuaded the inhabitants to exclude Tigranes.   So the Jewish ambassadors interceded with him, and entreated that he would decree nothing severe against the queen or nation.   He commended them for the court they paid

---

[1] On the east of the Jordan.  See Ant. xiv. 5, § 4; Jewish War, i. 8, § 5.   Perhaps 'Arak el-Emîr.

[2] Kefr Istûna, near Keriût, Coreæ.   Ant. xiv. 3, § 4; xiv. 5, § 2, 4 ; Jewish War, i. 6, § 4; i. 8, § 5.

[3] Mekaur, to the east of the Dead Sea.

[4] Tigranes II., 93-39 b.c.

[5] The number of 500,000, or even 300,000, as one Greek copy, with the Latin copies, have it, for Tigranes' army, that came out of Armenia into Syria and Judæa, seems much too large.   We have already had several such extravagant numbers in Josephus's present copies.   I incline to Dr. Hudson's emendation here, which supposes them but 40,000.—W.

him at so great a distance, and gave them good hopes
of his favour. But as soon as Ptolemais was taken, news
came to Tigranes that Lucullus, in his pursuit of Mithridates, could not light upon him (for he had fled into
Iberia), but was laying waste Armenia, and besieging its
cities. Now when Tigranes knew this, he returned home.

§ 5. After this, when the queen was fallen dangerously
ill, Aristobulus resolved to attempt to seize the kingdom, so he stole away secretly by night with only one
of his servants, and went to the fortresses wherein his
father's friends were settled. For as he had been a great
while displeased at his mother's conduct, so was he now
much more afraid that, upon her death, their whole family
would be in the power of the Pharisees, for he saw the
inability of his brother the heir apparent. Now no one
had any idea of what he was going to do except his wife,
whom he left at Jerusalem with their children. He went
first of all to Agaba,[1] where was Galæstes, one of the influential men before mentioned, and was received by him.
When it was day the queen perceived that Aristobulus
had fled ; and she did not for some time suppose that his
departure had any revolutionary intention ; but when
messengers came one after another with the news that he
had secured the first fortress, the second fortress, and all the
fortresses (for as soon as one began, they all submitted to
his disposal), then the queen and nation were in the greatest
alarm, for they were aware that it would not be long ere
Aristobulus would be able to settle himself firmly in the
government. What they were principally afraid of was
that he would inflict punishment upon them for the mad
treatment his house had had from them : so they resolved
to take his wife and children into custody, and kept them
in the fortress that was over the temple.[2] Now a mighty
conflux of people came to Aristobulus from all parts, inso-

[1] Not identified.
[2] This fortress, castle, citadel, or tower, whither the wife and children
of Aristobulus were now sent, and which overlooked the temple, could
be no other than what Hyrcanus I. built, Antiq. xviii. 4, § 3, and Herod
the Great rebuilt, and called the Tower of Antonia, Antiq. xv. 11, § 5.
—W.

much that he had a kind of royal retinue about him; for in little more than fifteen days he got twenty-two fortresses, which gave him the opportunity of raising an army from Libanus and Trachonitis and the monarchs. For men are easily led by majorities, and readily submit to them; and besides this they thought that by affording him their assistance when he could not expect it, they as well as he would enjoy the advantages that would come by his being king, because they had been the cause of his gaining the kingdom. Now Hyrcanus and the elders of the Jews went in to the queen, and desired that she would give them her views on the present state of affairs, for Aristobulus was already lord of almost all the kingdom, by possessing so many strongholds, and it was absurd for them to take any counsel by themselves, however ill she were, whilst she was alive, and the danger would be upon them in no long time. And she bade them do what they thought best to be done: for they had many circumstances in their favour still remaining, a nation in good heart, an army, and money in their several treasuries; but she had small concern for public affairs now, as the strength of her body already failed her.

§ 6. Now a little while after she had said this to them, she died, when she had reigned nine years, and had lived in all seventy-three. She was a woman who showed no signs of the weakness of her sex; for she was sagacious to the highest degree in her love of rule, and demonstrated at once by her doings her practical genius, and the little understanding that men show who make frequent mistakes in ruling. For she always preferred the present to the future, and ranked power above all things, and where that was at stake had no regard to what was good or right. However, she brought the affairs of her house to such an unfortunate condition, that she was the cause of its losing, and that at no distant date, that authority which she had obtained by much toil and danger, from a desire of interfering in what did not belong to a woman, and by siding in her opinions with those that bore ill-will to her family, and by leaving the administration destitute of proper support; and indeed her management during her administration,

while she was alive, was such as filled the palace after her
death with calamities and confusion.  However, although
this had been her fashion of governing, she preserved the
nation in peace.  Such was the conclusion of the reign of
Alexandra.

# BOOK XIV.

**FROM THE DEATH OF QUEEN ALEXANDRA TO THE DEATH OF ANTIGONUS.**

## CHAP. I.

*The War between Aristobulus and Hyrcanus about the King-
dom ; and how they made an Agreement that Aristobulus
should be King, and Hyrcanus live a private Life : as also,
how Hyrcanus, a little afterwards, was persuaded by Antipater to flee to Aretas.*

### § 1.

I HAVE related the reign of queen Alexandra and her
death in the previous book, and will now speak of what
followed next, having nothing so much at heart as this,
that I may omit no facts, either from ignorance or fault
of memory.  For I am upon the history and relation of
such things as most people are unacquainted with because
of their antiquity, and I aim to do it with a proper beauty
of style, so far as that is derived from words well arranged,
and from such ornaments of speech also as may contribute
to the pleasure of my readers, that they may imbibe the
knowledge of what I write with satisfaction and pleasure.
But the principal end that authors ought to aim at is to
speak accurately and truly, for the satisfaction of those
that are unacquainted with the transactions, and obliged
to believe what writers tell them.

§ 2. Now Hyrcanus began his high priesthood in the third

year of the hundred and seventy-seventh Olympiad, when
Quintus Hortensius and Quintus Metellus, who was also
called Creticus, were consuls at Rome. And Aristobulus
directly began to make war against him, and as it came to
a battle at Jericho, many of the soldiers of Hyrcanus deserted him, and went over to his brother; upon which
Hyrcanus fled into the citadel, where Aristobulus' wife
and children had been imprisoned by his mother, as I have
said already, and attacked and overcame his adversaries
that had fled to the temple precincts. And when he had
sent a message to his brother to treat with him, he
laid aside his enmity to him on these conditions, that
Aristobulus should be king, and that he should live without meddling in public affairs, and quiety enjoy his private
fortune. When they had agreed upon these terms in the
temple, and had confirmed the agreement with oaths, and
the giving one another their right hands, and embracing
one another in the sight of the whole multitude, they departed, Aristobulus to the palace, and Hyrcanus, as a
private man, to the house of Aristobulus.

§ 3. But there was a certain friend of Hyrcanus, an
Idumæan, called Antipater, who was very rich, and by
nature an energetic and factious man; he was at enmity with
Aristobulus, and had differences with him, from his good-
will to Hyrcanus. Nicolaus of Damascus says indeed that
Antipater was of the stock of the leading Jews who returned
from Babylon into Judæa; but that assertion of his was
made to gratify Herod, who was Antipater's son, and who,
by certain revolutions of fortune, came afterwards to be
king of the Jews, whose history I shall give in its proper
place. Now this Antipater was at first called Antipas, and
that was his father's name also, of whom they relate that
king Alexander and his wife made him governor of
all Idumæa, and that he made a league of friendship
with those Arabians and Gazites and Ascalonites that
thought as he did, and by many and large presents
made them his fast friends. But the younger Antipater
was suspicious of the power of Aristobulus, and was afraid
that he might do him some mischief because of his hatred
to him, so he stirred up the most powerful of the Jews
privately against him by detraction, and said that it was

wrong to overlook the conduct of Aristobulus, who had got the government unrighteously, and ejected his brother out of it, who was the elder, and ought to retain what belonged to him by primogeniture. And he perpetually made the same speeches to Hyrcanus, and told him, that his own life would be in danger, unless he was on his guard, and got rid of Aristobulus; for he said that the friends of Aristobulus omitted no opportunity of advising him to kill him, as being then, and not before, sure to retain the kingdom. Hyrcanus gave no credit to these words of his, being of a good disposition, and one that did not readily, owing to his mild character, listen to calumny. This temper of his, not disposing him to meddle in public affairs, and want of spirit, made him appear to spectators degenerate and unmanly; while Aristobulus was of a contrary temper, an active man and wide awake.

§ 4. When Antipater saw that Hyrcanus did not attend to what he said, he ceased not day by day to charge feigned crimes upon Aristobulus, and to calumniate him as desirous to kill him, and by being always at him he at last with great difficulty persuaded him to flee to Aretas, the king of Arabia, and promised, that if he would comply with his advice, he would also himself assist him. When Hyrcanus heard this, he said that it was for his advantage to flee to Aretas; for Arabia is a country that borders upon Judæa. However, Hyrcanus sent Antipater first to the king of Arabia, in order to receive assurances from him, that when he should come as a suppliant to him, he would not deliver him up to his enemies. And Antipater, having received such assurances, returned to Hyrcanus to Jerusalem. Not long afterwards he took Hyrcanus, and stole out of the city by night, and travelled fast, and brought him to the city called Petra,[1] where the palace of Aretas was; and as he was a very intimate friend of that king's he urged him to bring back Hyrcanus into Judæa, and continued his suit every day without intermission, and also offered him presents, and at last he prevailed with Aretas. Moreover, Hyrcanus promised him, that when he had been restored, and had recovered his kingdom, he would give back the territory and twelve cities which his father Alexander had

---

[1] Petra, near Mount Hor, to the east of the 'Arabah.

taken from the Arabians, namely, Medaba,[1] Naballo,[2] Libias,[3] Tharabasa,[2] Agalla,[4] Athone,[2] Zoara,[5] Oronæ,[6] Marissa,[7] Rydda,[2] Lusa,[2] and Oryba.[2]

## CHAP. II.

*How Aretas and Hyrcanus made an Expedition against Aristobulus, and besieged Jerusalem; and how Scaurus, the Roman General, raised the Siege. Concerning the Death of Onias.*

### § 1.

AFTER these promises had been made to Aretas, he marched against Aristobulus with an army of fifty thousand horse and foot, and beat him in battle. And as after that victory many went over to Hyrcanus as deserters, Aristobulus was left alone, and fled to Jerusalem. Upon this the king of Arabia took all his army, and made an assault upon the temple, and besieged Aristobulus therein, the people still supporting Hyrcanus and assisting him in the siege, while none but the priests continued with Aristobulus. So Aretas united the forces of the Arabians and Jews together, and pressed on the siege vigorously. As this happened at the time when the feast of Unleavened Bread, which we call the Passover, was being celebrated, the principal men among the Jews left the country and fled into Egypt. Now there was one whose name was Onias, a righteous man and beloved of God, who, in a certain drought, had prayed to God to put an end to the intense heat, and whose prayer God had heard, and had sent rain. This man had hid himself, because he saw that this civil

---

[1] *Medeba*, east of the Dead Sea.
[2] Site unknown.
[3] The Beth-Aram of Josh. xiii. 27, now *Tell er-Râmeh*, N.E. of the Dead Sea.
[4] Probably the Eglaim of Isaiah xv. 8, which Eusebius places eight miles S. of Ar of Moab.
[5] Apparently the later Zoar in the *Ghor es-Sâfi*, S.E. of the Dead Sea.
[6] Probably the Horonaim of Is. xv. 5, and Jer. xlviii. 3, 5, 34. Site unknown.
[7] Mareshah, *Kh. Mer'ash*.

war would last a long while.   However, they brought him
to the Jewish camp, and desired, that as by his prayers he
had once put an end to the drought, so he would in like
manner utter imprecations on Aristobulus and those of
his faction.   And when, upon his refusing and making excuses, he was still compelled to speak by the multitude, he
stood up in the midst of them, and said, " O God, the king
of the whole world, since those that stand now with me
are thy people, and those that are besieged are also thy
priests, I beseech thee, that thou wilt neither hearken to
the prayers of those against these, not bring to effect what
these pray against those."   And the wicked Jews who
stood around him, as soon as he had made this prayer,
stoned him to death.

§ 2. But God punished them immediately for this barbarity, and took vengeance on them for the murder of
Onias, in the manner following.   As the priests and Aristobulus were besieged, it happened that the feast called
the Passover was come, at which it is our custom to offer a
great number of sacrifices to God ; and those that were
with Aristobulus wanted victims, and desired that their
countrymen without would furnish them with such, and
assured them they should have as much money for them
as they wished ; and when they required them to pay a
thousand drachmæ for each head of cattle, Aristobulus and
the priests willingly undertook to pay for them accordingly,
and those within let down the money over the walls, and
gave it to them.   But when the others had received it, they
did not deliver the victims, but arrived at that height of
wickedness as to break the promises they had given, and
to be guilty of impiety towards God, by not furnishing
those that wanted them with victims.   And when the
priests found they had been cheated, and that the agreements that had been made were violated, they prayed to
God that he would avenge them on their countrymen.
Nor did he delay that punishment, but sent a strong and
vehement storm of wind, that destroyed the fruits of the
whole country, till a modius of wheat was bought for eleven
drachmæ.

§ 3. Meantime Pompey sent Scaurus into Syria, as he
was himself in Armenia making war against Tigranes : and

when Scaurus was come to Damascus, and found that
Lollius and Metellus had just taken that city, he pushed
on into Judæa.    And when he was come there, ambassadors came to him both from Aristobulus and Hyrcanus, for
both asked him to assist them.    And as both of them
promised to give him money, Aristobulus four hundred
talents, and Hyrcanus no less, he accepted of Aristobulus'
promise, for he was rich and had a great soul, and desired
to obtain nothing but what was fair, whereas the other was
poor, and mean, and made incredible promises for greater
advantages.    Nor was it the same thing to take a city by
storm, which was exceedingly strong and powerful, as it
was to eject out of the country some fugitives, with a
quantity of Nabatæans, who were no very warlike people.
He therefore made an agreement with Aristobulus for the
reasons before mentioned, and took his money, and raised
the siege, and ordered Aretas to depart, or else he should
be declared an enemy to the Romans.    Then Scaurus returned to Damascus again, and Aristobulus with a great
army marched against Aretas and Hyrcanus, and fought
them at a place called Papyron,[1] and beat them in the
battle, and slew about six thousand of the enemy, among
whom fell Phallion also, the brother of Antipater.


## CHAP.  III.

*How Aristobulus and Hyrcanus came to Pompey to discuss
who ought to have the Kingdom; and how, upon the Flight
of Aristobulus to the Fortress of Alexandrium, Pompey
led his army against him, and ordered him to deliver up
the Fortresses of which he was possessed.*


### § 1.

A LITTLE afterwards Pompey came to Damascus, and
marched over Cœle-Syria, and there came to him ambassadors from all Syria, and Egypt, and from Judæa
also.    For Aristobulus sent him a great present, which was a

---

[1] A town or river, the locality of which is unknown.   The battle took
place in 63 B.C.

golden vine,[1] and worth five hundred talents.  Now Strabo
of Cappadocia mentions this present in the following words.
"There came also an embassage out of Egypt and a crown
of the value of four thousand pieces of gold, and out of
Judæa there came another, whether you call it a vine or a
garden : they called it TERPOLE (*Delight*).  However, I
myself saw that present deposited at Rome in the temple
of Jupiter Capitolinus, with this inscription, ' The gift of
Alexander the king of the Jews.'  It was valued at five hundred talents, and the report is, that Aristobulus, the ruler
of the Jews sent it."

§ 2.  A little time afterwards came ambassadors again to
him, Antipater on behalf of Hyrcanus, and Nicodemus on
behalf of Aristobulus; which last also accused those who
had taken bribes, first Gabinius, and then Scaurus, the one
having had three hundred talents, and the other four hundred; by which proceeding he made those two his enemies,
besides those he had before.  And when Pompey had
ordered those that had differences with one another to
come to him in the beginning of the spring, he took his
army out of their winter quarters, and marched into the
country near Damascus ; and as he went along he demolished the citadel that was at Apamea,[2] that Antiochus
Cyzicenus had built, and subdued the country of Ptolemy
Mennæus (a wicked man, and not less so than Dionysius
of Tripolis, who had been beheaded, who was also his rela-

___

[1] This ' golden vine,' or ' garden,' seen by Strabo at Rome, has its
inscription here as if it were the gift of Alexander, the father of Aristobulus, and not of Aristobulus himself, to whom yet Josephus ascribes
it; and in order to prove the truth of that part of his history, introduces
this testimony of Strabo ; so that the ordinary copies seem to be here
either erroneous or defective, and the original reading seems to have
been either ' Aristobulus,' instead of ' Alexander,' with one Greek copy,
or else ' Aristobulus the son of Alexander,' with the Latin copies, which
last seems to me the most probable.   For as to Archbishop Usher's conjectures, that Alexander made it, and dedicated it to God in the temple,
and that thence Aristobulus took it, and sent it to Pompey, they are
both very improbable, and no way agreeable to Josephus, who would
hardly have avoided the recording both these uncommon points of history, had he known of them ; nor would either the Jewish nation, or
even Pompey himself, then have relished such a flagrant instance of
sacrilege.—W.
[2] *Kal'ât el-Medyk*, in Syria.

tion by marriage), who however bought off the punishment
of his crimes for a thousand talents, with which money
Pompey paid the soldiers their wages. He also razed to the
ground the fortress of Lysias,[1] of which Silas a Jew was
tyrant. And when he had passed by the cities of Heliopolis[2] and Chalcis,[3] and crossed over the mountain which is
the boundary of Cœle-Syria, he went from Pella[4] to Damascus; and there he carefully heard the Jews, and their
governors Hyrcanus and Aristobulus, who were at variance
with one another, as also the nation against them both, for
it did not desire to be under kingly government, because the
form of government they had received from their forefathers
was that of subjection to the priests of that God whom
they worshipped, whereas though Hyrcanus and Aristobulus were the posterity of priests, yet did they seek to
change the government of their nation to another form, in
order to enslave them. As to Hyrcanus, he complained,
that although he was the elder brother, he was deprived of
the prerogative of his birth by Aristobulus, and that he
had but a small part of the country under him, Aristobulus
having taken away the rest from him by force. He also
stated that the raids which had been made into their
neighbours' countries, and the piratical expeditions by sea,
were owing to him, and that the nation would not have
revolted, had not Aristobulus been a man given to violence
and disorder. And there were no fewer than a thousand
Jews, of the best reputation, who confirmed this accusation,
being suborned by Antipater. But Aristobulus alleged on
the other hand that it was Hyrcanus' own nature, which
was inactive, and so contemptible, that had caused him to
be deprived of the government; and that, as for himself, he
was necessitated to take it upon him, for fear it should be
transferred to others, and as to his title of king, it was no
other than the same title that his father had taken before
him. And he called as witnesses of this some persons who
were both young and insolent, whose purple garments,
fine heads of hair, and other ornaments, made them objec-
tionable, for they appeared not as though they were to

---

[1] Site unknown.
[3] Now *Kinnisrin*.
[2] Now *Ba'albek*.
[4] *Tubakât Fahil*, east of Jordan.

plead their cause in a court of justice, but as if they formed part of a triumphal procession.

§ 3. When Pompey had heard these two, and had condemned Aristobulus for his violent proceedings, he then spoke civilly to them, and sent them away, and told them that when he came into their country again he would settle all their affairs, after he had first taken a view of the affairs of the Nabatæans. Meantime he ordered them to be quiet, and at the same time paid great attention to Aristobulus, lest he should make the nation revolt, and hinder his return; which Aristobulus did: for without waiting for that further determination which Pompey had promised, he went to the city of Dium,[1] and thence marched into Judæa.

§ 4. Pompey was angry at this behaviour, and taking with him the army which he was leading against the Nabatæans, and the auxiliaries that came from Damascus and the rest of Syria, with the other Roman legions which he had with him, marched against Aristobulus. And as he passed by Pella and Scythopolis,[2] he came to Coreæ,[3] which is the first town in Judæa as one passes through the interior of the country, where he came to a most beautiful fortress (that was built on the top of a mountain), called Alexandrium,[4] to which Aristobulus had fled, and Pompey sent his commands to him, that he should come to him. Accordingly, as many urged him not to make war with the Romans, he came down, and when he had disputed with his brother the right to the government, he went up again to the citadel, as Pompey gave him leave to do. And this he did two or three times, flattering himself with the hopes of having the kingdom granted him, and pretending he would obey Pompey in whatever he commanded, although at the same time he retired to his fortress, that he might not depress himself too low, and that he might be prepared for war, in case Pompey, as he feared, should transfer the government to Hyrcanus. But when Pompey ordered Aristobulus to deliver up the fortresses he held, and to send written orders to their governors in his own hand-

---

[1] One of the towns of Decapolis, not yet identified.
[2] *Beisân.*                          [3] Now *Keriût.*
[4] Now *Kefr Istûna.*

writing for that purpose, for they had been forbidden to
deliver them upon any other conditions, he obeyed indeed,
but retired in dudgeon to Jerusalem, and made preparations for war.  A little after this certain persons came out
of Pontus, and informed Pompey, as he was on the way
and leading his army against Aristobulus, that Mithridates
was dead, having been slain by his son Pharnaces.

## CHAP. IV.

*How Pompey, when the Citizens of Jerusalem shut the Gates
against him, besieged the City and took it by Storm ; also
what other things he did in Judæa.*

### § 1.

NOW Pompey pitched his camp at Jericho (where the
palm-tree grows, and that balsam which is of all
ointments the most precious, which upon any incision
made in the wood with a sharp stone distils out like juice),
and marched next morning to Jerusalem.  Thereupon
Aristobulus repented, and went to Pompey, and offered
him money, and promised to receive him into Jerusalem,
and begged that he would leave off the war, and do what
he pleased peaceably.  Then Pompey, upon his entreaty,
forgave him, and sent Gabinius and some soldiers to receive
the money and take possession of the city.  But none of
these promises were performed, but Gabinius returned,
not only having been shut out of the city, but also having
received none of the money promised, because Aristobulus'
soldiers would not permit the agreement to be carried out.
At this Pompey was very angry, and put Aristobulus into
prison, and went himself to the city, which was strong on
every side, excepting the north, which was not well fortified ; for there was a broad and deep ditch that ran round
the city,[1] and included within it the temple, which was
itself surrounded with a very strong stone wall.

---

[1] The particular depth and breadth of this ditch whence the stones
for the wall about the temple were probably taken, are omitted in our
copies of Josephus, but set down by Strabo, xvi. p. 763, from whom we
learn, that this ditch was sixty feet deep, and 250 feet broad.—W.

§ 2. Now there was variance among the men that were within the city, for they did not agree as to what was to be done in their present circumstances, for some thought it best to deliver up the city to Pompey, but Aristobulus' party exhorted them to shut the gates and fight, because he was kept in prison. And these got the start of the others, and seized upon the temple, and cut off the bridge which reached from it to the city, and prepared themselves to stand a siege; but the others admitted Pompey's army in, and delivered up both the city and the king's palace to him. Then Pompey sent his lieutenant Piso with an army, and placed garrisons both in the city and in the palace to secure them, and fortified the houses that joined the temple, and all those that were outside but in the neighbourhood of it. And first he offered conditions to those within, but as they would not comply with what he invited them to, he fortified all the places thereabout, and Hyrcanus zealously assisted him in everything. And Pompey pitched his camp outside,[1] at the north end of the temple, where it was most open to attack, though even on that side great towers rose up, and a trench had been dug, and a deep ravine begirt it round about, for the parts towards the city were precipitous, and the bridge on which Pompey had entered in was broken down; however, a bank was raised day by day with a great deal of labour, as the Romans cut down the trees all round. And when this bank was sufficiently raised, and the trench filled up with difficulty owing to its immense depth, Pompey had his engines and battering rams brought from Tyre, and placing them on the bank, kept battering the temple with his catapults. Now had it not been our national practice to rest on the seventh days, this bank would never have been completed, owing to the opposition the Jews would have made; for though our law allows us to defend ourselves against those that commence a fight with us and assault us, it does not permit us to meddle with our enemies on the Sabbath-days while they do anything else.[2]

[1] So Dindorf.
[2] It deserves here to be noted, that this notion that offensive fighting was unlawful to the Jews, even under the utmost necessity, on the Sabbath-day, of which we hear nothing before the times of the

§ 3. Now when the Romans observed this, they threw no
missiles at the Jews on those days which we call Sabbaths,
nor did they come to a hand to hand fight, but raised up
their bank and towers, and brought forward their engines
that they might do execution the following day.   And one
may learn how very great piety we exercise towards God,
and how much we observe his laws, from the fact that the
priests were not at all hindered from their sacred ministra-
tions by fear during the siege, but did still twice a day, in
the morning and at the ninth hour, offer their sacrifices on
the altar, nor did they omit those sacrifices if any melancholy accident happened during the assaults.   Indeed when
the city was taken in the third month, on the day of the
fast, in the hundred and seventy-ninth Olympiad, when
Caius Antonius and Marcus Tullius Cicero were consuls,
and the enemy fell upon them, and cut the throats of those
that were in the temple, yet did not those that offered the
sacrifices leave them off, nor could they be compelled to run
away, either from the fear they were in for their own lives, or
from the numbers that had been already slain, thinking it
better to suffer whatever came upon them at the very altars,
than to omit anything that their laws required of them.
And that this is not a mere tale to pass an encomium upon
piety that was never displayed, but is the real truth, I
appeal to all those that have written of the acts of Pompey,
who bear me out, and among them to Strabo and Nicolaus,
and also to Titus Livius, the writer of the Roman history.

§ 4. Now when the battering engine was applied, the
greatest of the towers was shaken by it and fell down, and
opened a breach in the walls, so the enemy poured in
apace, and Cornelius Faustus, son of *the famous* Sulla, with
his soldiers, first of all scaled the wall, and after him Furius
the centurion, with those that followed him on the other
side, while Fabius, who was also a centurion, scaled it
in the middle, with a great body of men with him.   And
now all was full of slaughter, some of the Jews being slain
by the Romans, and some by one another; nay, there were
some who threw themselves down the precipices, or put
fire to their houses and burned them, not being able to

Maccabees, was the cause of Jerusalem's being taken by Pompey, by
Sosius, and by Titus.—W.

bear their miseries. Of the Jews there fell twelve thousand, but of the Romans very few. Absalom, who was at once both uncle and father-in-law of Aristobulus, was taken captive. And no small outrage was committed in the Holy of Holies, which before had been inaccessible and seen by none; for Pompey went into it, and not a few of those that were with him also, and saw all that it was unlawful for any men to see but the high priests. There were there the golden table, the holy candlestick, and the pouring vessels, and a great quantity of spices; and besides these there were among the treasures two thousand talents of sacred money; but Pompey touched nothing of all this,[1] on account of his regard to religion, but in this point also acted in a manner that was worthy of his virtue. The next day he gave order to those that had the charge of the temple to cleanse it, and to bring what offerings the law required to God; and he restored the high priesthood to Hyrcanus, not only because he had been useful to him in other respects, but also because he had hindered the Jews in the country from giving Aristobulus any assistance in the war. He also cut off the heads of those that had been the authors of the war, and bestowed fitting rewards on Cornelius Faustus and the others that had mounted the walls with such alacrity. And he made Jerusalem tributary to the Romans, and took away those cities of Cœle-Syria which the inhabitants of Judæa had formerly subdued, and put them under the government of the Roman prætor, and contracted the whole nation, which had elevated itself so high, within its own bounds. Moreover, he rebuilt Gadara (which had been razed to the ground a little before), to gratify Demetrius of Gadara,[2] who was his freedman, and restored the rest of the cities, as Hippos,[3] and Scythopolis, and Pella,[4] and Dium,[5] and Samaria,[6] as also Marissa,[7] Azotus,[8] Jamnia,[9] and Arethusa,[10] to their

---

[1] This is fully confirmed by the testimony of Cicero, who says in his oration for Flaccus, that "Cnæus Pompeius, when he was conqueror, and had taken Jerusalem, did not touch anything belonging to the temple."—W.

[2] *Umm Keis.*                         [3] *Sûsiyeh,* see Life, § 9.
[4] See note 4, p. 122.              [5] See note 1, p. 123.
[6] *Sebustieh.*        [7] *Kh. Mer'ash.*              [8] *Esdûd.*
[9] *Yebnah.*         [10] Now *Restan,* sixteen miles from *Homs,* Emesa.

own inhabitants. And these were in the interior of the country, except those that had been razed to the ground. As to the maritime cities, as Gaza and Joppa and Dora[1] and Strato's Tower (which last Herod rebuilt in a glorious manner, and adorned with havens and temples, and changed its name to Cæsarea[2]), Pompey left all of them free, and joined them to the province of Syria.

§ 5. Now the causers of this misery which came upon Jerusalem were Hyrcanus and Aristobulus, by their being at variance with one another; for we lost our liberty, and became subject to the Romans, and were deprived of the territory which we had gained by our arms from the Syrians. Moreover, the Romans exacted of us in a short time more than ten thousand talents. And the royal authority, which was a dignity formerly bestowed on those that were high priests by right of their family, became the property of common men. But of these matters I shall treat in their proper place. And Pompey handed over Cœle-Syria, as far as the river Euphrates and Egypt, to Scaurus, and two Roman legions, and then went away to Cilicia, and pushed on to Rome. He also bound Aristobulus and carried him and his children along with him, for he had two daughters, and as many sons; one of whom, Alexander, ran away, but the younger, Antigonus, was carried to Rome with his sisters.

## CHAP. V.

*How Scaurus made Peace with Aretas. And what Gabinius did in Judæa, after he had conquered Alexander, the Son of Aristobulus.*

### § 1.

SCAURUS now made an expedition against Petra[3] in Arabia, and ravaged all the places round about it, because of the great difficulty of access to it. And as his army was pinched by famine, Antipater furnished him with corn from Judæa, and with whatever else he wanted,

[1] *Tantûrah.*  [2] Cæsarea Palæstina, now *Kaisariyeh.*
[3] See note 1, p. 117

at the command of Hyrcanus. And Antipater, being
sent to Aretas as an ambassador by Scaurus, because they
were old friends, persuaded Aretas to give Scaurus a sum
of money to prevent the ravaging of his country, and
undertook to be his surety for three hundred talents. And
Scaurus, upon these terms, ceased to make war against him
any longer, for he wanted peace as much as Aretas.

§ 2. Some time after this, when Alexander, the son of
Aristobulus, overran Judæa, Gabinius came from Rome to
Syria, as commander of the Roman forces. He did many
other considerable actions, and marched against Alexander,
as Hyrcanus was no longer able to hold out against
Alexander's power, but was already attempting to rebuild
the walls of Jerusalem, which Pompey had overthrown,
although the Romans who were there restrained him from
that. However, Alexander scoured all the country-side,
and armed many of the Jews, and quickly got together
ten thousand foot and fifteen hundred horse, and fortified
Alexandrium[1] (a fortress near Coreæ) and Machærus[2] near
the mountains of Arabia. Gabinius therefore advanced
against him, having sent on Mark Antony and other commanders. They armed such Romans as followed them, and
besides them such Jews as were subject to them, who were
led by Pitholaus and Malichus, and they also took with
them the friendly contingent of Antipater, and met Alexander; and Gabinius himself followed with the heavy
armed troops. Thereupon Alexander retired to near Jerusalem, where they fell upon one another, and a pitched
battle ensued, in which the Romans slew about three
thousand of their enemies, and took as many alive.

§ 3. Meantime Gabinius went to Alexandrium, and
invited those that were in it to cessation of hostilities, and
promised that their former offences should be forgiven.
But as many of the enemy had pitched their camp before
the fortress, the Romans attacked them, and Mark Antony
fought bravely, and slew a great number, and seemed to
come off with the greatest honour. So Gabinius left part
of the army there to reduce the place, and he himself went
into the other parts of Judæa, and gave orders to rebuild

[1] See note 4, p. 123.
[2] *Mekaur*, see Jewish War, vii. 6, § 1.

all the cities that he came to that had been demolished.
So Samaria, Azotus, Scythopolis, Anthedon,[1] Raphia,[2] Dora,
Marissa, Gaza, and not a few others were rebuilt.   And
as the men acted according to Gabinius' command, it came
to pass at this time that those cities were safely inhabited,
which had been desolate for a long time.

§ 4.  When Gabinius had done thus throughout the
country, he returned to Alexandrium, and as he pressed on
the siege, Alexander sent an embassage to him, desiring
that he would pardon his former offences, and delivering
up to him the fortresses Hyrcania and Machærus, and at
last Alexandrium itself.  All these fortresses Gabinius razed
to the ground.  And when Alexander's mother, who was on
the side of the Romans, having her husband and other
children at Rome, came to Gabinius, he granted her whatever she asked ; and when he had settled matters with
her, he restored Hyrcanus to Jerusalem, and committed
the care of the temple to him.  And when he had appointed
five councils, he divided the nation into the same number
of parts, and these councils governed the people ; the first
was at Jerusalem, the second at Gadara, the third at
Amathus,[3] the fourth at Jericho, and the fifth at Sepphoris[4]
in Galilee.  So the Jews were now freed from kingly rule,
and were governed by an aristocracy.


## CHAP. VI.

*How Gabinius captured Aristobulus after he had fled from
Rome, and sent him back to Rome again ; also how
Gabinius, as he returned out of Egypt, overcame Alexander
and the Nabatœans in Battle.*


### § 1.

NOW Aristobulus escaped from Rome to Judæa, and
purposed to rebuild the fortress of Alexandrium,
which had been recently demolished : so Gabinius sent

---

[1] *Agrippias*, see Antiq. xiii. 13, § 3.
[2] Raphia was twenty-two miles S.W. of Gaza ; comp. Antiq. xiii. 13,
§ 3.
[3] Hamath, now *Hama.*                    [4] *Sefûrieh.*

soldiers against him, and Sisenna and Antony and Servilius as their commanders, to hinder him from making
himself master of the country again, and to recapture
him. For indeed many of the Jews flocked to Aristobulus, on account of his former glory, as also because they
were glad of a revolution. And one Pitholaus, lieutenant-
general at Jerusalem, deserted to him with a thousand
men, although many of those that joined him were unarmed. And when Aristobulus resolved to go to Machærus,
he dismissed these, because they were so badly equipped
(for they could not be useful to him in action), but he
took with him about eight thousand that were armed, and
set out. And as the Romans attacked them furiously, the
Jews were beaten in the battle, though they fought valiantly,
and were overcome by the enemy, and put to flight. And
about five thousand of them were slain, and the rest being
dispersed, tried, as well as they were able, to save themselves. However, Aristobulus had with him still above a
thousand, and with them he fled to Machærus, and fortified
the place, and though he had had ill success, he was still
sanguine about his affairs. But when he had held out two
days, and received many wounds, he was captured and
brought before Gabinius, with his son Antigonus, who had
also fled with him from Rome. Such was the fortune of
Aristobulus, who was sent back again to Rome, and there
retained in bonds, having been both king and high priest
for three years and six months, and being indeed a noble
person and one of a lofty soul. However, the senate let
his children go, upon Gabinius' writing to them that he
had promised their mother so much when she delivered up
the fortresses to him; and accordingly they then returned
to Judæa.

§ 2. Now when Gabinius was making an expedition
against the Parthians, and had already crossed over the
Euphrates, he changed his mind, and resolved to return
into Egypt, in order to restore Ptolemy to his kingdom.[1]
But this has been related elsewhere. However, Antipater

---

[1] This history is best illustrated by Dr. Hudson out of Livy, who
says, " That A. Gabinius, the proconsul, restored Ptolemy to his kingdom
of Egypt, and ejected Archelaus, whom they had set up for king," &c.
— W.

supplied the army which Gabinius despatched against
Archelaus with corn and weapons and money. He also
won over those Jews who were beyond Pelusium[1] to be his
confederates, who guarded the passes that led into Egypt.
But when he came back out of Egypt, he found Syria in
disorder sedition and confusion, for Alexander, the son of
Aristobulus, having seized on the government a second
time by force, made many of the Jews revolt to him, and
marched over the country with a great army, and slew all
the Romans he could light upon, and proceeded to besiege
them at the mountain called Gerizim,[2] where they had
retreated.

§ 3. Now when Gabinius found Syria in this condition, he
sent on Antipater, who was a sensible man, to those that were
rebellious, to try whether he could cure them of their madness, and persuade them to return to a better mind. And
when he came to them, he brought many of them to a
sound mind, and induced them to do what they ought to
do. But he could not restrain Alexander, for he had an
army of thirty thousand Jews, and met Gabinius, and
joining battle with him, was beaten, and lost ten thousand
of his men near mount Tabor.[3]

§ 4. Then Gabinius settled the affairs which belonged to
the city of Jerusalem, as was agreeable to Antipater's
wishes, and went against the Nabatæans, and overcame
them in battle. He also sent away in a friendly manner
Mithridates and Orsanes, who were Parthian deserters who
had come to him, though the report went abroad that they
had run away from him. And when Gabinius had performed great and glorious actions in his management of the
war, he returned to Rome, and handed over his province to
Crassus. Now Nicolaus of Damascus, and Strabo of Cappadocia, both describe the expeditions of Pompey and
Gabinius against the Jews, but neither of them say anything new which is not in the other.

---

[1] *Tineh*, not far from *Port Said*.
[2] Gerizim lay to the south of the valley in which Shechem, *Nablus*,
was situated.　　　　　　　　　　[3] Now *Jebel-et-Tor*.

## CHAP. VII.

*How Crassus went into Judœa, and pillaged the Temple ; and
marched against the Parthians, and perished with his army.
Also how Cassius made himself master of Syria, and put a
stop to the incursion of the Parthians, and then went into
Judœa.*

### § 1.

NOW Crassus, as he was going upon his expedition
against the Parthians, came into Judæa, and carried
off the money that was in the temple, which Pompey had left
(which amounted to two thousand talents), and was disposed
to spoil it of all the gold belonging to it (which was eight
thousand talents). He also took a beam, which was made
of solid beaten gold, of the weight of three hundred minæ.
Now each mina with us weighs two pounds and a half. It
was the priest who was guardian of the sacred treasures,
whose name was Eleazar, who gave him this beam, not out
of a wicked design, for he was a good and righteous man,
but being intrusted with the custody of the veils belonging
to the temple, which were of admirable beauty and of very
costly workmanship, and hung down from this beam, and
seeing that Crassus was bent on getting together money,
and being alarmed for the safety of all the ornaments of
the temple, he gave him this beam of gold as a ransom for
the whole, but not till he had given his oath that he would
remove nothing else out of the temple, but be satisfied with
this only, which he should give him, for it was worth many
ten thousand [shekels]. Now this beam was in a wooden
beam that was hollow, which was not known to anybody
else, for Eleazar alone knew of it. And Crassus took away
this beam, on condition of touching nothing else that belonged to the temple, but afterwards broke his oath, and
carried away all the gold that was in the Holy of Holies.

§ 2. Let no one wonder that there was so much wealth
in our temple, since all the Jews throughout the world,
and those that worshipped God, even in Asia and Europe,
sent their contributions to it, and that from very ancient
times. Nor is the largeness of these sums I have men-

tioned without attestation, nor is it due to our vanity, as
if we had without ground raised it to so great a height:
but there are many witnesses to it, especially Strabo of
Cappadocia, who speaks as follows. "Mithridates sent to
Cos,[1] and took the money which queen Cleopatra had deposited there, as also eight hundred talents belonging to
the Jews." Now, we have no public money but what
belongs to God. And it is evident that the Asiatic Jews
removed this money to Cos from fear of Mithridates,
for it is not probable that those in Judæa, who had a
strong city and temple, would send their money to Cos,
nor is it likely that the Jews, who were inhabitants of
Alexandria, would do so either, since they were in no fear
of Mithridates. And the same Strabo himself bears witness in another place, that at the time that Sulla passed
over into Greece to fight against Mithridates, he sent
Lucullus to put an end to a disturbance that our nation,
of whom the world is full, had raised in Cyrene,[2] for he
speaks as follows. "There were four classes of men in
Cyrene; the first composed of citizens, the second of hus-
bandmen, the third of resident aliens, and the fourth of
Jews. Now these Jews are already got into all cities, and
it is not easy to find a place in the world that has not received this tribe of men, and is not occupied by it. And it
has come to pass that Egypt and Cyrene (as having the
same governors), and a great number of other nations,
imitate their way of living, and especially cherish many
of these Jews, and grow to great prosperity with them,
following the Jewish customs. Accordingly, the Jews have
places assigned them in Egypt to dwell in, besides what is
peculiarly allotted to this nation at Alexandria, which is a
large part of that city. There is also an ethnarch allowed
them, who governs their nation, and dispenses justice, and
sees to their contracts and laws, as if he were the ruler of a
free republic. In Egypt indeed this nation is powerful,
because the Jews were originally Egyptians, and because
the land which they inhabit, since they went thence, is near
to Egypt. They also removed into Cyrene, because that
land adjoins the government of Egypt, as does Judæa, or

[1] Now *Stanco*, an island nearly opposite the gulf of Halicarnassus.
[2] *el-Krenna*, in the *Tripoli* district, west of Egypt.

rather was formerly under the same government." And this is what Strabo says.

§ 3. Now when Crassus had settled all things as he himself pleased, he marched into Parthia, where both he himself and all his army perished, as has been related elsewhere. But Cassius fled to Syria, and made himself master of it, and stopped the Parthians, who, because of their victory over Crassus, made incursions into Syria. And he went again to Tyre, and into Judæa also. And he attacked Taricheæ,[1] and captured it at once, and took about thirty thousand Jews captives, and slew Pitholaus (who had imitated Aristobulus in his rebellious practices), at the instigation of Antipater, who had great influence with him, and was at that time held in very great repute by the Idumæans also, out of which nation he married a wife, who was the daughter of one of their eminent men from Arabia, and her name was Cypros, and he had by her four sons, Phasaelus, and Herod (who afterwards became a king), and Joseph, and Pheroras, and one daughter called Salome. This Antipater cultivated also friendly relations with other potentates, and especially with the king of Arabia, in whose charge he placed his children, when he fought against Aristobulus. And Cassius removed his camp, and pushed on to the Euphrates, to meet those that were coming to attack him from that quarter, as has been related by others.

§ 4. But some time afterwards Julius Cæsar, when he had become master of Rome, and when Pompey and the senate had fled beyond the Ionian sea, freed Aristobulus from his bonds, and resolved to send him into Syria, and delivered two legions to him, that he might set matters right in that country, being an influential man. But Aristobulus had no enjoyment of what he hoped for from the power that was given him by Cæsar, for those of Pompey's party were too much for him, and carried him off by poison, but those of Cæsar's party buried him. His dead body also lay for a long time embalmed in honey, till Antony afterwards sent it to Judæa, and caused it to be buried in the royal sepulchres. And Scipio, upon Pompey's sending to him to slay Alexander the son of Aristobulus,

---

[1] *Kerak*, on the south shore of the Sea of Galilee.

accused the young man of offences he had been guilty of
earlier against the Romans, and cut off his head. And
thus did he die at Antioch; but Ptolemy, the son of
Mennæus, who was the ruler of Chalcis¹ under Mount
Libanus, welcomed his brothers, and sent his son Philippio
to Ascalon² to Aristobulus' wife, and bade her send back
with him her son Antigonus and her daughters, one of
whom, whose name was Alexandra, Philippio fell in love
with and married. But afterwards his father Ptolemy had
him put to death, and married Alexandra, and continued
to take care of her brothers.


## CHAP. VIII.

*How the Jews became Confederate with Cæsar when he fought
against Egypt. The glorious Actions of Antipater, and
his Friendship with Cæsar. The Honours which the Jews
received from the Romans and Athenians.*

### § 1.

NOW after Pompey was dead, and after the victory
Cæsar gained over him,³ Antipater, who managed the
Jewish affairs by the order of Hyrcanus, became very useful to Cæsar when he made war against Egypt. For when
Mithridates of Pergamus⁴ was bringing his auxiliary forces,
and was not able to continue his march by Pelusium,⁵ but
was obliged to stay at Ascalon, Antipater went to him
with three thousand armed Jews, and also got the principal men of the Arabians to come to his assistance; and
it was owing to him that all the Syrians joined him also,
being unwilling to appear behindhand in their zeal for Cæsar,
viz. Iamblichus the ruler, and Ptolemy his son, who dwelt
at Mount Libanus, and almost all the cities. So Mithridates marched out of Syria, and came to Pelusium, and as
its inhabitants would not admit him, he besieged the city.
And Antipater distinguished himself here, and was the first

---

¹ *Kinnisrin.*                ² *Ascalân.*                ³ At Pharsalia.
⁴ *Bergama*, on the west coast of Asia Minor, and north of Smyrna.
⁵ *Tineh.*

who pulled down a part of the wall, and so opened a way
for the others to enter into the city, and so Pelusium was
taken.   Now the Egyptian Jews, who dwelt in the district
of Onias, tried to prevent Antipater and Mithridates and
their soldiers passing over to Cæsar, but Antipater persuaded them to come over to his party, because he was of
the same race as them, and especially when he showed
them the letters of Hyrcanus the high priest, wherein he
exhorted them to cultivate friendship with Cæsar, and to
supply his army with presents and all things needful.
Accordingly, when they saw that Antipater and the high
priest were of the same sentiments, they did as they were
desired.   And when the Jews in the neighbourhood of
Memphis[1] heard that these Jews had come over to Cæsar,
they also invited Mithridates to come to them; and he
went and incorporated them also into his army.

§ 2. And when Mithridates had gone over the part called
Delta,[2] he came to a pitched battle with the enemy, near
the place called the Jewish camp.[3]   Now Mithridates was
on the right wing, and Antipater on the left; and when
the fight came on, the wing where Mithridates was gave
way, and would have suffered extremely, had not Antipater come running to him with his own soldiers along
the bank of the river, as he had already beaten the enemy
opposite him; and he delivered Mithridates, and put those
Egyptians to flight who had been too much for him.   He
also took their camp, and continued in the pursuit of them,
and called back Mithridates, who had retreated a great
way, and had lost eight hundred soldiers, while Antipater
had lost only forty.   And Mithridates wrote an account of
this battle to Cæsar, and declared that Antipater was the
author both of the victory and his safety, so that Cæsar
commended Antipater then, and made use of him during
all the rest of the war in the most hazardous undertakings; indeed he got wounded in some of the engagements.

§ 3. So when Cæsar, after some time, had finished the
war, and sailed to Syria, he honoured Antipater greatly,
and confirmed Hyrcanus in the high priesthood, and be-

---

[1]  *Mitrahamy*, on the left bank of the Nile above Cairo.
[2]  The modern Delta of Egypt, lying north of Cairo.
[3]  Possibly *Tell el-Yehúdi*.

stowed on Antipater the privilege of citizenship of Rome, and freedom from taxes everywhere. Now it is reported by many, that Hyrcanus joined Antipater in this expedition, and went himself into Egypt. And Strabo of Cappadocia bears me out, when he says as follows on the authority of Asinius. "After Mithridates and Hyrcanus the high priest of the Jews invaded Egypt." Nay, the same Strabo says again, in another place, on the authority of Hypsicrates, that "Mithridates at first set out alone, but Antipater, who had the care of Jewish affairs, was called by him to Ascalon, and mustered three thousand soldiers for him, and stirred up the other rulers, and Hyrcanus the high priest also took part in this expedition." This is what Strabo says.

§ 4. Now Antigonus, the son of Aristobulus, came at this time to Cæsar, and lamented his father's fate, and complained that it was owing to his loyalty to him that Aristobulus was taken off by poison, and his brother beheaded by Scipio, and desired that he would take pity on him, as he had been ejected from his dominions. He also accused Hyrcanus and Antipater of governing the nation by violence, and acting lawlessly to him. Antipater was present, and made his defence as to the accusations that were laid against him, and showed that Antigonus and his party were given to innovation, and were rebellious persons. He also reminded Cæsar of the labours he had undergone when he assisted him in his wars, relating what he had witnessed himself. He added, that Aristobulus was justly carried away to Rome, as one who was an enemy to the Romans, and could never be brought to be friendly to them, and that his brother had only his deserts from Scipio, being caught in the act of committing robberies; and that his punishment was not inflicted on him by way of violence or injustice by the perpetrator of it.

§ 5. When Antipater had made this speech, Cæsar appointed Hyrcanus to be high priest, and gave Antipater what position he himself should choose, and left the determination to himself, so he made him procurator of Judæa. He also gave Hyrcanus leave to raise up again the walls of his own city, on his asking that favour of him, for they had been demolished by Pompey. And

this grant he sent to the consuls at Rome, to be engraven
in the Capitol.  The decree of the senate was as follows.[1]
" Lucius Valerius (the son of Lucius) the prætor, referred
this to the senate, upon the Ides of December, in the
Temple of Concord.  There were present at the writing of
this decree Lucius Coponius (the son of Lucius) of the
Colline tribe, and Papirius of the Quirine tribe, concerning
the affairs which Alexander the son of Jason, and Numenius the son of Antiochus, and Alexander the son of
Dorotheus, ambassadors of the Jews, good men and our
allies, proposed, who came to renew that league of good-
will and friendship with the Romans which existed before.
They also brought a shield of gold, as a token of the
alliance, valued at fifty thousand pieces of gold ; and desired that letters might be given them, directed both to
free cities and to kings, that their country and their havens
might be in security, and that no one among them might
receive any injury.  It has therefore pleased [the senate]
to make a league of friendship and good-will with them,
and to bestow on them whatever they asked, and to accept
of the shield which was brought by them."  This happened in the ninth year of Hyrcanus the high priest and
ethnarch, in the month of Panemus.  Hyrcanus also received honours from the people of Athens, as having been
useful to them on many occasions, for they wrote and sent
him a decree as follows.  " Before the president and priest
Dionysius, the son of Asclepiades, on the fifth day of the
latter part of the month of Panemus, this decree of the
Athenians was given to their commanders, when Aga-
thocles was archon, and Eucles (the son of Menander) the

---

[1] Take Dr. Hudson's note upon this place, which I suppose to be the
truth : " Here is some mistake in Josephus : for when he had promised
us a decree for the restoration of Jerusalem, he brings in a decree of far
greater antiquity, and that a league of friendship and union only.  One
may easily believe that Josephus gave order for one thing, and his
amanuensis performed another, by transposing decrees that concerned
the Hyrcani, and as deluded by the sameness of their names, for that
belongs to the first high priest of this name [John Hyrcanus,] which
Josephus ascribes to one that lived later, [Hyrcanus the son of Alexander
Jannæus.]  However, the decree which he proposes to set down follows a
little lower, in the collection of Roman decrees that concerned the Jews,
and is that dated when Cæsar was consul the fifth time."  See chap. 10,
§ 5.—W.

Alimusian was the scribe. In the month of Munychion, on
the eleventh day of the Prytany, a council of the presidents
was held in the theatre. Dorotheus Erchieus and the
fellow presidents with him put it to the vote of the people.
Dionysius, the son of Dionysius, said: Since Hyrcanus, the
son of Alexander, the high priest and ethnarch of the Jews,
continues to bear good-will to our people in general, and to
every one of our citizens in particular, and treats them
with all sorts of kindness; and when any of the Athenians
come to him, either as ambassadors, or on any private
business, he receives them in an obliging manner, and
sees that they are conducted back in safety, of which we
have had several previous testimonies, it is now also decreed,
on the motion of Theodosius, the son of Theodorus of
Sunium,[1] who put the people in mind of the virtue of this
man, and that his purpose is to do us all the good that is
in his power, to honour this Hyrcanus with a crown of
gold, the usual reward according to the law, and to erect
his statue in brass in the temple of Demos and of the
Graces; and that this present of a crown shall be proclaimed publicly in the theatre at the Dionysia, while the
new tragedies are acting, and at the Panathenæan, Eleu-
sinian, and gymnastic contests also; and that the commanders shall take care, while he continues in his friendship, and maintains his good-will to us, to return all
possible honour and favour to the man for his affection
and generosity; that by this treatment it may appear how
our people receive the good, and repay them by suitable
return; and that he may be induced to continue in his affection to us, by the honours we have already paid him. Let
ambassadors be also chosen out of all the Athenians, who
shall carry this decree to him, and desire him to accept of
the honours we pay him, and to endeavour always to be
doing some good to our city." This much shall suffice as to
the honours that were paid to Hyrcanus by the Romans
and the people of Athens.

---

[1] One of the principal fortresses of Attica, on the promontory now
called *Cape Kolonnes.*

## CHAP. IX.

*How Antipater committed the care of Galilee to Herod, and that of Jerusalem to Phasaelus; as also, how Herod, because of the Jews' envy of Antipater, was accused before Hyrcanus.*

### § 1.

NOW when Cæsar had settled the affairs of Syria, he sailed away; and as soon as he had conducted Cæsar out of Syria, Antipater returned to Judæa, and immediately raised up the walls which had been thrown down by Pompey, and by his coming pacified the tumult which had been all over the country, both by threatening and advising the people to be quiet: for he told them if they would be on Hyrcanus' side, they would live happily, and pass their lives without disturbance in the enjoyment of their own possessions, but if they were influenced by hopes of what might come by revolution, and aimed to get gain thereby, they would find him a despot instead of a mild ruler, and Hyrcanus a tyrant instead of a king, and the Romans and Cæsar their bitter enemies instead of rulers; for they would never bear him to be set aside whom they had appointed to govern. And when Antipater had said this to them, he himself set in order the affairs of the country.

§ 2. And seeing that Hyrcanus was of a slow and sluggish temper, Antipater made Phasaelus, his eldest son, governor of Jerusalem and the places in its vicinity, and committed Galilee to Herod, his next son, who was then quite a young man, for he was but twenty-five years of age. But that youth of his was no impediment to him; but as he was a young man of noble spirit, he soon met with an opportunity of showing his courage. For finding that there was one Ezekias, a captain of a band of robbers, who overran the neighbouring parts of Syria with a great troop of them, he took him, and slew him, as well as a great number of the robbers that were with him. For this action he was greatly beloved by the Syrians, for they were very desirous to have their country freed from this nest of robbers, and he purged it of them: so they sung songs in his commendation in their villages and cities, for his having procured them peace, and the secure enjoyment of their possessions.   And on account of this he became known to Sextus Cæsar, who was a relation of the great Cæsar's, and was now procurator of Syria.   Now Phasaelus, Herod's brother, was moved with emulation at his actions, and envied the fame he had thereby got, and became ambitious not to be behind him in deserving the same, so he made the inhabitants of Jerusalem bear him the greatest good-will, as he governed the city himself, but did neither manage its affairs improperly, nor abuse his authority therein.   This conduct procured to Antipater from the nation such respect as is due to kings, and such honours as he might partake of if he were absolute lord of the country.   Yet did not this splendour of his, as frequently happens, diminish in the least in him his kindness and good faith to Hyrcanus.

§ 3.  But now the principal men among the Jews, when they saw Antipater and his sons growing so much in the good-will of the nation, and in the revenues which they received from Judæa and from Hyrcanus' own wealth, became ill disposed to him.   And indeed Antipater had contracted a friendship with the Roman emperors, and he had prevailed on Hyrcanus to send them money, but took it himself, and appropriated the intended present, and sent it as if it were his own, and not Hyrcanus', gift to them.   Hyrcanus heard of this but took no heed to it: nay rather he was very glad of it: but the chief men of the Jews were in fear, because they saw that Herod was a violent and bold man, and very desirous to play the tyrant, so they went to Hyrcanus, and now accused Antipater openly, and said to him, " How long wilt thou be quiet under such actions as are now done ?   Or dost thou not see that Antipater and his sons have already girded themselves with power ?  and that it is only the name of a king which is given thee ?   But do not thou suffer these things to be hidden from thee, nor think to escape danger by being so careless about thyself and the kingdom.   For Antipater and his sons are not now stewards of thine affairs: do not deceive thyself with such a notion, they are evidently absolute lords, for Antipater's son Herod has slain Ezekias

and those that were with him, and has thereby transgressed our law, which has forbidden to slay any man,
even though he were a wicked man, unless he had been first
condemned to suffer death by the sanhedrim; [1] yet has he
ventured to do this without any authority from thee."

§ 4. Upon Hyrcanus hearing this, he listened to it, and
the mothers also of those that had been slain by Herod
fanned his indignation; for every day in the temple they
continued to beseech the king and the people, that Herod
might undergo a trial before the sanhedrim for what he
had done. And Hyrcanus was so moved by all this, that he
summoned Herod to come to his trial, for what was charged
against him. Accordingly he came, but his father advised
him not to come like a private man, but with a body-guard
for the security of his person; and when he had settled
the affairs of Galilee in the best manner he could for his
own advantage, to come for his trial, but still with a
body of men sufficient for his security on the journey, yet
not with so great a force as might look formidable to
Hyrcanus, but still such a one as might not expose him
naked and unguarded [to his enemies]. However, Sextus
Cæsar, governor of Syria, wrote to Hyrcanus, and desired
him to discharge Herod from trial, and threatened him
also if he did not do so. And this letter of his was
the cause of Hyrcanus' delivering Herod from suffering
any harm from the sanhedrim, for he loved him as his
own son. But when Herod stood before the sanhedrim
with his band of men about him, he frightened them all,
and none of his former accusers durst after that bring any
charge against him, but there was a deep silence, and nobody knew what was to be done. When things were in this
posture, one whose name was Sameas, a righteous man and
for that reason above all fear, rose up, and said, "O king
and members of the sanhedrim, neither have I ever myself

---

[1] It is here worth our while to remark, that none could be put to
death in Judæa, but by the approbation of the Jewish sanhedrim, there
being an excellent provision in the law of Moses, that even in criminal
causes, and particularly where life was concerned, an appeal should lie
from the lesser councils of seven in the other cities, to the supreme
council of seventy-one at Jerusalem. And this is exactly according to
our Saviour's words, when he says, "It could not be that a prophet
should perish out of Jerusalem." Luke xiii. 33.—W.

known such a case, nor do I suppose that any one of you can name its parallel, that one who is called to take his trial by us ever stood in such a manner before us ; but every one, whoever he be, that comes to be tried by this sanhedrim, presents himself in a submissive manner, and like one that is in fear, and endeavours to move us to compassion, with his hair dishevelled, and in a black mourning garment : but this most excellent Herod, who is accused of murder, and called to answer so heavy an accusation, stands here clothed in purple, and with the hair of his head finely trimmed, and with armed men about him, that if we shall condemn him by our law, he may slay us, and by being too strong for justice may himself escape death.   Yet I do not blame Herod for this, if he is more concerned for himself than for the laws ; but I blame you and the king, who give him license to do so.   However, know that God is great, and that this very man, whom you wish to let go for the sake of Hyrcanus, will one day punish both you and the king himself also."   Nor was Sameas wrong in any part of this prediction ; for when Herod had got the kingdom, he slew Hyrcanus and all the members of this sanhedrim except Sameas, for he honoured him highly on account of his uprightness, and because, when the city was afterwards besieged by Herod and Sosius, he advised the people to admit Herod into it ; and told them that for their sins they would not be able to escape him. About all this I shall speak in its proper place.

§ 5.  Now when Hyrcanus saw that the members of the sanhedrim were ready to pronounce sentence of death upon Herod, he put off the trial to another day, and sent privately to Herod, and advised him to flee from the city, for by that means he might escape from danger.   So he retired to Damascus, as though he fled from the king : and when he had gone to Sextus Cæsar, and had put his own affairs in a sure posture, he resolved, if he were again summoned before the sanhedrim to take his trial, not to obey the summons.   Thereupon the members of the sanhedrim felt great indignation, and endeavoured to persuade Hyrcanus that all these things were against him. He was not ignorant that this was the case, but he was so unmanly and foolish, that he was able to do nothing at

all.   And when Sextus made Herod general of the army of
Cœle-Syria, for he sold him that post for money, Hyrcanus
was afraid that Herod would make war upon him ; nor
was the effect of what he feared long in coming upon him,
for Herod came with an army to fight against Hyrcanus,
being angry at the trial he had been summoned to undergo before the sanhedrim ; but his father Antipater, and
his brother [Phasaelus], met him, and hindered him from
assaulting Jerusalem. They also tried to pacify his vehement
temper, and begged him to do no overt action, but only
to frighten by threatening, and to proceed no further
against one who had given him the dignity he had ; they
also desired him, if he was vexed that he was summoned
and obliged to come to his trial, to remember also how
he was dismissed without condemnation, and to be grateful for that, and not to regard only what was disagreeable
to him, and so be unthankful for his deliverance. They
desired him also to consider, since it is God that turns
the scales of war, that there is great uncertainty in the
issues of battles, and therefore he ought not to expect
the victory, when fighting against his king and comrade,
who had bestowed many benefits upon him, and had done
nothing severe to him, for his accusation, which was
owing to evil counsellors and not to Hyrcanus, had rather
the suggestion and semblance of severity, than anything
really severe in it.   Herod listened to these arguments, and believed that it was sufficient for his future
hopes to have made a show of his strength before the
nation, and to have done nothing more. Such was the
state of affairs in Judæa at this time.


## CHAP. X.

*The Honours that were paid the Jews; and the Alliances*
*that were made by the Romans, and other Nations, with*
*them.*

### § 1.

NOW when Cæsar had returned to Rome, he was on
the eve of sailing for Africa to fight against Scipio and
Cato, when Hyrcanus sent to him, and besought him to

ratify the league of friendship and mutual alliance which was between them. And it seems to me to be necessary here to give an account of all the honours that the Romans and their emperors paid to our nation, and of the alliances they made with it, that all mankind may know what regard the kings of Asia and Europe have had to us, and that they have been abundantly satisfied with our courage and fidelity. Now since many owing to hostility to us do not believe what has been written about us by the Persians and Macedonians, because those writings are not everywhere to be met with, and are not stored up in public places, but are only among ourselves and certain other barbarous nations, while no one can gainsay the decrees of the Romans (for they are laid up in the public places of the cities, and are extant still in the Capitol, and engraven upon pillars of brass; moreover, Julius Cæsar made a pillar of brass for the Jews of Alexandria, and declared publicly that they were citizens of Alexandria), from these evidences I shall prove what I say. I shall also set down the decrees made both by the senate and Julius Cæsar, which relate to Hyrcanus and to our nation.

§ 2. "Caius Julius Cæsar, imperator, pontifex maximus, and dictator the second time, to the magistrates, senate, and people of Sidon, greeting. If you be in health, it is well. I also and the army are well. I have sent you a copy of the decree, registered on the tablet, which concerns Hyrcanus (the son of Alexander) the high priest and ethnarch of the Jews, that it may be laid up among the public records; and I will that it be engraved on a tablet of brass both in Greek and Latin. It is as follows. I Julius Cæsar, imperator the second time, and pontifex maximus, have made this decree with the approbation of the senate. Whereas Hyrcanus (the son of Alexander) the Jew, has demonstrated his fidelity and diligence in our affairs both now and in former times, both in peace and in war, as many of our generals have borne him witness, and came to our assistance in the last Alexandrian war with fifteen hundred soldiers, and when he was sent by me to Mithridates, showed himself superior in valour to all in the army, for these reasons I will that Hyrcanus the son of Alexander, and his children, be ethnarchs of the Jews and have the high priesthood of the Jews for ever according to the customs of their forefathers, and that he and his sons be our allies, and besides this that every one of them be reckoned among our particular friends. I also ordain that he and his children retain whatever privileges belong by their laws to the office of high priest, or whatever favours have been hitherto conceded to them. And if at any time hereafter there arise any questions about the Jewish customs, I will that he determine the same. And I do not approve of their being obliged to find us winter quarters, or of any money being required of them."

§ 3. "The decrees of Caius Cæsar, consul, containing what has been granted and determined, are as follows. That Hyrcanus and his sons bear rule over the nation of the Jews, and have the profits of the places granted to them, and that Hyrcanus himself, as high priest and ethnarch of the Jews, defend those that are injured. And that ambassadors be sent to Hyrcanus (the son of Alexander) the high priest of the Jews, to discourse with him about a league of friendship and alliance, and that a tablet of brass, containing all this, be openly set up in the Capitol, and at Sidon and Tyre and Ascalon, and in the temples, engraven in Roman and Greek letters: and that this decree be communicated to the quæstors and prætors of the several cities, and to the friends of the Jews : and that the ambassadors have presents made them, and that these decrees be sent everywhere."

§ 4. "Caius Cæsar, imperator, dictator, and consul, has granted, out of regard to the honour and virtue and kindness of the man, and for the advantage of the senate and people of Rome, that Hyrcanus, the son of Alexander, both he and his sons, be high priests and priests of Jerusalem and the Jewish nation, by the same right, and according to the same laws, by which their progenitors have held the priesthood."

§ 5. "Caius Cæsar, consul the fifth time, has decreed, that the Jews may keep Jerusalem, and fortify that city ; and that Hyrcanus (the son of Alexander), the high priest and ethnarch of the Jews, occupy it as he himself pleases ; and that the Jews be allowed to deduct out of their tribute every second year the land is let a cor of the tribute, and that the tribute they pay be not let to farm, and that they pay not always the same tribute."

§ 6. "Caius Cæsar, imperator the second time, has ordained, that all the country of the Jews, except Joppa, pay tribute for the city of Jerusalem every year except the seventh year, which they call the sabbatical year, because therein they neither receive the fruit of their trees, nor do they sow their land; and that they pay as their tribute in Sidon in the second year, the fourth part of what was sown: and besides this, they are to pay the same tithes to Hyrcanus and his sons, as they paid to their forefathers. And no one, either governor, or general, or ambassador, may raise auxiliaries within the bounds of Judæa, nor may soldiers exact money of them for winter quarters, or on any other pretext, but they are to be free from all sorts of injuries: and whatever they shall hereafter have, or get possession of, or buy, they shall retain. It is also our pleasure that the city of Joppa, which the Jews had originally, when they made a league of friendship with the Romans, shall belong to them, as it formerly did; and that Hyrcanus, the son of Alexander, and his sons, shall have as tribute for that city from those that occupy the land, for the country and for what they export every year to Sidon, twenty thousand six hundred and seventy-five modii every year, except the seventh year, which they call the sabbatical year, wherein they neither plough nor take the fruit off their trees. It is also the pleasure of the senate, as to the villages which are in the great plain, which Hyrcanus and his forefathers formerly possessed, that Hyrcanus and the Jews have them with the same privileges with which they formerly had them, and that the same original ordinances remain still in force which concern the Jews with regard to their high priests and priests, and that they enjoy the same benefits which they formerly had by the concession of the people and senate. And let them enjoy the like privileges at Lydda. It is the pleasure also of the senate, that Hyrcanus the ethnarch, and the Jews, retain those places, lands, and farm-steads, which belonged to the kings of Syria and Phœnicia, the allies of the Romans, and which they had bestowed on them as their free gift. It is also granted to

Hyrcanus, and to his sons, and to the ambassadors sent by them to us, that in the fights between gladiators, and in those with wild beasts, they shall sit among the senators to see those shows, and when they desire an audience, they shall be introduced to the senate by the dictator or master of the horse, and when they have introduced them, answers shall be returned them in ten days at the latest, after the decree of the senate is made."

§ 7. "Caius Cæsar, imperator [dictator] the fourth time, and consul the fifth time, declared to be perpetual dictator, made the following speech concerning the rights and privileges of Hyrcanus (the son of Alexander), the high priest and ethnarch of the Jews. 'Since those imperators[1] who have been in the provinces before me have borne witness to Hyrcanus, the high priest of the Jews, and to the Jews themselves, and that before the senate and people of Rome, when the people and senate returned their thanks to them, it is good that we now also remember the same, and provide that a requital be made to Hyrcanus, to the nation of the Jews, and to the sons of Hyrcanus, by the senate and people of Rome, and that suitably to the good-will they have shown us, and to the benefits they have bestowed upon us.'"

§ 8. "Julius Caius, prætor, consul of Rome, to the magistrates, senate, and people of the Parians, greeting. The Jews of Delos,[2] and some other Jews that sojourn there, signified to us, in the presence of your ambassadors, that you forbid them by a decree of yours to follow the customs of their forefathers and their sacred rites. Now it does not please me that such decrees should be made against our friends and allies, whereby they are forbidden to live according to their own customs, or to bring in contributions for common suppers and sacrifices, since they are not forbidden to do so even at Rome itself. For

[1] Dr. Hudson justly supposes, that the Roman imperators, or generals of armies, both here and § 2, who gave testimony to Hyrcanus' and the Jews' faithfulness and good-will to the Romans before the senate and people of Rome, were principally Pompey, Scaurus, and Gabinius; of all whom Josephus has already given us the history, as far as the Jews were concerned with them.—W.

[2] The well-known island, birthplace of Apollo and Artemis, on which was the celebrated Temple of Apollo, raised by the common contribution of the Greek States.

even Caius Cæsar, our imperator and consul, in the decree wherein he forbade other companies to meet in the city, did yet permit the Jews, and them only, both to bring in their contributions, and to make their common suppers. Accordingly, though I forbid other companies, I permit these Jews to gather themselves together, according to the customs and laws of their forefathers, and to continue therein. It will therefore be good for you, if you have made any decree against these our friends and allies, to abrogate the same, because of their virtue and good-will towards us."

§ 9. Now after Caius Cæsar was slain, when Marcus Antonius and Publius Dolabella were consuls, they assembled the senate, and introduced Hyrcanus' ambassadors into it, and discussed what they desired, and made a league of friendship with them. The senate also decreed to grant them all they desired. I add the decree itself, that those who read the present work may have at hand a proof of the truth of what I say. The decree was as follows.

§ 10. The decree of the senate copied out of the treasury from the public tablets belonging to the quæstors, when Quintus Rutilius and Caius Cornelius were city quæstors, and taken from the second tablet of the first class. "On the third day before the Ides of April, there were present in the temple of Concord, at the writing of this decree, Lucius Calpurnius Piso of the Menenian tribe, Servius Papinius Potitus of the Lemonian tribe, Caius Caninius Rebilius of the Terentine tribe, Publius Tidetius, Lucius Apulinus (the son of Lucius) of the Sergian tribe, Flavius (the son of Lucius) of the Lemonian tribe, Publius Platius (the son of Publius) of the Papirian tribe, Marcus Acilius (the son of Marcus) of the Mecian tribe, Lucius Erucius (the son of Lucius) of the Stellatine tribe, Marcus Quintus Plancillus (the son of Marcus) of the Pollian tribe, and Publius Serius. Publius Dolabella, and Marcus Antonius, the consuls, drew it up. As to those things which, by the decree of the senate, Caius Cæsar had determined about the Jews, and yet had not hitherto had that decree brought into the treasury, it is our will, as it is also the desire of Publius Dolabella and Marcus Antonius, our consuls, to have those decrees put on the public tablets, and brought to the city quæstors, that they may take care to have them put upon the double tablets. This was done in the temple of Concord the fifth day before the Ides of February. Now the ambassadors from Hyrcanus the high priest were these, Lysimachus the son of Pausanias, Alexander the son of Theodorus, Patroclus the son of Chæreas, and Jonathan the son of Onias."

§ 11. Hyrcanus also sent one of these ambassadors to Dolabella, who was then the governor of Asia, beseeching him to dismiss the Jews from military service, and to preserve to them the customs of their forefathers, and to permit them to live according to them. And when Dolabella had received Hyrcanus' letter, he sent without any further deliberation a letter to all in Asia, and to the city of the Ephesians (the metropolis of Asia), about the Jews, a copy of which here follows.

§ 12. "In the Presidency of Artemon, on the first day of the month Lenæon, Dolabella, imperator, to the senate and magistrates and people of the Ephesians sends greeting. Alexander the son of Theodorus, the ambassador of Hyrcanus (the son of Alexander), the high priest and ethnarch of the Jews, has shown to me that his countrymen cannot go into the army, because they are not allowed to bear arms or to travel on the Sabbath-days, nor to procure themselves then those sorts of food which they have been used to eat from the times of their forefathers. I do therefore grant them exemption from going into the army, as the governors before me have done, and permit them to use the customs of their forefathers, in assembling together for sacred and religious purposes, as their law requires, and for collecting oblations necessary for sacrifices: and my will is, that you write this to the several cities under your jurisdiction."

§ 13. Such were the concessions that Dolabella made to our nation when Hyrcanus sent an embassage to him. And Lucius Lentulus, the consul, said: "I have at my tribunal exempted those Jews, who are citizens of Rome, and follow the Jewish religious rites and perform them at Ephesus, from going into the army, on account of their religious scruples, on the twelfth day before the Calends of October, in the consulship of Lucius Lentulus and Caius Marcellus.

There were present Titus Appius Balgus (the son of Titus),
lieutenant of the Horatian tribe, Titus Tongius (the son of
Titus), of the Crustumine tribe, Quintus Ræsius, the son
of Quintus, Titus Pompeius Longinus, the son of Titus,
Caius Servilius (the son of Caius), of the Terentine tribe,
Bracchus the military tribune, Publius Clusius Gallus (the
son of Publius), of the Veturian tribe, and Caius Sentius
(the son of Caius), of the Sabatine tribe.  Titus Appius
Bulbus, the son of Titus, lieutenant and pro-prætor, to the
magistrates, senate, and people of the Ephesians, greeting.
Lucius Lentulus the consul exempted the Jews that are in
Asia from going into the army in consequence of my intercession for them.  And when I made the same petition
some time afterwards to Phanius the pro-prætor and to
Lucius Antonius the pro-quæstor, I obtained that privilege of them also ; and my will is, that you take care that
no one give them any trouble."

§ 14. The decree of the Delians.  " The answer of the
prætors, when Bœotus was archon, on the twentieth day of
the month Thargelion.  When Marcus Piso the lieutenant
lived in our city, who was also appointed head of the re-
cruiting of soldiers, he called us and many others of the
citizens, and gave order, if there were here any Jews who
were Roman citizens, that no one was to trouble them about
going into the army, because Cornelius Lentulus, the consul,
freed the Jews from going into the army on account of
their religious scruples.  You are therefore obliged to
submit to the prætor."  And the like decree was made by
the Sardians also about us.

§ 15. " Caius Phanius, the son of Caius, imperator and
consul, to the magistrates of Cos greeting.  I would have
you know that the ambassadors of the Jews have been with
me, and desired they might have those decrees which the
senate had made about them ; which decrees are here subjoined.  My will is that you take care of and see to these
men, according to the senate's decree, that they may be
safely conveyed home through your country."

§ 16. The declaration of Lucius Lentulus the consul : " I
have dismissed those Jews who are Roman citizens, and
who appeared to me to have their religious rites, and to
practise them at Ephesus, on account of their religious

scruples. This was done the thirteenth day before the Calends of October."

§ 17. "Lucius Antonius, the son of Marcus, pro-quæstor, and pro-prætor, to the magistrates, senate, and people of the Sardians, greeting. Those Jews that were our citizens came to me, and showed that they had an assembly of their own according to the laws of their forefathers, and that from the beginning, as also a place of their own, wherein they determined their suits and controversies with one another: upon their petition therefore to me, that these might be lawful for them, I gave order for their privileges to be preserved and permitted."

§ 18. The declaration of Marcus Publius, the son of Spurius, and of Marcus the son of Marcus, and of Lucius the son of Publius. "We went to the pro-consul Lentulus, and informed him of what Dositheus, the son of Cleopatrides, of Alexandria desired, that, if he thought good, he would dismiss those Jews who were Roman citizens, and were wont to observe the rites of the Jewish religion, on account of their religious scruples. Accordingly, he did dismiss them, on the thirteenth day before the Calends of October."

§ 19. "In the month Quintilis, when Lucius Lentulus and Caius Marcellus were consuls, there were present Titus Appius Balbus, the son of Titus, lieutenant of the Horatian tribe, Titus Tongius of the Crustumine tribe, Quintus Ræsius the son of Quintus, Titus Pompeius the son of Titus, Cornelius Longinus, Caius Servilius Bracchus (the son of Caius) military tribune, of the Terentine tribe, Publius Clusius Gallus (the son of Publius) of the Veturian tribe, Caius Teutius (the son of Caius) military tribune, of the Æmilian tribe, Sextus Atilius Serranus (the son of Sextus) of the Æsquiline tribe, Caius Pompeius (the son of Caius) of the Sabatine tribe, Titus Appius Menander the son of Titus, Publius Servilius Strabo the son of Publius, Lucius Paccius Capito (the son of Lucius) of the Colline tribe, Aulus Furius Tertius the son of Aulus, and Appius Menas. In the presence of these Lentulus pronounced the following decree: I have before my tribunal dismissed those Jews that are Roman citizens, and are accustomed to observe the sacred rites of the Jews at Ephesus, on account of their religious scruples."

§ 20. "The magistrates of the Laodiceans send greeting to Caius Rabilius (the son of Caius) the consul. Sopater the ambassador of Hyrcanus the high priest, has delivered us a letter from thee, whereby he lets us know that certain persons came from Hyrcanus the high priest of the Jews, and brought a letter written concerning their nation, wherein they desired that the Jews might be allowed to observe their Sabbaths, and other sacred rites, according to the laws of their forefathers, and that no one might lord it over them, because they were our friends and allies, or injure them in our province. Now although the Trallians there present replied that they were not pleased with these decrees, yet didst thou give order that they should be observed, and informedst us that thou wast desired to write this to us about them. We therefore, in obedience to the injunctions we have received from thee, have received the letter which thou sentest us, and have laid it up apart among our public records. As to the other things about which thou didst send to us, we will take care that no complaint be made against us."

§ 21. "Publius Servilius Galba (the son of Publius), proconsul, to the magistrates, senate, and people of the Milesians, sendeth greeting. Prytanis (the son of Hermes) a citizen of yours, came to me when I was at Tralles[1] and held a court there, and informed me that you used the Jews in a way different from our orders, and forbade them to celebrate their Sabbaths, and to perform the sacred rites received from their forefathers, and to manage the fruits of the land according to their ancient custom, and that he himself had promulgated the decree according to the laws. I would therefore have you know, that upon hearing the pleadings on both sides, I gave sentence that the Jews should not be prohibited to use their own customs."

§ 22. The decree of the people of Pergamus.[2] "When Cratippus was Prytanis, on the first day of the month Dæsius, the decree of the prætors was as follows. Since the Romans, following the conduct of their ancestors, undertake dangers for the common safety of all mankind, and

[1] Near *Aidin*, in the valley of the Mæander, on the west coast of Asia Minor.
[2] *Bergama*.

are ambitious to settle their allies and friends in happiness
and firm peace; and since the nation of the Jews, and their
high priest Hyrcanus, sent as ambassadors to them Strato
the son of Theodotus, and Apollonius the son of Alexander,
and Æneas the son of Antipater, and Aristobulus the son
of Amyntas, and Sosipater the son of Philip, all worthy
and good men, who gave a particular account of their
affairs, the senate thereupon passed a decree as to what
they asked of them, that Antiochus the king, the son of
Antiochus, should do no injury to the Jews, the allies of
the Romans; and that the fortresses and havens and territory, and whatever else he had taken from them, should
be restored; and that it should be lawful for them to export their goods out of their own havens: and that no
king or people should have leave to export any goods, either
from the country of Judæa or from their havens, without
paying customs, except Ptolemy the king of Alexandria,
because he is our ally and friend; and that according
to their desire, the garrison that was in Joppa should be
expelled. Now Lucius Pettius, one of our senators, a worthy
and good man, gave order that we should take care that
these things should be done according to the senate's decree; and that we should take care also that the Jewish ambassadors might return home in safety. And we admitted
Theodorus into our senate and assembly, and took the letter
from him as well as the decree of the senate; and as he
discoursed with great earnestness, and described Hyrcanus'
virtue and generosity, and how he was a benefactor to all
men in common, and to everybody that came to him in
particular, we laid up the letter in our public records, and
made a decree ourselves, since we also were allies of the
Romans, that we would do everything we could for the Jews
according to the senate's decree. Theodorus also, who
brought the letter, asked of our prætors, that they would
send Hyrcanus a copy of that decree, as also ambassadors
to signify to him the affection of our people to him, and to
exhort him to preserve and augment his friendship with
us, and to be ready to bestow other benefits upon us, as
we reasonably expected to receive a fit return, remembering that our ancestors were friendly to the Jews even
in the days of Abraham, who was the father of all the

Hebrews, as we have found it set down in our public records."

23. The decree of the Halicarnassians.[1] "Before Memnon the priest, the son of Orestides by descent, but of Euonymus by adoption, on the * * * day of the month Anthesterion, the decree of the people, upon the motion of Marcus Alexander, was as follows. Since we have ever a great regard to piety towards God and to holiness, following the people of the Romans, who are the benefactors of all men, and what they have written to us about a league of friendship and alliance between the Jews and our city, that their sacred rites and accustomed feasts and assemblies may be observed by them; we have decreed, that as many men and women of the Jews as wish to do so may celebrate their Sabbaths, and perform their holy rites, according to the Jewish laws, and have their places of prayer by the seaside, according to the customs of their forefathers; and if any one, whether a magistrate or private person, hinders them from so doing, he shall be liable to a fine, to be paid to the city."

§ 24. The decree of the Sardians.[2] "This decree was made by the senate and people, upon the representation of the prætors. Whereas those Jews, who are our fellow-citizens, and live in our city, have ever had great benefits heaped upon them by the people, and have come now to the senate, and requested of the people that, upon the restitution of their laws and liberty by the senate and people of Rome, they may assemble together according to their ancient customs, and that we will not bring any suit against them about it; and that a place may be given them where they may hold their congregations with their wives and children, and may offer, as their forefathers did, their prayers and sacrifices to God; the senate and people have decreed to permit them to assemble together on the days formerly appointed, and to act according to their own laws; and that such a place be set apart for them by the prætors for a building and habitation, as they shall esteem

[1] The people of Halicarnassus, now *Bûdrûm*, on the S.W. coast of Asia Minor.
[2] The people of Sardis, now *Sart*, in the valley of the Hermus, on the west coast of Asia Minor.

fit for that purpose.   And let those that see to provisions
for the city, take care that such sorts of food as they shall
esteem fit for their eating, may be introduced into the
city."

§ 25.  The decree of the Ephesians.  "When Menophilus
was Prytanis, on the first day of the month Artemisius,
this decree was made by the people.   Nicanor, the son of
Euphemus, pronounced it, upon the motion of the prætors.
As the Jews that dwell in this city petitioned Marcus
Julius Pompeius (the son of Brutus) the pro-consul, that
they might be allowed to observe their Sabbaths, and to
act in all things according to the customs of their forefathers, without impediment from anybody, the prætor
granted their petition.   So it was decreed by the senate and
people, as the affair concerned the Romans, that none of
them should be hindered from keeping the Sabbath-day,
nor be fined for so doing, but that they should be allowed
to do all things according to their own laws."

§ 26.  Now there are many other such decrees of the
senate and imperators of the Romans, made in favour of
Hyrcanus and our nation, and decrees for cities, and re-
scripts of the prætors to such letters as concerned our
rights and privileges: and certainly such as are not ill
disposed to what I write, may believe that they are all to
this purpose, from the specimens which I have inserted.
For as I have produced evident marks that may still be
seen of the friendship we have had with the Romans, and
shown that those marks are engraven upon pillars and
tablets of brass in the Capitol, that are still in existence and
will be so, I have omitted to set them all down as needless
and disagreeable; for I cannot suppose any one so perverse
as not to believe that we have had friendship with the
Romans, since they have demonstrated the same by such
a great number of their decrees relating to us, or to doubt
of our fidelity as to the rest of those decrees, since I have
shown a sample.   I have now sufficiently set forth the
friendship and alliance we had in those times with the
Romans.

## CHAP. XI.

*How Murcus succeeded Sextus, when he had been slain by*
*Bassus' treachery; and how, after the death of Cæsar,*
*Cassius came into Syria, and distressed Judæa; as also,*
*how Malichus slew Antipater, and was himself slain by*
*Herod.*

### § 1.

NOW it so fell out about this very time that the affairs
of Syria were in great disorder on the following
account. Cæcilius Bassus, one of Pompey's party, conspired
against Sextus Cæsar, and slew him, and then took his
army, and got the management of public affairs into his
own hand; so that there arose a great war about Apamea,[1]
for Cæsar's generals came against him with an army of
horse and foot. Antipater also sent succours with his sons
to them, calling to mind the kindnesses he had received
from Cæsar, and so he thought it but just to require
punishment for him, and to take vengeance on the man
that had murdered him. And as the war lasted a great
time, Murcus came from Rome to take Sextus' command,
and Cæsar was slain by Cassius and Brutus and the other
conspirators in the senate-house, after he had ruled three
years and six months. This is however related elsewhere.

§ 2. As the war that arose upon the death of Cæsar was
now begun, and the principal men all went, some one way,
some another, to raise armies, Cassius went from Rome
into Syria, to take the command of the army at Apamea,
and having raised the siege, he won over both Bassus and
Murcus to his party. He then visited the various cities,
and got together weapons and soldiers, and laid great taxes
upon the cities, and especially oppressed Judæa, exacting
from it seven hundred talents. But Antipater, when he saw
that affairs were in such great confusion and disorder,
divided the collection of that sum, and appointed his two
sons to gather some of it, and part of it was to be exacted
by Malichus, who was ill disposed to him, and part by

[1] *Kal'ât el-Medyk.*

others.  And because Herod did exact what was required
of him from Galilee before all others, he was in the greatest
favour with Cassius; for he thought it prudent to cultivate
a friendship with the Romans, and to gain their good-will
at the expense of others; whereas the rulers of the other
cities, with all the citizens, were sold for slaves; and
Cassius reduced four cities to slavery, the two most important of which were Gophna[1] and Emmaus,[2] and besides
them Lydda[3] and Thamna.[4]  Nay, Cassius was so very
angry at Malichus, that he would have killed him (for he
was mad at him), had not Hyrcanus sent him by Antipater
a hundred talents of his own, and so pacified his anger
against him.

§ 3.  But after Cassius had gone from Judæa, Malichus
conspired against Antipater, thinking his death would be
for the security of Hyrcanus' power; but his design was
not unknown to Antipater, who, when he perceived it,
retired beyond the Jordan, and got together an army,
partly of Arabs, and partly of his own countrymen.  However, Malichus, being a crafty fellow, denied that he had
laid any snares for him, and made his defence with an
oath both to him and his sons, and said, that as Phasaelus
had the garrison in Jerusalem, and Herod had the weapons
of war in his custody, he could never have thought of any
such thing.  So Antipater, perceiving the distress that
Malichus was in, was reconciled to him, and made an
agreement with him when Murcus was prætor of Syria,
who perceiving that this Malichus was raising disturbances
in Judæa, very nearly had him killed, but at the intercession of Antipater he saved his life.

§ 4.  However, Antipater little thought that in Malichus
he had saved his own murderer.  For when Cassius and
Murcus had got together an army, they intrusted the
entire care of it to Herod, and made him general of the
forces of Cœle-Syria, and gave him a fleet of ships, and an
army of horse and foot; and promised him, after the war
was over, to make him king of Judæa, for war was already
begun between them and Antony and the young Cæsar.[5]

---

[1] *Jifna*, N.W. of *Beitin*, Bethel.       [2] *'Amwâs*.       [3] *Ludd*.
[4] Now *Tibneh;* see Antiq. v. 1, § 29; xiv. 11, § 12.
[5] Octavius, afterwards the Emperor Augustus.

And as Malichus was now especially afraid of Antipater, he tried to get him out of the way; and, by the offer of money, persuaded the butler of Hyrcanus with whom they were about to feast, to kill him by poison. This being done, having armed men with him, he settled the affairs of the city. But when Antipater's sons, Herod and Phasaelus, got to know of this conspiracy against their father, and were indignant at it, Malichus denied all, and professed to have no knowledge of the murder. And thus died Antipater, a man that had distinguished himself for piety and justice and love for his country. And whereas one of his sons, Herod, resolved immediately to revenge his father's death, and marched against Malichus with an army, the elder of his sons, Phasaelus, thought it best rather to get round him by policy, lest they should appear to begin a civil war in the country. So he accepted Malichus' defence, and pretended to believe that he had had no hand in the death of Antipater his father, and erected a fine monument to him. Herod also went to Samaria,[1] and as he found it in great distress, he repaired the city, and composed the differences of its inhabitants.

§ 5. Not long after this, Herod, upon the approach of a festival at Jerusalem, went with his soldiers to that city; whereupon Malichus was afraid, and urged Hyrcanus not to permit him to enter the city. Hyrcanus listened to him, and alleged, as a pretext for excluding Herod, that a crowd of strangers ought not to be admitted when the multitude were purifying themselves. But Herod paid little regard to the messengers who were sent to him, and entered the city by night, and frightened Malichus, who however remitted nothing of his dissimulation, but wept for Antipater, and bewailed him with a loud voice as a friend of his. And Herod and his friends thought it well not to expose Malichus' hypocrisy, but to receive him kindly also, to prevent his feeling any suspicion.

§ 6. However, Herod sent to Cassius, and informed him of the murder of his father. And he, knowing the character of Malichus, sent him back word to revenge his father's death; and also sent privately to the commanders of the

[1] *Sebustieh.*

army at Tyre, ordering them to assist Herod in the execution of his very just design. Now when Cassius had taken Laodicea,[1] and they all went together to him, and carried him garlands and money, Herod expected that Malichus would be punished while he was there; but Malichus was somewhat apprehensive of some such thing when in the neighbourhood of Tyre in Phœnicia, and designed to make some great move, and as his son was then an hostage at Tyre, he went to that city, and resolved to steal him away privately, and to march thence into Judæa; and as Cassius was in haste to march against Antony, he thought to bring the country to revolt, and to procure the government for himself. But Providence opposed his counsels, for Herod being a shrewd man, and perceiving what his intention was, sent thither beforehand a servant, in appearance indeed to get a supper ready, (for he had said before that he would feast them all there,) but in reality to take a message to the commanders of the army, whom he urged to go out against Malichus with their daggers. So they went out, and met the man near the city, upon the sea-shore, and there stabbed him. Thereupon Hyrcanus was so astonished at what had happened, that his speech failed him; and when, after some difficulty, he came to himself, he asked Herod's men what the matter could be, and who it was that had slain Malichus? And when they said that it was done by command of Cassius, he commended the action; for he said Malichus was a very wicked man, and one that conspired against his country. And this was the punishment that was inflicted on Malichus for what he wickedly did to Antipater.

§ 7. But when Cassius had marched out of Syria, disturbances arose in Judæa: for Helix, who was left at Jerusalem with an army, made a sudden attack on Phasaelus, and the people themselves took up arms. And Herod went to Fabius, the prefect of Damascus, and desired to run to his brother's assistance, but was hindered by an illness that seized upon him, till Phasaelus by himself was too hard for Helix, and shut him up in the tower, and then dismissed him on conditions. Phasaelus also complained of

---

[1] *Latakieh*, on the coast of Syria.

Hyrcanus, on the ground that, although he had received a great many benefits from them, he yet acted with his enemies. For Malichus' brother at this time made many places to revolt, and kept garrisons in them, and especially at Masada,[1] the strongest fortress of all. Not long after this Herod recovered from his illness, and came and took from Malichus' brother all the places he had got, and, on certain conditions, let him go.

## CHAP. XII.

*Herod ejects Antigonus, the Son of Aristobulus, from Judæa, and gains the Friendship of Antony, who was now come into Syria, by sending him much Money; on which Account he would not hear those that would have accused Herod: and what it was that Antony wrote to the Tyrians in behalf of the Jews.*

### § 1.

NOW Ptolemy, the son of Mennæus, because he was akin to him, brought back into Judæa Antigonus the son of Aristobulus, who had already raised an army, and had by money made Fabius his friend. Marion also gave him assistance. Marion had been left by Cassius to tyrannize over Tyre, for Cassius having seized on Syria, then kept it under by tyrants. Marion also marched into Galilee, which lay in his neighbourhood, and took three of the fortresses, and put garrisons into them to keep them. But when Herod came against him he took them all from him, but he dismissed the Tyrian garrison in a very civil manner; nay he made presents to some from the good-will he bore to that city. When he had despatched these affairs, and had gone to meet Antigonus, he joined battle with him, and beat him, and drove him out of Judæa, when he was just come into its borders. And when he was come to Jerusalem, Hyrcanus and the people put garlands on his head; for he had already contracted an affinity with the family of Hyrcanus by having espoused a descendant of

[1] *Sebbeh,* on the west coast of the Dead Sea.

his, and for that reason Herod took the greater care of him, as he was about to marry the daughter of Alexander (the son of Aristobulus) and grand-daughter of Hyrcanus, by whom he eventually became the father of three sons and two daughters. He had also married before this another wife, of a lower family of his own nation, whose name was Doris, by whom he had his eldest son Antipater.

§ 2. Now Antony and Cæsar [1] had beaten Cassius near Philippi,[2] as others have related; and after that victory, Cæsar [1] went into Italy, and Antony set out for Asia, and, when he arrived at Bithynia,[3] ambassadors met him from all parts. The principal men also of the Jews came there to accuse Phasaelus and Herod, and said that Hyrcanus had indeed the semblance of reigning, but these men had all the power. But Antony paid great respect to Herod, who came to him to make his defence against his accusers, so that his adversaries could not so much as obtain a hearing; which favour Herod obtained of Antony by money. But when Antony was come to Ephesus, Hyrcanus the high priest, and our nation, sent an embassage to him, who carried a crown of gold with them, and begged that he would write to the governors of the provinces, to set those Jews free who had been carried captive by Cassius, though they had not fought against him, and to restore them the country which had been taken from them in the days of Cassius. Antony thought the Jews' requests were just, and wrote immediately to Hyrcanus and to the Jews. He also sent, at the same time, a decree to the Tyrians, the contents of which were as follows.

§ 3. "Marcus Antonius, imperator, to Hyrcanus the high priest and ethnarch of the Jews greeting. If you be in health, it is well; I also am in health and the army. Lysimachus the son of Pausanias, and Josephus the son of Mennæus, and Alexander the son of Theodorus, your ambassadors, met me at Ephesus, and have renewed that embassage which they had formerly been upon at Rome, and have diligently acquitted themselves in the present embas-

---

[1] That is Octavius, afterwards the Emperor Augustus.
[2] Now *Filibeh*, in Macedonia, not far from *Kavala*, Neapolis.
[3] The N.W. portion of Asia Minor.

sage on behalf of you and your nation, and have fully declared the good-will you have for us.    I am therefore
satisfied, both by your actions and words, that you are
well disposed to us, and I understand that your conduct of
life is constant and religious, so I reckon upon you as our
own.    But since those that were adversaries to you, and to
the Roman people, abstained neither from cities nor temples, and did not observe the agreements they had confirmed by oath, it was not only on account of our private
contest with them, but also on account of all mankind in
common, that we took vengeance on those who have been the
authors of great injustice towards men, and of great wickedness towards the gods ; for the sake of which we suppose
it was that the sun turned away its light,[1] being unwilling
to view the horrid crime they were guilty of in the case of
Cæsar.    We have also overcome their conspiracies, which
threatened the gods themselves, which Macedonia received,
as it is a climate peculiarly proper for impious and insolent
attempts, and we overcame that confused rout of men half
mad with spite against us, which they got together at
Philippi in Macedonia, when they occupied places fit for
their purpose, and, as it were, walled round with mountains to the very sea, and where approach was open only
through a single gate.    This victory we gained because
the gods had condemned those men for their wicked undertakings.    Now Brutus, when he had fled to Philippi,
was shut up by us, and partook of the same destruction
as Cassius ; and now that those men have received their
punishment, we hope that we may enjoy peace for the
time to come, and that Asia may be at rest from war. We,
therefore, make that peace which God has given us common to our allies also, so that the body of Asia is now recovered from its disease as it were owing to our victory.
I, therefore, bearing you in mind and hoping to aggran-
dize your nation, shall take care of what may be for your
advantage.    I have also sent letters to the several cities,

---

[1] This clause plainly alludes to that well known but unusual and very
long darkness of the sun, which happened upon the murder of Julius
Cæsar by Brutus and Cassius, which is taken notice of by Virgil,
Pliny, and other Roman authors.    See Virgil's Georgics, b. i. just
before the end ; and Pliny's Nat. Hist. b. ii. c. 30.—W.

that if any persons, whether freemen or bondmen, have been sold under the spear by Caius Cassius, or his subordinate officers, they are to be set free. And I will that you make use of the favours which I and Dolabella have kindly granted you. I also forbid the Tyrians to use any violence to you, and as to those places of the Jews they now possess, I order them to restore them. I have also accepted of the crown which you sent me."

§ 4. "Marcus Antonius, imperator, to the magistrates, senate, and people of Tyre, greeting. The ambassadors of Hyrcanus the high priest and ethnarch [of the Jews] have appeared before me at Ephesus, and have told me that you are in possession of part of their country, which you entered upon during the sway of our adversaries. Since, therefore, we have undertaken a war for obtaining the government, and have taken care to do what was agreeable to piety and justice, and have brought to punishment those that had neither any remembrance of the kindness they had received, nor kept their oaths, I will that you be at peace with those that are our allies, as also that what you have taken by means of our adversaries shall not be reckoned your own, but be returned to those from whom you took them. For none of our rivals took their provinces or their armies by the gift of the senate, but seized them by force, and gratified by violence such as served them in their unjust proceedings. Since, therefore, those men have received the punishment due to them, we desire that our allies may retain whatever they formerly possessed without disturbance, and that you restore all the places which you now have, which belonged to Hyrcanus the ethnarch of the Jews, even though only one day before Caius Cassius began an unjustifiable war against us, and entered our provinces. Neither use any force against the Jews in order to weaken them, that they may not be able to dispose of that which is their own. But if you have any plea to urge in defence against Hyrcanus, it shall be lawful for you to plead your case when we come to the places concerned, for we shall alike preserve the rights, and hear all the causes, of our allies."

§ 5. "Marcus Antonius, imperator, to the magistrates, senate, and people of Tyre, greeting. I have sent you my

decree, and I will that you take care that it be engraven on
the public tablets, in Roman and Greek letters, and that it
stand engraven in the most public place, that it may be
read by all. Marcus Antonius, imperator, one of the
triumvirs over public affairs, has spoken. Since Caius
Cassius, in the revolt he made, pillaged a province which
did not belong to him, and was held by garrisons there
encamped, and plundered our allies, and warred against
the nation of the Jews that was in friendship with the
Roman people, and since we have overcome his madness
by arms, we now correct by our decrees and judicial deter-
minations what he has laid waste, that all that may be
restored to our allies. And as for what has been sold of
the Jews, whether bodies or possessions, let them be released, the bodies into that state of freedom they were
originally in, and the possessions to their former owners.
I also will, that he who shall not comply with this decree
of mine, shall be punished for his disobedience; and if
such a one be caught, I will take care that the offender
shall suffer condign punishment."

§ 6. The same thing did Antony write to the Sidonians,
and the Antiochians, and the Aradians.[1]  I have produced
these decrees at a suitable place, as proofs of the truth of
what I said, namely that the Romans had a great concern
about our nation.


## CHAP. XIII.

*How Antony made Herod and Phasaelus Tetrarchs after they
had been accused to no purpose ; and how the Parthians,
when they brought Antigonus into Judœa, took Hyrcanus
and Phasaelus captives.  Herod's Flight ; and the Afflictions that Hyrcanus and Phasaelus endured.*

### § 1.

AFTER this when Antony came into Syria, Cleopatra
met him in Cilicia, and greatly captivated him. And
now again there came a hundred of the most influential

---

[1] The people of Aradus, Arvad, now the island *er-Ruad.*

of the Jews to accuse Herod and his party, and set the men of the greatest eloquence among them to speak. But Messala pleaded against them, on behalf of the young men, and in the presence of Hyrcanus, who was Herod's father-in-law already.[1]  When Antony had heard both sides at Daphne,[2] he asked Hyrcanus who governed the nation best? and he replied, Herod and his party. Thereupon Antony, because of the old friendship he had with Herod's father when he was with Gabinius, made both Herod and Phasaelus tetrarchs, and committed the public affairs of the Jews to them, and wrote letters to that purpose. He also put fifteen of their adversaries in bonds, and was going to kill them, but Herod obtained their pardon.

§ 2. Yet did not these men continue quiet when they returned from their embassage, but a thousand of the Jews went to Tyre to meet Antony there, as the report was that he would go there. But Antony was corrupted by the quantity of money which Herod and his brother had given him, and so he gave orders to the governor of the place to punish the Jewish ambassadors who were for making innovations, and to settle the government upon Herod. And Herod went out quickly to them, and Hyrcanus with him (for they stood upon the shore before the city), and charged them to go their ways, because great mischief would befall them if they went on with their pertinacity. But they would not listen, so the Romans ran upon them at once with their daggers, and slew some, and wounded others, and the rest fled away and went home, and remained quiet in great consternation. And when the people made a clamour against Herod, Antony was so provoked at it that he slew those fifteen that had been put in bonds.

§ 3. Now, in the second year, Pacorus, the king of Parthia's son, and Barzapharnes, a satrap of the Parthians, occupied Syria. Ptolemy, the son of Mennæus, was now

---

[1] We may here take notice, that espousals alone were of old esteemed a sufficient foundation for affinity, Hyrcanus being here called father-in-law to Herod, because his grand-daughter Mariamne was betrothed to him, although the marriage was not completed till four years afterwards. See Mat. i. 16.—W.

[2] *Beit el-Mâ*, near Antioch.

also dead, and Lysanias his son succeeded him, and made a
league of friendship with Antigonus, the son of Aristobulus,
and for that end made use of the satrap Barzapharnes, who
had great influence with him. Now Antigonus had promised
to give the Parthians a thousand talents and five hundred
women, if they would take the government away from
Hyrcanus, and bestow it upon him, and also kill Herod.
And although he did not give what he promised, yet did
the Parthians make an expedition into Judæa on that
account, and carried Antigonus with them. Pacorus went
along the maritime parts, and the satrap Barzapharnes
through the interior of the country. Now the Tyrians
excluded Pacorus, but the Sidonians and those of Ptolemais [1]
received him. However, Pacorus sent a troop of horse
into Judæa, to make a reconnaissance of the country, and
to assist Antigonus, and sent the king's butler as its commander, who had the same name as himself. And when
the Jews that dwelt about Mount Carmel came to Antigonus, and were ready to march with him into Judæa,
Antigonus hoped to get some part of the country by their
assistance; the place was called Drymi. [2] And when some
others came and met them, the men marched on Jerusalem; and when some more were come to them, they got
together in great numbers, and marched against the king's
palace and besieged it. But as Phasaelus' and Herod's
party came to the others' assistance, and a battle took
place between them in the market-place, the young men
beat their enemies, and pursued them into the temple,
and sent some armed men into the adjoining houses to
keep them in, who however being destitute of support
were burnt, houses and all, by the people who rose up
against them. But Herod was revenged on these seditious adversaries of his soon afterwards for this injury
they had done him, for he fought with them, and slew a
great number of them.

§ 4. But though there were daily skirmishes, the enemy
waited for the coming of the people out of the country
to Pentecost (a feast of ours so called), and when that

---

[1] 'Akka, St. Jean d'Acre.
[2] Comp. Jewish War, i. 13, § 2. Probably an oak-grove at the foot
of Carmel.

day was come, many myriads of the people were gathered
together near the temple, some in armour, and some unarmed.  Now those that came guarded both the temple
and the city, except near the palace, which Herod guarded
with a few of his soldiers ; and Phasaelus had the charge
of the wall, while Herod, with a body of his men, sallied
out upon the enemy, who lay in the suburbs, and fought
valiantly, and put many myriads to flight, some fleeing
into the city, and some into the temple, and some to the
outer vallum that was there.  Phasaelus also came to his
assistance.  And Pacorus, the general of the Parthians, at
the desire of Antigonus, was admitted into the city, with
a few of his horsemen, under pretext indeed of stilling
the sedition, but in reality to assist Antigonus in obtaining the government.  And when Phasaelus met him, and
received him kindly, Pacorus persuaded him to go himself as ambassador to Barzapharnes, which was done
treacherously.  And Phasaelus, suspecting no harm, complied with his proposal, while Herod did not approve of
what was done, because of the perfidiousness of the barbarians, but bade Phasaelus rather to fight against those
that were come into the city.

§ 5.  So both Hyrcanus and Phasaelus went on the embassage ; but Pacorus left with Herod two hundred horse,
and ten men who were called Freemen, and conducted the
others on their journey.  And when they got to Galilee,
the governors of the cities there met them in arms.  And
Barzarpharnes received them at first with cheerfulness,
and made them presents, though he afterwards conspired
against them ; and Phasaelus, with his horsemen, were
conducted to the seaside.  But when they heard that
Antigonus had promised to bribe the Parthians by a thousand talents and five hundred women to assist him against
them, they soon had a suspicion of the barbarians.  Moreover, there was one who informed them that snares were
laid for them by night, as a guard secretly surrounded
them.  And they would then have been seized upon, had
not they waited for the seizure of Herod by the Parthians
that were at Jerusalem, lest, upon the slaughter of Hyrcanus and Phasaelus, he should have an intimation of it,
and so escape out of their hands.  And these were the cir-

cumstances they were now in, and they saw who they were
that guarded them.  Some persons indeed advised Phasaelus to ride off immediately, and not to stay any longer;
and there was one Ophellius, who, above all the rest, was
urgent with him to do so, for he had heard of this treachery
from Saramalla, the richest of all the Syrians at that time,
who also promised to provide him ships for flight; for the
sea was near.  But he had no mind to desert Hyrcanus,
nor bring his brother into danger; but he went to Barzapharnes, and told him he did not act justly in plotting
thus against them, for if he wanted money, he would give
him more than Antigonus; and besides, it was monstrous
to slay ambassadors that came to him upon the security of
their oaths, and that when they had done no injury.  And
the barbarian swore to him that there was no truth in any
of his suspicions, but that he was troubled with nothing
but false fancies, and then went back to Pacorus.

§ 6.  But as soon as he was gone away, some of the Parthians came and bound Hyrcanus and Phasaelus, and
Phasaelus greatly reproached the Parthians for their perjury.  Now the butler who was sent against Herod had been
told to get him without the walls of the city and seize
upon him.  But messengers had been sent by Phasaelus to
inform Herod of the perfidiousness of the Parthians : and
when Herod knew that the enemy had seized Hyrcanus
and Phasaelus, he went to Pacorus, and to the most influential of the Parthians, as the lords of the rest.  And they,
although they knew the whole matter, dissembled with
him in a deceitful way; and said that he ought to go out
with them before the walls, and meet those who were
bringing him letters, for they had not yet been taken by
his adversaries, but were coming to give him an account of
the good success Phasaelus had had.  But Herod did not
credit what they said; for he had heard from others that
his brother had been seized.  And the daughter of Hyrcanus,
whose daughter he had espoused, advised him also [not to
credit them,] which made him still more suspicious of the
Parthians; for although other people did not give heed to
her, he believed her to be a woman of very great wisdom.

§ 7.  Now while the Parthians were in consultation what
was fit to be done (for they did not think it proper to make

an open attempt upon a person of his character), and put
off the matter to the next day, Herod was in great
anxiety; and rather inclining to believe the reports he
heard about his brother and the Parthians, than to give
heed to what was said on the other side, he determined
that, when evening came on, he would make use of it
for his flight, and not make any longer delay, as if danger
from the enemy was still uncertain. He therefore set out
with the armed men whom he had with him, and set the
women upon beasts of burden, as his mother and sister,
and her whom he was about to marry [Mariamne], the
daughter of Alexander (the son of Aristobulus), and her
mother the daughter of Hyrcanus, and his youngest
brother, and all their servants, and the rest of the multitude that was with him, and without the enemies' knowledge pursued his way to Idumæa[1]: nor could any enemy
of his, who had seen him then in this case, have been so
hard-hearted, as not to have commiserated his fortune, as
the women dragged along their infant children, and with
tears in their eyes, and sad lamentations, left their own
country, and their friends in prison, and expected nothing
but what was of a melancholy nature.

§ 8. But Herod raised his mind above the miserable
state he was in, and was of good courage in the midst of
his misfortunes, and, as he passed along, bade every one
be of good cheer, and not give way to sorrow, because that
would hinder them in their flight, which was now the only
hope of safety that they had. So they tried to bear with
patience the calamity they were in, as Herod exhorted them
to do; but he once almost killed himself, upon the overthrow of a waggon, and the danger his mother was then in
of being killed, not only because of his great concern for her,
but also because he was afraid lest, by this delay, the enemy
should overtake him in the pursuit. But as he was draw-
ing his sword, and going to kill himself with it, those that
were present restrained him, and being so many in number
were too much for him, and told him that he ought not to
desert them, and leave them a prey to their enemies, for
that it was not the part of a brave man to free himself

[1] The country south of Hebron and west of the Dead Sea is referred
to here.

from the distresses he was in, and to leave his friends to
struggle in the same. So he was compelled to let that
horrid attempt alone, partly from shame at what they said
to him, and partly from regard to the great number of
those that would not permit him to do what he intended.
And he revived his mother, and took all the care of her
the conjuncture would allow, and proceeded on the way he
proposed to go with the utmost haste, and that was to the
fortress of Masada.[1] And though he had many skirmishes
with such of the Parthians as attacked him and pursued
him, he was conqueror in them all.

§ 9. Nor indeed was he free from the Jews during
his flight; for by the time he had got sixty furlongs out of
the city, and was upon the road, they fell upon him, and
fought hand to hand with him, and he also put them to
flight and overcame them, not like one that was in distress
and in necessity, but like one that was excellently prepared for war, and had what he wanted in great plenty.
And in the very place where he overcame the Jews, some
time afterwards, when he became king, he built a most
fine palace, and a city round it, and called it Herodium.[2]
And when he was come to Idumæa, to a place called Thresa,[3]
his brother Joseph met him, and he then held a council to
take advice about all his affairs, and what was fit to be
done under the circumstances, as he had a great multitude
that followed him, besides his mercenary soldiers, and the
fortress of Masada, where he proposed to flee to, was too small
to contain so great a multitude. So he sent away the greater
part of his company, who were more than nine thousand, and
bade them go some one way and some another, and save
themselves in Idumæa, and gave them what would buy them
provisions on their journey; but he took with himself those
that were the least encumbered, and were most friendly to
him, and reached the fortress, and placed there his wives,
and his followers (who were eight hundred in number),
there being in the place a sufficient quantity of corn and
water and other necessaries, and himself set out directly
for Petra in Arabia. But when it was day, the Parthians

[1] *Sebbeh*, on the west shore of the Dead Sea.
[2] Probably *Jebel Fureidis*, south of Jerusalem.
[3] Comp. Jewish War, i. 13, § 8; Antiq. xiv. 15, § 2. Site not known.

plundered all Jerusalem, and the palace, and abstained
from nothing but Hyrcanus' money, which was three hundred talents.   A great deal of Herod's money escaped,
especially all that he had been so prudent as to send into
Idumæa beforehand.   However, what was in the city did
not suffice the Parthians, but they went out into the
country, and plundered it, and razed to the ground the
powerful city of Marissa.[1]

§ 10. Thus was Antigonus restored to Judæa by the
king of the Parthians, and received Hyrcanus and Phasaelus as prisoners; but he was greatly cast down because
the women had escaped, whom he intended to have given
the enemy, as he had promised they should have them,
with money, for their reward.   And being afraid that
Hyrcanus, who was guarded by the Parthians, would have
the kingdom restored to him by the multitude, he cut
off his ears, and so took care that the high priesthood
should never come to him any more, because he was thus
maimed, and the law required that this dignity should belong to none but such as had all their members entire.[2]
But one cannot but admire the fortitude of Phasaelus, who,
perceiving that he was to be put to death, did not think
death terrible at all; but he thought it a most pitiable
and dishonourable thing to die at the hands of the enemy,
and therefore, since he had not his hands at liberty, for
the bonds he was in prevented him from killing himself
with them, he dashed his head against a great stone, and
so took away his own life, which he thought to be the best
thing he could do in such straits as he was in, and so
put it out of the power of the enemy to put him to any
death he pleased.   It is also reported, that when he had
made a great wound in his head, Antigonus sent surgeons
as if to heal it, and ordered them to infuse poison into
the wound, and so killed him.   However, Phasaelus
hearing from a certain woman, before he was quite dead,
that his brother Herod had escaped the enemy, underwent
his death cheerfully, since he now left behind him one who
would revenge his death, and was able to inflict punishment on his enemies.

[1] *Kh. Mer'ash.*
[2] This law of Moses, that the priests were to be ' without blemish,' as
to all the parts of their bodies, is in Levit. xxi. 17-24.—W.

## CHAP. XIV.

*How Herod got away from the King of Arabia, and made haste to go into Egypt, and thence went away in haste also to Rome: and how, by promising a great deal of money to Antony, he was made by the Senate and Augustus King of the Jews.*

### § 1.

AS for Herod, the great hardships he underwent did not discourage him, but made him sharp in inventing bold plans. For he went to Malchus, king of Arabia, whom he had formerly been very kind to, in order to receive a return now he was in more than ordinary want of it, and desired he would let him have some money, either by way of loan or as a free gift, as he had received many benefits from him; for not knowing what had happened to his brother, he was in haste to ransom him out of the hands of his enemies, being willing to give three hundred talents as the price of his ransom. He also took with him the son of Phasaelus, who was a child of but seven years of age, in order that he might be a hostage to the Arabs for the repayment of the money; but there came messengers from Malchus to meet him, by whom he was desired to be off, for the Parthians had charged him not to receive Herod. This was only a pretext which he made use of that he might not be obliged to repay him what he owed him: and he was further induced to this by the principal men among the Arabians, that they might cheat him of the sums they had received from Antipater as a trust. He made answer, that he had not intended to be troublesome to them by his coming to them, but that he had desired only to discourse with them about certain affairs that were of the greatest importance to him.

§ 2. He then resolved to go away, and very prudently took the road to Egypt. And that night he lodged in a certain temple, for he had left a great many of his followers there, but on the next day he reached Rhinocurura,[1]

---

[1] *el-'Arísh*, on the coast between Egypt and Palestine.

and there heard what had befallen his brother. However, Malchus soon repented of what he had done, and came running after Herod, but with no success, for he had got a very great way off, making post haste on the road to Pelusium.[1] And when the ships that lay at anchor there hindered him from sailing to Alexandria, he went to the rulers of the place, by whom, in their reverence and great regard for him, he was conducted to the city, and was detained there by Cleopatra. However she was not able to prevail with him to stay there, because he was making haste to Rome, even though the weather was stormy, and he was informed that affairs in Italy were in great disorder and in a most unsettled condition.

§ 3. So he set sail from thence for Pamphylia,[2] and, falling in with a violent storm, had much ado to escape to Rhodes, with the loss of the ship's burden. And there two of his friends, Sappinas and Ptolemy, met him; and as he found Rhodes had been very much damaged in the war against Cassius, he neglected not to do it a kindness, though he was in necessity himself, but did what he could to restore it to its former state. He also built there a trireme, and set sail thence with his friends for Italy, and arrived at the port of Brundusium;[3] and when he had got from thence to Rome, he first related to Antony what had befallen him in Judæa, and how Phasaelus his brother had been seized by the Parthians, and put to death by them, and how Hyrcanus was detained captive by them, and how they had made Antigonus king, who had promised them no less a sum of money than a thousand talents, and five hundred women (who were to be of the principal families and of the Jewish stock), and how he himself had carried off the women by night, and by undergoing a great many hardships had escaped the hands of his enemies; as also, that his own relations were in danger of being besieged and taken, and that he had sailed through a storm, and despised all these terrible dangers, in order to come as soon as possible to him, who was his hope and only succour at this time.

§ 4. This account made Antony commiserate the change

---

[1] *Tineh.*    [2] On the south coast of Asia Minor.    [3] *Brindisi.*

that had happened in Herod's condition, and reasoning
with himself that this was a common case among those
that are placed in such great dignities, and that they too
are liable to fortune, he was very ready to give him the
assistance he desired, partly because he called to mind the
friendship he had had with Antipater, partly because
Herod offered him money to make him king, as he had
formerly done because he was made tetrarch, but chiefly
because of his hatred to Antigonus, for he took him to be
a seditious person, and an enemy to the Romans. Augustus
was also the forwarder to raise Herod's dignity, and to
give him his assistance in what he desired, on account of
the toils of war which his father had undergone with
Antipater in Egypt, and of the hospitable way in which
he had treated him, and the kindness he had always showed
him, as also to gratify Antony, who was very attached to
Herod. So the senate was convened, and Messala and after
him Atratinus introduced Herod, and enlarged upon the
benefits they had received from his father, and reminded
them of the good-will he had himself borne to the Romans.
At the same time they accused Antigonus, and declared him
an enemy, not only because of his former opposition to them,
but because he had now neglected the Romans, and taken
the government from the Parthians. Upon this the senate
was irritated, and Antony came forward and informed them
that it was for their advantage in the Parthian war that
Herod should be king. This seemed good to all the senators, and they made a decree to this effect accordingly.

§ 5. And this was the principal proof of Antony's affection for Herod, that he not only procured him a kingdom
which he did not expect (for he did not come with an
intention to ask the kingdom for himself, for he did not
suppose the Romans would grant it him, who generally
bestowed it on some of the royal family, but intended
to ask it for his wife's brother, who was grandson on the
father's side to Aristobulus, and to Hyrcanus on the
mother's side), but procured it for him so soon, little as he
expected it, that he left Italy in as few days as seven
in all. The young man his brother-in-law Herod afterwards took care to have slain, as I shall show in its proper
place. And when the senate was dissolved, Antony and

Augustus went out of the senate-house, with Herod between them, and with the consuls and other magistrates
before them, in order to offer sacrifices, and to lay up their
decrees in the Capitol. Antony also feasted Herod the
first day of his reign. And thus did he receive the kingdom, having obtained it in the hundred and eighty-
fourth Olympiad, when Caius Domitius Calvinus was
consul the second time, and Caius Asinius Pollio [the first
time].

§ 6. All this while Antigonus besieged those that were
in Masada, who had plenty of all other necessaries, and
were only in want of water, so that on that account
Joseph, Herod's brother, intended to desert from it with
two hundred of his men to the Arabians; for he heard
that Malchus repented of the offences he had been guilty
of with regard to Herod. But God, by sending rain in
the night-time, prevented his going away, for their cisterns
were thereby filled, and so he was under no necessity of
flight any longer, but they were now of good courage, and
the more so, because the sending that plenty of water
which they had been in want of, seemed a token of
divine providence; so they made a sally, and fought
with Antigonus' soldiers, some openly, others from ambush, and slew a great number of them. Meantime Ventidius, the general of the Romans, having been sent to
drive the Parthians out of Syria, marched after them
into Judæa, ostensibly to succour Joseph, but in reality
the whole affair was no more than a stratagem to get
money from Antigonus. So he pitched his camp very
near Jerusalem, and stripped Antigonus of a great deal
of money, and then retired himself with the greater part
of his army; but, that his motive might not be found
out, he left Silo there with a certain part of his soldiers;
and Antigonus also paid court to him, that he might
cause him no disturbance, though he still hoped that the
Parthians would come again and aid him.

## CHAP. XV.

*How Herod sailed from Italy to Judæa, and fought against*
*Antigonus ; also what other things happened in Judæa*
*about this Time.*

§ 1.

B Y this time Herod had sailed from Italy to Ptolemais,
and had got together no small army both of mercenaries and of his own countrymen, and marched through
Galilee against Antigonus. Silo also and Ventidius came
and assisted him, being urged by Dellius (who was sent
by Antony) to assist in restoring Herod. As for Ventidius, he was employed in settling the disturbances that
had been made in the cities because of the Parthians ;
and as for Silo he was in Judæa, having been bribed by
Antigonus. Now as Herod went along, his army increased
every day, and all Galilee, with some few exceptions,
joined him ; but as he was marching to those that were at
Masada (for he was obliged to endeavour to save those that
were besieged in that fortress because they were his relations) Joppa[1] was a hindrance to him, for it was necessary
for him to take that place first, it being a city hostile to
him, that no *point d'appui* might be left in his enemies'
hands on his rear, when he should go to Jerusalem. And as
Silo made this a pretext for departing and was thereupon
pursued by the Jews, Herod fell upon them with a small
body of men, and not only put the Jews to flight but saved
Silo, when he was very poorly able to defend himself.
And when Herod had taken Joppa, he made haste to set
free those of his friends that were in Masada.[2] Now some
of the people of the country joined him because of the
friendship they had had to his father, and some because of
his own reputation, and others by way of return for the
benefits they had received from both of them, but most
came to him in hope of getting something from him, if he
were once firmly settled in the kingdom.

§ 2. Herod had now a strong force, and as he marched

---

[1] *Jaffa.*                              [2] *Sebbeh.*

on, Antigonus laid snares and ambushes in the passes and places most proper for them, but in truth he did thereby little or no damage to his enemy. But Herod recovered his friends out of Masada, and took the fortress of Thresa,[1] and marched on for Jerusalem. The soldiers also that were with Silo accompanied him, as did many of the citizens, being awed at his power. And as soon as he had pitched his camp on the west side of the city, the soldiers that were set to guard that part shot their arrows, and threw their darts at him. And as some sallied out *en masse*, and fought hand to hand with the front ranks of Herod's army, he gave orders that they should, in the first place, make proclamation near the walls, that he came for the good of the people, and for the preservation of the city, and not to revenge any old grudge on even his most open enemies, but was ready to forget the offences which his greatest adversaries had done him. But Antigonus, by way of reply to what Herod had caused to be proclaimed, said to Silo and the Roman army, "That they would not do justly, if they gave the kingdom to Herod, who was only a private man, and an Idumæan, *i.e.*, only half a Jew, whereas they ought to bestow it on one of the royal family, as their custom was. For if they now bore ill-will to him (Antigonus), and had resolved to deprive him of the kingdom as having received it from the Parthians, yet were there many others of his family who might by their law take it, and those such as had no way offended against the Romans, and as they were priests, it would be an unworthy thing to pass them by." Now, as they said thus one to another, and fell to reproaching one another on both sides, Antigonus permitted his own men to repel the enemy from the walls. And they using their bows, and showing great energy against their enemies, easily drove them away from the towers.

§ 3. And now Silo made it plain that he had taken bribes. For he set many of his soldiers to complain aloud of their want of provisions, and to demand money to buy food, and to insist on being led into places proper for winter quarters, since the places near the city were a desert, because Antigonus' soldiers had looted everything, so he

[1] See Antiq. xiv. 13, § 9.

was for removing the army, and endeavoured to march away. But Herod pressed him not to depart, and exhorted Silo's captains and soldiers not to desert him, as Augustus and Antony and the senate had sent him there, for he would provide them plenty of all the things they wanted, and easily procure them a great abundance of what they required. After this entreaty he went immediately into the country, and left not the least pretext to Silo for departure, for he brought an unexpected quantity of provisions, and sent to those friends of his who dwelt near Samaria, to bring down corn, and wine, and oil, and cattle, and all other provisions, to Jericho, that there might be a plentiful supply for the soldiers for the time to come. Antigonus got to know this, and sent at once all over the country such as might hinder, and lie in ambush for, those that went out for provisions. And they obeyed the orders of Antigonus, and got together a great number of armed men in the neighbourhood of Jericho, and sat upon the mountains on the look out for those that brought provisions. However, Herod did not idly look on at their doing this, for he took ten cohorts of soldiers, of whom five were composed of Romans, and five of Jews, and some mercenaries also, and some few horsemen, and marched to Jericho ; and he found the city deserted, but five hundred occupied the tops of the hills with their wives and children, and these he took and sent away ; but the Romans fell upon the city and plundered it, and found the houses full of all sorts of good things. And the king left a garrison at Jericho, and returned, and sent the Roman army to take their winter quarters in the parts of the country that had come over to him, as Judæa and Galilee and Samaria. And so much did Antigonus gain of Silo for the bribes he gave him, that part of the army should be quartered at Lydda,[1] to please Antony. And the Romans now laid their weapons aside, and lived in plenty.

§ 4. But Herod was not pleased with being inactive, but despatched his brother Joseph against Idumæa with two thousand armed foot, and four hundred horse, while he himself went to Samaria, and left his mother and his other

---

[1] *Ludd.*

relations there, for they were already gone from Masada,
and set out for Galilee, to capture certain places which were
held by the garrisons of Antigonus. And he reached
Sepphoris [1] in a snow-storm, and as Antigonus' garrisons
had withdrawn, he had great plenty of provisions. He
also went thence, and resolved to destroy some robbers
that dwelt in the caves, and did much mischief in the
country, so he sent a troop of horse and three companies
of foot against them. They were very near to a village
called Arbela; [2] and on the fortieth day he came up himself with his whole army; and as the enemy sallied out
boldly against him, the left wing of his army gave way,
but he himself, coming up at the nick of time with a compact body of men, put those to flight who were already
conquerors, and rallied his men that had fled away. He
also pressed hard upon his enemies, and pursued them as
far as the river Jordan, though they fled by different roads.
And he brought over to him all Galilee, excepting those
that dwelt in the caves, and distributed money to every
one of his soldiers, giving them a hundred and fifty
drachmæ apiece, and much more to their commanders, and
sent them into winter quarters. Meantime Silo and the
commanders who were in winter quarters came to him,
because Antigonus would not give them provisions any
longer, for he supplied them for no more than one month.
Nay, he had sent to all the country round about, and
ordered them to carry off the provisions that were there,
and retire to the mountains, that the Romans might have
no provisions to live upon, and so might perish by famine.
But Herod committed the care of that matter to Pheroras,
his youngest brother, and ordered him to rebuild Alexandrium [3] also. And he quickly made the soldiers to abound
with great plenty of provisions, and rebuilt Alexandrium,
which had before been desolate.

§ 5. About the same time Antony continued some time
at Athens, and Ventidius, who was now in Syria, summoned Silo against the Parthians, and commanded him
first to assist Herod to finish the present war, and then to

[1] *Sefûrieh.*
[2] *Irbid,* on the hills west of the Sea of Galilee, and above *Mejdel*
Magdala.                                          [3] *Kefr Istûna.*

summon their allies to the war they were themselves engaged in. As for Herod, he went in haste against the
robbers that were in the caves, and sent Silo away to Ventidius, while he himself marched against them. These
caves were in mountains[1] that were exceedingly steep, and
in the middle had precipitous entrances, and were surrounded by sharp rocks, and the robbers lay concealed in
these caves with all their families about them. But the
king caused certain cases to be made bound about with
iron chains, and hung down by a mechanical contrivance
from the top of the mountain, it not being possible to get
up to them by reason of the sharp ascent of the mountain,
nor to creep down to them from above. Now these cases
were filled with armed men, who had long hooks in their
hands, by which they could pull out such as resisted them,
and then tumble them down the precipices, and kill them by
so doing. But the letting down the cases proved to be a
matter of great danger, because of the vast depth they were
to be let down; and they had their provisions inside with
them. But when the cases were let down, and not one of
those in the mouths of the caves durst come near them, but
remained quiet from fear, one of the armed men girt on his
armour, and with both of his hands took hold of the chain
by which the case was let down, and went into the mouth
of one of the caves, because he fretted that such delay was
made by the robbers not daring to come out. And when
he was at any of those mouths, he first killed many of
those that were in the mouths with his darts, and afterwards pulled to him those that resisted with his hook, and
tumbled them down the precipices, and afterwards went
into the cave and killed many more, and then returned to
his case again, and lay still there; and terror seized the
rest, when they heard the lamentations that were made, and
they despaired of escaping. However, when night came
on, that put an end to the whole work; and, as the king
permitted it, many made overtures and delivered up themselves to him as his subjects. The same method of assault
was made use of the next day, when Herod's men went
further, and got out in baskets to them, and fought them

[1] The caves are in the precipitous rocks of the gorge through which
*Wády Hammâm* runs down to the Plain of Gennesareth.

at their doors, and threw fire in among them, and set their caves on fire, for there was a great deal of wood inside them. Now there was one old man who was shut up in one of these caves with seven children and a wife, and they prayed him to give them leave to go out and yield themselves up to the enemy, but he stood at the cave's mouth, and still slew that son of his who went out, till he had killed them every one, and after that he slew his wife, and cast their dead bodies down the precipices, and himself after them, preferring death to slavery. But before he did this, he greatly reproached Herod with the meanness of his family, although Herod (who saw what he meant to do) stretched out his hand, and offered him all manner of security for his life. In this way all these caves were at length subdued entirely.

§ 6. And when the king had set Ptolemy over these parts of the country as his general, he went to Samaria, with six hundred horse and three thousand foot, intending to fight against Antigonus. But this command of the army did not succeed well with Ptolemy, for those that had been troublesome in Galilee before attacked him and slew him ; and when they had done this, they fled to the marshes and to places almost inaccessible, laying waste and plundering all that part of the country. But Herod soon returned, and punished them for what they had done ; for some of those rebels he slew, and others of them (who had fled to strongholds) he besieged, and both slew them and demolished their strongholds : and when he had thus put an end to their rebellion, he laid a fine upon the cities of a hundred talents.

§ 7. Meantime as Pacorus had fallen in battle, and the Parthians had been defeated, Ventidius sent Machæras to the assistance of Herod, with two legions and a thousand horsemen, at the instigation of Antony. But Machæras, at the invitation of Antigonus, without the approbation of Herod, being corrupted by money, went away as if to reconnoitre Antigonus' position. But Antigonus, suspecting the intention of his coming, did not admit him into the city, but kept him at a distance by hurling stones at him from slings, and so plainly showed what he himself meant. And when Machæras was sensible that Herod had given him good advice, and that he had made a mistake in not hearkening to it, he retired to the city of Emmaus ; [1] and whatever Jews he met on the road, he slew, whether they were enemies or friends, from the rage he was in at the hardships he had undergone. The king was provoked at this conduct of his, and went to Samaria, and resolved to go to Antony about these affairs, and to inform him that he stood in no need of such helpers, who did him more harm than they did his enemies, and that he was able of himself to beat Antigonus. But Machæras followed him, and begged that he would remain, or, if he was resolved to go, that he would join his brother Joseph to them, and let him fight against Antigonus. And he was reconciled to Machæras upon his earnest entreaties ; and he left Joseph there with his army, but charged him to run no hazards, and not to quarrel with Machæras.

§ 8. But he himself made haste to Antony (who was then besieging Samosata,[2] a place near the Euphrates), with troops both of horse and foot who went to his aid. And when he reached Antioch, and found there a great number of men got together, that were very desirous to go to Antony, but durst not venture to go from fear, because the barbarians fell upon them on the road, and slew many, he encouraged them, and became their conductor upon the road. Now when they were within two days' march of Samosata, the barbarians laid an ambush there for those who were going to join Antony ; and where the woods made the passes narrow to the plains, there they laid not a few of their cavalry, who were to lie still until those who were to pass by had got into a place where cavalry could manœuvre. Now as soon as their first ranks were gone by (for Herod brought up the rear), those that lay in ambush, who were about five hundred, fell upon them on the sudden, and when they had put the foremost of them to flight, the king came up riding hard, with the forces that were with him, and immediately drove back the enemy ; by which means he made the minds of his own men courageous, and emboldened them to go on, insomuch that those who ran away before now rallied, and the barbarians were slain on all sides. The king

[1] Emmaus-Nicopolis, *'Amwâs*.
[2] Now *Samsât*, on the Euphrates above *Birajik*.

also went on killing them, and recovered all the baggage (among which were a great number of beasts of burden and slaves) and proceeded on his march; and whereas there were a very great number of those in the woods that attacked them, and were near the outlet into the plain, he made a sally upon these also with a strong body of men, and put them to flight, and slew many of them, and thereby rendered the way safe for those that came after; and they called Herod their saviour and protector.

§ 9. And when he was near Samosata, Antony sent out his army in all their pomp to meet him, partly to pay Herod this respect, partly as a reinforcement, for he had heard of the attacks the barbarians had made upon him. He also was very glad to see him, having been made acquainted with the great actions he had performed upon the road, and he entertained him very kindly, and could not but admire his courage. Antony also embraced him as soon as he saw him, and saluted him in a most affectionate manner, and highly honoured him, as having himself lately made him a king. And in a little time Antiochus delivered up the fortress, and so the war was at an end; so Antony handed over the command to Sossius, and gave him orders to assist Herod, and himself went to Egypt. And Sossius sent two legions on to Judæa to the assistance of Herod, and followed himself with the main body of his army.

§ 10. Now Joseph had been already slain in Judæa in the following manner. He forgot the injunctions his brother Herod had given him when he went to Antony; and when he had pitched his camp among the mountains, as Machæras had lent him five regiments, he went hastily with them to Jericho, in order to reap the corn in that district; and as the Roman regiments were but newly raised, and were unskilled in war (for they were in great part collected out of Syria) he was attacked by the enemy, and entangled on difficult ground, and was himself slain fighting bravely, and lost his whole army, for six regiments were cut to pieces. And when Antigonus had got possession of the dead bodies, he cut off Joseph's head, although his brother Pheroras would have redeemed it for fifty talents. After this defeat the Galilæans revolted from their commanders, and drowned those of Herod's party in the lake, and a great part of Judæa became seditious; but Machæras fortified the place Gittha.[1]

§ 11. Meantime messengers came to Herod, and informed him of what had happened, and when he was come to Daphne near Antioch, they told him of the ill fortune that had befallen his brother; which he had indeed expected from certain visions that appeared to him in his dreams, which clearly foreshowed his brother's death. So he hastened his march, and when he came to mount Libanus, he took about eight hundred of the men of that neighbourhood, having already with him also one Roman legion, and went to Ptolemais. He also marched thence by night with his army, and proceeded through Galilee. Here the enemy met him, and fought him, and were beaten, and shut up in the same fortress whence they had sallied out the day before. So he attacked the place in the morning, but by reason of a great storm that then broke out, he was able to do nothing, but drew off his army into the neighbouring villages; but as soon as a second legion that Antony sent him had come, those that were in garrison in the place were afraid, and deserted it in the night-time. Then did the king march hastily to Jericho, intending to avenge himself on the enemy for the slaughter of his brother. And when he had encamped there, he made a feast for the principal people, and after this collation was over, he dismissed his guests, and retired to his own chamber. And here one may see what kindness God had for the king, for the upper part of the house fell down when nobody was in it, and so killed nobody, insomuch that all the people believed that Herod was beloved of God, since he had escaped such a great and surprising danger.

§ 12. But the next day six thousand of the enemy came down from the tops of the mountains to fight, which greatly terrified the Romans; and the soldiers that were in light armour came near, and pelted the king's guards who had come out with him with darts and stones, and one of them hit the king himself on the side with a dart. Antigonus also sent a commander whose name was Pappus, with some forces against Samaria, being desirous to show the

[1] Apparently the Gittah-Hepher, or Gath-Hepher, of Josh. xix. 13, and 2 Kings xiv. 25. Now *el-Mesh-hed*, three miles N.E. of Nazareth.

enemy how strong he was, and that he had men to spare
in his war with them : while he himself sat down to oppose
Machæras. But Herod, when he had taken five cities, slew
those who were left in them, who were about two thousand, and burnt the cities themselves, and then returned to
go against Pappus, who was encamped at a village called
Isanas;[1] and there flocked to him many from Jericho and
Judæa, near to which places he was, and the enemy fell
upon his men, so confident were they, and joined battle
with them, but he beat them in the fight, and in order to
be revenged on them for the slaughter of his brother, he
pursued them hotly, and killed them as they ran away.
And as the houses were full of armed men, and many of
them fled to the tops of the houses, he got possession of
these, and pulled down the roofs of the houses, and saw
the rooms below full of soldiers that were caught all together. And they threw stones down upon them as they
lay piled one upon another, and so killed them: nor
was there a more frightful spectacle in all the war than
outside the walls, where an immense number of dead
bodies lay heaped upon one another. It was this action
which chiefly broke the spirits of the enemy, who looked
anxiously to the future. For there appeared a mighty
number of people that came from places far distant, that
were now about the village, but ran away ; and had it not
been that the depth of winter prevented them, the king's
army would have gone to Jerusalem, being very courageous
at this good success, and would have brought the whole
war to an end. For Antigonus was already on the *qui
vive* to flee away and leave the city.

§ 13. Then the king gave order that the soldiers should
go to supper (for it was late at night) while he himself went
into a chamber to have a bath (for he was very weary), and
here it was that he was in the greatest danger, which yet
by God's providence he escaped. For as he was naked,
and had but one servant with him as he was bathing in
an inner room, some of the enemy, who were in their
armour, and had fled there out of fear, were then in the
place ; and as he was bathing, the first of them came out

---

[1] Possibly the Jeshanah of 2 Chron. xiii. 19 ; now *'Ain Sînia*, in the
valley N. of *Beitîn*, Bethel.

with his sword drawn, and went out at the doors, and after him a second and a third, armed in like manner, and were in such consternation that they did no hurt to the king, and thought themselves to have come off very well in suffering no harm themselves, but getting safe out of the house. On the next day Herod cut off the head of Pappus (for he was already slain) and sent it to Pheroras, in revenge for what their brother had suffered at his hands, for he had slain him with his own hand.

§ 14. When the winter was over, Herod removed his army, and came near to Jerusalem, and pitched his camp hard by that city. Now this was the third year since he had been made king at Rome. And as he removed his camp, and came near that part of the wall where it could be most easily assaulted, he pitched his camp before the temple, intending to make his attacks in the same manner as Pompey had done formerly. So he threw up three bulwarks round the place, and erected towers, and employed a great many hands in the work, and cut down the trees that were round about. And when he had appointed proper persons to oversee the works, while the army still lay before the city, he himself went to Samaria to marry Mariamne, the daughter of Alexander (the son of Aristobulus), to whom he was already betrothed, as I have before related.

## CHAP. XVI.

*How Herod, when he had married Mariamne, took Jerusalem, with the Assistance of Sossius, by Force, and how the Reign of the Asamonœans was put an end to.*

### § 1.

AFTER the wedding was over, came Sossius through Phœnicia, having sent on his army before him through the interior of the country. The commander also followed himself with a great number of horse and foot. The king also himself came from Samaria,[1] and brought with him

---

[1] *Sebustieh.*

no small army, besides that which had been there long
before, for they were about thirty thousand : and they all
mustered together at the walls of Jerusalem, and encamped
near the north wall of the city, being now an army of eleven
legions of foot, and six thousand horse, besides reinforcements from Syria. The generals were two, Sossius sent by
Antony to assist Herod, and Herod on his own account, in
order to take the government from Antigonus (who was
declared an enemy to Rome) and that he might himself
be king according to the decree of the senate.

§ 2. Now the Jews that were enclosed within the walls
of the city fought against Herod with great energy and
zeal (for the whole nation was gathered together); they
also gave out many prophecies about the temple, and foretold many things agreeable to the people, as if God would
deliver them out of the dangers they were in ; they had also
carried off whatever they could that was outside the city,
that they might not leave anything to afford sustenance
either to men or beasts, and by private robberies they made
the want of necessaries greater. When Herod observed
this, he set ambushes in the fittest places against their
private robberies, and sent legions of armed men to bring
in provisions, and that from remote places, so that in a little
time they had great plenty of necessaries. Now the three
bulwarks were easily erected, because so many hands were
continually at work upon them ; for it was summer time,
and there was nothing to hinder their erection, either from
the atmosphere or from the workmen: so they brought
their engines to bear, and shook the walls of the city, and
tried all manner of ways to get in. However, they did not
terrify those within, but they also contrived not a few
engines to oppose their engines with. They also sallied
out, and burnt not only those engines that were not completed, but those that were ; and when they fought hand to
hand, their daring was not less bold than that of the
Romans, though they were behind them in skill. They
also erected new works when the former ones were demolished, and making mines underground, met each other
in battle there; and in reckless daring rather than prudence, they persisted in this war to the very last : and that
though a mighty army lay round them, and they were dis-

tressed by famine and want of necessaries, for it happened to be a sabbatic year.  The first that scaled the walls were twenty picked men, the next were Sossius's centurions, for the first wall was taken in forty days, and the second in fifteen more, when some of the porticoes that were round the temple were burnt, which Herod alleged were burnt by Antigonus, in order to expose him to the hatred of the Jews.  And when the outer court of the temple and the lower part of the city were taken, the Jews fled into the inner court of the temple and into the upper part of the city : but fearing that the Romans would hinder them from offering their daily sacrifices to God, they sent an embassage, and begged that they would permit them only to bring in beasts for sacrifices, which Herod granted, hoping they were going to yield; but when he saw that they did nothing of what he expected, but bitterly opposed him, in order to preserve the kingdom to Antigonus, he made an assault on the city, and took it by storm.  And at once all parts of it were full of those that were slain by the rage of the Romans at the long duration of the siege, and by the zeal of the Jews that were on Herod's side, who were not willing to leave one of their adversaries alive.  So they were murdered continually in the narrow streets and in the houses by crowds, and as they were fleeing to the temple for shelter, and there was no pity taken either of infants or the aged, nor did they spare so much as the weaker sex; nay, although the king sent round, and besought them to spare the people, yet none restrained their hand from slaughter, but, as if they were a company of madmen, they fell upon persons of all ages without distinction.  At last Antigonus, without regard to either his past or present circumstances, came down from the citadel, and fell down at the feet of Sossius, who took no pity on him in this change of fortune, but insulted him beyond measure, and called him Antigone [*i.e.*, a woman and not a man]; however, he did not treat him as if he were a woman by letting him go free, but put him into bonds and kept him in close custody.

§ 3. And now Herod, having overcome his enemies, had to check those foreigners who had been his allies, for the crowd of strangers rushed to see the temple and the sacred things in the sanctuary.  But the king thinking victory a more severe affliction than defeat, if any of those things which it was not lawful to see should be seen by them, used entreaties and threatenings, and sometimes even force itself, to restrain them.  He also stopped the plundering that was going on in the city, and many times asked Sossius, whether the Romans would empty the city both of money and men, and leave him king of a desert? and told him, that he esteemed the dominion over the whole world as by no means an equivalent for such a wholesale murder of his citizens; and when Sossius said, that this plunder was justly permitted the soldiers in return for the siege they had undergone, he replied, that he would give every one a reward out of his own money, and so he redeemed what remained of the city from destruction.  And he performed what he promised, for he gave a handsome present to every soldier, and proportionably to their commanders, and a most royal present to Sossius himself, so that all went away with plenty of money.

§ 4.  This destruction befell the city of Jerusalem when Marcus Agrippa and Caninus Gallus were consuls at Rome, in the hundred and eighty-fifth Olympiad,[1] in the third month, on the solemn fast day, as if a cycle of calamity had come round since that which befell the Jews under Pompey, for the Jews were taken by Sossius on the same day twenty-seven years after.  And when Sossius had dedicated a crown of gold to God, he marched away from Jerusalem, taking Antigonus with him in bonds to Antony.  But Herod was afraid that Antigonus would be kept in bonds and carried to Rome by Antony, and might get his cause heard by the senate, and might show, as he was himself of the royal blood, and Herod but a private man, that it belonged to his sons to have the kingdom, on account of their family, if he had himself offended the Romans by what he had done.  Herod fearing this, by giving Antony a great deal of money, persuaded him to have Antigonus slain, which being done, he was free from fear.  And thus did the reign of the Asamonæans cease, a hundred and twenty-six years after it was first set up.  This family

[1] In B.C. 37.

was a splendid and an illustrious one, not only on account
of the nobility of its stock and the dignity of the high
priesthood, but also for the glorious actions its ancestors
had performed for our nation.   However they lost the
kingdom by their dissensions with one another, and it was
transferred to Herod the son of Antipater, who was of a
common family, and of private extraction, and a subject
of the kings.   And this is what history tells us of the end
of the Asamonæan family.

# BOOK XV.

### FROM THE DEATH OF ANTIGONUS TO THE FINISHING OF THE TEMPLE BY HEROD.

## CHAP. I.

*Concerning Pollio and Sameas.   Herod slays the principal
of Antigonus' Friends, and spoils the City of its Wealth.
Antony beheads Antigonus.*

### § 1.

HOW Sossius and Herod took Jerusalem by storm, and
   how they also took Antigonus captive, has been related by me in the previous book.   I shall now proceed
in the narrative.   Since Herod had now the government
of all Judæa put into his hands, he promoted such of
the private men in the city as had been of his party,
but never left off punishing and revenging himself every
day on those that had chosen the party of his enemies.
But Pollio the Pharisee, and Sameas a disciple of Pollio,
were honoured by him above all the rest, because when
Jerusalem was besieged, they had advised the citizens to
receive Herod, for which advice they were well requited.
Now this Sameas, at the time when Herod was once upon
his trial of life and death, foretold Hyrcanus and the other

judges reproachingly that this Herod, if they suffered him to escape, would afterwards avenge himself on them all. This prediction had its fulfilment in time, when God made good the words Sameas had spoken.

§ 2. At this time Herod, now that he had got Jerusalem in his power, carried off all the royal ornaments, and also spoiled the wealthy men of what they had got, and when he had heaped together by these means a great quantity of silver and gold, he gave it all to Antony and his friends that were about him. He also put to death forty-five of the principal men of Antigonus' party, and set guards at the gates of the city, that nothing might be carried out with their dead bodies. They also searched the dead, and whatever was found on them, either silver or gold or other treasure, was carried to the king. Nor was there any end of the miseries he brought upon them, and this distress was partly occasioned by Herod's own covetousness, who was still in want of more, and partly by the sabbatic year, which was on, which forced the country to lie uncultivated, since we are forbidden to sow the land in that year. Now when Antony had received Antigonus as his captive, he had determined to keep him in bonds till his triumph; but when he heard that the nation was growing rebellious, and that they continued to bear good-will to Antigonus, because of their hatred to Herod, he resolved to behead him at Antioch, for otherwise the Jews could no way be brought to be quiet. And Strabo of Cappadocia[1] bears out what I have said, where he speaks as follows. "Antony ordered Antigonus the Jew to be brought to Antioch, and there beheaded him: and this Antony seems to me to have been the first of the Romans that beheaded a king, supposing he could in no other way bend the minds of the Jews to receive Herod, whom he had made king in his stead; for by no torments could they be forced to call him king, so great a fondness had they for their former king. So he thought that this dishonourable death would diminish the value they had for Antigonus' memory, and at the same time would diminish the hatred they bore to Herod." Thus far Strabo.

---

[1] Strabo was born at Amasia, in Pontus.

## CHAP II.

*How Hyrcanus was set at liberty by the Parthians, and re-
turned to Herod, and what Alexandra did when she heard
that Ananelus was made High Priest.*

### § 1.

NOW after Herod got possession of the kingdom, Hyrcanus the high priest (who was then a captive among
the Parthians) hearing of it returned to him, being set free
from his captivity in the following manner. Barzapharnes
and Pacorus, the generals of the Parthians, took Hyrcanus,
who was first made high priest and afterwards king, and
Herod's brother Phasaelus, captives, and intended to carry
them away into Parthia. Phasaelus, indeed, could not
bear the reproach of being in bonds, and thinking that
death with glory was better than any life whatever, committed suicide, as I have formerly related.

§ 2. But when Hyrcanus was brought into Parthia, the
king Phraates treated him in a very kind manner, having
already learned of what an illustrious family he was; on
which account he set him free from his bonds, and allowed
him to dwell at Babylon,[1] where there was a quantity
of Jews. These Jews honoured Hyrcanus as their high
priest and king, as did all the Jewish nation that dwelt
as far as the Euphrates; which was very much to his
satisfaction. But when he was informed that Herod had
received the kingdom, new hopes came upon him as having
been himself from the beginning of a kind disposition
towards him, and he expected that Herod would bear in
mind the favour he had received from him when he was
upon his trial, for when he ran risk of a capital sentence
being pronounced against him, he delivered him from

---

[1] The city here called Babylon by Josephus, seems to be one which
was built by some of the Seleucidæ upon the Tigris, which long after
the utter desolation of Old Babylon was commonly so called, and I suppose not far from Seleucia; just as the latter adjoining city Bagdat
has been often called by the same old name of Babylon to this very
day.—W.

that risk and from all punishment. Accordingly, he talked of that matter with the Jews who often came to him from their great affection to him. But they endeavoured to retain him among them, and desired that he would stay with them, reminding him of the services and honours they had done him, and that those honours they paid him were not at all inferior to what they could pay to either their high priests or their kings; and what was a greater motive to determine him, they argued, was this, that he could not have those dignities [in Judæa] because of that mutilation on his body, which had been inflicted on him by Antigonus. They said also that kings did not usually re-quite men for those kindnesses which they received when they were private persons, the height of their fortune pro-ducing usually no small change in them.

§ 3. Now although they suggested these arguments to him for his own advantage, yet did Hyrcanus still desire to depart. Herod also wrote to him, and begged him to ask Phraates and the Jews that were there not to grudge him the royal authority, which he should have jointly with himself, for now was the proper time to make him a return for the favours he had received from him, having been brought up by him, and saved alive by him also, and for Hyrcanus to receive it. As he wrote thus to Hyrcanus, so did he also send his ambassador Saramallas to Phraates with many presents, and begged him in the most obliging way to be no hindrance to his gratitude towards his benefactor. But this zeal of Herod's did not flow from the principle of gratitude, but because he had been made king of Judæa without having any just claim to that posi-tion, he was afraid, and that upon reasons good enough, of a change in his condition, and so was anxious to get Hyr-canus into his power, or indeed to put him quite out of the way : which last thing he compassed eventually.

§ 4. However, when Hyrcanus came full of assurance, on the permission of the king of Parthia, and at the expense of the Jews who supplied him with money, Herod received him with all possible respect, and gave him the upper place at public meetings, and set him above all the rest at feasts, and thereby deceived him, calling him father, and endeavouring in all possible ways that he might have no suspicion of any treacherous design against him. He also did other things, in order to secure his power, which occasioned strife in his own family ; for being wary how he made any illustrious person the high priest of God, he sent for an obscure priest from Babylon, whose name was Ananelus, and bestowed the high priesthood upon him.

§ 5. Now Alexandra the daughter of Hyrcanus, and wife of Alexander (the son of king Aristobulus), who had children by Alexander, could not from the first bear this outrage. Her son was of the greatest comeliness, and was called Aristobulus; and her daughter, Mariamne, married to Herod, was eminent for her beauty also. Alexandra was much disturbed, and took this indignity offered to her son exceedingly ill, that while he was alive, any foreigner should have the dignity of the high priesthood conferred upon him. So she wrote to Cleopatra (a musician assisting her in taking care to have her letter transmitted) to desire her intercession with Antony, in order to gain the high priesthood for her son.

§ 6. But as Antony was slow in granting this request, his friend Dellius who came into Judæa upon some affairs, when he saw Aristobulus, marvelled at the tallness and handsomeness of the lad, and no less at Mariamne the king's wife, and was open in his commendations of Alexandra, as the mother of most beautiful children. And when she had a conversation with him, he urged her to get pictures drawn of them both, and to send them to Antony, for he said Antony, when he saw them, would deny her nothing that she should ask. And Alexandra was elated with these words of his, and sent their pictures to Antony. Dellius also talked extravagantly, and said, that those children seemed not derived from men, but from some god or other. His design in doing so was to entice Antony into lewd pleasures with them, who was ashamed to send for the damsel, as being the wife of Herod, and avoided it also because of the reproaches he would have from Cleopatra on that account, but he sent in the most decent manner he could for the young man, adding withal, " Unless it would give offence." When this letter was brought to Herod, he did not think it safe for him to send one so handsome as Aristobulus

was, in the prime of his life (for he was but sixteen
years of age) and of so noble a family, and particularly to
Antony, the principal man among the Romans, and one
that would abuse him in his amours, being a man that
openly indulged himself in pleasure (as his power allowed
him) without control. He therefore wrote back to him,
that if the lad should only go out of the country, all would
be in a state of war and uproar, because the Jews were in
hopes of a change in the government, and of having another
king over them.

§ 7. When Herod had thus excused himself to Antony,
he resolved that he would not leave either the lad or Alexandra entirely without honour, and his wife Mariamne was
vehemently at him to restore the high priesthood to her
brother, and he judged it was for his advantage so to do,
because, if he once had that dignity, he could not go out
of the country. So he called all his friends together, and
brought many charges against Alexandra, and said that
she had privately conspired against his royal authority, and
had endeavoured by means of Cleopatra so to bring it about
that he might be deprived of the government, and that by
Antony's means Aristobulus might have the management of
public affairs in his stead, and that this wish of hers was
unjust, since she would at the same time deprive her
daughter of the dignity she now had, and would bring disturbances upon the kingdom, for which he had taken a
great deal of pains, and had got it by undergoing extraordinary dangers. He said also that, though he well remembered her wicked practices, he would not leave off doing
what was right himself, but would even now give the youth
the high priesthood, and that he had formerly set up Ananelus, only because Aristobulus was then so very young a boy.
Now when he had said this, not at random, but (as he
meant) most advisedly, in order to deceive the women and
those friends whom he had taken into consultation, Alexandra, from the great joy she had at this unexpected
promise, and from fear at the suspicions she lay under,
fell a-weeping, and made the following apology for herself.
She said, that as to the high priesthood, she was very
much concerned at the slight put on her son, and so used
her utmost endeavours to procure it for him, but that as to

the kingdom she had made no attempts, and if it were offered her she would not accept it, for now she had enough honour, and as Herod himself occupied the throne, she had thereby security from his exceptional ability in governing for all her family. She added that she was now overcome by his benefits, and thankfully accepted the honour for her son, and would hereafter be entirely obedient; and she desired him to excuse her, if the nobility of her family and her freespokenness had made her act too precipitately from her indignation. When they had spoken thus to one another, they came to a mutual understanding, and all suspicion, as far as appearances went, vanished away.


## CHAP. III.

*How Herod, upon his making Aristobulus High Priest, took care that he should be murdered in a little time : and what apology he made to Antony about Aristobulus; as also concerning Joseph and Mariamne.*

### § 1.

SO king Herod immediately took the high priesthood away from Ananelus, who, as I said before, was not a native of our country, but was descended from one of those Jews that had been carried captive beyond the Euphrates. For not a few myriads of our people had been carried away captive, and dwelt in Babylonia, whence Ananelus came, who was of the stock of the high priests, and had been of old a particular friend of Herod; who when he was first made king, conferred that dignity upon him, and now took it away from him again, in order to quiet the troubles in his family, though what he did was plainly unlawful. For at no period had any one that had once been in that dignity been deprived of it, till Antiochus Epiphanes first broke the law, and deprived Jesus, and made his brother Onias high priest in his stead. Aristobulus was the second that did so, and took that dignity from his brother Hyrcanus : and Herod was the third, who took that high office away [from Ananelus], and gave it to the lad Aristobulus in his stead.

§ 2. And now Herod seemed to have healed the divisions in his family ; yet was he not without suspicion, as is frequently the case after an apparent reconciliation, for he thought that, as Alexandra had already made attempts tending to innovation, he had reason to fear that she would go on therein, if she found a fit opportunity for so doing. So he ordered her to dwell in the palace, and meddle with no public affairs : her guards also watched her so, that nothing she did in private life every day was concealed. All this put her out of patience, by little and little, and she began to hate Herod. For as she had the pride of a woman to the utmost degree, she had great indignation at this suspicious guard that was about her, being desirous rather to undergo anything that could befall her than to be deprived of her liberty of speech, and, under the specious pomp of a guard of honour, to live in a state of slavery and terror. She therefore sent to Cleopatra, and made a long complaint of the circumstances she was in, and entreated her to do her utmost for her assistance. Cleopatra thereupon advised her to take her son with her, and escape immediately to her into Egypt. This advice pleased her, and she planned the following contrivance for getting away : she got two coffins made, as if they were to carry away two dead bodies, and put herself into one, and her son into the other, and gave orders to such of her servants as knew of her intentions to carry them away in the nighttime. Now their road thence lay to the sea-side, and there was a ship ready to carry them into Egypt. Now Æsop, one of her servants, happened to fall in with Sabbion, one of her friends, and spoke of this matter to him, thinking he already knew of it. When Sabbion got to know this, (who had formerly been an enemy of Herod, and been esteemed one of those that had plotted against and given the poison to Antipater,) he expected that this discovery would change Herod's hatred into kindness, so he told the king of this stratagem of Alexandra. And he suffered her to proceed to the execution of her project, and caught her in the very act of flight, but still passed by her offence : for though he had a great mind to do so, he durst not inflict any severe treatment upon her (for he knew that Cleopatra would not bear that he should have her accused,

on account of her hatred to him), but made believe that it
was rather his generosity of soul, and great moderation,
that made him forgive her and her son. However, he fully
determined to put the young man out of the way, by one
means or other; but he thought he would probably evade
notice in doing so, if he did not do it quickly, or immediately after what had just happened.

§ 3. So upon the approach of the feast of Tabernacles
(which is a festival very much observed among us) he let
those days pass over, and both he and the rest of the
people were very merry therein. Nevertheless the envy
which at this time arose in him, caused him to make haste
to do what he was about, and provoked him to do it. For
when the youth Aristobulus, who was now in the seventeenth
year of his age, went up to the altar, to offer the sacrifices
according to the law, and that in the dress of the high
priest, as he performed the sacred offices, he seemed to be
exceeding comely, and taller than men of his age usually
were, and to exhibit in his countenance a great deal of the
high family he was sprung from, and a warm zeal and
affection towards him appeared among the people, and the
memory of the actions of his grandfather Aristobulus evidently came to their minds. And their affections got so far
the mastery of them, that they could not conceal their
feelings. They at once rejoiced and grieved, and mingled
with good wishes the joyful acclamations which they made
to him, till the good-will of the multitude was made too
evident, and they proclaimed the happiness they had received from his family more rashly than it was fit under a
monarchy to do. In consequence of all this Herod resolved
to carry out his intention against the young man. When,
therefore, the festival was over, and he was feasting at
Jericho with Alexandra, who entertained him there, he was
very pleasant with the young man, and drew him into a lonely
place, and at the same time played with him in a juvenile
and ludicrous manner. Now the temperature of that place
was hotter than ordinary; so they soon went out *en masse*
from languor, and as they stood by the fish ponds, of which
there were several large ones about the house, they proceeded to cool themselves [by bathing], because it was the
noon of a very hot day. At first they were only spectators

of Herod's servants and acquaintances as they were swimming, but after a while, the young man, at the suggestion of Herod, went into the water among them while such of Herod's acquaintances as he had appointed to do so ducked him, as he was swimming, and plunged him under water, as the darkness came on, as if it was in sport only, nor did they desist till he was entirely suffocated. And thus was Aristobulus murdered, having lived no more in all than eighteen years, and had the high priesthood one year only, and Ananelus now got back the high priesthood again.

§ 4. When what had happened was told the women, their joy was soon changed to lamentation at the sight of the dead body that lay before them, and their sorrow was immoderate. The city also on the spreading of this news was in very great grief, every family looking on this calamity as if it belonged not to another, but one of themselves had died. But Alexandra was more deeply affected, upon her knowledge of her son's death. Her sorrow was greater than that of others, by her knowing how the murder was committed, but she was under a necessity of bearing up under it, from the prospect of greater mischief that might otherwise follow. Indeed she often thought of killing herself with her own hands, but still she restrained herself, in hopes she might live long enough to revenge the unjust murder thus ingeniously committed; nay, she further resolved to endeavour to live longer, and to give no occasion to let it be thought she suspected her son was slain on purpose, and supposed that she might thereby be in a position to revenge it at a fit opportunity. Thus did she restrain herself, that she might not be thought to entertain any such suspicion. And Herod plausibly contrived that none abroad should believe that the lad's death was caused by malice prepense, so he not only used the ordinary signs of sorrow, but shed tears also, and exhibited a real confusion of soul: and perhaps his emotions overcame him, when he saw the lad's countenance, so young and so beautiful, although his death was supposed to tend to his own security; so far at least this grief served as to make some apology for him. Moreover he took care that his funeral should be very magnificent, by making great preparation for a sepulchre to lay his body in, and by provid-

ing a great quantity of spices, and by burying many ornaments with him, till the very women, who were in such
deep sorrow, were astonished at his conduct, and received
in this way some consolation.

§ 5. However, no such things could overcome Alexandra's grief, but the remembrance of this tragedy made
her sorrow both deep and obstinate. And she wrote an
account of Herod's treacherous behaviour to Cleopatra,
and how her son was murdered; and Cleopatra, who had
even formerly been desirous to give her what satisfaction
she could, commiserating Alexandra's misfortunes, made
the case her own, and would not let Antony be quiet, but
egged him on to punish the lad's murder; for she said it
was an unworthy thing that Herod, who had been made
king by him of a kingdom that no way belonged to him,
should be guilty of such horrid crimes against those that
were the kings *de jure*. Antony was persuaded by these
arguments, and when he went to Laodicea, he sent and
commanded Herod to come and make his defence as to
what he had done to Aristobulus, for he said that such a
treacherous design was not well done, if he had any hand
in it. Herod was now afraid both of this charge, and of
Cleopatra's ill-will to him, which was such, that she was
ever endeavouring to make Antony hate him. He, therefore, determined to obey his summons, for he had no
possible way to avoid it: and he left his uncle Joseph regent
and at the head of public affairs, and gave him a private
charge, that if Antony should kill him, he also should
kill Mariamne immediately; for he said he had a tender
affection for his wife, and was afraid of the injury that
would be offered him, if, after his death, she, for her
beauty, should be courted by some other man. But his
intimation was nothing but this at bottom, that Antony
had fallen in love with her because he had formerly
casually heard of her beauty. And when Herod had
given Joseph this charge, and had, indeed, no sure hopes
of escaping with his life, he set out for Antony.

§ 6. Now as Joseph administered the public affairs of
the kingdom, and for that reason was very frequently with
Mariamne, both because his business required it, and because of the respect he ought to pay to the queen, he fre-

quently fell into discourse about Herod's great love and affection towards her. And when the women, and especially Alexandra, rallied him on his words in feminine manner, Joseph was so over desirous to show the king's state of mind, that he proceeded so far as to mention the charge he had received, and thence drew his proof that Herod was not able to live without her, for if he should come to an ill end, he could not endure a separation from her, even after he was dead. Thus spoke Joseph. But the women, as was natural, did not take this to be a proof of Herod's strong affection for them, but of his savageness, that they could not escape destruction, nor a tyrannical death, even when he was dead himself, so that this communication made them entertain grave suspicion of Herod.

§ 7. Meantime a report went about the city of Jerusalem, set in motion by Herod's enemies, that Antony had tortured Herod and had him put to death. This report, as was natural, agitated those that were in the palace, but chiefly the women. And Alexandra endeavoured to persuade Joseph to go out of the palace, and flee to the ensigns of the Roman legion, which then lay encamped about the city as a guard to the kingdom, under the command of Julius; for so, if any disturbance should happen in the palace, they would be in greater security, having the Romans favourable to them ; they hoped also to obtain the highest authority, if Antony did but once see Mariamne, by whose means they might recover the kingdom, and want nothing which it was natural for them to hope for because of their royal extraction.

§ 8. But as they were in the midst of these deliberations, a letter arrived from Herod about all his affairs, and proved contrary to the report, and to what they had anticipated. For when he was come to Antony, he soon recovered his interest with him, through the presents he had brought for him from Jerusalem, and soon induced him, upon conversing with him, to leave off his indignation at him, so that Cleopatra's words had less force than the arguments and presents he brought to regain his friendship. And Antony said that it was not good to require an account of a king as to the management of his kingdom, for at this rate he could be no king at all, but those who had given him that authority ought to permit him to make use of it. He also said the same to Cleopatra, and told her that it would be best for her not to inquire too closely into the acts of princes. Herod wrote home an account of all this, and enlarged upon the other honours which he received from Antony, how he sat by him on the judgment seat, and feasted with him every day, and enjoyed those favours from him, notwithstanding the calumnies of Cleopatra, who having a great desire for his country, and earnestly entreating Antony that the kingdom might be given to her, laboured with the utmost diligence to get him out of the way. He added that he still found Antony just to him, and had no longer any apprehensions of harsh treatment from him; and that he should soon return, with a firmer assurance of his favour to him in his reign and management of public affairs; and that there was no longer any hope for Cleopatra's cupidity, as Antony had given her Cœle-Syria instead of what she desired, by which means he had at once pacified her, and got rid of the entreaties which she made to him for Judæa to be bestowed upon her.

§ 9. When this letter was brought, the women abandoned their project of fleeing to the Romans, when Herod was supposed to be dead, yet was not that purpose of theirs a secret; for when the king had conducted Antony on his way against the Parthians, he returned to Judæa, where both his sister Salome and his mother informed him at once of Alexandra's intentions. Salome also added further the calumny against her own husband Joseph that he had often had criminal connexion with Mariamne. The reason of her saying so was this, that she had for a long time borne her ill-will, for when they had had disputes with one another, Mariamne had with too much pride reproached her and her mother with the meanness of their birth. But Herod, whose affection to Mariamne was always very warm, was at once greatly agitated at this, and could not bear his torments of jealousy, but was restrained from doing any rash thing to her by the love he had for her, yet did his vehement affection and jealousy together make him question Mariamne by herself about this charge in connection with Joseph. And she denied it upon her oath, and said all that an innocent woman could possibly say in her own defence, so that by little and little the king was prevailed upon to drop his suspicion, and left off his anger at her; and being overcome with his passion for his wife, he made an apology to her for having seemed to believe what he had heard about her, and made her many acknowledgments of her modest behaviour, and confessed the great affection and love he had for her, till at last, as is usual with lovers, they both fell into tears, and embraced one another with the most tender affection.   But as the king gave more and more assurances of his belief in her fidelity, and endeavoured to draw her to a like confidence in him, Mariamne said, "The command thou gavest, that if any harm came to thee from Antony, I, who had been no oc- casion of it, should perish with thee, was no sign of thy love to me."   When these words had fallen from her, the king was in a violent rage, and at once let her go out of his arms, and cried out, and tore his hair with his hands, and said that now he had a clear proof that Joseph had had criminal connexion with her, for he would never have uttered what he had been privately told, unless there had been great familiarity and mutual understanding between them.   And while he was in this passion he had liked to have killed his wife, but being overcome by his love for her, he restrained this impulse, though not without lasting grief and disorder of mind.   However, he gave orders to slay Joseph, without permitting him to come into his sight; and as for Alexandra, he had her kept in custody, as the cause of all this mischief.

## CHAP. IV.

*How Cleopatra, when she had got from Antony some parts of Judæa and Arabia, came into Judæa; and how Herod gave her many Presents, and conducted her on her way back to Egypt.*

### § 1.

NOW at this time the affairs of Syria were in confusion owing to Cleopatra's constantly urging Antony to make an attempt upon everybody's dominions.   For she

kept urging him to take their dominions away from the
several princes, and bestow them upon her; and she had
a mighty influence upon him, because of his passion for
her.   She was also by nature very covetous, and stuck at
no wickedness.   She had already poisoned her brother,
because she knew that he would be king, when he was but
fifteen years old; and she got her sister Arsinoe to be
slain, by means of Antony, when she was a suppliant at
Diana's temple at Ephesus.   Indeed if there were but any
hopes of getting money, she would violate both temples
and sepulchres, nor was there any holy place, that was
esteemed the most inviolable, from which she would not
strip the ornaments it had in it; nor any place so profane,
but would suffer the most flagitious treatment possible
from her, if it could but contribute somewhat to the
covetous humour of this abandoned creature.   Yet did not
all this suffice so extravagant a woman, who was a slave
to her lusts, but she still imagined that she wanted everything she could think of, and did her utmost to gain it;
for which reason she was ever egging Antony on to deprive others of their dominions, and give them to her.
And as she went over Syria with him, she purposed getting
it into her possession; so she slew Lysanias, the son of
Ptolemy, accusing him of bringing the Parthians into
those parts.   She also petitioned Antony to give her
Judæa and Arabia, and desired him to take those countries
away from their present kings.   As for Antony, he was so
entirely enthralled by the woman, that one would not think
her intimacy with him only could do it, but that he was
some way or other bewitched to do whatever she would
have him;  yet did her injustice when manifest make him
so ashamed, that he would not always hearken to her, to
do those flagrant enormities she would urge him to.   That
therefore he might not either totally deny her, or, by
doing everything which she enjoined him, appear openly
to be an unjust man, he took some parts only of each of
those countries away from their rulers, and gave them to
her.   Thus he gave her the cities that were on this side
the river Eleutherus[1] as far as Egypt, except Tyre and

---

[1] The *Nahr el-Kelîr*, north of Tripolis.

Sidon, which he knew to have been free cities from their ancestors, although she pressed him very often to bestow those on her also.

§ 2. When Cleopatra had obtained thus much, and had accompanied Antony in his expedition to Armenia as far as the Euphrates, she returned back, and came to Apamea[1] and Damascus, and passed on to Judæa, where Herod met her, and hired from her those parts of Arabia that had been given to her, and those revenues that came to her from the region about Jericho. This country bears that balsam, which is the most precious thing that is there, and grows there alone, and also palm-trees, both numerous and excellent. When she was there, she was very often with Herod, and endeavoured to have criminal intercourse with him, nor did she affect secrecy in the indulgence of such sort of pleasures; and perhaps she had some passion for him, or rather (as is more probable) she laid a treacherous snare for him if adulterous intercourse with him resulted; however, upon the whole, she seemed overcome with love for him. Now Herod had a long while borne no good-will to Cleopatra, knowing that she was a woman troublesome to everybody, and at this time he thought her particularly worthy of hatred, if her attempt proceeded from lust; he also thought of preventing her intrigues, if such were her motives, by putting her to death. And he refused to comply with her proposals, and called a council of his friends to consult with them, whether he should not kill her, now he had her in his power? for he would thereby deliver from a multitude of evils all those to whom she was already troublesome, and was expected to be so also for the time to come; and this very thing would be much for the advantage of Antony himself, since she would certainly not be faithful to him, if any conjuncture or necessity should make him stand in need of her fidelity. But when he thought of this, his friends would not hear of it, but told him in the first place that it was not right to attempt so great a thing, and run himself thereby into the plainest danger; and they urged and begged of him to undertake nothing rashly, for

---

[1] *Kal'ât el-Medyk.*

Antony would never stand it, no, not though any one
should evidently lay before his eyes that it was for his own
advantage; and that the idea of having lost her by this
violent and treacherous method, would probably set his
affections more in a flame than before. Nor did it appear
that Herod could offer any thing of tolerable weight in
his defence, this attempt being against a woman of the
highest dignity of any of her sex at that time in the
world; and as to any advantage to be expected from such
an undertaking, if any such could be supposed in this case,
it would appear to deserve condemnation on account of the
insolence of carrying it out. These considerations made
it very plain that in so doing he would find his reign filled
with great and lasting mischiefs both to himself and his
posterity, whereas it was still in his power to reject the
wickedness she wanted to persuade him to, and to come
off honourably at the same time. By thus frightening
Herod, and representing to him the hazard he would, in
all probability, run by this undertaking, they restrained
him from it. So he paid court to Cleopatra, and made
her presents, and conducted her on her way to Egypt.

§ 3. But Antony subdued Armenia, and sent Artabazes,
the son of Tigranes, prisoner to Egypt with his sons and
satraps, and made a present of them and of all the royal
ornaments which he had taken out of that kingdom to
Cleopatra. But Artaxias, the eldest of his sons, who
escaped at that time, took the kingdom of Armenia, and was
afterwards ejected by Archelaus and Nero Cæsar, when
they restored Tigranes, his younger brother, to that kingdom : but this happened some time afterwards.

§ 4. Now as to the tribute which Herod was to pay
Cleopatra for the territory which Antony had given her,
ne acted fairly with her, not deeming it safe for him to
give Cleopatra any reason to hate him. As for the king
of Arabia, whose tribute Herod also received, for some
time indeed he paid him the two hundred talents, but he
afterwards became very disaffected to him and slow in his
payments, and could hardly be brought to pay some
portion of it, and was not willing to pay even that without
fraud.

## CHAP. V.

*How Herod made War with the King of Arabia, and after
they had fought many Battles, at length conquered him,
and was chosen by the Arabs to be Ruler of their Nation;
as also concerning a great Earthquake.*

### § 1.

THEREUPON Herod got ready to march against the
king of Arabia, because of his ill conduct, and because he would no longer do what was just, but made the
Roman war an occasion of delay. For the battle off
Actium was now expected, which came off in the hundred and eighty-seventh Olympiad, in which Augustus
and Antony were to fight for the sovereignty of the world:
and Herod having enjoyed now for a long time a country
that was very fruitful, and having got great taxes and
resources, enlisted a body of men, and carefully furnished
them with all necessaries, as auxiliaries for Antony. But
Antony said he had no need of his assistance, but commanded him to punish the king of Arabia (for he had
heard both from him and from Cleopatra of his perfidy).
And this was what Cleopatra desired, who thought it for her
own advantage that these two kings should mutually weaken
one another. On this message from Antony, Herod returned back, but kept his army with him, in order to invade Arabia immediately. And when his army of horse
and foot was ready, he marched to Diospolis,[1] where the
Arabians came to meet him, for they were not unapprised
of this war that was coming upon them; and after a well-
contested battle had been fought, the Jews had the victory.
But afterwards a numerous army of Arabians concentrated
at Cana, which is a place in Cœle-Syria. Herod was informed of this beforehand, so he marched against them
with most of the forces he had; and when he was come
near to Cana, he resolved to encamp himself, and began to
intrench his camp, that he might take an advantageous

[1] Lydda, *Ludd.*

season for attacking the enemy; but as he was giving those orders, the multitude of the Jews cried out, that he should make no delay, but lead them at once against the Arabians. They were impetuous for the fray because they believed in their excellent discipline, and especially those who had been in the former battle, and had been conquerors, and had not permitted the enemy so much as to come to close quarters with them. And as they were so tumultuous, and showed such great zeal, the king resolved to avail himself of the readiness the multitude then exhibited; and when he had assured them he would not be behindhand with them in courage, he led them on, and was at their head in his armour, all the men following him in their several ranks. And a panic fell at once upon the Arabians; for when they perceived that the Jews were not to be conquered, and were full of spirit, most of them after a short resistance ran away and avoided fighting, and they would have been cut to pieces, had not Athenion fallen upon the Jews and Herod. He was Cleopatra's general over the soldiers she had in those parts, and was at enmity with Herod, and very wistfully looked on to see what the event of the battle would be : for he had resolved, if the Arabians did anything that was brilliant, to remain still, but if they were beaten, as really happened, to attack the Jews with those forces he had of his own, and with those that had flocked to to him from that region. And he fell upon the Jews unexpectedly, and made a great slaughter of them, when they were fatigued, and thought they had already vanquished the enemy. For as the Jews had spent their courage upon their known enemies, and were about to enjoy themselves in fancied security after the victory, they were easily beaten by these that now attacked them, and received great loss in ground which was stony, and where their horses could not be of service, and where those that attacked them were better acquainted with the ground than themselves. And when the Jews had suffered this reverse, the Arabians plucked up their spirits again and returned back and slew those that were already routed : and indeed all sorts of slaughter were now frequent, and of those that fled only a few got back safe to the camp. And king Herod, as he despaired of the battle, rode off to them to bring them assistance, however he did not come up in time enough to do them any service, though he tried hard to do so, for the Jewish camp was taken, so that the Arabians had unexpectedly a most glorious success, having gained that victory which by themselves they were no way likely to have gained, and having slain a great part of the enemy's army. And thenceforward Herod could only act like a private robber, and make incursions into many parts of Arabia, and distress them by sudden raids, encamping among the mountains, and avoiding by any means coming to a pitched battle, yet greatly harassing the enemy by his assiduity and the pains he took in the matter. He also took great care of his own men, and used all the means he could to correct this reverse.

§ 2. Meantime the sea-fight happened off Actium,[1] between Augustus and Antony, in the seventh year of the reign of Herod;[2] and then it was also that there was an earthquake in Judæa, such as had not happened at any other time, and which brought a great destruction upon the cattle in that country. About thirty thousand men also perished by the fall of houses; but the army, which lodged in the field, received no damage by this sad accident. When the Arabians were informed of this, and when those that hated the Jews took pleasure in exaggerating the facts, they raised their spirits, as if their enemy's country was quite overthrown, and the men were utterly destroyed, and thought there now remained nothing that could oppose them. Accordingly, they seized on the Jewish ambassadors (who came to them after all this had happened to make peace with them) and slew them, and marched with great energy against their army. And the Jews durst not withstand them, and were so cast down by their calamities, that they took no care of their affairs, but gave up themselves to

[1] The promontory of Actium was at the entrance of the Ambraciot Gulf, now the *Gulf of Arta*, and opposite the modern town of *Preresa*.

[2] The reader is here to take notice, that this ' seventh ' year of the reign of Herod, and all. the other years of his reign, in Josephus, are dated from the death of Antigonus, or at the soonest from the conquest of Antigonus, and the taking of Jerusalem a few months before, and never from his first obtaining the kingdom at Rome above three years before, as some have very weakly and injudiciously done.—W.

despair, for they had no hope that they should be upon an
equality with them again in battle, nor obtain any assistance
elsewhere while their affairs at home were in such great
distress.   When matters were in this condition, the king
tried to animate the commanders by his words, and to
raise their spirits which were quite sunk.   And first he
endeavoured to encourage and embolden some of the better
sort, and then ventured to make a speech to the multitude,
which he had before avoided doing, lest he should find
them uneasy thereat, because of their reverses.   And he
made an hortatory speech to the multitude in the following
words.

§ 3. "You are not ignorant, fellow-soldiers, that we
have had not long since many reverses that have put a
stop to what we are about; and it is probable that even
those that are most distinguished above others for their
courage can hardly keep up their spirits in such circumstances; but since we cannot avoid fighting, and nothing
that has happened is of such a nature but it may by ourselves be restored to a good state by one brave action, I have
proposed to myself both to give you some encouragement
and at the same time some information, that you may still
continue in your fortitude.   I will then, in the first place,
prove to you that this war is a just one on our side, and
a war of necessity owing to the outrages of our adversaries,
for if you be once satisfied of this, it will be the greatest
cause of zeal in you, after which I shall further prove
that the misfortunes we are in are of no great consequence,
and that we have the greatest reason to hope for victory.
I shall begin with the first, and appeal to yourselves as
witnesses of what I say.   You are not ignorant certainly
of the lawlessness of the Arabians, who are as treacherous
to all other men, as barbarians wholly without conception
of God are likely to be.   They have mostly come into con-
flict with us from covetousness and envy, and they have
attacked us suddenly, when we were in disorder.   And what
need is there for me to give many proofs of such being
their procedure?   But when they were in danger of losing
their independence, and of being slaves to Cleopatra, who
but we freed them from that fear?   For it was the friendship I had with Antony, and the kind disposition he

was in towards us, that was the reason that even these Arabians were not utterly undone, Antony being unwilling to undertake anything which might be suspected by us. And when he had a mind to bestow some parts of each of our dominions on Cleopatra, I also managed that matter so, that by giving him many presents of my own, I might obtain security for both nations, while I undertook myself to answer for the money, and gave him two hundred talents, and became surety for two hundred more which were imposed upon the land that was subject to this tribute; and this they have defrauded us of. And yet it was not reasonable that Jews should pay tribute to any man living, or allow part of their land to be taxed, but even if it had been, yet ought we not to pay tribute for those Arabians, whom we ourselves preserved; nor is it fit that they, who have professed, and that with great effusion and sense of our kindness, that it is owing to us that they retain their independence, should injure us, and deprive us of what is our due, and that while we are not their enemies but their friends. And whereas observance of covenants takes place even among the bitterest enemies, and among friends is absolutely necessary, it is not observed among these men, who think gain to be the best of all things, let it be by any means whatever, and that injustice is no harm, if they can but get money by it. Is it therefore a question with you, whether the unjust are to be punished or not, when God wills this, and commands us ever to hate injuries and injustice, and that when people are pursuing a not only just but necessary war? For these Arabians have done what both the Greeks and barbarians own to be most lawless, for they have beheaded our ambassadors, though the Greeks declare that such ambassadors are sacred and inviolable, and for ourselves, we have learned from God the most excellent of our doctrines, and the most holy part of our law by angels; for this name brings God to the knowledge of mankind, and is able to reconcile enemies to one another. What wickedness then can be greater than the slaughter of ambassadors, who come to treat about doing what is right? And when such have been their actions, how is it possible they can enjoy a tranquil life, or be successful in war? In my opinion it is impossible. But perhaps some one will say, that what is holy and righteous is indeed on our side, but that the Arabians are more courageous, or more numerous than we are. Now as to this, in the first place, it is not fit for us to say so, for with whom is what is righteous, with them is God himself, and where God is, there are both numbers and courage. And to examine our own circumstances a little, we were conquerors in the first battle, and when we fought again, they were not able to oppose us, but ran away, and could not endure our attack and courage; but when we had conquered them, then came Athenion and made war against us without declaring it. Pray, is this an instance of their manhood, or a second instance of their wickedness and treachery? Why are we, therefore, of less courage, on account of what ought to inspire us with stronger hopes? and why are we terrified at those who, when they fight fairly, are continually beaten, and when they seem to be conquerors, gain the victory unfairly? And if any one should deem them to be men of real courage, will he not be excited by that very consideration to do his utmost against them? for true valour is not shown in fighting against weak persons, but in being able to overcome the strongest. But if the distresses we are ourselves now suffering from, and the miseries that have come from the earthquake dismay any one, let him consider in the first place, that this very thing will deceive the Arabians, who will think that what has befallen us is greater than it really is, and next that it is not right that the same thing that emboldens them should discourage us. For these men, you see, do not derive their courage from any advantage of their own, but from their hope, as to us, that we are quite cast down by our misfortunes; but if we boldly march against them, we shall soon abate their insolent self-conceit, and shall gain this by attacking them, that they will not be so valiant when we come to the battle. For our distresses are not so great, nor is what has happened an indication of the anger of God against us, as some imagine, for such things are accidental, and adversities that come in the usual course of things: and even if it happened by the will of God it is clear that it is now over by his will also, and that he is satisfied with what has already happened, for had he been willing to afflict us still more thereby, he would not have changed his mind so soon. And as for the war we are engaged in, he has himself shown that he is willing it should go on, and that he knows it to be a just war; for while some of the people in the country perished by the earthquake, all you who were in arms suffered nothing, but were all preserved alive: whereby God makes it plain that if you had all been in the army, with your children and wives, you would not have undergone anything that would have much hurt you. Consider these things, and, what is more than all the rest, that you have God at all times for your protector, and go out with a just bravery against these men, who in friendship are false, in their battles perfidious, towards ambassadors impious, and always inferior to you in valour."

§ 4. When the Jews heard this speech, they were much cheered in their minds, and more disposed to fight than before. So Herod, when he had offered the sacrifices appointed by the law, made haste, and took and led his men against the Arabians; and with a view to that, crossed over the Jordan, and pitched his camp near the enemy. He also thought it well to seize upon a certain fortress that lay between the two armies, hoping it would be for his advantage, and would the sooner pull on a battle, and if the battle had to be postponed, he should by it have his camp protected. And as the Arabians had the same intentions upon that place, a contest arose about it: at first they were but skirmishes, after which more soldiers came up, and it proved a sort of fight, and several fell on both sides, till those on the Arabian side were beaten and retreated. This was no small encouragement to the Jews immediately; and when Herod observed that the enemies' army was disposed to anything rather than to come to a general engagement, he ventured boldly to attack their earthworks and demolish them, so to get nearer to their camp, in order to fight them; for when they were forced out of their trenches, they went out in disorder, and had not the least vigour or hope of victory. Yet did they fight hand to hand, because they were more in number than the Jews, and because they were in such a strait that they were obliged to come on boldly: so a terrible battle ensued, wherein not a few fell on each side. However, at last the Arabians were routed and fled ; and so great a slaughter was made on their being routed, that they were not only killed by their enemies, but became the authors of their own deaths also, and were trodden down by the multitude, and by the great rush of people in disorder, and fell under the weight of their own armour. So five thousand men lay dead upon the spot, while the rest of the multitude soon ran within their intrenched camp, but had no firm hope of safety, because of their want of necessaries, and especially want of water. The Jews pursued them, but could not get in with them into their intrenched camp, but invested it, and prevented the entrance of any assistance to them, and also their coming out that desired.

§ 5. When the Arabians were in these circumstances, they sent ambassadors to Herod, first to propose terms of accommodation, and afterwards to offer him (so pressing was their thirst) to undergo whatever he pleased, if he would free them from their present distress. But he would hear of no ambassadors, or ransom, or any moderate terms whatever, being very desirous of revenge for their lawless conduct to his nation. So they were necessitated by other things, and particularly by their thirst, to come out, and deliver themselves up to him, to be carried away captives ; and in five days four thousand were taken prisoners so, while all the rest resolved to make a sally upon their enemies, and to fight it out with them, choosing rather, if it so must be, to die so, than to perish ingloriously by little and little. When they had taken this resolution, they came out of their trenches, but could no way sustain the fight, being too weak both in mind and body, and having no room to fight gloriously, so they thought it an advantage to be killed, and a misery to survive ; accordingly on the first onset there fell about seven thousand of them. After this stroke they lost all the courage they had before, and were amazed at Herod's warlike spirit under his calamities ; and thenceforward they yielded, and made him ruler of their nation ; whereupon he was greatly elevated at so seasonable a success, and returned home, having won prestige from this valiant exploit.

## CHAP. VI.

*How Herod slew Hyrcanus, and then hastened away to Augustus, and obtained the Kingdom from him also ; and how, a little time afterwards, he entertained Augustus in a most honourable manner.*

### § 1.

HEROD'S other affairs were now very prosperous, and he was not open to attack on any side, yet did there come upon him a danger that might hazard his entire dominions, after Antony had been beaten at the battle off Actium by Augustus. For at that time both Herod's enemies and friends thought his fortunes desperate, for it was not probable that he would remain without punishment, who had shown so much friendship for Antony. So it happened that his friends despaired and had no hopes of his escape, and as for his enemies, they all outwardly appeared to be troubled at his case, but were privately very glad at it, as hoping to obtain a change for the better. As for Herod himself, he saw that there was no one of royal rank left but Hyrcanus, and therefore he thought it would be for his advantage not to suffer him to be an obstacle in his way any longer ; for if he himself survived, and escaped the danger he was in, he thought it the safest way to put it out of the power of a man, who was more worthy of the kingdom than himself, to make any attempt against him at such a juncture of affairs; and if he himself should be put to death by Augustus, his envy prompted him to slay the only man that would be king after him.

§ 2. While Herod had these things in view, an opportunity was afforded him by Hyrcanus' family. Hyrcanus himself was of so mild a temper, both then and at other times, that he desired not to meddle with public affairs, nor to concern himself with innovations, but left all to fortune, and contented himself with what she afforded him. But Alexandra [his daughter] was a lover of contention, and was exceedingly desirous of change, and urged her father not to bear for ever Herod's injurious

treatment of their family, but to anticipate their future
hopes, as he safely might; and asked him to write about
the matters to Malchus, who was then governor of Arabia,
and to ask him to receive them and protect them; for if,
after their departure, Herod's affairs proved to be as it was
likely they would be because of Augustus' enmity to him,
they would then be the only persons that could take over the
kingdom, both on account of their royal blood, and the good
will of the multitude to them.   When she urged this,
Hyrcanus rejected her suit, but as she was a very woman,
and a contentious woman too, and would not desist either
night or day, but would always be speaking to him about
it, and about Herod's treacherous designs against them,
she at last prevailed on him to intrust Dositheus (one of
his friends) with a letter, wherein it was arranged that the
Arabian governor should send him some horsemen, who
should take and conduct him to the lake Asphaltites,[1]
which is three hundred furlongs from the bounds of
Jerusalem.   And he trusted Dositheus with this letter,
because he paid court to him and Alexandra, and had no
small reasons to bear ill-will to Herod: for he was a kinsman of Joseph, whom he had slain, and a brother of those
that had been formerly slain at Tyre by Antony.   However,
these motives could not induce Dositheus to serve Hyrcanus faithfully in this affair, for he gave Herod the letter,
preferring the hopes he had from the present king to
those he might have from him.   And he took his kindness
in good part, and bade him, besides doing what he had
already done, to go on serving him, by folding up the
letter and sealing it again, and delivering it to Malchus,
and then bringing back his letter in answer to it; for it
was very important for him to know Malchus' intentions
also.   And as Dositheus was very ready to serve him in this
point also, the Arabian governor returned back for answer,
that he would receive Hyrcanus and all his retinue, and
also all the Jews that were of his party: and that he
would, moreover, send forces sufficient to secure them on
their journey, and that he should be in no want of anything he should desire.   Now, as soon as Herod had re-

---

[1] The Dead Sea.

ceived this letter, he immediately sent for Hyrcanus, and questioned him about the agreement he had made with Malchus; and, when he denied it, he showed his letter to the sanhedrim, and had Hyrcanus put to death.

§ 3. We give the reader this account, because it is that contained in the commentaries of king Herod. But other historians do not agree with this, for they think that Herod did not find, but rather made this an opportunity for thus putting Hyrcanus to death, and that by treacherously laying a snare for him. For they thus write; that Herod and he were once at a supper-party, and that Herod had given no occasion to suspect [that he was displeased with him,] but put this question to Hyrcanus, whether he had received any letters from Malchus? and when he answered, that he had received letters, but only letters of civility, and when he asked further, whether he had not received any present from him? and when he replied, that he had received only four horses to ride on, which Malchus had sent him; they say that Herod charged this upon him as proof of bribery and treason, and gave order that he should be strangled. And in order to prove that he had been guilty of no offence, when he was thus brought to his end, they recount how mild his temper was, and how even in his youth he had never given any signs of boldness or rashness, and that the case was the same when he came to be king, for even then he committed the management of most public affairs to Antipater; and that now he was above fourscore years old, and knew that Herod's throne was in a secure state. He had also crossed the Euphrates, and left those who greatly honoured him beyond that river, to be entirely in Herod's power. So it was a most incredible thing that he should enterprise anything by way of innovation, and not at all agreeable to his temper, so they argue that the whole affair was a plot of Herod's contrivance.

§ 4. Thus did Hyrcanus end his life, after having undergone various and manifold turns of fortune in his lifetime. For he was made high priest of the Jewish nation in the beginning of the reign of his mother Alexandra, who held the government nine years; and when, after his mother's death, he took the kingdom himself, and held it three months, he was ejected from it by his brother Aristobulus. He was afterwards restored by Pompey, and received all sorts of honours from him, which he enjoyed forty years; but when he was again deprived by Antigonus, and mutilated in his body, he was made a captive by the Parthians, and thence returned home again after some time, on account of the hopes that Herod had given him; none of which came to pass according to his expectation, but he still battled with many misfortunes through the whole course of his life; and what was the heaviest calamity of all, as I have related already, he came to a bad end in his old age. He appears to have been a man of a mild and moderate disposition in all things, and to have suffered the administration of affairs to be generally done by others under him. He was averse to business, nor had he shrewdness enough to govern a kingdom: and both Antipater and Herod came to their greatness because of his mildness, and at last he met with such an end from them as was not agreeable either to justice or piety.

§ 5. Now Herod, as soon as he had put Hyrcanus out of the way, made haste to Augustus; and because he could not have any hopes of favour from him, on account of the friendship he had had for Antony, he felt suspicious about Alexandra, lest she should avail herself of this opportunity to bring the multitude to revolt, and introduce rebellion into the affairs of the kingdom; so he committed the care of everything to his brother Pheroras (placing his mother Cypros, and his sister [Salome,] and the whole family, at Masada [1]), and charged him, if he should hear any bad news about him, to seize the government. As to Mariamne his wife (because of the misunderstanding between her and his sister and mother, which made it impossible for them to live together), he placed her at Alexandrium [2] with her mother Alexandra, and left his treasurer Joseph, and Sohemus of Ituræa, [3] to take care of that fortress. These two had been very faithful to him from the beginning, and were now left to guard the women under pretext of paying them due respect. They also had it in charge,

---

[1] *Sebbeh.*                                    [2] *Kefr Istûna.*
[3] The present district of *Jedûr* extending from Mount Hermon towards the *Lejah.*

if they should hear any mischief had befallen Herod, to kill them both, and as far as they were able to preserve the kingdom for his sons, and for his brother Pheroras.

§ 6. When he had given them this charge he set out post haste to Rhodes to meet Augustus, and when he had sailed to that city, he took off his diadem, but remitted nothing else that marked his rank. And when, upon his meeting Augustus, he desired that he would let him speak to him, he therein exhibited much more the nobility of his great soul, for he did not betake himself to supplications, as men usually do upon such occasions, nor did he offer any petition as if he were an offender, but gave an account of what he had done with impunity. He made the following speech to Augustus. He said that he had had the greatest friendship for Antony, and done everything he could that he might be master of the world, that he was not indeed in the army with him, because the Arabians had diverted him, but that he had sent him both money and corn, which was but too little in comparison of what he ought to have done for him. "For," (he added) "if a man owns himself to be another's friend, and knows him to be a benefactor, he ought to hazard everything, to use every faculty of his soul, every member of his body, and all the wealth he has, for him, in which I confess I have been too deficient. However, I am conscious to myself that so far I have done right, in that I did not desert him after his defeat at Actium; nor upon the evident change of his fortunes did I transfer my hopes from him to another, but preserved myself, though not as a valuable fellow-soldier, yet certainly as a faithful counsellor to Antony, when I suggested to him that the only way that he had to save himself, and not to lose all his authority, was to put Cleopatra to death; for when she was once dead, there would have been room for him to retain his authority, and I recommended him rather to bring thee to make a composition with him, than to continue at enmity with thee any longer. None of which advice would he attend to, but preferred his own rash resolution, which has happened unprofitably for him, but profitably for thee. Now therefore, in case thou determinest about me, and my zeal in serving Antony, according to thy anger at him, I cannot deny what I have

done, nor will I disown, and that publicly too, that I had a
great kindness for him; but if thou wilt put him out of the
case, and only examine how I behaved myself to my benefactors in general, and what sort of friend I am, thou wilt
find by experience that I shall do and be the same to
thyself. For it is but changing the names, and the firmness of friendship that I shall bear to thee will not be
disapproved by thee."

§ 7. By this speech, and by his behaviour, which showed
Augustus the openness of his mind, he greatly gained upon
him, as he was himself of a generous and noble character,
insomuch that those very actions, which were the foundation of the accusation against him, won him Augustus'
favour. Accordingly, he restored him his diadem again,
and exhorted him to show himself as great a friend to him
as he had been to Antony, and held him in great esteem.
Moreover he added that Quintus Didius had written to him,
that Herod had very readily assisted him in the affair of
the gladiators. So when he had obtained such a kind reception, and had, beyond all his hopes, got his crown more
entirely and firmly settled upon him than ever by Augustus' gift, as well as by the decree of the Romans, which
Augustus took care to procure for his greater security, he
escorted Augustus on his way to Egypt, and made presents
even beyond his means to both him and his friends, and in
general behaved himself with great magnanimity. He also
begged that Augustus would not put to death one Alexander,
who had been a companion of Antony's; but Augustus had
sworn to put him to death, and so he could not obtain that
petition. And he returned to Judæa again with greater
honour and security than ever, and dismayed those that
had expected the contrary, acquiring from his very dangers
still greater splendour than before owing to the favour of
God to him. And he prepared at once for the reception of
Augustus, as he was going from Syria to invade Egypt; and
when he came, he entertained him at Ptolemais with all
royal magnificence. He also bestowed presents on the
army, and brought them provisions in abundance. He also
proved to be one of Augustus' most cordial friends, and put
the army in array, and rode along with Augustus, and had
a hundred and fifty chambers, well appointed in all respects

in a rich and sumptuous manner, for the better reception of him and his friends. He also provided them with what they would want especially as they passed over the desert, insomuch that they lacked neither wine nor water, which last the soldiers stood in the greatest need of. He also presented Augustus with eight hundred talents, and made all think that he was assisting them in a much greater and more splendid degree than the kingdom he had obtained could afford. Thus he more and more demonstrated to Augustus the firmness of his friendship, and his readiness to assist him; and what was the greatest advantage to him was that his liberality came at a seasonable time also. And when they returned back from Egypt, his assistance was no way inferior to the good offices he had formerly done.

## CHAP. VII.

*How Herod slew Sohemus, and Mariamne, and afterwards Alexandra, and Costobarus, and his most intimate Friends, and at last the Sons of Babas also.*

### § 1.

HOWEVER, when he returned to his kingdom again, he found his house all in disorder, and his wife Mariamne and her mother Alexandra very displeased. For, as they supposed (as was natural enough), that they were not put into that fortress [Alexandrium] for the security of their persons, but as into a garrison for their imprisonment, and that they had no power over anything, either of others or of their own, they were very displeased; and Mariamne supposing that the king's love to her was rather pretended, as advantageous to himself, than real, looked upon it as feigned. She was also grieved that he would not allow her any hopes of surviving him, if he should come to any harm himself, and recollected the commands he had formerly given to Joseph, so that she began to pay court to her keepers, and especially to Sohemus, being well apprised how all was in his power. And at first Sohemus was faithful to Herod, and neglected none of the things he had in-

trusted to him; but when the women, by kind words and
liberal presents, had gained his affections, he was by
degrees overcome, and at last disclosed to them all the
king's injunctions, chiefly because he did not expect that
Herod would come back with the same authority he had
before; so that he thought he would escape any danger
from him, and would not a little gratify the women, who
were not likely to lose their present rank, and so would be
able to make him abundant recompense, since they would
either reign themselves, or be very near to him that did
reign.    He had a further ground of hope also, in that,
though Herod should have all the success he could wish
for, and should return again, he could not contradict his
wife in what she desired, for he knew that the king's fondness for Mariamne was inexpressible.    These were the
motives that drew Sohemus to disclose the injunctions that
had been given him.    And Mariamne was greatly displeased
to hear that there was no end of the dangers she was in
from Herod, and was very vexed at it, and wished he might
obtain no favours [from Augustus,] and esteemed it almost
unbearable to live with him any longer.    Indeed she afterwards showed this very clearly, not concealing her resentment.

§ 2.  And now Herod sailed home, in great joy at the unexpected good success he had had, and went first of all, as
was likely, to his wife, and told her the good news before
the rest, on account of his fondness for her, and the intimacy
there had been between them, and embraced her.    But it
so happened, as he told her of the good success he had had,
that she was so far from rejoicing at it, that she was rather
sorry for it; nor was she able to conceal her resentment,
but, thinking of her dignity and the nobility of her birth,
on his embracing her she gave a groan, and showed evidently
that she rather grieved than rejoiced at his success, and
that till Herod was disturbed no longer by suspicion but
proof evident of her dislike to him.    It made him almost
mad to see that this unreasonable hatred of his wife to him
was not concealed, and he took it so ill, and was so unable
to bear it, on account of the fondness he had for her, that
he could not continue long in one mind, but sometimes was
angry at her, and sometimes reconciled to her; and by

always changing from one passion to another, he was in great discomfort. And thus was he entangled between hatred and love, and was frequently disposed to inflict punishment on her for her contemptuous behaviour to him; but being deeply in love with her in his soul, he had not the heart to get rid of her. In short, though he would gladly have had her punished, yet was he afraid lest, ere he were aware, he should, by putting her to death, bring unawares a heavier punishment upon himself.

§ 3. When Herod's sister and mother perceived that he was in this state of mind with regard to Mariamne, they thought they had now got an excellent opportunity to satisfy their hatred against her, so they provoked Herod to wrath by telling him such long stories and calumnies about her, as might at once excite both his hatred and jealousy. Now, though he willingly enough heard their words, yet he had not courage enough to do anything to her, as if he believed them. But still he became more ill-disposed to her, and their evil passions were more and more inflamed on both sides, as she did not hide her dislike to him, and he turned his love for her into wrath against her. But when he was just on the eve of putting matters past all remedy, he heard the news that Antony and Cleopatra were both dead, and that Augustus was victor in the war, and had conquered Egypt, whereupon he made haste to go and meet him, and left the affairs of his family *statu quo*. However, Mariamne recommended Sohemus to him, as he was setting out on his journey, and confessed that she owed him thanks for the care he had taken of her, and asked of the king a governorship for him, and accordingly that honour was bestowed upon him. Now, when Herod was come into Egypt, he enjoyed great freedom with Augustus, as already a friend of his, and received very great favours from him; for he made him a present of those four hundred Galatians who had been Cleopatra's body-guards, and restored to him again that territory which had by her been taken away from him. He also added to his kingdom Gadara[1] and Hippos[2] and Samaria[3]; and besides these, the

Umm Keis.                                      [2] Sûsiyeh.
                          [3] Sebustieh.

maritime cities of Gaza,[1] Anthedon,[2] Joppa,[3] and Strato's Tower.[4]

§ 4. Upon these new acquisitions, Herod grew more magnificent, and escorted Augustus as far as Antioch; but upon return, in proportion as his prosperity was augmented by the external additions that had been made to his kingdom, so much the greater were the distresses that came upon him in his own family, and chiefly in the affair of his marriage, wherein he formerly appeared to have been most fortunate. For the passion he had for Mariamne was no way inferior to such passions as are famous in history, and that on very good grounds; while as for her, she was in other respects chaste and faithful to him; but she had somewhat of the woman in her, and was haughty by nature, and treated her husband imperiously enough, because she saw he was so fond of her as to be her slave. She did not also consider (as would have been well) that she lived under a monarchy, and was at another's disposal, and so she would behave in a haughty manner to him, while he usually concealed his vexation, and bore her tantrums with moderation and good temper. She would also jeer at his mother and sister openly, and speak ill of them on account of the meanness of their birth, so that there was before this a disagreement and deadly hatred among the women, and it was now come to greater calumnies than formerly. And these suspicions increased, and lasted a whole year after Herod returned from Augustus. And this hatred, which had been kept under somewhat for a great while, burst out all at once upon the following occasion. As the king one day about noon was laid down on his bed to rest, he called for Mariamne out of the great affection he always had for her. She came to him accordingly, but would not lie with him though he was very desirous of her company, but showed her contempt of him; and also twitted him with having caused her father and brother to be slain.[5] And

---

[1] Ghuzzeh.
[2] Agrippias. Comp. Antiq. xiii. 13, § 3; xiv. 5, § 3.
[3] Jaffa.    [4] Cæsarea Palæstina, Kaisariyeh.
[5] Whereas Mariamne is here represented as reproaching Herod with the murder of her father [Alexander,] as well as her brother [Aristobulus,] while it was her grandfather Hyrcanus, and not her father

as he took this contemptuous treatment very unkindly, and was inclined to use violence to her, the king's sister Salome, observing that he was more than ordinarily put out, sent to the king his cup-bearer, who had been prepared long beforehand for such a design, and bade him tell the king that Mariamne had asked him to give his assistance in preparing a love potion for him; and if he appeared to be troubled, and asked what that love potion was, he was to tell the king that she had the potion, and that he was asked only to supply it, but in case he did not appear to be much concerned about this potion, he was to let the matter drop, for no harm would come to him. When she had given him these instructions, she then sent him in to say this. So he went in with a plausible and earnest manner, and said that Mariamne had given him presents, and had urged him to give the king a love potion. And when this greatly moved the king, he said, that this love potion was a composition she had given him, whose properties he did not know, which was the reason of his resolving to give him this information, as the safest course he could take, both for himself and for the king. When Herod heard this, being prejudiced against Mariamne before, his indignation grew more violent, and he ordered the eunuch of Mariamne's who was most faithful to her to be brought to torture about this potion, well knowing that it was not possible that anything great or small could be done without him. And when this man was in the utmost agony he could say nothing concerning the matter he was tortured about, but that Mariamne's hatred against Herod was occasioned by something that Sohemus had told her. Now, while he was still saying this, Herod cried out aloud, and said that Sohemus, who had been at all other times most faithful to him and to his throne, would not have disclosed the injunctions he had given him, unless he had been unduly intimate with Mariamne. So he gave orders that Sohemus should be arrested and put to death immediately, but he put his wife on her trial, and got together those

Alexander, whom he caused to be slain, (as Josephus himself informs us, chap. 6, § 2,) we must either take Zonara's reading, which is here grandfather rightly, or else we must, as before, chap. 1, § 1, allow a slip of Josephus' pen or memory in the place before us.—W.

who were most faithful to him, and made a formal accusation against her as to this love potion and composition, which had been laid to her charge calumniously. And he was intemperate in his words, and was in too great a passion for judging right about the matter; and so, when the court was at last satisfied that he was so resolved, they passed sentence of death upon her: but when sentence had been passed upon her, it was suggested by himself, and by some others of the court, that she should not be thus hastily put to death, but be imprisoned in one of the fortresses belonging to the kingdom. But Salome and her party laboured hard to have the poor woman put to death, and they prevailed upon the king to do so, urging that the multitude would be riotous if she were suffered to live. And so Mariamne was led out to execution.

§ 5. When Alexandra saw how things went, and that there was small hope that she herself would escape the like treatment from Herod, she changed her behaviour to quite the reverse of her former boldness, and that in a very unseemly manner. For wishing to show how entirely ignorant she was of the crimes laid against Mariamne, she jumped up, and reproached her daughter in the hearing of all the people; and cried out, that she had been peevish and ungrateful to her husband, and that her punishment came justly upon her for such insolent behaviour, for she had not made a proper return to him who had been their common benefactor. And when she had for some time acted in this hypocritical manner, and even gone so far as to tear her hair, this unseemly dissembling, as was to be expected, was greatly condemned by the rest of the spectators, as was manifested still more by the poor woman who was to suffer; for she spoke to her not a single word, nor did she seem disturbed or to regard her unfriendliness, yet did she, in her greatness of soul, discover her concern for her mother's offence, and especially for her exposing herself in a manner so unbecoming. As for herself, she went to her death with unshaken firmness of mind, and without changing colour, and so evidently showed the nobility of her descent to the spectators even in the last moments of her life.

§ 6. And thus died Mariamne, a woman of an excellent

character both for chastity and greatness of soul ; but she wanted moderation, and had too much of contentiousness in her nature, but she surpassed all the women of her time more than can be said in the beauty of her body and charm of her society, which was the principal reason why she did not prove so agreeable to the king, nor live so pleasantly with him, as she might otherwise have done ; for as she was most indulgently used by the king, from his fondness to her, and did not expect that he could do any hard thing to her she took too excessive liberty.   But what most distressed her was what Herod had done to her relations, and she ventured to speak out of all they had suffered at his hands, and at last greatly provoked both the king's mother and sister (till they became enemies to her), and also the king himself, on whom alone she relied to escape extreme punishment.

§ 7. But when she was once dead, the king's passion for her was kindled more than before, he being such as I have already described.   For his love to her was not of a calm nature, nor such as we usually meet with in other husbands, for at its commencement it was enthusiastic, nor was it weakened by long cohabitation and free intercourse.   And now his love for Mariamne seemed to seize him in such a peculiar way as looked like divine vengeance upon him for taking away her life, for he would frequently call for her, and frequently lament for her in a most unseemly manner.   Moreover, he bethought him of everything he could make use of to divert his mind from thinking of her, and contrived feasts and company for that purpose, but nothing would suffice ; he therefore laid aside the administration of public affairs, and was so overcome by his passion, that he would order his servants to call for Mariamne, as if she were still alive, and could hear.   And when he was in this way, there arose a pestilential disease, that carried off many of the people, and his most esteemed friends, and made all men suspect that this was brought on them by the anger of God, for the injustice that had been done to Mariamne.   This circumstance affected the king still more, till at length he went into retirement, and, under a pretence of going a hunting, bitterly mourned, and had not borne his grief there many days before he fell into a most dangerous illness. He had an inflammation upon him, and a pain in the hinder part of his head, joined with madness; and the remedies that were used did him no good at all, but proved contrary to his case, and so at last his life was despaired of. All the physicians also that were about him, partly because the medicines they brought for his recovery could not at all conquer the disease, and partly because his diet could be no other than what his disease inclined him to, desired him to take whatever he had a mind to, and so left the small hopes they had of his recovery to the power of that diet, and left him to fortune. And thus was he ill at Samaria, now called Sebaste.[1]

§ 8. Now Alexandra lived at Jerusalem, and being informed of the condition Herod was in, endeavoured to get possession of the fortified places that were about the city, which were two, the one belonging to the city itself, the other belonging to the temple; for whoever could get them into their hands had the whole nation ever in their power, for without the command of them it was not possible to offer the sacrifices; and to think of leaving off those sacrifices is to all Jews plainly impossible, for they are more ready to lose their lives than to leave off the divine worship which they have been wont to pay to God. So Alexandra told those that had the keeping of those strongholds, that they ought to deliver up the same to her and to Herod's sons, lest, upon his death, any other person should seize upon the government; and if he recovered none could keep them more safely for him than those of his own family. These words were not taken by them at all in good part; and as they had been in former times faithful [to Herod], they resolved to continue so more than ever, not only because they hated Alexandra, but also because they thought it a sort of impiety to despair of Herod's recovery while he was yet alive. For they had been his old friends, and one of them, whose name was Achiabus, was his cousin. They therefore sent messengers to acquaint Herod with Alexandra's design; and he without any delay gave orders to have her put to death. And it was only with difficulty, and after he

<hr />

[1] *Sebustieh.*

had endured great pain, that he got rid of this illness.  He
was still sorely afflicted both in mind and body, so that he
was very morose, and readier than ever upon all occasions
to inflict punishment upon those that fell under his power.
He also slew the most intimate of his friends, as Costobarus, and Lysimachus, and Gadias, who was also called
Antipater, as also Dositheus, for the following reason.

§ 9.  Costobarus was an Idumæan by birth, and one of
principal dignity among them, and his ancestors had been
priests to the Koze, whom the Idumæans esteem a god ;
but after Hyrcanus had made a change in their polity, and
made them receive the Jewish customs and law, Herod
after he got the kingdom made Costobarus governor of
Idumæa and Gaza, and gave him his sister Salome to wife,
after putting to death Joseph, who had that government
before, as I have related already.  When Costobarus had got
so highly advanced, it pleased him, being more than he had
hoped for, and he was more and more puffed up by his good
fortune, and in a little while he exceeded all bounds, and
did not think fit to obey what Herod his ruler commanded him, or that the Idumæans should adopt the
Jewish customs, or be subject to the Jews.  He therefore sent
to Cleopatra, and informed her that the Idumæans had been
always under her progenitors, and for that reason it was but
just that she should ask that country of Antony, and added
that he himself was ready to transfer his friendship to her.
This he did, not because he was better pleased to be under
Cleopatra's government, but because he thought that, upon
the diminution of Herod's power, it would not be difficult
for him to obtain himself the entire rule over the Idumæans,
and somewhat more also; for he raised his hopes still
higher, as having no small advantages both from his
birth and those riches which he had got by his constant
attention to filthy lucre, and it was no small matter that
he aimed at.  So Cleopatra asked this country of Antony,
but did not get it.  An account of this was brought to
Herod, who was thereupon inclined to kill Costobarus, but
upon the entreaties of his sister and mother he let him
go, and vouchsafed to pardon him, though he was suspicious of him ever afterwards for this attempt of his.

§ 10.  But some time afterwards, when Salome happened

to be at variance with Costobarus, she sent him at once a bill of divorce,[1] and dissolved her marriage with him, though this was not according to the Jewish laws. For with us it is lawful for a husband to do so, but a wife, if she departs from her husband, cannot herself marry another, unless her former husband put her away. However, Salome chose to follow not the law of her country, but the law of her own will, and so renounced her wedlock, and told her brother Herod that she left her husband out of good-will to him, because she had found out that Costobarus and Antipater and Lysimachus and Dositheus were raising a rebellion against him : as an evidence whereof she alleged the case of the sons of Babas, who had been preserved alive by him twelve years, as proved to be the case. But when Herod thus unexpectedly heard of this, he was greatly surprised at it, and the more so because the affair appeared incredible to him. For Herod had formerly taken great pains to bring those sons of Babas to punishment, as being enemies to his government, but they were now forgotten by him, on account of the length of time between. Now, the cause of his ill-will and hatred to them was because, when Antigonus was king, Herod with his army besieged the city of Jerusalem, where the distress and miseries that the besieged endured were so harassing, that many invited Herod into the city, and already placed their hopes on him. But the sons of Babas, who occupied a high position and had much influence with the multitude, were faithful to Antigonus, and were always calumniating Herod, and encouraging the people to preserve the kingdom to the royal family who held it by inheritance. Now they acted thus for their own advantage, as they thought; but when the city was taken, and

---

[1] Here is a plain example of a Jewish lady giving a bill of divorce to her husband, though in the days of Josephus it was not esteemed lawful for a woman so to do. See alike among the Parthians, Antiq. xviii. 9, § 6. However, the Christian law, when it allowed divorce for adultery, Matt. v. 32, allowed the innocent wife to divorce her guilty husband, as well as the innocent husband to divorce his guilty wife, as we learn from the shepherd of Hermas, Mand. iv., and from the second Apology of Justin Martyr, where a persecution was brought upon the Christians upon such a divorce ; and I think the Roman laws permitted it at that time, as well as the laws of Christianity.—W.

Herod had become master of the position, and Costobarus was appointed to hinder men from passing out at the gates, and to guard the city, that those citizens that were guilty, and of the party opposite to the king, might not get out of it, Costobarus, knowing that the sons of Babas were held in respect and honour by the whole multitude, and supposing that their preservation might be of great advantage to him in any changes of government afterwards, took them out of the way, and concealed them on his own estate. And when the thing was suspected, he assured Herod upon oath that he really knew nothing of the matter, and so allayed his suspicions. Moreover after that, when the king had publicly proposed a reward for their discovery, and devised all sorts of methods for searching out the matter, he would not confess, but being persuaded that, owing to his having at first denied it, he would not escape unpunished, if the men were found, he was forced to keep them secret, not only from his goodwill to them, but from necessity. But when the king knew the facts of the case from his sister's information, he sent men to the places where he had intimation they were concealed, and ordered both them, and those that were accused as guilty with them, to be slain, so that now there were none at all left of the kindred of Hyrcanus, and the kingdom was entirely in Herod's own power, and there was nobody remaining of such high position as could interfere with what he did against the Jewish laws.

## CHAP. VIII.

*How ten of the Citizens [of Jerusalem] made a Conspiracy against Herod, because of the foreign Practices he had introduced, which was a Transgression of the Laws of their Country. Concerning the building of Sebaste and Cæsarea, and other Erections of Herod.*

### § 1.

THIS was why Herod revolted from the laws of his country, and corrupted our ancient polity, which ought to have been preserved inviolable, by the intro-

duction of foreign practices; by which we became guilty
of great wickedness afterwards, as those religious observances which used to lead the multitude to piety
were now neglected.  For, in the first place, he appointed
solemn games to be celebrated every fifth year, in honour
of Augustus, and built a theatre at Jerusalem, as also a very
great amphitheatre in the plain.  Both of them were indeed
costly works, but opposite to the Jewish notions; for we have
had no such shows handed down to us by tradition as fit
to be used or exhibited by us; yet did Herod celebrate these
games every five years in the most splendid manner.  He
also made proclamation to the neighbouring people, and
called men together out of all the nation.  Wrestlers also,
and the rest of those that strove for the prizes in such
games, were invited out of all the land, both by the hopes
of the rewards there to be bestowed, and by the glory of
victory there to be gained.  So the principal persons that
were most renowned for these sorts of exercises were got
together, for there were very great rewards proposed
for victory, not only to those who performed gymnastic
exercises, but also to those who were professional musicians,
and who were called Thymelici; indeed Herod spared no
pains to induce all persons, the most famous for such exercises, to come to the contest. He also proposed no small rewards for those who contended for the prizes in chariots
drawn by four horses, or by a pair, or with race-horses. He
also imitated everything, though ever so costly or magnificent, that was practised by other nations, being ambitious
to give public demonstration of his grandeur.  Inscriptions
also of the great actions of Augustus, and trophies of
the nations which he had got in his wars, all made of
the purest gold and silver, were all round the theatre.
Nor was there anything that could conduce to display,
whether precious garments or precious stones set in order,
which was not also exposed to sight in these games.  He
also got together a great quantity of wild beasts, and of
lions in very great abundance, and of such other beasts as
were either of uncommon strength, or of such a sort as
were rarely seen.  These were trained either to fight one
with another, or men who were condemned to death were
to fight with them.  And truly foreigners were greatly

surprised and delighted at the vast expense of the shows, and at the great danger of the spectacles, but to the Jews it was a palpable breaking up of those customs for which they had so great a veneration. It appeared also no better than barefaced impiety to throw men to wild beasts, to afford delight to the spectators, and it appeared no less impiety to change their own laws for such foreign practices. But above all the trophies gave most distaste to the Jews, for as they imagined them to be images inclosed in the armour that hung round about them, they were sorely displeased at them, because it was not the custom of their country to pay honour to such things.

§ 2. Nor was Herod unacquainted with their emotion, and as he thought it unseasonable to use violence, he tried to conciliate and console some of them, and to free them from their religious scruples, but he could not satisfy them, but they cried out with one accord, from their great uneasiness at the offences they thought he had been guilty of, that although they might bear all the rest, yet would they never bear images of men in their city (meaning the trophies), because this was against the laws of their country. Now when Herod saw them so put out, and that they would not easily change their sentiments unless they received satisfaction on this point, he called to him the most eminent men among them, and brought them to the theatre, and showed them the trophies, and asked them what sort of things they took these trophies to be? And when they cried out, that they were the images of men, he ordered that they should be stripped of the ornaments which were about them, and showed them the bare wood; which wood, now without any ornament, became matter of great sport and laughter to them, as indeed they had always before had the ornaments of images in derision.

§ 3. When Herod had thus baffled the multitude, and dissipated the vehemence of passion under which they laboured, most of the people were disposed to change their ideas, and not to be displeased at him any longer; but some of them still continued to be offended with him for his introduction of new customs, and esteemed the violation of the laws of their country as likely to be the origin of very great mischiefs to them, so that they deemed it an instance of piety rather to run any risk than to seem as if they took no notice of Herod's action in changing their polity, and violently introducing such customs as they had never been used to before; for he was indeed to appearance a king, but in reality one that showed himself an enemy to their whole nation. So ten men that were citizens conspired together against him, and swore to one another to undergo any dangers in the attempt, and took daggers with them under their garments [for the purpose of killing Herod]. Now there was a certain blind man among these conspirators, who was moved by indignation in consequence of what he heard had been done; he was not indeed able to afford the rest any assistance in the undertaking, but was ready to undergo any suffering with them, if they should come to any harm, insomuch that he became a very great encouragement to the conspirators.

§ 4. When they had taken their resolution, they went by common consent into the theatre, hoping that Herod himself would not escape them, as they would fall upon him so unexpectedly, and supposing that, if they missed him, they should anyhow kill a great many of those who were about him; and feeling they would be satisfied, even though they should die for it, if they brought home to the king what injuries he had done to the multitude. These conspirators, therefore, being thus prepared beforehand, went about their design with great zeal. But there was one of Herod's spies, who were appointed to fish out and inform him of any conspiracies that were made against him, who found out the whole affair, and told the king of it, as he was about to enter the theatre. And when he reflected on the hatred which he knew most of the people bore him, and on the disturbances that arose upon every occasion, he thought this plot against him not improbable. Accordingly, he retired into his palace, and called those that were accused of this conspiracy before him by their names; and as, by his guards falling upon them, they were caught in the very act, and knew they could not escape, they prepared themselves for their deaths with all the decency they could, and so as not to recede at all from their resolute behaviour. For they showed no shame at their act, nor did they deny it, but when they were seized, they showed their daggers, and professed that their conspiracy was a holy and pious action, that what they intended to do was not for gain, or to indulge their passions, but rather for those common customs of their country, which all Jews were obliged to observe or to die for them. This is what these men boldly said, in their undaunted courage evinced in this conspiracy, as they were led away to execution by the king's guards that surrounded them, and patiently underwent all the torments inflicted on them till they died. Nor was it long before the spy who had informed against them was seized on by some of the people, from the hatred they bore to him, and was not only slain by them, but pulled to pieces limb by limb, and given to the dogs. This action was seen by many of the citizens, but not one of them would discover the doers of it, till upon Herod's making a strict and severe search for them, certain women that were tortured confessed what they had seen done; and the authors of the act were so terribly punished by the king, that their entire families were destroyed for their rash attempt. But the obstinacy of the people, and the undaunted constancy they showed in the defence of their laws, made Herod afraid unless he strengthened himself in a more secure manner. So he resolved to hem in the multitude on all sides, lest faction should end in open rebellion.

§ 5. When therefore he had fortified the city by the palace in which he lived, and the temple by a strong fortress rebuilt by himself, called Antonia,[1] he contrived to make Samaria also a *point d'appui* for himself against all the people, and called it Sebaste,[2] supposing that it would overawe the country as much as the other. So he fortified the place, which was a day's journey distant from Jerusalem, so as to be useful to him both in keeping the country and city in awe. He also built another fortress for the whole nation, which was of old called Strato's Tower, but was by him called Cæsarea.[3] Moreover, he chose out some

---

[1] The castle of Antonia was on the north side of the Temple, and is supposed to have partly occupied the site on which the Turkish Barracks stand at Jerusalem.

[2] *Sebustieh.*					[3] Cæsarea Palæstina, *Kaisariyeh.*

picked cavalry to wait upon him in the great plain, and built [for them] a place in Galilee called Gaba,[1] and Esebonitis in Peræa.[2] And these were the places which he particularly built, as he was always inventing something fresh for his own security, and surrounding the whole nation with garrisons, that they might by no means get out of his power, nor fall into tumults, which they did continually upon any small commotion; and that if they did make any commotions he might know of it, as some of his spies would be upon them from the neighbourhood, and would both be able to know what they were attempting, and to prevent it. And when he started fortifying Samaria, he took care to convey there many of those that had assisted him in his wars, and many of the people in that neighbourhood also, whom he made fellow-citizens with the others. This he did partly from an ambitious desire of building a temple, and making the city more eminent than it had been before, but chiefly that it might at once be for his own security, and a monument of his magnificence. He also changed its name, and called it Sebaste. Moreover, he parcelled out the adjacent country, which was excellent in its kind, among the inhabitants of Samaria, that they might be in a prosperous condition on their first coming to inhabit it. He also surrounded the city with a wall of great strength, and availed himself of the steepness of the place to make its fortifications stronger; nor was the compass of the place made now so small as it had been before, but it was such as rendered it not inferior to the most famous cities; for it was twenty furlongs in compass. And within in about the middle of it he built a sacred enclosure, a furlong and a half in circumference, and adorned it with all sorts of decorations, and erected a temple in it, which was most notable both on account of its size and beauty. And as to the several parts of the city, he adorned them with decorations of all sorts also: and seeing what was necessary to provide for his own safety, he made the walls very strong for that purpose, and made it for the most part a citadel; and as to elegance of building, that was

[1] Now *Jebâta*. See Life, § 24; Jewish War, iii. 3, § 1.
[2] Heshbon, now *Hesbân;* near the border between Reuben and Gad.

looked after also, that he might leave a memorial of the
fineness of his taste, and of his beneficence, to future
ages.

## CHAP. IX.

*Concerning the Famine that happened in Judæa and Syria ;
and how Herod, after he had married another Wife, rebuilt
Cæsarea, and other Greek Cities.*

### § 1.

NOW in this very year, which was the thirteenth year
of the reign of Herod, very great calamities came
upon the country, whether from the anger of God, or
whether this evil recurs naturally in certain periods of
time.  For in the first place there were perpetual droughts,
and for that reason the ground was barren, and did not
bring forth the same quantity of fruits that it usually produced ; and next to this the change of food which the want
of corn occasioned produced diseases in the bodies of men,
and a pestilence prevailed, one misery following hard upon
the back of another.  And the circumstance that they were
destitute both of methods of cure and of food, made the
pestilence, which began in a violent manner, the more intense, and the death of men in such a manner deprived
those that survived of all their courage, because they had
no way to provide remedies sufficient to meet the distress
they were in.  As therefore the fruits of that year were
spoiled, and whatever they had laid up beforehand was expended, there was no hope of relief remaining, but the evil,
contrary to what they expected, still increased upon them;
and not only in that year, when they had nothing for themselves left at the end of it, but the seed they had sown
perished also, because of the ground not yielding its fruits
in the second year.  The distress they were in made them
also out of necessity eat many things that were not usually
eaten ; nor was the king himself free from this distress any
more than other men, as he was deprived of the tribute he
used to have from the fruits of the ground, and had already

expended what money he had in his liberality to those whose cities he had built. Nor had he any people that were worthy of his assistance, for this miserable state of things had procured him the hatred of his subjects, for it is a constant rule that misfortunes are laid to the account of those that govern.

§ 2. Under these circumstances he considered with himself how to procure some relief; which was a difficult matter, as their neighbours had no food to sell them, as they had suffered as much themselves, and their money also was gone, had it been possible to purchase a little food at a great price. However, he thought it well not to leave off by any means his endeavours to assist his people; so he cut off the rich furniture both of silver and gold that was in his palace, nor did he spare the finest vessels he had, or those that had been made with the most elaborate skill of the artificers, but sent the money to Petronius, who had been made prefect of Egypt by Augustus. And as not a few had already fled to him in their necessities, and as he was a particular friend of Herod, and desirous to have his subjects preserved, Petronius gave them first leave to have corn from Egypt, and assisted them every way both in purchasing and conveying it to Judæa, so that he was the principal, if not the only person, who afforded them help in this matter. And Herod took care the people should know that this help came from himself, and so not only changed the bad opinions of those that formerly hated him, but gave the greatest proof of his good-will to them and care of them. For, in the first place, to those who were able to provide their own food, he distributed their proportion of corn in the exactest manner, while for those many that were not able to provide food for themselves, either because of old age or any other infirmity, he made this provision for them, seeing that the bakers made their bread for them. He also took care that they should not be hurt by the dangers of winter, as they were in great want of clothing also, because of the utter destruction and loss of their flocks, so that they had no wool to make use of, nor anything else to cover themselves with. And when he had procured these things for his own subjects, he also attempted to provide necessaries for the neighbouring cities, and gave seed to the Syrians, which thing turned as much to his own advantage, this charitable assistance being afforded most seasonably to their fruitful soil, so that every one had now a plentiful provision of food. And when the harvest of the land was generally approaching, he sent no less than fifty thousand men, whom he had sustained, into the country; by which means he not only repaired the afflicted condition of his own kingdom with great generosity and diligence, but also very much lightened the afflictions of his neighbours, who were suffering from the same calamities. For there was nobody who had been in want, that was left destitute of a suitable assistance from him: nor were there either any peoples or cities or private persons, who had to make provision for multitudes and so were in want, who had recourse to him, without receiving what they stood in need of, insomuch, that it appeared upon computation, that the number of cors of wheat (now a cor is ten Attic medimni) that was given to foreigners amounted to ten thousand, and the number that was given in his own kingdom was about fourscore thousand. Now it happened that this care of his, and this seasonable benevolence, had such influence on the Jews, and was so cried up among other nations, that it wiped off that old hatred which his violation of some of their customs, during his reign, had procured him among all the nation, and this liberality of assistance in their greatest necessity was reckoned full requital. It also procured him great fame among foreigners, and it seems as if those calamities, that afflicted his kingdom to a degree plainly incredible, came in order to raise his glory, and to be to his great advantage. For the greatness of his liberality in those distresses, which he displayed beyond all expectation, did so change the disposition of the multitude towards him, that they were ready to suppose he had been from the beginning not such a one as they had found him long ago by experience, but such a one as the care he had taken of them in supplying their necessities now showed him to be.

§ 3. About this time it was that he sent five hundred picked men of his body-guards as auxiliaries to Augustus, whom Ælius Gallus conducted to the Red Sea, and who were of great service to him there. And when his affairs

were in a good and flourishing condition again, he built
himself a palace in the upper part of the city, raising the
rooms to a very great height, and adorning them with the
most costly furniture of gold and precious stones and decorations, and built apartments so large that they could contain very many men, and had particular names given them
according to their size, for one apartment was called
Augustus', another Agrippa's.   He also fell in love again,
and married another wife, not suffering his reason to
hinder him from living as he pleased.   The occasion of this
marriage was as follows.   There was one Simon, a native
of Jerusalem (the son of one Boethus, an Alexandrian),
who was a priest of great note, and had a daughter who
was esteemed the most beautiful woman of her time; and
as the people of Jerusalem talked much about her, it happened that Herod was much affected first with what was said
about her, and afterwards when he saw the damsel he was
deeply smitten with her beauty, yet did he entirely reject the
thoughts of using his authority to abuse her, believing, as
was the truth, that if he did so he would be stigmatized for
violence and tyranny, so he thought it best to take the
damsel to wife.   And as Simon was of a rank too low to
be allied to him, but still too considerable to be despised,
he followed his inclination in the most prudent manner,
by augmenting the dignity of his family, and making it
more honourable.   So he forthwith deprived Jesus, the
son of Phabes, of the high priesthood, and conferred that
dignity on Simon, and then married his daughter.

§ 4. When the wedding was over, he built another citadel
in the place where he had conquered the Jews when he was
driven out of his kingdom, when Antigonus was at the
head of affairs.   This citadel[1] is about threescore furlongs
from Jerusalem.   It is a place strong by nature, and fit
for such a building.   It is a sort of a moderate hill, raised
to a greater height by the hand of man, so that its circuit
is like the shape of a woman's breast.   It has circular
towers at intervals, and a steep ascent up to it, composed
of two hundred steps of polished stones.   Within it are
royal and very costly apartments, constructed both for

[1] The ruins are still to be seen on the summit and at the base of
*Jebel Fureidis*, south of Jerusalem.

security and beauty.  At the bottom of the hill there are
habitations of such a structure as are well worth seeing,
both on other accounts, and also on account of the water
which is brought there from a great way off,[1] and at vast
expense, for the place itself is destitute of water.  The plain
below is full of buildings, and not inferior to any city in
size, having the hill above it as a citadel.

§ 5. And now, when all Herod's designs had succeeded
according to his hopes, he had not the least suspicion that
any troubles would arise in his kingdom, because he kept
his people obedient, as well by the fear they stood in of
him, for he was implacable in his punishments, as by the
provident care he had showed towards them, in the most
magnanimous manner, when they were in their distresses.
Still he took care to have external security as a fortress
against his subjects.  For to the cities he was courteous and
full of kindness, and cultivated a seasonable good understanding with their governors, and bestowed presents on
every one of them, inducing them thereby to be more
friendly to him, and using his magnificent disposition, so
that his kingdom might be the better secured to him, and
all his affairs be every way more and more augmented.
But that magnificent temper of his, and the court which he
paid towards Augustus and the most powerful men of Rome,
obliged him to transgress the customs of his nation, and to
set aside many of their laws, both by building cities in an
ambitious manner, and erecting temples; not in Judæa
indeed (for that would not have been borne, it being forbidden for us to pay any honour to images, or representations of animals, like the Greeks), but he did thus in the
country and cities out of our bounds.  The apology which
he made to the Jews for this was that all was done, not
by his own inclination, but by command and order, to
please Augustus and the Romans, as though he had not
the Jewish customs so much in his eye as he had paying
honour to the Romans, while yet he had himself in view
entirely all the while, and indeed was very ambitious to
leave great monuments of his reign to posterity; whence

----

[1] The water was brought from the *Wâdy Ûrtâs*, in which are the
' Pools of Solomon.'

it was that he was so zealous in building such fine cities, and spent such vast sums of money upon them.

§ 6. Now upon his observing a place near the sea, which was very well adapted for a city, and was before called Strato's Tower, he set about planning a magnificent city there, and erected many edifices with great care all over it of white stone. He also adorned it with most sumptuous palaces, and edifices for containing the people; and what was the greatest and most laborious work of all, he adorned it with a haven sheltered from the waves of the sea, in size not less than the Piræus [at Athens,] and containing inside two stations for ships.[1] It was excellently constructed, which was the more remarkable from its being built in a place that of itself was not suitable for such a noble structure, but had to be brought to perfection by materials fetched from other places at very great expense. The city is situate in Phœnicia, in the passage by sea to Egypt, between Joppa[2] and Dora,[3] which are smaller maritime cities, and not fit for havens, on account of the fierce south winds that beat upon them,—which, rolling the sand that comes from the sea against the shore, do not give good anchorage for ships, but merchants are generally forced to ride at anchor out at sea. This inconvenience Herod endeavoured to rectify, and laid out such a compass towards the land as might be sufficient for a haven, wherein great fleets might lie in safety; and this he effected by putting down huge stones of above fifty feet in length, and not less than eighteen in breadth, and nine in depth, twenty fathoms deep, and as some stones were less, so others were bigger than those dimensions. This mole which he built by the sea-side was two hundred feet long, and half of it was opposed to the force of the waves, so as to keep them off (and so was called break-water), and the other half had upon it a wall, with several towers at intervals, the largest of which was called Drusus, and was a work of very great excellence, and had its name from Drusus, the step-son of Augustus, who died young. There were also a great number of arches, where the mariners dwelt; there was also in front

---

[1] The ruins of *Kaisariyeh* and of its ancient port are still very extensive.

[2] *Jaffa.*                                        [3] *Tantûrah.*

of them a quay which ran round the entire haven, and was a most agreeable walk to such as had a mind for exercise. And the entrance or mouth of the port faced north, which wind brings the clearest sky. And the basis of the whole circuit on the left hand, as you sail into the port, supported a round turret, which was made very strong, in order to resist the greatest waves; while on the right hand stood two huge stones, each of them larger than the turret which was opposite them, which stood upright, and were joined together. And there were edifices all along the circular haven, made of the most polished stone, with a certain elevation in the middle, whereon was erected a temple of Cæsar,[1] visible a great way off to those who were sailing for that haven, which had in it two statues, one of Rome, the other of Cæsar.[1] The city itself was called Cæsarea, and was itself built of fine materials, and handsomely constructed; nay, the very subterranean vaults and cellars had as much care bestowed on them as the buildings above ground. Some of these vaults carried things at regular distances to the haven and to the sea; but one of them ran obliquely, and undergirt all the rest, that both the rain and sewage of the citizens were conveyed away with ease, and the sea itself at full tide entered the city, and washed it all clean. Herod also built therein a theatre of stone; and on the south side of the harbour behind an amphitheatre also, capable of holding a vast number of men, and conveniently situated for a sea view. This city was finished thus in twelve years;[2] during which time the king did not fail both to go on with the work, and to pay the necessary expenses.

[1] Augustus.
[2] It is ten years in Antiq. xvi. 5, § 1.—W.

## CHAP. X.

*How Herod sent his Sons to Rome; also how he was accused by Zenodorus and the Gadarenes, but was cleared of what they accused him of, and withal gained to himself the Good-will of Augustus. Also concerning the Pharisees, the Essenes, and Manahem.*

### § 1.

WHEN Herod was engaged in these matters, and had already built Sebaste [Samaria], he resolved to send his sons Alexander and Aristobulus to Rome, to visit Augustus. And they, when they got there, lodged at the house of Pollio,[1] who was very proud of Herod's friendship; and they had leave to lodge in Augustus' own palace, for he received these sons of Herod with all kindness, and gave Herod leave to give his kingdom to which of his sons he pleased: and moreover he bestowed on him Trachon,[2] and Batanæa,[3] and Auranitis,[4] which he gave him for the following reason. One Zenodorus had hired the house of Lysanias, and, as he was not satisfied with its revenues, he became a partner with the robbers that infested Trachon, and so got a larger income; for the inhabitants of that region lived in a mad way, and pillaged the country of the Damascenes, and Zenodorus did not restrain them, but shared himself in the booty. Now, as the neighbouring people were thereby great sufferers, they complained to Varro, who was then president [of Syria], and entreated him to write to Augustus about this wrong-doing of Zenodorus. When these matters were laid before Augustus, he wrote back to Varro to destroy those nests of robbers, and to give the land to Herod, that so by his care the neighbouring

[1] This Pollio, with whom Herod's sons lodged at Rome, was not Pollio the Pharisee, already mentioned by Josephus, chap. 1, § 1, and again presently after this, chap. 10, § 4, but Asinius Pollio, the Roman, as Spanheim here observes.—W.

[2] Now *el-Lejah.*

[3] The name is still retained in *Ard el-Bathanyeh.*

[4] *Haurân.* Trachon, Batanæa, and Auranitis were three of the four districts into which Bashan was divided.

countries might be no longer disturbed by these doings of the Trachonites. For it was no easy thing to restrain them, since this habit of robbery had been their usual practice, and they had no other way to get their living, because they had neither any city of their own, nor lands in their possession, but only some dens and caves in the earth, and there they and their cattle lived in common together. However, they had made contrivances to get water, and laid up corn for themselves, and were able to make great resistance, by issuing out on the sudden against any that attacked them. For the entrances of their caves were narrow, so that but one could go in at a time, and the places within were incredibly large and roomy; and the ground over their habitations was not very high, but rather on a plain. And the rocks were altogether hard and difficult of access, unless any one followed the track of another, for these roads are not straight, but have many windings. And when those men were hindered from their wicked preying upon their neighbours, their custom was to prey upon one another, so that no sort of wrong-doing came amiss to them. But when Herod had received this grant of land from Augustus, and went into this country, he procured skilful guides, and put a stop to their wicked robberies, and gave peace and quietness to the neighbouring people.

§ 2. Thereupon Zenodorus was angry, first because his district was taken away from him, and next even still more because he envied Herod who had got it; so he went up to Rome to accuse him, but returned back again without success. Now Agrippa was [about this time] sent to govern in the name of Augustus the countries beyond the Ionian Sea, and Herod visited him when he was wintering at Mitylene, for he had been his particular friend and companion, and then returned to Judæa again. And some of the Gadarenes went to Agrippa, and accused Herod, but he sent them back bound to the king, without giving them a hearing. And the Arabians, who of old bore ill-will to Herod's sway, were excited, and now attempted to raise a rebellion in his dominions; and, as they thought, for a justifiable reason. For Zenodorus, despairing already of success as to his own affairs, anticipated [his enemies] by

selling to those Arabians a part of his district, called
Auranitis, for fifty talents; and as this was included in
the grant of Augustus, they contested the point with Herod,
as being unjustly deprived of what they had bought.
Sometimes they did this by making incursions upon him,
and sometimes by attempting force against him, and sometimes by going to law with him. Moreover, they persuaded the poorer soldiers to help them, and were hostile
to Herod in the constant hope of an insurrection, a thing
which those that are in the most miserable circumstances
of life most rejoice in. And although Herod had been a
long time aware of this, yet did he not act with severity
to them, but by reason tried to conciliate them, being unwilling to give any handle for tumults.

§ 3. Now when Herod had already reigned seventeen
years, Augustus came into Syria: at which time most of
the inhabitants of Gadara[1] clamoured against Herod, as im-
perious in his orders, and tyrannical. These reproaches
they mainly ventured upon by the encouragement and
calumny of Zenodorus, who swore that he would never
desert them till he had got them severed from Herod's
kingdom, and joined to Augustus' jurisdiction. The
Gadarenes were induced thereby, and raised no small out-
cry against Herod, and that the more boldly, because
those that had been delivered up by Agrippa to him were
not punished by Herod, who let them go, and did them no
harm; for indeed he (if anyone) appeared inexorable in
punishing crimes in his own family, but very generous in
remitting offences that were committed elsewhere. And
as they accused Herod of violence and plunder and over-
throwing of temples, he stood unconcerned, and was ready
to make his defence. However Augustus gave him his
right hand, and remitted nothing of his kindness to him,
upon this uproar of the multitude; and indeed these
things were alleged the first day, but the hearing proceeded
no further on the following days. For as the Gadarenes
saw the bias of Augustus and of his assessors, and expected,
as they had reason to do, that they would be delivered up
to the king, some of them, in dread of the torments they

---

[1] *Umm Keis.*

might undergo, cut their own throats in the night, and
some of them threw themselves down precipices, and others
of them cast themselves into the river, and committed
suicide; which seemed a sufficient condemnation of the
rashness and fault they had been guilty of; and thereupon Augustus without any further delay acquitted Herod
of what he was accused of. Another fortunate event also
befriended Herod at this time; for Zenodorus' belly burst,
and a great quantity of blood issued from him in his illness, and he departed this life at Antioch in Syria. And
Augustus bestowed his district, which was no small one,
upon Herod; it lay between Trachon and Galilee, and contained Ulatha [1] and Paneas,[2] and the country round about.
He also made him one of the procurators of Syria, and
commanded that nothing should be done without his approbation; in short, he arrived at that pitch of felicity,
that whereas there were but two men that governed the
Roman empire, first Augustus, and then Agrippa, who was
Augustus' principal favourite, Augustus preferred no one
to Herod after Agrippa; and Agrippa made no one his
greater friend than Herod except Augustus. And when
he had acquired such great influence, he begged of
Augustus a tetrarchy[3] for his brother Pheroras, and himself bestowed upon him a revenue of a hundred talents out
of his own kingdom, that if he came to any harm himself,
his brother might be in safety, and his sons might not
have dominion over him. And when he had escorted
Augustus to the sea, and had returned home, he built in
his honour a most beautiful temple of white stone, in
Zenodorus' district, near the place called Panium;[4] where
there is a very fine cave in a mountain, under which there
is a great cavity in the earth, and the cavern is precipitous, and prodigiously deep, and full of stagnant water;

[1] The district round the Lake Semechonitis, Merom, now *Baheiret
el-Hûleh*.
[2] *Bâniâs*, Cæsarea Philippi.
[3] A *tetrarchy* properly and originally denoted *the fourth part of an
entire kingdom or country;* and a *tetrarch*, one that was *a ruler of such
fourth part;* which always implies somewhat less extent of dominion
and power than belong to a kingdom and to a king.—W.
[4] The cavern at *Bâniâs* from which one of the sources of the Jordan
issues; there are still several niches with inscriptions cut in the rock.

over it hangs a vast mountain; and under the cavern
arise the springs of the river Jordan. Herod still further
adorned this place, which was already a very remarkable
one, by the erection of this temple, which he dedicated to
Augustus.

§ 4. At this time Herod remitted to his subjects the
third part of their taxes, under pretext indeed of relieving
them after the dearth they had had; but his main reason
was, to recover their good-will, for they were vexed at
him because of the innovations he had introduced in their
practices, to the dissolution of their religion, and to the
disuse of their own customs; and the people everywhere
talked against him, like people who were still provoked and
put out. Against these discontents he greatly guarded
himself, taking away the opportunities the people might
have to disturb him, and enjoining them to be always at
work; nor did he permit the citizens either to meet together,
or to walk or eat together, but watched everything they
did. And when any were caught they were severely
punished, and there were many who were brought to the
citadel Hyrcania,[1] both openly and secretly, and were there
put to death; and there were spies set everywhere, both
in the city and in the roads, who watched those that met
together. Nay, it is reported, that he did not himself
neglect this part, but that he would often himself put
on the dress of a private man, and mix among the multitude in the night-time, and so find out what opinion
they had of his government. And as for those that could
no way be induced to acquiesce in his scheme of government, he persecuted them in all manner of ways, while for
the rest of the multitude, he required that they should be
obliged to take an oath of fidelity to him, and compelled
them to swear that they would bear him good-will in his
government. And indeed most, either to please him, or
out of fear of him, yielded to what he required of them,
but such as had more spirit, and were indignant at force,
he by one means or other made away with. He endeavoured also to persuade Pollio the Pharisee, and Sameas,
and most of their scholars, to take this oath; but they

---

[1] See Antiq. xiii. 16, § 3.

would not submit to do so, nor were they punished with the rest, from the regard he had to Pollio. The Essenes also, as we call a sect of ours, were excused from this necessity. These men live the same kind of life as do those whom the Greeks call Pythagoreans, concerning whom I shall speak more fully elsewhere. However, it is but fit to set down here the reason why Herod held these Essenes in such honour, and thought higher of them than their mortal nature warranted; nor will this account be unsuitable to the nature of this history, as it will show the opinion men had of these Essenes.

§ 5. One of these Essenes, whose name was Manahem, had this testimony, that he not only conducted his life in an excellent manner, but had also the foreknowledge of future events given him by God. This man once saw Herod when he was but a lad, and going to school, and saluted him as king of the Jews; but he thinking that either he did not know him, or that he was in jest, reminded him that he was but a private person; but Manahem quietly smiled and clapped him on the backside with his hand, and said, "However that be, thou wilt be king, and wilt begin thy reign happily, for God finds thee worthy of it. And do thou remember the blows that Manahem has given thee, as a token to thee of the change of thy fortunes. And truly this will be the best determination for thee, that thou love justice and piety towards God, and clemency towards the citizens; yet do I know thy whole conduct, that thou wilt not be such a one. For thou wilt excel all men in good fortune and obtain an everlasting reputation, but wilt forget piety and justice. And these crimes will not be concealed from God, for at the conclusion of thy life thou wilt find that he will be mindful of them, and punish thee for them." Now at the time Herod did not attend at all to what Manahem said, having no hopes of such advancement; but afterwards, when he was so fortunate as to be advanced by degrees to the dignity of king, and was at the height of his power, he sent for Manahem, and asked him, How long he should reign? Manahem did not tell him the full length of his reign, so upon his silence he asked him further, Whether he should reign ten years, or not? when he replied, "Yes, twenty, nay,

thirty years," but did not state the precise period of his
reign.   Herod was satisfied with this answer however, and
gave Manahem his hand, and dismissed him, and from
that time he continued to honour all the Essenes.   I have
thought it proper to relate this to my readers, however
strange it seems, and to declare what has happened among
us, because many of the Essenes have, by their excellent
virtue, been honoured [by God] by the knowledge of divine
things.


## CHAP. XI.

*How Herod rebuilt the Temple, and raised it higher, and*
*made it more magnificent than it was before; as also con-*
*cerning the Tower which he called Antonia.*


### § 1.

AND now Herod, in the eighteenth year of his reign,
and after the acts already mentioned, undertook a
very great work, that is to build at his own expense the
temple of God, and to make it larger in compass, and to
raise it to a most magnificent height, esteeming it to be the
most glorious of all his actions, as it really was, to bring it
to perfection, and thinking this would be sufficient for an
everlasting memorial of him.   But as he knew the multitude were not ready nor willing to assist him in so great a
design, he thought to prepare them first by making a
speech to them, and then set about the work itself, so he
called them together, and spoke to them as follows.   " I
think I need not speak to you, fellow countrymen, about
such other works as I have done since I came to the kingdom, although I may say they have been performed in
such a manner as to bring more security to you than glory
to myself: for I have neither been negligent in the most
difficult times about what tended to ease your necessities,
nor have the buildings I have erected been so much to
preserve me as yourselves from injuries; and I imagine
that, with God's assistance, I have advanced the nation of
the Jews to a degree of prosperity which they never had
before.   And as for the particular edifices belonging to

your own country, and your own cities, that we have lately acquired, which we have erected and greatly adorned, and so augmented the dignity of your nation, it seems to me a needless task to enumerate them to you, since you well know them yourselves. But as to the undertaking which I have a mind to set about at present, and which will be a work of the greatest piety and excellence in our power, I will now speak about it to you. Our fathers, indeed, when they returned from Babylon, built this temple to Almighty God, yet does it want sixty cubits in height compared with the first temple which Solomon built. But let no one condemn our fathers for negligence or want of piety herein, for it was not their fault that the temple was no higher; for it was Cyrus and Darius (the son of Hystaspes) who determined the measures for its rebuilding; and because of the subjection of those fathers of ours to them and to their posterity, and after them to the Macedonians, they had not opportunity to follow the archetype of this holy edifice, nor could they raise it to its ancient height. But since I am now, by God's will, your governor, and have had peace a long time, and have gained great riches, and large revenues, and, what is the principal thing of all, am at amity with and favourably regarded by the Romans, who, if I may so say, are the rulers of the whole world, I will do my endeavour to correct that imperfection which has arisen from necessity and the slavery which we were under formerly, and to make a thankful return in the most pious manner to God, for the blessings I have received from him in giving me this kingdom, by rendering his temple as complete as I am able."

§ 2. Such was the speech which Herod made to them, but still it astonished most of the people, being unexpected by them; and because it seemed incredible to hope, it did not encourage them, but put a damper upon them, for they were afraid that he would pull down the whole edifice, and not be able to bring his intentions for rebuilding it to perfection, and this danger appeared to them to be very great, and the vastness of the undertaking to be such as could hardly be accomplished. But while they were in this disposition, the king encouraged them, and told them, he would not pull down their temple till

all things were got ready for building it up entirely again.
And as he promised them this beforehand, so he did not
break his word with them, but got ready a thousand
waggons, that were to bring stone for the building,[1] and
chose out ten thousand of the most skilful workmen, and
bought a thousand sacerdotal garments for as many of the
priests, and had some of them taught how to be builders,
and others how to be carpenters, and then began to build,
but not till everything was well prepared for the work.

§ 3. And Herod took up the old foundations, and laid
others, and erected the temple upon them, which was in
length a hundred cubits, and in height twenty additional
cubits, which [twenty,] upon the sinking of their foundations,[2] fell down; and this part it was that we decreed to
raise again in the days of Nero. Now the temple was
built of stones that were white and strong, and the length
of each was twenty-five cubits, the height eight, and the
breadth about twelve.[3] And the whole structure, as was
also the structure of the royal portico, was on each side
much lower, but the middle was much higher, so that it
was visible to those that dwelt in the country for many
furlongs, but chiefly to such as lived opposite, or approached

[1] The stones for the Temple were apparently taken from the large
subterranean quarry near the Damascus Gate.

[2] Some of our modern students in architecture have made a strange
blunder here, when they imagine that Josephus affirms the entire
foundation of the temple, or holy house, sunk down into the rocky
mountain on which it stood, no less than twenty cubits; whereas he is
clear, that they were the foundations of the additional twenty cubits
only above the hundred, (made perhaps weak on purpose, and only for
show and grandeur,) that sunk or fell down, as Dr. Hudson rightly
understands him; nor is the thing itself possible in the other sense.
Agrippa's preparation for building the inner parts of the temple twenty
cubits higher, (Jewish War, v. 1, § 5,) must, in all probability, refer
to this matter, since Josephus says here, that this which had fallen
down was designed to be raised up again under Nero, under whom
Agrippa made that preparation. But what Josephus says presently,
that Solomon was the first king of the Jews, appears by the parallel
place, Antiq. xx. 9, § 7, and other places, to be meant only the first of
David's posterity, and the first builder of the temple.—W.

[3] Josephus here gives the size of one or two of the largest stones in
the wall, and has rather exaggerated the height of the courses. The
stones have weathered a yellowish brown; when fresh from the quarry
they must have been of a pearly white colour.

it. The temple had doors also at the entrance, and lintels over them, of the same height as the temple itself. They were adorned with embroidered veils, with flowers of purple, and pillars interwoven; and over these, but under the cornices, was spread out a golden vine, with its clusters hanging down from a great height, the size and fine workmanship of which was a surprising sight to the spectators to see, such vast materials were there, and with such great skill was the workmanship done. He also surrounded the entire temple with very large porticoes, contriving them all in due proportion, and he laid out larger sums of money than had ever been done before, till it seemed that no one else had so greatly adorned the temple as he did. There was a large wall to both the porticoes, which wall was itself the most prodigious work that was ever heard of by man. The hill was a rocky ascent, that sloped gradually towards the east of the city up to its topmost peak. This hill it was which Solomon, who was the first of our kings, surrounded by divine revelation with a wall of excellent workmanship above and round the top of it.[1] He also built a wall below, beginning at the bottom, which was encompassed by a deep valley; and on the south side he laid rocks together, and bound them to one another with lead, and included some of the inner parts, till it proceeded to a great depth, and till both the size of the square edifice, and its altitude, were immense, and till the vastness of the stones in the front were plainly visible on the outside, and the inward parts were fastened together with iron, and preserved the joints immoveable for all time. When this work was joined together to the very top of the hill, he wrought it all into one outward surface, and filled up the hollow places which were about the wall, and made it a level on the external upper surface, and a smooth level also. This hill was walled all round, and in compass four furlongs, each angle containing a furlong in length;[2] but

[1] This sentence should be read as a parenthesis. The following 'He' refers to Herod.

[2] This direct statement of Josephus that each side of Herod's temple measured a furlong, or 600 feet, agreeing as it does with his statement below (§ 5) that the royal cloister was also a furlong, is of great importance in connection with the controversy relating to the site of the Temple at Jerusalem.

within this wall, and on the very top of all, there ran another wall of stone also, having on the east ridge a double
portico of the same length as the wall; in the midst
of which was the temple itself. This portico faced the
gates of the temple; and it had been adorned by many
kings in former times. And round about the entire temple
were fixed the spoils taken from barbarous nations; all
these were dedicated to the temple by Herod, who added
those he had taken from the Arabians.

§ 4. Now in an angle on the north side [of the temple]
was built a citadel, well fortified and of extraordinary
strength. This citadel was built before Herod by the
kings of the Asamonæan race, who were also high priests,
and they called it the Tower, and in it were deposited the
vestments of the high priest, which the high priest only put
on at the time when he was to offer sacrifice.[1] These vestments king Herod kept in that place, and after his death
they were in the power of the Romans, until the days of
Tiberius Cæsar; in whose reign Vitellius, the governor of
Syria, when he visited Jerusalem, and was most magnificently received by the multitude, had a mind to make them
some requital for the kindness they had showed him; so,
upon their petition to have those holy vestments in their
own power, he wrote about them to Tiberius Cæsar, who
granted his request; and this power over the sacerdotal
vestments continued with the Jews till the death of king
Agrippa. And after him Cassius Longinus, who was
governor of Syria, and Cuspius Fadus, who was procurator
of Judæa, bade the Jews deposit those vestments in the
Tower of Antonia, on the plea that the Romans ought to
have them in their power, as they had formerly had. However, the Jews sent ambassadors to Claudius Cæsar, to
intercede with him as to this matter, on whose coming king
Agrippa, junior, being then at Rome, asked for and obtained power over them from the emperor, who ordered
Vitellius, who was then commander in Syria, to give it them
accordingly. Before that time, they were kept under the
seal of the high priest, and of the treasurers of the temple,
which treasurers, the day before a festival, went up to the

---

[1] The castle of Antonia; it is that to which St. Paul was taken for
safety. Acts xxiii. 10.

Roman commander of the fortress, and viewed their own seal, and received the vestments; and again, when the festival was over, brought them back to the same place, and showed the commander of the fortress their seal, which corresponded with his seal, and deposited them there. And that these things were so, the afflictions that happened to us afterwards [about them] are sufficient evidence. As for the tower itself, when Herod the king of the Jews had fortified it more firmly than before, in order to secure and guard the temple, he gave the Tower the name of Antonia, to gratify Antony, who was his friend and a ruler of the Romans.

§ 5. Now in the western part of the enclosure of the temple there were four gates; the first led to the king's palace, and went to a passage over the intermediate valley; two more led to the suburbs of the city; and the last led to the rest of the city, where the road descended down into the valley by a great number of steps, and thence up again to the ascent.[1] For the city lay opposite the temple like a theatre, and was encompassed with a deep valley along the entire south quarter. But the fourth front of the temple, facing south, had indeed itself gates in its midst, and over it the royal portico, which was triple and reached in length from the east valley unto that on the west, for it was impossible it should reach any further: and this portico deserves to be mentioned better than any other under the sun. For as the valley was very deep, and its bottom could not be seen if you looked from above into the depth, the high elevation of the portico stood upon that height, that if any one looked down from the top of the roof to those depths, he would be giddy, while his sight could not reach down to such an abyss. And there were pillars that stood in four rows one over-against the other all along (for the fourth row was interwoven into the wall, which was built of stone), and the thickness of each pillar was such, that three men might with their arms extended span it, and its length was twenty-seven feet, with a double spiral

[1] The first gate is that which led over 'Wilson's Arch' to the Upper City and Herod's palace; the last led over 'Robinson's Arch;' the remaining two are probably 'Barclay's Gate' and 'Warren's Gate,' in the west wall of the *Harâm Area* at Jerusalem.

at its base.   And the number of all the pillars was a hundred and sixty-two.   Their chapiters were made with
sculptures in the Corinthian style, that caused amazement
from the grandeur of the whole.   These four rows of pillars
included three intervals for walking in the middle of the
portico ; two of which walks were made parallel to each
other, and were contrived in the same manner ; the breadth
of each of them was thirty feet, the length a furlong,[1]
and the height above fifty feet, but the breadth of the
middle part of the cloister was one and a half of the other,
and the height was double, for it was much higher than
those on each side.   And the roofs were adorned with deep
carving in wood, representing many sorts of figures : the
middle was much higher than the rest, and the wall in front
was adorned with lintels, resting upon pillars that were
interwoven into it, and the front was all of polished stone ;
insomuch, that its fineness, to such as had not seen it, was
incredible, and to such as had seen it, was marvellous.
Such was the first enclosure, and in the midst, not far from
it, was the second, to be ascended to by a few steps ; this
was surrounded by a stone wall for a partition, with an
inscription forbidding any foreigner to enter under pain of
death.   Now, this inner enclosure had on its south and
north sides three gates, equi-distant from one another ; but
on the east side, towards the sunrising, there was one large
gate, through which such as were pure went in with
their wives.   But within was a sanctuary not open to the
women ; and still further within was there a third sanctuary, which it was not lawful for any but the priests to
enter.   The temple itself was within this, and before it was
the altar, upon which we offer our sacrifices and burnt-
offerings to God   Into none of these three did king Herod
enter, for he was forbidden because he was not a priest.
However, he laboured at the porticoes, and the outer en-
closures, and these he built in eight years.

§ 6.  And the temple itself was built by the priests in a
year and six months, upon which all the people were full

---

[1] The royal cloister commenced at the S.W. angle of the *Harâm
Area*, and ran for 600 feet along its southern wall.   The approach to
the central aisle, from the west, was over ' Robinson's Arch,' the ruins
of which were found by Sir C. Warren during his excavations.

of joy, and returned thanks in the first place to God for the speed with which it was finished, and in the next place for the zeal the king had shown, feasting and celebrating this rebuilding of the temple. As for the king, he sacrificed three hundred oxen to God, as did the rest, every one according to his ability; the number of which sacrifices is not possible to be set down, for it cannot be that we should truly relate it. For at the same time as this celebration of the work about the temple, fell also the day of the king's inauguration, which he kept of old as a festival, and it now coincided with the other, which coincidence of both made the festival most notable.

§ 7. There was also an underground passage built for the king, which led from Antonia to the inner temple to its eastern gate, above which he also erected for himself a tower, that he might have the opportunity of an underground ascent to the temple, in order to guard against any rebellion which might be made by the people against their kings. It is also reported that, during the time that the temple was building, it did not rain in the daytime, but showers fell in the night, so that the work was not hindered. And this our fathers have handed down to us, nor is it incredible, if any one looks to the other manifestations of God. And thus was performed the work of the rebuilding of the temple.

# BOOK XVI.

## CHAP. I.

*A Law of Herod about Housebreakers. Salome and Phe-
roras calumniate Alexander and Aristobulus upon their
Return from Rome, for whom Herod yet provides Wives.*

### § 1.

AS king Herod was very zealous in the administration
of all his affairs, and desirous to put a stop to particular acts of injustice which were done by criminals in
the city and country, he made a law no way like our
original laws, which he enacted of himself, to sell housebreakers to be taken out of his kingdom, which punishment
was not only grievous to be borne by the offenders, but
contained in it an infringement of the customs of our
forefathers. For slavery to foreigners and such as did
not live after the manner of the Jews, and necessity to do
whatever such men should command, was an offence
against our religion rather than a punishment to such as
were found to have offended, such a punishment being
avoided in our original laws. For those laws ordained
that the thief should restore fourfold, and if he had not so
much, he should be sold indeed, but not to foreigners, nor
so as to be in perpetual slavery, for he had to be released
after six years. But this law, thus enacted in order to
introduce a severe and illegal punishment, seemed to be a
piece of arrogance in Herod, as he did not act as a king
but as a tyrant, and thus contemptuously, and without
any regard to his subjects, ventured to introduce such a
punishment. Now this penalty, thus brought into practice, was like Herod's other actions, and became one of

the charges brought against him, and caused hatred to himself.

§ 2. Now at this time it was that he sailed to Italy, being very desirous to meet Augustus, and to see his own sons who lived at Rome. And Augustus was not only very obliging to him in other respects, but delivered him his sons again, that he might take them home with him, as they had already completed their education. And as soon as the young men returned from Italy, the people were very desirous to see them, and they became the observed of all observers, being adorned with great blessings of fortune, and having the countenances of persons of royal dignity. So they at once appeared to be the objects of envy to Salome the king's sister, and to those who had done Mariamne to death with their calumnies; for they were suspicious, that when these sons of her's came to the throne, they should be punished for the wickedness they had been guilty of against their mother. So they made this very fear of theirs a motive to raise calumnies against them also; and gave it out that they were not pleased with their father's company, because he had put their mother to death, as if it did not appear agreeable to piety to live with their mother's murderer. Now, by retailing these stories, that were untrue [1] and only built on probabilities, they were able to do them mischief, and to take away that kindness from his sons which Herod had before borne to them. For they did not say these things to him outright, but scattered abroad such words among the multitude generally; from which words, when carried to Herod, hatred was by degrees generated, which natural affection itself, even by length of time, was not able to overcome. Yet did the king at this period prefer the natural affection of a father to all the suspicions and calumnies his sons lay under; and he honoured them as he ought to do, and married them to wives, now they were grown up. To Aristobulus he gave for wife Berenice Salome's daughter, and to Alexander Glaphyra, the daughter of Archelaus king of Cappadocia.

[1] I read ἄπο.

## CHAP. II.

*How Herod twice sailed to Agrippa; and how, upon the complaint of the Jews in Ionia against the Greeks, Agrippa confirmed the Laws of the Jews to them.*

### § 1.

WHEN Herod had despatched these affairs, on hearing that Marcus Agrippa had sailed again from Italy to Asia, he hasted to him, and besought him to come to his kingdom, and receive that welcome he might justly expect from one that had been his guest and friend. This request he urgently pressed, and Agrippa agreed to it, and came into Judæa. And Herod omitted nothing that might please him, but entertained him in his new-built cities, and showed him the edifices he had built, and provided all sorts of the best and most costly dainties for him and his friends, and showed him Sebaste, and the port that he had built at Cæsarea, and the fortresses which he had erected at great expense, as Alexandrium [1] and Herodium [2] and Hyrcania. He also conducted him to the city of Jerusalem, where all the people met him in their festival garments, and received him with acclamations. Agrippa also offered a hecatomb to God, and feasted the people, without omitting any of the greatest dainties. As for himself he enjoyed himself so much there, that he abode many days with them, and would willingly have stayed longer, but that the season of the year made him haste away; for, as winter was coming on, he thought it not safe to sail later, as he was obliged to return again to Ionia.

§ 2. So Agrippa sailed away, after Herod had bestowed many presents on him, and on the chief persons of his suite. And king Herod, when he had passed the winter in his own dominions, made haste to join him again in the spring, as he knew he meant to go on a campaign to the Bosphorus. So when he had sailed by Rhodes and Cos, he touched at Lesbos,[3] thinking he should find

---

[1] *Kefr Istûna.*                    [2] *Jebel Fureidis.*
[3] The island now called Mytilene, from the name of its principal town.

Agrippa there, but he was delayed there by a north wind,
which hindered his ship from entering port. So he continued many days at Chios, and there he kindly treated a
great many that came to him, and obliged them by giving
them royal gifts; and when he saw that the portico of the
city was fallen down (which, as it was overthrown in the
Mithridatic war, and was a very large and fine building,
was not so easy to rebuild as the rest) he furnished
a sum not only large enough for that purpose, but
more than sufficient to finish the building, and ordered
them not to neglect that portico, but to rebuild it quickly,
that so the city might recover its principal ornament.
And when the wind ceased, he sailed to Mytilene,[1] and
thence to Byzantium;[2] and when he heard that Agrippa
had sailed beyond the Cyanean rocks,[3] he made all the
haste possible to overtake him, and came up with him
at Sinope[4] in Pontus. He was sighted by the fleet most
unexpectedly, but appeared to their great joy; and many
friendly greetings passed between Agrippa and him, for
Agrippa thought he had received the greatest marks of
Herod's kindness and affection towards him possible, since
he had come so long a voyage, and at a very fit season for
his assistance, and had left the administration of his own
dominions, and thought it better worth his while to come to
him. Accordingly, Herod was all in all to Agrippa in the
management of the war, and a great assistant in civil
affairs, and in giving advice as to particular matters. He
was also a pleasant companion for Agrippa when he relaxed
himself, and a partner with him in all things, in difficulties because of his good-will, and in prosperity because
of the respect Agrippa had for him. Now as soon as they
had finished those affairs in Pontus, for which Agrippa
was sent there, they did not think fit to return by sea, but
passed through Paphlagonia and Cappadocia, and travelled

---

[1] The chief town of Lesbos; it is now called *Castro*, and faces the
mainland.

[2] The old name of Constantinople.

[3] The islands off the mouth of the Bosphorus; Strabo calls them
"two little isles, one upon the European, and the other on the Asiatic
side of the strait, separated from each other by twenty stadia."

[4] On the north coast of Asia Minor, now *Sinúb*.

thence by land over great Phrygia, and came to Ephesus, and then sailed across from Ephesus to Samos. And indeed Herod bestowed a great many benefits on every city that he came to, according as they stood in need of them; for as for those that wanted either money or kind treatment, he was not wanting to them, but supplied the former himself at his own expense; he also became an intercessor with Agrippa for all such as sought after his favour, and he so managed that the petitioners failed in none of their suits to him, Agrippa being himself of a good disposition, and of great generosity, and ready to grant all such requests as might be advantageous to the petitioners, provided they were not to the detriment of others. The inclination of Herod was of very great weight to stimulate Agrippa, who was himself not slow to do good; for he made a reconciliation between him and the people of Ilium,[1] with whom he was angry, and paid the money the people of Chios owed Augustus' agents, and relieved them of their tribute; and helped all others according as their several necessities required.

§ 3. But now when Agrippa and Herod were in Ionia, a great number of Jews, who dwelt in their cities, came to them, and seizing the opportunity and freedom now given them, laid before them the injuries which they suffered, as they were not permitted to use their own laws, but were compelled to prosecute their lawsuits by the ill-usage of the judges upon their holy days, and were deprived of the money they used to send to Jerusalem, and were forced into the army and into other services, and obliged to spend their sacred money, from which burdens they always used to be freed by the Romans, who had still permitted them to live according to their own laws. As they vociferated this, the king desired of Agrippa that he would hear their cause, and assigned Nicolaus, one of his friends, to plead for their privileges. Accordingly, when Agrippa had called the principal of the Romans, and such of the kings and rulers as were there, to be his assessors, Nicolaus stood up, and pleaded for the Jews as follows.

§ 4. "It is of necessity incumbent, most mighty

---

[1] Troy, *Hissarlik*.

Agrippa, on all who are in distress to have recourse to those that have it in their power to free them from injury, and those that are now your suppliants, approach you with great assurance. For as they have formerly often found you what they wished, they now only entreat that you, who have been the donors, will take care that those favours you have already granted them shall not be taken away from them. We have received these favours from you, who alone have power to grant them, but have them taken from us by such as are no greater than ourselves, and by such as know they are as much subjects as we are. And certainly, if persons have been vouchsafed great favours, it is to their commendation who have obtained them, as having been found deserving of such great favours; and if those favours be but small ones, it is dishonourable for the donors not to confirm them. And as to those that thwart the Jews and use them ill, it is evident that they affront not only the receivers of these favours, as they will not allow those to be worthy men to whom their excellent rulers themselves have borne testimony, but also the donors, as they desire that those favours already granted may be abrogated. Now if any one were to ask them which of the two they would rather part with, their lives, or the customs of their forefathers, as their solemn processions, their sacrifices, and their festivals, which they celebrate in honour of those they suppose to be gods, I know very well that they would choose to suffer anything whatever, rather than to give up any of the customs of their forefathers. For most choose rather to go to war on that account, being very solicitous not to transgress in such matters: and indeed we measure that happiness which all mankind do now enjoy owing to you by this very thing, that we are allowed every one to worship and live as our institutions require. And although they would not like to be thus treated themselves, yet do they endeavour to compel others to comply with them, as if it were not as great an instance of impiety, to profanely dissolve the religious solemnities of others, as to be negligent in the observance of their own duty towards their gods. And now let us consider another case. Is there any people or city, or community of men, to whom your

government and the Roman power does not appear to be
the greatest blessing? Is there any one that can desire to
make void the favours thence proceeding? No one is
certainly so mad: for there are no men who have not been
partakers of those favours both publicly and privately;
and indeed those that take away what you have granted,
can have no assurance but that every one of their own
grants made them by you may be taken from them also.
And yet these grants of yours can never be sufficiently
valued; for if people were to compare the old government
under kings with the present government, besides the
great number of benefits which this government has bestowed on them for their happiness, this is above all the
rest, that they appear to be no longer in a state of slavery
but of freedom. Now our circumstances, even at the
best, are not such as deserve to be envied, for we are
indeed in a prosperous state through you, but only in
common with all others; and we desire no more than this,
to preserve our national religion without any prohibition;
which as it appears not in itself a privilege to be grudged
us, so is it for the advantage of those that grant it to us;
for if the divinity delights in being honoured, he delights
also in those that permit him to be honoured. And there
are none of our customs which are inhuman, but all are
pious and devoted to the preservation of justice; nor do
we conceal these precepts of ours, by which we govern our
lives, as they are suggesters of piety, and of friendliness
to men: and the seventh day we set apart from labour for
the learning of our customs and laws,[1] as we think it proper
to reflect on them, as well as on any [good] thing else, in
order to avoid sin. If any one, therefore, examine our
customs, he will find that they are good in themselves, and
that they are ancient also, though some think otherwise,
so that those who have received them cannot easily be
brought to depart from them, from the honour they pay
to the length of time they have religiously observed them.

---

[1] We may here observe the ancient practice of the Jews, of dedicating
the Sabbath-day not to idleness, but to the learning their sacred rites
and religious customs, and to meditation on the law of Moses. The
like to which we meet with elsewhere in Josephus, as Against Apion,
i. § 22.—W.

Now our adversaries are for unjustly taking our privileges
away, they violently seize upon that money of ours which
is offered to God, and called sacred money, and that
openly in a sacrilegious manner; and they impose tribute
upon us, and bring us before tribunals and make us do
other services on holy days, not because the laws require
it, or for their own advantage, but because they would put
an affront on our religion, which they know as well as we,
indulging themselves in an unjust and involuntary hatred.
For your government over all your subjects is one, and tends
to the establishing of benevolence and abolishing of ill-
will among such as are disposed to it.  This then is what
we implore of thee, most mighty Agrippa, that we may not
be ill-treated; that we may not be abused; that we may
not be hindered from following our own customs; nor be
despoiled of our goods; nor be forced by these men to do
what we ourselves do not force them to do: for these
privileges of ours are not only according to justice, but
have also been granted us by you.  And we are able to
read to you many decrees of the senate, and the tablets
that contain them, which are still extant in the Capitol,
concerning these things, which it is evident were granted
after you had experience of our fidelity towards you, and
which would be valid, even if no such fidelity had previously been shown by us.  For you have hitherto preserved
what people were in possession of, not to us only but to
almost all men, and have added greater advantages than
they could have hoped for, and thereby your sway has become a great advantage to them.  And if any one were to
enumerate the benefits you have conferred on every nation,
he would never put an end to his discourse; but that we
may prove that we are not unworthy of all those advantages we have obtained, it will be sufficient for us to say
nothing of other things, but to speak freely of the king
who now governs us, and is one of thy assessors.  For
indeed, in what instance of good-will, as to your house,
has he been deficient?  What mark of fidelity to it has
he omitted?  What token of honour has he not devised?
What occasion of assisting you has he not regarded first?
What hinders, therefore, but that your kindnesses may be
as numerous as his so great benefits to you have been?

It may also perhaps be fit here not to pass over in silence the valour of his father Antipater, who, when Cæsar made an expedition into Egypt, assisted him with two thousand armed men, and proved second to none, either in the battles on land, or in the management of the fleet. And what need to say anything of the great importance those soldiers were at that juncture? or how many and how great presents they were vouchsafed by Cæsar? And truly I ought before now to have mentioned the letters which Cæsar wrote to the senate at that time, and how Antipater had public honours, and the freedom of the city of Rome bestowed upon him. For these are proofs that we have received these favours by our own deserts, and so we petition thee for thy confirmation of them, from whom we should have had reason to hope for them, even though they had not been given us before, looking both to our king's disposition towards you, and your disposition towards him. We have also been informed by those Jews, that were there, with what kindness thou camest into our country, and how thou offeredst perfect sacrifices to God, and honoured him with perfect vows, and how thou gavest the people a feast, and didst accept their own hospitable presents to thee. We ought to esteem all these kind entertainments made both by our nation and city to a man who has management of so much of the public affairs, as indications of that friendship which thou feelest in return to the Jewish nation, and which has been procured them by the family of Herod. So we put thee in mind of these things, in the presence of the king now sitting by thee, and make our request for no more but this, that what you have given us yourselves, you will not see taken away from us by others."

§ 5. When Nicolaus had made this speech, there was no opposition made to it by the Greeks, for this was not an inquiry made as in a court of justice, but a petition to prevent violence being offered to the Jews any longer. Nor did the Greeks deny that they had done so, but their excuse was that as the Jews inhabited their country, they were entirely unjust to them [in not joining in their worship]. But the Jews proved that they were natives, and that, though they worshipped according to their own institu-

tions, they did nothing to harm them. So Agrippa, perceiving that they had been oppressed by violence, made
the following answer: that because of Herod's good-will
and friendship, he was ready to grant the Jews whatever
they should ask him, and that their requests seemed to
him in themselves just; and that if they requested anything further, he should not scruple to grant it them,
provided it was no way to the detriment of the Roman
empire; and that, while their request was no more than
this, that the privileges they had already had given them
might not be abrogated, he confirmed this to them, that
they might continue in the observance of their own customs, without any one offering them injury." And when
he had said this, he dissolved the assembly; upon which
Herod stood up, and saluted him, and gave him thanks
for the kind disposition he showed to them. Agrippa took
this in a very obliging manner, and saluted him back, and
embraced him, and then left Lesbos.[1] But Herod determined to sail homewards, and when he had taken his leave
of Agrippa, he set sail, and landed at Cæsarea[2] in a few
days' time, having favourable winds, from whence he went
to Jerusalem, and there gathered all the people together to
an assembly, not a few being there from the country also.
So he came forward, and gave a particular account of all his
journey, and of the affairs of all the Jews in Asia, and how
owing to him they would live without injurious treatment
for the time to come. He also told them of all the good
fortune he had met with, and how he had administered the
government, and had not neglected anything which was
for their advantage; and as he was very joyful, he now
remitted to them the fourth part of their taxes for the last
year. And they were so pleased with his favour and
speech to them, that they went their ways with great
gladness, and wished the king all manner of happiness.

[1] The island of *Mytilene.*
[2] Cæsarea Palæstina, *Kaisariyeh.*

## CHAP. III.

*How great Disturbances arose in Herod's Family because of*
*his preferring Antipater, his eldest Son, to the rest, and*
*how Alexander took that Injury very much to heart.*

### § 1.

BUT now the affairs in Herod's family grew to more disorder, and became worse and worse, from the hatred
of Salome to the young men [Alexander and Aristobulus],
which descended as it were by inheritance [from their mother
Mariamne]; and as she had completely succeeded against
their mother, so she proceeded to that degree of reckless
daring as to endeavour that none of her posterity might
be left alive, who might have it in their power to revenge
her murder. The young men had also somewhat of a
haughty and ill-affected air towards their father, occasioned
by the remembrance of what their mother had unjustly
suffered, and by their own desire for reigning. The old
grudge was again renewed, and they cast reproaches on
Salome and Pheroras, who requited the young men with
malice and laid treacherous snares for them. As for this
hatred, it was equal on both sides, but the manner of
showing it was different; for as for the young men they
were rash, reproaching and affronting Salome and Pheroras
openly, being inexperienced enough to think it most noble
to declare their minds in that frank manner; but Salome
and Pheroras did not take that method, but made use of
calumnies in subtle and spiteful manner, provoking the
young men on every occasion, and imagining that their boldness might in time come to offering violence to their father.
For inasmuch as they were not ashamed of the pretended
crimes of their mother, and thought she suffered unjustly,
Salome and Pheroras supposed that their feelings might at
length exceed all bounds, and might induce them to think
they ought to be avenged on their father, even though
they despatched him with their own hands. At last it
came to this, that the whole city was full of talk of this
kind, and, as is usual in such contests, the inexperience of
the young men was pitied, but the contrivance of Salome

was too much for them, and the imputations she laid upon them came to be believed owing to their own conduct. For they were so deeply affected at the death of their mother, that while they said both she and themselves were in a miserable case, they vehemently complained of her pitiable end, which indeed was truly such, and said that they were themselves in a pitiable case also, because they were forced to live with those that had been her murderers, and likely to experience the same treatment.

§ 2. These family feuds increased greatly, and the king's absence abroad afforded a fit opportunity for their increase. And as soon as Herod had returned, and had made his speech to the multitude, Pheroras and Salome immediately let fall words as if he were in great danger, and as if the young men openly threatened that they would not spare him any longer, but revenge their mother's death upon him. They also added another circumstance, that their hopes were fixed on Archelaus, the king of Cappadocia, that they should be able through him to go to Augustus and accuse their father. Herod was immediately disturbed at hearing such things, and indeed was the more dismayed because the same things were related to him by some other persons also. This recalled to his mind his former calamity, and he reflected that family troubles had hindered him from enjoying any comfort from those that were dearest to him, and from his wife whom he loved so well; and suspecting that his future troubles would be even heavier and greater than those that were past, he was in great confusion of mind. For divine Providence had indeed conferred upon him a great many outward advantages for his happiness, even beyond his hopes, but the troubles he had at home were such as he had never expected to have met with, and rendered him unfortunate; nay, both good and bad fortune happened to him more than one could have anticipated, and made it a doubtful question, whether, upon the comparison of both, it was desirable to have had so much success in outward things with such great misfortunes at home, or whether it would not have been better to avoid family troubles, though he had never possessed the admired grandeur of a kingdom.

§ 3. As he was thus embarrassed and unhappy, in order to put down these young men, he summoned to his court another of his sons, that was born to him when he was a private individual (whose name was Antipater), but he did not indulge him then as he did afterwards, when he was quite mastered by him, and let him do everything he pleased, but rather in the design of repressing the insolence of the sons of Mariamne, and managing this elevation of his so, that it might be for a warning to them; for their audacity would not (he thought) be so great, if they were once persuaded that the succession to the kingdom did not appertain to them alone, or need of necessity come to them. So he introduced Antipater as their rival, and imagined this a good plan for abating their pride, and that after this was done to the young men, there might be a likelihood of their being of a better disposition. But the event proved other than he expected. For the young men thought he had done them a very great injury, and as Antipater was a shrewd man, when he had once obtained this position, and begun to expect greater things than he had before hoped for, he had but one design, and that was to hurt his brothers, and not to yield them the pre-eminence, but to stick to his father, who was already alienated from them by calumnies, and easy to be worked upon in any way his zeal against them urged him to pursue, that he might be continually more and more severe against them. Accordingly, all the reports that were spread abroad came from him, while he avoided himself the suspicion of those discoveries coming from him, for he mainly used those persons as his creatures who were unsuspected, and such as might be believed to speak truth because of the good-will they bore to the king. And indeed there were already not a few who paid court to Antipater in hopes of gaining somewhat by him, and these were the men who most of all persuaded Herod, because they appeared to speak thus out of their good-will to him. And while these accusations from various sources corroborated each other, the young men themselves afforded further occasion for suspicion. For they were observed to shed tears often, on account of the dishonour that was done them, and often had their mother in their mouths, and among their friends

openly ventured to reproach their father as not acting
justly by them; all which things were with an evil intention kept in memory by Antipater for a fit season, and
when they were repeated to Herod with exaggerations,
increased very much the family troubles. For as the king
was very angry at what was alleged against the sons of
Mariamne, and was desirous to humble them, he still increased the honours that he bestowed on Antipater; and
was at last so much under his influence that he actually
brought his mother to court. He also wrote frequently to
Augustus in his favour, and most earnestly recommended
him to him. And when Agrippa was returning to
Rome, after he had finished his ten years' government in
Asia, Herod sailed from Judæa, and when he met with
Agrippa, he had none with him but Antipater, whom he
delivered to him, that he might take him along with him,
together with many presents, that so he might become
Augustus' friend; insomuch, that things already looked as
if he had all his father's favour, and that the young men
were entirely shut out of any hopes of the kingdom.


## CHAP. IV.

*How, during Antipater's Abode at Rome, Herod brought
Alexander and Aristobulus before Augustus, and accused
them. Alexander's Defence of himself before Augustus,
and Reconciliation with his Father.*

### § 1.

AND now what happened during Antipater's absence
augmented the honour to which he had been promoted,
and his apparent eminence above his brothers, for he made
a great figure in Rome, because Herod had recommended
him by letter to all his friends there. Only he was grieved
that he was not at home, and had no opportunities for
perpetually calumniating his brothers; and his chief fear
was, lest his father should alter his mind, and entertain
a more favourable opinion of the sons of Mariamne.
And as he had this in his mind, he did not desist from his

purpose, but continually sent from Rome any such stories
as he hoped might grieve and irritate his father against his
brothers, under pretence indeed of a deep concern for his
preservation, but in truth, such as his malignity suggested,
in order to add to his hope of the succession, which yet
was already great in itself; and thus he did till he had
excited such a degree of anger and indignation in Herod,
that he was already become very ill-disposed towards the
young men. But as he shrank from publicly showing his
violent disgust with them, that he might not either be too
remiss or too rash, and so offend, he thought it best to sail
to Rome, and there accuse his sons before Augustus, and
not to indulge himself in any such act as might from its
enormity be suspected of impiety. And on his going up
to Rome, it happened that he hastened to meet Augustus
at the city of Aquileia; [1] and when he came to speech with
Augustus, he asked for a time for hearing this great cause,
wherein he thought himself very miserable, and produced
his sons there, and accused them of their desperate conspiracy against him. He said that they were enemies to
him, and did their utmost to show their hatred to him their
father, and wished to take away his life in the most barbarous manner, and so obtain his kingdom, which he had
authority from Cæsar to dispose of, not by necessity but
by choice, to him who should show the greatest piety towards him. He said also that his sons were not so desirous of ruling, as they were (upon being disappointed
thereof) to expose their own lives, if they might but deprive
their father of his life, so wild and polluted had their minds
become from their hatred to him. And whereas he had a
long time borne this misfortune, he was now compelled (he
said) to lay it before Augustus, and to pollute his ears with
the hearing of it. And yet what severity had they ever
suffered from him? or what hardships had he ever laid
upon them to make them complain of him? and how could
they think it just, that he should not be lord of that kingdom, which he had gained in a long time and with great
danger, and that they should not allow him to keep it,
and dispose of it to him who should deserve best? And

[1] The modern *Aquileia*, near the head of the Adriatic. It was the
capital of the province of Venetia.

that, with other advantages, he proposed as a reward for
the piety of such a one as would hereafter imitate the
care he had taken of it, and such a one would gain so
great a requital. But it was an impious thing for them
to intrigue for it beforehand, for he who had ever the
kingdom in his view, at the same time reckoned on the
death of his father, because otherwise he could not come
to the throne. As for himself, he had hitherto given
them all that he was able, and all that was fit for such as
were subject to royal authority, and were the sons of a
king, pomp and servants, and delicate fare, and had married them into the most illustrious families, Aristobulus
to his sister's daughter, and Alexander to the daughter
of king Archelaus. And what was the greatest favour of
all, though their crimes were so very bad, and he had
authority to punish them, yet had he not made use of it
against them, but had brought them before Augustus, their
common benefactor, and had not used the severity which
he might have done, either as a father who had been impiously treated, or as a king who had been conspired against,
but made them stand upon the same level as himself in
judgment. Lastly he said that it was necessary that all
this should not be passed over without punishment, nor he
himself live in the greatest fears; nay, that it was not for
their own advantage to see the light of the sun after what
they had aimed at, even if they should escape that time,
since they had done the vilest things that ever were known
among mankind, and would certainly suffer the greatest
punishment.

§ 2. These were the accusations which Herod brought
with great vehemence against his sons before Augustus.
Now the young men wept and were in confusion while he
was speaking, and still more at his concluding. As to themselves, they knew in their own consciences that they were
innocent, but because they were accused by their father, they
knew, as was indeed the case, that it was hard for them to
make their apology, since though they were at liberty to
speak their minds freely as the occasion required, and
might with force and earnestness refute their father's
accusation, yet it was not now decent so to do. There was
therefore a difficulty how they should be able to speak,

and tears and at last deep groans followed, for they were
afraid, if they said nothing, that they should seem to be in
this difficulty from a consciousness of guilt, nor had they
any defence ready because of their youth and the alarm
they were in.   Nor did Augustus fail to perceive, when
he saw the confusion they were in, that their delay to make
their defence did not arise from any consciousness of
crime, but from their unskilfulness and modesty.   They
were also commiserated by those who were present, nay
they privately moved their father with genuine emotion.

§ 3. So when they saw there was a kind disposition both in
him and Augustus, and that every one else present did
either shed tears, or at least sympathize with them, the
one of them, whose name was Alexander, addressed his
father, and attempted to answer his accusations, and said,
" O father, the benevolence thou hast shown to us is
evident, even in this very judicial procedure, for hadst
thou had any bad intentions in regard to us, thou wouldst
not have produced us here before the common saviour of all.
For it was in thy power, both as a king and as a father, to
punish the guilty, but by thus bringing us to Rome, and
making Augustus himself a witness to what is done, thou
intimatest that thou intendest to save us, for no one that
has a design to slay a man will bring him to temples and
sanctuaries.   But our circumstances are still worse, for
we cannot endure to live any longer, if it be believed
that we have injured such a father; nay, perhaps, it
would be worse for us to live with this suspicion upon
us, that we have injured him, than to die innocent.   But
if our bold defence be received as true, we shall be happy,
both in persuading thee, and in escaping the danger we are
in, but if this calumny still prevails, it is more than enough
for us that we have seen the sun this day, for why should
we see it with this suspicion fixed upon us?   Now, it is easy
to say of young men, that they desire to reign, and to add
charges about our unhappy mother, is abundantly sufficient
to produce our present misfortune out of the former.   But
consider well, whether such an accusation does not suit all
young men, and may not be said of them all promiscuously?
For nothing can hinder him that reigns, if he have children, and their mother be dead, but that he may have

a suspicion of all his sons, as intending some treachery against him; but a mere suspicion is not sufficient to prove such impiety. Now let any man say, whether we have actually dared to attempt any such things as would make actions otherwise incredible to appear credible. Can anyone prove the preparation of poison, or a conspiracy of our comrades, or the corruption of servants, or letters written against thee? though indeed there are none of those things but have sometimes been invented by calumny, though they were never done. For a royal family that is at variance with itself is a terrible thing; and the throne, which thou callest a reward of piety, often excites in very wicked men such hopes as make them draw back from no criminality. However no one will actually lay any crime to our charge. And as to calumny, how can he put an end to it, who will not hear what we have to say? Have we talked with too great freedom? not against thee, for that would be wrong, but against those that never conceal anything that is spoken to them. Have either of us lamented our mother? yes, but not because she is dead, but because she was ill spoken of by unworthy persons. Are we desirous of the throne which we know our father is possessed of? For what reason can we be so? if we already have royal honours, as we have, should we not labour in vain? And if we have them not, yet are not we in hope of them? Or supposing that we had killed thee, could we expect to obtain thy kingdom? why, neither the earth would let us tread upon it, nor the sea let us sail upon it, after such an action as that: nay, the religion of all your subjects, and the piety of the whole nation, would have prevented parricides from being at the head of affairs, and from entering into the most holy temple built by thee. And suppose we had made light of other dangers, can any murderer go off unpunished, while Augustus is alive? We are thy sons, and not so impious or thoughtless as that, though perhaps more unfortunate than was well for thee. But if thou neither findest any causes of complaint, nor any treacherous designs, what sufficient evidence hast thou to make such wickedness credible? Our mother is dead indeed, but what befell her would be an instruction to us to caution, and not an incitement to wickedness.  We are willing to make a longer apology for ourselves, but actions never done do not admit of argument.  Wherefore we make this agreement with thee before Augustus, the lord of all, as mediator now between us : if thou, O father, canst bring thyself by the evidence of truth to have a mind free from suspicion concerning us, let us live, though even then we shall not be happy ; for to be accused of great acts of wickedness, though falsely, is a terrible thing ; but if thou hast any fear remaining, continue thou in thy pious life, we will see to ourselves,[1] our life is not so desirable to us as for us to wish to have it, if it tend to the harm of our father who gave it us."

§ 4. When Alexander had thus spoken, Augustus, who did not even before believe so grave a charge, was still more moved, and looked intently upon Herod, and perceived he was a little confused ; and the persons present were in anxiety about the young men, and the fame that was spread abroad at court made the king hated.  For the incredibility of the charge, and the pity felt for the young men, who were in the flower of youth and beauty of body, inspired sympathy, and the more so because Alexander had made his defence with dexterity and prudence.  Nay, the young men themselves did not any longer continue in their former guise, bedewed with tears and with eyes cast down to the ground, for now there arose in them a hope of better things, and the king himself appeared not to have had foundation enough to build such an accusation upon, he having no real evidence to convict them, so that some apology seemed required from him.  But Augustus, after some delay, said, that although the young men were innocent of that with which they had been charged, yet they had been to blame for not having demeaned themselves towards their father so as to prevent the suspicion which was spread abroad concerning them.  He also exhorted Herod to lay aside all such suspicion and to be reconciled to his sons ; for it was not just to give any credit to such reports concerning his own children ; and this change of mind on both sides might not only heal those breaches that had happened between them, but might even

---

[1] A euphemism for committing suicide.

improve their good-will to one another, whereby on both sides, apologizing for the rashness of their suspicions, they might resolve to feel more affection towards each other than they had before. After Augustus had given them this admonition, he beckoned to the young men, and when they were disposed to fall down at their father's feet, he took them up, and embraced them, in tears as they were, and took each of them in turn into his arms, till not one of those that were present, whether freeman or slave, but was deeply affected.

§ 5. Then did they return thanks to Augustus, and went away together, and with them went Antipater, who hypocritically pretended that he rejoiced at this reconciliation. And on the following days Herod made Augustus a present of three hundred talents, as he was then exhibiting shows, and bestowing largesses on the people of Rome; and Augustus made him a present of half the revenue of the copper mines in Cyprus, and committed the care of the other half to him, and honoured him with other gifts and incomes: and as to his kingdom, he left it in his own power to appoint which of his sons he pleased as his successor, or to distribute it in parts to each, that the royal rank might so come to them all. And when Herod was disposed to make such a settlement at once, Augustus said that he would not give him leave to deprive himself, while he was alive, of the power over his kingdom, or over his sons.

§ 6. After this Herod returned to Judæa again. But during his absence from home, the Trachonites, no small part of his dominions, had revolted, but the commanders he left there had vanquished them, and compelled them to submission again. Now, as Herod was sailing with his sons, and put in near Cilicia at Elæusa, which has now had its name changed to Sebaste,[1] he met with Archelaus king of Cappadocia, who received him kindly, and rejoiced that he was reconciled to his sons, and that the accusation against Alexander, who had married his daughter, was at an end. They also made one another such presents as it became

[1] The island and town of Elæusa, called Sebaste, was near the river *Lamas*, on the south-east coast of Asia Minor. It is now a small peninsula covered with ruins, and connected with the main land by an isthmus of sand.

kings to make. From thence Herod went to Judæa, and
to the temple, where he made a speech to the people, concerning what had been done during his absence from home,
telling them about Augustus' kindness to him, and about as
many of the particular things he had done, as he thought
it for his advantage they should be acquainted with. At
last he turned his speech to the admonition of his sons, and
exhorted the courtiers and the multitude to concord, and
informed them, that his sons were to reign after him,
Antipater first, and then Alexander and Aristobulus, the
sons of Mariamne; but at present he desired that they
should all pay court to himself, and esteem him king and
lord of all, since he was not yet effete from old age, but
was at that period of life when he was most skilful in
governing, and that he was not deficient in other arts that
might enable him to govern the kingdom well, and to rule
over his children also. He also told the rulers and soldiers, that in case they looked to him alone, they would
pass their lives in tranquillity, and would make one another
happy. And when he had said this, he dismissed the assembly. His speech was acceptable to most of the audience,
but not to some, for the contention among his sons, and
the hopes he had given them, occasioned thoughts and
desires of innovation among some of them.

## CHAP. V.

*How Herod celebrated Games, to take place every fifth Year,
upon the Building of Cæsarea; and how he built and
adorned many other Places in a magnificent manner; and
how he did many other Actions gloriously.*

### § 1.

ABOUT this time Cæsarea Sebaste, which Herod had
built, was finished. The entire building being concluded in the tenth year, the solemnity of it fell in the
twenty-eighth year of Herod's reign, and in the hundred
and ninety-second Olympiad. There was accordingly a
great festival, and most sumptuous preparations were made

at once for its dedication.  For the king appointed contests in music and athletic exercises, and also got ready a
great number of gladiators, and of beasts for like purpose :
horse races also, and the most costly of such sports and
shows as used to be exhibited at Rome and in other places.
He consecrated these contests to Cæsar Augustus, and
ordered them to be celebrated every fifth year.  He also
provided all the apparatus for it at his own expense, to set
off his liberality; and Julia, the Emperor's wife, sent a
great part of her most costly things privately from Rome,
insomuch that he had no want of anything.  The sum of
them all was estimated at five hundred talents.  Now
when a great multitude was come to Cæsarea, to see the
shows, as well as the ambassadors whom various people
sent because of the benefits they had received from Herod,
he entertained them all in the public inns, and at public
tables, and with perpetual feasts, the festival having in
the day-time the attractions of the fights, and in the night-
time such merry-making as cost vast sums of money, and
publicly demonstrated the greatness of his soul, for in all
his undertakings he was ambitious to exhibit what exceeded
whatever had been done before.  And they say that
Augustus himself and Agrippa often said, that the dominions of Herod were too little for the greatness of his
soul, for he deserved to have the kingdom of all Syria, and
of Egypt also.

§ 2.  After this solemnity and these festivals were over,
Herod erected another city in the plain which is called
Capharsaba, where he chose out a fit place, both for plenty
of water and goodness of soil for what was there planted,
as a river encompassed the city itself, and a grove of the
best trees for size was round about it.  This he named
Antipatris after his father Antipater.[1]  He also built, upon
another spot of ground above Jericho, a place of great
security, and very pleasant for habitation, and called it
Cypros [2] after the name of his mother.  He also dedicated
the finest monument to his brother Phasaelus, on account of

---

[1] Now *Râs el-'Ain*, near the point at which the Roman road from
Jerusalem to Cæsarea left the hills for the plain
[2] Possibly *Beit Jubr et-Tahtâni*.  See Jewish War, i. 21, §§ 4, 9; ii.
18, § 6.

the great natural affection there had been between them, by
erecting a tower in the city itself, not smaller than the
tower of Pharos,[1] which he called Phasaelus, which was at
once a part of the defences of the city and a memorial of
him that was deceased, because it bore his name. He also
built a city which he called after him in the valley of
Jericho, as you go from it northwards, whereby he rendered
the neighbouring country more fruitful, by the cultivation
which its inhabitants introduced; and this he called
Phasaelis.[2]

§ 3. As for his other benefits, it is impossible to reckon
up those which he bestowed on cities both in Syria and in
Greece, and in all the places he went to in his travels. For
he seems to have contributed very liberally to many public
burdens and to the building of public works, and furnished the money that was necessary for such works as
wanted it upon the failure of their revenues. But the
greatest and most illustrious of all his works was the
erection of Apollo's temple at Rhodes at his own expense,
and his giving the people of Rhodes a great many talents
of silver to build a fleet. He also built the greatest part
of the public edifices for the inhabitants of Nicopolis[3] near
Actium : and for the inhabitants of Antioch, the principal
city of Syria, where a broad street cuts through the place
lengthways, he built porticoes along it on both sides, and
paved the open road with polished stone, which was of
very great advantage to the inhabitants. And as to the
Olympian games, which were in a very low condition
because of want of money, he revived their reputation, and
appointed revenues for keeping them up, and made that
general festival more stately as to the sacrifices and other
displays. And because of this great liberality, he was
almost unanimously registered as one of the perpetual
judges of those games.

§ 4. Now there are some who stand amazed at the diver-
sity of Herod's nature and purposes. For when we look at
his magnificence, and at the benefits which he bestowed on

---

[1] The present 'Tower of David' at Jerusalem.
[2] Now *Fusâil*.
[3] Built by Augustus in commemoration of the victory of Actium ; the
ruins are near *Prévesa*.

all people, there is no possibility even for those that had the least respect for him to deny, or not to admit, that he had a nature vastly beneficent; but when any one looks upon the punishments he inflicted, and the injuries he did not only to his subjects but to his nearest relations, and takes notice of his severe and unrelenting disposition, he will be forced to allow that he appears brutish, and a stranger to all humanity; whence some people suppose his nature to be various and sometimes self-contradictory. But I am myself of another opinion, and imagine that the cause of both these sort of actions was one and the same. For being an ambitious man, and quite overcome by that passion, he was induced to be magnificent, wherever there appeared any hopes either of future memory or of present reputation; and as his expenses were beyond his means, he was necessitated to be harsh to his subjects. For the persons on whom he expended his money were so many that they made him a very bad procurer of it; and as he was conscious that he was hated by those under him for the injuries he had done them, he thought it no easy thing to amend his offences, for that was inconvenient for his revenue; he therefore strove on the other hand to make their ill-will an opportunity to add to his gains. As to his own people, therefore, if anyone was not very obsequious to him in language, and would not confess himself to be his slave, or seemed to think of any innovation in his realm, he was not able to contain himself, but prosecuted his very kindred and friends, and punished them as if they were his enemies; and he committed such faults from a desire that he might himself alone be honoured. Now for this my assertion about that feeling of his, we have the greatest evidence, by what he did to honour Augustus and Agrippa and his other friends; for those honours he paid to those who were his superiors he desired also to be paid to himself; and what he thought the most excellent present he could make another, he showed an inclination to have also presented to himself. But the Jewish nation is by their law a stranger to all such things, and accustomed to prefer righteousness to glory; for which reason that nation was not agreeable to him, because it was out of their power to flatter the king's ambition with statues or temples, or any

other such things.  And this seems to me to have been at
once the cause of Herod's harsh acts to his own courtiers
and counsellors, and of his benefits to foreigners and to
those that had no relation to him.


## CHAP. VI.

*An Embassage of the Jews in Cyrene and Asia to Augustus,
concerning the Complaints they had to make against the
Greeks; with Copies of the Letters which Augustus and
Agrippa wrote to the Cities for them.*

### § 1.

NOW the Greek cities ill-treated the Jews in Asia, and
also all those of the same nation who lived in Libya [1]
near Cyrene, though the former kings had given them
equal privileges with the other citizens; but the Greeks
oppressed them at this time, and that so far as to take
away their sacred money, and to do them mischief on
particular occasions.  As therefore they were thus evil
intreated, and found no end of the barbarous treatment
they met with among the Greeks, they sent ambassadors
to Augustus about these matters.  And he gave them the
same privileges as they had before, and sent letters to the
same purpose to the governors of the provinces, copies of
which I subjoin here, as testimonies of the favourable disposition the Roman emperors formerly had towards us.

§ 2.  "Cæsar Augustus, Pontifex Maximus, and tribune
of the people, ordains as follows.  Since the nation of the
Jews has been found friendly to the Roman people, not only
at this time, but in time past also, and especially Hyrcanus
the high priest, under my father Cæsar the emperor,[2] it
has seemed good to me and my council, according to the
wish and oath of the people of Rome, that the Jews should

---

[1] Libya was that portion of Africa which lay to the west of Lower
and Middle Egypt.

[2] Augustus here calls Julius Cæsar his 'father,' though by birth he
was only his 'uncle,' on account of his adoption by him.  See the same,
Antiq. xiv. 14, § 4.—W.

have liberty to follow their own customs, according to the law of their forefathers, as they did under Hyrcanus the high priest of Almighty God; and that their sacred money be not touched, but be sent to Jerusalem, and that it be committed to the care of the receivers at Jerusalem; and that they be not obliged to appear in court either on the Sabbath-day, or on the day of preparation before it, after the ninth hour.[1]  And if any one be caught stealing their holy books, or their sacred money, whether it be out of the synagogue, or from the men's apartments, he shall be deemed a sacrilegious person, and his goods shall be confiscated to the public treasury of the Romans.  And I give order, that the decree which they have given me, on account of the piety which I exercise to all mankind, and out of regard to Caius Marcus Censorinus, and the present edict, be put up in the most eminent place consecrated to me by the community of Asia at Ancyra.[2]  And if any one transgress any part of what is above decreed, he shall be severely punished."  This was inscribed upon a pillar in the temple of Cæsar Augustus.

§ 3.  "Cæsar Augustus sends greeting to Norbanus Flaccus.  Let those Jews, however numerous they be, who have been used according to their ancient custom to send their sacred money to Jerusalem, do the same freely."  These were the decrees of Cæsar Augustus.

§ 4.  Agrippa also himself wrote in the following manner on behalf of the Jews.  "Agrippa, to the magistrates, senate, and people of the Ephesians, greeting.  I will that the care and custody of the sacred money that is carried to the temple at Jerusalem be left to the Jews of Asia, to do with it according to their ancient custom; and that such as steal that sacred money of the Jews, and flee to a sanctuary, shall be torn from thence and delivered to the Jews, by the same law that sacrilegious persons are torn from thence.  I have also written to Silanus the

---

[1] This is authentic evidence, that the Jews, in the days of Augustus, began to prepare for the celebration of the Sabbath at the ninth hour on Friday, as the tradition of the elders did, it seems, then require of them.—W.

[2] *Angora* in Asia Minor; the inscription was on one of the walls of the Temple.

prætor, that no one compel the Jews to appear in court on the Sabbath-day."

§ 5. "Marcus Agrippa, to the magistrates, senate, and people of Cyrene, greeting. The Jews of Cyrene have petitioned me for the performance of what Augustus sent orders about to Flavius, who was then prætor of Libya, and to the other procurators of that province, that the sacred money should be sent to Jerusalem without hindrance, as has been their custom from their forefathers, for they complain that they are harassed by certain informers, and, under pretence of taxes which are not due, are hindered from sending them; which I command to be restored them without any diminution or trouble; and if any of that sacred money in the cities be taken from their proper receivers, I further enjoin, that the same be duly returned to the Jews in that place."

§ 6. "Caius Norbanus Flaccus, proconsul, sends greeting to the magistrates and senate of the Sardians. The Emperor has written to me, and commanded me not to forbid the Jews, however numerous they be, from assembling together according to the custom of their forefathers, or from sending their money to Jerusalem. I have therefore written to you, that you may know that both the Emperor and I would have you act accordingly."

§ 7. Nor did Julius Antonius, the proconsul, write otherwise. "To the magistrates, senate, and people of the Ephesians, greeting. As I was dispensing justice at Ephesus on the Ides of February, the Jews that dwell in Asia pointed out to me, that Cæsar Augustus and Agrippa had permitted them to use their own laws and customs, and to offer those their first fruits, which every one of them freely offers to the Deity on account of piety, and to carry them in a company together to Jerusalem without let or hindrance. They also petitioned me, that I would also confirm what had been granted by Augustus and Agrippa by my own decree. I would therefore have you take notice, according to the will of Augustus and Agrippa, that I permit them to use, and do according to, the customs of their forefathers without let or hindrance."

§ 8. I have felt obliged to set down these decrees, because the history of our acts will go generally among the

Greeks, and I have thus shown them that we were formerly held in great esteem, and were not prohibited by those governors we were under from keeping any of the laws of our forefathers; nay, that we were supported by them in following our own religion and worship of God. And I frequently mention these decrees to reconcile other people to us, and to remove any reasons for that hatred which inconsiderate men seem naturally to bear to us. As for our customs, there is no nation which always makes use of the same, and in every city almost we meet with different ones; but justice is most for the advantage of all men equally, both Greeks and barbarians, to which our laws pay the greatest regard, and so render us, if we observe them rightly, benevolent and friendly to all men. On which account we have reason to expect the like return from others, nor ought they to esteem difference of institutions a sufficient cause of alienation, but should look rather to virtue and probity, for this belongs to all men in common, and is sufficient of itself alone for the preservation of human life. I now return to the thread of my history.

## CHAP. VII.

*How, upon his going down into David's Tomb, the Troubles in Herod's Family greatly increased.*

### § 1.

AS for Herod, he had spent vast sums on the cities both without and within his own kingdom: and as he soon heard how Hyrcanus, who had been king before him, had opened David's tomb, and taken out of it three thousand talents of silver, and how there was much more left, indeed enough to suffice for all his wants, he had long intended to make an attempt on it, so now he opened the tomb by night, and went into it, and to prevent its being known in the city took only his most faithful friends with him. As for money, he found none, as Hyrcanus had done, but golden ornaments and various treasures laid up there, all of which he took away. However, he had a

great desire to make a more diligent search, and to go
further in, even as far as the very coffins of David and
Solomon.  But two of his body-guards were slain, by a
flame that burst out upon those that went in, as the report
went, so he was terribly frightened, and went out and
built a propitiatory memorial in white stone at the mouth
of the tomb at great expense, to mark the fright he had
been in.  Even Nicolaus his historiographer makes mention of this building of Herod, though he does not mention
his going down into the tomb, as he knew that action
was indecorous.  And many other things he treats in the
same manner in his history.  For he wrote in Herod's lifetime, and during his reign, and so as to please and serve
him, touching upon nothing but what tended to his glory,
and openly excusing many of his notorious crimes, and
very diligently concealing them.  And as he was desirous
to put a good colour on the murder of Mariamne and her
sons, which were barbarous actions on the part of the
king, he tells falsehoods about the incontinence of Mariamne, and the treacherous plots of her sons, and thus he
proceeded in his whole work, passing excessive encomiums
upon the just actions Herod did, and earnestly apologizing
for his unjust ones.  However, as I said, one might say a
great deal by way of excuse for Nicolaus; for he did not
so much write a history for others, as what might serve
the king himself.  As for ourselves, who come of a family
nearly allied to the Asamonæan kings, and so have the
honour of the priesthood, we think it unbecoming to say
anything that is false about them, and accordingly we have
described their actions in an honest and upright manner.
And although we reverence many of Herod's posterity who
still reign, yet do we pay a greater regard to truth than to
them, and that though it has sometimes happened that we
have incurred their displeasure by so doing.

§ 2. Now Herod's family troubles seemed to be augmented by the attempt he made upon David's tomb,
whether divine vengeance increased the calamities he suffered from, in order to render them incurable, or whether
fortune made an assault upon him in those cases, wherein
the opportuneness of the case made it strongly believed
that the calamities came upon him for his impiety.  For

the quarrels were like a civil war in his palace, and their hatred towards one another was such that each strove to exceed one another in calumnies. And Antipater was always undermining his brothers, and that very cunningly: he got them loaded with accusations, but took upon himself frequently to apologize for them, that this seeming benevolence to them might make him get believed, and forward his attempts against them. By this means he in various ways circumvented his father, who believed that all he did was for his preservation. Herod also recommended Ptolemy, who was the manager of the affairs of his kingdom, to Antipater, and consulted with his mother about important matters also. And indeed these were all in all, and did what they pleased, and made the king angry with any other persons, as they thought would be to their own advantage. So the sons of Mariamne got in a worse and worse condition perpetually, and as they were passed over, and set in a more dishonourable rank, though by birth the most noble, they could not bear the dishonour. As for the women, Alexander's wife Glaphyra, the daughter of Archelaus, was hated by Salome, both because of her love to her own husband, and because of Glaphyra's seeming to behave herself somewhat insolently towards her daughter,[1] who was the wife of Aristobulus, which equality of rank to herself Glaphyra took very impatiently.

§ 3. Now, besides this second strife that had fallen out among them, neither did the king's brother Pheroras keep himself out of trouble, but gave private grounds for suspicion and hatred. For he was overcome by the charms of his wife to such a degree of madness, that he despised the king's daughter, to whom he had been betrothed, and wholly adhered to his wife, who had been but a slave. So Herod was vexed at the dishonour done him, because he had bestowed many favours upon him, and had advanced him to that height of power that he was almost a partner with him in the kingdom, and saw that he did not make him a due return for his favours, and esteemed himself unhappy on that account. So upon Pheroras' refusal,

---

[1] Berenice, the daughter of Salome.

he gave the damsel to Phasaelus's son: but after some
time, when he thought the heat of his brother's affection
for his wife was abated, he blamed him for his former
conduct, and asked him to take his second daughter,
whose name was Cypros.  Ptolemy also advised him to
leave off affronting his brother, and to put away her whom
he loved, for it was disgraceful to be so enamoured of a
slave, as to deprive himself of the king's good-will to him,
and become an occasion of his trouble, and make himself
hated by him.  Pheroras knew that this advice was for his
good, particularly as he had been accused before, and
forgiven; so he put the poor woman away, although he
had already a son by her, and promised the king that he
would take his second daughter, and agreed that the thir-
tieth day after should be the day of marriage; and swore
he would have no further intercourse with her whom he
had put away.  But when the thirty days were over, he
was such a slave to his affections, that he no longer performed anything he had promised, but continued still with
his former wife.  This plainly grieved Herod and made
him angry, so that the king dropped one word or other
against Pheroras perpetually; and many made the king's
anger an opportunity for calumniating him.  Nor had the
king any longer a single quiet day or hour, but some fresh
quarrel or other arose among his relations and those that
were dearest to him.  For Salome was of a harsh temper,
and ill-natured to Mariamne's sons, nor would she suffer
her own daughter, who was the wife of Aristobulus, one of
those young men, to live happily with her husband, but persuaded her to tell her if he said anything to her in private;
and when any misunderstanding happened, as is common,
she raised a great many suspicions out of it; by which
means she learned all their concerns, and made the damsel
ill-natured to the young man.  And in order to gratify her
mother, she often said that the young men used to mention
Mariamne when they were by themselves, and that they
hated their father, and were continually threatening, if
they once got the kingdom, that they would make Herod's
sons by his other wives village-clerks, for the present
education which was given them, and their diligence in
learning, fitted them for such an employment; while as

for the women, whenever they saw them adorned with their mother's clothes, they threatened, that instead of their present gaudy apparel, they should be clothed in sackcloth, and confined so closely that they should not see the light of the sun. These stories were at once carried by Salome to the king, who was troubled to hear them, and endeavoured to make up matters; but these suspicions afflicted him, and becoming more and more uneasy, he believed everybody against everybody. However, upon his rebuking his sons, and hearing their defence, he was easier for a while, though a little afterwards much worse troubles came upon him.

§ 4. For Pheroras went to Alexander, the husband of Glaphyra, who was the daughter of Archelaus, as I have already stated, and said, that he had heard from Salome, that Herod was enamoured of Glaphyra, and that his passion for her was vehement. When Alexander heard that, he was all on fire from his youth and jealousy, and put the worst interpretation on Herod's attentions to her, which were very frequent, from the suspicions he had on account of what fell from Pheroras. Nor could he conceal his grief at the thing, but went to his father and informed him of what Pheroras had said. Upon this Herod was more put out than ever, and not being able to bear such a false calumny, which tended to his shame, was much disturbed at it: and often did he complain of the wickedness of his relations, and how good he had been to them, and what ill return they had made him. And he sent for Pheroras, and reproached him, and said, "Thou vilest of all men! art thou come to that unmeasureable and extravagant degree of ingratitude, as not only to suppose but to speak such things of me? I now indeed perceive what thy intentions are, it is not thy aim only to reproach me, in using such words to my son, but thereby to tempt him to plot against me, and take me off by poison. For who, if he had not a good genius like my son, would have such a suspicion of his father, and not revenge himself upon him? Dost thou suppose that thou hast only dropped a word for him to think of, and not rather put a sword into his hand to slay his father? And what dost thou mean, when thou really hatest both him and his brother, by pretending kindness to them, only

to raise calumnies against me, and by talking of such
things as no one but such an impious wretch as thou art
could either devise in mind or declare in words.  Begone,
thou that art such a vile plague to thy benefactor and
brother, and may that evil conscience of thine go along
with thee ; and may I still overcome my relations by kindness, and be so far from avenging myself on them as they
deserve, as to bestow greater benefits upon them than they
are worthy of."

§ 5.  Thus did the king speak.  Whereupon Pheroras,
who was caught in the very act of his villainy, said, that
Salome had concocted this plot, and that the words came
from her.  And as soon as she heard that (for she happened
to be at hand), she cried out plausibly that no such word ever
came out of her mouth, and that they all earnestly endeavoured to make the king hate her, and to get rid of her,
because of the good-will she bore to Herod, and because
she was always foreseeing the dangers that were coming
upon him ; and that at present there were more plots
against him than usual ; and as she was the only person
who had urged her brother to put away the wife he now
had, and to marry the king's daughter, it was no wonder if
she was hated by him.  As she said this, and often tore her
hair, and often beat her breast, her countenance made her
denial somewhat plausible, but the malignity of her
character argued her dissimulation.  But Pheroras was in
a fix, and had nothing plausible to offer in his own defence,
for he confessed that he had said what was charged against
him, but was not believed when he said he had heard it from
Salome.  So the confusion among them, and their quarrelsome words to one another, increased.  At last the king,
out of his hatred to his brother and sister, sent them both
away ; and when he had commended the moderation of his
son in himself telling him of the report, as it was now late
he went to rest.  After such a contest as this had fallen
out among them, Salome's reputation suffered greatly,
since she was supposed to have first raised the calumny ;
and the king's wives hated her, knowing she was a very ill-
natured woman and unreliable, as she would sometimes
be a friend, and sometimes an enemy.  So they perpetually
said one thing or other against her to Herod, and some-

thing that now happened made them the bolder in speaking against her.

§ 6. There was one Obodas, king of Arabia, an inactive and slothful man in his nature; and Syllæus managed most of his affairs for him. He was an able man, although but young, and was handsome also. This Syllæus upon some occasion coming to Herod, and supping with him, saw Salome, and set his heart upon her; and understanding that she was a widow he made up to her. Now because Salome was at this time less in favour with her brother, and looked upon Syllæus with some passion, she was very earnest to be married to him; and on the following days, as they went to supper, there appeared many and very great indications of their mutual understanding. Now the women carried this news to the king, and laughed at the unseemliness of it; whereupon Herod inquired further about it of Pheroras, and desired him to observe at supper how they behaved to one another; and he told him that by their nods and looks they were both evidently in love. After this the Arabian being suspected went away, but came again two or three months afterwards, as if on that very design, and spoke to Herod about it, and asked that Salome might be given him to wife; for he said that affinity with him might be not unprofitable to Herod through his connection with Arabia, the government of which country was already in effect in his hands, and would be still more so hereafter. And when Herod discoursed with his sister about it, and asked her, whether she were disposed to the match, she quickly agreed to it. But when Syllæus was asked to conform to the Jewish religion, and then he should marry her (for it was impossible to do so on any other terms), he would not hear of it, but went his way, for he said if he should do so, he would be stoned by the Arabs. Then did Pheroras twit Salome with her lust, as did the women much more, who said that Syllæus had had connection with her. As for the damsel, whom the king had betrothed to his brother Pheroras, who had not taken her, as I have before stated, because he was enamoured of his wife, Salome asked Herod that she might be given to her son by Costobarus, which match Herod had no objection to, but was dissuaded from it by Pheroras,

who pleaded that this young man would not be kind to
her, because of the murder of his father, and that it was
much more just that his son should have her, who was to
be his successor in the tetrarchy. So he sued for pardon,
and the king's wrath was over. And the damsel, upon
this change of her espousals, was disposed of to this young
man, the son of Pheroras, the king giving her also as her
portion a hundred talents.

## CHAP. VIII.

*How Herod arrested Alexander, and put him in prison, and
how Archelaus, King of Cappadocia, reconciled him to his
Father Herod again.*

### § 1.

HOWEVER affairs in Herod's family grew no better, but
were every day more troublesome. And the following
circumstance happened, which arose from no decent occasion, and proceeded so far as to bring great difficulties
upon him. There were certain eunuchs whom the king
was very fond of on account of their beauty; and the
care of bringing him drink was intrusted to one of
them, of bringing him his supper to another, and of
putting him to bed to the third, who almost managed the
principal affairs of the kingdom. Now some one told the
king that these eunuchs had been corrupted by Alexander
the king's son with great sums of money. And when
Herod asked them if Alexander had had criminal dealings
with them, they confessed that he had, but said they knew
of no further criminality on his part against his father. But
when they were tortured, and were in the utmost extre-
mity, for the tormentors to gratify Antipater stretched the
rack to the very utmost, they said that Alexander bore
great ill-will and innate hatred to his father: and that he
had told them, that Herod despaired of living much longer,
and that in order to cover his great age, he dyed his hair
black, and endeavoured to conceal what would discover
how old he was; but if they would join him, when he
should attain the kingdom, which, in spite of his father,

would come to no one else, they should quickly have the first place in the kingdom under him; and he was now ready to take the kingdom, not only as his birthright, but by the preparations he had made for obtaining it, because a great many of the rulers, and a great many of his friends were zealous partisans of his, ready both to do and to suffer anything.

§ 2. When Herod heard this confession, he was all over anger and fear, some parts of it seeming to him insulting, and some making him suspicious of dangers that awaited him, insomuch that on both accounts he was provoked, and bitterly afraid lest some worse plot should be actually laid against him than he should be able to escape from now. So he did not any longer make any open search, but sent about spies to watch such as he suspected, for he was now overrun with suspicion and hatred against everybody, and indulging his suspicions, in order to his preservation, he continually suspected those that were innocent. Nor did he set any bounds to himself, but supposing that those who were near him had the most power to hurt him, they were his bugbears; and for those that were not used to come to him, it seemed enough generally to name them [to make them suspected], and he thought himself safer when they were at once put to death. At last his courtiers were come to that pass, that being no way secure of escaping themselves, they fell to accusing one another, imagining that he who first accused another was most likely to save himself. Yet, when any had thus overthrown others, they were hated, and they were thought to suffer justly, who unjustly accused others only thereby to anticipate being accused themselves. Nay, at last they avenged their own private enmities by this means, and when they were caught they were punished in the same way, using this opportunity as an instrument and snare against their enemies, yet when they tried it often themselves caught in the same snare which they laid for others. And the king soon repented of what he had done, because he had no clear evidence of the guilt of those whom he had slain; and yet what was still more severe in him, he did not make use of his repentance in order to leave off doing the like again, but in order to in-flict the same punishment upon their accusers.

§ 3. And in this troubled state were the affairs of the palace; and Herod had already told many of his friends not to appear before him, nor come into the palace; and the reason of this injunction was that [when they were there] he had less freedom of action, or greater restraint on himself on their account. And at this time it was that he dismissed Andromachus and Gemellus, men who had been very old friends of his, and been very useful to him in the affairs of his kingdom, and been of advantage to his family in their embassages and counsels; and had been tutors to his sons, and had in a manner the first degree of freedom with him. He dismissed Andromachus, because his son Demetrius was intimate with Alexander, and Gemellus, because he knew that he wished Alexander well, which arose from his having been with him in his youth when he was at school, and also with him when he was absent at Rome. These he expelled from his palace, and would have liked to have done worse to them; but that he might not seem to take such liberty against men of so great reputation, he contented himself with depriving them of their rank and power to hinder his wicked proceedings.

§ 4. Now Antipater was the cause of all this, who when he saw the mad and licentious conduct of his father, as he had been a great while one of his counsellors, egged him on, and thought he would gain his own ends more, when everyone that could oppose him was removed out of the way. When therefore Andromachus and his friends were driven away, and had no freedom of access or speech with the king any longer, the king in the first place examined by torture all whom he thought faithful to Alexander, to see whether they knew of any plot against him; but they died under the torture without having anything to say, which made the king more furious, that he could not find out the evil proceedings he suspected. As for Antipater, he was very clever in raising calumny against those that were really innocent, as if their denial was only their constancy and fidelity [to Alexander,] and instigated Herod by the torture of more persons to discover any hidden plots. Now a certain person among the many that were tortured, said that he knew that Alexander had often said (when he was commended as a tall man in his body, and a skilful marksman, and told that in his exercises he exceeded all men), that these qualifications given him by nature, though good in themselves, were not advantageous to him, because his father was grieved at them, and envied him for them; so that when he walked with his father he endeavoured to depress and shorten himself, that he might not appear too tall, and that when he shot at anything as he was hunting, he missed his mark on purpose when his father was by, for he knew how ambitious his father was of being first in such exercises. So when the man was tormented about this saying, and had his body given ease after, he added, that Alexander had his brother Aristobulus as his assistant, and that they resolved to lie in wait for their father, as he was hunting, and kill him: and when they had done so, to flee to Rome, and ask to have the kingdom given to Alexander. There were also letters of the young man found written to his brother, wherein he complained, that his father did not act justly in giving Antipater a country, whose [yearly] revenues amounted to two hundred talents. Upon these confessions Herod at once thought he had something to depend on as to his suspicion about his sons; so he arrested Alexander and put him in prison. Yet did he still continue to be uneasy, and was not quite satisfied of the truth of what he had heard; and when he considered the matter, he found that they had only exhibited juvenile complaints and contentions, and that it was an incredible thing, if his son should slay him, that he should go openly to Rome; so he was desirous to have some surer proof of his son's wickedness, and was very solicitous about it, that he might not appear to have condemned him to be put in prison too rashly. So he tortured the principal of Alexander's friends, and put not a few of them to death, without getting out of them any of the things which he suspected. And as Herod was very busy about this matter, and the palace was full of terror and trouble, one of the young men, when he was in the utmost agony, said that Alexander had sent to his friends at Rome, and asked that he might be quickly invited there by Augustus, and that he could discover a plot against him, for Mithridates, the king of Parthia, was joined in a friendship with his father against the Romans;

he also added that Alexander had a poisonous potion ready prepared at Ascalon.

§ 5. To this Herod gave credit, and enjoyed thereby, in his miserable case, some sort of consolation for his rashness, in flattering himself with finding things in so bad a condition. But as for the poisonous potion, though he was anxious to find it, he could find none. As for Alexander, he was desirous from a contentious spirit to aggravate the great misfortunes he was in, so he denied not the accusation, but punished the rashness of his father with a greater fault of his own; and perhaps he wished to make his father thereby ashamed of his easy belief of such calumnies : he aimed especially, if he could gain belief to his story, to plague him and his whole kingdom. For he wrote four letters, and sent them to Herod to tell him, that he need not torture any more persons, nor search any further, for he had himself plotted against him, and that he had as his partners Pheroras and the most faithful of the king's friends; and that Salome came to him by night, and lay with him against his will; and that all men were come to be of one mind to make away with the king as soon as they could, and so get rid of the continual fear of him they were in. Among others he accused Ptolemy and Sapinnius, who were the most faithful friends of the king. And what more can be said, but that those who were before the most intimate friends were become wild beasts to one another, as if a certain madness had fallen upon them, and there was no room for defence or refutation, in order to the discovery of the truth, but all were at random doomed to destruction; so that some lamented those that were in prison, others those that had been put to death, others that they were in the expectation of the same miseries : and dejection and solitude rendered the kingdom quite the reverse of the happy state it formerly enjoyed. Herod's own life also was bitter to him, so greatly alarmed was he ; and because he could trust nobody, he was sorely punished by the expectation of further misery, for he often fancied in his imagination, that his son had made an insurrection against him, or even stood by him with a sword in his hand. Thus was his mind night and day intent upon this thing, and he revolved it over and over, just as if he were distracted.  Such was the sad condition Herod was now in.

§ 6.  But when Archelaus, king of Cappadocia, heard of the state that Herod was in, being in great distress about his daughter, and the young man [her husband,] and sorry for Herod as a man that was his friend, on account of the great trouble he was in, he came [to Jerusalem] on purpose to arrange matters.  And when he found Herod in such a state, he thought it wholly unseasonable to reprove him, or to say that he had acted rashly, for he would thereby naturally bring him to dispute the point with him, and make him the more irritated by his having still more to apologize for himself.  He went therefore another way to work, in order to improve matters, and appeared angry with the young man, and said, that Herod was so very mild a man, that he had not acted a rash part at all.  He also said he would dissolve his daughter's marriage with Alexander, for he could not in justice spare his own daughter, if she were conscious of anything, and did not inform Herod of it.  When Archelaus appeared in this mood, far otherwise than Herod expected, and in the main angry on Herod's account, the king abated his harshness, and took occasion, from his appearing to have acted justly hitherto, to come by degrees to put on the affection of a father; and was on both sides to be pitied, for when some persons refuted the calumnies that were laid on the young man, he fell into a passion, but when Archelaus joined in the accusation, he was dissolved into tears and great sorrow; and begged that he would not dissolve his son's marriage, or be so angry at his offences.  So when Archelaus had brought him to a more moderate temper, he shifted the charges to his friends, and said, it must be owing to them that so young a man, and one without a touch of malice, was corrupted, and thought there was more reason to suspect the brother than the son.  Upon this Herod was very much displeased at Pheroras, who indeed had now no one that could reconcile him and his brother; so when he saw that Archelaus had the greatest influence with Herod, he betook himself to him in the guise of a mourner, and like one that had all the signs upon him of a ruined man.  Upon this Archelaus did not neglect the intercession he made to him, but said that he could not change the king's disposition to him immediately, and said that it was best for him to go himself to the king, and confess himself the occasion of all the trouble, and beg the king's pardon, for that would mitigate the king's anger towards him, and he would be present to assist him. When he had persuaded him to this, he gained his point with both of them, and the calumnies raised against the young man were contrary to all expectation wiped off. And Archelaus, as soon as he had made this reconciliation between Pheroras and Herod, went away to Cappadocia, having proved at this critical juncture the most acceptable person to Herod in the world; on which account he gave him the richest presents as tokens of his respect to him, being on all occasions magnificent, and esteemed him as one of his dearest friends. He also made an agreement with him that he would go to Rome, because he had written to Augustus about these affairs, and they went together as far as Antioch. And there Herod made a reconciliation between Archelaus and Titus (the president of Syria), who had been greatly at variance, and then returned to Judæa.


## CHAP. IX.

*Concerning the Revolt of the Trachonites; how Syllœus accused Herod before Augustus; and how Herod, when Augustus was angry with him, resolved to send Nicolaus to Rome.*

### § 1.

WHEN Herod had been at Rome, and had come back again, a war broke out between him and the Arabians, for the following reason. The Trachonites,[1] after Augustus had taken their country away from Zenodorus, and added it to Herod, were no longer permitted to rob, but were forced to plough the land, and to live quietly, which was a thing they did not like: and though they took pains, the ground did not produce much profit.

---

[1] The inhabitants of Trachonitis, *el-Lejah.*

However, from the first, the king would not permit them
to rob, and so they abstained from that unjust way of
living upon their neighbours, which got Herod a great
reputation for his pains; but when he sailed to Rome (it
was when he went to accuse his son Alexander, and to
commit his son Antipater to Augustus' protection), the
Trachonites spread a report that he was dead, and revolted from his sway, and betook themselves again to their
accustomed way of robbing their neighbours. For the
time the king's commanders subdued them during Herod's
absence, but about forty of the principal robbers, being
terrified by the punishment of those that had been taken,
left the country, and retired into Arabia, Syllæus enter-
taining them now he had missed of marrying Salome, and
giving them a place of strength, in which they dwelt. And
they overran and pillaged not only Judæa but all Cœle-Syria
also, while Syllæus afforded *points d'appui* and security to
these illdoers. But when Herod came back from Rome,
he perceived that his dominions had greatly suffered at
their hands, and since he could not reach the robbers
themselves, because of the security which the protection
of the Arabians afforded them, being very angry at the
injuries they had done him, he went over all Trachonitis,
and slew their relations. Thereupon these robbers were
more angry than before, it being a law among them to
be avenged on the murderers of their relations by all
possible means, so they continued to harry and plunder
all Herod's dominions with impunity. Then did Herod
speak about these robbers to Saturninus and Volumnius,
and demanded that they should be punished; upon which
they waxed stronger, and became more numerous, and
by their rising threw everything into confusion, laying
waste the countries and villages that belonged to Herod's
kingdom, and butchering men whom they took prisoners,
till these unjust proceedings came to be like a real war,
for the robbers were now become about a thousand. At
which Herod was sore displeased, and demanded the
surrender of the robbers, as well as the money which
he had lent Obodas through Syllæus, which was sixty
talents, and since the time of payment was now past, he
desired to have it paid him. But Syllæus, who had set

Obodas aside, and managed everything himself, denied
that the robbers were in Arabia, and put off the payment
of the money : about which there was a discussion before
Saturninus and Volumnius, who were then the governors
of Syria. At last he, on their decision, agreed that within
thirty days Herod should be paid his money, and that
each of them should deliver up the other's subjects. Now,
as to Herod, there was not one of the other's subjects
found in his kingdom, either for committing any crime or
on any other account, but it was proved that the Arabians
had the robbers amongst them.

§ 2. When the day appointed for payment of the money
was past, Syllæus, without performing any part of his
agreement, set out for Rome. So Herod demanded the
payment of the money, and that the robbers that were in
Arabia should be delivered up, and, by permission of
Saturninus and Volumnius, took the law into his own
hands against those that were refractory. He took the
army that he had, and led it into Arabia ; and in three
days' time, by forced marches, he arrived at the garrison
wherein the robbers were, and took it by storm, and captured them all, and demolished the place, which was called
Raipta,[1] but did no harm to any others. But as the Arabians came to the assistance of the robbers, under Nacebus
their captain, a battle ensued, wherein a few of Herod's
soldiers, and Nacebus, the captain of the Arabians, and
about twenty of his men fell, while the rest betook themselves to flight. So when Herod had punished them, he
settled three thousand Idumæans in Trachonitis, and so
restrained the robbers that were there. He also sent an account of these things to the captains that were in Phœnice,[2]
showing that he had done nothing but what he ought
to do, in punishing the refractory Arabians, which, upon
exact inquiry, they found to be true.

§ 3. However, messengers hurried away to Syllæus to
Rome, and informed him of what had been done, and, as
is usual, exaggerated everything. Now Syllæus had already wormed himself into the acquaintance of Augustus,
and was then about the palace, and as soon as he heard of

---

[1] Site unknown.                          [2] Phœnicia.

these things, he changed his dress to black, and went in, and told Augustus that Arabia was afflicted with war, and that all his kingdom was in great confusion, because of Herod's laying it waste with his army : and added, with tears in his eyes, that two thousand five hundred of the principal men among the Arabians had fallen, and that their captain Nacebus, his familiar friend and kinsman, had been slain ; and that the riches that were at Raipta had been carried off ; and that Obodas was despised, as his infirm state of body rendered him unfit for war ; on which account neither he, nor the Arabian army, were present. When Syllæus had said this, and added invidiously that he would not himself have left the country, unless he had believed that Augustus would have provided that they should all have peace with one another, and that, had he been there, he would have taken care that the war should not have been to Herod's advantage ; Augustus was nettled at what was said, and asked only this one question, both of Herod's friends that were there, and of his own friends, who were come from Syria, "Whether Herod had led an army there?" And as they were forced to admit this, Augustus, without staying to hear why and how he did so, grew very angry, and wrote to Herod sharply. The sum of his letter was that, whereas of old he had treated Herod as his friend, he should now treat him as his subject. Syllæus also wrote an account of this to the Arabians. And they were so elated at it, that they neither delivered up the robbers that had fled to them, nor paid the money that was due, and retained those pastures also which they had hired, and kept them without paying their rent, and all this because the king of the Jews was now humiliated because of Augustus' anger with him. The inhabitants of Trachonitis also seized their opportunity, and rose up against the Idumæan garrison, and followed the same way of robbing as the Arabians, who had pillaged their country, and were more active in their unjust proceedings, not only for gain, but for revenge also.

§ 4. Now Herod was forced to bear all this, that confidence of his being quite gone with which Augustus' favour used to inspire him, and his spirit failed him. For Augustus would not so much as receive an embassage from him to make an apology, and when the envoys came a second time, he sent them away without success. So Herod was in dejection and fear, and Syllæus grieved him exceedingly, as he was now trusted by Augustus, and was present at Rome, nay, aspired even higher. For Obodas was dead, and Æneas, whose name was now changed to Aretas,[1] took over the rule over the Arabians. And Syllæus endeavoured by calumnies to get him turned out of his kingdom that he might himself take it: with which design he gave much money to the courtiers, and promised much money to Augustus, who indeed was angry that Aretas had not written to him first before he took the kingdom. But Aretas afterwards himself also sent a letter and presents to Augustus, and a golden crown of the weight of many talents. And his letter accused Syllæus of having been a wicked servant, and of having killed Obodas by poison, and while he was alive, of having governed him as he pleased, and of having also debauched the wives of the Arabians, and of having borrowed money, in order to obtain the kingdom for himself. But Augustus did not listen to these accusations, but sent his ambassadors back, without receiving any of his presents. And meantime affairs in Judæa and Arabia became worse and worse, partly because of the disorder they were in, and partly because, bad as they were, nobody had power to bring them round. For of the two kings, the one was not yet confirmed in his kingdom, and so had not authority sufficient to restrain evildoers; and as for Herod, Augustus was angry with him, for having so soon avenged himself, and so he was compelled to bear all the injuries that were offered him. At last, when he saw no end of the evils which surrounded him, he resolved to send an ambassador to Rome again, to see whether through his friends he could mitigate the wrath of Augustus, and to have an interview with Augustus himself. And the ambassador he sent was Nicolaus of Damascus.

---

[1] This Aretas was now become so established a name for the kings of Arabia, that when the crown came to this Æneas, he changed his name to Aretas, as Havercamp here justly observes. See Antiq. xiii. 15, § 2.—W.

## CHAP. X.

*How Eurycles falsely accused Herod's Sons, and how their Father put them in prison, and wrote to Augustus about them. Of Syllæus, and how he was accused by Nicolaus.*

### § 1.

THE troubles in Herod's family and about his sons at this time grew much worse; for it now appeared certain, nor was it unforeseen beforehand, that fortune threatened the greatest and most insupportable misfortunes possible to his kingdom. Their progress and increase at this time was due to the following cause. One Eurycles, a Lacedæmonian (a person of note in his own country, but a man of perverse mind, and so cunning in his pleasures and flattery, as to indulge both, and yet seem to indulge neither), visited Herod's court, and made him presents, but so that he received more presents from him. He also seized such opportunities of worming himself into Herod's friendship, that he became one of the most intimate of the king's friends. He lodged in Antipater's house, but he had access to and intimacy with Alexander, for he told him that he was in great favour with Archelaus the king of Cappadocia. He also pretended much respect to Glaphyra, and secretly cultivated a friendship with them all, but always observed what was said and done, that he might with calumnies please them all. In short, he behaved himself so to everybody as to appear to be his particular friend, and he made others believe that his associating with any one was for that person's advantage. So he won over Alexander, who was but young, and persuaded him that he might open his grievances to him with safety, but to nobody else. So he declared his grief to him, and how his father was alienated from him, and related also the affairs of his mother, and how Antiochus had driven him and his brother from their proper honour, and had the power over everything himself. He added that all this was intolerable, as his father had already come to hate them, and would neither admit them to his table, nor to his presence. Such were the complaints, as was but natural, of Alexander, as to the things that troubled him ; and Eurycles retailed these words to Antipater : and told him, he did not inform him of them on his own account ; but that, being overcome by his kindness, the great importance of the matter obliged him to do so, and he warned him to have a care of Alexander, for what he said was spoken with vehemence, and in the words themselves lay murder. So Antipater, thinking him to be his friend by this advice, gave him great presents upon all occasions, and at last persuaded him to inform Herod of this. So when he related to the king Alexander's displeasure, as discovered by the words he had heard him speak, he was easily believed, and brought the king to that pass, turning him about by his words and irritating him, that he made his hatred implacable : as he showed at that very time, for he immediately gave Eurycles a present of fifty talents. And he, when he had received them, went to Archelaus king of Cappadocia, and commended Alexander to him, and told him that he had been many ways useful to him in making reconciliation between him and his father. So he got money from him also, and went away, before his pernicious practices were found out ; and when Eurycles returned to Lacedæmon, he did not leave off mischief making, and at last for his many acts of injustice was banished from his own country.

§ 2. As for Herod, he was not now in the temper he was in formerly towards Alexander and Aristobulus, when he had been content with only hearing calumnies of them when others told him, for he was now come to that pass of hatred as to urge men to speak against them, though they did not do it of themselves. He also observed all that was said, and put questions, and gave ear to everyone that would but speak, if they could but say anything against them, till at length he heard that Euaratus of Cos was a conspirator with Alexander, which news was to Herod the most agreeable and sweetest imaginable.

§ 3. But a still greater misfortune came upon the young men, for new calumnies against them were continually being fabricated, and, so to speak, as if it was everyone's task to lay some grievous thing to their charge, which might appear to be for the king's safety. There were two body-guards of Herod held in honour for their strength and height, Jucundus and Tyrannus, who had been cast off by Herod, who was displeased with them, and now used to ride with Alexander, and for their skill in their exercises were held in honour by him, and had some gold and other gifts bestowed upon them. Now the king having at once suspicion of these men, had them tortured, and they endured the torture courageously for a long time, but at last confessed that Alexander urged them to kill Herod when he was hunting wild beasts; for it could be said he fell from his horse, and was run through with his own spear, for he had once met with such a misfortune formerly. They also showed where there was money hidden in a stable under ground, and convicted the king's chief hunter of having given them the royal hunting spears, and weapons to Alexander's attendants, at Alexander's command.

§ 4. Next to these the commander of the garrison of Alexandrium [1] was arrested and tortured; for he was accused of having promised to receive the young men into his fortress, and to supply them with money of the king which was stored up in that fortress. He confessed nothing himself; but his son came forward, and said it was so, and delivered up a letter which, so far as could be guessed, was in Alexander's hand-writing. Its contents were as follows. "When we have finished, by God's help, all that we have proposed to do, we will come to you : but endeavour, as you have promised, to receive us into your fortress." After this writing was produced, Herod had no longer any doubt about the treacherous designs of his sons against him. But Alexander said that Diophantus the scribe had imitated his hand-writing, and that the letter was a forgery of Antipater. For Diophantus appeared to be very clever in such practices, and was afterwards convicted of forging other papers, and therefore put to death.

§ 5. And the king produced before the multitude at Jericho those that had been tortured, in order to have them accuse the young men; and many of the people

---

[1] *Kefr Istûna.*

stoned these accusers to death. But when they were going to kill Alexander and Aristobulus likewise, the king would not permit them to do so, but restrained the multitude by the help of Ptolemy and Pheroras. However, the young men were put under a guard, and kept in custody, and nobody might any longer have access to them: and all that they did or said was observed, and the reproach and fear they were in was little or nothing different from that of condemned criminals. And one of them, Aristobulus, was so deeply affected, that he induced Salome, who was his aunt and mother-in-law, to sympathize with him in his calamities, and to hate him who had been persuaded to let things come to that pass; when he said to her, "Are not you also in danger of destruction, as the report goes that you disclosed beforehand all our affairs to Syllæus, when you were in hopes of being married to him?" But she immediately carried these words to her brother. And he, being no longer able to control his rage, gave command to bind them and keep them apart from one another, to write down the ill things they had done against their father, and send them on to Augustus. And when this was enjoined them, they wrote that they had laid no treacherous design, nor formed any plot against their father, but that they had intended to flee away, and that from the distress they were in, their lives being now suspected and full of anxiety.

§ 6. About this time there came an ambassador out of Cappadocia[1] from Archelaus, one Melas, who was a ruler under him. And Herod wishing to show Archelaus' ill-will to him, sent for Alexander, as he was in his bonds, and asked him again concerning their proposed flight, as to whither and how they had resolved to flee? Alexander replied, "To Archelaus, who had promised to send them thence to Rome, but that they had no wicked nor mischievous designs against their father, and that none of the charges fabricated against them by their adversaries was true; and that they wished Tyrannus and his associates were yet alive that they might have been examined more strictly, but that they had been suddenly slain by means

[1] The portion of Asia Minor lying west of the Anti-Taurus range. The principal town was Mazaca, Cæsarea, *Kaisariyeh.*

of Antipater, who put his own friends among the multitude [for that purpose."]

§ 7. When he had said this, Herod commanded that
both Alexander and Melas should be carried to Glaphyra,
the daughter of Archelaus, and that she should be asked
whether she did not know anything of plots against Herod?
Now as soon as they came to her, and she saw Alexander
in bonds, she beat her head, and in great consternation
gave a deep and moving groan. The young man also fell
into tears. This was so miserable a sight to those present, that, for a great while, they were not able to say or
do anything; but at last Ptolemy, who had been ordered
to bring Alexander, bade him say, if his wife were privy to
his actions? He replied, "How is it possible, that she,
whom I love better than my own soul, and by whom I have
had children, should not know what I do?" Upon which
she cried out, that "she knew of no wicked designs of his;
but yet, if accusing herself falsely would tend to his preservation, she would confess all." Then Alexander said,
"There is no such wickedness as those (who ought least
to do so) suspect, which either I have intended, or you
know of, but this only, that we had resolved to retire to
Archelaus, and from thence to Rome." And when she
also confessed this, Herod, supposing that Archelaus' ill-
will to him was fully proved, gave a letter to Olympus and
Volumnius, and bade them, as they sailed by, to touch at
Elæusa[1] in Cilicia, and give it to Archelaus, and when they
had expostulated with him for having a hand in his sons'
plot against him, to sail thence to Rome; and if they found
Nicolaus had gained any ground, and that Augustus was
no longer displeased with Herod, to give him the letters
and proofs which he sent ready prepared against the young
men. As to Archelaus, he made this defence for himself,
that he had promised to receive the young men, because it
was both for their own and their father's advantage to do
so, lest he should take some violent step in the anger he
was in because of his present suspicions; but that he had
not promised to send them to Augustus, nor had he
promised anything else to the young men that could show
ill-will to him.

[1] See Antiq. xvi. 4, § 6; Jewish War, i. 23, § 4.

§ 8. When Olympus and Volumnius reached Rome, they had a good opportunity of delivering their letters to Augustus, because they found him reconciled to Herod. For Nicolaus' embassage had gone off as follows. As soon as he was come to Rome, and was about the court, he did not first only set about what he was come for, but he thought fit also to accuse Syllæus. Now the Arabians, even before he came to talk with them, openly quarrelled with one another, and some of them left Syllæus' party, and joined themselves to Nicolaus', and informed him of all the wicked things that had been done; and showed him evident proofs of the slaughter of a great number of Obodas' friends by Syllæus, for when they left Syllæus' party, they had carried off with them letters whereby they could convict him. When Nicolaus saw such an opportunity offered him, he made use of it in order to gain his own ends afterwards, being anxious to reconcile Augustus and Herod. For he knew very well that if he should desire to make a defence for Herod's acts, he would not be allowed that liberty; but that, if he desired to accuse Syllæus, an opportunity would present itself of speaking on Herod's behalf. So when the case was ready for hearing, and the day appointed, Nicolaus, in the presence of Aretas' ambassadors, accused Syllæus of various other things, and imputed to him the destruction of his king and of many others of the Arabians, and said he had borrowed money for no good purpose, and proved that he had been guilty of adultery, not only with women in Arabia but in Rome also. And he added, as the heaviest charge, that he had estranged Augustus from Herod, having said nothing true about the actions of Herod. When Nicolaus was come to this point, Augustus stopped him from going on, and desired him only to say as to Herod that he had not led an army into Arabia, nor slain two thousand five hundred men there, nor taken prisoners, nor pillaged the country. To this Nicolaus answered that he could prove conclusively that either none at all or but very few of those imputations of which he had been informed were true, for had they been true, he might justly have been angry at Herod. At this unexpected assertion Augustus was very attentive, and Nicolaus said, that there was a debt due to Herod of five hundred talents, and a bond, wherein it was written, that if the time appointed for payment had elapsed, it should be lawful to make reprisals in any part of the country.  As for the expedition into Arabia, he said it was no hostile expedition, but a just demanding back of his own money, and that not immediately, nor so soon as the bond allowed, but that Herod had frequently gone to Saturninus and Volumnius, the governors of Syria ; and that at last Syllæus had sworn at Berytus,[1] by the Emperor's fortune, that he would certainly pay the money within thirty days, and deliver up those that had fled from Herod's dominions.  " And when Syllæus performed nothing of this, Herod went again before those governors, and upon their permission to make reprisals for the money, he went reluctantly out of his own dominions with a party of soldiers for that purpose.  And this is all the war which these men so tragically describe ; this was the expedition into Arabia.  And how can this be called a war, when thy governors permitted it, and the bond allowed it, and it was not executed till thy name, O Cæsar Augustus, with that of the other gods, had been profaned ?  And now I must speak in order about the captives.  There were robbers that dwelt in Trachonitis ;[2] at first their number was no more than forty, but they became more numerous afterwards, and they escaped the punishment Herod would have inflicted on them, by making Arabia their head-quarters.  Syllæus received them, and supported them with food to the detriment of all men, and gave them a country to inhabit, and received himself the gains they made by robbery.  But he promised on oath that he would deliver up these men on the day that he fixed for payment of his debt ; nor can he show that any other persons besides these were at this time taken out of Arabia, and indeed not all these either, but only so many as could not conceal themselves.  And thus does the odious calumny of the captives appear to be no better than a fiction and lie, made on purpose to provoke thy indignation.  For I say, that when the forces of the Arabians came upon us, and one or two of Herod's party fell, Herod only defended

---

[1]  *Beirût* in Syria.            [2]  The district *el-Lejah.*

himself, and Nacebus the Arabian general fell, and about
twenty-five others in all, and no more ; whereas Syllæus,
by multiplying every single soldier by a hundred, reckons
the slain to have been two thousand five hundred."

§ 9. This speech greatly moved Augustus, and he turned to
Syllæus full of rage, and asked him how many Arabians
had been slain ?   And as he hesitated, and said he had been
imposed upon, the conditions about the borrowed money
were read, and the letters of the governors of Syria, and
the complaints of all the cities that had been injured by
the robbers.  The conclusion of the matter was this, that
Syllæus was condemned to die, and that Augustus was reconciled to Herod, and owned his repentance for the severe
things he had written to him occasioned by calumny, and
told Syllæus that he had induced him by his lying account
to be guilty of ingratitude to a man that was his friend.
In fine Syllæus was sent away to answer Herod's suit, and
to repay the debt that he owed, and after that to be
executed.  But Augustus was still offended with Aretas, that
he had taken upon himself the kingdom, without his consent being first obtained, for he had determined to bestow
Arabia upon Herod ;  but the letters Herod had sent hindered him from doing so now.  For Olympus and Volumnius,
on finding that Augustus was now become favourable to
Herod, thought fit immediately to deliver him the letters
they were commanded by Herod to give him concerning
his sons and the proofs of their crimes.  When Augustus
had read them, he thought it would not be proper to add
another kingdom to him, now he was old, and on bad
terms with his sons, so he admitted Aretas' ambassadors;
and after he had just reproved his rashness, in not waiting till he received the kingdom from him, he accepted his
presents, and confirmed him in his kingdom.

## CHAP. XI.

*How Herod, by Permission of Augustus, accused his sons before a Council of Judges at Berytus; and what Tero suffered for using too much Liberty of Speech. Concerning also the Execution of the young Men, and their Burial at Alexandrium.*

### § 1.

AND Augustus being now reconciled to Herod wrote to him that he was grieved for him on account of his sons, and said if they had been guilty of any grave crimes against him, it would behove him to punish them as parricides (and he gave him authority to do so), but if they had only designed to flee away, he would have him give them an admonition, and not proceed to extremities with them. He also advised him to appoint and convene a council at Berytus, where the Romans had a colony, and to include the governors *of Syria* and Archelaus the king of Cappadocia, and as many more as he thought remarkable for their merit and friendship to him, and determine what should be done by their advice. These were the directions that Augustus gave. And Herod, when the letter was brought to him, was very glad of Augustus' reconciliation to him, and very glad also that he had complete authority given him over his sons. And somehow it happened that whereas before, in his adversity, though he had indeed shown himself severe, he had not been very rash or precipitate in procuring the destruction of his sons, he now, in his prosperity, took advantage of this change for the better, and the freedom he now had, to glut his hatred against them. He therefore sent round and invited whom he thought fit to this council, except Archelaus, for he would not invite him, either out of hatred to him, or because he thought he would be an obstacle to his designs.

§ 2. When the governors *of Syria* and the others whom he invited from the various cities were come to Berytus, he kept his sons in a certain village belonging to Sidon, called

Platana,[1] but near Berytus, that if they were called he
might produce them, for he did not think fit to bring them
before the council. And when there were one hundred and
fifty persons present, Herod came in by himself alone, and
accused his sons, and that in such a way as if it were
not a melancholy accusation, and painful necessity in
consequence of misfortune, but in such a way as was very
indecent for a father to accuse his sons in. For he was
very vehement and impassioned when he came to the demonstration of the crime they were accused of, and gave
the greatest signs of fury and barbarity: nor would he
suffer the council to judge of the weight of the evidence,
but played the part of advocate himself in a manner most
indecent in a father against his sons, and read what they
had written, wherein there was no mention of any plot or
contrivance against him, but only a confession that they
had meant to flee away, containing also certain reproaches
against him because of the ill-will he bore them. And when
he came to those reproaches, he bellowed out most of all,
and exaggerated what was said, as if they had confessed
plotting against him, and swore that he would rather lose
his life than hear such words. Lastly he said that he had
sufficient authority both by nature and by Augustus' permission [to do what he thought fit.] He also mentioned
a law of their country which enjoined that, if parents laid
their hands on the head of him that was accused, the bystanders were obliged to cast stones at him, and so to
kill him. But though he was ready to do this in his own
country and kingdom, yet he said he waited for their determination; though they came not thither so much as judges,
to condemn his sons for such manifest designs against him,
whereby he had almost perished, bu t as persons who had an
opportunity of joining him in his anger, for it was unworthy in any, even the most remote, to pass over such
conspiracy [without punishment.]

§ 3. When the king had said this, and the young men
had not been produced to make any defence for themselves, the members of the council perceived there was no

[1] See Jewish War, i. 27, § 2. Apparently a castle guarding a narrow
pass between the sea and Lebanon, near the river Damuras, *Nahr
Damûr.*

chance of mildness and reconciliation, so they confirmed his authority. And Saturninus, a person who had been consul, and one of great influence, first pronounced his sentence, but with great moderation and considering the circumstances. He said, "That he condemned Herod's sons, but did not think they should be put to death. He had sons of his own, and to put one's son to death was a greater misfortune than any that could befall one by them." After him Saturninus' sons (for he had three sons that accompanied him, and were his lieutenants) pronounced the same sentence as their father. Volumnius' sentence, on the contrary, was to inflict death on such as had been so impiously undutiful to their father; and most of the rest said the same, insomuch that the conclusion was that the young men were condemned to die. Immediately afterwards Herod went away from thence, and took his sons to Tyre, where Nicolaus met him, having sailed back from Rome; of whom Herod inquired, after he had related to him what had passed at Berytus, what his friends at Rome thought about his sons. He answered, "What they had resolved to do to thee is impious, and thou oughtest to keep them in prison : and if thou thinkest anything further necessary, thou mayest indeed so punish them, that thou appear not to indulge thy anger more than to govern thyself by judgment; but if thou inclinest to the milder side, thou mayest absolve them, lest perhaps thy misfortunes be rendered incurable; and this is the opinion of most of thy friends at Rome." On this Herod was silent and very thoughtful, and bade Nicolaus sail along with him.

§ 4. On Herod's reaching Cæsarea,[1] everybody there was talking of his sons, and the kingdom was in suspense, and the people in great expectation as to what would become of them. For a terrible fear seized upon all men, lest the old dissensions of the family should come to a sad conclusion, and they were in great anxiety about their sufferings; nor was it without danger to say any hasty thing about the matter, or even to hear another saying it; but men's pity was forced to be shut up in themselves, which made their

[1] *Kaisarîyeh.*

sorrow silent. But there was an old soldier of Herod's,
whose name was Tero (who had a son of the same age as
Alexander, and his friend), who was so bold as openly to
speak out what others silently thought about the matter,
and felt forced to cry out often among the multitude, saying in the most unguarded manner that truth had perished,
and that justice was taken away from men, and that lies
and malice prevailed, and brought such a mist upon public
affairs, that offenders were not able to see the greatest ills
that could befall men. And as he was so bold, he seemed
to bring himself into danger by speaking so freely; but
the reasonableness of what he said moved men to regard
him as having behaved with great courage and seasonably.
So every one heard what he said with pleasure; and although
they provided for their own safety by keeping silent themselves, yet did they approve of the great freedom he took;
for the expected tragedy constrained them to speak in
behalf of Tero whatever they pleased.

§ 5. This man thrust himself into the king's presence
with the greatest freedom, and desired to speak with
him by himself alone, which the king permitted him to
do, when he spoke as follows. "Since I am not able,
O king, to bear the great concern I am in, I have preferred the use of this bold liberty that I now take (which
is necessary and advantageous to you) to my own safety.
Where is your understanding gone, and left your soul
empty? Where is that extraordinary sagacity of yours
gone, whereby you performed so many and such glorious
actions? Whence comes this absence of friends and relations, though I judge those neither friends nor relations
who overlook such horrid wickedness in your once happy
kingdom. Do you not perceive what is doing? Will you
slay these two young men, your sons by your queen, who
are proficients in every virtue, and leave yourself destitute
in your old age, and in the power of one son, who has
very ill sustained the confidence placed in him, and to relations whose death you have so often resolved on yourself? Will you not take notice that the silence of the
multitude at once sees the crime and abhors the case, and
that the whole army and its officers have commiseration
on the poor unhappy youths, and hatred to those that are

the authors of this?" The king heard these words, and for some time with good temper. But what can one say? When Tero plainly touched upon the tragedy and the perfidiousness of Herod's domestics, he was moved at it: but when Tero went on further, and by degrees used an unbounded military freedom of speech, (for he was too boorish to accommodate himself to the occasion,) Herod was greatly vexed, and seeming to be rather reproached by his speech, than to be hearing what was for his advantage, as he learned thereby that the soldiers abhorred what he was about, and the officers were indignant at it, he gave orders that all whom Tero had named, and Tero himself, should be bound and kept in prison.

§ 6. When this was done, one Trypho, who was the king's barber, took the opportunity, and came and told the king, that Tero often urged him, when he shaved the king, to cut his throat with the razor, for so he should be among the chief of Alexander's friends, and receive great rewards from him. When he had said this, the king gave orders that Tero and his son and the barber should be tortured, which was done accordingly. And though Tero bore up himself, his son seeing his father already in a sad case, and without hope of deliverance, and perceiving what would be the consequence of his terrible sufferings, said that if the king would free him and his father from those torments for what he should say, he would tell the truth. And when the king had given his word to do so, he said that there was an agreement made, that Tero should lay violent hands on the king, because it was easy for him to approach him when he was alone; and if, when he had done so, he should suffer death for it, as was not unlikely, it would be an act of generosity done on behalf of Alexander. This was what Tero's son said, and thereby freed his father from the torture, but it is uncertain whether he had been thus forced by the torture to speak what was true, or whether it was a contrivance of his own to procure his own and his father's deliverance from their pain.

§ 7. As for Herod, if he had before any doubt about putting his sons to death, there was now no longer any room left in his soul for it; but as he had rejected whatever might afford him the least suggestion of reasoning

better about the matter, so he made haste at once to bring
his purpose to a conclusion. He therefore brought three
hundred of the officers that were accused, as also Tero and
his son, and the barber that accused them, before an
assembly, and brought charges against them all; and the
multitude stoned them with whatever came to hand, and
so killed them. Alexander also and Aristobulus were
brought to Sebaste [1] by their father's command, and there
strangled; and their dead bodies were carried by night
to Alexandrium, where their uncle on the mother's side,
and most of their ancestors, had been buried.

§ 8. And now perhaps it may not seem strange to some
that such a long-standing hatred should so grow, and
proceed so far as to overcome nature: but it may justly
deserve consideration, whether it is to be laid to the
charge of the young men, that they gave such a handle
to their father's anger, and led him to do what he did, and
by going on long in the same way made things past remedy,
and caused him to use them so unmercifully; or whether
it is to be laid to the father's charge, that he was so hard-
hearted, and so very greedy in the desire of power and of
other kinds of glory, that he would take no one into part-
nership with him, that so whatever he wished might be
law; or indeed, whether Fortune has not greater power
than all prudent forecasting, whence we are persuaded
that human actions are determined beforehand by her by
an inevitable necessity, and we call her Fate, because
there is nothing which is not done by her. However, I
suppose it will be sufficient to compare this notion with
that other, which attributes somewhat to ourselves, and
renders men not unaccountable for the perversity of their
lives, which notion is no other than the philosophical
view of our ancient law. As to the other two causes
of this sad event, anybody may partly lay the blame
on the young men, who under the influence of youthful
vanity, and pride at their royal birth, listened to the
calumnies that were raised against their father, while certainly they were not kindly judges of the actions of his
life, but ill-natured in suspecting, and intemperate in

[1] *Sebustieh.*

speaking of them, and so on both accounts easily led away by those who observed them, and informed of them to gain favour. However, their father cannot be thought worthy of excuse as to his impiety to them, seeing that, without any certain evidence of their treacherous designs against him, and without any proofs that they had made preparation for such an attempt, he had the heart to kill his own sons, who were of very comely bodies and the great darlings of all other men, and no way deficient in their pursuits, whether hunting, or warlike exercises, or speaking upon occasional topics. For in all these things they were skilful, and especially Alexander, who was the eldest. And certainly it would have been sufficient, even though Herod had condemned them, to have kept them alive in bonds, or to have let them live at a distance from his dominions in banishment, as he was surrounded by the Roman forces, which were a strong security to him, and would prevent his suffering anything from either a sudden attack or from open force. But for him to kill them so quickly, in order to gratify a passion that mastered him, was a proof of excessive impiety; especially as he was guilty of so great a crime in his old age. Nor will the delay that he made, and the late time in which the crime was done, plead at all for his excuse. For when a man is taken by surprise and moved to commit a wicked action, although it be a grave crime, yet it is a thing that is always happening; but to do it deliberately, and after frequent attempts, and as frequent delays, to undertake and accomplish it at last, was the action of a murderous mind, and one not easily moved from what is evil. Moreover Herod showed this temper in what he did afterwards, when he did not spare those that seemed to be the best beloved of his friends that were left, in regard to whom, though the justice of their punishment caused those that perished to be the less pitied, yet was the barbarity of the man as great, in that he did not abstain from their slaughter either. But of these persons I shall have occasion to speak more hereafter.

# BOOK XVII.

FROM THE DEATH OF ALEXANDER AND ARISTOBULUS TO
THE BANISHMENT OF ARCHELAUS.

## CHAP. I.

*How Antipater was hated by all the Nation for the Death
of his Brothers; and how, for that Reason, he courted his
Friends at Rome, by giving them many Presents; as he
did also to Saturninus, the Governor of Syria, and to
others. Also concerning Herod's Wives and Children.*

### § 1.

WHEN Antipater had thus got rid of his brothers, and
brought his father into the highest degree of impiety, till he was haunted by the Furies for what he had
done, his hopes did not succeed to his mind as to his
future. For although he was delivered from the fear of
his brothers being his rivals as to the government, yet did
he find it a very hard thing, and almost impracticable, to
come at the kingdom, because the hatred of the nation was
become very great against him. And besides this very
disagreeable circumstance, the alienation of the soldiers
from him grieved him still more, for these kings derived
from them all the safety which they had, whenever they
found the nation desirous of innovation; and he had drawn
all this danger upon himself by his destruction of his
brothers. However, he governed the nation jointly with
his father, being indeed no other than a king already;
and he was the more trusted by Herod and got his greater
good-will for what it would have been well for him to have
been put to death, as he seemed to have informed against
his brothers from his concern for the preservation of
Herod, and not rather out of his ill-will to them, and
still more to his father himself. Such was the accursed
state he was in. Now, all Antipater's contrivances tended

to pave the way to take off Herod, that he might have
nobody to accuse him in the vile practices he was devising,
and that Herod might have no refuge, nor any to afford
him assistance, if Antipater became his open enemy; insomuch that the very plots he had laid against his brothers
were occasioned by the hatred he bore his father.   And at
this time he was more than ever set upon the carrying out
of his attempts against Herod, because, if he were once
dead, the kingdom would now be firmly secured to him;
but, if Herod were to live any longer, he would himself be
in danger upon discovery of the wickedness of which he
had been the contriver, and his father would of necessity
then become his enemy.   And so he became very bountiful
to his father's friends, and bestowed great sums on several
of them, in order so to take off men's hatred against him.
He also sent great presents to his friends especially at
Rome, to gain their good-will, and above all to Saturninus,
the governor of Syria.   He also hoped to gain the favour
of Saturninus' brother by the large presents he bestowed
on him; and also used the same treatment to [Salome]
the king's sister, who had married one of Herod's chief
friends.   And as he counterfeited friendship to those with
whom he conversed, he was very clever in gaining their
belief, and very cunning in hiding his hatred against any
that he really did hate.   But he could not impose upon
his aunt, who had understood him a long time, and was a
woman not easily to be deluded, as she had already used
every possible caution to prevent his malicious designs.
And although Antipater's maternal uncle had married her
daughter, and that by Antipater's contrivance and management, as she had before been married to Aristobulus,
while Salome's other daughter was married to Callias the
son of her husband, yet that marriage was no obstacle to
her discovering his wicked designs, any more than her
former relationship to him could prevent her hatred of
him.   Now Herod had compelled Salome, when she was in
love with Syllæus the Arabian, and had a great fondness
for him, to marry Alexas, which match was arranged by
Julia, who persuaded Salome not to refuse it, lest there
should be open enmity between the brother and sister, as
Herod had sworn that he would never be friends with

Salome, if she would not accept Alexas for her husband.
And she listened to Julia as being the Emperor's wife, and
also because she advised her to nothing but what was very
much for her advantage. At this time, also, Herod sent
back king Archelaus' daughter, who had been Alexander's
wife, to her father, returning the portion he had with her
out of his own estate, that there might be no dispute
between them about it.

§ 2. Now Herod himself brought up his sons' children
with very great care; for Alexander had two sons by
Glaphyra; and Aristobulus had three sons and two
daughters by Berenice, Salome's daughter; and once when
his friends were with him, he produced the children
before them, and deploring the fortune of his own
sons, prayed that no such ill fortune might befall their
children, but that they might improve in virtue, and
obtain what they justly deserved, and so might make him
return for his care of their education. He also promised
them in marriage when they should come to the proper
age, the elder of Alexander's sons to Pheroras' daughter,
and Antipater's daughter to Aristobulus' son. He also
allotted one of Aristobulus' daughters to Antipater's son,
and Aristobulus' other daughter to Herod, a son of his
own by the high priest's daughter; for it is the ancient practice among us to have several wives at the
same time. Now, the king made these betrothals for
the children out of commiseration of them now they
were fatherless, endeavouring to render Antipater kind
to them by these intermarriages. But Antipater did
not fail to continue in the same temper of mind to his
brothers' children as he had been in to his brothers themselves; and his father's affection for them irritated him,
as he thought that they would become greater than ever
his brothers had been, especially when they came to men's
estate, as Archelaus, a king, would support his daughter's
sons, and Pheroras, a tetrarch, would have one of the
daughters as wife for his son. What provoked him further
was that all the multitude commiserated these fatherless
children, and so hated him, and he feared that all would
come out, since they were no strangers to his malignity
to his brothers. He manœuvred, therefore, to upset his

father's arrangements, thinking it a terrible thing that
they should be so related to him, and be powerful. And
Herod yielded to him, and changed his resolution at his
entreaty: and the arrangement now was, that Antipater
himself should marry Aristobulus' daughter, and Antipater's son Pheroras' daughter. And the betrothals were
changed in this manner against the king's real wishes.

§ 3. Now Herod the king had at this time nine wives,
one of them Antipater's mother, and another the high
priest's daughter, by whom he had a son of his own name.
He had also one who was his brother's daughter, and another his sister's daughter, but these two had no children.
One of his wives also was of the Samaritan nation, and her
sons were Antipas and Archelaus, and her daughter Olympias, who afterwards married Joseph, the king's brother's
son; but Archelaus and Antipas were brought up at the
house of a certain private man at Rome. Herod also had as
wife Cleopatra of Jerusalem, and by her he had Herod and
Philip, which last was also brought up at Rome. Pallas
also was another of his wives, who bore him a son Phasaelus. And besides these, he had for wives Phaedra and
Elpis, by whom he had two daughters, Roxane and Salome.
As for his elder daughters by the same mother as Alexander
and Aristobolus, and whom Pheroras had refused to marry,
he gave the one in marriage to Antipater, the king's sister's
son, and the other to Phasaelus, his brother's son. And
this was the posterity of Herod.


# CHAP. II.

*Concerning the Babylonian Jew Zamaris. Also concerning
the Plots laid by Antipater against his Father. Also about
the Pharisees.*

§ 1.

AND now Herod, being desirous of securing himself
against the Trachonites, resolved to build a village as
large as a city for the Jews between him and them, which
might make his own country difficult of access, and which
he might make a *point d'appui* to make sudden sallies

upon the enemy from a short distance, and so do them a mischief. So when he heard that there was a man that was a Jew come out of Babylonia with five hundred horsemen (all of whom could shoot their arrows as they rode on horseback) who with a hundred of his relations had crossed over the Euphrates, and now dwelt at Antioch near Daphne in Syria, where Saturninus, who was then governor of Syria, had given them a place to dwell in called Valatha, he sent for this man and his companions, and promised to give him land in the toparchy called Batanæa, which is bounded by Trachonitis, wishing to make his settlement a *point d'appui* against the enemy. He also promised to let him hold the country free from tribute, and that they should dwell there without paying any such customs as used to be paid, and gave it them tax free.

§ 2. This Babylonian was induced by these offers to settle there, and took possession of the land, and built fortresses in it and a village, which he called Bathyra.[1] And he became a protection to the inhabitants against the Trachonites, and also kept those Jews who came out of Babylon to offer their sacrifices at Jerusalem from being hurt by the Trachonite robbers; so that many came to him from all those parts where the ancient Jewish laws were observed, and the country became full of people because of the universal freedom from taxes. This continued during the life of Herod; but when Philip, who was [tetrarch] after him, took over the government, he made them pay a few taxes, but for a little while only; and although Agrippa the Great, and his son of the same name, harassed them greatly, yet they would not take their liberty away. And though the Romans have now taken the government into their own hands from them, they still give them the privilege of their freedom, and oppress them merely with the imposition of taxes. But I shall treat these matters more fully in the progress of this history.

§ 3. At length Zamaris, the Babylonian, to whom Herod had given that country for a possession, died, having lived virtuously, and left good children behind him, one of whom was Jacimus, who was famous for his valour, and

---

[1] *el-Bethirra;* probably the same place as Batthora, one of the Roman military stations east of Jordan.

taught the Babylonians under him how to ride their horses, and a troop of them were body-guards to the forementioned kings. And when Jacimus died in old age, he left a son whose name was Philip, one of great strength in his hands, and in other respects also more eminent for his valour than any one; so that there was a firm friendship and lasting good-will between him and king Agrippa; and whatever army the king kept he constantly trained and led wherever they had occasion to march.

§ 4. The affairs of Herod being in the condition I have described, everything depended upon Antipater; and his power was such, that he could do what he pleased, by his father's concession, who believed in his good-will and fidelity to himself, and he ventured to use his powers still further, because his wicked designs were concealed from his father, and he made him believe everything he said. He was also formidable to all, not so much because of the power and authority he had as for his cunning malice; and Pheroras especially paid court to him, and received the like friendship in return. And Antipater had cunningly surrounded him by a company of women, whom he placed about him; for Pheroras was completely under the influence of his wife, and her mother, and her sister; and that notwithstanding the hatred he bore them for the indignities they had offered to his virgin daughters. Yet did he put up with them, and nothing was to be done without the women, who had got round this man, and continued still to assist each other in all things, so that Antipater was entirely under their influence, owing both to himself and his mother, for these four women[1] all said the same thing; and the opinions of Pheroras and Antipater only differed in a few points of no consequence. But the king's sister [Salome] was their antagonist, who for a good while had pried into all their affairs, and knew that this friendship of theirs was made in order to do Herod some harm, and was disposed to inform the king of it. And as they knew that their friendship did not please Herod, they contrived that their meetings should not be discovered, and pretended to hate one another, and

[1] Pheroras' wife, and her mother and sister, and Doris, Antipater's mother.—W.

abused one another as time and opportunity allowed, and especially when Herod was present, or when any one was there that would tell him; but their intimacy was greater than ever in secret. This was the course they took; but they could not conceal from Salome either their contrivance when first they set about this plan, or when they had made some progress in it, but she searched out everything; and, exaggerating the matter to her brother, disclosed to him their secret meetings and compotations, and counsels taken in a clandestine manner, which, if they were not in order to destroy him, might well enough have been open and public. And though to appearance they were at variance, and spoke about one another as if they intended one another a mischief, they agreed well enough together when they were out of the sight of people; for when they were alone by themselves, they acted in concert, and professed that they would never leave off their friendship, but would fight against those from whom they concealed their designs. And thus did she search out these things, and get a perfect knowledge of them, and then told her brother of them; who was himself aware of a great deal of what she said, but still durst not act upon it, because of the suspicion he had that much of his sister's tales was calumny. Now there was a certain sect of Jews, who valued themselves highly upon the strict observance of the law of their fathers, and made men believe they were highly favoured by God, and had great influence over women. They were called Pharisees, and ventured even to oppose kings. They were a cunning set, and prompt to open fighting and mischief. And when all the rest of the Jewish people gave assurance by oath of their good-will to the Emperor and to the king's government, these very men would not swear, who were more than six thousand; and when the king imposed a fine upon them, Pheroras' wife paid the fine for them. And they to requite that kindness of hers (for they were believed to have fore-knowledge of things to come by divine inspiration) foretold that God had decreed that Herod's sway should cease, and that his posterity should be deprived of it, and that the kingdom should come to her and Pheroras and their children. These predictions (for they were not concealed from Salome) were told the king; as also how they had corrupted some persons about the palace itself: and the king slew such of the Pharisees as were chiefly accused, and the eunuch Bagoas, and one Carus the royal catamite, who excelled all his contemporaries in beauty. He slew also those of his own household who had consented to what the Pharisees foretold. As for Bagoas, he had been puffed up by them as though he should be called father and benefactor of him who was by the prediction to be their king: for this king would have all things in his power, and would enable Bagoas to marry and beget children.

## CHAP. III.

*Of the Enmity between Herod and Pheroras ; how Herod sent Antipater to Augustus ; and of the Death of Pheroras.*

### § 1.

WHEN Herod had punished those Pharisees who had been convicted of these crimes, he gathered together an assembly of his friends, and accused Pheroras' wife ; and ascribing the outrages done to the virgins to the audacity of the woman, brought an accusation against her for the dishonour she had brought upon him. He added that she had stirred up strife between him and his brother, and had by her ill temper brought them into a state of war, to the best of her power, both by her words and actions ; and that the fines which he had imposed had not been paid, for the offenders had escaped punishment by her means ; and that nothing which had of late been done had been done without her. "And so Pheroras will do well, if he will, of his own accord, and at his own initiative, and not at my entreaty, or as following my opinion, put this his wife away, as one that will still be the occasion of strife between us. And now Pheroras, if thou valuest thy relation to me, put this wife of thine away ; for so thou wilt continue to be a brother to me, and wilt abide in thy love to me." Then said Pheroras, (although moved by the force of Herod's words,) that he would neither do so unjust a thing as renounce his brotherly relation to him, nor leave off his

affection for his wife; that he would rather choose to die
than live and be deprived of a wife that was so dear to
him.   Thereupon Herod put off his anger against Pheroras
on these accounts, although he exacted a severe punishment,
for he forbade Antipater and his mother to associate with
Pheroras, and bade them take care to avoid the assemblies of
the women : which they promised to do, but still got together when an opportunity presented itself, and both Pheroras and Antipater had their own merry meetings.   The
report went also, that Antipater had criminal connection
with Pheroras' wife, and that they were brought together
by Antipater's mother.

§ 2.  But Antipater was now suspicious of his father, and
afraid that his hatred to him would increase: so he wrote
to his friends at Rome, and bade them signify to Herod,
that he was to send Antipater without delay to Augustus.
And Herod did this, and sent most handsome presents with
Antipater, as also his testament, wherein he appointed Antipater to be his successor : and if Antipater should die first,
Herod his son by the high priest's daughter was to succeed.
And Syllæus the Arabian went with Antipater to Rome,
though he had done nothing of all that Augustus had enjoined, and Antipater accused him of the same crimes as
he had been formerly accused of by Nicolaus.  Syllæus
was also accused by Aretas of having without his consent
slain many of the chief Arabians at Petra, and particularly
Sohemus, a man that deserved to be honoured by all men,
and of having slain Fabatus a slave of Augustus.  Syllæus
was also accused on the following account.  Corinthus was
one of Herod's body-guards, and greatly trusted by him.
Syllæus had tempted this man by the offer of a great sum
of money to kill Herod, and he had promised to do so.
When Fabatus learnt of this, for Syllæus himself told him
of it, he informed the king of it; and he had Corinthus
arrested and put to the torture, and so wormed the whole
conspiracy out of him.  He also got two other Arabians
arrested, trusting to the information of Corinthus ; the one
the head of a tribe, and the other a friend of Syllæus, who
were both put by the king to the torture, and confessed
that they had come to encourage Corinthus not to fail in
courage, and to assist him with their own hands in the

murder, if need should require their assistance. And Saturninus, upon Herod's discovering the whole matter to him, sent them to Rome.

§ 3. Herod also commanded Pheroras, since he was so obstinate in his affection for his wife, to retire to his own tetrarchy; which he did very willingly, and swore many oaths that he would not come back again, till he heard that Herod was dead. Indeed, when Herod was ill, and Pheroras was asked to come to him before he died, that he might intrust him with some injunctions, he had such a regard to his oath, that he would not come to him. But Herod did not imitate Pheroras in his conduct, but changed his purpose [not to see him,] which he before had, and as soon as Pheroras began to be ill, went to him without being sent for. And when he was dead, he took care of his funeral, and had his body brought to Jerusalem and buried there, and appointed a solemn mourning for him. Now this [death of Pheroras] became the beginning of Antipater's misfortunes, although he had already sailed for Rome, God being now about to punish him for the murder of his brothers. I shall narrate this matter very fully, that it may be a warning to mankind, that they take care to conduct their whole lives by the rules of virtue.

## CHAP. IV.

*Pheroras' Wife is accused by his Freedmen of poisoning him; and how Herod, upon examining the Matter by Torture, found the Poison; but also that it had been prepared for himself by his son Antipater; and how, upon Inquiry by Torture, he discovered the dangerous Designs of Antipater.*

### § 1.

AS soon as Pheroras was dead, and his funeral was over, two of Pheroras' freedmen, who were much esteemed by him, went to Herod, and entreated him not to leave the murder of his brother unavenged, but to examine into the cause of his strange and unhappy death. As he was moved by these words, for they seemed to him to be true,

they said that Pheroras had supped with his wife the day
before he fell ill, and that a certain potion was brought
him in a kind of food he was not used to eat, and that when
he had eaten it he died of it; that this potion was brought
out of Arabia by a woman, nominally as a love potion, (for
it was called a philter,) but in reality to kill Pheroras; for
the Arabian women were skilful in making such poisons,
and the woman to whom they ascribed this, was con-
fessedly a most intimate friend of one of Syllæus' mis-
tresses, and both the mother and sister of Pheroras' wife
had been to the places where she lived, and had persuaded
her to sell them this potion, and had returned with it the
day before Pheroras' last supper.  At these words the king
was exasperated, and put the women slaves and also some
free women to the torture, and as the matter was by no
means clear, because none of them would speak out, at last
one of them, after suffering extreme agonies, said no more
but that she prayed that God would send the like agonies
upon Antipater's mother, who had been the cause of these
miseries to all of them.   This prayer induced Herod to increase the women's tortures, till thereby all was discovered:
the merry-makings, the secret meetings, and the disclosing
of what he had said to his son alone unto Pheroras' women.[1]
(Now what Herod had charged Antipater to conceal, was
the gift of a hundred talents to him not to have any
dealings with Pheroras.)   It also came out what hatred
Antipater bore to his father, and how he complained to his
mother how very long his father lived, and that he was
himself almost an old man, insomuch, that if the kingdom
ever came to him, it would not afford him the same pleasure; and that there were a great many of his brothers, or
brothers' children, being reared in hopes of the kingdom, as
well as himself, all which made his own hopes of it uncertain; and even now, if he should himself not live, Herod
had ordered that the kingdom should be conferred, not on
his son, but rather on his brother.   He had also accused
the king of great barbarity, and of the slaughter of his
sons, and had said that it was the fear he was in, lest he
should do the like to him, that made him contrive his

---

[1] His wife, her mother and sister.—W.

journey to Rome, and made Pheroras contrive to go to his own tetrarchy.

§ 2. All this tallied with what Herod's sister had told him, and tended greatly to corroborate her testimony, and to free her from the suspicion of unfaithfulness to him. And the king having satisfied himself of the spite which Doris, Antipater's mother, as well as Antipater himself, bore to him, took away from her all her fine ornaments, which were worth many talents, and then sent her away, and entered into friendship with Pheroras' women. But he who most of all irritated the king against his son was one Antipater, a Samaritan, the steward of Antipater the king's son, who, when he was tortured, said among other things that Antipater had prepared a deadly potion, and given it to Pheroras, bidding him give it to his father during his own absence, and when he was too remote to have the least suspicion cast upon him as to it: and that Antiphilus, one of Antipater's friends, brought the potion out of Egypt, and that it was sent to Pheroras by Theudion, the brother of the mother of the king's son Antipater, and so came to Pheroras' wife, her husband having given it her to keep. And when the king questioned her about it, she confessed, and as she was running to fetch it, she threw herself down from the house-top, but did not kill herself, because she fell upon her feet. And so, when the king comforted her, and promised her and her domestics pardon, upon condition of their concealing nothing of the truth from him, but threatened her with the utmost tortures if she obstinately determined to conceal anything, she promised and swore that she would speak out and tell how everything was done; and said what most took to be entirely true. "The potion was brought out of Egypt by Antiphilus, and his brother, who is a physician, procured it; and when Theudion brought it us, I kept it upon Pheroras' committing it to me, and it was prepared by Antipater for you. So when Pheroras was fallen ill, and you came to him and took care of him, and when he saw the kindness you had to him, his mind was broken thereby. So he called me to him, and said to me; 'Antipater has deluded me, wife, in this affair of his father and my brother, by persuading me to have a murderous intention to him, and

procuring a potion for that purpose. Go therefore and
fetch the potion, (since my brother appears to have still
the same kind disposition to me as he had formerly, and
I do not expect to live long myself), and, that I may
not defile my forefathers by the murder of a brother,
burn it before my face:' and I immediately brought
it, and did as my husband bade me, and burnt most of the
potion, but left a little of it, that if the king, after Pheroras'
death, should treat me ill, I might poison myself, and so
get rid of my miseries." Upon her saying this, she
brought out the potion, and the box it was in, before them
all. And another brother of Antiphilus, and his mother
also, under the agony of pain and torture, confessed the
same things, and recognised the box. The high priest's
daughter also, who was the king's wife, was accused of
having been privy to all this, and of having resolved to
conceal it ; so Herod divorced her, and blotted her son out
of his testament, wherein he had been mentioned as one to
reign after him ; and he took the high priesthood away
from his father-in-law, Simon the son of Boethus, and
appointed Matthias the son of Theophilus, who was born
at Jerusalem, to be high priest in his room.

§ 3. Meantime Bathyllus, Antipater's freedman, also
came from Rome, and upon being tortured, was found to
have brought another potion, to give to Antipater's mother
and to Pheroras, that if the former potion did not operate
upon the king, this at least might carry him off. There
came also letters from Herod's friends at Rome, by the
advice and at the suggestion of Antipater, to accuse
Archelaus and Philip, as if they calumniated their father
on account of the slaughter of Alexander and Aristobulus,
and as if they commiserated their deaths; and as if they
concluded, because they were sent for home (for their
father had already recalled them), that they themselves
were also to be put to death. These letters were concocted
for great rewards by Antipater's friends. And Antipater
himself also wrote to his father about Archelaus and Philip,
and laid the heaviest things to their charge ; yet did he
entirely excuse them of any guilt, for he said they were
but striplings, and so imputed their words to their youth.
He added that he had himself been very busy in the affair

relating to Syllæus, and in paying court to great men, and
on that account had bought splendid ornaments to present
them with, which had cost him two hundred talents. Now,
one may wonder how it came about, while so many accusations were laid against Antipater in Judæa for seven
months before this, that he was not made acquainted with
any of them. The explanation of this is that the roads
were carefully guarded, and that men hated Antipater: for
there was nobody who would run any hazard himself to
procure Antipater's safety.

# CHAP. V.

*Antipater sails Home from Rome to his Father; and how he
was accused by Nicolaus of Damascus, and condemned to
die by his Father, and by Quintilius Varus, who was then
Governor of Syria; and how he was imprisoned till
the Emperor should decide on the Case.*

## § 1.

NOW Herod, upon Antipater's writing to him, that
having done all that he was to do, and as he was
to do it, he would soon return, concealed his anger
against him, and wrote back to him, and bade him not delay his journey, lest any harm should befall himself in his
absence. At the same time also he made some little complaints about Antipater's mother, but promised that he
would drop those complaints on Antipater's return. He
also expressed his entire affection for him, fearing lest he
should have some suspicion of him, and defer his journey
home, and lest, while he lived at Rome, he should plot for
the kingdom, and do him some harm. Antipater got this
letter in Cilicia, but had received an account of Pheroras'
death before at Tarentum,[1] which news affected him deeply,
not out of any affection for Pheroras, but because he had
died without having murdered Herod, as he had promised
to do. And when he was at Celenderis[2] in Cilicia, he began

---

[1] *Taranto* in Italy.
[2] *Kilindria*, on the south coast of Asia Minor, opposite Cyprus.

to deliberate whether he should sail home, as he was much
put out at the banishment of his mother. Now, some of
his friends advised him to tarry a while and wait for
further information. But others advised him to sail home
without delay, for if he were once arrived there, he would
soon put an end to all accusations, and nothing now
afforded any weight to his accusers but his absence. He
was persuaded by these last and set sail, and landed at the
haven called Sebastus,[1] which Herod had built at vast expense, and called Sebastus in honour of Cæsar Augustus.[2]
And now Antipater was evidently in a sorry plight, as nobody
came to him or saluted him, as they did at his going away,
with good wishes or joyful acclamations ; nor was there now
anything to hinder the people from receiving him, on the
contrary, with bitter curses, as they supposed he was come
to receive punishment for the murder of his brothers.

§ 2. Now, Quintilius Varus was at this time at Jerusalem,
being sent to succeed Saturninus as governor of Syria, and
was come as an adviser to Herod, who had asked his advice in the present state of affairs ; and as they were sitting
together, Antipater came in, without knowing anything of
the matter ; so he entered the palace clothed in purple.
The porters received him indeed in, but excluded his friends.
And now he was in great alarm, and clearly perceived the
position he was in, for upon going to salute his father he
was repulsed by him, and Herod called him a murderer of
his brothers, and a plotter of destruction against himself,
and told him that Varus should hear everything and be his
judge the very next day. So he found that the misfortune he now first heard of was already upon him, the
greatness of which dismayed him, and his mother and
wife soon had an interview with him (his wife was the
daughter of Antigonus, who was king of the Jews before
Herod), from whom he learned everything, and prepared
for his defence.

§ 3. The following day Varus and the king sat together
in judgment, and both their friends were also called in, as
also the king's relations, and his sister Salome, and as
many as could discover anything, and all those who had

---

[1] The harbour of Cæsarea Palæstina, *Kaisarîyeh.*
[2] Sebastus would be Greek for Augustus.

been tortured; and besides these, some slaves of Antipater's mother, who had been arrested a little before Antipater's coming, having on them a letter, the sum of which was that Antipater was not to return home, as all was come to his father's knowledge, and that Augustus was the only refuge he had left to prevent both him and her falling into Herod's hands. Then did Antipater fall down at his father's feet, and besought him not to prejudge his case, but that his father would first hear him, and not decide against him except upon evidence. Then Herod ordered him to be brought into the midst, and then lamented that he had had children, from whom he had suffered such great misfortunes before, and now Antipater plotted against him in his old age. He also touched on the maintenance and education he had given his sons, and what seasonable supplies of wealth he had afforded them as they desired, though none of those favours had hindered them from plotting against him, and from bringing his very life into danger, in order to gain his kingdom in an impious manner, by taking away his life before either the course of nature, or their father's wishes, or justice, required that the kingdom should come to them. As to Antipater, he wondered what hopes could bring him to such a pass as to be bold enough to attempt such things; for he had by his testament declared him in writing his successor in the kingdom, and while he was alive he was in no respect inferior to him either in his splendid dignity or in power and authority, as he had no less than fifty talents for his yearly income, and had received for his journey to Rome no less than thirty talents. He also accused him as to his brothers, saying if they were guilty he had imitated their example, and if they were innocent, he had brought him groundless accusations against his near relations; for he had been informed of all those things by him, and by nobody else, and had done what he had done by his advice, and he now absolved them from all that was criminal, as he had become the inheritor of the guilt of their parricide.

§ 4. When Herod had thus spoken, he fell a-weeping, and was not able to say any more; but at his desire Nicolaus of Damascus, who was the king's friend, and very intimate with him, and well acquainted with all his affairs,

proceeded to what remained, and stated all that concerned
the proofs and evidences of the facts.   Upon which Antipater, in his defence, turned to his father, and enlarged
upon the many indications he had given of his good-will
to him ; and enumerated the honours that had been done
himself, which would not have been done, had he not
deserved them by his regard to his father ; for he had
made provision for everything that could be foreseen, as
to giving his father the wisest advice ; and whenever there
was occasion for the labour of his hands, he had not
grudged any such pains for him.   He added that it was
unlikely that he who had delivered his father from so many
treacherous contrivances of others against him, should
himself plot against him, and so lose all the reputation he
had gained for his virtue then by the wickedness which
succeeded it, and that though he was already appointed
his successor, and had nothing to prevent his enjoying
the royal honour with his father at present ; nor was it
likely that a person who had half the royal authority
without any danger, and with a good character, should
hunt after the whole with infamy and danger, and that
when it was doubtful whether he could obtain it or not,
and when he had seen the punishment of his brothers, and
was both the informer and accuser against them when
otherwise their guilt would not have been discovered ; nay,
was himself the author of the punishment inflicted upon
them, when it appeared evident that they were guilty of a
wicked attempt against their father ; and even the contentions there were in the king's family, were proofs that he
had ever managed affairs in the sincerest affection to his
father.   And as to what he had done at Rome Augustus
was a witness, who was no more to be imposed upon than
God himself : of whose opinion his letters sent there were
sufficient evidence, and it was not reasonable to prefer the
calumnies of such as proposed to raise disturbances to
those letters ; most of which calumnies had been raised
during his absence, which gave opportunity to his enemies
to forge them, which they would not have been able to do
if he had been at home.   Moreover, he descanted on the
weakness of evidence obtained by torture, which was commonly false ; because the distress men were in under

such torture naturally obliged them to say many things in order to please those in power.  He also offered himself to the torture * * *.

§ 5. Hereupon there was a change observed in the assembly, as they greatly pitied Antipater, who, by weeping and putting on a countenance suitable to his sad case, moved even his enemies to compassion ; and it appeared plainly that Herod himself was affected in his own mind, although he was not willing it should be taken notice of. Then did Nicolaus begin to recapitulate what the king had begun, and that with great bitterness ; and summed up all the evidence which arose from the tortures, or from the witnesses.  He mainly enlarged upon the king's virtue, which he had exhibited in the maintenance and education of his sons, though he had never gained any advantage thereby, but had still fallen from one misfortune to another. And although he owned that he was not so much surprised at the thoughtless behaviour of Herod's other sons, who were younger, and were besides corrupted by wicked counsellors, who had caused them to wipe out of their minds all the righteous dictates of nature, and that from a desire of coming to the throne sooner than they ought to do ; yet he could not but justly stand amazed at the horrible wickedness of Antipater, who, although he had had great benefits bestowed on him by his father, yet was not more tamed in mind than the most envenomed serpents, and even those creatures admitted of some mitigation, and would not bite their benefactors ; and Antipater had also not let the misfortunes of his brothers be any hindrance to him, but had gone on to imitate their barbarity none the less.  "Yet wast thou (he continued) O Antipater! the informer as to the wicked actions they had dared, and the searcher out of the evidence against them, and the author of the punishment they underwent upon their detection. Nor do we say this as accusing thee for being so zealous in thy anger against them, but we are astounded at thy endeavours to imitate their wicked behaviour ; and we discover thereby that thou didst not act thus for the safety of thy father, but for the destruction of thy brothers, that by thy expressed hatred of their impiety thou mightest be believed to be a lover of thy father, and mightest so get power enough to do mischief with the greater impunity; which design thy actions indeed demonstrate. It is true thou tookest thy brothers off, because thou didst convict them of their wicked designs, but thou didst not yield up to justice those who were their fellow-conspirators, and so didst make it evident to all men, that thou madest covenant with them against thy father, as thou chosest to be the accuser of thy brothers, wishing to gain for thyself alone the advantage of laying plots to kill thy father, and so to enjoy double pleasure, which is truly worthy of the evil disposition which thou didst openly show against thy brothers; on which account thou didst rejoice, as having done a most famous exploit, nor was that thought unworthy of thee. But if thy intention was otherwise, then art thou worse than they; for while thou didst contrive to hide thy treachery against thy father, thou didst hate them, not as plotters against thy father, for in that case thou wouldst not thyself have fallen into the like crime, but as successors to his throne, and more worthy of that succession than thyself. Thou wouldst kill thy father after thy brothers, lest thy lies raised against them might be detected; and lest thou shouldst suffer the punishment thou hadst deserved, thou hadst a mind to exact that punishment from thy unhappy father, and didst devise such an uncommon sort of parricide as the world never yet saw. For thou, who art his son, didst not only plot against a father, but against one who loved thee, and had been thy benefactor, and had made thee in reality his partner in the kingdom, and had openly declared thee his successor, so that thou wast not forbidden to taste the sweetness of authority already, and hadst sure hope of what was to come by thy father's determination and the security of a written testament. But certainly thou didst not estimate these things according to thy father's virtue, but according to thy own wicked thoughts, and wert desirous to take away the part of the kingdom that remained from thy too indulgent father, and soughtest to destroy with thy deeds him whom thou in words pretendedst to preserve. Nor wast thou content to be wicked thyself, but thou also filledst thy mother's head with thy devices, and raisedst disturbances among thy brothers, and hadst the boldness to call thy father a wild

beast; whilst thou hadst thyself a mind more cruel than
any serpent, whence thou sentest out that poison among
thy nearest kindred and greatest benefactors, and invitedst
them to assist thee and guard thee, and didst hedge thyself in on all sides by the artifices of both men and women
against an old man; as though that mind of thine was not
sufficient of itself to support so great a hidden hatred as
thou didst bear to him. And now thou appearest here, after
the tortures of freemen and domestics and men and women
on thy account, and after the informations of thy fellow-
conspirators, as anxious to contradict the truth, and hast
thought on ways not only to take thy father out of the
world, but to set aside that law which is written against
thee, and the virtue of Varus, and the nature of justice.
Nay, so great is that impudence in which thou confidest,
that thou desirest to be put to the torture thyself, though
thou allegest that the tortures of those already examined
thereby have made them tell lies; that those that have saved
thy father from thee may not be thought to have spoken
the truth, but that thy tortures forsooth may be esteemed
the discoverers of truth! Wilt not thou, O Varus! deliver
the king from the injuries of his kindred? Wilt not thou
destroy this wicked wild beast, who has pretended kindness to his father in order to destroy his brothers, while yet
he is himself alone ready to take the kingdom immediately,
and appears to be the most deadly enemy to his father of
them all? For thou art well aware that parricide is an
injury alike to nature and life, and that the intention of
parricide is as great a crime as its perpetration : and he who
does not punish it does an injury to nature itself."

§ 6. Nicolaus added further what concerned Antipater's
mother, as whatever she had prattled with womanish gar-
rulity, and also about the predictions and sacrifices relating to the king; and whatever Antipater had done
lasciviously in his cups and amours with Pheroras' women.
He touched also upon the result of the examinations by
torture, and the testimonies of the witnesses, which were
many and of various kinds, some prepared beforehand, and
others sudden answers, which confirmed the foregoing
evidence. For those men who were acquainted with any
of Antipater's practices, but had concealed them out of

fear, lest if he got off he would avenge himself on them,
when they saw that he was exposed to the accusations of
those who had begun to accuse him, and that fortune,
which had often supported him before, had now evidently
betrayed him into the hands of his enemies, who were
insatiable in their hatred to him, now told all they knew
of him.    And his ruin was now hastened, not so much by
the enmity of those who were his accusers, as by the great
audacity of his wicked contrivances, and by his ill-will to
his father and brothers, as he had filled their house with
dissension, and caused them to murder one another; and
was neither fair in his hatred, nor kind in his friendship,
but only so far as was likely to serve his own turn.    Now
there were many who had for a long time observed all this,
and especially those who were naturally disposed to judge
of matters by the rules of virtue, because they were used
to decide about facts without passion, but had been restrained from making any open complaints before, who
now, upon the leave given them, produced all that they
knew before the public.    There were also various wicked
crimes alleged against him, which could no way be refuted, because the many witnesses did neither speak out
of favour to Herod, nor were they obliged to keep back
what they had to say from suspicion of any danger they
were in, but they spoke what they knew, because they
thought such actions very wicked, and that Antipater
deserved every punishment, not so much indeed for
Herod's safety, as on account of his own wickedness.
Many things were also said by a great number of persons
who were not called upon to say them, so that Antipater, who
used generally to be very clever in his lies and brazen-faced
impudence, was not able to say one word to the contrary.
When Nicolaus had left off speaking, and had finished pro-
ducing his evidence, Varus bade Antipater betake himself
to his defence, if he had prepared any whereby it might
appear that he was not guilty of the crimes he was accused
of; for as he was himself desirous, so did he know that
his father was in like manner desirous also, to find him
entirely innocent.    But Antipater fell down on his face, and
appealed to God and to all men to testify to his innocency,
desiring that God would declare, by some evident signs,

that he had not laid any plot against his father. This is
the usual method of all men destitute of virtue; when they
set about any wicked undertakings, they fall to work
according to their own inclinations, as if they believed that
God did not interfere in human affairs; but when once
they are found out, and are in danger of undergoing the
punishment due to their crimes, they endeavour to upset
all the evidence against them by appealing to God; which
was the very thing which Antipater now did. For whereas
he had done everything as if there was no God in the
world, now that he was on all sides hemmed in by justice,
and was destitute of proofs by which he might rebut the
accusations laid against him, he impudently abused the
majesty of God, and ascribed it to his power that he had
been preserved hitherto, and enumerated before them all
the bold acts he had never failed to do for his father's
safety.

§ 7. But when Varus, upon frequently asking Antipater
what he had to say for himself, found he had nothing to
say besides appealing to God, and saw that there would
be no end of all this, he bade them bring the potion before
the court, that he might see what virtue still remained in
it; and when it was brought, and one that was condemned
to die had drunk it by Varus' command, he died at
once. Then Varus got up, and left the court, and the
day following went away to Antioch, where his usual residence was, because that was the royal city of the Syrians.
And Herod at once put his son in prison. Now what
Varus said to Herod was not known to the generality,
nor his last words before he went away: though it was
generally supposed that whatever Herod did afterwards
to Antipater was done with his approbation. But when
Herod had imprisoned his son, he sent letters to Rome
to Augustus about him, and messengers also to inform
Augustus by word of mouth of Antipater's crimes. Now, at
this very time there was intercepted a letter of Antiphilus,
written to Antipater from Egypt (where Antiphilus lived),
and, when it was broken open by the king, it was found to
contain what follows. "I have sent thee Acme's letter,
and hazarded my own life; for thou knowest that I am in
danger from two families, if I am discovered. I wish thee

good success in thy affair." These were the contents of
this letter; but the king made inquiry about the other
letter also, for it did not appear, and Antiphilus' slave,
who brought the letter which was read, denied that
he had received any other. But while the king was in
doubt about it, one of Herod's friends, seeing a seam upon
the inner coat of the slave (for he had two coats on),
guessed that the letter might be hidden within the lining,
which proved to be the case. So they took out the letter,
and its contents were as follows. "Acme to Antipater.
I have written to thy father such a letter as thou desiredst
me. I have also taken a copy and sent it, as if it came
from Salome to my mistress; and when he reads it, I
know that Herod will punish Salome, as plotting against
him." Now, this pretended letter of Salome's to her mistress was composed by Antipater, in the name of Salome
as to its meaning, but in the words of Acme. The letter
was as follows. "Acme to king Herod. I have done my
endeavour that nothing that is done against thee should be
concealed from thee. So upon my finding a letter of
Salome written to my mistress against thee, I have written
out a copy, and sent it to thee, with risk to myself, but for
thy advantage. The reason why she wrote it was because
she had a mind to be married to Syllæus. Do thou therefore tear this letter in pieces, that I may not come into
danger of my life." Now Acme had written to Antipater
himself, to inform him that, in compliance with his command, she had not only herself written to Herod, as if
Salome was intensely eager to plot against him, but had
also sent a copy of a letter, as coming from Salome to her
mistress. This Acme was a Jewess by birth, and a slave to
Julia, the Emperor's wife; and she did this out of friendship to Antipater, having been bought by him with a large
sum of money, to assist in his evil designs against his
father and aunt.

§ 8. Thereupon Herod was so amazed at the prodigious
wickedness of Antipater, that he was eager to have him
slain immediately, as a turbulent person in the most important concerns, and as one that had laid a plot not only
against himself, but against his sister also, and even corrupted the Emperor's household. Salome also incited him

to it, beating her breast, and bidding him kill her, if he could produce any credible testimony that she had acted in that manner. Herod also sent for his son, and questioned him, and bade him contradict it if he could, and not suppress anything he had to say from mistrust. But as he did not speak one word, he asked him, since he was every way detected of villany, at least to discover without delay his associates in his wicked designs. And he laid all upon Antiphilus, and discovered nobody else. Thereupon Herod was in such great grief, that he was eager to send his son to Rome to Augustus, there to give an account of these his wicked contrivances. But afterwards he feared lest he might there, by the assistance of his friends, escape the danger he was in; so he kept him in prison as before, and sent more ambassadors and letters [to Rome] to accuse his son, as also an account of the assistance Acme had given him in his wicked designs, with copies of the letters before mentioned.

## CHAP. VI.

*Concerning the Illness that Herod had, and the Rebellion which the Jews raised in consequence, as also the Punishment of the Rebellious.*

### § 1.

NOW Herod's ambassadors made haste to Rome, having been instructed beforehand, what answers they were to make to the questions put to them. They also carried the letters with them. But Herod now fell ill, and made his will, and bequeathed his kingdom to [Antipas], his youngest son; and that out of hatred to Archelaus and Philip owing to the calumnies of Antipater. He also bequeathed a thousand talents to the Emperor, and five hundred to Julia, the Emperor's wife, and to the Emperor's children, and friends, and freedmen. He also distributed his money revenues and lands among his sons and grandsons. He also made Salome his sister very rich, because she had continued faithful to him in all his circumstances, and had never ventured to do him any harm. And as he despaired of recovering, for he was in the seventieth year of his age, he grew very fierce, and indulged the bitterest anger upon all occasions; the reason whereof was that he thought himself despised, and that the nation was pleased with his misfortunes; besides which, he resented a rebellion which some of the people excited against him, the occasion of which was as follows.

§ 2. Judas, the son of Sariphæus, and Matthias, the son of Margalothus, were two of the most eloquent men among the Jews, and the most celebrated interpreters of the Jewish laws, and men well beloved by the people, because of their education of the youth; for all those youths that were studious of virtue frequented their lectures every day. These men, when they heard that the king's illness was incurable, incited the young men to pull down all those works which the king had erected contrary to the law of their fathers, and so obtain the rewards which the law would confer on them for such actions of piety, for it was truly on account of Herod's rashness in making such things as the law had forbidden that his other misfortunes, which were so unusual among mankind, and this illness also, with which he was now afflicted, had come upon him. For Herod had caused some things to be made which were contrary to the law, for which he was accused by Judas and Matthias. For example the king had erected over the great gate of the temple a large golden eagle, of great value, as an offering to the temple. Now, the law forbids those that propose to live according to it to erect images or representations of any living creatures. So these wise men bade [their scholars] pull down the golden eagle; saying that, though they might incur danger, which might bring them to their deaths, the virtue of the action now proposed to them was evidently far more advantageous to them than the pleasure of living, since they would die for the preservation and maintenance of the law of their fathers, and would also acquire everlasting fame and commendation, and would be commended not only by the present generation, but leave an example of life that would never be forgotten to posterity. And as death could not be avoided by living to escape danger, it was well for those who aimed after virtue to accept their fate so as to go out of the world with praise and honour; and it would alleviate death to a great degree,

thus to come at it by noble actions which danger brought,
and, at the same time, to leave that reputation behind
them to their children, and to all their relations, whether
men or women, which would be of great advantage to them
afterwards.

§ 3. With such words did they incite the young men,
and a report having come to them that the king was dead
co-operated with the wise men's arguments.   So at midday
they went and pulled down the eagle and cut it in pieces
with axes, while a great many people were in the temple.
And now the king's captain, hearing of the affair, and supposing it was more serious than it proved to be, went to the
spot with a large force, such as was sufficient to put a stop
to the multitude of those who were trying to pull down
what was dedicated to God : and he attacked them unexpectedly, as they were upon this bold attempt in foolish
presumption rather than cautious prudence (as is usual
with the multitude), and while they were in disorder and
incautious of what was for their advantage ; and he arrested
no fewer than forty of the young men, who had the courage
to wait his attack when the rest ran away, as also the in-
stigators of this bold attempt, Judas and Matthias, (who
thought it an ignominious thing to retire upon his approach,)
and led them to the king.   And when they were come to
the king, and he asked them if they had been so bold as to
pull down what he had dedicated to God, " Yes, (said
they,) we contrived what was contrived, and we performed
what has been performed, and that with such virtue as be-
comes men; for we have given our assistance to those
things which are dedicated to the honour of God, and we
have paid heed to the hearing of the law ; and it ought not
to be wondered at at all, if we esteem those laws which
Moses had suggested and taught to him by God, and which
he wrote and left behind him, more worthy of observation
than thy commands.   And we will with pleasure undergo
death, or whatever punishment thou mayst inflict upon us,
since we are conscious to ourselves that we shall not die for
any unrighteous actions, but for our love to religion."
And thus they all said, and their courage was equal to their
words, as also to the spirit with which they had set about
their bold action.   And the king ordered them to be bound,

and sent them to Jericho, and summoned the principal men
of the Jews. And when they were come, he assembled them in
the theatre, and as he could not himself stand, he lay upon
a couch, and enumerated the many labours that he had
long endured on their account, and how he had built the
temple at great expense, though the Asamonæans, during
the hundred and twenty-five years of their rule, had not
been able to perform so great a work for the honour of
God; and how he had also adorned it with very valuable
votive offerings, so that he hoped he had left himself a
memorial and fair fame after his death. He then cried out
that these men had not abstained from affronting him even
in his life-time, but in the very day-time, and in the sight
of the multitude, had outraged him to that degree, as to
lay their hands upon what he had dedicated, and by way
of abuse to pull it down to the ground. They pretended,
indeed, that they had done so to affront him, but if any one
considered the matter, he would find that they were really
guilty of sacrilege against God.

§ 4. But those present, because of Herod's temper, and
for fear he would be so cruel as to inflict punishment on
them, said that what was done was done without their approbation, and that it seemed to them that the deed deserved
punishment. But Herod dealt more mildly with the others,
but he deprived Matthias of the high priesthood, as in part
the cause of this action, and made Joazar, who was Matthias'
wife's brother, high priest in his stead. Now it happened,
during the time of the high priesthood of this Matthias,
that another person was made high priest for a single day,
which the Jews observed as a fast, for the following reason.
This Matthias the high priest, during the night before the
day when the fast was to be celebrated, seemed in a dream to
have connection with his wife; and because he could not
officiate himself on that account, Joseph, the son of Ellemus,
his kinsman, performed the sacred duties for him. Herod
now deprived this Matthias of the high priesthood, and
burnt alive the other Matthias, who had raised this insurrection, with his companions. And that very night there
was an eclipse of the moon.[1]

---

[1] This eclipse of the moon (which is the only eclipse of either of the
luminaries mentioned by our Josephus in any of his writings) is of the

§ 5. And now Herod's disease greatly increased upon him, God inflicting judgment upon him for his sins; for a slow fire consumed him, which did not so much appear to the touch outwardly, as it augmented his pains inwardly; and brought on him a vehement appetite for eating, which he could not but satisfy. His intestines were also ulcerated, and he had especial pain in his colon; an aqueous and transparent humour was also in his feet, and a similar ailment afflicted him in his abdomen. His privy-member also was putrified, and bred worms; and when he sat upright, he had a difficulty of breathing, which was very unpleasant, on account of the foulness of his breath, and his frequent panting; he had also convulsions in all parts of his body, which made him preternaturally strong. It was said by those who practised divination, and were endued with wisdom to foretell such things, that God inflicted this punishment on the king on account of his great impiety. And though his afflictions seemed greater than any one could bear, yet had he some hopes of recovering, and sent for physicians, and did not refuse to follow what they prescribed for his relief, and he crossed the river Jordan, and bathed in the warm baths that were at Callirrhoe,[1] which, besides their other general virtues, were also fit to drink; these waters run into the lake called Asphaltites.[2] And when the physicians thought fit to revive him there, by placing him in a vessel full of oil, it was supposed that he was dying; but upon the lamentable cries of his domestics, he came round, and having no longer the least hopes of recovery, gave orders that every soldier should be paid fifty drachmæ. He also gave a great deal of money to their commanders, and to his friends, and returned to Jericho, where he grew so choleric, that it made him do all things savagely, and though he was near his death, he contrived the following wicked design. Having commanded that all the principal men of the entire

greatest consequence for the determination of the time for the death of Herod and Antipater, and for the birth and entire chronology of Jesus Christ. It happened March 13th, in the year of the Julian period 4710, and the 4th year before the Christian era.—W.

[1] The hot-springs in the *Wâdy Zerka Ma'in*, on the east of the Dead Sea.

[2] The Dead Sea.

Jewish nation, wherever they lived, should come to him (and a great number came, because the whole nation was called, and all men heard of this decree, and death was the penalty of such as should neglect the letters sent to call them), the king was in a wild rage against them all, as well innocent as guilty, and ordered them to be all shut up in the hippodrome, and sent for his sister Salome, and her husband Alexas, and spoke to them as follows. " I shall die at no distant time, so great are my pains ; and death ought to be cheerfully borne, and to be welcomed by all men ; but what principally troubles me is this, that I shall die without being lamented, and without such mourning as usually takes place at a king's death." He added that he was not unacquainted with the temper of the Jews, and knew that his death would be a thing very desirable and exceedingly acceptable to them, for even during his lifetime they were ready to revolt from him and despise his measures. He told them it was therefore their duty to resolve to afford him some alleviation of his great sorrow under these circumstances. For if they did not refuse him their consent in what he desired, he would have a great mourning at his funeral, and such as never any king had had before him, for then the whole nation would mourn from their very soul, which otherwise would be done in sport and mockery only. He desired therefore that as soon as they saw he had given up the ghost, they should place soldiers round the hippodrome, who did not know that he was dead, and that they should not announce his death to the multitude till this was done, and that they should give orders to have those that were in the hippodrome shot with these soldiers' darts ; and this slaughter of them all would cause him not to fail to rejoice on two accounts, first at their performing what he charged them with his dying breath to do, and secondly at his having the honour of a memorable mourning at his funeral. So he deplored his condition with tears in his eyes, and appealed to them by the kindness due from kindred, and by their faith in God, and conjured them not to debar him of this honourable mourning at his funeral. And they promised him to do what he wished.

§ 6. Now one may easily discover the temper of this

man's mind, even if one were satisfied with his former
acts, as having been done to his relations from love of life,
by these last commands of his which savoured of great in-
humanity, since he took care, when he was departing out
of this life, that the whole nation should be put into
mourning by the loss of their dearest ones, as he gave orders
that one out of every family should be slain, although
they had done nothing that was unjust, or that was against
him, nor were they accused of any other crimes; though it
is usual for those who have any regard to virtue to lay
aside at the hour of death their hatred even to those whom
they justly esteem their enemies.


## CHAP. VII.

*Herod has thoughts of killing himself with his own hands, and
a little afterwards orders Antipater to be slain.*


A S he was giving these instructions to his relations, there
came letters from his ambassadors who had been sent
to Rome to Augustus, and when they were read, their pur-
port was as follows: that Acme had been put to death by
Augustus, in consequence of his indignation at the hand
she had had in Antipater's wicked practices; and that,
as to Antipater himself, Augustus left it to Herod to act
as became a father and king, and either to banish him
or take away his life, which he pleased.   When Herod
heard this, he felt somewhat better from the pleasure he
had at the contents of the letters, and was elated at the
death of Acme, and at the power that was given him
over his son; but as his pains became very great, he was
now ready to faint for want of something to eat; so he
called for an apple and a knife; for it was his custom
even formerly to pare an apple himself, and gradually to
cut it and eat it.   When he had got the knife, he looked
about, and had a mind to stab himself with it; and would
have done so, had not his cousin Achiabus prevented him,
and held his hand, and cried out loudly.   Whereupon a

woeful lamentation echoed through the palace, and a great
noise was made, as if the king was dead.   Upon this
Antipater, who verily believed his father was dead, grew
bold in his language, hoping to be immediately and entirely
released from his bonds, and to take the kingdom into his
own hands without any more ado ; so he talked with the
jailor about letting him go, and promised him great things,
both now and hereafter, as if that were the only thing now in
question.  But the jailor not only refused to do what Antipater would have him, but informed the king of his intentions, and of the many solicitations he had had from him.
Thereupon Herod, who had not formerly been overpowered
by good-will towards his son, when he heard what the
jailor said, cried out, and beat his head, although he was
at death's door, and raised himself upon his elbow, and
sent for some of his body-guards, and commanded them to
kill Antipater without any further delay, and to do it quickly,
and to bury him in an ignoble manner at Hyrcania.[1]


# CHAP. VIII.

### *Concerning Herod's Death, Testament, and Burial.*

## § 1.

A ND now Herod changed his testament again upon the
alteration of his mind ; for he appointed Antipas, to
whom he had before left the kingdom, to be tetrarch of
Galilee and Peræa,[2] and granted the kingdom to Archelaus.
And Gaulonitis, and Trachonitis, and Batanæa,[3] and Panias,[4]
he gave to Philip, his son, and own brother to Archelaus.[5]

---

[1] See Antiq. xiii. 16, § 3 ; xiv. 5, § 4 ; Jewish War, i. 8, § 5.
[2] Peræa extended from Pella in the north to Machærus in the south,
and from the Jordan eastward to Philadelphia, Rabboth Ammon.  Jewish
War, iii. 3, § 3.
[3] See Life, § 11.
[4] Cæsarea Philippi, now *Bâniâs.*
[5] When it is said that Philip and Archelaus were own brothers, or
born of the same father and mother, there must be here some mistake ;
because they had indeed the same father Herod, but different mothers ;
the former Cleopatra, and Archelaus, Malthace.   They were indeed

by the name of a tetrarchy ; and bequeathed Jamnia,[1] and Azotus,[2] and Phasaelis,[3] to his sister Salome, as also five hundred thousand [drachmæ] of coined silver. He also made provision for all the rest of his kindred, by giving them sums of money and revenues, and so left them all in a wealthy condition. He bequeathed also to Augustus ten millions of [drachmæ] of coined silver, besides vessels both of gold and silver, and to Julia, Augustus' wife, exceedingly costly garments, and to some others five millions. When he had done these things, he died, the fifth day after he had caused his son Antipater to be slain ; having reigned thirty-four years since he had had Antigonus slain, and thirty-seven since he had been declared king by the Romans. He was a man of great cruelty to all men alike, and a slave to his anger, and indifferent to justice, yet was he favoured by fortune as much as any man ever was, for from a private man he became a king, and though he was surrounded by ten thousand dangers, he got clear of them all, and protracted his life to a very old age. But as to the affairs of his family and sons, in which indeed, according to his own opinion, he was also very fortunate, because he was able to conquer his enemies, he was in my opinion very unfortunate.

§ 2. However Salome and Alexas, before the king's death was generally known, dismissed those that were shut up in the hippodrome to their own homes, and told them that the king ordered them to go away to their own lands, and look after their own affairs. They thus conferred on the nation a great benefit. And now the king's death was made public, and Salome and Alexas gathered the soldiers together in the amphitheatre at Jericho ; and the first thing they did was to read Herod's letter written to the soldiers, thanking them for their fidelity and good-will to him, and exhorting them to treat his son Archelaus, whom he had appointed as their king, with like fidelity and good-will. After this Ptolemy, who had the king's seal intrusted to him, read the king's testament, which was not to be of force till Augustus had inspected it. And there was accla-

brought up all together at Rome like own brothers, which is perhaps all that Josephus intends by the words before us.—W.

[1] *Yebnah.*          [2] *Esdûd.*          [3] *'Ain Fusâil.*

mation made at once to Archelaus as king, and the soldiers
came by bands, and their commanders with them, and
promised the same good-will to him, and zeal in serving
him, as they had exhibited to Herod, and they prayed God
to be his helper.

§ 3. After this was over, they prepared for the king's
funeral, Archelaus taking care that his father should be
buried in a very sumptuous manner. Accordingly, he
brought out all his ornaments to add to the pomp of the
funeral. The body was carried upon a golden bier, embroidered with very precious stones of great variety, and
the bier was covered over with purple, as well as the body
itself, which had a diadem upon its head, and above it a
crown of gold, and a sceptre in its right hand. Round the
bier were Herod's sons and numerous relations; next to
these were the soldiers, disposed according to their several
countries and names, and placed in the following order:
first of all went the body-guards, then the band of Thracians, after them the Germans, and next them the Galatians, every one in their habiliments of war; and behind
these marched the whole army in the same manner as they
used to go out to war, preceded by their commanders and
centurions; and these were followed by five hundred domestics carrying spices. And they went eight furlongs on
the road to Herodium;[1] for there by his own command
Herod was to be buried. And thus did he end his life.

§ 4. Now Archelaus paid his father so much respect, as
to continue his mourning till the seventh day; for so many
days are appointed by the custom of our country. And
when he had feasted the multitude, and left off his mourning,
he went up into the temple; and he had acclamations and
praises given him, whichever way he went, every one vying
with one another who should appear to use the loudest
acclamations. And he ascended a high platform made for
him, and took his seat on a throne made of gold, and spoke
kindly to the multitude, and declared with what joy he
received their acclamations and marks of good-will and
returned them thanks for not remembering to his disad-
vantage the injuries his father had done them, and pro-

---

[1] *Jebel Fureidis.*

mised them he would endeavour not to be slack in reward-
ing their zeal to him.  He said he should abstain at present
from the name of king, but he would have the honour of
that dignity if the Emperor should confirm the testament
his father had made; and that was the reason why, when
the army would have put the diadem on his head at Jericho,
he would not accept of that honour, which is usually so
much desired, because it was not yet evident that he who
had the authority of bestowing it would give it him.  But
if he got the kingdom he would not (he said) come short in
the virtue of gratitude for their good-will; for it should be
his endeavour, in all things wherein they were concerned,
to prove in every respect better than his father.  Whereupon the multitude, as is usual with them, supposed that
the first days show the intentions of those that enter upon
such sovereignty, and the more gently and civilly Archelaus spoke to them, so much the more highly did they
commend him, and made application to him to grant what
they desired.  Some cried out to him to ease them of some
of their annual payments, others to release those that had
been put into prison by Herod (who were many, and had
been there a long time); others asked that he would do
away with those heavy taxes which had been laid upon
what was publicly sold or bought.  And Archelaus contra-
dicted them in nothing, as he was anxious to do all things
so as to conciliate the good-will of the multitude, looking
upon that good-will as a great step towards the preservation of his power.  He then went and offered sacrifice to
God, and afterwards betook himself to feasting with his
friends.

## CHAP. IX.

*How the People raised a Rebellion against Archelaus, and
how he Sailed to Rome.*

### § 1.

MEANTIME some of the Jews assembled together out
of desire of innovation, and lamented Matthias, and
those that were slain with him by Herod, who had not had

at the time any respect paid them by mourning, from the
fear men were in of Herod, and had been condemned for
pulling down the golden eagle. These people made a great
clamour and lamentation, and threw out some reproaches
against the king also, as if that was a solace to the
deceased. They assembled together, and demanded of
Archelaus, that, to avenge them, he would inflict punishment on those who had been honoured by Herod : and
first and foremost that he would deprive the high priest
whom Herod had made, and would choose one more agreeable to the law, and of greater purity, to officiate as high
priest. To this Archelaus assented, although he was
mightily offended at their importunity, because he proposed to himself to go to Rome shortly, to see what the
Emperor had determined about him. However, he sent
his general to use persuasion, and to tell them that the
death which was inflicted on their friends was according
to the law, and to represent to them that their petitions
about these things were highly insulting to him, and that
the time was not now fit for such petitions, but rather required their unanimity until he should be established on
the throne by the consent of the Emperor, and should
have come back to them ; for he would then consult
with them in common as to what they asked ; but they
ought at present to be quiet, lest they should seem factious.

§ 2. When the king had suggested this line of argument, and instructed his general what he was to say, he
sent him to the people. But they made a clamour, and
would not let him speak, and put him in danger of his
life, as they also did to all who ventured upon saying
openly anything which might bring them to a sober mind,
and prevent their going on in their present courses ; because they had more desire to have all their way than to
yield obedience to their rulers, thinking it monstrous that,
while Herod was alive, they should have lost those who
were most dear to them, and that now he was dead, they
should not get their revenge. So they went on with their
designs in a violent manner, and thought all to be lawful
and right which tended to please them, being unskilful in
foreseeing what danger they ran, and if they had suspicion

of any such thing, the present pleasure they took in the idea of the punishment of those they deemed their very great enemies outweighed all such considerations. And although Archelaus sent many to speak to them, they treated them not as messengers sent by him, but as persons who came of their own accord to mitigate their anger, and would not suffer one of them to speak. The rebellion was also set in motion by such as were in a great passion, and it was evident that it would grow, as the people joined the movement in great numbers.

§ 3. Now on the approach of the feast of Unleavened Bread, which the law of their fathers had appointed for the Jews (which feast is called the Passover,[1] and is a memorial of their deliverance out of Egypt, when they offer sacrifices with zeal, and when it is customary to slay more victims than at any other festival, and when an innumerable multitude come out of the country—nay, from beyond its limits also, to worship God), the innovators lamented Judas and Matthias, those teachers of the laws, and kept together in the temple, having plenty of food, because those factious persons were not ashamed to demand it. And as Archelaus was afraid that some terrible thing would happen owing to these men's madness, he sent a regiment of armed men, and with them a captain of a thousand, to suppress the violence of the rebellious, before the whole population should be infected with the like madness; and charged them, if they found any more openly rebellious than others, to bring them before him. But those that were rebellious because of those dead teachers of the law, incited the people by noise and clamour, so they made an assault upon the soldiers, and went up to them, and stoned most of them, but a few ran away wounded, and their captain with them. And when they had thus done, they attended to the sacrifice again. Now Archelaus thought there was no way to keep his throne but by cutting off those of the people who made this attempt upon it; so he sent out his whole army against them, and despatched his cavalry to prevent those that had

[1] This Passover, when the rebellion here mentioned was moved against Archelaus, was not one, but thirteen months after the eclipse of the moon already mentioned.—W.

their tents outside the temple from assisting those that were within the temple, and to kill such as fled from the infantry when they thought themselves out of danger. And the cavalry slew some three thousand men, and the rest betook themselves to the neighbouring mountains. Then did Archelaus order proclamation to be made that all should go to their own homes; so they went away, and left the festival fearing that something worse might follow, although they had been so bold because of their stupidity. Then Archelaus went down to the sea with his mother, and took with him Nicolaus and Ptolemy, and many of his friends, and left his brother Philip governor of all things belonging both to his family and the realm. There also went with him Herod's sister Salome, who took with her her children, and many of her kindred went with her, under pretext of assisting Archelaus in gaining the kingdom, but in reality to oppose him, and chiefly to make loud complaints of what he had done in the temple. But Sabinus, the Emperor's administrator in Syrian affairs, as he was making haste to Judæa to take charge of Herod's money, met with Archelaus at Cæsarea; but Varus came up and restrained him from meddling with it, for he had been sent for there by Archelaus through Ptolemy. And Sabinus, to gratify Varus, did neither seize upon any of the fortresses that were among the Jews, nor seal up the treasures in them, but permitted Archelaus to have them, till the Emperor should declare his will about them, and having promised that, he remained at Cæsarea. But after Archelaus had sailed for Rome, and Varus had removed to Antioch, Sabinus went to Jerusalem, and seized on the king's palace He also sent for the keepers of the garrisons, and for all those who had had the charge of Herod's affairs, and declared publicly that he should call them to account, and disposed of the fortresses as he pleased. However, those who kept them did not neglect what Archelaus had commanded them, but continued to keep all things in the manner that had been enjoined them; and their pretext was that they kept them all for the Emperor.

§ 4. At the same time, also, did Antipas, another of Herod's sons, sail to Rome, to claim the kingdom, being buoyed up by Salome with promises that he should have

it, as [1] being much fitter than Archelaus for that authority;
since Herod had, in his former testament, which ought to
be esteemed most valid, deemed him the worthiest to be
made king.   Antipas also took with him his mother, and
Ptolemy the brother of Nicolaus, who had been Herod's
most honoured friend, and was now zealous for Antipas;
but it was Irenæus the orator, who, on account of his
reputation for sagacity, was intrusted with the affairs of
the kingdom, who most of all encouraged him to think of
claiming the kingdom.   That was why, when some advised
him to yield to Archelaus, as his elder brother, who had
been declared king by their father's last will, he would not
do so.   And when he was come to Rome, all his relations
came over to him, not out of good-will to him, but out of
hatred to Archelaus, though indeed they were most desirous
of gaining their liberty, and of being put under a Roman
governor; but if opposition were made to that, they thought
Antipas preferable to Archelaus, and so tried to get the
kingdom for him.   Sabinus also accused Archelaus to the
Emperor in a letter.

§ 5.  Now, when Archelaus had despatched a letter to
the Emperor, wherein he pleaded his right to the kingdom,
and his father's testament, and sent Ptolemy with Herod's
seal and the accounts of Herod's money, he waited the
event.   And when the Emperor had read Archelaus' letter,
and Varus' and Sabinus' letters, and the accounts of the
money, and the statement of the annual revenues of the
kingdom, and understood that Antipas had also sent a letter
laying claim to the kingdom, he summoned his friends together to give their opinions, and among them Caius, the son
of Agrippa and his daughter Julia whom he had adopted,
whom he made to sit first of all, and bade such as pleased
speak their minds about the affairs now before them.   And
Salome's son Antipater, a very clever orator, and a very
bitter enemy to Archelaus, spoke first, and said that it was
jesting of Archelaus to plead now to have the kingdom
given him, since he had in reality assumed the authority
already, before Augustus had granted it.   He also in-
veighed against his bold action in slaying so many at the

---

[1] For καὶ I read ὡς.   It is well known how similar the abbreviation
of these two words is, and how frequently this mistake is made in MSS.

Jewish festival, for if the men had acted unjustly, it was
but fit the punishing of them should have been reserved
to those who were out of the country, and had the right to
punish them, and not been executed by a man who, if he
pretended to be a king, wronged Augustus by ignoring his
authority, and if he owned himself a private person, his
case was much worse, since he who put in claim to the
kingdom, could by no means expect to have that power
granted him over the Jews, of which he had already deprived Augustus. He also charged and upbraided him with
changing some commanders in the army, and sitting on the
royal throne, and deciding lawsuits, just as if he were king,
and assenting to the requests of those that publicly petitioned him, and indeed his management of all things,
which could in his opinion be no greater if he had been
already settled in the kingdom by Augustus. He also
ascribed to him the releasing of the prisoners that were
in the hippodrome, and many other things, that had either
been done by him, or might be believed to have been done,
because they were of such a nature as were done by young
men, and by such as in desire of ruling grasped at power
too soon. He also charged him with neglect in mourning
for his father, and with revelling the very night he died;
and said that was why the multitude began raising a tumult; and if Archelaus could thus requite his dead father,
who had bestowed such benefits upon him, and bequeathed
such great things to him, pretending to shed tears for him
in the day-time like an actor on the stage, but every night
making merry at having got the kingdom, he would show
himself the same Archelaus to Augustus, if he granted
him the kingdom, as he had been to his father; for he
had then danced and sung, as though an enemy of his had
fallen, and not as though a man was being carried to his
funeral, that was so nearly related to him, and had been
so great a benefactor. But he said that the most monstrous thing of all was, that he came now before Augustus
to obtain the kingdom by his grant, when he had before
acted in all things as he would have acted if the Emperor
himself had already fixed him firmly in the kingdom. And
what he most exaggerated in his pleading was the slaughter
of those in the temple, and the impiety of its being done

at festival time, and how they were slain like sacrifices themselves, some of them foreigners, and others of their own country, till the temple was full of dead bodies: and all this was not done by an alien, but by one who laid claim to the lawful title of king, that he might fulfil the wicked tyranny which his nature prompted him to, and which was hated by all men. That was no doubt the reason why his father had never so much as dreamed of making him his successor in the kingdom, when he was of a sound mind, because he knew his character, and in his former and more authentic testament had appointed his enemy Antipas to succeed; for Archelaus was called by his father to the kingdom, when Herod was in an ailing condition both of body and mind, while Antipas was called when Herod was ripest in his judgment, and of such strength of body as made him capable of managing his own affairs. And even if his father had had the like notion of him formerly that he had now showed, yet Archelaus had given a sufficient specimen of what sort of a king he was likely to be, when he deprived Augustus of the power which he justly had of disposing of the kingdom, and had not abstained from making a terrible slaughter of his fellow-citizens in the temple when he was but as yet a private person.

§ 6. When Antipater had said thus much, and had confirmed what he said by producing many witnesses from among his own relations, he ended his speech. Upon which Nicolaus rose up on behalf of Archelaus, and said that what had been done in the temple was rather to be attributed to the behaviour of those who had been killed than to the authority of Archelaus; for those who were the authors of such things, were not only wicked in the injuries they themselves did, but in forcing sober persons to avenge themselves upon them. And it was evident that their hostile action was taken in pretext, indeed, against Archelaus, but in reality against the Emperor himself, for those riotous persons attacked and slew those who were sent by Archelaus, and who came only to put a stop to their doings, having no regard either to God or to the custom of the festival; and yet Antipater was not ashamed to advocate their cause, whether to indulge his enmity against Archelaus, or because of his own hatred of virtue and justice. For those who began such tumults, and attacked people who little expected it, forced men even against their will to betake themselves to arms to punish them. Nicolaus also ascribed all the rest that was done to all those who had acted in counsel with the accusers, for nothing which was here accused of as unjust had been done, but what had been approved of by them; nor were those things bad in themselves, but only so represented to harm Archelaus. So great was these factious persons' desire to do injury to a man that was of their kindred, and their father's benefactor, and one familiarly acquainted with them, who had ever lived in friendship with them. And as to Herod's testament, it was made by the king when he was in a sound mind, and so ought to be more valid than his former testament, for Augustus was left by it the judge and sole disposer of all its contents. And certainly Augustus would not imitate the unjust proceedings of those men, who, during Herod's life, had on all occasions been benefited by his power, and yet now zealously endeavoured to hinder his will, though they had not themselves deserved as well of Herod as Archelaus had. Augustus would not therefore disannul the testament of a man who had put everything at his disposal, and had been his friend and ally, and had committed everything to him in trust. Nor would Augustus' virtuous and upright disposition, which was known and uncontested throughout all the world, imitate the wickedness of these men in condemning a king as having lost his reason, and as a madman, for having bequeathed the succession to a good son, who fled to Augustus' uprightness for refuge. Nor could Herod ever have been mistaken in his judgment about his successor, when he showed so much prudence as to submit all things to the decision of Augustus.

§ 7. When Nicolaus had laid these arguments before Augustus, he ended his speech. And Augustus kindly raised Archelaus up when he threw himself down at his feet, and said that he was most worthy of the kingdom, and showed that he was not disposed to act otherwise than his father's testament directed, which was for the advantage of Archelaus. However, though he gave this encouragement to Archelaus to rely on him and banish all fear, he made no full determination about him.    And, when the assembly was broken up, he debated with himself, whether he should confirm the kingdom to Archelaus, or whether he should divide it among all Herod's posterity, as these too stood in need of much assistance.

## CHAP. X.

*An Insurrection of the Jews against Sabinus; and how
Varus brought the Authors of it to Punishment.*

### § 1.

BUT before these things could be brought to a settlement, Archelaus' mother, Malthace, fell ill and died, and letters came from Varus, the governor of Syria, informing Augustus of a revolt of the Jews.    For, after Archelaus had sailed, the whole nation was in an uproar, and Varus himself, as he was on the spot, brought the authors of the disturbance to punishment; and when he had mostly composed this rising, which was a formidable one, he set out for Antioch, leaving one legion of his army at Jerusalem to keep the Jews quiet, if they made any new rising.    But this did not at all avail to put an end to their rebellion; for after Varus was gone away, Sabinus, Augustus' procurator, stayed behind, and greatly harassed the Jews, believing that the forces that were left there would by their numbers be too many for the Jews.    For he made use of them, and armed them as his guards, so oppressing and troubling the Jews, that they rebelled; for he used force to seize the citadels, and zealously made violent search for the king's money, on account of his love of gain, and extraordinary covetousness.

§ 2.  Now on the approach of Pentecost (which is a festival of ours, so called from the days of our forefathers) a great many myriads of men assembled together not only to keep the festival, but also in consequence of their indignation at the mad insolence of Sabinus.    They were chiefly Galilæans and Idumæans, and from Jericho, and those who inhabited the districts on the other side of the river Jordan, who all banded together, and were more zealous than the others to avenge themselves on Sabinus. And they divided themselves into three bands, and encamped in the following places, some of them seized upon the hippodrome, and one of the other two bands encamped on the east quarter from the north part of the temple to the south, while the third band occupied the west part of the city where the king's palace was. Their action tended to besiege entirely the Romans, and to shut them in on all sides. Now Sabinus was afraid of these men's numbers and spirit, for they had little regard to their lives from their desire not to be overcome, and they thought it virtue to conquer their enemies; so he sent immediately a letter to Varus, and, as was usual with him, was very urgent with him, and entreated him to come quickly to his assistance, as the forces he had left were in imminent danger, and would probably, in no long time, be intercepted and cut to pieces. But he himself occupied the highest tower of the fortress Phasaelus (which had been built in honour of Phasaelus,[1] king Herod's brother, and so called when the Parthians had brought him to his death[2]), and thence gave a signal to the Romans to attack the Jews, and although he did not himself venture even to come down to his friends, expected that all the others should expose themselves to death for his greediness. And as the Romans ventured to make a sally, a terrible battle ensued; and though the Romans beat their adversaries, yet were not the Jews cowed in spirit even at the sight of the terrible slaughter that was made of many of them, but they made a circuit, and got upon those porticoes which surrounded the outer court of the temple, where a great fight was still maintained, and they cast stones at the Romans, partly with their hands, and partly from slings, being very expert in that kind of warfare. All the archers also drawn up in battle-array did the Romans a great deal of mischief, because they were on higher ground, and so not easy to get at, for when the Romans tried to shoot their arrows against the Jews upwards, these arrows could not reach them, so that the

[1] The 'Tower of David' at Jerusalem.
[2] See Antiq. xiv. 13, § 10, and Jewish War, ii. 12, § 9.—W.

Jews were too much for their enemies here. And this sort
of fight lasted a great while, till at last the Romans, who
were greatly enraged at what was done, set fire to the
porticoes so stealthily, that those Jews who were upon
them did not perceive it. This fire being fed by a great
deal of combustible matter,[1] soon caught the roof of
the porticoes; and the wood, which was full of pitch and
wax, especially as its gold was smeared over with wax,
yielded to the flames at once; and those vast works, which
were so worthy of esteem, were destroyed utterly, and
those that were on the roof unexpectedly perished at the
same time; for, as the roof tumbled in, some of these
men fell down with it, and others were killed by their
enemies who surrounded them. Many also, in despair of
saving their lives, and dismayed at the fate that awaited
them, either cast themselves into the fire, or threw themselves upon their own swords, and so got out of their
misery. And as to those that endeavoured to escape by
the same way by which they ascended, they were all killed
by the Romans, being unarmed, and their courage failing
them; their reckless fury being now unable to serve them,
as they were destitute of armour; so that not one of those
that ascended to the roof escaped. The Romans also
rushed through the fire, where it was practicable, and
seized on the treasure where the sacred money was; a
great part of which was stolen by the soldiers, but Sabinus
got openly four hundred talents.

§ 3. Now the loss of their friends, who fell in this
battle, grieved the Jews, as did also the plundering of the
money dedicated to God in the temple. So that body of
them which was most compact and most warlike surrounded the palace, and threatened to set fire to it, and
kill all that were in it, and commanded them to go out
quickly, and promised, if they would do so, that they
would not hurt them, or Sabinus either. And most of the
king's troops deserted to them, while Rufus and Gratus.

---

[1] These great devastations made about the temple here, and Jewish
War, ii. 3, § 3, seem not to have been fully repaired in the days of Nero;
till whose time there were 18,000 workmen continually employed in
rebuilding and repairing the temple, as Josephus informs us, Antiq.
xx. 9, § 7.—W.

who had three thousand of the most warlike of Herod's army with them, who were men of bodily activity, went over to the Romans. There was also a troop of horse under the command of Rufus, which itself went over to the Romans also. However, the Jews went on with the siege, and dug mines under the walls, and besought those that had gone over to the other side not to hinder them, now they had such an opportunity for the recovery of their country's ancient liberty. As for Sabinus, he was desirous of going away with his soldiers, but dared not trust himself with the enemy on account of the mischief he had already done them, and this great clemency of theirs (*which he suspected*) made him reject their offer. He also expected that Varus was coming, and so endured the siege.

§ 4. At this time there were myriads of other troubles in Judæa, many people in many places stirring up war either in hope of gain to themselves, or from enmity to the Jews. And two thousand of Herod's old soldiers, who had been already disbanded, mustered in Judæa itself, and fought against the king's troops, and Achiabus, Herod's cousin, opposed them; but as he was driven out of the plains into the mountainous parts by their military skill, he kept on ground not easy of approach, and saved what he could.

§ 5. There was also one Judas, the son of that Ezekias who had been a robber-chief, a very strong man, who had with great difficulty been taken by Herod. This Judas having got together a multitude of men of profligate cha-racter at Sepphoris [1] in Galilee, made an assault upon the palace [there,] and seized upon all the weapons that were stored up in it, and armed with them every one of his men, and made off with all the money that was left there, and became terrible to all men by plundering those that came near him, in consequence of a thirst for power, and an ambitious desire for royal rank, which he hoped to obtain, not as the reward of his virtue, but of his power to do harm.

§ 6. There was also one Simon, who had been a slave of

---

[1] *Sefûrieh.*

Herod the king, but was in other respects a comely person, tall and of a robust body, and had had great things committed to his trust. He, being elated at the disorderly state of affairs, was so bold as to put a diadem on his head, and a certain number of the people stood by him, and by their madness he was hailed as king, and he thought himself more worthy of that dignity than any one else, and burnt down the royal palace at Jericho, and plundered what was left in it, and also set fire to many other of the king's houses in various parts of the country, and utterly destroyed them, and permitted those who were associated with him to take what was left in them as spoil. And he would have done greater things, if care had not been taken to repress him quickly ; for Gratus, after he had joined himself to the Roman soldiers, took the forces he had with him, and met Simon, and after a great and obstinate fight, most of those that came from Peræa, who were a disorderly body of men, and fought in rather a bold than skilful manner, were cut to pieces, and although Simon tried to save himself by flight through a certain defile, yet Gratus overtook him, and cut off his head. The royal palace at Amatha,[1] near the river Jordan, was also burnt down by a party of men that mustered together, like those belonging to Simon. Thus did a great and wild fury spread itself over the nation, because they had no king of their own to keep the multitude in virtue, and because those foreigners, who came to reduce the rebellious to order, did, on the contrary, set them more in a flame, because of their avarice and outrageous treatment of them.

§ 7. At this time also Athronges, a person eminent neither for the dignity of his progenitors, nor for any great virtue or wealth of his own, as he was only a shepherd, and obscure in all respects, because he was a tall man, and excelled others in the strength of his hands, was so bold as to set up for king, and thought it so sweet a thing to do injuries to others, that although he should be killed, he did not much care if he lost his life in such actions. He had also four brothers, who were tall men themselves, and were believed to be superior to others in

---

[1] *'Amateh,* east of the Jordan and north of the Jabbok.

the strength of their hands, and he thought that strength of theirs would aid him in retaining his kingdom. Each of them ruled over a band of men of their own; for those who mustered to them were very numerous. They were also every one of them commanders, but when they came to fight, they were subordinate to Athronges, and fought for him, and he put a diadem on his head, and assembled a council to debate about what things were to be done, and all things were done according to his pleasure. And he retained his power a great while, being called king, and having nothing to hinder him from doing what he pleased, and he and his brothers slew a great many both of the Romans and of the king's forces, acting with the like hatred to each of them, to the king's forces because of their outrageous conduct during Herod's reign, and to the Romans because of the injuries they had so lately received from them. But in process of time they grew more cruel to all sorts of men alike, nor could any one escape, for they slew some in the hope of gain, and others from the mere habit of slaying men. They once attacked a company of Romans at Emmaus,[1] who were bringing corn and weapons to the army, and surrounded Areus, the centurion, who commanded the company, and shot down him and forty of the best of his foot-soldiers; and the rest of them were dismayed at their slaughter, and left their dead behind them, but escaped themselves by the aid of Gratus, who came with the king's troops that were with him to their assistance. They continued such guerilla warfare a long while, and much harassed the Romans, but did their own nation also a great deal of injury. But they were afterwards put down, one of them in a fight with Gratus, another with Ptolemy; and Archelaus took the eldest of them prisoner, when the last of them was so dejected at the others' misfortune, and saw so plainly that he had no way now left to save himself, being left alone and worn out with continual labours, and having lost his men, that he also delivered himself up to Archelaus, upon his promise and oath to God [to preserve his life.] But these things happened some time afterwards.

---

[1] Emmaus Nicopolis, 'Amwâs.

§ 8. And now Judæa was full of bands of robbers, and, as the several companies of the seditious lit upon any one to head them, he was created a king immediately, in order to do mischief to the community.  They did some small harm to a few of the Romans, but their murders of their own people lasted the longest.

§ 9. Directly Varus was informed of the state of Judæa by Sabinus' writing to him, he was afraid for the legion he had left; so he took the two other legions (for there were three legions in all in Syria), and four troops of horse, and all the auxiliary forces that either the kings or any of the tetrarchs supplied him with, and made what haste he could to assist those who were then besieged in Judæa. He also gave orders to all who were sent forward to hasten to Ptolemais.  The citizens of Berytus [1] also gave him fifteen hundred auxiliaries, as he passed through their city.  Aretas also, the king of Arabia Petræa,[2] from his hatred to Herod, and in order to purchase the favour of the Romans, sent no small assistance, besides foot and horse.  And when Varus had concentrated all his forces at Ptolemais,[3] he committed part of them to his son, and to a friend of his, and sent them upon an expedition into Galilee, which lies in the neighbourhood of Ptolemais; and they attacked the enemy, and put them to flight, and took Sepphoris, and made its inhabitants slaves, and burnt the city.  But Varus himself pushed on to Samaria [4] with the main army : but he did not meddle with the city of that name, because it was not accused of rebellion, but pitched his camp at a certain village that belonged to Ptolemy, called Arus,[5] which the Arabians burnt from their hatred to Herod, and from the enmity they bore to his friends.  The Arabians marched thence to another village called Sampho,[5] which they plundered and burnt, although it was a very strong and fortified place ; and all along this march nothing escaped them, but all places were full of fire and slaughter.  Emmaus was also burnt by Varus' order, after its inhabitants had deserted it, that he might avenge those that had been

[1] *Beirût.*
[2] The desert of Petra and the Peninsula of Sinai.
[3] *'Akka.*                              [4] *Sebustieh.*
[5] Not identified.

slain there. From thence Varus marched at once to Jerusalem, and those Jews whose camp lay there, and who were
besieging the Roman legion, at first sight of the approach
of his army raised the siege and fled. But as to the Jews in
Jerusalem, when Varus reproached them bitterly, they
cleared themselves of the charges laid against them, and
said that the conflux of the people was occasioned by the
feast, and that the war was not made with their approbation, but came from the rashness of the strangers, for they
were on the side of the Romans, and rather besieged with
them, than desirous at all to besiege them. Now Joseph,
the cousin of king Herod, had also come before this to
meet Varus, as had also Gratus and Rufus (who brought
their soldiers with them), and those Romans who had been
besieged. But Sabinus did not come into Varus' presence,
but stole out of the city privately, and went to the sea-
side.

§ 10. Next Varus sent a part of his army all over the
country, to seek out the authors of the revolt; and when
they were discovered, he punished some of those that were
most guilty, and some he dismissed: the number of those
that were crucified on this account was two thousand.
After this he disbanded his army, which he found not at
all useful, for the soldiers behaved themselves very disorderly, and disobeyed Varus' orders and wishes, being
intent on the gain which they made by malpractices. As
for himself, when he was informed that ten thousand Jews
had mustered together, he made haste to crush them; but
they did not venture to fight him, but, at the advice of
Achiabus, surrendered to Varus. Thereupon he forgave
the multitude their crime of revolting, but sent their
several commanders to Augustus. The Emperor dismissed
many of them, and the only persons whom he punished
were those relations of Herod who had joined these men in
this war, who, without the least regard to justice, had
fought against their own kindred.

## CHAP. XI.

*An Embassy of the Jews to Augustus, and how he confirmed Herod's Testament.*

§ 1.

WHEN Varus had settled these affairs, and left the legion that had been formerly there to garrison Jerusalem, he set out for Antioch. As for Archelaus, he had new sources of trouble come upon him at Rome from the following circumstances. An embassy of the Jews came to Rome (Varus having permitted the nation to send it) to petition for the liberty of living according to their own laws. Now, the number of the ambassadors that were sent by the will of the nation was fifty, who were joined by more than eight thousand Jews who dwelt at Rome. And Augustus assembled his friends, and the chief men among the Romans, in the temple of Apollo, which he had built at great expense, and the ambassadors came there, and the multitude of Jews that lived at Rome with them, as did also Archelaus and his friends. But as for the various kinsmen of the king, they would not join themselves with Archelaus, from their hatred to him; and yet they thought it monstrous to vote with the ambassadors against him, supposing it would be a disgrace to them in Augustus' opinion to think of thus acting in opposition to a man of their own kindred. Philip also had arrived there from Syria, at the instigation of Varus, with the principal intention of assisting his brother (for Varus was his great friend), but still so, if any change should happen in the form of government (for Varus expected the kingdom would be divided, because of the many who desired the liberty of living in accordance with their own laws), that he might not be behind, but might have his share of it.

§ 2. Now upon liberty being given to the Jewish ambassadors to speak, they who hoped by their words to put down kingly government betook themselves to accusing Herod of various lawless acts, and declared that he had been nominally indeed a king, but had usurped that absolute

authority which tyrants exercise over their subjects,
and had made use of that authority for the destruction of the Jews, and had not abstained from introducing
many innovations among them besides, according to his
own inclination. And although a great many had perished
during his reign by various kinds of deaths, so many
indeed as no previous history related, they that had survived were far more miserable than those that had suffered,
not only from the anxiety they were in as to his look and
disposition, but also from the danger their estates were in.
They said Herod had never ceased adding to the beauty of
those neighbouring cities that were inhabited by foreigners,
but the cities belonging to his own kingdom were ruined
and utterly destroyed, and whereas when he took the kingdom, it was in an extraordinarily flourishing condition, he
had afflicted the nation with extreme poverty, and when he
had slain any of the nobility upon unjust pretexts, he had
taken away their estates, and when he permitted any of
them to live, he had condemned them to the forfeiture of
what they possessed. And, besides the annual impositions
which he laid upon every one of them, they had had to
make liberal presents to him and his domestics and
friends, and to such of his slaves as were vouchsafed the
favour of being his tax-gatherers, because there was no
way of obtaining freedom from unjust violence, without
giving either gold or silver for it. They would say nothing
of the deflowering of their virgins, or the debauching of
their wives, and that carried out in a wanton and inhuman
manner, because it was almost equal pleasure to the sufferers to have such things concealed as not to have suffered
them. They said Herod had ill treated them worse than
a wild beast would have done, if he had had power
given him to rule; and although their nation had passed
through many vicissitudes and changes, their history gave
no account of any calamity it had ever undergone, that
could be compared with what Herod had brought upon
the nation. And so they had thought they might
reasonably and gladly hail Archelaus as king, upon the
supposition that whoever should be set over the kingdom
would appear more mild to them than Herod had been;
and they had joined with him in the mourning for his

father, in order to gratify him, and were ready to oblige
him in other points also, if they found him mild in his
dealings with them.  But he seemed to be afraid lest he
should not be deemed Herod's own son; and so, without
any delay, he immediately let the nation understand his
disposition, and that before his position on the throne was
secure, since Augustus could either give it him or not, as
he pleased.  Moreover he had given his subjects a specimen of his future virtue, and of the kind of moderation
and good administration with which he would govern
them, by his first action in the sight of the citizens and
God himself, when he slaughtered three thousand of his
own countrymen in the temple.  How, then, could they
help justly hating him who, besides his other barbarity,
had alleged as one of their crimes that they had opposed
and thwarted him in the exercise of his authority?   They
concluded by saying that the main thing they desired was
that they might be delivered from kingly and similar
governments, and might be added to Syria, and be put
under the authority of such chief magistrates as should be
sent to them; for it would thereby be made evident,
whether they were really rebellious people, and generally
fond of innovations, or whether they would live in an
orderly manner, if they had mild rulers set over them.

§ 3. Now when the Jews had said this, Nicolaus vindi-
cated the kings from those accusations, and said that as
for Herod, since he had never been thus accused during
his life, it was not right for those that might during his
lifetime have accused him before just judges, and procured
his punishment, to bring an accusation against him now
that he was dead.  He also attributed the actions of
Archelaus to the Jews' insolence, who, striving after what
was contrary to the laws, and beginning to kill those who
would have hindered them from their insolence, now complained of just reprisals.  He also accused them of their
love of innovation, and of the pleasure they took in sedition, because of their not having learned to submit to
justice and the laws, through their desiring to have their
way in all things.  This was what Nicolaus said.

§ 4. When Augustus had heard these pleadings, he dissolved the assembly, and a few days afterwards appointed

Archelaus not indeed king, but ethnarch of half the
country that had been subject to Herod, and promised to
give him the royal dignity subsequently, if he deserved it.
As for the other half, he divided it into two parts, and
gave it to two other of Herod's sons, to Philip and to that
Antipas who disputed with Archelaus the whole kingdom.
Now Peræa and Galilee paid their tribute, which amounted
annually to two hundred talents, to Antipas, while
Batanæa and Trachonitis and Auranitis, with a certain
portion of what was called the house of Zenodorus, paid
the tribute of one hundred talents to Philip. But Idumæa,
and Judæa, and Samaria, paid tribute to Archelaus, but
had a fourth part of their tribute taken off by order of
Augustus, who decreed them that abatement because they
had not joined in revolt with the rest of the multitude.
There were also other cities which paid tribute to Archelaus, as Strato's tower,[1] and Sebaste,[2] and Joppa, and Jerusalem; for as to Gaza and Gadara[3] and Hippos,[4] they are
Greek cities, which Augustus separated from Archelaus'
jurisdiction, and added to the province of Syria. And
the tribute-money that came to Archelaus every year from
his dominions amounted to six hundred talents.

§ 5. So much of their father's inheritance came to
Herod's sons. As to Salome, besides what her brother left
her by his testament, namely, Jamnia,[5] and Azotus,[6] and
Phasaelis,[7] and five hundred thousand [drachmæ] of coined
silver, Augustus made her a present of the royal habitation at Ascalon;[8] her revenues in all amounted to sixty
talents a year, and her dwelling-house was within Archelaus' jurisdiction. The rest also of the king's relations
received what his testament allotted them. Moreover,
Augustus made a present to each of Herod's two virgin
daughters, besides what their father left them, of two hundred and fifty thousand [drachmæ] of silver, and married
them to Pheroras' sons; he also granted all that was bequeathed to himself to the king's sons, which was one
thousand five hundred talents, except a few of the vessels,

---

[1] Cæsarea Palæstina, *Kaisarîyeh.*          [2] Samaria, *Sebustieh.*
[3] *Umm Keis.*          [4] *Sûsiyeh.* See Life, § 9.          [5] *Yebnah.*
[6] *Esdûd.*          [7] *'Ain Fusâil.*          [8] *'Ascalân.*

which he reserved for himself; and they were acceptable
to him, not so much for their great value as because they
were memorials to him of king Herod.

# CHAP. XII.

*Concerning a spurious Alexander.*

### § 1.

WHEN these affairs had been thus settled by Augustus,
a certain young man, by birth a Jew, but brought up
by a Roman freedman in the city of Sidon, palmed himself
off as akin to Herod, by the resemblance of countenance,
which those who saw him attested him to have to Alexander the son of Herod, whom Herod had had put to death.
And this was an incitement to him to endeavour to seize
the kingdom. So he took to him as an assistant a man
of his own tribe (one who was well acquainted with the
affairs of the palace, but in other respects a bad man, and
one whose nature made him capable of causing great mischief, and who taught this wicked contrivance to the other),
and declared himself to be Alexander the son of Herod, who
had been stolen away by one of those that were sent to slay
him, who slew two others to deceive the spectators, but saved
both him and his brother Aristobulus alive. Thus was this
man puffed up, and proceeded to impose on all that saw
him, and when he landed at Crete, he made all the Jews
that came into his company believe his story. And when
he had got much money, which was presented to him there,
he crossed over to Melos,[1] where he got much more money
than he had before, from the belief the people of Melos had
that he was of the royal family, and from their hopes that
he would recover his father's kingdom, and reward his
benefactors: so he made haste to Rome, and was escorted
there by his private friends. He was also so fortunate,
upon landing at Dicæarchia,[2] as to bring the Jews that
were there into the same delusion; and not only other

---

[1] This island, now *Milo*, is the most westerly of the Cyclades.
[2] Puteoli, now *Pozzuoli*, near *Naples*.

people, but also all those who had been intimate with Herod, or had good-will to him, joined themselves to him as their king. The reason was that men gladly listened to his tale, which was confirmed by his appearance, which made those who had been intimately acquainted with Alexander believe that he was no other but the very same person, which they also confirmed to others by oath. And so, when the report went about him that he was come to Rome, the whole multitude of the Jews that were there went out to meet him, ascribing it to divine providence that he had so unexpectedly escaped, and being very joyful because of their affection to his mother's family. And wherever he went, he was carried in a litter through the streets, and all the ornaments about him were such as kings wore, and all this was done at the expense of his private friends. The multitude also flocked about him perpetually, and made auspicious acclamations to him, and nothing was omitted which could be thought proper treatment for such as had been so unexpectedly preserved alive.

§ 2. When news of this was told Augustus he did not believe it, because Herod was not so easily to be imposed upon in affairs of great concern to him; yet, having some suspicion it might be so, he sent Celadus, one of his freedmen, who had intimately known the young men, and bade him bring Alexander into his presence. And he brought him, being no better in judging about him than the rest of the multitude. However the young man did not deceive Augustus, for although there was a resemblance between him and Alexander, yet was it not so exact as to impose on such as had good discernment. For this spurious Alexander had his hands rough from the labour he had undergone, and instead of that softness of body which the other had, derived from his delicate and noble bringing up, this man, for the contrary reason, had a hard body. When, therefore, Augustus saw how the master and scholar agreed in this lying story, and in their audacious fiction, he inquired about Aristobulus, and asked what had become of him, who (according to his story) was stolen away also, and why he had not come with him, and endeavoured to recover the rights due to his high birth also? And he said, that he had been left in the island of Cyprus, for fear of the dangers of the sea, that, in case anything should happen to himself, the posterity of Mariamne might not utterly perish, but that Aristobulus might survive, and punish those that had plotted against them.    And as he perse-vered in his affirmations, and the author of the imposture bore him out, Augustus took the young man aside and said to him, " If thou wilt not impose upon me, thou shalt have this for thy reward, that thou shalt escape with thy life ; tell me, then, who thou art, and who it was that had bold-ness enough to contrive such a cheat as this ; for this con-trivance is too great a piece of villany to have been under-taken by one of thy age."    And as he had no other course to take, he told Augustus of the contrivance, and how, and by whom, it was made up.    Then Augustus, observing the spurious Alexander to be a strong active man, and fit to work with his hands (for he would not break his promise to him) put him to row in his gallies, but had him executed who had induced him to do what he had done.    As for the people of Melos, he thought them sufficiently punished, in having thrown away so much of their money upon this spurious Alexander.    Such was the ignominious conclu-sion of this bold contrivance in regard to this spurious Alexander.

## CHAP. XIII.

*How Archelaus, upon a second Accusation, was banished to Vienne.*

### § 1.

WHEN Archelaus had taken over his ethnarchy, and returned to Judæa, he accused Joazar, the son of Boethus, of having assisted the rebellious, and took away the high priesthood from him, and put Eleazar his brother into his place.    He also magnificently rebuilt the royal palace at Jericho, and diverted half the water with which the village of Neara[1] used to be watered, and drew off that water into the plain, which he had planted with palm-

---

[1] Probably the Naarah or Naarath of Josh. xvi. 7, now *Kh. el-'Aûjah*, in the Jordan valley.

trees.  He also built a village which he called Archelais;[1]
and he transgressed the law of our fathers[2] by marrying
Glaphyra, the daughter of Archelaus, who had been the
wife of his brother Alexander, who had three children
by her, though it was a thing detestable among the Jews
to marry their brothers' wives.  But Eleazar did not continue long in the high priesthood; Jesus, the son of Sie,
being put in his room while he was still living.

§ 2.  Now in the tenth year of Archelaus' rule, the
principal men of Judæa and Samaria, not being able to
bear his barbarous and tyrannical usage of them, accused
him to Augustus, especially as they knew he had broken
the commands of the Emperor, namely to behave himself
with moderation among them.  And Augustus, when he
heard this accusation, was very angry, and called for Archelaus' agent, who looked after his affairs at Rome, and whose
name was Archelaus also, and thinking it beneath him to
write to Archelaus, he bade this agent sail away as soon as
possible, and bring him to Rome : and he made haste in his
voyage, and when he reached Judæa, found Archelaus
feasting with his friends; and he told him what Augustus
had sent him for, and hurried him off.  And when he
reached Rome, Augustus, upon hearing what his accusers
had to say, and his reply, banished him, and appointed
Vienne,[3] a city of Gaul, to be the place of his habitation,
and took his money away from him.

§ 3.  Now, before Archelaus had gone up to Rome upon
being summoned by Augustus, he related the following
dream to his friends, that he saw ten ears of corn full
of wheat, perfectly ripe, which ears, as it seemed to
him, were devoured by oxen.  And when he woke (for
the vision appeared to be of great importance to him) he
sent for the wise men who understood dreams.  And while
some were of one opinion, and some of another, (for all
their interpretations did not agree,) Simon, a man of the

---

[1] *Tell el-Mazâr*, in the Jordan valley.
[2] Spanheim seasonably observes here, that it was forbidden the Jews
to marry their brother's wife, when she had children by her first
husband, and that Zenoras interprets the clause before us accordingly.
—W.
[3] *Vienne*, on the left bank of the *Rhone*.

sect of the Essenes, desired leave to speak his mind freely, and said that the vision denoted a change in the affairs of Archelaus, and that not for the better; that oxen, because that animal takes uneasy pains in its labours, denoted afflictions, and indeed denoted further a change of affairs, because the land which was ploughed by oxen could not remain in its former state: and that the ears of corn being ten marked the same number of years, because an ear of corn grows in one year; and that the time of Archelaus' rule was over. Thus did this man expound the dream. Now, on the fifth day after this dream came first to Archelaus, the other Archelaus, that was sent to Judæa by Augustus to recall him, arrived also.

§ 4. Something similar befell Glaphyra his wife, who was the daughter of king Archelaus, and was married, as I said before, while she was a virgin, to Alexander the son of Herod, and brother of Archelaus; but after Alexander was put to death by his father, she married Juba, the king of Libya, and when he was dead, and she living in widowhood in Cappadocia with her father, Archelaus divorced his former wife Mariamne, and married her, so great was his affection for this Glaphyra. And she, during her marriage to him, had the following dream. She thought she saw Alexander standing by her, at which she rejoiced, and embraced him with great affection, but he complained of her, and said, "O Glaphyra! thou provest that saying to be true, which assures us that women are not to be trusted. Didst not thou pledge thy faith to me? and wast not thou married to me when thou wast a virgin? and had we not children? Yet hast thou forgotten the affection I bore to thee, in thy desire for a second husband. Nor wast thou satisfied with that injury thou didst me, but thou hast been so bold as to procure thee a third husband to lie by thee, and in an indecent and impudent manner hast entered into my house, having married Archelaus, thy husband, and my brother. However, I will not forget thy former kind affection for me, but will set thee free from all reproach, and cause thee to be mine again, as thou once wast." When she had related this dream to her female companions, a few days after she departed this life.

§ 5. Now, I do not think these stories unsuitable in my

present history, because my narrative is now concerning kings; and besides I thought them fit to be set down, as they confirm the immortality of the soul, and the providence of God over human affairs. But if any one does not believe such relations, let him indeed enjoy his own opinion, but let him not hinder another, that would thereby encourage himself in virtue. However Archelaus' country was added to the province of Syria; and Cyrenius, who had been consul, was sent by Augustus to take a valuation of property in Syria, and to sell the house of Archelaus.

# BOOK XVIII.

### FROM THE BANISHMENT OF ARCHELAUS, TO THE DEPARTURE OF THE JEWS FROM BABYLON.

## CHAP. I.

*How Cyrenius was sent by Augustus to take a Valuation of Syria and Judæa; and how Coponius was sent to be Procurator of Judæa; also of Judas of Galilee, and the Sects that were among the Jews.*

### § 1.

NOW Cyrenius, a Roman senator, and one who had gone through other offices, and had passed through all till he became consul, and one who, on other accounts, was of great merit, came at this time into Syria with a few others, being sent by Augustus to be a judge of that nation, and to take a valuation of their substance. Coponius also, a man of the equestrian order, was sent with him, to have the supreme power over the Jews. Cyrenius also came into Judæa, which was now added to the province of Syria, to take a valuation of their substance, and to dispose of Archelaus' money. But the Jews, although at first they took the report of a taxation very ill, yet left off any further opposition to it, at the persuasion of Joazar, who

was high priest, and the son of Boethus.  For they listened
to Joazar's words, and gave an account of their estates
without any dispute.  But one Judas,[1] a Gaulanite, of a
city whose name was Gamala,[2] joining himself to Sadduc
a Pharisee, was eager to draw them to a revolt.  Both
said that this taxation was nothing but a direct introduction of slavery, and exhorted the nation to assert their
liberty, as if they could procure them happiness and security for what they possessed, and if they failed in the happiness that would result from this, they would acquire
honour and glory for magnanimity.  They also said that
God would not assist them unless they joined with one
another energetically for success, and still further set
about great exploits, and did not grow weary in executing
the same.  And the men heard what they said with pleasure, and so this bold attempt proceeded to a great height.
All sorts of misfortunes also sprang from these men, and
the nation was infected by them to an incredible degree :
one violent war came upon us after another, and we lost
our friends who used to alleviate our pains ; there were
also very great robberies, and murders of our principal
men, under pretext indeed of the public welfare, but in
reality from the hopes of private gain.  Hence arose seditions, and owing to them political murders, which sometimes fell on their own people, (from the madness of these

[1] Since St. Luke once, Acts v. 37, and Josephus four times, here,
§ 6, and xx. 5, § 2 ; Jewish War, ii. 8, § 1, and 17, § 8, calls this
Judas, who was the pestilent author of that seditious doctrine and temper which brought the Jewish nation to utter destruction, a Galilæan,
but here, § 1, Josephus calls him a Gaulanite, of the city of Gamala,
it is a great question where this Judas was born, whether in Galilee
on the west side, or in Gaulanitis, on the east side of the river Jordan;
while in the place just now cited out of the Antiquities, xx. 5, § 2,
he is not only called a Galilæan, but it is added to his story, ' as I
have signified in the books that go before these,' as if he had called
him a Galilæan in those Antiquities before, as well as in that particular
place, as Dean Aldrich observes, Jewish War, ii. 8, § 1.  Nor can one
well imagine why he should here call him a Gaulanite, when in the 6th
sect. following here, as well as twice in Jewish War, he still calls him a
Galilæan.  As for the city of Gamala, whence this Judas was derived, it
determines nothing, since there were two of that name, the one in
Gaulanitis, the other in Galilee.  See Reland on the city or town of that
name.—W.

[2] *Kul'at el-Husn.*

men towards one another, and their desire that none of their rivals should be left,) and sometimes on their enemies; a famine also came upon us, and reduced us to the last degree of despair, as did also the taking and demolishing of cities, nay, faction at last increased so high, that the very temple of God was burnt down by the enemies' fire. So greatly did the alteration and change from the customs of our fathers tend to bring all to destruction who thus banded together, for Judas and Sadduc, who introduced a fourth philosophic sect among us, and had a great many followers therein, filled our state with tumults at the time, and laid the foundations of future miseries by their system of philosophy which we were before unacquainted with, concerning which I shall discourse a little, and that the rather, because the infection which spread thence among our younger men, who were zealous for it, brought our nation to destruction.

§ 2. The Jews had had for a great while three sects of philosophy peculiar to themselves, the sect of the Essenes, and the sect of the Sadducees, and the third sort of opinions was that of those called Pharisees. And although I have already spoken of these sects in the second book of the Jewish War, yet will I touch a little upon them also now.

§ 3. As for the Pharisees, they live simply, and despise delicacies, and follow the guidance of reason, as to what it prescribes to them as good, and think they ought earnestly to strive to observe its dictates. They also pay respect to such as are in years; nor are they so bold as to contradict them in anything which they have introduced. And when they say that all things happen by fate, they do not take away from men the freedom of acting as they think fit; since their notion is, that it has pleased God to mix up the decrees of fate and man's will, so that man can act virtuously or viciously. They also believe, that souls have an immortal power in them, and that there will be under the earth rewards or punishments, according as men have lived virtuously or viciously in this life; and the latter souls are to be detained in an everlasting prison, but the former will have power to live again. On account of these doctrines they have very great influence with the people, and whatever they do about divine worship, or prayers, or sacrifices, they perform according to their direction. Such great testimony do the cities bear them on account of their constant practice of virtue, both in the actions of their lives, and in their conversation.

§ 4. But the doctrine of the Sadducees is that souls die with the bodies; nor do they pretend to regard anything but what the law enjoins on them; for they think it virtue to dispute with the teachers of the philosophy which they follow, and their views are received by only a few, but those are of the highest rank. But they are able to do hardly anything so to speak, for when they become magistrates, as they are unwillingly and by force sometimes obliged to do, they addict themselves to the notions of the Pharisees, because the people would not otherwise put up with them.

§ 5. The doctrine of the Essenes is that all things are left in the hand of God. They teach the immortality of souls, and think that the rewards of righteousness are to be earnestly striven for. And when they send what they have dedicated to God to the temple, they do not offer sacrifices, because they have more pure lustrations of their own; on which account they are excluded from the common court of the temple, and offer their sacrifices by themselves. But their course of life is better than that of other men, and they entirely addict themselves to husbandry. It also deserves our admiration, how much they exceed in justice all other men that addict themselves to virtue, to such a degree as has never appeared among any other men, either Greeks or barbarians, and that not for a short time, but it has endured for a long while among them. This is shown by that institution of theirs, which will not suffer anything to hinder them from having all things in common, so that a rich man enjoys no more of his wealth than he who has nothing at all. There are more than four thousand men who live in this way, and they neither marry wives, nor are desirous to keep slaves, thinking that the latter tempts men to be unjust, and that the former gives a handle to domestic quarrels; but as they live by themselves, they minister to one another. They also appoint good priests to receive their revenues, and the fruits of the ground, so as to get their corn and food. They live all alike, and mostly resemble those Dacæ who are called Polistæ.[1]

§ 6. But Judas the Galilæan was the author of the fourth sect of Jewish philosophy. Its pupils agree in all other things with the Pharisaic notions, but they have an inviolable attachment to liberty, and say that God is their only ruler and lord. They also do not mind dying any kinds of death, nor indeed do they heed the tortures of their relations and friends, nor can any such fear make them call any man lord. And since this immovable resolution of theirs is well known to a great many, I shall speak no further about that matter; for I am not afraid that anything I have said of them should be disbelieved, but rather fear that what I have said comes short of the resolution they show when they undergo pain. And it was in Gessius Florus' time, who was our procurator, that the nation began to suffer from this madness, for by the abuse of his authority he made the Jews go wild and revolt from the Romans. And these are the sects of Jewish philosophy.

## CHAP. II.

*How Herod and Philip built several Cities in Honour of Cæsar Augustus. Concerning the Succession of Priests and Procurators; also concerning Phraates and the Parthians.*

### § 1.

WHEN Cyrenius had now disposed of Archelaus' money, and when the taxings were come to a conclusion, which were made in the thirty-seventh year after Augustus' victory over Antony off Actium,[2] he deprived Joazar of the high priesthood, which dignity had been conferred on him by the multitude, and appointed Ananus, the son of Seth, to be high priest. Now Herod and Philip had each of them received their own tetrarchy, and settled

---

[1] Founders of cities, that is. Possibly communists might be the best rendering. But the matter is very obscure.
[2] At the entrance of the *Gulf of Arta.*

affairs therein.   Herod also fortified Sepphoris,[1] (which is the ornament of all Galilee,) and dedicated it to the emperor.   He also built a wall round Betharamptha,[2] which was itself a city also, and called it Julias, from the name of the emperor's wife.[3]   Philip also built Paneas,[4] a city at the springs of the Jordan, and called it Cæsarea.   He also advanced the village Bethsaida,[5] situate near the lake of Gennesar, to the dignity of a city, both from the number of inhabitants it contained, and its opulence in other respects, and called it by the name of Julias, from the name of the emperor's daughter.[6]

§ 2.  As Coponius, who I said was sent out with Cyrenius, was administrating Judæa, the following event happened.   When the Jews celebrate the feast of Unleavened Bread, which we call the Passover, it is customary for the priests to open the temple gates just after midnight.   When, therefore, these gates were first opened at this Passover, some of the Samaritans who had come privately to Jerusalem threw about dead men's bones in the porticoes; so the Jews afterwards excluded them all from the temple, which they had not used to do at such festivals; and on other accounts also watched the temple more carefully than they had formerly done.   Soon after this event Coponius returned to Rome, and Marcus Ambivius came to be his successor in the government; under whom Salome, the sister of king Herod, died, and left to Julia Jamnia[7] and all its toparchy, and Phasaelis in the plain, and Archelais,[8] where is a great plantation of palm-trees, whose fruit is most excellent.   His successor was Annius Rufus, during whose term of office died Augustus, the second emperor of the Romans, the duration of whose reign was fifty-seven years six months and two days, (of which time Antony ruled with him fourteen years,) and the duration of his life was seventy-seven years; and on his

---

[1] *Sefûrieh.*

[2] The Beth-Haram of Josh. xiii. 27; afterwards called Livias; it is now *Tell Râmeh*, east of Jordan, and near the mouth of *Wâdy Hesbân.*

[3] Julia.                                        [4] Cæsarea Philippi, now *Bâniâs.*

[5] Possibly *et-Tell*, on the left bank of the Jordan, near the Sea of Galilee.

[6] Julia.                  [7] *Yebnah.*                  [8] See Antiq. xvii. 13, § 1.

death Tiberius Nero, his wife Julia's son, succeeded. He was now the third emperor, and he sent Valerius Gratus as procurator of Judæa, to succeed Annius Rufus. He deprived Ananus of the high priesthood, and appointed Ishmael, the son of Phabi, to be high priest. He also deprived him in a little time, and appointed Eleazar, the son of Ananus (who had been high priest before) to be high priest; which office, when he had held it for a year, Gratus deprived him of, and gave the high priesthood to Simon, the son of Camithus, and, when he had held that dignity only a year, Joseph, also called Caiaphas, was made his successor. When Gratus had done all these things, he returned to Rome, after he had stayed in Judæa eleven years, and Pontius Pilate came as his successor.

§ 3. And Herod the tetrarch, who was in great favour with Tiberius, built a city of the same name as him, and called it Tiberias.[1] He built it in the best part of Galilee near the lake of Gennesar. There are warm baths at no great distance from it, in a village called Emmaus.[2] Strangers came and inhabited this city, a great number of the inhabitants were Galilæans also; and many were made to go there from the country belonging to Herod, and were by force compelled to be its inhabitants, some of these being persons of condition. Herod also admitted poor people, gathered from all parts, to dwell in it. Nay, some of them were not quite freemen, and these he was a great benefactor to, and made them free in great numbers; but obliged them not to forsake the city, by building them very good houses at his own expense, and by giving them land also; for he knew that to colonize this place was to transgress the ancient Jewish laws, because many sepulchres there had to be taken away to make room for this city of Tiberias, and our laws pronounce that such inhabitants are unclean for seven days.[3]

§ 4. About this time died Phraates, king of the Parthians, by the treachery of Phraataces his son, for the following reason. Though Phraates had legitimate sons of his own, he had an amour with an Italian maid (whose name was

[1] *Tubariya.*
[2] The Hammath of Josh. xix. 35. Now *Hummâm Tubariya.*
[3] Numb. xix. 11-14.—W.

Thermusa, who had been formerly sent to him among other presents by Julius Cæsar), and being a great admirer of her beauty, and in process of time having a son by her, whose name was Phraataces, he eventually made her his legitimate wife, and held her in great honour.  Now, though she was able to persuade him to do any thing that she said, and strove to procure the throne of Parthia for her son, she saw that her endeavours would not succeed, unless she could contrive to remove Phraates' legitimate sons.  So she urged him to send those sons of his as pledges of his fidelity to Rome; and they were sent to Rome accordingly, because it was not easy for him to contradict her commands.  Now, as Phraataces was alone brought up to succeed to the throne, he thought it very tiresome and tedious to wait for that throne by his father's donation as his successor; he therefore formed a treacherous design against his father, by his mother's assistance, with whom (so the report went) he had also criminal relations.  And he was hated for both these things, as his subjects esteemed this incestuous love of his mother to be as bad as his parricide; and he was expelled out of the country by them, in an insurrection, before he grew too great, and so died.  But, as the noblest of the Parthians agreed that it was impossible they could be governed without a king, while it was also their constant practice to choose one of the descendants of Arsaces (nor did their law allow of any others, and they thought the kingdom had been sufficiently injured already by the marriage with an Italian concubine, and by her issue,) they sent ambassadors and invited Orodes [to take the crown;] for though the multitude did not like him, and though he was accused of very great cruelty, and was of an intractable temper, and prone to wrath, yet he was one of the descendants of Arsaces.  However, a conspiracy was made against him, and he was slain, as some say, at a festival and at table (for it is the universal custom there to carry swords); but the more general report is that he was slain when he was induced to go a-hunting.  They then sent ambassadors to Rome, and asked for one of those that were pledges there to be their king.  And Vonones was preferred before the rest, and sent to them, for he seemed capable of such great fortune, which two of the greatest kingdoms under the sun now offered him, his own and a foreign one. However, the barbarians soon changed their minds, being naturally of a fickle disposition, and supposing that he was not worthy to be their king (for they could not think of obeying the commands of one that had been a slave, for so they called those that had been hostages, nor could they bear the ignominy of that name); and this was the more intolerable, because the Parthians were now to have a king set over them, not by right of war, but by insolence in time of peace. So they forthwith invited Artabanus, king of Media, to be their king, who was one of the descendants of Arsaces. Artabanus complied with the offer that was made him, and came to them with an army. And Vonones met him, and at first the multitude of the Parthians stood on his side, and he put his army in battle array, and Artabanus was beaten, and fled to the mountains of Media; but a little while after he gathered a great army together, and fought again with Vonones, and beat him; whereupon Vonones fled away on horseback, with a few of his attendants about him, to Seleucia.[1] And when Artabanus had slain a great number in the rout from the very great dismay the barbarians were in, he betook himself to Ctesiphon[2] with a great number of his people. And so he now reigned over the Parthians. But Vonones fled away to Armenia, and as soon as he got there, he desired to have the government of that country given him, and sent ambassadors to Rome about it. But as Tiberius refused it him, partly because he wanted courage, partly because of the Parthian king's threats (who sent ambassadors to threaten war), and as he had no other way to get the kingdom (for the people of authority among the Armenians near Niphates[3] joined themselves to Artabanus), he delivered himself up to Silanus, the president of Syria, who, out of regard to his education at Rome, kept him in Syria,

---

[1] Near the junction with the Tigris of the great dyke which crossed Mesopotamia from the Euphrates to the Tigris, and was called the 'Royal River.'

[2] On the left bank of the Tigris, in the south part of Assyria. The ruins are opposite those of Seleucia, about sixteen miles below *Baghdad*.

[3] The mountain country east of Commagene, near the present Persian frontier.

and Artabanus gave Armenia to Orodes, one of his own sons.

§ 5. At this time died Antiochus, the king of Commagene,[1] whereupon the people disputed with the aristocracy, and both sent ambassadors to Rome, for the men in power were desirous that their form of government might be changed into that of a Roman province ; but the people desired to be under kings, as their fathers had been. And the senate made a decree, that Germanicus should be sent out to settle affairs in the East, fortune hereby taking opportunity to deprive him of his life. For when he had gone to the East, and settled all affairs there, he was taken off by poison by Piso, as has been related elsewhere.

## CHAP. III.

*Insurrection of the Jews against Pontius Pilate. Concerning Christ, and what befell Paulina and the Jews at Rome.*

### § 1.

NOW Pilate, the procurator of Judæa, removed the army from Cæsarea, and put it in winter quarters at Jerusalem, in order to abolish the Jewish laws. And he thought of introducing into the city the Emperor's busts, which were upon the standards, whereas our law forbids us the very making of images ; on which account former procurators were wont to make their entry into the city with such standards as had not such ornaments. Pilate was the first who brought those images to Jerusalem, and set them up there; which was done without the knowledge of the people, because it was done in the night-time. But as soon as they knew it, they flocked in great numbers to Cæsarea, and besought Pilate many days that he would remove the images. And when he would not grant their request, because it would seem an insult to the Emperor, as they persevered in their request, he ordered his soldiers on the sixth day to take their weapons privately, and

---

[1] Between Cilicia and the Euphrates; its capital was Samosata, now *Samsât*.

himself came and sat upon his judgment-seat, which was
so prepared in the open part of the city, that it concealed
the army that lay in ambush.   And when the Jews petitioned him again, he gave a signal to the soldiers to
surround them, and threatened that their punishment
should be no less than speedy death, unless they left off
disturbing him, and went their ways home.   But they
threw themselves upon the ground, and bared their necks,
and said they would welcome death rather than that the
wisdom of their laws should be transgressed.   Thereupon
Pilate was astonished at their determination to keep their
laws inviolable, and instantly commanded the images to
be carried back from Jerusalem to Cæsarea.

§ 2.  Pilate also introduced water into Jerusalem, paying
for the work with the sacred money, and brought the
water a distance of two hundred furlongs.   However, the
Jews were not pleased with what was done about this
water; and many myriads of the people assembled together and made a clamour against him, and insisted that
he should abandon his intention.   Some of them also used
reproaches, and abused Pilate, as crowds love to do.   So
he dressed a great number of his soldiers in the Jewish
dress, who carried daggers under their garments, and sent
them to a place where they might surround the Jews, and
then himself bade the Jews go away.   But as they began
to abuse him, he gave the soldiers the signal which had
been agreed on beforehand, and they laid about them with
much greater vigour than Pilate had commanded, and
equally punished those that were riotous, and those that
were not.   But the Jews abated not a whit their obstinacy,
and as they were unarmed, and roughly handled by men
provided with weapons, a great number of them were slain
by this means, and others of them ran away wounded.
Thus an end was put to this insurrection.

§ 3.  Now about this time lived Jesus, a wise man, if indeed it be lawful to call him a man.   For he was a doer of
wonderful works, a teacher of men who receive the truth
with pleasure ; and drew over to him many of the Jews,
and many of the Gentiles.   He was the Christ.   And when
Pilate, at the information of the leading men among us,
had condemned him to the cross, those who had loved him

at first did not cease to do so.  For he appeared to them alive again the third day, as the divine prophets had foretold this and ten thousand other wonderful things concerning him.  And the tribe of Christians, so named from him, are not extinct at this day.

§ 4. About the same time, also, another sad calamity troubled the Jews, and certain shameful practices took place in the temple of Isis that was at Rome.  I shall first relate the wickedness done in the temple of Isis, and will then give an account of what befell the Jews.  There was at Rome a woman whose name was Paulina, who, on account of the rank of her ancestors, and because of the regular conduct of a virtuous life, had a great reputation ; she was also very rich, and although she was of a beautiful countenance, and in that flower of her age wherein women are the most gay, she led a life of great modesty.  She was married to Saturninus, who well assorted in every way to her from his excellent character.  Decius Mundus, a man very high in the equestrian order, fell in love with Paulina, and as she was of too great rank to be caught by presents, and had already rejected them, though they had been sent her in great abundance, he was still more inflamed with love for her, insomuch that he promised to give her two hundred thousand Attic drachmæ for one enjoyment of her.  And as not even this would prevail upon her, and he was not able to bear this ill success in his amours, he thought it the best way to starve himself to death, on account of his trouble at Paulina's refusal.  And he determined to die in this manner, and went on with his purpose accordingly.  Now, Mundus had a freed-woman, who had been made free by his father, whose name was Ide, a woman up to all sorts of mischief.  She was very much grieved at the young man's resolution to kill himself (for he did not conceal his intention to destroy himself), and went to him, and encouraged him by her words, and made him hope that he might yet enjoy Paulina.  And when he joyfully listened to her entreaty, she said she wanted no more than fifty thousand drachmæ to entrap Paulina.  Now when she had encouraged in this way the young man, and got as much money as she asked for, she did not take the same methods as had been taken

before, because she perceived that the lady was by no
means to be tempted by money; but knowing that she was
very much given to the worship of the goddess Isis, she
devised the following stratagem. She went to some of Isis'
priests, and told them the passion of the young man, and
with the strongest promises of concealment urged them
by words, but chiefly by the offer of money, twenty-five
thousand drachmæ in hand, and as much more when the
thing had been done, to use all possible means to seduce
the woman. And they were induced to promise to do so
by the large sum of gold they were to have. So the
oldest of them went immediately to Paulina, and upon
his being admitted desired to speak with her by herself.
When that was granted him, he told her that he was sent
by the god Anubis, who had fallen in love with her, and
bade her visit him. And she took the message very
kindly, and boasted to her lady friends of this condescension
of Anubis, and told her husband, that she had a message
sent her, and was to sup and sleep with Anubis. And he
agreed to her acceptance of the offer, being fully satisfied
of the chastity of his wife. Accordingly, she went to the
temple, and after she had supped there, and it was the
hour to go to sleep, the priest shut the doors of the temple,
when the lights were also put out in the inner sanctuary.
Then did Mundus leap out, (for he was hidden there,)
and did not fail to enjoy her, and she was at his service all
the night long, supposing he was the god; and when he had
gone away, which was before the priests who knew not of
this stratagem were stirring, Paulina went home early in the
morning to her husband, and told him how the god Anubis
had appeared to her, and also boasted about the matter to
her lady friends. And they partly disbelieved the thing
when they reflected on its nature, and partly were amazed
at it, but had no pretext for not believing it, when they
considered her modesty and merit. But on the third day
after what had been done, Mundus met Paulina, and said,
"Truly, Paulina, thou hast saved me two hundred thousand
drachmæ, which sum thou mightest have given thine
own family; yet hast thou not failed to be at my service
in what I asked of thee. As for the reproaches thou hast
heaped upon Mundus, I care not about names; but I rejoice

in the pleasure I reaped by what I did, when I took to myself the name of Anubis." When he had said this, he went his way, but she rent her garments, now first knowing what she had done, and told her husband of this wicked and black contrivance, and prayed him not to neglect to assist her. And he discovered the matter to the emperor; whereupon Tiberius inquired into it thoroughly, examining the priests about it, and ordering them to be crucified, as well as Ide, who was the cause of their ruin, and had contrived the whole matter, which was so injurious to Paulina. He also demolished the temple of Isis, and gave orders that her statue should be thrown into the river Tiber. But he only banished Mundus, and did no more to him, because he supposed that the crime he had committed was done from the violence of his love. These were the circumstances as to the temple of Isis, and the outrage done by her priests. I now return to the relation of what happened about this time to the Jews at Rome, as I said before I should.

§ 5. There was a man who was a Jew, but had been driven away from his own country by an accusation of transgressing the laws, and by the fear he was in of punishment for the same, but he was in all respects a wicked man. He, then living at Rome, professed to instruct men in the wisdom of the laws of Moses, and also got three other men, entirely of the same character as himself, to be his partners. These men persuaded Fulvia, a woman of great rank, who had become a disciple of theirs, and embraced the Jewish religion, to send purple and gold to the temple at Jerusalem, and, when they had got these, they employed them to their own use, and spent the money themselves, which was the very reason why they had first asked it of her. Whereupon Tiberius (who had been informed of the thing by his friend Saturninus, the husband of Fulvia, who desired inquiry might be made about it) ordered all the Jews to be banished from Rome. And the consuls enlisted four thousand of them, and sent them to the island of Sardinia; [1] but punished very many, who were unwilling to become soldiers, because of their respect

---

[1] Of the banishment of these 4,000 Jews into Sardinia by Tiberius, see Suetonius, Tiber. § 36.—W.

for the laws of their forefathers. Thus were these Jews banished from Rome owing to the wickedness of four men.

## CHAP. IV.

*How the Samaritans made a Tumult, and how Pilate slew many of them: also how Pilate was accused, and what was done by Vitellius as regarded the Jews and the Parthians.*

### § 1.

BUT the nation of the Samaritans did not escape without tumult. The man who excited them to it was one who thought lying a thing of little consequence, and who contrived everything to please the multitude. So he bade them assemble together upon Mount Gerizim, which is by them looked upon as the most holy of all mountains, and assured them, that when they came there, he would show them the sacred vessels that were buried there, because Moses had them put there. And they went there armed, and thought the statement of the man probable; and as they encamped at a certain village, which was called Tirathana,[1] they got together as many as they could, desiring to go up the mountain *en masse*. But Pilate prevented them by occupying the ascent with a band of horse and foot, who attacked those who were concentrated in the village; and when it came to an action, they slew some, and put others to flight, and took a great many alive, the leaders of whom, and also the most influential of those that fled away, Pilate ordered to be put to death.

§ 2. But when this tumult was appeased, the Samaritan senate sent an embassy to Vitellius, a man that had been consul, and was now president of Syria, and accused Pilate of the murder of those that had been killed, for they said they had gone to Tirathana not to revolt from the Romans, but to escape the violence of Pilate. And Vitellius sent Marcellus, a friend of his, to see to the affairs of Judæa, and ordered Pilate to go to Rome, to answer the accusa-

---

[1] Not identified.

tions of the Jews before the emperor.   And Pilate, who
had spent ten years in Judæa, hasted to Rome in obedience
to the orders of Vitellius, which he durst not contradict.
But before he got to Rome, Tiberius was dead.

§ 3. But Vitellius came into Judæa, and went up to
Jerusalem ; it was at the time of that festival which is called
the Passover. And as he was magnificently received there,
Vitellius released the inhabitants of Jerusalem from all
the taxes upon the fruits that were bought and sold, and
allowed the high priest's vestments, with all their ornaments, to be under the charge of the priests in the temple,
as they had been in old times, although at this time they
were laid up in the fortress called Antonia,[1] and that for the
following reason.  One of the high priests called Hyrcanus,
the first of many of that name, built a tower near the
temple, and when he had so done, he generally dwelt in it,
and kept these vestments (which were in his charge) there,
because it was lawful for him alone to put them on, and he
deposited them there when he went down into the city, and
took his ordinary garments ; and the same practice was continued by his sons, and by their sons after them.  But when
Herod came to be king, he rebuilt this tower, which was
very conveniently situated, in a magnificent manner ; and
because he was a friend of Antony, he called it by the name
of Antonia.  And as he found these vestments lying there,
he retained them in the same place, believing that the people
would not rise against him because he had them in his
custody.  The same as Herod did was done by his son
Archelaus, who was appointed king after him ; after
whom the Romans, when they took over the government,
took possession of these vestments of the high priest, and
had them deposited in a stone chamber, under seal of the
priests and keepers of the treasury, the commandant of the
fortress lighting a lamp there every day.  And seven days
before a festival they were delivered to them by the commandant of the fortress, when the high priest having
purified them, and used them, laid them up again in the
same chamber where they had been laid up before the very
day after the feast was over.  This was the practice at the

---

[1] On the north side of the Temple.

three yearly festivals, and on the fast day.[1]  But Vitellius put these vestments into our own power, as in the days of our forefathers, and ordered the commandant of the fortress not to trouble himself to inquire where they were laid, or when they were to be used; and this he did as an act of kindness, to oblige the nation to him.  He also deprived Joseph, who was also called Caiaphas, of the high priesthood, and appointed Jonathan (the son of Ananus, the former high priest,) to succeed him.  After this he returned to Antioch.

§ 4. And Tiberius sent a letter to Vitellius, and commanded him to negotiate a friendship with Artabanus, the king of Parthia; for he was his enemy, and terrified him, as he had seized Armenia, lest he should proceed further, and Tiberius said he should only trust him upon Artabanus giving him hostages, and especially his son.  Upon Tiberius' writing thus to Vitellius, by the offer of great presents of money, he persuaded both the king of Iberia,[2] and the king of Albania,[3] to make no delay, but to fight against Artabanus; and although they would not do so themselves, yet they gave the Scythians a passage through their country, and opened the Caspian gates[4] to them, and brought them upon Artabanus.  So Armenia was again taken from the Parthians, and the country of Parthia was filled with war, and their leading men were slain, and all things were in disorder among them: the king's son also himself fell in these wars, together with many ten thousands of his army.  Vitellius had also sent such great sums of money to the kinsmen and friends of his father Artabanus, that he had almost got him slain by those who had taken the bribes.  And when Artabanus

---

[1] This mention of the high priest's **sacred** garments received seven days before a festival, and purified in those days against a festival, as having been polluted by being in the custody of heathens, in Josephus, agrees well with the traditions of the Talmudists, as Reland here observes.  Nor is there any question but the three feasts here mentioned were the Passover, Pentecost, and Feast of Tabernacles; and the Fast, so called by way of distinction, as Acts xxvii. 9, was the great day of expiation.—W.

[2] Iberia corresponds very nearly with the modern *Georgia*.

[3] On the S.W. shore of the Caspian, and embracing a portion of the Caucasus.

[4] The *Pass of Derbend*.

perceived that the plot laid against him was not to be avoided, because it was laid by many persons and by the leading men, so that it would certainly take effect, and compared the number of those who were truly faithful to him with those that were already corrupted, and deceitful in the kindness they professed to him, and were likely, if any attempt were made upon him, to go over to his enemies, he made his escape to the upper satrapies. And he afterwards raised a great army out of the Dahæ and Sacæ, and fought with his enemies, and recovered his throne.

§ 5. When Tiberius heard of these things, he desired to have friendship negotiated between himself and Artabanus. And when, upon this invitation, Artabanus received the proposal kindly, he and Vitellius met at the Euphrates, and as a bridge was laid over the river, they each of them, attended by their guards, had an interview with one another in the middle of the bridge. And when they had agreed upon the terms of peace, Herod the tetrarch erected a rich tent in the middle of the passage, and feasted them there. Artabanus also, not long afterwards, sent his son Darius to Tiberius as a hostage, with many presents, among which was a man seven cubits in height, a Jew by race, whose name was Eleazar, and who for his height was called Giant. After this Vitellius went to Antioch, and Artabanus to Babylonia. And Herod, wishing to give Tiberius the first information that they had obtained hostages, sent letter-carriers, and accurately described all the particulars, and left nothing for the consular Vitellius to inform him of. So when Vitellius' letters were sent, and Tiberius let him know that he was acquainted with the affair already, because Herod had given him an account of them before, Vitellius was very much vexed at it; and supposing that he had been thereby more injured than was really the case, he nourished a secret anger for it, till he could be revenged on Herod, which was after Caius had succeeded to the empire.

§ 6. About this time Philip, Herod's brother, departed this life, in the twentieth year of the reign of Tiberius,[1]

---

[1] This calculation is exactly right: for since Herod died about Sep-

after he had been tetrarch of Trachonitis, and Gaulanitis, and Batanæa also, thirty-seven years. He had shown himself a person of moderation and quietness in his rule. He always lived in the country which was subject to him, and used to make his progresses with a few chosen friends; his tribunal also, on which he sat in judgment, followed him in his progresses, and when any one met him who wanted his assistance, he made no delay, but had his tribunal set down immediately, wherever he happened to be, and sat down upon it, and heard the case; and ordered the guilty that were convicted to be punished, and absolved those that were accused unjustly. He died at Julias,[1] and when he was carried to the tomb which he had already had erected for himself beforehand, he was buried with great pomp. Tiberius took his dominions, for he left no sons behind him, and added them to the province of Syria, but gave orders that the tribute collected in his tetrarchy should be kept in it.


## CHAP. V.

*Herod the Tetrarch makes War with Aretas, the King of Arabia, and is beaten by him; also concerning the Death of John the Baptist; and how Vitellius went up to Jerusalem; together with some Account of Agrippa, and of the Posterity of Herod the Great.*

### § 1.

ABOUT this time Aretas, the king of Arabia Petræa, and Herod, had a quarrel on the following account. Herod the tetrarch had married the daughter of Aretas, and had lived with her a long time. But on his journey to Rome, he lodged with Herod, who was his brother indeed, but

tember, in the fourth year before the Christian era, and Tiberius began, it is well known, August 19, A.D. 14, it is evident that the thirty-seventh year of Philip, reckoned from his father's death, was the twentieth of Tiberius, or near the end of A.D. 33 (the very year of our Saviour's death also), or, however, in the beginning of the next year, A.D. 34. This Philip seems to have been the best of all the posterity of Herod, for his love of peace and love of justice.—W.

[1] Bethsaida. Julias. See p. 383, note 5.

not by the same mother; for this Herod [1] was the son of the high priest Simon's daughter. And he fell in love with Herodias, this last Herod's wife, (who was the daughter of Aristobulus their brother, and the sister of Agrippa the Great,) and ventured to talk to her of marriage. And as she agreed to his proposal, it was arranged that she should change her habitation, and come to him as soon as he should return from Rome: it was also stipulated that he should divorce Aretas' daughter. When he had made this agreement, he sailed to Rome; and when he had done there the business he went about, and returned home again, his wife having heard of the agreement he had made with Herodias, and having learned of it before her husband was aware of her knowledge of his whole design, she desired him to send her to Machærus,[2] a fortress on the borders of the dominions of Aretas and Herod, without informing him of any of her intentions. Accordingly Herod sent her there, not thinking his wife had any inkling of his arrangement with Herodias. Now she had sent various things a good while before to Machærus, which was at that time subject to her father, and so all necessary preparations for her journey were made by the general of Aretas' army; and so she soon started and reached Arabia, passed on by one general to another, and soon got to her father, and told him of Herod's intentions. And Aretas made this a *casus belli*, having previously had some difference with Herod about their frontiers in the district of Gamalitis.[3] So they raised armies on both sides, and prepared for war, and sent their generals to fight instead of themselves; and, when they joined battle, all Herod's army was destroyed by the treason of some fugitives, who, as they were of the tetrarchy of Philip, served under Herod. And Herod wrote about this to Tiberius, who, being very angry at the aggression of Aretas, wrote to Vitellius to make war upon him, and either to

---

[1] This Herod seems to have had the additional name of Philip, as Antipas was called Herod Antipas, and as Antipas and Antipater seem to be in a manner the very same name, yet were the names of two sons of Herod the Great; so might Philip the tetrarch and this Herod Philip be two different sons of the same father.—W.

[2] *Mekaur*, east of the *Dead Sea*.

[3] The district of Gamala, now *Kul'at el-Hu n*.

take him alive, and bring him to him in bonds, or to kill him, and send him his head. This was the charge that Tiberius gave the president of Syria.

§ 2. Now some of the Jews thought that the destruction of Herod's army came from God, and that very justly, as a punishment for what he did against John, who was called the Baptist. For Herod had had him put to death, though he was a good man, and commanded the Jews to exercise virtue, both as to justice towards one another, and piety towards God, and so to come to baptism; for baptism would be acceptable to God, if they made use of it, not in order to expiate some sins, but for the purification of the body, provided that the soul was thoroughly purified beforehand by righteousness. Now, as many flocked to him, for they were greatly moved by hearing his words, Herod, fearing that the great influence John had over the people might lead to some rebellion, (for the people seemed likely to do any thing he should advise,) thought it far best, by putting him to death, to prevent any mischief he might cause, and not bring himself into difficulties, by sparing a man who might make him repent of his leniency when it should be too late. Accordingly, he was sent a prisoner, in consequence of Herod's suspicious temper, to Machærus, the fortress I before mentioned, and was there put to death. So the Jews had an opinion that the destruction of this army was sent as a punishment upon Herod, and was a mark of God's displeasure at him.

§ 3. Now Vitellius prepared to make war upon Aretas, having with him two legions of armed men: he also took with him all the light-armed troops and cavalry with them, which were drawn from those kingdoms which were under the Romans, and pushed on for Petra,¹ and arrived at Ptolemais. And when he was going to lead his army through Judæa, the principal men met him, and desired that he would not march through their land; for the laws of their country would not permit them to overlook images being brought into it, of which there were a great many on their standards. And he listened to what they said, and changed the resolution which he had before taken in

¹ The present Petra, east of the *Arabah.*

the matter, and ordered the army to march along the
great plain, while he himself with Herod the tetrarch and
his friends went up to Jerusalem to offer sacrifice to God,
as an ancient festival of the Jews was then at hand.
And when he arrived there, and was honourably received
by the people of the Jews, he stayed there for three days,
during which time he deprived Jonathan of the high
priesthood, and gave it to his brother Theophilus; but
on the fourth day, when letters came to him informing
him of the death of Tiberius, he obliged the people to take
an oath of fidelity to Caius; he also recalled his army, and
made them every one go home to their winter quarters,
because, as the empire had devolved upon Caius, he had
not the same authority for making this war as he had
before. It was also reported, that when Aretas heard of
the coming of Vitellius to fight him, he said, upon his
consulting the auguries, that it was impossible that this
army of Vitellius' should enter Petra ; for one of the
rulers would die, either he that gave orders for the war,
or he that was marching at the other's desire to carry out
his will, or else he against whom this army was prepared.
And Vitellius retired to Antioch.  Now Agrippa, the son of
Aristobulus, had gone to Rome a year before the death of
Tiberius, in order to treat of some affairs with the
emperor, if he might be permitted to do so.  I have now
a mind to describe at some length Herod and his family,
and how it fared with them, partly because it concerns
this history to speak of the matter, and partly because
Herod's family history is a signal proof that a great number of children is of no advantage, any more than any
other strength that mankind set their hearts upon, apart
from piety towards God : for it happened, within a hundred years, that the posterity of Herod, who were very
numerous, with but few exceptions completely died out.[1]
One may well apply this for the instruction of mankind, to

[1] Whether this sudden extinction of almost the entire lineage of
Herod the Great, which was very numerous, as we are both here and in
the next section informed, was not in part as a punishment for the gross
incests they were frequently guilty of, in marrying their own nephews
and nieces, well deserves to be considered.  See Levit. xviii. 6, 7 ; xxi.
10.—W.

learn thence how unhappy they were; it will also be well to relate the history of Agrippa, who, as he was a person most worthy of admiration, so was he from a private man, beyond the expectation of all that knew him, advanced to great power and authority. I have said something of them formerly, but I shall now speak more in detail.

§ 4. Herod the Great had two daughters by Mariamne, the daughter of Hyrcanus; one was Salampsio, who married Phasaelus her cousin, who was himself the son of Herod's brother Phasaelus, her father making the match; the other was Cypros, who herself married her cousin Antipater, the son of Herod's sister Salome. Phasaelus had three sons by Salampsio, Antipater, Herod, and Alexander, and two daughters, Alexandra and Cypros. Agrippa, the son of Aristobulus, married this Cypros, and Timius of Cyprus married Alexandra; he was a man of note, but had by her no children. Agrippa had by Cypros two sons and three daughters; the daughters were called Berenice, Mariamne, and Drusilla; and the names of the sons were Agrippa and Drusus, of whom Drusus died before he came to the years of puberty. And their father, Agrippa, was brought up with his other brothers Herod and Aristobulus, who were also the sons of *Aristobulus the son of* Herod the Great by Berenice; this Berenice was the daughter of Costobarus and of Herod's sister Salome. Aristobulus left these infants, when he and his brother Alexander were put to death by their father, as I have already related. But when they arrived at years of puberty, this Herod, the brother of Agrippa, married Mariamne, the daughter of Olympias (who was the daughter of Herod the king), and of Joseph (the son of Joseph, who was brother to Herod the king), and had by her a son, Aristobulus. And Aristobulus, the third brother of Agrippa, married Jotape, the daughter of Sampsigeramus, king of Emesa;[1] they had a daughter who was deaf, whose name also was Jotape. These so far are the children of the male line. And Herodias, their sister, was married to Herod [Philip], the son of Herod the Great by Mariamne the daughter of Simeon the high priest, and they had a daughter

---

[1] Now *Homs.*

Salome; after her birth Herodias took upon her to con-
found the laws of our country, and divorced herself
from her husband while he was alive, and married
Herod [Antipas], (her husband's brother on the father's
side,) who was tetrarch of Galilee. And her daughter
Salome married Philip (the son of Herod), tetrarch of
Trachonitis. And, as he died childless, Aristobulus (the
son of Herod, the brother of Agrippa) married her; they
had three sons, Herod, Agrippa, and Aristobulus. This
was the posterity of Phasaelus and Salampsio. And the
daughter of Antipater by Cypros was Cypros, who married
Alexas Helcias, the son of Alexas, and they had a daughter
Cypros; but Herod and Alexander, who, as I said, were the
brothers of Antipater, died childless. As to Alexander, the
son of Herod the king, who was put to death by his father, he
had two sons, Alexander and Tigranes, by the daughter of
Archelaus the king of Cappadocia; Tigranes, who was king
of Armenia, was accused at Rome, and died childless;
but Alexander had a son of the same name as his brother
Tigranes, who was sent out as king of Armenia by Nero;
and he had a son, Alexander, who married Jotape, the
daughter of Antiochus, the king of Commagene;[1] Vespasian made him king of an island[2] in Cilicia. But these
descendants of Alexander, soon after their birth, deserted
the Jewish religion, and went over to that of the Greeks.
And the rest of the daughters of Herod the king all died
childless. And as the descendants of Herod, whom I have
enumerated, were in existence when Agrippa the Great got
the kingdom, and I have now given an account of their
pedigree, it now remains that I relate the various vicissitudes that befell Agrippa, and how he lived through
them, and was advanced to the greatest height of dignity
and power.

[1] See Antiq. xviii. 2, § 5.
[2] Probably the island of Elæusa, near the river *Lamas*.

## CHAP. VI.

*How Agrippa sailed for Rome to Tiberius; and how, upon his being accused by his own freedman, he was put in prison; and how he was set at liberty by Caius, after Tiberius' death, and was made King of the Tetrarchy of Philip.*

### § 1.

A LITTLE before the death of Herod the king, Agrippa living at Rome, and being brought up with and very intimate with Drusus, the emperor Tiberius' son, also contracted a friendship with Antonia (the wife of the elder Drusus), who held his mother Berenice in great esteem, and was very desirous of advancing her son.   Now though Agrippa was by nature magnanimous and very generous in respect to giving, he did not manifest this inclination of his mind  while  his  mother was alive, thinking  it best to avoid her anger for such extravagance; but when Berenice was dead, and he was his own master, he spent a great deal extravagantly in his daily course of living, and a great deal in the immoderate presents he made, and those chiefly to the emperor's freedmen, hoping for their support, so that in a little time he was reduced to poverty, and could not live at Rome any longer.   Tiberius also forbade the friends of his deceased son to come into his sight, because on seeing them he should be put in mind of his son, and his grief would be thereby revived.

§ 2.  For these reasons he went away from Rome, and set sail for Judæa, but in evil circumstances, being dejected by the loss of the money which he once had, and because he had not wherewithal to pay his creditors, who were many in number, and gave him no chance of avoiding them; so that he knew not what to do, and in shame at the state of his affairs, retired to a certain tower at Malatha [1] in Idumæa, and had thoughts of killing himself. But his wife Cypros perceived his intention, and tried all sorts of methods to divert him from taking such a course.

---

[1] Apparently *Tell el-Milh*, thirteen miles east of Beersheba.

So she sent a letter to his sister Herodias, who was now
the wife of Herod the tetrarch, and let her know Agrippa's
present design, and the necessities that drove him to it,
and desired her, as a kinswoman of his, to help him and
to engage her husband to do the same, as Herodias could
see how she (Cypros) alleviated her husband's troubles
all she could, although she had not the means they had.
And they sent for him, and allotted him Tiberias for
his habitation, and assigned him some money for his
maintenance, and made him a magistrate of that city, by
way of honouring him.   However, Herod did not long
continue in the resolution of supporting him, though even
that support was not sufficient for him.   For as they were
once at a feast at Tyre, and in their cups abused one
another, Agrippa thought it was not to be borne, that
Herod threw in his teeth his poverty, and his owing his
necessary food to him.   So he went to Flaccus, who had
been consul, and a very great friend to him at Rome
formerly, and was now president of Syria.

§ 3. And Flaccus received him kindly, and he lived
with him.   Flaccus had also with him there Aristobulus,
who was Agrippa's brother, but was at variance with
him; yet did not their enmity to one another hinder the
friendship of Flaccus to them both, but they both received equal honour from him.   However, Aristobulus did
not abate his ill-will to Agrippa, till at length he got
him to be on bad terms with Flaccus, bringing on the
estrangement as follows. The Damascenes had a difference
with the Sidonians about their frontiers, and when Flaccus
was about to hear the case pleaded, on hearing that Agrippa
had great influence with him, they begged that he would be
on their side, and promised him a great deal of money.   So
he was zealous in assisting the Damascenes as far as he was
able; but Aristobulus (who had got intelligence of this promise of money) accused him to Flaccus. And when, upon a
thorough examination of the matter, it appeared plainly
to be so, Flaccus discontinued his friendship to Agrippa.
So he was reduced to the utmost straits, and went to
Ptolemais,[1] and because he knew not where else to get

---

[1] *'Akka.*

a livelihood, he thought of sailing to Italy. But as he was prevented from doing so by want of money, he desired Marsyas, who was his freedman, to find some method of procuring him as much money as he wanted for that purpose, by borrowing it of some person or other. So Marsyas desired Peter, who was the freedman of Agrippa's mother Berenice, but by virtue of her testament belonged to Antonia, to lend Agrippa money upon his own bond and security; but he accused Agrippa of having defrauded him of certain sums of money, and so obliged Marsyas, when he made the bond for 20,000 Attic drachmæ, to accept 2,500 drachmæ less than that sum. This the other allowed because he could not help it. Upon the receipt of this money, Agrippa went to Anthedon,[1] and took shipping, and was going to set sail; but Herennius Capito, who was the procurator of Jamnia,[2] sent a band of soldiers to demand of him 300,000 drachmæ of silver, which were owing by him to the emperor's treasury at Rome, and tried to force him to stay. He pretended at the time that he would do as he was told, but when night came on, he cut cables, and went off, and sailed to Alexandria, where he desired Alexander the Alabarch to lend him 200,000 drachmæ; but he said he would not lend it him, but did not refuse it to Cypros, as he greatly admired her affection to her husband, and all her other virtue; and she undertook to repay it. And Alexander gave them five talents at Alexandria, and promised to pay them the rest of the sum at Dicæarchia,[3] and this he did from the fear he was in that Agrippa would soon spend it. And Cypros, having thus set her husband free to sail on to Italy, returned to Judæa with her children.

§ 4. And when Agrippa reached Puteoli, he wrote a letter to Tiberius Cæsar, who then lived at Capreæ,[4] and told him that he was come so far to wait on him and pay him a visit, and asked that he would give him leave to come over to Capreæ. And Tiberius made no difficulty, but wrote to him in an obliging way in other respects, and also told him he was glad of his safe return, and desired him to come to Capreæ; and when he was come he did not

---

[1] Agrippias. See Antiq. xiii. 13, § 3.  [2] *Yebnah.*
[3] Puteoli, *Pozzuoli.*  [4] The island of *Capri.*

fail to welcome him and treat him as kindly as he had promised him in his letter to do.   But the next day came a letter to the emperor from Herennius Capito, informing him, that Agrippa had borrowed 300,000 drachmæ, and not paid it at the time appointed; but, when it was demanded of him, had run away like a fugitive from the places in his jurisdiction, and had put it out of his power to get the money from him.  When Tiberius had read this letter he was much vexed at it, and gave orders that Agrippa should be excluded from his presence until he had paid the debt.  But he, being no way dismayed at the emperor's anger, entreated Antonia, the mother of Germanicus, and also of Claudius, who was afterwards emperor himself, to lend him those 300,000 drachmæ, that he might not lose Tiberius' friendship.  And she, out of regard to the memory of Berenice his mother (for these two women had been very intimate with one another), and out of regard to his having been brought up with Claudius, lent him the money, and, upon the payment of his debt, his friendship with Tiberius continued as before.   After this, Tiberius Cæsar recommended to him his grandson,[1] and ordered that he should always accompany him when he went out.  But Agrippa, after the kind treatment of Antonia, paid great court to Caius, who was her grandson, and was held in very high honour because of the popularity of his father.[2]  Now there was one Thallus, a freedman of Tiberius, a Samaritan by race, of whom Agrippa borrowed a million drachmæ, and so repaid Antonia the debt he owed her, and by spending the overplus in paying his court to Caius, he became a person of great influence with him.

§ 5.  Now as the friendship which Agrippa had with Caius rose to a great height, they once had a conversation about Tiberius, as they were in a chariot together, Agrippa praying (for they two sat by themselves) that Tiberius might soon go off the stage, and leave the empire to Caius, who was in every respect more worthy of it.   Now Eutychus, who was Agrippa's freedman, and drove his chariot, heard these words, and at the time said nothing about them : but when Agrippa accused him of stealing some

---

[1] Tiberius junior.—W.            [2] Germanicus.—W.

garments of his (which he really did steal) he ran away
from him; and when he was captured and brought before
Piso, who was governor of the city, and asked why he ran
away? he replied, that he had something private to say to
Tiberius, that regarded his security and safety: so Piso
sent him in bonds to Capreæ. And Tiberius, according
to his usual custom, kept him in bonds, being a procras-
tinator, if ever king or tyrant was so; for he did not
receive ambassadors quickly, and no successors were despatched to governors or procurators of provinces that
had been formerly sent, unless they were dead. This made
him also negligent in hearing prisoners. And when he was
once asked by his friends, what was the reason of his delay
in such cases? he said, that he delayed to hear ambassadors, lest, upon their quick dismissal, other ambassadors
should be appointed, and return to him; and so he should
bring trouble upon himself by their receptions and dis-
missals. He said also that he permitted those governors
who had been once sent to their governments to stay there
a long time from regard to the subjects that were under
them; for all governors were naturally disposed to get as
much as they could, and those who were not to remain
there, but to stay a short time only, and that in uncertainty
when they would be turned out, were all the more tempted to
fleece the people. Whereas, if their government was long
continued to them, they were at last satiated with their spoil,
as having got a great deal, and so became less keen in their
pillaging; but if a rapid succession of governors took place,
the poor subjects, who were exposed to them as a prey, would
not be able to bear the new ones, for they would not have the
same time allowed them, as their predecessors had filled
themselves in, and so grown indifferent to getting more,
because they would be recalled too soon for making a rich
harvest otherwise. He gave them an illustration to show his
meaning. A great number of flies swarmed about the sore
places of a man that had been wounded; upon which one
of the bystanders pitied the man's misfortune, and thinking he was not able to drive those flies away himself, was
going to drive them away for him. But he prayed him to
let them alone, and when the other asked him in rejoinder
the reason of such indiscretion in not getting relief from

his present misery, he replied, " If thou drivest these
flies away, thou wilt hurt me worse. For as these are
already full of my blood, they do not crowd about me, nor
pain me so much as before, but are somewhat more remiss,
while fresh ones that came almost famished, and found me
quite tired out already, would be my destruction." Tiberius said this was why he was himself careful not to send
new governors perpetually to his subjects (who were already
sufficiently harassed by many oppressions), who, like these
flies, would further distress them, and, besides their natural
desire of gain, would have this additional incitement to
it, that they expected to be soon deprived of the pleasure
which they derived from it. And, as a further attestation
to what I say of the character of Tiberius, I appeal to his
practice itself; for, although he was emperor twenty-two
years, he sent in all only two procurators to govern the
nation of the Jews, namely Gratus, and his successor in the
government, Pilate. Nor had he one way of acting with
respect to the Jews, and another with respect to the rest of
his subjects. He also gave out that he made such delay in
hearing prisoners, because immediate death to those that
were condemned to die would be an alleviation of their
present miseries, whereas those wicked wretches did not
deserve any such favour ; but their being harassed by the
anticipation of calamity would make them undergo greater
misery.

§ 6. This was why Eutychus could not obtain a hearing,
but was kept still in bonds. However, some time afterwards, Tiberius went from Capreæ[1] to Tusculanum,[2] which
is about a hundred furlongs from Rome, and Agrippa
asked Antonia to procure a hearing for Eutychus, let the
matter whereof he accused him prove what it would. Now
Antonia was greatly esteemed by Tiberius on all accounts,
not only from her connexion with him (for she was his brother
Drusus' wife), but also from her eminent chastity ; for though
she was still a young woman, she continued in her widowhood,
and refused all other matches, although Augustus had enjoined her to marry somebody, and all her life long preserved
her reputation free from reproach. She had also been privately

[1] The island of *Capri*.    [2] The villa of Tiberius at Tusculum.

the greatest benefactress to Tiberius when there was a very
dangerous plot laid against him by Sejanus, a man who
had been her husband's friend, and who had the greatest
power at that time because he was in command of the
army, and when many members of the senate, and many of
the freedmen joined with him, and the soldiers were tampered
with, and the plot became very formidable, and Sejanus
would certainly have gained his point, had not Antonia's
boldness been more wisely conducted than Sejanus' villainy.
For when she had discovered his designs against Tiberius,
she wrote him an exact account of the whole, and gave the
letter to Pallas, the most faithful of her slaves, and sent him
to Capreæ to Tiberius; and Tiberius, when he heard of it,
slew Sejanus and his fellow-conspirators, and though he had
held Antonia in great esteem before, now looked upon her
with still greater respect, and regarded her as trustworthy
in all things. So, when Tiberius was desired by this Antonia
to examine Eutychus, he answered, "If indeed Eutychus
has falsely accused Agrippa in what he has said of him, he
has had sufficient punishment by what I have done to him
already; but if, upon examination, the accusation appears
to be true, let Agrippa have a care, lest, in desire of
punishing his freedman, he do not rather bring a punishment upon himself." Now when Antonia told Agrippa of
this, he was still much more pressing that the matter might
be examined into; so Antonia, upon Agrippa's continually
importuning her to beg for this, seized the following opportunity. As Tiberius once reclined in his litter, and
was being carried about in it, and Caius, her grandson, and
Agrippa walked before him, after dinner, she went close to
the litter, and begged Tiberius to call Eutychus, and have
him examined; to which he replied, "O Antonia! the
gods are my witnesses, that I am induced to do what I am
going to do, not by my own inclination, but because I am
forced to it by thy entreaty." When he had said this, he
ordered Macro, who had succeeded Sejanus, to bring Eutychus to him; and he was brought without any delay. Then
Tiberius asked him what he had to say against a man who
had given him his liberty. Upon which he said, "O my
lord! this Caius, and Agrippa with him, were once riding
in a chariot, and I sat at their feet, and among other con-

versation that passed, Agrippa said to Caius, ' O that the
day would come, when this old man would die, and appoint
thee as master of the world! for Tiberius, his grandson,
would be no hindrance to us, if taken off by thee, and the
world would be happy, and I should be happy still more.'"
Now Tiberius took these to be truly Agrippa's words, and
having an old grudge also at Agrippa, because, when he
had commanded him to pay court to Tiberius his grandson, and the son of Drusus, Agrippa had neglected him,
and disobeyed his commands, and transferred all his
homage to Caius, he said to Macro, " Bind this person."
But Macro, not distinctly knowing whom it was he bade
him bind, and not expecting that he would wish any such
thing done to Agrippa, delayed until he should know more
distinctly what Tiberius meant.   But, when Tiberius had
gone round the hippodrome, he found Agrippa standing
there, and said " Why, Macro, here is the person I meant
to have bound; " and when he still asked, " Which of
them?" he said " Agrippa."   Then Agrippa betook himself to making supplication for himself, reminding him of
his son, with whom he was brought up, and of Tiberius
[his grandson] whom he had educated: but all to no purpose, for they took him off bound in his purple robe.   It
was also very hot weather, and they had had but little
wine to their meal, so that he was very thirsty; he was
also distressed and vexed at this treatment.   Seeing therefore one of Caius' slaves, whose name was Thaumastus,
carrying some water in a vessel, he desired that he would
let him drink.   And as he readily gave him some water
to drink, he drank, and said, " Boy! this service of thine
to me will be for thy advantage; for, if I once get rid of
these my bonds, I will soon procure thee thy freedom from
Caius, seeing thou hast not been wanting to minister to
me, though I am in bonds, in the same manner as when
I was in my former state and dignity."   Nor did he
deceive him in what he promised him, but requited him
for what he had done, for, when Agrippa afterwards came
to be king, he took particular care of Thaumastus, and
got him his liberty from Caius, and made him manager of
his affairs, and when he died, left him to Agrippa his son,
and to Berenice his daughter, to minister to them in the

same capacity. Thaumastus also grew old in that honour-able post, and died in it. But all this happened some time afterwards.

§ 7. Now Agrippa stood in his bonds before the royal palace, with many others who were in bonds also, and leaned against a certain tree in dejection, and as a certain bird sat upon the tree against which Agrippa leaned, (the Romans call this bird bubo,[1]) one of those that were bound, a German by nation, seeing the bird, asked a soldier who that man in purple was. And when he was informed that his name was Agrippa, and that he was by race a Jew, and one of the principal men of that nation, he asked leave of the soldier to whom he was bound,[2] to let him come nearer to him, to speak with him; for he had a mind to inquire of him about some things relating to his country. And when he had obtained leave, he stood near him, and spoke as follows to him by an interpreter. "This sudden change of thy condition, young man! troubles thee, as bringing on thee a manifold and very great adversity; nor wilt thou believe me, when I foretell how thou wilt get rid of this present misery, and how divine Providence will provide for thee. Know therefore (and I appeal to my own country's gods, as well as to the gods of this place, who have awarded these bonds to us,) that all I am going to say about thy concerns, shall neither be said to please thee by its babbling, nor in the endeavour to cheer thee without cause, for such predictions, when they come to fail, make the grief in the end more bitter than if one had never heard them at all. However, though I expose myself to danger by so doing, I think it fit to declare to thee the prediction of the gods. It cannot be that thou shalt continue long in these bonds, but thou wilt soon be delivered from them, and wilt be promoted to the highest dignity and power, and wilt be envied by all who now pity thy fortunes, and wilt be happy in thy death, and wilt leave happiness to thy children. But remember, whenever thou seest this bird again, thou wilt then live but five days

---

[1] That is, owl.

[2] Dr. Hudson here takes notice, out of Seneca, Epistle v., that this was the custom of Tiberius, to couple the prisoner, and the soldier that guarded him, together with the same chain.—W.

longer. This event will be brought to pass by that God
who has sent this bird here to be a sign unto thee. I
think it wrong to conceal from thee what I foresee concerning thee, that by thy knowing beforehand what happiness
is coming upon thee, thou mayest lightly regard thy
present misfortunes. But when this happiness shall come
to thee, do not forget what misery I am in myself, but
endeavour to deliver me." When the German had said
this, he made Agrippa laugh at him as much as he afterwards appeared worthy of admiration. But Antonia took
Agrippa's misfortune to heart: however, to speak to
Tiberius on his behalf, she saw to be a very difficult thing,
and indeed quite impracticable; but she got leave of
Macro, that the soldiers that guarded him should be of a
gentle nature, and that the centurion who was over them,
and was bound to him, should be of the same disposition, and that he might bathe every day, and that his
freedmen and friends might have access to him, and that
other things that tended to ease his body might be allowed
him. So his friend Silas had access to him, and two of
his freedmen, Marsyas and Stœcheus, brought him such
kind of food as he was fond of, and indeed took great care
of him; they also brought him garments, under pretence
of selling them, and, when night came on, laid them under
him, and the soldiers assisted them, as Macro had ordered
beforehand. Such was Agrippa's condition for six months,
and such was the state of his affairs.

§ 8. As for Tiberius, on his return to Capreæ, he fell ill.
At first his illness was but mild, but as it increased upon
him, he was anxious about his condition, and bade Euodus,
who was the freedman whom he most of all valued,
to bring the children to him; for he said he wanted to
talk to them before he died. Now he had no longer any
sons of his own alive; for Drusus, who was his only son, was
dead; but Drusus' son Tiberius was still living, who was
also called Gemellus. There was also living Caius, the
son of Germanicus, who was the son of his brother
[Drusus]. He was now grown up, and had finished his
education, and was in esteem and favour with the people
because of the excellent character of his father Germanicus, who had attained the highest honour among the

multitude by his consistent behaviour, and the easiness
and affability of his intercourse with the multitude, for
the rank he had did not hinder his treating all persons as if
they were his equals. In consequence of this behaviour he
was not only greatly esteemed by the people and the senate,
but also by every one of the nations that were subject to
the Romans ; some of whom were captivated, when they
met him, with the grace of their reception by him, and
others by the report of those who had met him. So upon
his death there was a lamentation made by all men, not
counterfeit sorrow such as is made in flattery to rulers, but
real sorrow, for everybody grieved at his death, as if they
had lost one that was near to them. So affable was he to all
men, that it turned greatly to the advantage of his son
among all ; and the soldiers in particular were so devoted
to him, that they reckoned it a gain, if need were, to die, if
he might but become emperor.

§ 9. Now when Tiberius had given orders to Euodus
to bring the children to him the next day in the morning, he prayed to his country's gods to show him a manifest sign which of the two should be his successor, being
very desirous to leave it to his son's son, but still intending
to depend more upon what God should foreshow concerning
them, than upon his own opinion and inclination. So he
made this to be the omen, that the empire should belong
to him who should come first to him the next day. When
he had thus resolved, he sent to his grandson's tutor, and
ordered him to bring the child to him early in the morning,
supposing that God would not interfere about who should
be made emperor. But God thwarted his intention. For
as Tiberius was thus contriving matters, directly it was
day, he bade Euodus to call in the child which should be
ready there first. And he went out, and found Caius
before the door, (for Tiberius was not yet come, for his
breakfast was late, and Euodus knew nothing of what his
lord intended,) so he said to Caius, "Thy father calls
thee," and brought him in. As soon as Tiberius saw
Caius, he reflected then first on the power of God, and how
the power of bestowing the empire on whom he would
was entirely taken from him, and so he was not able to
make good what he had intended. And he greatly lamented

that the power of carrying out his intention was taken from
him, and that his grandson Tiberius was not only to lose
the Roman empire by his mode of divination, but his own
safety also, because his preservation would now depend upon
such as would be more powerful than himself, who would
think it a thing insufferable that a kinsman should live with
them, and so his relationship would not be able to protect
him, but he would be feared and hated by him who had the
supreme authority, partly on account of his being next to
the empire, partly because he would be perpetually plotting,
not only to preserve himself, but also to be at the head of
affairs. Now Tiberius was very much given to the casting of
nativities, and had spent his life more successfully in the
science than those whose profession it was. For example,
when he once saw Galba coming to him, he said to his
most intimate friends, that there came a man that would
one day have the rank of Roman emperor. And Tiberius
was more addicted to all sorts of divinations than any
other of the Roman emperors, because he had found
them to reveal the truth about his own affairs. And indeed he was now in great distress at this chance that
had befallen him, and was very much grieved about his
grandson as if he were already murdered, and vexed with
himself that he should have made use of such a method of
divination, when it was in his power to have died without
grief in ignorance of the future, whereas he must now die
tormented by his foreknowledge of the misfortunes of such
as were dearest to him. But although he was troubled at
this unexpected succession to the empire of those for whom
he did not intend it, he spoke as follows to Caius, though
unwillingly and against his inclination : "O child ! though
Tiberius is nearer related to me than thou art, I, by my
own determination and the vote of the gods, do give, and
put into thy hand, the Roman empire. And I desire thee
never to be unmindful when thou comest to it, either of
my kindness to thee, in setting thee in so high a dignity,
or of thy relationship to Tiberius; and as thou knowest that
I am, together with and after the gods, the procurer of
such great blessings to thee, so I desire that thou wilt
make me a return for my readiness to assist thee, and wilt
take care of Tiberius because of his near relationship to

thee. Besides which, thou art to know, that, while Tiberius is alive, he will be a bulwark to thee, both as to the empire and as to thy own preservation ; but, if he die, that will be but a prelude to thy own misfortunes; for to be alone under the weight of such vast affairs is very dangerous ; nor will the gods suffer those actions which are unjustly done, contrary to the law which directs men to act otherwise, to go unpunished." This was the speech which Tiberius made, which did not persuade Caius to act accordingly, although he promised to do so, for when he was settled in the empire, he took off this Tiberius, as was predicted by his grandfather, as he was also himself, no long time afterwards, slain by a conspiracy formed against him.

§ 10. After Tiberius had at this time appointed Caius to be his successor, he lived only a few days, and then died, after he had been emperor twenty-two years, five months, and three days. Now Caius was the fourth emperor. And when the Romans heard that Tiberius was dead, they rejoiced at the good news, but had not courage to believe it, not because they were unwilling it should be true, for they would have given large sums of money that it might prove to be so, but because they were afraid, if they showed their joy prematurely, and the news proved false, they would be accused and ruined. For this Tiberius had brought a vast load of misery on the patrician families of the Romans, for he was easily inflamed with passion in all cases, and was of such a temper as rendered his anger uncontrollable till he had wreaked it, even though he hated anyone without reason, for he was by nature fierce in all the sentences he gave, and made death the penalty for the slightest offences. And so, though the Romans heard the rumour about his death gladly, they were restrained from the full enjoyment of that pleasure by the dread of such miseries as they foresaw would follow, if their hopes proved ill grounded. Now as soon as Marsyas, Agrippa's freedman, heard of Tiberius' death, he came running to tell Agrippa the news ; and finding him going out to the bath, he gave him a nod, and said in the Hebrew tongue, " The lion is dead."[1] And he, understanding his meaning, and being

---

[1] The name of a lion is often given to tyrants, especially by the Jews, such as Agrippa, and probably his freedman Marsyas, in effect were,

delighted at the news, said, "All thanks and happiness
attend thee for this news of thine: I only hope that what
thou sayest may prove true." Now the centurion, who
was set to guard Agrippa, when he saw with what haste
Marsyas came, and what joy Agrippa had at what he said,
suspected that his words announced something startling,
and asked them about the subject of their conversation.
They at first turned the subject, but, upon his further
pressing, Agrippa, without more ado, told him (for he was
already his friend), and he joined with him in the pleasure
which this news occasioned, because it would be fortunate
to Agrippa, and made him a supper. But, as they were
feasting and drinking merrily, there came one who said,
that Tiberius was still alive, and would return to the city
in a few days. At this news the centurion was exceedingly troubled, because he had done what might cost him
his life, in feasting so jovially a prisoner, and that upon
the news of the death of the emperor; so he thrust Agrippa
from the couch whereon he reclined, and said, " Dost thou
think to cheat me by a lie about the emperor without
punishment? and shalt not thou pay for this report at the
price of thine head?" When he had so said, he ordered
Agrippa to be bound again, (for he had loosed him before,)
and kept a severer guard over him than formerly. In that
evil condition was Agrippa that night; but the next day
the rumour increased in the city, and confirmed the news
that Tiberius was certainly dead, insomuch that men durst
now openly and freely talk about it; nay, some offered
sacrifices on that account. Several letters also came from
Caius, one of them to the senate, informing them of the
death of Tiberius, and of his own succession to the empire,
another to Piso, the governor of the city, which announced
the same thing. Caius also gave orders that Agrippa should
be removed out of the camp, and go to the house where he
lived before he was put in prison; so that he was now out
of fear as to his own affairs; for, although he was still in
custody, yet he had considerable freedom. And as soon as
Caius was come to Rome, and had brought Tiberius' body

Ezek. xix. 1, 2; Esth. xiv. 13; 2 Tim. iv. 17. They are also som etimes
compared to or represented by wild beasts, of which the lion is the
principal. Dan. vii. 3, 8; Apoc. xiii. 1, 2.—W.

with him, and had made a sumptuous funeral for him, according to the laws of his country, he was much disposed to set Agrippa at liberty that very day, but Antonia hindered him, not out of any ill-will to the prisoner, but from regard to decency in Caius, lest it should make men believe that he heard of the death of Tiberius with pleasure, if he set free so soon one whom Tiberius had put in bonds. However, not many days elapsed before Caius sent for Agrippa to his house, and had him shaved, and made him change his raiment, after which he put a diadem upon his head, and appointed him king of the tetrarchy of Philip. He also gave him the tetrarchy of Lysanias,[1] and changed his iron chain for a golden one of equal weight. He also sent out Marullus to be master of the horse in Judæa.

§ 11. Now, in the second year of the reign of Caius Cæsar, Agrippa asked for leave to sail home, and settle affairs in his kingdom, and promised to return again when he had put everything in order, as it ought to be put. And, upon the emperor's permission, he returned to his own country, and appeared before all men unexpectedly as king, and thereby demonstrated to those that saw him the power of fortune, when they compared his former poverty with his present prosperity. And some called him a happy man, because he had not been foiled of his hopes, others could scarce believe what had happened.


## CHAP. VII.

*How Herod the Tetrarch was exiled to Lugdunum.*

### § 1.

BUT Herodias, Agrippa's sister, who was wife of that Herod who was tetrarch of Galilee and Peræa, was envious of this authority of her brother, particularly as she saw that he had far greater dignity bestowed on him than her husband had, though, when he ran away, he

---

[1] Although Caius now promised to give Agrippa the tetrarchy of Lysanias, yet was it not actually conferred upon him till the reign of Claudius, as we learn, Antiq. xix. 5, § 1.—W.

was not able to pay his debts, but now he was come back,
he had great position and prosperity.  She was therefore
grieved, and much displeased at so great a change, and especially when she saw him walking about among the multitude
with the usual marks of royal authority, and was not able
to conceal how miserable she was from her envy, but she
incited her husband, and begged him to sail to Rome, to
court honours equal to Agrippa's : for she said life was
unbearable for them, if Agrippa (the son of that Aristobulus who was condemned to death by his father), who
came to her husband in such extreme poverty, that all the
necessaries of life had to be supplied him day by day, and
had fled away from his creditors by sea, now returned a
king, while he himself, the son of a king, whom his near
relationship to royalty called upon to claim the same
dignity, sat still, and was contented with a private life.
"And if," she continued, " before, Herod, you did not
mind being in a lower condition than your father, who
begot you, had, yet now at any rate seek after a similar
dignity ; and do not bear this come down that a man
who has paid court to your riches should be in greater
honour than yourself, nor suffer his poverty to show itself
able to purchase greater things than our abundance ; nor
esteem it other than a shameful thing to be inferior to one,
who, the other day, lived upon your charity.  But let us
go to Rome, and let us spare no pains or expenditure of
silver or gold, since they cannot be kept for any better use
than for procuring a kingdom."

§ 2. As for Herod, he opposed her request for a time,
from his love of ease, and a suspicion that he would have
trouble at Rome, and he tried to instruct her better.  But
the more she saw him draw back, the more she pressed
him to it, and desired him to leave no stone unturned to
be king: and at last she left not off till she engaged him,
whether he would or not, to be of her sentiments, because
he could no otherwise avoid her importunity.  So he got
all things ready, in as sumptuous a manner as he was
able, and spared for nothing, and went up to Rome, and
took Herodias with him.  And Agrippa, when he heard of
their intention and preparations, also made his preparations.  And as soon as he heard they had set sail, he sent

Fortunatus, one of his freedmen, to Rome, to carry presents to the emperor, and letters against Herod, and to speak to Caius himself, if he should have an opportunity. This man followed Herod so quick, and had so prosperous a voyage, and came so little time after Herod, that while Herod was with Caius, he also arrived, and delivered his letters; for they both sailed to Dicæarchia,[1] and found Caius at Baiæ,[2] which is itself a little town in Campania, about five furlongs from Dicæarchia. There are in that place royal palaces with sumptuous apartments, each emperor still endeavouring to outdo his predecessor's magnificence; the place also has warm baths that spring out of the ground of their own accord, which are of advantage for the recovery of the health of those that make use of them, and also minister to men's luxury. Now Caius simultaneously addressed Herod (it was the first time he had met with him) and looked at the letters which Agrippa had sent him, and which were written in accusation of Herod, wherein he was accused of having been in conspiracy with Sejanus against Tiberius' government, and of being now confederate with Artabanus, the king of Parthia, in opposition to the government of Caius, as a proof of which Agrippa said that Herod had armour sufficient for seventy thousand men ready in his armoury. Caius was moved at this information, and asked Herod, whether what was said about the armour was true. And when he admitted there was such armour there (for he could not deny it, the truth of it being too notorious), Caius took that as a sufficient proof of the accusation that he intended to revolt. So he took away from him his tetrarchy, and gave it by way of addition to Agrippa's kingdom; he also gave Herod's money to Agrippa, and punished Herod by perpetual exile, and appointed Lugdunum,[3] a city of Gaul, to be his place of habitation. But when he was informed that Herodias was Agrippa's sister, he made her a present of the money that was her own, and told her, that it was only her brother who prevented her sharing the calamity of her husband. But she replied, "You, indeed, O emperor! say this in a magnificent manner, and as be-

---

[1] Puteoli, *Pozzuoli*.          [2] *Baja*.          [3] *Lyon*.

comes you, but the love which I have for my husband
hinders me from partaking of the favour of your gift; for
it is not right that I, who have been a partner in his prosperity, should forsake him in his misfortunes." Thereupon Caius was angry at her pride, and sent her into exile
with Herod, and gave her estate to Agrippa. And thus
did God punish Herodias for her envy of her brother, and
Herod for giving ear to the vain discourses of a woman.
Now Caius administered public affairs with great magnanimity during the first and second year of his reign, and
behaved himself with such moderation, that he gained the
good-will of the Romans themselves, and of his other subjects. But, in process of time, he thought himself because
of the vast extent of his dominions as something more
than a man, and made himself a god, and took upon himself to act in all things so as to insult the Deity.


## CHAP. VIII.

*Concerning the Embassage of the Jews to Caius, and how
Caius sent Petronius into Syria to make War against the
Jews, unless they would receive his Statue.*

### § 1.

NOW a tumult having arisen at Alexandria between
the Jewish inhabitants and the Greeks, three ambassadors were chosen out of each party that were at
variance, who came to Caius. Now one of these ambassadors from the people of Alexandria was Apion, who
greatly slandered the Jews, and, among other things that
he said, charged them with neglecting the honours that
belonged to the emperor; for while all who were subject to
the Roman empire built altars and temples to Caius, and
in all other respects treated him as one of the gods, these
Jews alone thought it unseemly to erect statues in honour
of him, or to swear by his name. When Apion had said
many of these severe things, by which he hoped to exas-
perate Caius against the Jews, as was likely to be the case,
Philo, the principal person of the Jewish embassage, a

man eminent on all accounts, and the brother of Alexander the Alabarch,[1] and not unskilled in philosophy, was ready to betake himself to make his defence against those accusations. But Caius prohibited him, and bade him be gone, and was also in such a rage, that it was clear he was about to do them some very great mischief. And Philo having been thus ill treated went out, and said to those Jews who were about him, that they ought to be of good courage, for Caius' words indeed showed anger at them, but in reality he had already set God against him as an enemy.

§ 2. Then Caius, indignant that he should be thus despised by the Jews only, sent Petronius as his lieutenant to Syria, and as successor in the government to Vitellius, and gave him orders to invade Judæa with a large force, and, if they would admit his statue willingly, to erect it in the temple of God, but, if they were obstinate, to conquer them by war, and then to do it. Accordingly, Petronius took over the government of Syria, and made haste to obey Caius' injunctions. He got together as great a number of auxiliaries as he possibly could, and took with him two legions of the Roman army, and went to Ptolemais[2] to winter there, intending to set about the war in the spring. He also wrote word to Caius what he had determined to do, and he commended him for his energy, and ordered him not to be slack in the work, but to make war with them, if they would not obey his commands. Then many ten thousands of the Jews went to Ptolemais to Petronius, to offer their petitions to him, that he would not compel them to transgress and violate the law of their forefathers. "But if (said they) you are absolutely determined to bring this statue and erect it, first kill us, and then do what you have resolved on; for while we are alive, we cannot permit such things to be done as are forbidden us by the authority of our legislator and our forefathers, who have decided that such prohibitions are proofs of virtue." But Petronius was angry with them, and said,

---

[1] This Alexander the Alabarch, or governor of the Jews at Alexandria, and brother to Philo, is supposed by Bishop Pearson to be the same as that Alexander who is mentioned by St. Luke, as of the kindred of the high priests, Acts iv. 6.—W.

[2] 'Akka, St. Jean d'Acre.

"If I were myself emperor, and meant to follow my own will in acting thus, these words of yours would be properly spoken to me, but now the emperor has sent me, I am under the necessity of carrying out his decrees, because disobedience to them would bring upon me inevitable destruction." Then the Jews replied, "Since, therefore, you are so disposed, O Petronius, that you will not disobey Caius' commands, neither will we transgress the bidding of our law; and as we, relying on God and virtue, and the efforts of our ancestors, have continued hitherto without suffering them to be transgressed, we dare not by any means suffer ourselves to be so timorous as to transgress those laws, which God has ordered for our advantage, from the fear of death. And if we fall into misfortunes, we will bear them in order to preserve our laws, knowing that those who expose themselves to dangers have good hope of escaping them, because God will stand on our side, if, out of regard to him, we undergo afflictions, and sustain the uncertainties of fortune. But, if we should submit to you, we should be greatly reproached for our cowardice, as thereby showing ourselves ready to transgress our law; and we should incur the great anger of God also, who, even in your own judgment, is superior to Caius."

§ 3. When Petronius saw by their words that their determination was fixed, and that he would not be able without a war to obey Caius in the dedication of his statue, and that there would be a great deal of bloodshed, he took his friends and retinue, and pushed on to Tiberias, wishing to know in what posture the affairs of the Jews were. And many ten thousands of the Jews met Petronius again, when he was come to Tiberias, for they thought they would run a mighty hazard if they should have war with the Romans, but judged that the transgression of the law was of much greater consequence, and made supplication to him, that he would by no means reduce them to such straits, nor defile their city with the erection of Caius' statue. Then Petronius said to them, "Will you war then with the emperor, without considering his great preparations for war, and your own weakness?" And they replied, "We will not by any means war with him, but we will die before we see our laws transgressed." Then they threw them-

selves down upon their faces, and stretched out their
throats, and said they were ready to be slain. And this
they did for forty days together, and in the meantime left
off the tilling of their ground, though the season of the
year required them to sow it. Thus firm did they continue
in their resolution, and proposal to die willingly, rather
than to see the erection of Caius' statue.

§ 4. When matters were in this state, Aristobulus, king
Agrippa's brother, and Helcias the Great, and the other
principal men of that family, and the leading Jews with
them, went in unto Petronius, and besought him, since
he saw the determination of the multitude, not to
drive them to despair, but write to Caius, that the
Jews had an insuperable aversion to the reception of
his statue, and how they assumed a hostile attitude, and
left off the tillage of their ground: and that they were not
willing to go to war with him, because they were not able
to do it, but were ready to die with pleasure, rather than
suffer their laws to be transgressed: and how, if the land
continued unsown, robberies would be on the increase, from
their inability of paying tribute. They added that perhaps
Caius would be thereby moved to pity, and not entertain
any savage idea, or think of destroying the nation, but if
he continued inflexible in his former opinion to war against
them, he might then set about it himself. Thus did Aristobulus, and the rest with him, supplicate Petronius. And
Petronius,[1] partly on account of the earnest entreaties of
Aristobulus and the rest, and because of the great importance of what they asked, and the skilful way in which
they made their supplication; partly because he saw the
firmness of the opposition made by the Jews, and thought
it monstrous for him so to carry out the madness of Caius,
as to slay so many ten thousand men, only because of
their religious disposition towards God, and to pass all

---

[1] This Publius Petronius was after this still president of Syria,
under Claudius, and, at the desire of Agrippa, published a severe decree
against the inhabitants of Dora, who, in a sort of imitation of Caius,
had set up a statue of Claudius in a Jewish synagogue there. This
decree is extant, xix. 6, § 3, and greatly confirms the present accounts
of Josephus, as do the other decrees of Claudius, relating to the like
Jewish affairs, xix. 5, § 2, 3.—W.

his life after that in remorse; Petronius, I say, thought it much better to write to Caius, although he knew what intolerable rage he would be in against him for not obeying sooner his commands. But perhaps he thought he might persuade him, or if this mad resolution continued, he might then begin the war against them; nay, even if Caius should turn his anger against him (Petronius), it was good for persons who laid claim to virtue even to die for such vast multitudes of men. So he determined to hearken to the petitioners in this matter.

§ 5. He then called the Jews together to Tiberias (who came many ten thousands in number), and went up to them, and pointed out that the present expedition was not undertaken at his own option, but at the commands of the emperor, whose wrath would immediately and without delay be executed on such as had the temerity to disobey what he had commanded; nor was it fit for him, who had obtained such great honour by his favour, to contradict him in any thing. "Yet," added he, "I do not think it just to have such a regard to my own safety and honour, as to refuse to sacrifice them for your preservation, as you are so many in number, and endeavour to preserve the respect due to your law (which because it has come down to you from your forefathers, you esteem worth fighting for) and to the supreme authority and power of God, whose temple I will not venture to allow to fall into contempt by the imperial authority. I will, therefore, send to Caius, and let him know what your determination is, and will assist your suit as far as I am able, that you may not suffer on account of the virtuous designs you have proposed to yourselves. And may God be your helper (for his authority is beyond all the contrivance and power of men), and may he procure you the preservation of your ancient laws, and not be deprived, by the unreasonable wishes of men, of his accustomed honours! But if Caius be irritated, and turn the violence of his rage upon me, I will rather undergo all the danger and affliction that may come either upon my body or soul, than see so many of you perish, while you are acting in so excellent a manner. Do you, therefore, every one of you, go your ways about your own occupations, and fall to the cultivation of your land. I will myself send to Rome, and will not refuse to serve you in all things, either by myself or by my friends."

§ 6. When Petronius had said this, and had dismissed the assembly of the Jews, he desired those in authority to see to the cultivation of the fields, and to encourage the people to hope for better things. Thus did he soon make the multitude cheerful again. And now did God show his presence to Petronius, and signify to him, that he would afford him his assistance in his whole design; for he had no sooner finished the speech that he made to the Jews, but God sent down at once great showers of rain, contrary to human expectation, for the day was a clear day in the morning, and gave no indication by the appearance of the sky of any rain; nay, the whole year had been subject to a great drought, and made men despair of any rain from above, even if at any time they saw the heavens overcast with clouds; so that when such a great quantity of rain fell then, and that in an unusual manner, and without any expectation of it, the Jews hoped that Petronius would not fail in his supplication for them. And as to Petronius, he was amazed, evidently seeing that God took care of the Jews, and gave very plain signs of his appearance, so that those that were actually much inclined to a contrary opinion were unable to contradict it. This also among other particulars he wrote to Caius, all tending to dissuade him from his purpose, and entreating him by all means not to drive so many ten thousands of these men mad, whom if he should slay (for without war they would by no means suffer the laws of their worship to be set aside,) he would lose the revenue they paid him, and would be publicly cursed by them through all future ages. He added that God, who was their protector, had shown his power most clearly, and that such a power as left no room for doubt about it. Such was the business that Petronius was now engaged in.

§ 7. Now king Agrippa, who at this time chanced to be living at Rome, grew more and more in favour with Caius; and when he had once made him a feast, and was careful to exceed all others, both in the expense of the feast, and in such preparations as might contribute to his pleasure, which were not only far out of the means of all others, but such as Caius himself could never equal, much less exceed (such care did Agrippa take to exceed all men, and particularly to do all he could to please the emperor), Caius admired his generous disposition and magnificence, that he should strive to do every thing to please him even beyond his means, and wished to imitate the generosity which Agrippa exhibited in order to please him.    So Caius, when he had drunk wine plentifully, and was merrier than usual, said during the feast, when Agrippa urged him to drink, " I knew before now what great regard you had for me, and what great kindness you showed me, though with risk to yourself from Tiberius, nor have you omitted anything to show your good-will towards me, even beyond your means.   So, as it would be a base thing for me to come short of you in affection, I am desirous to make you amends for every thing in which I have been formerly deficient.   For all that I have bestowed on you, that may be called my gifts, is but little; every thing therefore that may contribute to your happiness shall be at your service, and that gladly, and as far as my power will reach."    And this Caius said to Agrippa, thinking he would ask for some province or the revenues of certain cities.    But, although he had made up his mind beforehand what he would ask, yet did he not discover his intentions, but made answer to Caius immediately, that it was not out of any expectation of gain that he formerly paid court to him, contrary to the commands of Tiberius, nor did he now do any thing to please him with an eye to his own advantage, and in order to receive any thing from him : for the gifts he had already bestowed upon him were great, and beyond the hopes of even a grasping man ; for, although they might be beneath the emperor's power, they were greater than the expectation and merit of the receiver.    And, as Caius was amazed at Agrippa's virtue, and pressed him still more to make his request for something which he might gratify him with, Agrippa replied, " Since, my lord ! you declare, such is your liberality, that I am worthy of **your** gifts, I will ask nothing that will contribute to my own happiness, for what you have already bestowed on me has made me remarkable for that ; but I ask something which may make you glorious for piety, and render the Deity a helper of your designs,

and may be an honour to me among those that hear of it,
as showing that I never fail to obtain what I ask of you.
Now my petition is this, that you will no longer think of
the dedication of the statue which you have ordered Petronius to set up in the Jewish temple."

§ 8. Thus did Agrippa venture to cast the die upon this
occasion, so important was the matter in his opinion, though
he knew how dangerous a thing it was so to speak ; for, had
not Caius approved of his request, it would have tended to
no less than the loss of his life.  But Caius, who was mightily
taken with Agrippa's obliging behaviour, and also thought
it unseemly to break his word before so many witnesses,
as he had with such eagerness forced Agrippa to become a
petitioner, and thought it would look as if he soon repented
of his offer, and because he greatly admired Agrippa's
virtue, in not desiring him at all to augment his own
dominions, either with large revenues, or greater authority,
but in thinking of the public tranquillity, of the laws, and
of the Deity, granted him what he requested, and wrote
as follows to Petronius, commending him for mustering
his army, and consulting him about this affair.  " If (he
said,) thou hast already erected my statue, let it continue
up ; but, if thou hast not yet done so, do not trouble thyself further about it, but dismiss thy army, and go to
the business which I sent thee about first, for I have now
no occasion for the erection of the statue.  I have granted
this as a favour to Agrippa, a man whom I honour so
very greatly, that I am not able to refuse him what he
would have, or what he has desired me to do for him."
Now Caius wrote this to Petronius, before he received
his letter, informing him that the Jews were ripe for revolt
about the statue, and that they seemed absolutely resolved
to threaten war against the Romans.  Upon receipt of this
letter Caius was much displeased that any attempt should
be made against his supreme authority, being as he was a
slave to base and vicious actions on all occasions, and paying
no regard to what was virtuous and honourable, and if he
resolved to show his anger against any one for any reason
whatever, suffering not himself to be restrained by any
advice, but thinking the indulging his anger a real pleasure.  So he wrote as follows to Petronius.  " Seeing thou

esteemest the presents made thee by the Jews to be of greater value than my commands, and art grown insolent enough to be subservient to their pleasure, I charge thee to become thy own judge, and to consider what thou art to do, now thou art under my displeasure; for I will make thee an example to the present and to all future ages, that none may dare to contradict the commands of their emperor."

§ 9. This was the letter which Caius wrote to Petronius, but Petronius did not receive it while Caius was alive; the ship which carried it sailing so slow, that other letters came to Petronius before it, by which he learned that Caius was dead. For God would not forget the dangers Petronius had undertaken to gratify the Jews, and to do him honour, but when he had taken Caius off in indignation at his so insolently attempting to claim for himself divine worship, he discharged his debt to Petronius. And Rome and all the empire co-operated with Petronius, especially those of the senators that were of most merit, because Caius had been unmercifully severe to them. For Caius died not long after he had written to Petronius the letter which threatened him with death; but as to the cause of his death, and the nature of the plot against him, I shall relate them in the progress of my narrative. Now the letter which informed Petronius of Caius's death came first, and a little afterwards came that which commanded him to kill himself with his own hands. And Petronius rejoiced at this circumstance of the death of Caius, and at the same time marvelled at the providence of God, who without the least delay, and immediately, gave him a reward for the regard he had had to the temple, and for the assistance he had afforded the Jews. Thus easily and unexpectedly did Petronius escape the danger of death.

## CHAP. IX.

*What befell the Jews that were in Babylon, because of two*
*Brothers, Asinœus and Anilœus.*

### § 1.

A DREADFUL calamity now befell the Jews that were
in Mesopotamia, and especially those that dwelt in
Babylonia. It was inferior to none, and accompanied by
great slaughter of them, and that greater than any recorded before; concerning all which I shall speak explicitly,
and set forth the causes of their calamity. There was a city
in Babylonia called Naarda,[1] not only a populous one, but
one that had a fertile and large territory round it, and,
besides its other advantages, was full of men also. It was
also not easy to be assaulted by enemies, because the river
Euphrates encompassed it all round, and because it had
strong walls. There was also the city Nisibis,[2] situate on
the same current of the river. So the Jews, depending on
the natural strength of these places, deposited in them that
half shekel which every one, by the custom of our country,
offers to God, as well as they did other things devoted to
him, for they made use of these cities as a treasury, whence,
at the proper time, they were transmitted to Jerusalem;
and many ten thousand men undertook to carry those
donations, from fear of the ravages of the Parthians,
to whom Babylonia was then subject. Now, there were
two brothers, Asinæus, and Anilæus, natives of the city of
Naarda, who had lost their father, and their mother put
them to learn the art of weaving, it not being esteemed a
disgrace among those people for men to spin wool. Now,
he that taught them that art, and was set over them, complained that they came too late to their work, and punished
them with stripes: and they took this punishment as an
outrage, and carried off all the weapons which were kept
in that house, which were not a few, and went into a cer-

---

[1] Called in the Peutinger, Table Naharra; it was not far from Sippara.
[2] Now *Nisibin*.

tain place where was a partition of the rivers, a place naturally very fit for the feeding of cattle, and for getting hay to be stored up for the winter. The poorest sort of the young men also resorted to them, whom they armed with the weapons they had got, and became their captains, and nothing hindered them from being their leaders in mischief. And they soon became invincible, and built a citadel, and sent to such as fed cattle, and ordered them to pay so much tribute out of them as might be sufficient for their maintenance, and stated that they would be their friends if they would submit to them, and that they would defend them from all their enemies on every side, but that they would kill all the cattle of those that refused to obey them. So they hearkened to their proposals (for they could do nothing else), and sent them as many sheep as were required of them, so that their forces grew greater, and they became lords over all they pleased, because they made sudden and unexpected raids, so that everybody who had to do with them chose to pay them court, and they became formidable to such as came to assault them, till the report about them came to the ears of the king of Parthia himself.

§ 2. Now when the satrap of Babylonia heard of this, desiring to nip them in the bud, before greater mischief should arise from them, he got together as great an army as he could, both of Parthians and Babylonians, and marched against them, thinking to attack them and destroy them, before any one should carry them the news that he had got an army together. He then encamped in the marshes, and lay still, but on the next day, (which was the Sabbath, which is among the Jews a day of rest from all work,) supposing that the enemy would not dare to fight him thereon, but that he could take and carry them off prisoners without fighting, he advanced stealthily, and thought to take them by surprise. Now Asinæus was sitting with the rest, and their weapons lay beside them, and he said, " Men, I hear a neighing of horses, not of such as are feeding, but such as have riders on their backs, for I also hear the noise of their bridles, and am afraid that some enemies are stealing upon us to surround us. However, let somebody go and reconnoitre,

and make a sure report of the present state of things; and
may what I have said prove a false alarm!" And when he
had said this, some of them went to spy out what was the
matter, and soon came back and said to him, "Neither
were you mistaken in telling us what our enemies were
doing, nor will they permit us to do harm to people any
longer. We are caught by their stratagem, like brute
beasts, for there is a large body of cavalry marching upon
us, while we are destitute of hands to defend ourselves
with, because we are restrained from doing so by the prohibition of our law, which obliges us to rest [on this day."]
But Asinæus did not by any means agree with the opinion
of his spy as to what was to be done, but thought it more
agreeable to the law to pluck up their spirits in this emergency, and break their law by avenging themselves, even if
they should die in the action, than by doing nothing to
please their enemies by submitting to be slain by them.
Accordingly, he took up his weapons, and infused courage
in those that were with him to act as bravely as himself.
So they engaged with their enemies, and slew a great many
of them, (because they despised them, and came as to a
certain victory,) and put the rest to flight.

§ 3. Now when the news of this fight came to the king of
Parthia, he was surprised at the boldness of these brothers,
and was desirous to see them, and speak with them. He
therefore sent the most trusty of all his body-guards
to say to them, " King Artabanus, although he has
been wronged by you, as you have invaded his kingdom,
yet has more regard to your courageous behaviour than
to the anger he bears to you, and has sent me to offer
you his right hand and friendship, and he permits you
to come to him safely and without any injury on the road,
and he wants you to address yourselves to him as friends,
and means no guile or deceit to you. He also promises to make you presents, and so to honour you as by
his power to augment your present fame." But Asinæus
himself put off his journey there, but sent his brother
Anilæus with all such presents as he could procure. So he
went, and was admitted to the king's presence; and when
Artabanus saw Anilæus coming alone, he inquired why
Asinæus had not come with him. And when he learnt

that he was afraid, and stayed in the marshes, he took an oath by the gods of his country, that he would do them no harm, if they came to him upon the assurances he gave them, and offered Anilæus his right hand, which is the greatest pledge of security with all those barbarians to those who converse with them ; for none of them will deceive you, when once they have given you their right hands, nor will any one doubt of their fidelity, when that is once given, even though they were before suspected of an intention to harm you. When Artabanus had done this, he sent away Anilæus to try to persuade his brother to come to him. Now the king acted in this way, because he wanted by the courage of these Jewish brothers to curb his own satrapies, lest they should violate their friendship with him, for they were ripe for revolt, and disposed to rebel, and he was about to make an expedition against them. He was also afraid that, while he was engaged in a war in order to subdue those satrapies that revolted, the party of Asinæus and the Babylonians would be augmented, and either make war upon him when they should hear of their revolt, or, if they should be disappointed in that, would not fail of doing him very much harm.

§ 4. With these intentions the king sent away Anilæus, and Anilæus prevailed on his brother [to go to the king,] when he had related to him the king's good-will, and the oath that he had taken ; accordingly, they made haste to go to Artabanus. And he received them, when they were come, with pleasure, and marvelled at Asinæus' courage in the actions he had done, and that because he was a little man to look at, and at first sight appeared contemptible also to such as met him, so that they might deem him of no value at all, and he said to his friends that, upon both being compared together, Asinæus showed his soul to be superior to his body. And, as they were once drinking together, he·showed Asinæus to Abdagases, one of the generals of his army, and told him his name, and described the great courage he had exhibited in war. And when Abdagases desired leave to kill him, and so to inflict punishment on him for the injuries he had done to the Parthian kingdom, the king replied, "I will never give leave to kill a man who has trusted in my good faith, especially after I have sent

him the offer of my right hand, and endeavoured to gain
his confidence by oaths by the gods. But if you are a good
warrior, you stand not in need of my perjury to avenge the
outraged Parthian kingdom. Attack this man, when he is
gone home, and conquer him by the forces that are under
your command, without my privity." And the king sent
for Asinæus early in the morning, and said to him, "It is
time for you, young man! to return home, and not to
provoke the indignation of my generals here any more,
lest they attempt to murder you, and that without my
approbation. I commit to you the country of Babylonia
in trust, that it may, by your care, be preserved free
from robbers, and from other mischief. I have kept my
faith inviolable to you, and that not in trifling matters, but
in such as concerned your safety, and I therefore deserve
your kindness in return." When he had said this, and
given Asinæus some presents, he sent him away immediately. And he, when he was come home, built fortresses,
and made those that were previously built stronger, and
became great in a little time, and managed affairs with
such courage and success, as no other person, that had
had no higher a beginning, ever did before him. Those
Parthian governors also, who were sent that way, paid him
great respect; for the honour that was paid him by the
Babylonians seemed too small, and beneath his deserts,
although he was in no small dignity and power there: nay,
indeed, all the affairs of Mesopotamia depended on him,
and he flourished more and more in this happy condition
for fifteen years.

§ 5. But as the two brothers were in so flourishing a
condition, the beginning of calamity came upon them for
the following reason, after they had deviated from that
course of virtue whereby they had gained so great power,
and affronted and transgressed the laws of their forefathers, and fallen under the dominion of their lusts and
pleasures. A certain Parthian, who came as general of an
army into those parts, was accompanied by his wife, who had
a great reputation for other accomplishments, and was particularly admired above all other women for her great
beauty; and Anilæus, the brother of Asinæus, either heard
of her beauty from others, or perhaps saw her himself

also, and so at once became her lover and her enemy;
partly because he could not hope to enjoy her but by obtaining power over her as his captive, partly because he
thought he could not conquer his passion for her.  As
soon therefore as her husband had been declared an enemy
of theirs, and had fallen in a battle forced on him, the
widow of the deceased was captured and married to her
lover.   However, she did not come into their house without
causing great misfortune not only to Anilæus himself, but
also to Asinæus, for she brought great mischief upon them
both from the following cause.  When she was led away
captive, upon the death of her husband, she concealed the
images of those gods which were her and her husband's
national gods, for it is the custom in that country for all to
keep the idols they worship in their own houses, and to
carry them along with them when they go into a foreign
land, according to which custom of theirs she carried her
idols with her.   And at first she performed her worship of
them privately, but when she became Anilæus' wife, she
worshipped them in her accustomed manner, and with the
same ceremonies which she used in her former husband's
life.   Thereupon their most esteemed friends first blamed
him for not acting after the manner of the Hebrews,
and for doing what was not agreeable to their laws,
in marrying a foreign wife, and one that neglected the
observance of their sacrifices and religious ceremonies ; and
bade him look to it, lest by conceding too much to the pleasures of the body, he might lose his position and the power
which, by God's blessing, he had arrived at.   But, as they
prevailed not with him at all, he slew one of them, who was
most highly esteemed, because of the liberty he took with
him ; and he, as he was dying from regard to the laws,
imprecated curses upon his murderer Anilæus, and upon
Asinæus also, and prayed that all their companions might
come to a like end from their enemies; the two first
as the principal actors in this lawlessness, and the rest
because they would not assist him when he suffered in
defending their laws.   Now these latter were sorely
grieved, yet did they tolerate these doings, because they
remembered that they had arrived at their present happy
state by no other means than the bravery of the two

brothers. But when they also heard of the worship of those gods whom the Parthians honour, they thought the outrage that Anilæus offered to their laws could be borne no longer; so a great number of them came to Asinæus, and loudly complained of Anilæus, and told him, if he had not previously noticed what was advantageous to them, that now it was high time anyhow to correct what had been done amiss, before the crime that had been committed proved the ruin of himself and all the rest of them. They added that the marriage of this woman took place without their consent, and without regard to their laws; and that the worship which she paid to her gods was an outrage to the God whom they worshipped. Now, Asinæus knew that his brother's offence had been already the cause of great mischiefs, and would continue to be so, but he tolerated it because of the good-will he had to so near a relative, and made allowance for him, considering that his brother was quite overcome by his wicked passion which mastered him. But as more and more came to him every day, and the clamours became greater, he at last spoke to Anilæus about the matter, reproving him for his former actions, and desiring him for the future to leave them off, and send the woman back to her relations. But nothing was gained by these reproofs. And as the woman perceived what a tumult was made among the people on her account, and was afraid for Anilæus, lest he should come to any harm for his love to her, she put poison into Asinæus' food, and so took him off, and was now free from fear, as her lover was now sole judge of what should be done about her.

§ 6. When Anilæus had thus got all the power himself alone, he led out his army against the villages of Mithridates, who was a leading man in Parthia, and had married king Artabanus' daughter, and plundered them. So he got much money, and many slaves, and much cattle, and many other things, which, when gained, make men's condition happy. Now, when Mithridates, who was in that region at the time, heard that his villages were taken, he was very enraged that Anilæus had begun to injure him, and to affront him in his present dignity, though he had not offered any injury to him previously; so he got together the largest body of cavalry he was able, and picked out of that number those who were in their prime, and went to fight Anilæus. And when he was arrived at a certain village of his own, he rested there, intending to fight Anilæus on the day following, because it was the sabbath, the day on which the Jews rest. And when Anilæus was informed of this by a Syrian stranger from another village, who not only gave him an exact account of other circumstances, but told him where Mithridates would feast, he took his supper betimes, and marched by night, intending to fall upon the Parthians while they were ignorant of what he was going to do; and fell upon them about the fourth watch of the night, and slew some of them while they were asleep, and put others to flight, and took Mithridates alive, and set him naked upon an ass, which is esteemed the greatest reproach possible among the Parthians. And when he had brought Mithridates into a wood in such guise,[1] and his friends desired him to kill him, he soon told them his own mind to the contrary; for he said it was not well to kill a man who was one of the principal families among the Parthians, and still more honoured by contracting a royal marriage; that so far as they had hitherto gone was tolerable; for although they had insulted Mithridates, yet if they preserved his life, this benefit would be remembered by him to the advantage of those that had conferred it on him; but if he were once put to death, the king would not rest till he had made a great slaughter of the Jews that dwelt at Babylon, whose safety they ought to regard, both on account of their relationship to them, and because, if any misfortune befell them, they had no other place to retire to, since the king had got the flower of their youth. By this suggestion and speech of his made in council he persuaded them, so Mithridates was let go. But when he returned home, his wife reproached him, that, although he was son-in-law to the king, he neglected to avenge himself on those who had insulted him, and took no heed of it, but was contented to have been made captive by the Jews, and to have escaped them. And she bade him either go back like a man of courage, or

---

[1] I read πορίσματος. What can ὁρίσματος mean here?

else she swore by the gods of their royal family, that she
would certainly dissolve her marriage with him. Upon
this, partly because he could not endure the annoyance of
her daily taunts, partly because he was afraid of her high
spirit, lest she should in earnest dissolve her marriage with
him, he unwillingly, and against his inclinations, got
together again as large an army as he could, and marched
along with them, himself now thinking it insufferable that
he, a Parthian, should be defeated by a Jew who warred
against him.

§ 7. Now as soon as Anilæus heard that Mithridates was
marching with a large force against him, he thought it
ignoble to remain in the marshes, and not to be first in
meeting his enemies, and he hoped to have the same
success, and to beat the enemy as he had done before; so he
ventured boldly upon the like attempt. Accordingly, he
led out his army, and a great many more men joined themselves to his army, to betake themselves to plunder other
persons' property, and to terrify the enemy again first by
their appearance. But when they had marched ninety furlongs, as their road lay through waterless places, they became very thirsty about the middle of the day, and Mithridates suddenly appeared, and fell upon them, as they were
in distress for want of water, on which account, and on
account of the time of day, they were not able to bear
their weapons. So Anilæus and his men were put to an
ignominious rout, as they were faint and yet had to attack
men that were fresh and in good plight; so a great
slaughter was made, and many ten thousands killed. Now
Anilæus and all that remained round him fled as fast
as they were able into a wood, and gave Mithridates
the pleasure of having gained a great victory over them.
And now there flocked unto Anilæus a countless number of
bad men, who regarded their own lives very little, if they
might but gain some present ease, so that, by their
thus coming to him, they compensated for the number of
those that had perished in the fight. But they were not
equal in quality to those that had fallen, because they had
had no practice in war; however, with them Anilæus attacked the villages of the Babylonians, and a mighty destruction of all things there was made by his violence. So

the Babylonians, and those that joined in the war, sent to
Naarda to the Jews there, and demanded them to deliver
up Anilæus. And although they did not obey their demand
(for if they had been willing to deliver him up, it was not
in their power to do so), yet did they desire to make peace
with them. To which the others replied, that they
also wanted conditions of peace, and sent envoys with
the Babylonians, to treat with Anilæus about peace. But
the Babylonians, having made a reconnaissance, and
found out where Anilæus and his men were encamped,
fell secretly upon them as they were drunk and had fallen
asleep, and slew with impunity all of them they fell in
with, and killed Anilæus himself also.

§ 8. The Babylonians were now freed from Anilæus'
raids (which had been a great hindrance to their carrying
out their hatred to the Jews, for they were almost always
at variance because of the difference of their laws, and
whichever party grew boldest attacked the other first), and
so now, upon the slaughter of Anilæus' party, they attacked the Jews. And they, dreading the injuries they
received from the Babylonians, and being unable to fight
them, and thinking it intolerable to live with them,
migrated to Seleucia,[1] the principal city in those parts,
which was built by Seleucus Nicator; and was inhabited
by many Macedonians, but principally by Greeks, and not
a few Syrians also dwelt there. And there did the Jews
take refuge, and lived there five years without any misfortunes. But in the sixth year a pestilence came upon
those at Babylon, and because of it a stampede took place
to Seleucia. And a still heavier calamity came upon them
for the reason which I am going to relate.

§ 9. The life of the Greeks and Syrians in Seleucia was
mostly quarrelsome, and full of strife, though the Greeks
had the best of it. But when the Jews came there and
dwelt among them, there arose a sedition, and the Syrians
were too much for the Greeks, owing to the assistance of
the Jews, who are men that despise dangers, and are very
ready to fight upon any occasion. Now, as the Greeks had
the worst in this sedition, and saw that they had but one

---

[1] See Antiq. xiii. 7, § 1.

way of recovering their former authority, and that was, if they could prevent the unity of the Jews and Syrians, they each talked with such of the Syrians as were formerly acquainted with them, and offered to be at peace and friendship with them. And they gladly agreed to this, and a conference was held by both parties; and as the principal men of both nations agreed to a reconciliation, it was soon brought about. And when they were so agreed. they both felt that the chief token of such a union would be common hostility to the Jews; so they fell upon them suddenly, and slew about fifty thousand of them. Indeed the Jews were all destroyed, except a few who escaped from the compassion of their friends or neighbours, and migrated to Ctesiphon,[1] a Greek city near Seleucia, where the king winters every year, and where the greatest part of his treasures are deposited. But the Jews had no certain settlement here, those of Seleucia having little concern for the king's honour. For the whole nation of the Jews were afraid both of the Babylonians and Seleucians, because all the Syrians that lived in those places agreed with the Seleucians to war against the Jews: so most of them gathered themselves together, and went to Naarda and Nisibis,[2] and obtained security there from the strength of those cities; and also their inhabitants, who were a great many, were all warlike men. Such was the state of the Jews in Babylonia.

[1] On the left bank of the Tigris.   See Antiq. xviii. 2, § 4.
[2] See Antiq. xviii. 9, § 1.

# BOOK XIX.

**FROM THE DEPARTURE OF THE JEWS OUT OF BABYLON, TO FADUS, THE ROMAN PROCURATOR.**

## CHAP. I.

*How Caius was slain by Chœrea Cassius.*

### § 1.

NOW Caius showed his outrageous madness not only to the Jews at Jerusalem, or to those that dwelt in Judæa, but also exhibited it in every land and sea that was subject to the Romans, and filled the empire with ten thousand woes, such as no former history relates. But Rome itself felt the most dire effects of his acts, as he held it in not a whit more honour than all other cities, but savagely oppressed all its citizens, and especially the senate and patricians, and such as were honoured for their illustrious ancestors. He also found out ten thousand devices against those of the equestrian order, as it was called, who were esteemed by the citizens equal in dignity and wealth to the senators, because out of them the senators were themselves chosen; he treated these in an ignominious manner, and degraded them from their position, and they were not only slain, but their wealth plundered, for he slew men generally in order to seize on their riches. He also asserted his own divinity, and insisted on greater honours being paid him by his subjects than are due to mankind, for he frequented the temple of Jupiter which they call the Capitol, which is among the Romans the most honoured of all their temples, and had the audacity to call Jupiter his brother. And other things he did like a madman, as when he laid a bridge from the city of

Dicæarchia¹ in Campania to Misenum,² another city upon
the seaside, a distance of thirty furlongs by sea from
one promontory to the other.   And this he did because
he disliked crossing over in a trireme, and thought also
that it became him to make that bridge, since he was lord
of the sea, and might demand from it as much as from
the land, so he enclosed the whole bay within his bridge,
and drove his chariot over it, and thought that, as he was
a god, it was fit for him to make such roads as this was.
Nor did he abstain from the plunder of any of the Greek
temples, but gave orders that all the paintings and sculptures, and the rest of the ornaments of the statues and
votive offerings should be brought to him, saying that
beautiful things ought to be set nowhere but in the best
place, and that was the city of Rome.   He also adorned
his own house and gardens with what was brought from
those temples, as also his houses which he occasionally
stayed at when he travelled in Italy ; and he did not scruple
to command that the statue of Olympian Zeus, the work
of Phidias the Athenian, which was honoured by the Greeks,
should be transferred to Rome.   But he did not compass
his end in this, for the architects told Memmius Regulus,
who was commanded to remove that statue of Zeus, that it
would be broken if it were removed.   It is also reported
that Memmius, both on that account, and on account of
some mighty prodigies such as are of an incredible nature,
deferred the removing it, and wrote these circumstances
to Caius, as his apology for not having done what his
letter required of him ; and when he was in consequence
in danger of his life, he was saved by Caius dying himself,
before he had him put to death.

§ 2. Nay, Caius' madness rose to such a height, that when
he had a daughter born, he carried her into the Capitol,
and put her upon the knees of the statue, and said that
the child was common to him and to Jupiter, and affirmed
that she had two fathers, but which of these fathers was
the greatest he left undetermined.   And yet men put
up with such actions !   He also gave leave to slaves to

¹ Puteoli.   *Pozzuoli.*
² Now *Casaluce,* on the south side of the *Porto di Miseno,* at the
northern limit of the Bay of Naples.

accuse their masters of any crimes whatever they pleased; for all such accusations were terrible, because they were in great part made to please him and at his suggestion, insomuch that Pollux, Claudius' slave, had the boldness to lay an accusation against Claudius himself, and Caius was not ashamed to be present, and to hear the trial for his life of his own uncle, in hope of being able to take him off, although the result did not turn out to his mind. But when he had filled the whole world which he governed with false accusations and miseries, and had made slaves in a great measure their masters' masters, many plots were laid against him, for some conspired against his life in rage and to revenge themselves for the miseries they had already undergone from him, and others to take him off before they should fall into such great miseries. And so his death happened very opportunely for the preservation of the laws of all nations, and had a great influence upon the public welfare, and happened most happily for our nation in particular, which would almost have utterly perished if he had not been soon slain. I intend to give a complete account of his murder, especially as it affords great proof of the power of God, and great comfort to those who are in afflictions, and soberness to those who think their happiness will never end, instead of bringing them at last to the most enduring miseries, if they do not conduct their lives by the principles of virtue.

§ 3. Now there were three conspiracies made to murder Caius, and each of these three was headed by excellent persons. Æmilius Regulus, a native of Corduba[1] in Iberia, got some men together, and was desirous to take Caius off either by them, or by himself. Another conspiracy was laid under the lead of Chærea Cassius, a tribune [of the Prætorian guard]. Minucianus Annius was also one of great consequence among those that were prepared to put an end to Caius' tyranny. Now the reasons of these men's hatred and conspiracy against Caius were as follows. Regulus had indignation and hatred against all injustice (for he was by nature hot-tempered and frank, which made him not conceal his counsels; so he communicated them

---

[1] *Cordova* in *Spain*.

to many of his friends, and to others who seemed to
him men of action); and Minucianus entered into conspiracy, because of the injustice done to Lepidus his particular friend, and one of the best of all the citizens, whom
Caius had slain, and also because he was afraid of him
himself, as Caius' wrath revelled in the slaughter of all
alike: and as for Chærea, he thought it no illiberal deed
to kill Caius, being ashamed of Caius constantly twitting
him with being effeminate,[1] as also because he was himself in danger every day from his friendship with Caius,
and the observance he paid him.   These men opened their
plot to all who saw the injuries that were done them, and
who were desirous that by Caius' death they might escape
all this: for perhaps they would succeed, and it would
be a happy thing if they should to have so many excellent fellow-conspirators, who earnestly wished to share
in their design for the delivery of the city and empire, even
at the hazard of their own lives.   But Chærea was the
most zealous of them all, not only from a desire of getting
himself the greatest name, but also because of his access
to Caius' presence with less danger, because he was a
tribune [of the Prætorian guard], and so could the more
easily kill him.

   § 4. Now at this time came on the horse-races, the view
of which games is eagerly desired by the people of Rome,
for they come with great alacrity into the Circus at such
times, and crowd round in great multitudes, and petition
their emperors for what they stand in need of; and they
usually do not think fit to deny them their requests, but
readily and graciously grant them.   Accordingly now they
most importunately desired that Caius would ease them in
their tributes, and abate somewhat of the rigour of the taxes
imposed upon them.   But he would not listen to their petition,
and, as their clamours increased, he sent soldiers, some one
way, and some another, and gave orders that they should
arrest those that made the clamours, and without any
more ado, bring them out, and put them to death.   These
were Caius' commands, and those who were commanded
carried them out, and the number of those slain on this

---

[1] See Suetonius, *Caligula*, 56.

occasion was very great.  Now the people saw this, and
bore it, and soon left off clamouring, because they saw
with their own eyes that this petition to be somewhat
relieved of the payment of their taxes brought immediate death upon them.  These things made Chærea more
resolute to go on with his plot, in order to put an end
to this savageness of Caius against men.  Frequently
he thought to fall upon Caius as he was feasting, but
he restrained himself by some considerations, not that he
had any doubt about killing him, but because he watched
for a proper season, that the attempt might not be in vain,
but might be carried out effectually.

§ 5.  Chærea had been in the army a long time, but was
not pleased with much intercourse with Caius.  And
when Caius appointed him to exact the tribute and other
dues, which, when not paid in due time, were forfeited to the
emperor's treasury, he made some delay in exacting them,
because those burdens had been doubled, and rather indulged his own mild disposition than carried out Caius'
commands, and indeed provoked Caius to anger by his
sparing men, and pitying the hard fortunes of those from
whom he demanded the taxes, and Caius upbraided him
with his sloth and effeminacy in being so long about collecting the money.  And indeed he not only affronted
him in other respects, but whenever he gave him the word
for the day in his turn, he gave him feminine words,[1] and
those of a very reproachful nature.  And this he did,
having been initiated in the secrets of certain mysteries
which he had himself invented : for as he sometimes put
on women's clothes, and devised false curls, and did a
great many other things, in order to get taken for a woman,
so he ventured to taunt Chærea with the like womanish
behaviour.  And whenever Chærea received the word for the
day from him, he was indignant at it, but still more whenever he had to pass it on to others, being laughed at by those
that received it, insomuch that his fellow-tribunes made him
their sport.  For they would foretell that he would bring
them some of his usual amusing words whenever he was to
bring the word for the day from the emperor.  For these

[1] See Suetonius, *Caligula*, 56.

reasons he took the bold step of joining to him certain associates, having just reasons for his indignation against Caius.
Now there was one Pompedius, a senator, who had gone
through almost all offices, but was in other respects an Epi-
curean, and one who for that reason loved to lead an inactive
life.   Now Timidius, an enemy of his, informed Caius that
Pompedius had used unseemly reproaches against him, and
called Quintilia as a witness, a woman who was much run
after by many that frequented the theatre, and also by Pompedius, because of her great beauty.   Now as this woman
thought it monstrous to bear witness to a lying accusation
that touched the life of her lover, Timidius desired to
have her put to the torture.   And Caius in his exasperation
commanded Chærea without any delay to torture Quintilia,
as he used to employ Chærea in such bloody matters, and
whenever the rack was required, because he thought he
would do it the more severely to avoid the imputation of
effeminacy.   But Quintilia, when she was brought to the
rack, trod upon the foot of one of her associates, and let
him know, that he might be of good courage, and not be
afraid of any consequences from her tortures ; for she would
bear them bravely.   And Chærea tortured her in a cruel
manner, unwillingly indeed, and only because he was
compelled to act so for his own safety, and then brought
her, without her being the least moved at what she had
suffered, into the presence of Caius, and that in such a
condition as was sad to behold. And Caius, being somewhat affected by the sight of Quintilia, who had her body
miserably racked with pain, acquitted both her and Pompedius of the crime laid to their charge.   He also gave
her money to make her honourable amends, and comfort
her for the injury to her body which she had suffered,
and for her glorious patience under such dreadful
torments.

§ 6. This matter sorely grieved Chærea, as having been
the cause, as far as he could be, of such miseries to human
beings as seemed worthy of consolation to Caius himself ;
and he said to Clemens and to Papinius (of whom Clemens
was commander of the Prætorian body-guard, and Papinius
tribune,) "Certainly, Clemens, we have no way failed in
guarding the emperor ; for as to those that have con-

spired against his government, some have been slain by
our forethought and pains, and some have been tortured
by us, and that to such a degree, that he has himself pitied them. How great then is our virtue in submitting to lead his armies!" Clemens was silent, but
showed the shame he felt in obeying Caius' orders both
by his looks and blushing countenance, though he thought
it by no means right to accuse the emperor in ex-
press words, lest his own safety should be endangered
thereby. Upon this Chærea took courage, and spoke to
him without fear of danger, and descanted on the sore
calamities under which the city and empire then laboured,
and said, "We may indeed pretend in words that
Caius is the person to whom such miseries ought to be
imputed; but in the opinion of such as try to investi-
gate the truth, it is I, O Clemens, and Papinius here, and
before us both you yourself, who bring these tortures upon
the Romans and upon all mankind, not by our being subservient to the commands of Caius, but by following our
own wish, for whereas it is in our power to put an end to
the life of this man, who has so terribly outraged the
citizens and his subjects, we are his body-guards and
executioners rather than soldiers, and are the instru-
ments of his cruelty. We carry weapons not for our liberty,
nor for the Roman empire, but only for his preservation,
who has enslaved both the bodies and minds of his subjects, and we are every day polluted with the blood that
we shed, and the torments we inflict upon them, until somebody shall become Caius' instrument in bringing the like
miseries upon ourselves. Nor does he thus employ us out
of good-will to us, but rather because he is suspicious of
us, as also because when many more have been killed
(for Caius will set no bounds to his wrath, since he acts thus
not out of regard to justice, but to his own pleasure,) we
shall also ourselves be a mark for his cruelty; whereas we
ought to be the means of confirming the security and
liberty of everybody, and at the same time we ought to resolve to free ourselves from dangers."

§ 7. Then Clemens openly commended Chærea's intention, but bade him be silent, for in case his words should
get out among many, and such things should spread abroad

as were well to be concealed, the plot would be discovered
before it was executed, and they would be brought to
punishment : so he recommended that they should leave
all to the future and the hope which arose thence that
some fortunate event would aid them ; as for himself,
his age would not permit him to take any active part
in the attempt. " Although perhaps," he added, " I could
suggest what might be safer than what you, Chærea, have
contrived and urged, yet how is it possible for any one to
suggest what is more for your reputation ? " And Clemens
went his way home, reflecting on what he had heard, and
what he had himself said. Chærea was also in anxiety,
and went quickly to Cornelius Sabinus (who was himself
also a tribune, and one whom he also knew to be a
worthy man and lover of liberty, and so very much opposed to the present management of public affairs), being
desirous to carry out quickly what had been determined,
and thinking it well for him to propose it to him, not only
being afraid lest Clemens should inform against them, but
also looking upon procrastination and delay as next door
to abandoning the enterprise.

§ 8. Now all this was agreeable to Sabinus, who had himself the same design as Chærea, but had been silent for
want of a person to whom he could safely communicate
his views, so now having met with one, who not only promised to conceal what he heard, but who also opened his
mind to him, he was much more encouraged, and desired
of Chærea that no delay might be made. So they went to
Minucianus, who was as virtuous a man, and as zealous to
do glorious actions, as themselves, and was suspected by
Caius on account of his murder of Lepidus ; for Minucianus
and Lepidus had been intimate friends, and both in fear
of their common dangers. For Caius was terrible to all
great men, not ceasing to rage against each of them in
particular, and all of them in general ; and men were
afraid of one another, while yet uneasy at the posture of
affairs, and hesitated to let one another see their mind
and hatred against Caius, from fear of danger, although
they perceived in other ways their mutual hatred of Caius,
and so did not cease to feel mutual good-will.

§ 9. When Minucianus and Chærea met together, and

saluted one another, as they had been used in former
intercourse to give the first place to Minucianus, both on
account of his eminent merit (for he was the noblest of
all the citizens) and because he was highly commended by
all men, especially when he made speeches, Minucianus
began first, and asked Chærea, what was the word he had
received for that day from Caius. For the insults which were
offered Chærea in giving the words for the day were notorious
all over the city. And Chærea made no delay to reply to that
question, from the joy he had that Minucianus had such
confidence in him as to discourse with him. "And do
you," said he, "give me Liberty as the word! And I return you my thanks for having so greatly encouraged me
to exert myself in an extraordinary manner; nor do I
stand in need of many words to embolden me, if you and
I are of the same mind, and sharers in the same resolution, even before this conversation. I have indeed but
one sword girt on, but it will be enough for us both.
Come on, therefore, let us set about the work. Do you go
first, if so minded, and bid me follow you, or else I will
go first, and you shall assist me, and I will rely on your
co-operation. Nor is there a necessity for even one sword
to such as have a mind disposed to action, for by the mind
the sword is wont to be sharpened. I am zealous about
this action, nor am I solicitous as to what I may myself
undergo; for I am not at leisure to consider the dangers
that may come upon myself, so deeply am I troubled at
the slavery of our once free country, and at the abeyance
of our excellent laws, and at the destruction which hangs
over all men's heads owing to Caius. I hope that I may in
your judgment be esteemed worthy of credit in these matters,
seeing that we are both of the same opinion, and that there
is no difference between us."

§ 10. When Minucianus saw the vehemence with which
Chærea delivered himself, he gladly embraced him, and
encouraged him in his bold attempt, commending and
embracing him, and so let him go with his good wishes
and prayers. And some affirm that Minucianus confirmed
him in the execution of what had been agreed among
them. For, as Chærea entered the senate-house, they say
that a voice came from among the multitude to encourage

him, which bade him finish what he was about, and take
the opportunity that providence afforded : and that Chærea
at first suspected that one of the conspirators had turned
traitor, and that he was detected, but at last perceived
that it was by way of exhortation, whether someone who
knew what he was about gave a signal for his encouragement, or whether God himself, who looks upon
the actions of men, encouraged him to go on boldly in his
design.   The plot had now been communicated to a great
many, and the conspirators were all armed, some of them
being senators, and some of the equestrian order, and all
the rest soldiers who were privy to the plot.   For there was
not one of them who did not reckon it happiness to remove
Caius, and so they were all very zealous in the affair, however
they might compass it, and resolved not to be behindhand
in these virtuous designs, but to be ready with all their
alacrity and power, both in words and actions, to slay the
tyrant.   Another conspirator was Callistus (who was a
freedman of Caius), and was the only man who had arrived
at a very great degree of power under him, such a power,
indeed, as was in a manner equal to the power of the
tyrant himself, from the dread that all men had of him,
and from the great riches he had acquired; for he took
bribes most freely, and insolently treated everybody, using
his power contrary to equity; he also knew the disposition of Caius to be implacable, and never to be turned
from what he had once resolved on; he had also many
other reasons why he thought himself in danger, and not
least the vastness of his wealth.   So he privately ingratiated himself with Claudius, and transferred his court to
him, hoping if, after the removal of Caius, the empire
should come to him, his interest in such changes would
lay a foundation for his preserving his position under
Claudius, as he would have laid in beforehand a stock of
gratitude and good-will.   He had also the audacity to pretend that he had been ordered to kill Claudius by poison,
but had contrived ten thousand ways of delaying to do it.
But it seems probable to me that Callistus only pretended
this to ingratiate himself with Claudius, for if Caius had
resolved in earnest to take off Claudius, he would not have
admitted of excuses from Callistus, nor would Callistus have

put it off, if he had been enjoined to do such an act because it was desired by Caius, or, if he had disobeyed those injunctions of his master, he would have had immediate punishment: so that Claudius was preserved from the madness of Caius by a certain divine providence, and Callistus pretended to have done him such a kindness as he never had done.

§ 11. However, the execution of Chærea's design was put off from day to day, from the hesitation of many of the conspirators: for as to Chærea himself, he did not willingly make any delay in carrying it out, thinking every time a fit time for it. For frequent opportunities offered themselves, as when Caius went up to the Capitol to sacrifice for his daughter, or when he stood on the roof of his royal palace, and threw pieces of gold and silver among the people, he might be pushed down headlong, because the roof of the palace overlooking the forum was very high; and also when he celebrated the mysteries which he had himself instituted, *he might easily be attacked,* for he was then no way secluded from the people, but solicitous to do every thing formally and duly, and was free from all suspicion that he would then be attacked by any body. And although the gods should afford Chærea no indication that he would be able to take away Caius' life, yet had he strength sufficient to despatch him even without a sword. So Chærea was angry with his fellow-conspirators, fearing they would suffer opportunities to slip by; and they were sensible that he had just cause to be angry at them, and that his eagerness was for their advantage; however, they desired that he would have a little longer patience, lest, if their attempt failed, they should agitate the city, and when search should be made for the conspirators, should make the courage of those that were to attack Caius ineffectual, as he would then secure himself more carefully than ever against them. They thought therefore that it would be best to set about the work when the shows were exhibited in the palace. These shows were acted in honour of that Cæsar [1] who first changed the common-

[1] Here Josephus supposes that it was Augustus, and not Julius Cæsar, who first changed the Roman commonwealth into a monarchy; for these shows were in honour of Augustus, as we shall learn in the next section but one.—W.

wealth into a monarchy; galleries being fixed before the palace, where the Romans that were patricians sat as spectators, with their children and wives, and the emperor himself also; and the conspirators reckoned, as many ten thousands would be crowded there in a narrow space, that they would have a favourable opportunity to make their attack upon Caius as he came in; because his body-guards, even if any of them had a mind to do so, would not be able to give him any assistance.

§ 12. Chærea consented to this delay, and it was resolved to do the deed the first day that the shows were exhibited. But fortune, which allowed a further delay, was too much for their preconcerted plan, and, as three days of the regular time usual for these shows were now over, they had much ado to get the business done on the last day. So Chærea called the conspirators together, and spoke to them as follows. "So much time passed away without effect is a reproach to us, for delaying to go through such a virtuous design as we are engaged in; but this delay will prove more fatal, if we be discovered and the design be frustrated; for Caius will then become much more savage. Do we not see how long we deprive all our friends of their liberty, and give Caius leave still to tyrannize over them, whereas we ought to have procured them security for the future, and by laying a foundation for the happiness of others, have gained for ourselves great admiration and honour for all time to come?" Now, as the conspirators had nothing particular to say by way of contradiction, and yet did not quite relish what they were doing, but were silent and seemed dazed, he said further, "O my brave comrades! why do we delay? Do not you see that this is the last day of these shows, and that Caius is about to go to sea?" (for he had made preparations to sail to Alexandria in order to visit Egypt.) "Is it then for your honour to let a man go out of your hands who is a reproach to mankind, and to permit him to go about in a magnificent procession of Romans both by land and sea? Shall we not be justly ashamed of ourselves, if some Egyptian or other, who shall think his injuries insufferable to freemen, shall kill him? As for myself, I will no longer bear your procrastination, but will expose myself to the dangers of the enterprise this very day, and bear cheerfully whatever shall be the consequences of the attempt, let them be ever so great, for I will not put off the affair any longer. For what can be more miserable to a man of spirit than the thought that, while I am alive, any one else should kill Caius, and deprive me of the honour of so virtuous an action."

§ 13. When Chærea had spoken thus, he zealously set about the work, and inspired courage into the rest to go on with it, and they were all eager to fall to it without further delay. And he was at the palace early in the morning, with his equestrian sword girt on, for it was the custom that the tribunes should ask for the word for the day from the emperor with their swords on, and this was the day on which Chærea's turn was to receive the word. And the multitude had already come to the palace, in great crowds and jostling one another, to get a good place early for seeing the shows; and Caius was delighted with this eagerness of the multitude, so no peculiar seats were appointed for the senators, or for the equestrian order, but all sat promiscuously, men and women together, and free men mixed up with slaves. So a way was made for Caius, and he offered sacrifice to Cæsar Augustus, in whose honour indeed these shows were celebrated. Now it happened, as one of the victims was slain, that the toga of Asprenas, a senator, was sprinkled with blood, which made Caius laugh, and was an evident omen to Asprenas, for he was slain at the same time with Caius. It is also stated that Caius was that day, contrary to his usual nature, so very affable and courteous in his conversation, that every one of those that were present were astonished. After the sacrifice was over, Caius betook himself to see the shows, and sat down for that purpose, and his chief friends sat round him. Now the theatre was constructed as follows, as it was put together every year. It had two doors, one leading to the open air, the other for going in or out of the portico, that those within the theatre might not be thereby disturbed; but out of one gallery there was an inward passage, parted into partitions also, which led into another gallery, to give room to the combatants, and to the musicians, to go out as occasion served. When the multitude had sat down,

and Chærea and the other tribunes were not far from
Caius (now the right corner of the theatre was allotted to
the emperor), one Vatinius, a senator, and commander of the
Prætorian band asked of Cluvius, who sat near him, and
was of consular dignity, whether he had heard any news
or not, but took care that nobody should hear what he
said. And when Cluvius replied, that he had heard no
news, "Know then," said Vatinius, "that the play of
tyrannicide is to be played to-day." And Cluvius said,
"Brave comrade! hold thy peace, lest some other of the
Achæans hear thy tale." [1]  And as there was much fruit
scrambled among the spectators, as also a great number
of birds of great value to such as got them on account of
their rarity, Caius was amused with the fights and scuffles
of the spectators for them. Here also I understand [2] there
were two omens. For a Mime was introduced, in which
a leader of robbers was crucified, and the pantomimic
dancer brought in a play called Cinyras, wherein he himself was slain and his daughter Myrrha, and wherein a
great deal of sham blood seemed to flow, both round
him that was crucified, and also round Cinyras. It is also
admitted, that this was the same day whereon Pausanias, a
friend of Philip (the son of Amyntas), king of Macedonia,
slew him as he was entering the theatre. And now
Caius was in doubt whether he would stay to the end of
the shows, as it was the last day, or whether he would not
go first to bathe and dine, and then return as on previous
days, when Minucianus, who sat above Caius, afraid that
the opportunity would fail them, got up, because he saw
that Chærea had already gone out, and was hastening out
to confirm him in his resolution, when Caius took hold of
his garment in a free and easy way, and said to him, " My
good fellow, where are you going?" Whereupon, out of
reverence to the emperor apparently, he sat down again,
but his fear prevailed, and in a little time he got up again,
and this time Caius did not at all oppose his going out,
thinking he went out to do some necessary act of nature.
And Asprenas, who was one of the conspirators also, persuaded Caius to go out to bathe and dine, as he had done

---

[1] An allusion to Homer, Iliad, xiv. 90.
[2] I read μανθάνω.

on previous days, and then to come in again, being desirous that what had been resolved on might be brought to a conclusion immediately.

§ 14. And Chærea and his associates posted themselves as conveniently as they could, but it was not without great effort that they could keep the place which was appointed them. And they were put out by having to wait so long to carry out their purpose, for it was already about the ninth [1] hour of the day, and Chærea, upon Caius' tarrying so long, had a great mind to go in to him and attack him on his seat. He foresaw however that this could not be done without much bloodshed, both of the senators, and of those of the equestrian order that were present ; but although he knew this must result, yet had he a great mind to do so, thinking it right to procure security and freedom to all, even at the expense of such as might perish at the same time. And as they were just going back to the entrance to the theatre, the great applause told them that Caius had risen up. Then the conspirators turned and thrust back the crowd, on the pretext that they annoyed Caius, but in reality being desirous to murder him securely through depriving him of any to defend him. Now Claudius, his uncle, and Marcus Vinicius, his sister's husband, as also Valerius Asiaticus, preceded him, and though the conspirators would have liked to thrust them out of the way too, respect to their dignity hindered them from doing so, and Caius came last with Paulus Arruntius. And when Caius got within the palace, he left the direct road, along which his servants stood that were in waiting, and which Claudius and those with him had taken, and turned aside into a private narrow passage, in order to go to the baths, as also to look at some boys that had come from Asia, who had been sent from thence partly to sing hymns in the mysteries which were now being celebrated, partly to dance the Pyrrhic dance at the theatres. And Chærea met him, and asked him for the word ; and upon Caius' giving him one of his mocking words, Chærea immediately reproached him, and drew his sword, and gave him a terrible but not

---

[1] Suetonius says Caius was slain about the seventh hour of the day ; Josephus, about the ninth. The series of the narration favours Josephus. —W.

mortal stroke with it.   And although some say that it was
so contrived on purpose by Chærea, that Caius should not
be killed at one blow, but should be punished more severely
by a number of wounds, yet this story appears to me incredible, because the fear men are in in such actions does
not allow them to use their reason.   And if Chærea was of
that mind, I esteem him the greatest of all fools, for so
indulging his spite against Caius, rather than immediately
procuring safety to himself and his fellow-conspirators
from the danger they were in; for many things might still
happen for Caius' help, if he had not already given up the
ghost.   For certainly Chærea would not regard so much
the punishment of Caius as himself and his friends, when
it was in his power after such success to keep silent, and to
escape the wrath of Caius' defenders; far less, when it was
uncertain whether he had gained the end he aimed at or
not, would he in a stupid way have been likely to act as if
he had a mind to ruin himself, and lose the opportunity.
But every one may conjecture as he pleases about this
matter.   However, Caius staggered from the pain that the
blow gave him (for the sword wounded him between the
shoulder and the neck, but was prevented by the collar-
bone from proceeding any further,) but did not either cry
out in his astonishment, or call out for any of his friends;
whether he had no confidence in them, or because he was
lightheaded, but he groaned from the excessive pain, and
moved forward to flee.   Then Cornelius Sabinus, who had
already made up his mind, received him and thrust him
down upon his knee, and many others stood round about
him with one consent, and hacked at him with their swords,
and encouraged one another to repeat their blows.   And all
agree that Aquila gave him the finishing stroke, which
instantly killed him.   But one may justly ascribe this
murder to Chærea, for although many had a hand in the
act itself, yet was he the first contriver of it, and began
long before all the rest to prepare for it, and was the first
that spoke boldly of it to the rest; and upon their approv-
ing of the project, he got the dispersed conspirators together, and prepared every thing in a clever manner, and
by suggesting good advice showed himself far superior
to the rest, and conciliated them by clever speeches, inso-

much that he compelled even the timid to go on with the enterprise, and when the time came for action, he appeared ready first and gave the first blow, and also brought Caius easily into the power of the rest, and almost killed him himself, insomuch that it is but just to ascribe all that the rest did to the advice and bravery of Chærea, and to the labours of his hands.

§ 15. Thus did Caius come to his end, and lay dead from the many wounds which had been given him. And Chærea and the other conspirators, now Caius was dead, saw that it was impossible for them to save themselves if they should all go the same way. For not only were they unnerved by what they had done (for they had incurred no small danger by killing an emperor who was honoured and loved by the madness of the people, and the soldiers were likely to make a bloody inquiry after his murderers), but the road was narrow where the deed was done, and also crowded with a great number of Caius' attendants, and with such of the soldiers as were the emperor's guard that day. So they went by different ways, and reached the house of Germanicus, the father of Caius whom they had just killed (which house joined on to the palace; for though the palace was one edifice, it had been built in its several parts by previous emperors, and those parts bore the names of those that built them, or the name of him who had begun to build any of them), and so they got away from the attack of the multitude, and were for the present out of danger, as long as what had happened to the emperor was not known. The Germans were the first that perceived that Caius was slain. These Germans were his body-guards, and had their name from the country where they had been enlisted, and composed the Celtic legion. The men of that country are naturally passionate, which is not unfrequently the temper of some other of the barbarous nations also, as they do not much reason about what they do, but are strong in their bodies, and rush upon their enemies at the first onset, and wherever they go perform great exploits. When, therefore, they knew that Caius was slain, they were very sorry for it, because they did not judge public affairs on their merits, but measured them by the advantages they themselves received, (Caius being beloved by them because

of the money he gave them, by which he had purchased
their good-will,) so they drew their swords, and Sabinus
led them on.   He was their tribune, not because of the
virtue and nobility of his ancestors, for he had only been a
gladiator, but he had obtained that position over these men
by his strength of body.   Now these Germans marched along
the houses in quest of Caius' murderers, and cut Asprenas
to pieces, because he was the first man they fell in with,
whose garment the blood of the sacrifice had stained, as I
have stated already, which was ominous that his meeting with
the soldiers would not be for his good.   The next that met
them was Norbanus, who was one of the noblest of the
citizens, and could show many generals of armies among
his ancestors, but they paid no regard to his rank, but
he was of such great strength, that he wrested the sword
of the first of those that assaulted him out of his hands,
and showed plainly that he would not die without a fight
for his life, but he was surrounded at last by a great number of assailants, and died in consequence of the many
wounds which he received.   The third they met was
Anteius, a senator, and a few others were with him.   He
did not meet these Germans by chance, as the rest did before, but came to show his hatred to Caius, and to feast
his eyes with seeing Caius lie dead, and took a pleasure in
the sight, because Caius had banished Anteius' father, who
was of the same name as himself, and, not being satisfied
with that, had despatched soldiers to slay him.   So he
had come to rejoice at the sight of him, now he was dead;
but as the house was now all in confusion, though he tried
to hide himself, he could not escape the careful search
which the Germans made, for they barbarously slew alike
those that were guilty and those that were innocent.   And
thus were these persons slain.

§ 16.   But when the news that Caius was slain reached
the theatre, there was both panic and incredulity.   For
some that heard of his destruction with great pleasure,
and were more desirous of its happening than of almost
any other satisfaction that could come to them, could
not believe it for fear.   There were also others who greatly
distrusted it, because they were unwilling that any such
thing should happen to Caius, nor could they believe it,

though ever so true, because they thought no one able to
kill Caius. These were the women, and youths, and slaves,
and some of the soldiers. These last had taken his pay,
and in a manner tyrannized with him, and had ill-treated
the best of the citizens, in obedience to his outrageous commands, and to gain honours and advantages to themselves ; and the women and youths had been captivated, as
crowds are, with shows, and the fightings of gladiators,
and distributions of meat, all which things were done
nominally to please the multitude, but in reality to
glut the savage madness of Caius. The slaves also were
loath to believe the news, because they were allowed by
Caius to accuse and despise their masters, and they could
have recourse to his assistance when they had acted insolently to them ; for he was very easy in believing them
against their masters, even when they accused them falsely ;
and, if they would discover what money their masters had,
they might soon obtain both liberty and riches as the
reward of their accusations, because the eighth part of
their masters' substance was assigned to these informers.[1]
As to the patricians, although the report appeared credible
to some of them, either because they knew of the plot
beforehand, or because they wished it might prove true,
they concealed not only the joy they felt at the news, but that
they had heard any news at all. These last acted so from
the fear they had that, if the report proved false, they
would be punished for having so soon let men know their
minds. And those that knew Caius was dead, because
they were privy to the conspiracy, concealed it still more,
not knowing one another's minds, and fearing lest they
should speak of it to some of those to whom the continuance
of tyranny was advantageous, and if Caius should prove
after all to be alive, they might be informed against and
punished, for another report went about, that although
Caius had been wounded indeed, he was not dead, but still
alive, and under the surgeon's hands. Nor was any one
looked upon by another as one to be trusted, and to whom
one might boldly open one's mind ; for he was either a

[1] The reward proposed by the Roman laws to informers was sometimes an eighth part of the criminal's goods, as here, and sometimes a
fourth part, as Spanheim assures us from Suetonius and Tacitus.—W.

friend to Caius, and therefore suspected to favour his
tyranny, or he was one that hated him, and therefore
might be suspected to deserve the less credit for what he
said, because of his ill-will to him.   It was also reported by
some, (who deprived the patricians of all their hopes, and
made them sad indeed), that Caius despised the danger
he had been in, and took no care to heal his wounds,
but had got away to the forum, bloody as he was, and was
making an harangue to the people.   And these were the
conjectural reports of those that were so unreasonable as
to endeavour to raise tumults, which were received different
ways according to the opinions of the hearers.   However,
they did not leave their seats, for fear of being accused if
they should go out before the rest ; for they would not be
judged by the real intention with which they went out, but
by the conjectures of the accusers and judges.

§ 17. But when the multitude of Germans surrounded
the theatre with their swords drawn, all the spectators
looked for nothing but death, and upon every one's coming
in a fear seized upon them, as if they would be cut in
pieces immediately; and they were in great anxiety, not
having courage enough to go out of the theatre, and yet
not believing themselves safe from danger if they stayed
there.   And when the Germans rushed in, the theatre
rang again with the cries and entreaties of the spectators to the soldiers, for they pleaded that they were
entirely ignorant of every thing that related to an insurrection, and if any insurrection had been raised, they knew
nothing of what had happened.   They therefore begged
that they would spare them, and not punish those that had
not the least hand in such bold crimes of other persons,
while they neglected to search after those who had really
done whatever had been done.   Then did they appeal to
God, and deplore their infelicity with shedding of tears
and beating of their faces, and said every thing that the
most imminent danger, and the utmost concern for their
lives, could dictate to them.   This broke the fury of the
soldiers, and made them repent of what they had intended
to do to the spectators, for that would have been barbarous,
and so it appeared even to these savages, who fixed the heads
of those that were slain with Asprenas upon the altar.   At

this dreadful sight the spectators were sorely afflicted, both from the consideration of the rank of the persons, and commiseration at their sufferings; nay, indeed, they were almost in as great terror at the prospect of the danger they themselves were in, seeing it was still uncertain whether they should to the end escape the like calamity. And thus it came about that such as thoroughly and justly hated Caius, were yet robbed of pleasure at his death, because they were themselves in jeopardy of perishing with him, nor had they as yet any firm assurance of surviving.

§ 18. There was at this time one Euaristus Arruntius, a public crier in the market, and therefore of a powerful voice, who vied in wealth with the richest of the Romans, and was able to do what he pleased in the city both now and afterwards. This man made himself look as mournful as he could, (although he had greater hatred against Caius than any one else, but his fear and astuteness to secure his own safety taught him to conceal his present pleasure) and put on such mourning as he would have done had he lost his dearest friend in the world, and went to the theatre, and announced the death of Caius, and so put an end to the state of ignorance as to what had happened that people were in. Paulus Arruntius also went round, and called out to the Germans, as did the tribunes with him, bidding them put up their swords, and telling them that Caius was dead. And this most certainly saved the lives of those that were assembled together in the theatre, and all the rest who any way met the Germans; for, while they had hopes that Caius had still any breath in him, they abstained from no sort of mischief; and such an abundant kindness had they still for Caius, that they would willingly have prevented the plot against him, and purchased his escape from such an end at the expense of their own lives. But they left off their eagerness to punish his enemies, now they were fully satisfied that Caius was dead, because it was now in vain for them to show their zeal and kindness to him, as he that would reward them had perished. They were also afraid, if they went on doing such injuries, that they would be punished by the senate, if the authority devolved on them, or by the next emperor. And thus at last a stop was put, though not without difficulty, to the rage which possessed the Germans on account of Caius' death.

§ 19. Now Chærea was so much afraid for Minucianus, lest he should fall in with the Germans, now they were in their fury, and be killed by them, that he went and spoke to every one of the soldiers, and prayed them to take care of his preservation, and made himself great inquiry about him, lest he should have been slain. As for Clemens, he let Minucianus go (for he was brought to him) and, with many other of the senators, affirmed the deed was right, and commended the virtue of those that had contrived it, and had had courage enough to execute it; and said that tyrants did indeed please themselves with tyranny and look big for a while, but did not, however, go happily out of the world, because they were hated by the virtuous, and perished miserably like Caius, who had become a conspirator against himself, before those men who attacked him had plotted against him, and by becoming intolerable in his outrages, and by setting aside the wise provision the laws had made, had taught his dearest friends to treat him as an enemy, so that, though in common parlance the conspirators had slain Caius, yet in reality it was by his own act that he now lay dead.

§ 20. Now by this time the people in the theatre had risen from their seats, and those that were within made a very great disturbance, the reason of which was that the spectators were in too great a hurry to get away. There was also one Halcyon, a surgeon, who hurried away, as if to cure those that were wounded, and on that pretext sent those that were with him to fetch what things were necessary for the healing of those wounded persons, but in reality to free them from the imminent danger they were in. Meantime the senate had met, and the people also had assembled in the forum where they held their comitia, and both were employed in searching after the murderers of Caius. The people did this very zealously, but the senate in appearance only; for Valerius Asiaticus, a man of consular authority, went to the people, as they were troubled and very uneasy that they could not yet discover who had murdered the emperor, and when he was earnestly asked by them all, who it was that had done it, he replied, "I wish I had." The consuls also published an edict, wherein they accused Caius, and ordered the people and soldiers to go home, and gave the people hopes of abatement of their grievances, and promised the soldiers if they kept quiet as they used to do, and went not abroad to do mischief, that they would bestow rewards upon them. For there was reason to fear that the city would suffer harm from their wild behaviour, if they should once betake themselves to spoiling the citizens or plundering the temples. And now the whole multitude of the senators were assembled together, and especially those that had conspired to take away the life of Caius, who put on at this time an air of great assurance and great contempt of others, as if the administration of public affairs had already devolved upon them.

## CHAP. II.

*How the Senators wished to restore the Republic; but the soldiers were for preserving the Monarchy. The Murder of Caius' Wife and Daughter. The character of Caius.*

### § 1.

WHEN public affairs were in this condition, Claudius was suddenly hurried away out of his house. For the soldiers held a meeting, and when they had debated about what was to be done, they saw that a democracy was incapable of managing such a vast weight of public affairs, and that if it should be set up it would not be for their advantage: and if one of those already in power should become emperor, it would in all respects be unsatisfactory to them, if they did not assist him in his advancement: it would therefore be well for them, while public affairs were still unsettled, to choose Claudius as emperor, who was uncle to the deceased Caius, and of greater dignity than any of those senators who were assembled together, both on account of the virtue of his ancestors, and the attention he had paid to learning, and who, if once made emperor, would reward them according to their deserts, and bestow largesses upon them. This was their

462                                           [BOOK XIX.

plan, and they executed it immediately. Claudius was
therefore seized upon by the soldiers. But Cnæus Sentius
Saturninus, although he had heard of the seizing of Claudius, and that he intended to claim the throne, unwillingly
indeed in appearance, but in reality with his consent, stood
up in the senate, and, without being dismayed, addressed
them in a manner suitable to free and noble men, and spoke
as follows.

§ 2. "Although it seems incredible, O Romans, because
of the great length of time since so unexpected an event
has happened, yet are we now in possession of liberty.
How long indeed it will last is uncertain, and lies at the
disposal of the gods, whose grant it is, yet is it sufficient to
make us rejoice, and be happy for the present, although
we may soon be deprived of it ; for to those that love virtue
one hour is sufficient spent in freedom in our country, which
is now independent and governed by such laws as it once
flourished under.   As for myself, I cannot remember our
former time of liberty, for I was born after it had passed
away, but I am beyond measure filled with joy at the
thought of our present freedom, and esteem those happy
men that were born and bred up in it, and I think these
men worthy of no less honour than the gods themselves,
who have, though late, given us a taste of it in this age.
May secure enjoyment of it continue to all ages : though
this single day may suffice for our youth, as well as for our
old men.   It will seem an age to our old men, if they die
during its happy duration ; it will also instruct our younger
men what kind of virtue those men had from whom we
are sprung.   As for ourselves, nothing will be more to
our advantage in the present than to live virtuously, for it is
virtue alone that can preserve men their liberty.   As to our
ancient state I have heard from others, but as to our later
state, I have personally seen and known what mischiefs
tyrannies have brought upon our polity, discouraging all
virtue, and depriving persons of magnanimity of their
liberty, and teaching flattery and fear, because they leave
public affairs to be governed not by the wisdom of the laws,
but by the caprice of our rulers.   For since Julius Cæsar
took it into his head to overthrow our democracy, and, by
violating the regular system of our laws, brought disorders

into our polity, and got above right and justice, and was a
slave to his own inclinations, there is no evil that has not
plagued our state, as all those that have succeeded him
have vied with one another to overthrow the ancient laws
of our country, and to leave it destitute of all citizens of
noble principles, because they thought it for their safety to
have only vicious men to deal with, and not only to break
the spirits of those that were best esteemed for their virtue,
but to resolve upon their utter destruction.  Of all these
tyrants, who have been many in number, and who have
laid upon us an insufferable burden during their reigns,
this Caius, who has been slain to-day, has brought more
terrible calamities upon us than did all the rest, not only
by wreaking his ungovernable rage upon his fellow-citizens,
but also upon his kindred and friends, inflicting upon all
alike still greater miseries by exacting unjust punishments, being equally furious against men and against the
gods.  For tyrants are not content to gain their pleasure
by doing injuries, or by tampering both with men's estates and wives, but they look upon it as entire gain when
they can utterly overthrow the entire families of their
enemies.  So hateful to tyrants is all liberty, nor can even
those gain their friendship that patiently endure whatever
miseries they bring on them.  For as they are conscious of
the abundant evils they have brought on several, and how
nobly they have borne their hard fortune, they cannot but
be sensible what evils they have done them, and so only
think they can get security, so suspicious are they, by
putting them entirely out of the world.  Since, then, we are
now got clear of so great a plague, and are only account-
able to one another (which form of government affords us
the best assurance of present concord and future security
from evil designs, and will be most for our own glory in
putting the state in good order), you ought every one of
you personally to look to the public interests of everybody,
nay, even to oppose measures which have been proposed that
you dislike, and that without any danger, because there
is now no irresponsible despot to do mischief to the state,
with absolute power to take off those that freely declare their opinions.  Nor has any thing so much contributed to the increase of tyranny of late as sloth and timi-

dity in contradicting the emperor's will; for men had too great love for the sweets of peace, and had learned to live like slaves. And as many of us as either suffered intolerable calamities, or saw the miseries of our neighbours, because we dreaded dying virtuously, had the prospect of death with the utmost infamy. We ought, then, in the first place, to decree the greatest honours we are able to those that have taken off the tyrant, especially to Chærea Cassius. For this one man, with the aid of the gods, has by his counsel and actions been the procurer of our liberty, nor ought we to be ungrateful to him, seeing that he under a tyranny conspired and hazarded his life for our liberty, but we ought to decree him honours, and exhibit this as our first spontaneous act. And certainly it is a very excellent thing, and one well becoming freemen, to requite benefactors, such as this man has been to us all, though unlike Cassius and Brutus who slew Caius Julius [Cæsar]; for they laid the foundations of sedition and civil war in our city, but this man by his tyrannicide has set our city free from all the mischiefs that came therefrom."

§ 3. This was the gist of Sentius' oration, which was received with pleasure by the senators, and by as many of the equestrian order as were present. And now one Trebellius Maximus rose up hastily, and took off Sentius' finger a ring, which had a stone with the image of Caius engraven upon it, and which, in his zeal in speaking, and earnestness in what he was about, he had forgotten (it was supposed) to take off himself. The intaglio was broken immediately. And, as it was now far in the night, Chærea demanded of the consuls the word, and they gave him Liberty. What had happened seemed wonderful to them and almost incredible. For it was a hundred years since the democracy had been set aside, when this giving the word for the day returned to the consuls; for, before the city was governed by tyrants, they were the commanders of the soldiers. And when Chærea had received the word, he passed it on to those soldiers who were on the senate's side, which were four regiments, who esteemed government without emperors to be preferable to tyranny. And these went away with their tribunes. The people also now departed very joyful, full of hope and courage at having recovered their former power, and being no longer under an emperor. And Chærea was everybody with them.

§ 4. And now Chærea was very uneasy that Caius' wife and daughter were still alive, and that all his family had not perished with him, since whoever was left of them would be left for the ruin of the city and the laws. So, being anxious to complete his work, and satisfy his hatred of Caius, he sent Julius Lupus, one of the tribunes, to kill Caius' wife and daughter. They proposed this office to Lupus, as a kinsman of Clemens, that he might be so far a partaker in the tyrannicide, and might get credit for his virtue among the citizens, and might seem to have been one of the original conspirators. But it appeared to some of the conspirators cruel to use such severity to a woman, because Caius, in all that he did, indulged his own ill-nature more than used her advice, and it was owing to him (*and not her*) that the city was in such a desperate condition of misery, and the flower of the citizens destroyed. But others accused her of giving her consent to these things, nay, they ascribed all that Caius had done to her as the cause of it, and said that she had given a philtre to Caius, which had made him enslaved to her will, and had tied him down to love her, so that she, having made him mad, was herself the author of all the misfortunes that had befallen the Romans and the world that was subject to them. So that at last it was determined that she must die, for those of the contrary opinion could not at all prevail to have her saved, and Lupus was sent accordingly. Nor did he make any delay in executing his errand, but he took the first opportunity to obey those that sent him, being desirous to be no way blamable in what was done for the advantage of the people. So he went to the palace, and found Cæsonia, Caius' wife, lying by her husband's dead body, which also lay on the ground, and was destitute of all such things as the law allows to the dead, and herself besmeared all over with the blood of her husband's wounds, and in the greatest affliction, her daughter lying by her side also: and nothing else was heard from her in these circumstances but blaming Caius for not having attended to what she had so often told him beforehand; which words of hers were taken in two

senses even at that time, and are now esteemed equally
ambiguous by those that hear them, and are still interpreted
according to the different inclinations of people. For some
said that the words denoted, that she had advised him to
leave off his mad behaviour and cruelty to the citizens, and
to govern the public with moderation and virtue, lest he
should perish by their using him as he had used them.
Others said, as certain words had passed concerning the
conspirators, that she desired Caius to make no delay, but
immediately to put them all to death, and that whether
they were guilty or not, and so he would be out of fear of
any danger; and that this was what she now blamed
him for, for being too tender in the matter when she had
advised him to slay them all. And this was what Cæsonia
said, and what the opinions of men were about it. But
when she saw Lupus approach, she showed him Caius'
dead body, and begged him to come near with lamentation
and tears; and when she noticed that Lupus seemed unsettled in his purpose, and approached her as if to do something disagreeable to himself, she was well aware for what
purpose he came, and bared her throat very readily, be-
wailing her case like people who utterly despair of their
life, and bidding him not delay to end the tragedy they
had resolved upon relating to her. So she boldly received
her death at the hand of Lupus, as did her daughter after
her. Then Lupus made haste to inform Chærea of what
he had done.

§ 5. Such was the end of Caius, after he had reigned
four years all but four months. Even before he came to
be emperor he was ill-natured, and one that had arrived at
the utmost pitch of wickedness; a slave to pleasure, and a
lover of calumny; greatly afraid of what was formidable,
and of a very murderous disposition, where he durst show
it. He enjoyed his power to this only purpose, to injure
those that least deserved it with unreasonable arrogance,
and he got his wealth by murder and injustice. He laboured
to appear above the gods and the laws, but was a slave to
the praises of the populace; and whatever the laws determined to be shameful, and censured, that he esteemed
more honourable than virtue. He was unmindful of his
friends, however intimate, and though they were persons of

the highest character ; and, if he was once angry at any
of them, he would inflict punishment upon them for the
most trifling matters, and esteemed every man that endeavoured to lead a virtuous life his enemy.   And whatever
he commanded, he would admit of no contradiction to his
desires, so it was that he committed incest with his own
sister,[1] on which account chiefly it was that a bitter hatred
first sprang up against him among the citizens, that sort
of incest not having been known for a long time, and so it
provoked men to distrust and hate him that was guilty of
it.   As for any great or royal work that he ever did, which
might be for the advantage of his contemporaries or
posterity, nobody could name any such, except the haven
that he made about Rhegium [2] and Sicily, for the ships that
brought corn from Egypt ; which was indeed indisputably
a very great work in itself, and of very great advantage for
navigation.   Yet this work was not brought to perfection
by him, but was left only half finished because of his
want of application to it ; the reason was that he dissipated
his energy on useless matters, and as he spent his money
upon pleasures such as tended to no one's benefit but his
own, he could not be liberal in things that were undeniably
of greater consequence.   In other respects he was an excellent orator, and thoroughly acquainted with the Greek
tongue, as well as with his own mother-tongue, the Latin.
He was also able, off-hand and readily, to give answers to
compositions made by others of considerable length.   He
was also more skilful in persuading others in important
cases than any one else in consequence of a natural facility,
which had been improved by much exercise and pains-
taking.   For as he was the grandson [3] of the brother of
Tiberius, whose successor he was, this was a strong com-
pulsion to his prosecution of learning, because Tiberius

[1] Spanheim here notes from Suetonius, that the name of Caius'
sister, with whom he was guilty of incest, was Drusilla ; and that
Suetonius adds, he was guilty of the same crime with all his sisters also.
He notes further, that Suetonius omits the mention of the haven for
ships, which our author esteems the only great public work which Caius
left behind him, though in an imperfect condition.—W.

[2] *Reggio*, on the east side of the Straits of *Messina*.

[3] This Caius was the son of that excellent person Germanicus ; who
was the son of Drusus, the brother of Tiberius the emperor.—W.

was eminent for his success in learning, and Caius aspired
after the like glory for eloquence, being induced thereto by
the letters of his kinsman and emperor. He was also foremost of the citizens of his own age, but the advantages he
received from his learning did not counterbalance the mischief he brought upon himself by his license; so difficult
is it for those to get the virtue of self-control who have
irresponsible freedom of action. At first he got himself
such friends as were in all respects most worthy, and was
greatly beloved by them, in consequence of his learning
and emulating the glory of the best men; until from his
excessive injuries to them, they laid aside the kindness
they had for him, and began to hate him, from which hatred
came the plot which they raised against him, in which he
perished.

## CHAP. III.

*How Claudius was seized, and brought out of his House, and
taken to the Camp, and how the Senate sent an Embassage
to him.*

### § 1.

NOW Claudius, as I said before, had taken a different road
from Caius, and, as the royal family were greatly put out
by the sad murder of the emperor, he was in great anxiety
how to save himself, and was found to have hidden himself
in a certain narrow passage, though he had no reason for
suspicion of danger besides the dignity of his birth. For
he lived privately and behaved himself with moderation,
and was contented with his present fortune, applying
himself to learning, and especially to that of the Greeks,
and holding himself entirely aloof from every thing that
might bring trouble. But as at this time the multitude
were in consternation, and the whole palace was full of the
fury of the soldiers, and the emperor's body-guards seemed
in the same panic and confusion as private persons, the
band called Prætorian, which was the purest part of the
army, held a consultation as to what was to be done at this
juncture. Now all those that were present at this consultation, had little regard to the punishment Caius had suffered,

because he justly deserved his fate, but rather considered their own fortunes, how they might take the best care of themselves, especially as the Germans were busy in punishing the murderers of Caius, rather to gratify their own savage temper, than for the good of the public. All these things troubled Claudius, who was afraid for his own safety, especially when he saw the heads of Asprenas and his fellow-conspirators carried about. He stood in a certain place ascended by a few steps, where he had retired in the dark. And when Gratus, who was one of the soldiers that belonged to the palace, saw him, but could not well tell by his countenance who he was, because it was dark, though he could see that it was some one who was hiding, he went nearer to him, and when Claudius desired that he would retire, he discovered who he was, and said to his followers, "This is a Germanicus;[1] come, let us choose him for our emperor." And when Claudius saw that they were preparing to take him away by force, and was afraid they would kill him, as they had killed Caius, he besought them to spare him, reminding them how quietly he had demeaned himself, and that he was unacquainted with all that had been done. Thereupon Gratus smiled upon him, and took him by the right hand, and said, "Leave off these humble thoughts of saving yourself, while you ought to have greater thoughts, even of obtaining the empire, which the gods, in their concern for the world, have committed to your virtue by taking Caius out of the way. Go, therefore, and take the throne of your ancestors." So he lifted him up and carried him, because he was unable to walk, such was his mingled dread and joy at what Gratus said to him.

§ 2. Now there were already gathered round Gratus a great number of the body-guards, and when they saw Claudius carried off, they looked sad, supposing that he was being dragged to execution for the mischief that had been lately done, though he was a man who had never meddled with public affairs all his life long, and had been

---

[1] How Claudius, son of Drusus, and brother of Germanicus, could be here himself called Germanicus, Suetonius informs us, when he tells us that by a decree of the senate, the surname of Germanicus was bestowed upon Drusus and his posterity also. Sueton. *Claud.* i.—W.

in great danger during the reign of Caius; and some of
them thought it well that the consuls should take cogni-
zance of the matter. And, as more and more of the soldiers got together, the crowd gave way, and Claudius could
hardly go forward from weakness of body, and those who
carried his litter, when they heard of his being carried off,
ran away and saved themselves, despairing of their lord's
safety. But when they were come into the large court of
the palace (which, as the report goes about it, was the first
part inhabited in the city of Rome), and had just got to
the public treasury, many more soldiers flocked to him,
being glad to see Claudius' face, and thought it exceeding
right to make him emperor, on account of their kindness
for Germanicus, who was his brother, and had left behind
him a great reputation among all that were acquainted
with him. They reflected also on the covetousness of the
leading men of the senate, and what great errors they had
been guilty of formerly, when they were in power. They
also considered the difficulty of the situation, as also what
danger they would be in, if the government should devolve
upon any individual but Claudius, who would take it as
their grant and favour, and would be grateful for the
benefit they had done him, and make them a sufficient
recompense for the same.

§ 3. These were the discourses the soldiers had with
one another and by themselves, and they communicated
them to all such as came near them. And they, on hearing it, willingly embraced the proposal, and they carried
Claudius to the camp, crowding round him as his guard,
and bearing him aloft in a litter, that their impatience
might not be thwarted. As to the populace and senate
they differed in their opinions. The latter were very
desirous to recover their former dignity, and anxious to
get rid of the slavery that had been imposed on them by
the insolence of their tyrants, now that they had an opportunity afforded them; but the people, who were envious
of them, and knew that the emperors were able to curb
their arrogance, and were a protection to themselves, were
very glad that Claudius had been carried off by the army,
and thought that if he were made emperor, he would prevent such a civil war as there was in the days of Pompey.

But when the senate knew that Claudius had been taken to the camp by the soldiers, they sent to him those of their body who had the best character for virtue, to recommend him to do nothing to gain power by violence, but to submit to the senate, as he was either already, or would hereafter be, one of their body, which consisted of so many persons, and to submit to the law in all that related to public order, and to remember how greatly previous tyrants had afflicted their state, and what dangers both he and they had run under Caius, for they said he ought not to hate the heavy burden of tyranny, when the injury was done by others, and yet be himself willing to play havock with his country. They added that if he would hearken to them, and show that his determination was to live quietly and virtuously as before, he would have the greatest honours decreed to him that a free people could bestow, and by subjecting himself in part to the law, would obtain this commendation, that he acted like a man of virtue both as a ruler and subject; but if he would act recklessly, and learn no wisdom by Caius' death, they would not permit it. For a great section of the army (they added) sided with them, and they had plenty of weapons, and a great number of slaves to make use of: and hope played a great part in such cases, and fortune and the gods never assisted any but those that exerted themselves with virtue and goodness, who could only be such as fought for the liberty of their country.

§ 4. Such was the speech that the envoys, Veranius and Brocchus, who were both tribunes of the people, made to Claudius, and falling down upon their knees, begged of him, that he would not bring the city into wars and misfortunes. But when they saw what a multitude of soldiers surrounded and guarded Claudius, and that the consuls were totally inadequate to cope with them, they added that, if he desired the empire, he should accept it as given by the senate, for he would be happier in it and take it under better auspices, if he did not seize it by violence, but accepted it from the good-will of those who offered it to him.

## CHAP. IV.

*What King Agrippa did for Claudius, and how Claudius,*
*when he had become Emperor, commanded the Murderers*
*of Caius to be slain.*

### § 1.

NOW Claudius, though he was not blind to the presumption of this message from the senate, yet behaved himself for the present with moderation, as they
advised. However, he recovered from his fright, being
encouraged partly by the boldness of the soldiers, and
partly by king Agrippa, who exhorted him not to let
such an empire slip out of his hands, when it came thus
spontaneously to him. King Agrippa acted also to Caius
as became one who had been so much honoured by him;
for he embraced Caius' body after he was dead, and laid it
upon a bed, and laid it out as well as he could, and went
to the body-guards, and told them that Caius was still
alive, but bade them fetch surgeons, for he was very ill of
his wounds. But when he learned that Claudius had been
carried off by the soldiers, he pushed through the crowd
to him, and when he found that he was in a condition of
terror, and ready to yield to the senate, he encouraged him,
and bade him stick to the empire. And when he had
said this to Claudius, he returned home, and, upon the
senate's sending for him, he anointed his head with oint-
ment, as if he had just come from a festive party, and so
went to them, and also asked the senators what Claudius
had done. And when they told him the present state of
affairs, and further asked his opinion on the whole matter,
he at once told them that he was ready to lose his life for
the honour of the senate, but desired them to consider
what was for their advantage, without any regard to their
personal desires. For those who grasped at government,
stood in need of weapons, and soldiers to guard them,
lest being unprepared they should fall into danger. And
when the senate replied, that they could bring weapons
and money in abundance, and that as to an army, part of it
was already mustered together, and they could raise a larger

one by giving the slaves their liberty, Agrippa made the following answer. "O senators! may you be able to do what you desire; but I will without any hesitation tell you my thoughts, because they tend to your preservation. Know, then, that the army which will fight on behalf of Claudius has been long trained in war, while our army will be no better than a mob and rabble, as it is composed of such as have been unexpectedly freed from slavery, and are without discipline; we shall therefore bring up against those who are skilful in war men who know not so much as how to draw their swords. My opinion therefore is, that we should send some persons to Claudius, to urge him to lay down the government, and I am ready to be one of your ambassadors."

§ 2. Upon this speech of Agrippa, the senate complied with him, and he was sent with others, and privately informed Claudius of the alarm of the senate, and advised him to answer them in a somewhat commanding strain, and as one invested with dignity and authority, So Claudius replied that he did not wonder the senate did not wish to have an emperor over them, because they had been harassed by the savageness of those who had formerly been at the head of affairs; but they should enjoy an equitable government and good times under him, for he would only be their ruler in name, but the authority should be common to all. And since he had passed through many and various scenes of life before their eyes, it would be well for them not to distrust him. The ambassadors, upon receiving this answer, were dismissed. And Claudius harangued the army which was gathered together, and made them swear that they would remain faithful to him, and gave the body-guards five thousand drachmæ apiece,[1] and a proportionable quantity to their captains, and promised to give the same to the rest of the armies wherever they were.

§ 3. And now the consuls convoked the senate to the temple of Jupiter Stator, while it was still night. But

[1] This number of drachmæ to be distributed to each private soldier, 5,000 drachmæ, equal to 20,000 sesterces, or £161 sterling, seems much too large, and directly contradicts Suetonius, chap. x., who makes them in all but fifteen sesterces, or 2s. 4d.—W.

some of the senators concealed themselves in the city, being uncertain what to do on the hearing of this summons, and some of them retired to their estates in the country, foreseeing the issue of public affairs, and despairing of liberty, supposing it much better for them to be slaves without danger to themselves, and to live a lazy and inactive life, than, by trying to gain the glory of their forefathers, to hazard their own safety. So a hundred and no more met together, and as they were deliberating about the present posture of affairs, a sudden clamour was raised by the soldiers that were on their side, bidding the senate to choose an emperor, and not to ruin the state by setting up a multitude of rulers. Thus they fully declared themselves to be for giving the government not to all, but to one; but they gave the senate leave to look out for a person worthy to be set over them. And now the situation of the senate was much worse than before; because they had not only failed in the recovery of their vaunted liberty, but were afraid of Claudius also. Yet there were some of them that hankered after the chief power, both on account of the dignity of their families, and that accruing to them by their marriages. For Marcus Minucianus was illustrious, both from his own nobility, and from his having married Julia, the sister of Caius, and accordingly was very ready to claim the government, although the consuls discouraged him on one pretext or another. And Minucianus, who was one of Caius' murderers, restrained Valerius Asiaticus from thinking of such things. And indeed there would have been a prodigious slaughter, if those men who desired to be emperors had been permitted to set up themselves in opposition to Claudius. There were also a considerable number of gladiators, and of those soldiers who kept watch by night in the city, and of rowers who flocked to the camp; so that of those who claimed the empire, some gave up their pretensions to spare the city, and others from fear for their own safety.

§ 4. Now at first dawn of day Chærea, and those that were associated with him, went to the senate, and attempted to make speeches to the soldiers. However, the mass of the soldiers, when they saw that they were making signals for silence with their hands, and were going to begin to speak to them, grew tumultuous, and would not let them speak at all, because they all desired to be under the rule of one; and they demanded of the senate an emperor, for they would endure no longer delays. But the senate were in a fix about either their own governing, or how they should be governed, for the soldiers would not allow them to govern, and the murderers of Caius would not permit the soldiers to dictate to them. As affairs were in this posture, Chærea was not able to contain his anger at their demand for an emperor, and promised that he would give them a leader, if any one would bring him the word for the day from Eutychus. Now this Eutychus was charioteer of the green faction in the Circus at Rome,[1] and a great friend of Caius, who used to tire out the soldiers with building stables for his horses, and put them to ignominious labours. Chærea reproached them with this, and other similar things, and told them, he would bring them the head of Claudius, for it was monstrous after a madman to have a fool for emperor. But they were not moved with his words, but drew their swords, and took up their standards, and went to Claudius, to join in taking the oath of fidelity to him. So the senate were left without anybody to defend them, and the consuls had no more authority than private persons: and there was great consternation and dejection, men not knowing what would become of them, because Claudius was irritated by them; so they fell to reproaching one another, and repented of what they had done. At this juncture Sabinus, one of Caius' murderers, came forward and threatened to kill himself sooner than consent to make Claudius emperor, and see slavery returning upon them; and also rebuked Chærea for loving life, since he, who was first in his contempt of Caius, could think it good to live, now that (after all they had done) they found it impossible to recover their liberty. But Chærea said he had not changed his mind at all about killing himself, but he would sound the intentions of Claudius first.

§ 5. Such was the posture of affairs in the senate. But in the camp every body was pushing their way from all

---

[1] See Juvenal, xi. 196.

sides to pay their court to Claudius, and one of the consuls, Quintus Pomponius, was especially reproached by the soldiers for having exhorted the senate to recover their liberty, and they drew their swords, and rushed at him, and would have murdered him, if Claudius had not hindered them. For he snatched the consul out of the danger he was in, and set him by his side; but he did not receive those of the senate who had sided with Quintus in the like honourable manner; for some of them received blows, and were thrust away as they came to salute Claudius, and Aponius went away wounded, and all were in danger. Then king Agrippa went up to Claudius, and desired he would treat the senators more gently; for if any mischief should come to the senate, he would have no others over whom to rule. And Claudius listened to him, and called the senate together to the palace, and was carried there himself in his litter through the city, the soldiers escorting him not without injuring the multitude a good deal. And Chærea and Sabinus, two of Caius' murderers, went about openly, though Pollio, whom Claudius had a little before made captain of his body-guards, had sent them a letter, forbidding them to appear in public. So Claudius, upon his reaching the palace, got his friends together, and desired their opinion as to Chærea. They said that the deed done seemed a glorious one, but they accused the doer of disloyalty, and thought it just to inflict condign punishment upon him, to discountenance such actions for the time to come. So Chærea was led out to execution, and Lupus and many other Romans with him. And it is reported that Chærea bore his fate nobly, as was evidenced not only by the firmness of his own behaviour under it, but by his reproach to Lupus, who fell into tears; for when Lupus had laid his garment aside and complained of the cold,[1] Chærea said that cold never hurt lupus [i.e. a wolf]. And as a great multitude followed to see the sight, when Chærea came to the place of execution, he asked the soldier who was to be their executioner whether the office was one he was used to, or

---

[1] This piercing cold here complained of by Lupus, agrees well to the time of the year when Claudius began his reign: that being a few days after January 24th, the day on which Caius was murdered.—W.

whether this was the first time of his using his sword in
that manner, and bade him fetch the very sword with
which he himself had slain Caius.  And he was happily
killed at one stroke; but Lupus did not meet with such
good fortune in going out of the world, as he was timid,
and had many blows levelled at his neck, because he did
not stretch it out boldly.

§ 6.  Now, a few days after this, as the festival called the
Parentalia[1] was just at hand, the Roman multitude made
their usual offerings to their dead relatives, and put por-
tions into the fire in honour of Chærea, and besought him
to be propitious to them, and not angry with them for their
ingratitude.  Such was the end of Chærea.  As for Sabinus,
although Claudius not only set him at liberty, but gave him
leave to retain his former command in the army, he thought
it would be unjust in him to fail in good faith to his fellow-
conspirators, so he fell upon his sword and killed himself,
driving his sword up to the very hilt in the wound.

## CHAP. V.

*How Claudius restored to Agrippa his Grandfather's King-
doms, and augmented his Dominions, and how he published
an Edict in behalf of the Jews.*

### § 1.

NOW, when Claudius had speedily got rid of all the
soldiers whom he suspected, he published an edict,
wherein he confirmed to Agrippa the kingdom which Caius
had given him, and commended the king highly.  He also
added to it all the territory over which his grandfather
Herod had reigned, that is, Judæa and Samaria : and this
he restored to him as due to his family.  As for Abila,[2]
that had belonged to Lysanias, and all the country near

---

[1] A festival at Rome in honour of dead relatives.  Our All Souls'
Day.

[2] The capital of the tetrarchy of Abilene (Luke iii. 1).  The ruins
are near *Nebi Habil*, not far from the remarkable gorge called *Sûk
Wâdy Barada*.

Mount Libanus, he bestowed them upon him, as out of his
own territory. He also made a league with Agrippa, confirmed by oaths, in the middle of the forum, in the city of
Rome. He also took away from Antiochus the kingdom
which he had, but gave him a portion of Cilicia and Commagene.[1] He also set at liberty Alexander Lysimachus, the
Alabarch, who had been his old friend, and steward to his
mother Antonia, but had been imprisoned by the anger of
Caius. Now Marcus, Alexander's son, had married Berenice, the daughter of Agrippa; and when Marcus died,
who had married her when she was a virgin, Agrippa gave
her in marriage to his brother Herod, and begged of
Claudius the kingdom of Chalcis[2] for him.

§ 2. Now, about this time, there was strife between
the Jews and Greeks in the city of Alexandria. For
when Caius was dead the nation of the Jews, which had
been very much oppressed under his reign, and very badly
treated by the people of Alexandria, recovered courage and
immediately took up arms. And Claudius sent an order to
the governor of Egypt to quiet the tumult. He also sent
an edict, at the requests of king Agrippa and king Herod,
both to Alexandria and to Syria, whose contents were as
follows. "Tiberius Claudius Cæsar, Augustus, Germanicus,
Pontifex Maximus, and Tribune of the people, ordains as
follows. Since I have long known that the Jews of Alexandria, called Alexandrians, have been joint colonists from
the earliest times with the Alexandrians, and have obtained
from their kings equal privileges with them, as is evident
from the public records that are in their possession, and
the edicts, and since, after Alexandria was made part
of our empire by Augustus, their rights and privileges
have been preserved by those who have at divers times
been sent there as governors, and since no disputes were
raised about those rights and privileges, when Aquila was
governor of Alexandria, and since, when the Jewish ethnarch
was dead, Augustus did not prohibit making ethnarchs,
wishing that all nations subject to the Romans should
continue in the observance of their own customs, and

---

[1] The district of Antiochiane in Cappadocia, in which Derbe, Laranda,
Kybistra, &c., were situated.
[2] *Kinnisrin*, in Northern Syria.

not be forced to transgress their country's religion; and since, in the reign of Caius, the Alexandrians became excited against the Jews that were among them, and Caius, from his great madness and want of understanding, oppressed the nation of the Jews, because they would not transgress their national worship, and call him a god, I decree that the nation of the Jews be not deprived of their rights and privileges on account of the madness of Caius, but that those rights and privileges which they formerly enjoyed, be preserved to them, and that they may continue in their customs. And I charge both parties to take very great care that no trouble arises after the promulgation of this edict."

§ 3. Such were the contents of the edict on behalf of the Jews that was sent to Alexandria. But the edict that was sent to the rest of the world was as follows. "Tiberius Claudius Cæsar, Augustus, Germanicus, Pontifex Maximus, Tribune of the people, chosen Consul the second time, ordains as follows. Upon the petition of king Agrippa and king Herod, who are persons very dear to me, that I would grant the same rights and privileges to be preserved to the Jews throughout all the Roman empire, as I have granted to the Jews of Alexandria, I very willingly comply therewith, not only to gratify my petitioners, but also judging those Jews for whom I have been petitioned worthy of such a favour, on account of their fidelity and friendship to the Romans. I think it also very just that no Greek city should be deprived of such rights and privileges, since they were preserved to them under the great Augustus. It is therefore right to permit the Jews throughout all our empire to keep their ancient customs without let or hindrance. And I do charge them also to use this my kindness to them with moderation, and not to show contempt at the superstitious observances of other nations, but to observe their own laws only. And I will that the rulers of cities and colonies and municipal towns, both within and without Italy, and kings and governors by their ambassadors, post up this decree publicly for full thirty days, in a place ¹ where it may plainly be read from the ground."

¹ This form was so known and frequent among the Romans, as Dr.

## CHAP. VI.

*What was done by Agrippa at Jerusalem, when he had re-*
*turned to Judæa : and what Petronius wrote in behalf of*
*the Jews to the Inhabitants of Doris.*

### § 1.

NOW Claudius Cæsar showed by these decrees, which
were sent to Alexandria and to all the world, what
opinion he had of the Jews.  And he soon sent Agrippa
away to administer his kingdom, advanced as he was to
more illustrious dignity than before, and sent letters to the
governors and procurators of the provinces to treat him with
attention.   And he returned in haste, as it was likely he
would, now he returned in greater prosperity than before.
He also went to Jerusalem, and offered thank-offerings, and
omitted nothing that the law required.  So he ordered
that many of the Nazarites should have their heads shorn,
and as for the golden chain which had been given him by
Caius, of the same weight as the iron chain wherewith his
royal hands had been bound, he hung it up within the
temple precincts above the treasury, as a memorial of his
sad fortune, and a testimony of his change for the better,
that it might be a proof how the greatest prosperity may
have a fall sometimes, and that God can raise up what is
fallen down.   For this chain thus dedicated reminded all
men, that king Agrippa had once been bound with a chain
for a small matter, but had recovered his former rank again,
and soon afterwards had got out of his bonds, and was
advanced to be a more illustrious king than he was before.
Whence men may understand that all that partake of
human nature, however great, may fall; and that those
that fall may gain their former illustrious rank again.

§ 2. And when Agrippa had discharged all his religious
duties to God, he removed Theophilus, the son of Ananus,

---

Hudson here tells us, from the great Selden, that it used to be thus
represented at the bottom of their edicts by the initial letters only *U. D.*
*P. R. L. P.   Unde De Plano Recte Legi Possit.*  " Where it may plainly
be read from the ground."—W.

from the high-priesthood, and bestowed his office on
Simon (the son of Boethus) also called Cantheras. This
Simon had two brothers, and a sister who married king
Herod, as I have related before. Simon, then, had the
high-priesthood with his brothers, and with his father, in
like manner as the three sons of Simon, the son of Onias,
had it formerly under the rule of the Macedonians, as I
have related in a former book.

§ 3. When the king had settled the high-priesthood in
this manner, he returned the kindness which the inhabitants
of Jerusalem had shown him; for he released them from
the tax upon every house, thinking it a good thing to
requite the affections of those that loved him. He also made
Silas, who had shared with him in many of his troubles,
the general of his forces. But very soon afterwards the
young men of Doris,[1] preferring audacity to piety, and being
naturally bold and insolent, carried a statue of the emperor
into a synagogue of the Jews, and erected it there. This
action of theirs greatly provoked Agrippa; for it plainly
tended to the dissolution of the laws of his country. So
he went without delay to Publius Petronius, who was then
governor of Syria, and accused the people of Doris. Nor
did he less resent what was done than did Agrippa; for he
judged it a piece of impiety to transgress the laws. So he
wrote the following letter to the people of Doris, in angry
strain. "Publius Petronius, the lieutenant of Tiberius
Claudius Cæsar, Augustus, Germanicus, to the magistrates
of Doris, ordains as follows. Since some of you have had
the boldness, or madness rather (after the edict of Claudius
Cæsar, Augustus, Germanicus, was published, permitting
the Jews to observe the laws of their country,) not to obey
the same, but have acted in entire opposition thereto, forbidding the Jews to assemble together in the synagogue, and
setting up the emperor's statue therein, and thereby have
offended not only the Jews, but also the emperor himself,
whose statue is more properly placed in his own temple
than in a foreign one, and that too in a place of assembling
together, seeing that it is but a part of natural justice, that
everyone should have power over the places belonging to

---

[1] Dor, now *Tantûrah*, on the sea coast north of Cæsarea Palæstina,
*Kaisarîyeh*.

themselves, according to the decree of the emperor (to say nothing of my own decree, which it would be ridiculous to mention after the emperor's edict, which gives the Jews leave to make use of their own customs, and also orders that they are to enjoy the same rights of citizens as the Greeks themselves); I therefore order Proculus Vitellius, the centurion, to bring those men before me, who, contrary to the emperor's edict, have been so insolent as to do this thing, (at which the men, who appear to be of principal reputation among them, are indignant also themselves, and allege that it was not done with their consent, but by the violence of the multitude,) to give account of what has been done. I also advise the principal magistrates, unless they wish to have this outrage supposed to have been done with their consent, to point out to the centurion the guilty persons, and to take care that no handle be thence taken for raising a sedition or quarrel, which those who encourage such doings seem to me to hunt after; for both I myself, and king Agrippa, whom I hold in the highest honour, are more anxious about nothing than that the nation of the Jews may have no opportunity given them of gathering together and becoming tumultuous under the pretext of defending themselves. And that what the emperor has determined about the whole matter may be more publicly known, I have subjoined the edicts which he has lately caused to be published at Alexandria, and which, although they may be well known to all, Agrippa, for whom I have the highest esteem, read nevertheless at that time before my tribunal, and pleaded that the Jews ought not to be deprived of the benefits which the emperor had granted them. I therefore charge you, that you do not, for the time to come, seek for any occasion of sedition or disturbance, but that everybody be allowed to follow their own religious customs."

§ 4. Thus did Petronius make provision that such lawlessness might be corrected, and that no such thing might be attempted afterwards against the Jews. And now king Agrippa took the high-priesthood away from Simon Cantheras, and was for putting Jonathan, the son of Ananus, back into it again, and owned that he was more worthy of the dignity. But it did not seem to him de-

sirable to resume so great a dignity.  So he refused it, and
said, " O king! I rejoice in the honour you show me, and
take it kindly that you are inclined to give me such a
dignity, though God has judged that I am not at all worthy
of the high-priesthood.  I am satisfied with having once
put on the sacred garments; for I put them on then in
a more holy manner  than I should now resume them.
But if you desire that a person more worthy than myself
should have this honour, give me leave to name such a
one to you.  I have a brother that is pure from all sin
against God, and of all offences against yourself; I recommend him to you, as one that is fit for this dignity."  And
the king was pleased with these words of his, and approved
of the advice of Jonathan, and bestowed the high-priesthood upon his brother Matthias.  And not long after
Marsus succeeded Petronius as governor of Syria.


## CHAP. VII.

*Concerning Silas, and why King Agrippa was angry with him.
How Agrippa began to surround Jerusalem with a wall;
and what Benefits he bestowed on the Inhabitants of
Berytus.*

### § 1.

NOW Silas, the general of the king's army, because he
had been faithful to him in all his misfortunes, and
had never declined sharing with him in any of his dangers,
but had often undertaken the most perilous services for
him, was full of assurance, and thought he might expect a
sort of equality with the king, because of the constant friendship he had shown him.  Accordingly he would not sit
lower than the king at table, and used similar freedom in
all his intercourse with him, and became troublesome to the
king, when they were merry together, by extolling himself
beyond measure, and by often reminding the king of the
misfortunes he had undergone, that he might bring up his
own faithfulness to him in those days; and he was continually harping upon this string, what he had gone through
for him.  The repetition of this so frequently seemed a

reproach to the king, insomuch that he took this uncontrolled liberty of speech very ill at his hands. For the bringing up times when men have been under a cloud is by no means agreeable to them; and he is a very silly man, who is perpetually relating to a person the good services he has done him. At last, therefore, Silas so thoroughly provoked the king's indignation, that he acted rather from passion than reason, and not only turned Silas out of his place as general of his army, but sent him in bonds into his own country. But the edge of his anger wore off in time, and made room for more just reasonings as to his judgment about the man, and he considered how many labours he had undergone for his sake. So when Agrippa kept his birthday, and all his subjects partook of the mirth, he sent for Silas straightway to be his guest. But as he was a very frank man, he thought he had now a very just handle given him for his anger, which he could not conceal from those who came to fetch him, but said to them, "What honour is this the king invites me to, which will soon be over? for the king has not let me keep my first rewards for the good-will I bore him, but has plundered and ill-treated me. Does he think that I can leave off that liberty of speech, which, upon the consciousness of my deserts, I shall use more loudly than before, and shall relate how many dreadful things I have delivered him from, how many labours I have undergone for him, whereby I procured for him safety and honour, as a reward for which I have borne the hardship of bonds and a dark prison. I shall never forget these things; nay, perhaps my very soul, when it is departed out of the body, will not forget the glorious actions I did on his account." This was what he vociferated, and ordered the messengers to repeat to the king. So he perceived that Silas was incurable in his folly, and suffered him to continue in prison.

§ 2. As for the walls of Jerusalem, that looked to the new city, he repaired them at the public expense, and made them wider in breadth, and higher in altitude, and would have made them too strong for all human power to demolish, had not Marsus, the governor of Syria, informed Claudius Cæsar by letter of what he was doing. And as Claudius had some suspicion he meant innovation, he ordered Agrippa to leave off the building of those walls at once; and he thought it inexpedient to disobey.

§ 3. Now king Agrippa was by nature very liberal in his gifts, and very ambitious to oblige people with large donations, and to get celebrity by his great expenditure, as he took delight in giving, and rejoiced in living with a good reputation, being very unlike the Herod who reigned before him. For that Herod was ill-natured, and severe in his punishments, and had no mercy on those that he hated, and it is admitted that he was more friendly to the Greeks than to the Jews; for he adorned foreign cities with large grants of money, and baths, and theatres; nay, in some of those places he erected temples, and in others porticoes, but he did not vouchsafe to raise one of the least edifices in any Jewish city, or make them any donation that was worth mentioning. But Agrippa's temper was mild, and he was equally liberal to all men. He was humane to foreigners, and displayed to them his munificence, while to his own countrymen he was equally kind, but more sympathetic. Accordingly, he loved to live continually at Jerusalem, and was strict in the observance of the laws of his country. He therefore kept himself entirely pure, nor did any day pass over his head without its appointed sacrifice.

§ 4. Notwithstanding, a certain man of the Jewish nation at Jerusalem, called Simon, who was thought to be skilled in the knowledge of the law, called the multitude together in assembly, while the king was absent at Cæsarea, and had the insolence to accuse him of not living holily, and said he might justly be excluded from entrance into the temple, since it belonged only to native Jews. And the captain of the city informed Agrippa by letter that Simon had said this to the people. So the king sent for him, and, as he was sitting in the theatre at the time, he bade him sit down by him, and said to him in a low and gentle voice, "What is there done here that is contrary to the law?" But he had nothing to say for himself, and begged for pardon. And the king was more easily reconciled to him than one would have imagined, as he esteemed mildness a better quality in a king than anger, and knew that moderation is more becoming in great men than passion. So he gave Simon a present, and dismissed him.

§ 5. Now, Agrippa was a great builder in many places, but paid peculiar regard to the people of Berytus.[1] For he erected a theatre for them, superior to many both in sumptuousness and elegance, as also an amphitheatre built at great expense, and besides these he built them baths and porticoes, and spared no cost in any of his edifices to render them both handsome and large. He also spent a great deal upon their dedication, and exhibited shows in the theatre, and brought there musicians of all sorts, and such as made delightful music in great variety. He also showed his magnificence in the amphitheatre by a great number of gladiators, and there too he exhibited fighting on a large scale to please the spectators, indeed he sent no fewer than seven hundred men to fight with seven hundred other men, using all the malefactors he had for this purpose, that both they might receive punishment, and that this operation of war might give delight in peace. Thus he destroyed all these criminals at once.

## CHAP. VIII.

*What other Acts were done by Agrippa until his Death ; and how he died.*

### § 1.

WHEN Agrippa had completed what I have just stated at Berytus, he removed to Tiberias,[2] a city in Galilee. Now he was held in great esteem by other kings. Accordingly, there came to him Antiochus, king of Commagene,[3] and Sampsigeramus, king of Emesa,[4] and Cotys, who was king of Lesser Armenia, and Polemo, who was king of Pontus,[5] as also Herod his brother, who was king of Chalcis.[6] All these he treated with agreeable entertainments and in an obliging manner, and so as to exhibit the greatness of his

[1] *Beirût.*
[2] *Tubariya,* on the western shore of the Sea of Galilee.
[3] Between Cilicia and the Euphrates. See Antiq. xviii. 2, § 5.
[4] *Homs.*
[5] On the north coast of Asia Minor.          [6] *Kinnisrin.*

mind, and to appear worthy of the respect which these kings paid to him, by thus coming to see him. However, while these kings stayed with him, Marsus the governor of Syria came to visit him. And Agrippa, to show the respect that was due to the Romans, went out of the city as far as seven furlongs to meet him. But this proved to be the beginning of a difference between him and Marsus; for Agrippa took with him in his chariot those other kings seated with him. And Marsus was suspicious what the meaning could be of so great a friendship of these kings with one another, and did not think so close an agreement of so many kings for the benefit of the Romans. He therefore sent some of his friends to each of them, and enjoined them to go to their own countries without delay. This was very ill taken by Agrippa, who after that became Marsus' enemy. And he took the high-priesthood away from Matthias, and made Elionæus, the son of Cantheras, high priest in his stead.

§ 2. Now, when Agrippa had reigned three years over all Judæa, he went to the city of Cæsarea,[1] which was formerly called Strato's Tower; and there he exhibited shows. n honour of Claudius Cæsar, upon his being informed that this festival was one instituted for his safety. At this festival a great multitude assembled together of the principal persons, and such as were of dignity throughout the province. On the second day of the shows Agrippa put on a garment made wholly of silver, and of a contexture truly wonderful, and came into the theatre at daybreak; at which time the silver of his garment being illumined by the early rays of the sun's beams upon it, glittered in a surprising manner, and was so resplendent as to inspire fear and trembling in tho se that looked intently upon him. And straightway his flatterers cried out, one from one place, and another from another, (though not really for his good,) that " he was a god;" and they added, " Be thou merciful to us; for although we have hitherto reverenced thee only as a man, yet do we hence-forth own thee as superior to mortal nature." Upon this the king did neither rebuke them, nor reject their impious flattery. But soon afterwards he looked up, and saw an

---

[1] Cæsarea Palæstina, *Kaisariyeh.*

owl sitting on a certain rope over his head, and immediately understood that this bird was the messenger of ill tidings, as it had once been the messenger of good tidings, and felt heart-piercing grief. A severe pain also seized his belly, and began in a most violent manner. He therefore jumped up from his seat and said to his friends, "I whom ye call a god, am now commanded to depart this life ; fate thus reproving the lying words you just now said to me ; and I, who was by you called immortal, am now hurried off to death. But I am bound to accept my destiny, as it pleases God ; for I have lived no paltry life, but in a splendid and happy manner." When he had said this, his pain became intense. So he was carried quickly into the palace, and the rumour went abroad every where, that he would certainly die soon. And the multitude at once sat in sackcloth, with their wives and children, according to the law of their country, and besought God for the king's recovery ; and all places were full of mourning and lamentation. Now the king rested in a high chamber, and as he saw them below lying prostrate on the ground, he could not himself forbear weeping. And when he had been quite worn out by the pain in his belly for five days, he departed this life, being in the fifty-fourth year of his age, and in the seventh year of his reign ; for he reigned four years under Caius Cæsar ; three of them over Philip's tetrarchy only, but in the fourth he had that of Herod added to it ; and he reigned also three years under the reign of Claudius Cæsar, during which time he reigned over the forementioned countries, and also had Judæa and Samaria and Cæsarea added to them. The revenues that he received out of them were very great, being no less than twelve millions of drachmæ.[1] However, he borrowed great sums from others ; for he was so very liberal that his expenses exceeded his income, and his generosity was boundless.

§ 3. But before the multitude knew of Agrippa's having expired, Herod the king of Chalcis, and Helcias the commander and friend of the king, sent Aristo, one of the king's

---

[1] This sum, which is equal to £425,000 sterling, was Agrippa the Great's yearly income, or about three quarters of his grandfather Herod's income ; he having abated the tax upon houses at Jerusalem, and not being so tyrannical as Herod had been to the Jews.—W.

most faithful servants, and slew Silas (who was their
enemy), as if it had been done by the king's own command.


## CHAP. IX.

*What happened after the Death of Agrippa; and how*
*Claudius, on account of the Youth and Unskilfulness of*
*Agrippa Junior, sent Cuspius Fadus to be Governor of*
*Judæa, and of the entire Kingdom of Agrippa.*

### § 1.

THUS did king Agrippa depart this life. But he left
behind him a son Agrippa, a youth in the seventeenth year of his age, and three daughters; one of whom,
Berenice, was married to Herod her father's brother,
and was sixteen years old; the other two, Mariamne and
Drusilla, were still virgins, Mariamne was ten years old,
and Drusilla six. Now these daughters had been betrothed
by their father, Mariamne to Julius Archelaus, the son of
Chelcias, and Drusilla to Epiphanes, the son of Antiochus
the king of Commagene. Now when it was known that
Agrippa had departed this life, the inhabitants of Cæsarea
and of Sebaste [1] forgot the kindnesses he had bestowed on
them, and acted the part of the bitterest enemies. For
they cast such reproaches upon the deceased as were not fit
to be spoken, and as many of them as were then soldiers
(who were a great number), went to his house, and carried
off the statues [2] of the king's daughters, and with one accord
carried them into the brothels, and, when they had set them
on the roofs of those houses, abused them to the utmost of
their power, and did such things to them as are too indecent
to be related. They also reclined in public places and
celebrated general feastings, with garlands on their heads,
and anointed themselves, pouring out libations to Charon,
and drinking to one another for joy that the king had expired. And they were not only unmindful of Agrippa, who

---

[1] *Sebustieh.*
[2] Photius says, they were not the statues or images, but the ladies
themselves, who were thus basely abused by the soldiers.—W.

had lavishly extended his liberality to them, but of his grand-father Herod also, who had himself rebuilt their cities, and had raised them havens and temples at vast expense.

§ 2. Now Agrippa, the son of the deceased, was at Rome at this time, being brought up with Claudius Cæsar. And when the emperor heard that Agrippa was dead, and that the inhabitants of Sebaste and Cæsarea had acted so insolently to his memory, he was sorry for the death of Agrippa, and was displeased with the ingratitude of those cities. He was therefore disposed to send Agrippa Junior away at once to succeed his father in the kingdom, and wished to make good his oaths. But those freedmen and friends of his, who had the greatest influence with him, tried to dissuade him from it, and said that it was a dangerous experiment to permit so large a kingdom to come into the hands of so very young a man, and one hardly yet arrived at years of discretion, who would not be able to take sufficient care of its administration, for the weight of a kingdom was heavy enough to a grown man. And the emperor thought what they said reasonable. So he sent out Cuspius Fadus to be governor of Judæa, and of the entire kingdom of Agrippa, and paid that respect to the deceased, not to introduce Marsus, who had been at variance with him, into his kingdom. But he determined before everything to give injunctions to Fadus to chastise the inhabitants of Cæsarea and Sebaste for the insults they had offered to the memory of him that was deceased, and their licentious conduct to his daughters that were still alive; and to remove the body of soldiers that were at Cæsarea and Sebaste, and the five cohorts, to Pontus, that they might do military duty there, and to choose an equal number of soldiers out of the Roman legions that were in Syria, to supply their place. However those that had such orders were not actually removed; for by sending messengers to Claudius, they mollified him, and got leave to stay in Judæa still; and these were the very men that became the source of very great calamities to the Jews in after times, and sowed the seeds of the war which began under Florus. And so, when Vespasian had subdued the country, he removed them out of the province, as I shall relate hereafter.

# BOOK XX.

## CHAP. I.

*A Quarrel between the Philadelphians and the Jews ; also concerning the Vestments of the High Priest.*

### § 1.

UPON the death of king Agrippa, which I related in the previous book, Claudius Cæsar sent Cassius Longinus as successor to Marsus, out of regard to the memory of king Agrippa, who had often desired of him by letters, while he was alive, that he would not suffer Marsus to be any longer governor of Syria. But Fadus, as soon as he was come into Judæa to administer affairs, found a quarrel going on between the Jews that dwelt in Peræa [1] and the people of Philadelphia, [2] about their borders, at a village called Mia, [3] that was filled with men of war ; for the Jews of Peræa had taken up arms without the consent of their principal men, and had slain many of the Philadelphians. When Fadus was informed of this, it provoked him very much that they had not left the decision of the matter to him, if they thought the Philadelphians had done them any wrong, but had rashly taken up arms against them. So he seized upon three of their principal men, who were also the causes of this strife, and ordered them to be bound, and afterwards had one of them slain, whose name was Annibas, and banished the other two, Amaramus and Eleazar. Tholomæus also, the arch robber, was, in a little time, brought to him bound, and slain, but not till he had done a great deal of mischief to Idumæa and the Arabians. And indeed all Judæa was cleared of robberies from that time by the care and forethought of Fadus. He also at this time sent for

[1] See Antiq., xvii. 8, § 1.
[2] Rabboth Ammon, *'Ammân.*                                    [3] Unknown.

the high priests and principal persons in Jerusalem by command of the emperor, and bade them place the long garment, and the sacred vestment, which it was customary for only the high priest to wear, in the fortress of Antonia,[1] that it might be under the power of the Romans as it had been formerly. Now the Jews durst not contradict what he said, but nevertheless begged Fadus and Longinus (which last had come to Jerusalem with a great army, from fear that the injunctions of Fadus would force the Jews to rebel,) first to give them leave to send ambassadors to the emperor, to petition him that they might have the holy vestments in their own power, and next to wait till they knew what answer Claudius would give to their request. And they replied that they would give them leave to send their ambassadors, provided they would give them their sons as hostages. And when they had agreed to do so and had given them the hostages they desired, the ambassadors were sent accordingly. And when, upon their coming to Rome, Agrippa Junior, the son of the deceased, knew of the reason why they came (for he dwelt with Claudius Cæsar, as I said before,) he besought the emperor to grant the Jews their request about the holy vestments, and to send a message to Fadus accordingly.

§ 2. Thereupon Claudius summoned the ambassadors, and told them he granted their request, and bade them return their thanks to Agrippa for this favour which had been bestowed on them upon his entreaty. And, besides these answers of his, he sent the following letter. " Claudius Cæsar, Germanicus, tribune of the people the fifth time, and consul designate the fourth time, and imperator the tenth time, the father of his country, to the magistrates, senate, and people, and whole nation of the Jews, greeting. Upon the presentation of your ambassadors to me by my friend Agrippa (whom I have brought up, and have now with me, and who is a person of very great piety), who are come to give me thanks for the care I have taken of your nation, and have entreated me in an earnest and solemn manner, that they may have the holy vestments and the crown in their own power, I grant their

---

[1] On the north side of the Temple.

request, as that excellent person Vitellius, who is very dear to me, did before me. And I have complied with your desire, first in regard to my own piety and because I would have every one worship God according to the laws of their own country; and next because I know I shall hereby gratify king Herod and Aristobulus Junior, whose piety to me and good-will to you I am well acquainted with, and for whom I have the greatest friendship, as I highly esteem them and value them. I have also written about these affairs to Cuspius Fadus my procurator. The carriers of the letter are Cornelius the son of Cero, Trypho the son of Theudio, Dorotheus the son of Nathanael, and John the son of John. Dated the fourth day before the Calends of July, Rufus and Pompeius Silvanus being consuls."

§ 3. Herod also, the brother of the deceased Agrippa, who was at this time possessed of the royal authority over Chalcis, petitioned Claudius Cæsar for authority over the temple, and the sacred money, and the choice of the high priests, and obtained all that he petitioned for; so that after this time that authority continued [1] with all his descendants till the end of the war. Accordingly, Herod removed the high priest called Cantheras, and bestowed that dignity on his successor Joseph, the son of Camei.

## CHAP. II.

*How Helena, Queen of Adiabene, and her son Izates, embraced the Jewish Religion; and how Helena supplied the Poor with Corn when there was a great Famine at Jerusalem.*

### § 1.

ABOUT this time Helena, queen of Adiabene,[2] and her son Izates, changed their course of life, and embraced the Jewish customs, for the following reason. Monobazus,

---

[1] Here is some error in the copies, or mistake in Josephus; for the power of appointing high priests, after Herod king of Chalcis was dead, and Agrippa Junior was made king of Chalcis in his room, belonged to him, and he exercised the same all along till Jerusalem was destroyed. —W.

[2] A district on the greater *Zab*, which formed a vassal state respec-

the king of Adiabene, who had also the name of Bazæus, fell in love with his sister Helena, and took her to be his wife, and got her with child. And as he was in bed with her one night, having laid his hand upon his wife's belly, he fell asleep, and seemed to hear a voice bidding him take his hand off his wife's belly, and not hurt the infant that was therein, which, by God's providence, would be safely born, and have a happy end. This voice troubled him, and he woke immediately, and told the matter to his wife, and when his son was born, he called him Izates. He had also had Monobazus, an elder son, by Helena, and other sons by other wives. But he openly placed all his affections on this his only begotten [1] son Izates, which was the origin of the envy of his brothers, who on this account hated him more and more, and all grieved that their father should prefer Izates to them. Now although their father was well aware of this, yet did he forgive them, as not feeling envy from an evil disposition, but from the desire each of them had to be beloved by their father. However, he sent Izates with many presents to Abennerigus, the king of Charax-Spasini,[2] because of the great dread he was in for him, lest he should come to some misfortune from the hatred of his brothers, and he committed his son's safety to him. And Abennerigus gladly received the young man, and had a great affection for him, and married him to his own daughter, whose name was Symacho : he also bestowed a province upon him, from which he might receive large revenues.

§ 2. But when Monobazus was grown old, and saw that he had but a little time to live, he wished to see his son before he died. So he sent for him, and embraced him in the most affectionate manner, and bestowed on him the region called Carræ ;[3] it was a soil that bore amomum in great plenty : there are also in it the remains of the ark, wherein

---

tively of Armenia, Parthia, and Rome. At one period it extended west of the Tigris to Nisibis, *Nisibin.* See xx. 3, § 3.

[1] Josephus here uses the word μογογενῆ, only begotten son, for best beloved, as do both the Old and New Testament : I mean where there were one or more sons besides (Gen. xxii. 2, Heb. xi. 17).—W.

[2] Between the mouths of the Euphrates and Tigris. See Antiq., i. 6, § 4.

[3] Now *Harran.* See Antiq., i. 16, § 1 ; i. 19, § 4.

it is related that Noah escaped the deluge, which are still shown to such as desire to see them.[1] And Izates abode in that region until his father's death. And the very day that Monobazus died, queen Helena sent for all the grandees and satraps of the kingdom, and for those in command of the forces; and when they were come, she made the following speech to them. "I believe you are not ignorant that my husband desired Izates to succeed him in the kingdom, and thought him worthy to do so. However, I wait your determination; for happy is he who receives a kingdom not from a single person only, but from the willingness of many." She said this in order to try to discover the sentiments of those whom she had summoned together. Upon the hearing of this, they first of all paid their homage to the queen, as their custom was, and then they said that they confirmed the king's determination, and would submit to it, and rejoiced that Izates' father had preferred him before the rest of his brothers, as it was agreeable to all their wishes. But they said they were desirous first of all to slay his brothers and kinsmen, that so the kingdom might come securely to Izates; for if they were once destroyed, all the fear would be over which might arise from their hatred and envy to him. Helena replied to this, that she returned them her thanks for their good-will to herself and to Izates; but desired that they would defer the execution of this proposed slaughter of Izates' brothers till he should be there himself, and give his approbation to it. But as these men prevailed not with her to slay them, as they had advised, they exhorted her at least to keep them in bonds till Izates should come for their own security; they also counselled her to appoint some one whom she put the greatest trust in, as regent of the kingdom in the mean time. Helena complied with this counsel of theirs, and appointed Monobazus, the eldest son, to be king, and put the diadem upon his head, and gave him his father's signet ring, as also the sword of state which they call Sampsera, and exhorted him to administer the affairs of the kingdom till his brother should come. But Izates returned quickly, on hearing that his father was

[1] It is here very remarkable, that the remains of Noah's ark were believed to be still in existence in the days of Josephus. See i. 3, § 5.—W.

dead, and succeeded his brother Monobazus, who resigned
up the kingdom to him.

§ 3. Now, during the time that Izates abode at Charax-
Spasini, a certain Jewish merchant, whose name was Ananias,
got among the king's women, and taught them to worship
God according to the Jewish religion.  Moreover through
them he became known to Izates, and persuaded him in like
manner to embrace the Jewish religion, and also, at his
earnest entreaty, accompanied Izates when he was sent for
by his father to Adiabene.  It also happened that Helena
was instructed similarly by another Jew, and went over also
to the Jewish religion.  Now when Izates had taken over the
kingdom, and had come to Adiabene, and there saw his
brothers and other kinsmen in bonds, he was displeased at
what had been done ; and as he thought it impious either
to slay or imprison them, but still thought it hazardous to
let them have their liberty at his court, as they would
remember the injury that had been done them, he sent
some of them with their children as hostages to Rome to
Claudius Cæsar, and sent the others to Artabanus, the
king of Parthia, on the like pretext.

§ 4. And when he found that his mother was highly
pleased with the Jewish customs, he was fain to embrace
them entirely ; and, as he supposed that he could not be
thoroughly a Jew unless he were circumcised, he was ready
to undergo that operation.  But when his mother heard of
his intention, she endeavoured to hinder him from it, and
told him that it would bring him into danger; for as
he was king, he would get himself into great odium
among his subjects, when they should learn that he was so
fond of rites to them strange and foreign, and they would
never submit to be ruled over by a Jew.  She said this to
him, and tried every way to dissuade him from his purpose.
And when he had repeated what she had said to Ananias,
he confirmed what his mother had said, and also threatened
to leave the king, unless he complied with him, and
actually departed.  For he said he was afraid lest, if such
an action were once made public to all, he should himself be in danger of punishment, as having been the cause
of it, and having been the king's instructor in actions that
were ill thought of.  He also said that the king might wor-

ship God without being circumcised, even though he did
resolve to follow the Jewish law entirely, for the worship of
God was of more importance than circumcision.   He added
that God would forgive him, though he did not perform the
operation, as it was omitted out of necessity, and from fear of
his subjects.   And the king for the time listened to these
arguments, but afterwards (for he had not quite left off his
desire of doing this thing) another Jew that came out of
Galilee, whose name was Eleazar, and who was esteemed
very skilful in the knowledge of his country's laws, urged
him to do it.   For as he entered his palace to salute him,
and found him reading the law of Moses, he said to him,
"You are ignorant, O king, of the immense injury you are
doing to the laws, and through them to God himself, for it
is necessary not only to read them, but also still more to practise what they enjoin.   How long will you continue uncircumcised?   But, if you have not yet read the law on the
matter, that you may know what great impiety you are
guilty of in neglecting it, read it now."   When the king
heard these words, he delayed the thing no longer, but retired to another room, and sent for a surgeon, and did what
he was commanded to do.   He then sent for his mother,
and Ananias his original instructor in Jewish principles,
and informed them that he had done the thing, upon
which they were at once seized with astonishment and
fear, and that to a great degree, lest the matter should
be openly discovered and censured, and the king should
hazard the loss of his kingdom, as his subjects might not
submit to be governed by a man who was so zealous for
a strange religion ; and lest they should themselves run
some hazard, because they would be supposed the cause
of his having so done.   But God himself hindered what
they feared from happening: for he preserved both Izates
himself, and his sons, when they fell into many dangers,
and procured their deliverance when it seemed to be
impossible, and showed thereby, that the fruit of piety
does not perish for those that look to him, and fix their
faith upon him only.   But I shall relate these events hereafter.

§ 5.  Now Helena, the king's mother, when she saw that
the affairs of the kingdom were in peace, and that her son

was a happy man, and an object of envy to all men, even to
foreigners, owing to God's providence over him, desired to
go to the city of Jerusalem, to worship at that temple
of God which was so very famous among all men, and
to offer her thank-offerings there. So she asked her son
to give her leave to go there, upon which he gave his
very willing consent to what she asked, and made great
preparations for her departure, and gave her a great deal of
money, and she went down to the city of Jerusalem, her son
conducting her a great way on her journey. Now her
visit was of very great advantage to the people of Jerusalem,
for as a famine oppressed their city at that time, and many
people died for want of money to procure necessaries with,
queen Helena sent some of her servants to Alexandria with
a great quantity of money to buy corn, and others of them
to Cyprus to bring a cargo of dried figs. And as soon
as they had come back with those provisions very quickly,
she distributed food to those that were in want of it, and
left an excellent memorial behind her of this beneficence to our whole nation. And when her son Izates was
informed of this famine, he sent great sums of money
to the principal men in Jerusalem, which being distributed
amongst those that were in want relieved many from
the griping pangs of hunger. However, what favours this
king and queen conferred upon our city of Jerusalem, and
what resources came from her to our citizens, shall be further related hereafter.

## CHAP. III.

*How Artabanus, King of Parthia, afraid of the Plots of his
Subjects against him, went to Izates, and was by him rein-
stated in his Kingdom; as also how Vardanes, his son,
denounced War against Izates.*

### § 1.

NOW Artabanus, king of the Parthians, on learning that
his satraps had formed a plot against him, did not
think it safe to remain among them, but resolved to go

to Izates, wishing to find some way of preservation through him, and, if possible, to get his return to his own dominions. So he went to Izates, and took a thousand of his kindred and servants with him, and met him upon the road, and he well knew Izates, but Izates did not know him.   When Artabanus stood near him, and had first prostrated himself before him, according to the custom of his country, he then said to him, " O, king, do not overlook me thy servant, nor proudly reject the suit I make thee: for as I am reduced to a low estate by reverse of fortune, and from a king am become a private man, I stand in need of thy assistance. Look then at the uncertainty of fortune, and consider the case as one that might be thine, and esteem the care thou shalt take of me to be taken of thyself also; for if I be neglected, and my subjects go unpunished, many subjects will become more insolent towards other kings also." Now Artabanus made this speech with tears in his eyes, and with a dejected countenance.   And as soon as Izates heard Artabanus' name, and saw him stand as a suppliant before him, he leapt down from his horse quickly, and said to him, " Take courage, O king, and be not disturbed at thy present calamity, as if it were incurable ; for a change from thy sad condition shall be speedy, for thou shalt find me to be more thy friend and assistant than thou hopest ; for I will either reinstate thee in the kingdom of Parthia, or lose my own kingdom."

§ 2. When he had said this, he set Artabanus upon his horse, and himself accompanied him on foot, honouring him as a greater king than himself.   But when Artabanus saw this, he was very uneasy at it, and swore by his present fortune and honour that he would dismount, unless Izates would get upon his horse again, and go before him. So he complied with his desire, and leaped upon his horse ; and when he had brought him to his royal palace, he showed him every honour when they sat together, and gave him the chief place at festivals, regarding not his present fortune, but his former dignity, and considering also that changes in fortune are common to all men.   He also wrote to the Parthians, urging them to receive Artabanus again, and gave them his right hand and faith, that Artabanus would forget what was past and done, and offered himself

as mediator between them.  Now the Parthians did not themselves refuse to receive him again, but pleaded that it was
now out of their power to do so, because they had given the
kingdom to another person, who had accepted it, whose
name was Cinnamus, and that they were afraid lest a civil
war should arise on this account.   When Cinnamus heard
of their views, he wrote to Artabanus himself, for he had
been brought up by him, and was by nature good and
gentle, and besought him to put confidence in him, and
come and take his own dominions again.   Accordingly,
Artabanus trusted him, and returned home, and Cinnamus
met him, and prostrated himself before him, and saluted
him as king, and took the diadem off his own head, and put
it on the head of Artabanus.

§ 3.  Thus was Artabanus restored to his kingdom again
through Izates, after he had previously lost it owing to his
grandees.   Nor was he unmindful of the benefits Izates had
conferred upon him, but rewarded him with the greatest
honours among them; for he allowed him to wear his
tiara upright,[1] and to sleep upon a golden bed, which are
privileges and marks of honour allowed only to the kings
of Parthia.   He also cut off a large and fruitful country
from the king of Armenia, and bestowed it upon him.
The name of the country is Nisibis,[2] and the Macedonians
had formerly built there the city of Antioch, which they
called in Mygdonia.   These were the honours that were paid
Izates by the king of the Parthians.

§ 4.  But no long time after Artabanus died, and left
the kingdom to his son Vardanes.  Now this Vardanes
came to Izates, and urged him to join him with his army,
and to assist him in the war he was preparing to make against
the Romans, but he could not prevail upon him to do so.
For Izates knew so well the strength and good fortune of
the Romans, that he thought Vardanes was attempting
what was impossible.  And having besides sent his sons,
five in number, and those but young also, to learn accurately the language and learning of our nation, as he had

---

[1] This privilege of wearing the tiara upright, or with the tip of the
cone erect, is known to have been of old peculiar to great kings, from
Xenophon and others, as Dr. Hudson observes here.—W.

[2] *Nisibin*, in Mesopotamia.

sent his mother to worship at our temple, as I have related already, he was still more reluctant, and tried to restrain Vardanes, telling him perpetually of the great armies and famous actions of the Romans, and thinking thereby to frighten him, and hinder him from his desire for an expedition against them. But the Parthian king was provoked at this behaviour, and proclaimed war immediately against Izates. Yet did he gain no advantage by this war, because God cut off all his hopes therein; for the Parthians, perceiving Vardanes' intention, and how he had determined to war against the Romans, slew him, and gave his kingdom to his brother Cotardes. He also in no long time perished by a plot made against him, and Vologeses, his brother, succeeded him, who intrusted his kingdoms to two of his brothers by the same father, Media to the elder Pacorus, and Armenia to the younger Tiridates.

## CHAP. IV.

*How Izates was betrayed by his own Subjects, and fought against by the Arabians; and how, by the Providence of God, he was delivered out of their hands.*

### § 1.

NOW when the king's brother, Monobazus, and his other kinsman, saw how Izates, owing to his piety to God and inherent goodness of character, was become greatly esteemed by all men, they also had a desire to leave the religion of their country, and to embrace that of the Jews, and they carried out their intention. But this act of theirs was discovered by Izates' subjects, and the grandees were much displeased at it, but dissembled their anger, only they intended, when they could find a convenient opportunity, to inflict punishment upon them. Accordingly, they wrote to Abias, king of the Arabians, and promised him great sums of money, if he would make an expedition against their king: and further promised him that on the first onset they would desert their king, for they wished to punish him because of the hatred he had to their religion, and they bound themselves by oaths to be faithful to each other, and begged that he would lose no time in the matter. The king of Arabia complied with their request, and brought a great army into the field, and marched against Izates without delay; and at the first onset, and before they came to close fight, all those grandees, as if in a panic, deserted Izates, as they had agreed to do, and turned their backs upon their enemies, and ran away. But Izates was not dismayed at this, but as he saw that the grandees had betrayed him, he also retired to his camp, and made inquiry into the matter; and as soon as he knew who they were that had made this conspiracy with the king of Arabia, he put to death those that were found guilty, and renewed the fight the next day, and slew most of his enemies, and forced all the rest to betake themselves to flight. He also pursued their king, and drove him into a fortress called Arsamus,[1] and, following up the siege vigorously, he took that fortress. And, when he had plundered it of all the spoil that was in it, which was not small, he returned to Adiabene, but he did not take Abias alive; because, as he found himself surrounded on every side, he slew himself, before he could fall into the hands of Izates.

§ 2. But although the grandees of Adiabene had failed in their first attempt, being delivered up by God into their king's hands, yet would they not be quiet even then, but wrote again to Vologeses, who was now king of Parthia, and begged that he would kill Izates, and set over them some other potentate, who should be a Parthian by race; for they said they hated their own king for changing the laws of their forefathers, and being enamoured of foreign customs. When the king of Parthia heard this, he was elated at the idea of war, and as he had no just pretext for it, he sent and demanded back those honours which had been bestowed on Izates by Artabanus, and threatened, on his refusal, to war against him. Upon hearing this, Izates was in no small trouble of mind, thinking it would be a reproach upon him to appear to resign those honours that had been bestowed upon him from fear; but because he knew that the king of Parthia would not be quiet, even if

---

[1] Site unknown.

he should receive back those honours, he resolved to commit himself to God, his protector, in the present danger he was in of his life: and as he esteemed God his principal help, he placed his children and wives in a very strong fortress, and stored up his corn in citadels, and set the hay and grass on fire. And when he had thus put things in order as well as he could, he awaited the coming of the enemy. And when the king of Parthia was come with a great army of foot and horse, which he did sooner than was expected, (for he marched in great haste,) and had intrenched himself at the river that separated Adiabene from Media, Izates also pitched his camp not far off, having with him six thousand horse. But a messenger, sent by the king of Parthia, came to Izates, and told him, how great the power of the king of Parthia was, as his dominions extended from the river Euphrates to Bactria,[1] and enumerated the king's subjects. He also threatened him, that he should be punished, as a person ungrateful to his master, and added, that the God whom he worshipped could not deliver him out of the king's hands. When the messenger had delivered this message, Izates replied that he knew the king of Parthia's power was much greater than his own, but he knew also that God was much more powerful than all men. And when he had returned this answer, he betook himself to make supplication to God, and threw himself upon the ground, and defiled his head with ashes, and fasted with his wives and children, and called upon God, and said, "O Lord and Governor, if I have not in vain committed myself to thy goodness, but have justly esteemed thee the only Lord and chief protector and master of all beings, come now to my assistance, and defend me from my enemies, not only on my own account, but on account of their insolent behaviour with regard to thy power, for they have not feared to lift up their proud and arrogant tongue against thee." Thus did he lament with weeping and wailing. And God heard his prayer, for immediately, that very night, Vologeses received letters, the contents of which were that a great band of Dahæ and Sacæ, despising him now he had gone so long a journey from home, had

---

[1] *Balkh*, south of the Oxus in Afghan Turkistan.

made an expedition, and laid Parthia waste, so he went home again without effecting his purpose. And thus Izates escaped the threatenings of the Parthian by the providence of God.

§ 3. And not long after Izates died, when he had completed fifty-five years of his life, and had ruled his kingdom twenty-four years. He left behind him twenty-four sons and twenty-four daughters. And he gave orders that his brother Monobazus should succeed him as king, thereby requiting him, because, when he was himself absent after his father's death, he had faithfully preserved the kingdom for him. But when his mother Helena heard of her son's death, she was in great heaviness, as was but natural upon the loss of a most dutiful son; yet was it a comfort to her to hear that the succession came to her eldest son. Accordingly, she went to him in haste, and when she had reached Adiabene, she did not long outlive her son Izates, but soon expired, being worn out with old age and grief. And Monobazus sent her bones and those of Izates his brother to Jerusalem, and gave orders that they should be buried in the pyramids which their mother had erected; they were three in number,[1] and three furlongs from the city of Jerusalem. As for the actions of Monobazus the king, which he did during the rest of his life, I shall relate them hereafter.[2]

## CHAP. V.

*Concerning Theudas, and the Sons of Judas the Galilæan; as also what calamity fell upon the Jews on the Day of the Passover.*

### § 1.

NOW when Fadus was administrator of Judæa, a certain impostor, whose name was Theudas,[3] urged a great part of the people to take their effects with them, and

---

[1] The tomb of Helena, Queen of Adiabene, is usually identified with the ' Tombs of the Kings,' north of Jerusalem. No traces of the three pyramids remain.

[2] This account is now wanting.—W.

[3] This Theudas, who arose under Fadus the procurator, about A.D. 45 or 46, could not be the Theudas who arose in the days of the taxing, under Cyrenius, or about A.D. 7, Acts v. 36, 37.—W.

follow him to the river Jordan; for he told them he was a prophet, and that he would, by his own command, divide the river, and afford them an easy passage over it: and many were deluded by his words. However, Fadus did not permit them to reap any advantage from their folly, but despatched a troop of horse against them, who, falling upon them unexpectedly, slew many of them, and took many of them alive. They also took Theudas himself alive, and cut off his head, and carried it to Jerusalem. This was what befell the Jews in the time of Cuspius Fadus' administration.

§ 2. Tiberius Alexander came as successor to Fadus; he was the son of Alexander the Alabarch of Alexandria, who was foremost among his contemporaries both for his family and wealth: he was also more eminent for piety than his son Alexander, for he did not continue in the religion of his country. Under these administrators it was that that great famine happened in Judæa, when queen Helena bought corn in Egypt at a great expense, and distributed it to those that were in want, as I have related already. Moreover the sons of that Judas of Galilee were now slain, who caused the people to revolt from the Romans, when Cyrenius came to assess the estates of the Jews, as I have shown in a previous book. The names of these sons were James and Simon, and Alexander commanded them to be crucified. And Herod, king of Chalcis,[1] removed Joseph, the son of Cemede, from the high priesthood, and made Ananias, the son of Nebedæus, his successor. And Cumanus came as successor to Tiberius Alexander, and Herod, brother of Agrippa the Great, departed this life in the eighth year of the reign of Claudius Cæsar. He left behind him three sons, Aristobulus, whom he had by his first wife, and Berenicianus and Hyrcanus, who were both by Berenice his brother's daughter. But Claudius Cæsar bestowed his dominions on Agrippa Junior.

§ 3. Now while the Jewish affairs were under the administration of Cumanus, there happened a great tumult at the city of Jerusalem, and many of the Jews perished therein. I shall first explain the reason why it happened. When the feast, which is called the Passover, was at hand,

[1] *Kinnisrin.*

(at which time our custom is to use unleavened bread), and a great multitude had gathered together from all parts to that feast, Cumanus was afraid lest some disturbance should then be made by them; so he ordered that one regiment of soldiers should take their arms, and stand in the temple porticoes, to suppress any riot which might occur, which was no more than what former governors of Judæa had done at such festivals. But on the fourth day of the feast a certain soldier exposed his person to the multitude, which put those that saw him into a furious rage, and made them cry out, that this shameful action was not done to insult them, but God himself. Nay, some of the bolder ones reproached Cumanus, and pretended that the soldier was set on to act so by him, and when Cumanus heard that, he was not a little provoked at such reproaches, yet did he exhort them to leave off the desire for riot, and not to raise a tumult at the festival. But as he could not induce them to be quiet, for they still went on the more reproaching him, he gave order that the whole army should take their entire armour, and go to Antonia, which was a fortress, (as I have said already), which overlooked the temple; but when the multitude saw the soldiers there, they were frightened at them, and ran away hastily: but as the passages out were narrow, and as they thought their enemies followed them, they crowded together in their flight, and a great number were pressed to death in these narrow passages. So that no fewer than twenty thousand perished in this tumult. Thus, instead of a festival, they had at last mourning, and they all forgot their prayers and sacrifices, and betook themselves to lamentation and weeping; so great an affliction did the obscene conduct of a single soldier bring upon them.[1]

§ 4. Now before this their first mourning was over, another mischief befell them also; for some of those that had raised this riot robbed Stephanus, a slave of Cæsar, as

---

[1] This and many more tumults and seditions, which arose at the Jewish festivals, illustrate the cautious procedure of the Jewish governors, when they said, Matt. xxvi. 5, "Let us not take Jesus on the feast-day, lest there be an uproar among the people;" as Reland well observes on this place. Josephus also takes notice of the same thing, Jewish War, i. 4, § 3.—W.

he was journeying along the public road, about a hundred furlongs from the city, and plundered him of all that he had with him. And when Cumanus heard of this, he sent soldiers immediately, and ordered them to plunder the neighbouring villages, and to bring the most eminent persons among them in bonds to him, for he would exact vengeance for this audacious act. Now, as these villages were being ravaged, one of the soldiers seized the laws of Moses that lay in one of the villages, and brought them out before the eyes of all present, and tore them to pieces, and did this with reproachful language and much scurrility. Now when the Jews heard of this, they ran together in great numbers, and went down to Cæsarea, where Cumanus then was, and besought him that he would avenge, not themselves, but God himself, whose laws had been insulted, for they could not bear to live any longer, if the laws of their forefathers must be insulted in this manner. Then Cumanus, fearing that the multitude would go in for another riot, following also the advice of his friends, had the soldier beheaded who had offered this insult to the laws, and so put a stop to the riot which was likely to burst out a second time.

## CHAP. VI.

*How a Quarrel happened between the Jews and the Samaritans, and how Claudius put an End to their Differences.*

### § 1.

A QUARREL also arose between the Samaritans and the Jews for the following reason. It was the custom of the Galilæans, when they came to the holy city for the festivals, to journey through the country of the Samaritans ; [1] and at this time there lay in the road they

---

[1] This constant passage of the Galilæans through the country of Samaria, as they went to Judæa and Jerusalem, illustrates several passages in the Gospels to the same purpose, as Dr. Hudson rightly observes. See Luke xvii. 11 ; John iv. 4. See also Josephus' Life, § 52, where the journey is said to take three days.—W.

took a village that was called Ginæa[1] (which was situated
on the borders of Samaria and the great plain,) some inhabitants of which fought with the Galilæans, and killed
many of them. And when the leading Galilæans heard of
what had been done, they went to Cumanus, and desired
him to avenge the murder of those that had been killed :
but he was bribed with money by the Samaritans to do nothing in the matter. And the Galilæans were much displeased at this, and urged the multitude of the Jews to
betake themselves to arms, and to regain their liberty, and
said that slavery was in itself a bitter thing, but when it
was joined with injuries, it was perfectly intolerable. And
when their principal men endeavoured to pacify them, and
tried to stop the tumult, and promised to endeavour to
persuade Cumanus to avenge those that were killed, they
would not hearken to them, but took their weapons, and
entreated the assistance of Eleazar, the son of Dinæus (a
robber, who had many years made his abode in the mountain), and set on fire and plundered several villages of the
Samaritans. When Cumanus heard of this action of theirs,
he took the troop of horse at Sebaste,[2] and four regiments
of foot, and armed the Samaritans, and marched out against
the Jews, and came up with them, and slew a great number
of them, but took more alive ; whereupon those that were
the most eminent persons at Jerusalem in reputation and
family, as soon as they saw to what a height of calamity
things had come, put on sackcloth, and heaped ashes upon
their heads, and in all kind of ways besought and urged
the insurgents to consider the utter ruin of their country,
the conflagration of their temple, and the slavery of themselves their wives and children, which would be the result
of what they were doing, and to alter their minds, and
cast away their weapons, and for the future be quiet, and
return to their own homes. These arguments prevailed
with them. So the people dispersed, and the robbers went
away again to their strongholds. And from this time all
Judæa was overrun with bands of robbers.

§ 2. But the leading persons of the Samaritans went to
Ummidius Quadratus, the governor of Syria, who was at this

---

[1] *Jenin*, on the borders of the plain of Esdraelon.
[2] *Sebustieh.*

time at Tyre, and accused the Jews of setting their villages on fire, and plundering them. They also said that they were not so much displeased at what they had themselves suffered, as they were at the contempt thereby shown to the Romans, for if the Jews had received any injury, they ought to have made the Romans the judges of what had been done, and not overrun the country, as if they had not the Romans for their governors. So they now came to him to obtain satisfaction. This was the accusation which the Samaritans brought against the Jews. But the Jews affirmed that the Samaritans were the authors of this tumult and fighting, and before everything maintained that Cumanus had been bribed by their gifts, and so passed over in silence the murder of those that had been slain. When Quadratus heard this, he put off the hearing of the case, and said he would give sentence after he went into Judæa, and got a more exact knowledge of the truth. So they went away without effecting their object: but not long afterwards Quadratus came to Samaria, where, upon hearing the case, he came to the conclusion that the Samaritans were the authors of the disturbance. But, when he was informed that some of the Jews were for revolution, he ordered those whom Cumanus had taken captive to be crucified. From thence he went to a certain village called Lydda,[1] which was as big as a city, and there heard the Samaritans a second time before his tribunal, and there learned from a certain Samaritan, that one of the chief of the Jews, whose name was Dortus, and some other riotous persons with him, four in number, had urged the multitude to revolt from the Romans. And Quadratus ordered them to be put to death, but he sent Ananias the high priest and Ananus the commander in bonds to Rome, to give account for what they had done to Claudius Cæsar. He also ordered the principal persons both of the Samaritans and the Jews, as also Cumanus the governor, and Celer the tribune, to go to Italy to the emperor, to be judged before him as to their differences with one another. He next went to the city of Jerusalem, fearing that the multitude of the Jews would again attempt

[1] *Ludd.*

a riot, but he found the city in a peaceable state, and celebrating one of their usual festivals to God. So he believed
that they would not attempt any rioting, and left them
celebrating the festival, and returned to Antioch.

§ 3. Now Cumanus, and the principal Samaritans, who
were sent to Rome, had a day appointed them by the
emperor, on which they were to plead their cause about their
differences with one another. But the Emperor's freedmen and friends were very zealous on behalf of Cumanus
and the Samaritans, and they would have prevailed over
the Jews, had not Agrippa Junior, who was then at Rome,
observing that the principal of the Jews were hard set,
earnestly entreated Agrippina, the emperor's wife, to urge
her husband to hear the case, as was agreeable to his
justice, and to condemn those to be punished who were
really the authors of the insurrection. And Claudius was
moved by this request and heard the case, and when he
found that the Samaritans had been the ringleaders in
these troubles, he gave orders that those who had come
up to him should be slain, and that Cumanus should be
banished. He also gave orders that Celer the tribune
should be carried back to Jerusalem, and should be drawn
through the city in the sight of all the people, and then
put to death.


## CHAP. VII.

*Felix is made Governor of Judæa; also concerning Agrippa
Junior and his Sisters.*


### § 1.

THEN Claudius sent Felix, the brother of Pallas, to administer affairs in Judæa. And when he had already
completed the twelfth year of his reign, he bestowed upon
Agrippa the tetrarchy of Philip and Batanæa,[1] and added
thereto Trachonitis [2] and Abila,[3] which last had been the
tetrarchy of Lysanias, but he took from him Chalcis,
when he had reigned over it four years. And when

---

[1] See Antiq. xvii. 8, § 1.    [2] *el-Lejah.*    [3] See Antiq. xix. 5, § 1.

Agrippa had received these gifts from the Emperor, he gave his sister Drusilla in marriage to Azizus, king of Emesa, upon his consent to be circumcised. For Epiphanes, the son of king Antiochus, refused to marry her, not wishing to come over to the Jewish religion, though he had promised her father formerly he would do so. Agrippa also gave Mariamne in marriage to Archelaus, the son of Helcias, to whom she had formerly been betrothed by her father Agrippa; of which marriage came a daughter, whose name was Berenice.

§ 2. As for the marriage of Drusilla and Azizus, it was no long time afterwards dissolved for the following reason. When Felix was governor of Judæa, he saw this Drusilla, and fell in love with her, for she did indeed excel all other women in beauty, and he sent to her a person whose name was Simon, one of his friends, a Jew, born in Cyprus, who pretended to be a magician, and endeavoured to persuade her to forsake her present husband, and marry Felix, and promised, that if she would not refuse Felix, he would make her a happy woman. Accordingly she acted wickedly, and because she was desirous to avoid her sister Berenice's envy (for she was very ill treated by her on account of her beauty), was prevailed upon to transgress the laws of her forefathers, and to marry Felix. And she had a son by him, whom she called Agrippa. And how that young man and his wife perished at the conflagration of Mount Vesuvius, in the days of Titus Cæsar, shall be related hereafter.[1]

§ 3. As for Berenice, she lived a widow a good while after the death of Herod [king of Chalcis], who was both her husband and uncle, but when the report went that she committed incest with her brother [Agrippa Junior], she urged Polemo, who was king of Cilicia,[2] to be circumcised and to marry her, supposing that by this means she should prove those calumnies to be false; and Polemo listened to her chiefly on account of her riches. But this marriage did not continue long, for Berenice soon left Polemo, owing, as was said, to her licentiousness. And he left simultaneously

[1] This is now wanting.—W.
[2] The south-eastern portion of Asia Minor; now the *Vilayet* of *Adana*.

both his marriage and the Jewish religion.  At the same time
Mariamne put away Archelaus, and married Demetrius,
the principal man among the Alexandrian Jews, both for
his family and wealth; and indeed he was then their
Alabarch.  And she named the son whom she had by him
Agrippinus.  But of all these particulars I shall hereafter
speak more exactly.[1]


## CHAP. VIII.

*How, upon the Death of Claudius, Nero succeeded as Em-
peror, as also what barbarous things he did.   Concerning
the Robbers, Murderers, and Impostors that arose while
Felix and Festus were Governors of Judæa.*

### § 1.

NOW Claudius Cæsar died when he had reigned thirteen years, eight months, and twenty days; and a
report went about from some that he was poisoned by his
wife Agrippina.  Her father was Germanicus, the Emperor's
brother, and her first husband was Domitius Ænobarbus,
one of the most illustrious persons in the city of Rome; after
whose death, when she had long continued in widowhood,
Claudius married her, and she brought with her a son,
Domitius, of the same name as his father.   Claudius
before this had his wife Messalina slain out of jealousy,
by whom he had had a son Britannicus and a daughter
Octavia; their eldest sister was Antonia, whom he had by
Petina his first wife.   And he married Octavia to Nero;
for that was the name that Claudius gave Domitius after
adopting him as his son.

§ 2.  But Agrippina being afraid that, when Britannicus
should come to man's estate, he would succeed his father
as emperor, and desiring to secure the empire beforehand
for her own son Nero, according to report contrived the
death of Claudius, and immediately sent Burrus, the
general of the army, and the tribunes with him, and such
also of the freedmen as had the greatest influence, to take
Nero away to the camp, and salute him emperor.   And

---

[1] This is now wanting.—W.

when Nero had thus obtained the empire, he got Britannicus poisoned so that the multitude should not know of it, but publicly put his own mother to death not long afterwards, making her this requital, not only for being her son, but by bringing it about by her intrigues that he obtained the Roman empire. He also slew his wife Octavia and many other illustrious persons, under the pretext that they plotted against him.

§ 3. But I omit any further discourse about these affairs, for many have composed the history of Nero, some of whom have neglected the truth out of favour to him, having received benefits from him, while others, out of hatred to him, and from the great ill-will which they bore him, have so impudently raved against him with their lies, that they justly deserve to be condemned. But I do not wonder at such as have told lies of Nero, since they have not in their writings preserved the truth of history as to facts earlier than his time, even when the persons concerned could have no way incurred their hatred, since those writers lived a long time after them. But as to those that have no regard to truth, they may write as they please; for in that they seem to take delight: but as to ourselves, who have made truth our direct aim, we shall briefly touch upon what only belongs remotely to our undertaking, but shall relate what has happened to us Jews with great fulness, and shall not shrink from giving an accurate account both of the calamities we have suffered, and of the faults we have been guilty of. I will now therefore return to the relation of our affairs.

§ 4. In the first year of the reign of Nero, upon the death of Azizus, king of Emesa, his brother Sohemus succeeded him in the kingdom. And Aristobulus, the son of Herod, king of Chalcis, was intrusted by Nero with the government of Lesser Armenia. The emperor also bestowed on Agrippa a certain part of Galilee, ordering Tiberias [1] and Tarichææ [2] to submit to his jurisdiction. He gave him also Julias, [3] a city in Peræa, and fourteen villages that lay about it.

---

[1] *Tubariya.*
[2] Probably Kerak, at the south end of the Sea of Galilee.
[3] Bethsaida-Julias. See Antiq. xviii. 2, § 1, and 4, § 6.

§ 5. Now the affairs of the Jews grew worse and worse continually. For the country was again full of bands of robbers, and of impostors who deluded the multitude. Yet did Felix capture and put to death many of these impostors every day, as well as the robbers. He also took alive Eleazar, the son of Dinæus, who had got together a company of robbers, and this he did by treachery, for he gave him assurance that he should suffer no harm, and so persuaded him to come to him; but when he came he bound him, and sent him to Rome. Felix was also vexed with the high priest Jonathan, because he frequently gave him admonitions about governing the Jewish affairs better than he did, lest he should himself have complaints made of him by the multitude, since it was he who had asked Claudius to send him as governor of Judæa. So Felix contrived a method whereby he might get rid of him, now he was become so continually troublesome to him; for continual admonition is grievous to those who are disposed to act unjustly. So in consequence of this Felix persuaded one of Jonathan's most trusted friends, a native of Jerusalem, whose name was Doras, to bring the robbers upon Jonathan to kill him; and this he did by promising to give him a great deal of money for so doing. Doras complied with the proposal, and contrived matters so, that the robbers might murder him in the following manner. Certain of those robbers went up to the city, as if they were going to worship God, but with daggers under their garments, and mingling themselves with the multitude slew Jonathan. And as this murder was never punished, the robbers went up with the greatest security to the festivals after this time, and having their weapons concealed in like manner as before, and mingling themselves with the multitude, they slew both their own enemies and those whom other men wanted them to kill for money, not only in other parts of the city, but some even in the temple itself, for they had the boldness to murder men there, without thinking of the impiety of which they were guilty. And this seems to me the reason why God, out of his hatred of these men's wickedness, rejected our city, and no longer judged the temple sufficiently pure for him to dwell therein, but brought the Romans upon us, and threw a fire upon the

city to purge it, and brought slavery upon us and our
wives and children, being desirous to sober us by our
calamities.

§ 6. With such impiety did the actions that were done
by the robbers fill the city. And impostors and deceivers
urged the multitude to follow them into the wilderness,
and pretended that they would exhibit manifest wonders
and signs, that should be performed by the providence of
God. And many that were persuaded by them suffered
the punishment of their folly: for Felix brought them
back, and then punished them. There also came out of
Egypt about this time to Jerusalem one that said he was
a prophet, and advised the multitude of the common people
to go along with him to the Mount of Olives, as it was
called, which lay opposite the city at five furlongs distance: for he said he wished to show them from thence,
how, at his command, the walls of Jerusalem would fall
down, through which he promised to procure them an entrance into the city. Now, when Felix was informed of this,
he ordered his soldiers to take their weapons, and himself set
out from Jerusalem with a great number of horse and foot,
and attacked the Egyptian and those that were with him,
and slew four hundred of them, and took two hundred
alive. But the Egyptian himself escaped out of the fight,
and did not appear any more. And again the robbers
stirred up the people to make war against the Romans,
and said they ought not to obey them at all, and if any
persons would not comply with them, they set fire to their
villages, and plundered them.

§ 7. And now a great quarrel arose between the Jews
and Syrians who inhabited Cæsarea, as to their equal right
to the privileges of citizenship. For the Jews claimed
the pre-eminence, because Herod their king, the founder
of Cæsarea, was by birth a Jew. Now the Syrians did
not deny what was stated about Herod, but they said
that Cæsarea was formerly called Strato's Tower, and that
then there was not one Jewish inhabitant in the city.
When the rulers of that district heard of this, they arrested
the ringleaders of this dispute on both sides, and tormented
them with stripes, and so put a stop to the disturbance for
a time. But the Jewish citizens, relying on their wealth,

and on that account despising the Syrians, reproached
them again, and hoped to provoke them by their reproaches.  However, the Syrians, though they were inferior
in wealth, valued themselves highly because most that
served there as soldiers under the Romans were from
Cæsarea[1] or Sebaste,[2] so they also for some time used reproachful language to the Jews, till at last they came to
throwing stones at one another, and several were wounded
and fell on both sides, though the Jews were the conquerors.
But when Felix saw that this quarrel was become a kind of
war, he sprung forward and desired the Jews to desist, and
when they refused so to do, he armed his soldiers, and sent
them out at them, and slew many of them, and took more
of them alive, and permitted his soldiers to plunder some
of the houses of many of the citizens, which were full of
riches.  And now the Jews that were more moderate, and
of principal dignity among them, were afraid for themselves, and begged of Felix that he would sound a retreat
to his soldiers, and spare them for the future, and give
them opportunity to repent of what they had done ; and
Felix was prevailed upon to do so.

§ 8.  About this time king Agrippa gave the high priesthood to Ishmael, who was the son of Fabi.  And now
arose dissension between the high priests and the leading
men of the multitude of Jerusalem, each of whom got
about them a company of the boldest sort of men, and of
those that loved innovation, and became leaders to them,
and when they met together, they cast reproachful words and
threw stones at one another.  And there was nobody to punish
them, but these things were done with impunity as in a
city without a government.   And such shamelessness and
boldness seized on the high priests, that they ventured to
send their slaves to the threshing floors, to take the tithes
that were due to the priests, so that the poorest sort of the
priests died for want.  To this degree did the violence of
faction prevail over all right and justice!

§ 9.  Now, when Porcius Festus was sent as successor to
Felix by Nero, the principal of the Jewish inhabitants of
Cæsarea went up to Rome to accuse Felix ; and he would

---

[1] *Kaisarlyeh.*                    [2] *Sebustieh.*

certainly have been brought to punishment for his offences against the Jews, had not Nero yielded to the importunate solicitations of his brother Pallas, who was at that time held in the greatest honour by him. And two of the principal Syrians in Cæsarea bribed Burrus (who was Nero's tutor, and secretary for his Greek letters), by a great sum of money, to disannul the equality of the privileges of citizenship which the Jews enjoyed with the Syrians. And Burrus by his solicitations obtained leave of the emperor that a letter should be written to that purpose. This letter became the occasion of the subsequent miseries that befell our nation; for, when the Jews of Cæsarea were informed of the contents of this letter to the Syrians, they were more disorderly than ever, till they kindled a war.

§ 10. Upon Festus' coming into Judæa, it happened that Judæa was afflicted by the robbers, as all the villages were set on fire, and plundered by them. And now it was that the Sicarii, as they were called (who were robbers) grew numerous. They made use of small swords, very similar in size to the Persian acinaces, but somewhat crooked, and like the Roman sicæ, as they were called, and from these weapons these robbers got their denomination, and with these weapons they slew a great many. For they mingled themselves among the multitude at their festivals, as I said before, when they came up in crowds from all parts to the city to worship God, and easily slew those they had a mind to slay. They also came frequently with their weapons to the villages belonging to their enemies, and plundered them, and set them on fire. And Festus sent forces both of horse and foot, to fall upon those that had been seduced by a certain impostor, who promised them deliverance and freedom from the miseries they suffered from, if they would but follow him as far as the wilderness. And the forces that were sent destroyed both the impostor and his followers.

§ 11. About this time king Agrippa built himself a very large dining-room in the royal palace at Jerusalem, near the portico. This palace had been erected of old by the sons of Asamonæus, and was situated upon an elevation, and afforded a most delightful prospect to those who wished to overlook the city, which prospect was desired by the king, for there he could recline and see what was being done in the temple. Now when the chief men of Jerusalem observed this, they were very much displeased; for it was not agreeable to the habits or laws of our country, that what was done in the temple should be overlooked, especially what belonged to the sacrifices. They therefore erected a high wall before the hall in the inner part of the temple towards the west, and this wall, when it was built, did not only intercept the view from the dining-room in the palace, but also the view from the western portico in the outer part of the temple, where the Romans kept guard near the temple at the festivals. At these doings king Agrippa was much displeased, and still more Festus the governor, and Festus ordered them to pull the wall down again; but the Jews petitioned him to give them leave to send an embassage about this matter to Nero; for they said they could not endure to live, if any part of the temple were demolished; and when Festus had given them leave to do so they sent ten of their principal men to Nero, as also Ishmael the high priest, and Helcias the keeper of the sacred treasure. And when Nero had heard what they had to say, he not only forgave them what they had already done, but also gave them leave to let the wall they had built stand, in order to gratify his wife Poppæa, who was a religious woman, and had requested these favours of Nero, and who gave orders to the ten ambassadors to go their way home, but retained Helcias and Ishmael as hostages with herself. As soon as the king heard this news, he gave the high priesthood to Joseph (who was called Cabi), the son of Simon who was formerly high priest.

## CHAP. IX.

*Concerning Albinus, under whose Governorship James was slain, also what Edifices were built by Agrippa.*

### § 1.

AND Nero, upon hearing of the death of Festus, sent Albinus into Judæa, as governor. And king Agrippa deprived Joseph of the high priesthood, and bestowed the succession to that dignity on the son of Ananus, who was

also himself called Ananus. They say that this older
Ananus was a most fortunate man; for he had five sons,
who were all high priests to God, and he had himself enjoyed that dignity a very long time formerly, which had
never happened to any other of our high priests. But the
younger Ananus, who, as I have said already, succeeded to
the high priesthood, was a bold man in his temper, and
very audacious, and followed the sect of the Sadducees,
who are more severe in punishing offenders than all
other Jews, as I have already shown. As therefore
Ananus was of such a disposition, he thought he had now
a good opportunity [to exercise his authority,] as Festus
was now dead, and Albinus was still on the road, so he assembled the sanhedrim of judges, and brought before them
the brother of Jesus who was called Christ, whose name
was James, and some others, and having accused them as
breakers of the law, he delivered them over to be stoned.
But those who seemed the most moderate of the citizens,
and strict in the observance of the laws, disliked what was
done; and secretly sent to king Agrippa, beseeching him to
bid Ananus to act so no more, for what he had already done
was not done rightly. Nay, some of them also went to meet
Albinus, as he was upon his journey from Alexandria, and
informed him that it was not lawful for Ananus to assemble
a sanhedrim without his consent. And Albinus listened to
what they said, and wrote in anger to Ananus, and threatened that he would bring him to punishment for what he
had done. And king Agrippa took the high priesthood
from him, when he had ruled but three months, and made
Jesus the son of Damnæus high priest.

§ 2. Now as soon as Albinus was come to the city of
Jerusalem, he used all his endeavours and care that the
country might be kept in peace, so he slew many of the
Sicarii. As for the high priest Ananias, he increased in
credit every day, and obtained the favour and esteem of the
citizens in a signal manner. For he was a great maker of
money; so he daily courted the friendship of Albinus and
the high priest by making them presents. But he had
servants who were very wicked, who joined themselves to
the boldest sort of the people, and went to the threshing-
floors, and took away by violence the tithes that belonged

to the priests, and did not refrain from beating such as would not give these tithes to them. And the high priests acted in the same manner as Ananias' servants did, without any one's being able to prevent them. And so [some of the] priests that were wont of old to be supported with those tithes, died for want of food.

§ 3. And the Sicarii again went into the city by night just before the festival, for one was now at hand, and took alive the scribe belonging to Eleazar the governor of the temple (who was the son of Ananus the high priest), and bound him, and carried him away with them. They then sent to Ananias, and said that they would send the scribe to him, if he would persuade Albinus to release ten of their party whom he had captured and put in bonds. So Ananias was forced to beg Albinus to do so, and gained his request. This was the beginning of greater calamities; for the robbers perpetually contrived to take alive some of Ananias' servants, and when they had captured them, they would not let them go except in exchange for some of their own Sicarii. And as they were again become no small number, they grew bold again, and ravaged the whole country.

§ 4. About this time king Agrippa built Cæsarea Philippi [1] larger than it was before, and, in honour of Nero called it Neronias. And when he had built a theatre at Berytus [2] at vast expense, he exhibited shows to the people there every year, and spent therein many ten thousand [drachmæ]; for he gave the people corn and distributed oil among them. And he adorned the entire city with statues of his own donation, and with original images made by ancient hands, nay, he almost transferred there all that was most ornamental in his own kingdom. This made him greatly hated by his subjects, because he took away the things that belonged to them to adorn a foreign city. And now Jesus the son of Gamaliel became the successor of Jesus, the son of Damnæus, in the high priesthood, which the king had taken from the latter; and so a quarrel arose between the high priests, and they got together bodies of the boldest sort of people, who frequently from reproaches proceeded to throwing stones at each other. But Ananias got the best of it, as by his riches he gained over those that were most

[1] *Bâniâs.*                                [2] *Beirût.*

ready to receive. Costobarus also and Saulus got together a multitude of wicked wretches, for they were of the royal family, and obtained favour because of their kindred to Agrippa, but they were violent and ready to plunder those who were weaker than themselves. And from that time chiefly it came to pass, that our city greatly suffered, and that all things grew worse and worse among us.

§ 5. Now when Albinus heard that Gessius Florus was coming to succeed him, he was desirous to appear to have done something for the people of Jerusalem, so he brought out all those prisoners who seemed to him to be most plainly deserving of death, and ordered them to be put to death accordingly; but as for those who had been put into prison for some trifling matter, he took money of them, and dismissed them. So the prisons were emptied, but the country was filled with robbers.

§ 6. Now as many of the Levites (a tribe of ours) as were singers of hymns urged the king to assemble a sanhedrim, and to give them leave to wear linen garments as well as the priests; for they said it would be a work worthy the times of his government, to date from them the commencement of such a novelty. Nor did they fail to obtain their desire; for the king, with the suffrages of those who came to the sanhedrim, granted the singers of hymns this privilege, that they might lay aside their former garments, and wear such a linen one as they desired; and as part of this tribe ministered in the temple, he also permitted them to learn the hymns as they had besought him. Now all this was contrary to the laws of our country, and whenever they have been transgressed, we have never been able to escape the punishment of such transgressions.

§ 7. And now the temple was quite finished. So, when the people saw that the workmen, who were above eighteen thousand, were unemployed, and as they received no wages were in want, because they had earned their bread by their labours about the temple, and as they were unwilling to keep them out of the treasures deposited there from fear of the Romans, though as they desired to make provision for the workmen, they had a mind to expend those treasures upon them (for if any one of them did but labour for a single hour, he received his pay immediately), they urged the king to rebuild the east portico. This portico was on the outer part of the temple, and lay in a deep valley, and had walls four hundred cubits [in length], built of square and very white stones, the length of each stone being twenty cubits, and the height six cubits. This was the work of king Solomon, who first of all built the entire temple. But king Agrippa (who had the care of the temple committed to him by Claudius Cæsar), considering that it is easy to demolish any building, but hard to build it up again, and that it was particularly so in the case of this portico (for it would require a considerable time and great sums of money), denied the petitioners their request about this matter; but he did not prevent their paving the city with white stone. He also deprived Jesus the son of Gamaliel of the high priesthood, and gave it to Matthias, the son of Theophilus, under whom the war between the Jews and Romans began.

## CHAP. X.

### An enumeration of the High Priests.

I NOW think it necessary and proper for this history to give an account of our high priests; how they began, who had that dignity, and how many of them there were to the end of the war. They say then that Aaron, the brother of Moses, first officiated to God as high priest, and that after his death his sons immediately succeeded him, and that this dignity has been continued down from them to all their posterity. Hence it is a custom of our country, that no one should take the high priesthood of God, but he who is of the blood of Aaron, while every one that is of another stock, though he were a king, can never obtain that high priesthood. Accordingly, the number of all the high priests from Aaron, who was (as I have said) first of them, until Phinees, who was made high priest during the war by the seditious, was eighty-three. Thirteen of these officiated as high priests from the days of Moses in the wilderness, while the tabernacle was standing, until the people came into Judæa, when king Solomon erected the temple to God: for at first they held the high priesthood till the end of their life, though afterwards they had successors even while they were alive. And these thirteen, who were descendants of the two sons of Aaron, received this dignity by succession, one after another. Now their first form of government was an aristocracy, and after that a monarchy, and in the third place the government was regal. Now the number of years during the rule of these thirteen, from the day when our fathers departed out of Egypt, under Moses as their leader, until the building of the temple which king Solomon erected at Jerusalem, was six hundred and twelve. After those thirteen high priests, eighteen took the high priesthood at Jerusalem, one in succession to another, from the days of king Solomon, until Nebuchadnezzar, king of Babylon, made an expedition against Jerusalem and burnt the temple, and removed our nation to Babylon, and took Josedek the high priest captive. The time of these high priests was four hundred and sixty-six years six months and ten days, while the Jews were still under kingly government. But after the period of seventy years' captivity under the Babylonians, Cyrus, king of Persia, sent the Jews from Babylon to their own land again, and gave them leave to rebuild their temple; at which time Jesus, the son of Josedek, took the high priesthood over the captives when they had returned home. Now he and his posterity, who were in all fifteen, lived under a democratical government for four hundred and fourteen years, until king Antiochus Eupator, and then the forementioned Antiochus, and Lysias the general of his army, deprived Onias, who was also called Menelaus, of the high priesthood, and slew him at Berœa,[1] and putting his son out of the succession appointed Jacimus as high priest, who was indeed of the stock of Aaron, but not of the family of Onias. On which account Onias, who was cousin of the Onias that was dead, and had the same name as his father, went into Egypt, and became friendly with Ptolemy Philometor and his wife Cleopatra, and persuaded them to

---

[1] *Aleppo.*

make him high priest of the temple [1] which they had built to God in the district of Heliopolis, in imitation of that at Jerusalem; and as to that temple which was built in Egypt, I have spoken of it frequently. Now, when Jacimus had retained the priesthood three years, he died, and there was no one that succeeded him, but the city continued seven years without a high priest. After that the posterity of the sons of Asamonæus, who had the government of the nation conferred upon them, when they had beaten the Macedonians in war, appointed Jonathan to be their high priest, who ruled over them seven years. And when he had been slain by the treacherous contrivance of Trypho, as I have before related, Simon his brother took the high priesthood; and when he was killed at a feast by the treachery of his son-in-law, his son, whose name was Hyrcanus, succeeded him, after he had held the high priesthood one year longer than his brother. This Hyrcanus enjoyed the dignity thirty years, and died an old man, leaving the succession to Judas, who was also called Aristobulus, whose brother Alexander succeeded him; this Judas died of illness, after he had held the priesthood together with the royal authority (for this Judas was the first that put on his head a diadem, which he wore for one year). And when Alexander had been both king and high priest for twenty-seven years, he departed this life, and permitted his wife Alexandra to appoint the next high priest; so she gave the high priesthood to Hyrcanus, but retained the kingdom herself nine years, and then departed this life. For the same period only did her son Hyrcanus enjoy the high priesthood; for after her death his brother Aristobulus fought against him, and beat him, and deprived him of his high priesthood, and did himself not only reign, but perform the office of high priest to God. But when he had reigned three years and as many months, Pompey came and took the city of Jerusalem by storm, and put him and his children in bonds, and sent them to Rome. He also restored the high priesthood to Hyrcanus, and made him ruler of the nation, but forbade him to wear a diadem. This Hyrcanus ruled, besides his first nine years, twenty-four years more, when Barzapharnes and Pacorus, rulers of the Parthians, crossed over the

[1] Possibly at *Tell el-Yehûdi.*

Euphrates, and fought with Hyrcanus, and took him alive, and made Antigonus, the son of Aristobulus, king; and when he had reigned three years and three months, Sossius and Herod besieged and captured him, and Antony had him brought to Antioch and slain there. And Herod, who was then made king by the Romans, did no longer appoint high priests out of the descendants of Asamonæus, but appointed to that office men of no note, and barely priests, with the single exception of Aristobulus. For he made this Aristobulus high priest, who was the grandson of Hyrcanus who was taken by the Parthians, and married his sister Mariamne, only to win the good-will of the people, because of their remembrance of Hyrcanus. But afterwards, being afraid that all would fall away to Aristobulus, he put him to death, contriving to have him suffocated as he was swimming at Jericho, as I have already related; and after him he never intrusted the high priesthood to the posterity of the sons of Asamonæus. Herod's son Archelaus also acted like his father in the appointment of high priests, as did the Romans also, who took the government over the Jews into their own hands after Archelaus. And the number of the high priests, from the days of Herod until the day when Titus took and burnt the temple and the city, was in all twenty-eight, and the period they were high priests was a hundred and seven years. Some of them took part in affairs in the reigns of Herod and Archelaus his son, but after their death the government became an aristocracy, and the high priests were intrusted with dominion over the nation. Thus much may suffice to say concerning our high priests.

## CHAP. XI.

*Concerning Gessius Florus the Governor, who forced the Jews to take up arms against the Romans.   Conclusion of the Antiquities of the Jews.*

### § 1.

NOW Gessius Florus, who was sent as successor to Albinus by Nero, filled Judæa with many miseries. He was a native of Clazomenæ, and brought with him his wife

Cleopatra, (by whose friendship with Nero's wife Poppæa he obtained this government,) who was as wicked as he was. This Florus was so bad and violent in the exercise of his authority, that the Jews cried up Albinus as their bene- factor, so excessive were the evils that Florus brought upon them. For Albinus concealed his wickedness, and was careful that it might not be discovered by anybody ; but Gessius Florus, as though he had been despatched to Judæa on purpose to display his crimes, ostenta- tiously showed his lawlessness to our nation, never omitting any rapine or unjust punishment ; for he was not to be moved by pity, and was never satisfied with any amount of gain, nor did he pay any more regard to great than to small acquisitions, but went shares even with the robbers. For many pursued that calling without fear, feeling perfect security, because he went shares in their robberies ; so that there were no bounds set to the nation's miseries ; but the unhappy Jews, being unable to bear the devasta- tions which the robbers made among them, were all forced to leave their own habitations and flee away, as if they could dwell better any where else in the world among foreigners. And why need I say any more, for it was Florus who forced us to take up arms against the Romans, as we thought it better to be destroyed at once than by little and little. For this war began in the second year of the government of Florus, and in the twelfth year of the reign of Nero. And what actions we were forced to do, or what miseries we had to suffer, may be accurately known by such as will peruse those books which I have written about the Jewish war.

§ 2. I shall now, therefore, make an end here of my Antiquities, after which I began to write my account of the war. Now these Antiquities contain what has been delivered down to us from the original creation of man to the twelfth year of the reign of Nero, as to what has befallen us Jews, as well in Egypt as in Syria and in Palestine, and what we have suffered from the Assyrians and Babylonians, and what afflictions the Persians and Macedonians brought upon us, and after them the Romans. And I think I may say that I have composed this history with all accuracy. I have attempted to enumerate

the high priests that we have had during the interval of
two thousand years. I have also accurately recorded the
succession of our kings, and related their actions and
polity, as also the power of our monarchs, and all according to what is written in our sacred books; for this is
what I promised to do in the beginning of this history.
And I make bold to say, now I have completed the work I
proposed to myself to do, that no other person, whether
Jew or foreigner, had he ever so great an inclination to it,
could have given so accurate an account to the Greeks as
I have done. For those of my own nation freely acknow-
ledge, that I far exceed them in the learning belonging to
Jews; I have also taken a great deal of pains to obtain
the learning of the Greeks, and understand the elements
of the Greek language, although I have so long accustomed myself to speak our own tongue, that I cannot pronounce Greek with sufficient exactness. For our nation
does not encourage those that learn the languages of many
nations, and so adorn their discourses with the smooth-
ness of their periods, because they look upon this sort of
accomplishment as common not only to all sorts of free
men, but to as many servants as please to learn them, and
they give those only the testimony of being wise men who
are fully acquainted with our laws, and able to interpret
the meaning of the holy writings. And so, though there
have been many who have done their endeavours with
great patience to obtain this learning, there have been
hardly as many as two or three that have succeeded therein,
and immediately got the fruit of their labours.

§ 3. And now perhaps it will not be invidious or unapt,
if I treat briefly of my own family, and of the actions of
my own life, while there are still living such as can either
prove what I say to be false, or attest that it is true. So
I shall here put an end to these Antiquities, which are
contained in twenty books and sixty thousand lines. And
if God permit me, I shall briefly run over the war again,
and what befell us to this very day, which is the thirteenth
year of the reign of the Emperor Domitian, and the fifty-
sixth year of my own life. I intend also to write four

books concerning our Jewish opinions about God and his being and concerning our laws, and why, according to them, some things are permitted us to do, and others are prohibited.

# SELECTED BIBLIOGRAPHY

Allon, G. "The Attitude of the Pharisees toward Roman Rule and the Herodian Dynasty" (in Hebrew), *Zion*, III (1935), 300–322.

―――. "On the History of the High-Priesthood at the Close of the Second Temple" (in Hebrew), *Tarbiz*, XIII (1941–42), 1–24.

Aptowitzer, V. *Parteipolitik der Hasmonäerzeit im rabbinischen und pseudepigraphischen Schrifttum*. Vienna and New York, 1927.

Arnold , W. T. *The Roman System of Provincial Administration* (3d ed., rev. by E. S. Bouchier). London, 1914.

Avi-Yonah, M., *et al*. "The Archaeological Survey of Masada, 1955–1956," *Israel Exploration Journal*, VII (1957).

Balsdon, J. P. V. D. *The Emperor Gaius*. Oxford, 1934.

Baron, Salo W. *A Social and Religious History of the Jews* (2d ed.), II, *passim*. Philadelphia, 1952.

Bell, H. I. *Jews and Christians in Egypt*. Oxford, 1924.

Bentwich, Norman. *Josephus*. Philadelphia, 1914.

Bevan, E. R. *Jerusalem under the High Priests*. London, 1924.

Bickerman, Elias. *Der Gott der Makkabäer*. Berlin, 1937.

―――. *From Ezra to the Last of the Maccabees*. New York, 1962.

――― "Les Herodéens." *Revue Biblique*, XLVII (1938), 184–97.

Braun, Martin. "King Herod as Oriental Monarch," *Commentary*, XXV (1958), 48–53.

Burrows, Millar. *The Dead Sea Scrolls*. New York, 1955.

―――. *More Light on the Dead Sea Scrolls*. New York, 1958.

―――. "On the Fortress Antonia and the Praetorium," *Biblical Archaeologist*, I (1938), 17 ff.

Debevoise, N. C. *A Political History of Parthia*. Chicago, 1938.

Derenbourg, J. *Essai sur l'histoire et la géographie de la Palestine*. Paris, 1867.

Driver, G. R. *The Judaean Scrolls*. New York, 1965.

Eisler, Robert. "Flavius Josephus on Jesus Called the Christ," *Jewish Quarterly Review*, XXI (1930), 1–60.

―――. *Iesous Basileus ou Basileusas*. Heidelberg, 1929. English abridgment by A. H. Krappe, *The Messiah Jesus and John the Baptist according to Flavius Josephus' Recently Discovered Capture of Jerusalem, etc.* London, 1931.

Farmer, W. R. *Maccabees, Zealots, and Josephus: An Inquiry into Jewish Nationalism in the Greco-Roman Period.* New York, 1956.

Feldman, L. H. "The Sources of Josephus' *Antiquities*, Book 19," *Latomus*, XXI (1962), 320–33.

Finkelstein, Louis. *The Pharisees: The Sociological Background of Their Faith* (3d ed.). 2 vols. Philadelphia, 1962.

Foakes-Jackson, F. J. *Josephus and the Jews.* New York, 1930.

Fritsch, C. T. "Herod the Great and the Qumran Community," *Journal of Biblical Literature*, LXXIV (1955), 173–81.

Glatzer, N. N., ed. *Jerusalem and Rome: The Writings of Josephus.* New York, 1960.

Glueck, Nelson. *The Other Side of the Jordan.* New Haven, 1940.

———. "Nabataean Syria and Nabataean Transjordan," *Journal of the Palestine Oriental Society*, XVIII (1938), 1–6.

Goodenough, Erwin R. *Jewish Symbols in the Greco-Roman World.* 8 vols. New York, 1953–58.

Hengel, Martin. *Die Zeloten.* Leiden, 1961.

Herford, R. Travers. *Pharisaism.* London and New York, 1912.

Hollis, F. J. *The Archeology of Herod's Temple.* London, 1934.

Jeremias, Joachim. *Jerusalem zur Zeit Jesu.* 2 vols., Leipzig, 1923–37.

Jones, A. H. M. *The Herods of Judaea.* Oxford, 1938.

———. *The Cities of the Eastern Roman Provinces.* London, 1937.

Juster, Jean. *Les Juifs dans l'Empire romain.* 2 vols. Paris, 1914.

Kennard, J. S. "Judas of Galilee and His Clan," *Jewish Quarterly Review*, XXXVI (1945–46), 281–86.

Klausner, Joseph. *History of the Second Commonwealth*, vols. II-V. Jerusalem, 1952.

Kraeling, Carl H. "The Episode of the Roman Standards at Jerusalem," *Harvard Theological Review*, XXXV (1942), 263–89.

Laqueur, Richard. *Der jüdische Historiker Flavius Josephus.* Giessen, 1920.

Levy, Hans. "Josephus the Physician," *Journal of the Warburg Institute*, I, No. 3 (1938), 221–42.

Lichtenstein, Hans. "Megillat Taanit: Die Fastenrolle, etc.," *Hebrew Union College Annual*, VIII–IX (1931–32), 257–351.

Lieberman, Saul. *Hellenism in Jewish Palestine*. New York, 1950.

Maisler (Mazar), Benjamin. "The House of Tobiah," *Tarbiz*, XII (1941–42), 109–23.

Marcus, Ralph. "Pharisees, Essenes, and Gnostics," *Journal of Biblical Literature*, LXXIII (1954), 157–61.

Mazar, Benjamin. "The Tobiads," *Israel Exploration Journal*, VII (1957), 137–45, 229–38.

Momigliano, Arnaldo. "Josephus as a Source for the History of Judaea," *Cambridge Ancient History*, X (1934), 884–87.

Montgomery, James Alan. "The Religion of Flavius Josephus," *Jewish Quarterly Review*, XI (1920–21), 277–305.

———. *The Samaritans, the Earliest Jewish Sect*. Philadelphia, 1907.

Moore, G. F. *Judaism in the First Centuries of the Christian Era*. 2 vols. New York, 1971.

Neusner, Jacob. *A History of the Jews in Babylonia*. 5 vols. Leiden, 1965–70.

Niese, Benedictus. *Flavii Josephi Opera Omnia*. 6 vols. Berlin, 1890–1904.

———. "Josephus," *Encyclopaedia of Religion and Ethics*. Edinburgh, 1914.

Otto, Walter. *Herodes*. Stuttgart, 1913.

Parrot, André. *The Temple of Jerusalem*. London, 1957.

Perowne, Stewart. *The Life and Times of Herod the Great*. London, 1956.

———. *The Later Herods: the Political Background of the New Testament*. London, 1958.

Reifenberg, A. *Ancient Hebrew Arts*. New York, 1950.

———. *Ancient Jewish Coins*. Jerusalem, 1947.

———. "Caesarea, A Study in the Decline of a Town," *Israel Exploration Journal*, I (1950–51), 20–32.

Rengstorf, Karl Heinrich, ed. *A Complete Concordance to Flavius Josephus*. 3 vols. Leiden, 1968.

Roth, Cecil. "The Jewish Revolt against Rome," *Commentary*, XXVII (1959), 513–22.

Roth, Otto. *Rom und die Hasmonäer*. Leipzig, 1914.

Rowley, H. H., "The Herodians in the Gospels," *Journal of Theological Studies*, XLI (1940), 14–27.

Schalit, Abraham. *Roman Administration in Palestine* (in Hebrew). Jerusalem, 1937.

———. "Herod and Mariamne: Josephus' Description in the Light of Historiography," *Molad*, XIV (1956), 95–102.

————. *Herod the King* (in Hebrew). Jerusalem, 1960.

Schreckenberg, Heinz. *Bibliographie zu Flavius Josephus.* Leiden, 1968.

Schürer, Emil. *A History of the Jewish People in the Time of Jesus.* New York, 1963.

Shutt, R. J. H. *Studies in Josephus.* London, 1961.

Starcky, Jean. "The Nabataeans, a Historical Sketch," *Biblical Archeologist,* XVIII (1955), 84–106.

Stern, M. "The Death of Onias III," *Zion,* XXV (1960), 1–16.

Strugnell, J. "Flavius Josephus and the Essenes: Antiquities XVIII. 18–22," *Journal of Biblical Literature,* LXXXVII (1958), 106–15.

Tcherikover, Victor. *Hellenistic Civilization and the Jews.* Philadelphia, 1959.

Thackeray, H. St. John. *Josephus, the Man and the Historian.* New York, 1929.

————; Marcus, Ralph; Wikgren, Allen; and Feldman, L. H. *Josephus, with an English Translation.* (Loeb Classical Library.) 9 vols. London, New York, and Cambridge, Mass., 1926–65.

Weber, Wilhelm. *Josephus und Vespasian.* Berlin, 1921.

Yadin, Yigael. *Masada. First Season of Excavations, 1963–1964* (in Hebrew). Jerusalem, 1965.

Zeitlin, Solomon. *Megillat Taanit, etc.* Philadelphia, 1922.

————. *Josephus on Jesus.* Philadelphia, 1931.

————. *The Rise and Fall of the Judaean State.* 2 vols. Philadelphia, 1962 and 1967.

————. "The Tobias Family and the Hasmoneans," *Proceedings of the American Academy for Jewish Research,* IV (1933), 169–233.

# INDEX